THE OXFORD HANDBOOK OF

SOCIOLOGY AND ORGANIZATION STUDIES

CLASSICAL FOUNDATIONS

THE OXFORD HANDBOOK OF

SOCIOLOGY AND ORGANIZATION STUDIES

CLASSICAL FOUNDATIONS

Edited by

PAUL S. ADLER

OXFORD
UNIVERSITY PRESS

OXFORD
UNIVERSITY PRESS

Great Clarendon Street, Oxford OX2 6DP

Oxford University Press is a department of the University of Oxford.
It furthers the University's objective of excellence in research, scholarship,
and education by publishing worldwide in

Oxford New York

Auckland Cape Town Dar es Salaam Hong Kong Karachi
Kuala Lumpur Madrid Melbourne Mexico City Nairobi
New Delhi Shanghai Taipei Toronto

With offices in

Argentina Austria Brazil Chile Czech Republic France Greece
Guatemala Hungary Italy Japan Poland Portugal Singapore
South Korea Switzerland Thailand Turkey Ukraine Vietnam

Oxford is a registered trade mark of Oxford University Press
in the UK and in certain other countries

Published in the United States
by Oxford University Press Inc., New York

First published 2009

British Library Cataloguing in Publication Data
Data available

Library of Congress Cataloging in Publication Data
Data available

Typeset by SPI Publisher Services, Pondicherry, India
Printed in Great Britain
on acid-free paper by
CPI Antony Rowe, Chippenham, Wiltshire

ISBN 978–0–19–953523–1

1 3 5 7 9 10 8 6 4 2

Preface

The genesis of this volume lies in conversations with numerous colleagues over several years about our shared frustration with the growing divorce between organization studies and one of its key source disciplines, sociology. I took a proposal for an edited volume aimed at bridging that gap to David Musson at Oxford University Press: David's strong encouragement and wise counsel helped give it its current form. Over the course of 2006–7, I reached out to potential contributors, and the response was overwhelmingly positive.

Draft chapters benefited from discussion at a conference held at Wharton in August 2007. Along with the chapter authors, the participating faculty were: Mie Augier (Stanford), Peter Bryant (Macquarie), Jordi Comas (Bucknell), Marlese Durr (Wright State), Isabel Fernandez-Mateo (London Business School), Michal Frenkel (Hebrew Univ.), Zeke Hasenfeld (UCLA), Roberta Iversen (Pennsylvania), Candace Jones (Boston College), Shamus Khan (Columbia), Brayden King (Brigham Young), Sheen Levine (Singapore Mgt. Univ.), Marshall Meyer (Pennsylvania), Ilya Okhmatovskiy (McGill), Sean Safford (Chicago), Samps Samila (Brock), Russell Schutt (Univ. Mass., Boston), Wesley Sine (Cornell), Klaus Weber (Northwestern), and Ray Zammuto (Melbourne). Graduate students too participated in this discussion: Ebony Bridwell-Mitchell (NYU), Ed Carberry (Cornell), Jay Chok (Univ. of Southern Calif.), Anne Fleischer (Michigan), Steve Hoffman (Northwestern), Maksim Kokushkin (Missouri), Andrew Parker (Stanford), Renee Rottner (UC Irvine), Laura Singleton (Boston College), Elizabeth Terrien (Chicago), Matt Vidal (UCLA ILRE), and Peggy Wallace (St Marys). We thank all these colleagues for their immensely helpful constructive criticism.

We also thank the National Science Foundation and in particular Jacqueline Meszaros for funding the conference under Grant No. 0706814. Generous financial support also came from my home department, the Management and Organization Department of the Marshall School at the University of Southern California. My department colleagues there, notably Tom Cummings, Mark Kennedy, and Peer Fiss, provided essential encouragement and guidance throughout. Jay Chok provided crucial research and administrative assistance. Our editor, Lynn Deanne Childress, was exceptionally helpful in structural revision and copyediting.

Paul S. Adler
Los Angeles, August 2008

Contents

PART III AMERICAN PERSPECTIVES

PART IV AFTERWORD

List of Figures

List of Tables

Notes on Contributors

Andrew Abbott is the Gustavus F. and Ann M. Swift Distinguished Service Professor at the University of Chicago. Known for his ecological theories of occupations, Abbott has also pioneered algorithmic analysis of social sequence data. He has written on the foundations of social science methodology and on the evolution of the social sciences and the academic system. He is the author of five books and sixty articles and chapters.

Paul S. Adler is a Professor in the Department of Management and Organization, Marshall School of Business, University of Southern California. He has published four edited volumes, *Technology and the Future of Work* (1992), *Usability: Turning Technologies into Tools* (1992), *Remade in America: Transplanting and Transforming Japanese Management Systems* (1999), and *The Firm as a Collaborative Community: Reconstructing Trust in the Knowledge Economy* (2006), all with Oxford University Press.

Christopher Ansell is an Associate Professor of Political Science at the University of California, Berkeley, and holds a Ph.D. in Political Science from the University of Chicago. His research focuses on understanding conflict and cooperation in interorganizational and intergovernmental systems. He is the author of *Schism and Solidarity in Social Movements* (Cambridge, 2001) and co-editor of *Restructuring Territoriality: Europe and the United States Compared* (Cambridge, 2004) and *What's the Beef? The Contested Governance of European Food Safety* (MIT Press, 2006).

Markus C. Becker holds a Ph.D. in Management from the Judge Business School, Cambridge University. He has held positions with the Centre National de Recherche Scientifique (CNRS) at the University of Strasbourg, France, and with the University of Southern Denmark. He currently is Professor of Organization Theory at the Strategic Organization Design Unit, Department of Marketing & Management, University of Southern Denmark.

Arne Carlsen is a Senior Scientist at SINTEF Technology and Management in Norway. Much of his research has been linked to practical development processes in and with professional service organizations. He has published in journals and books about knowledge management, professional service work, and identity formation at work. He is broadly interested in temporality, narrative theory, pragmatism, and positive psychology, and is presently most curious about the various practices of 'idea work' in organizations.

Stewart Clegg is Professor at the University of Technology, Sydney, and Research Director of the Centre for Management and Organization Studies. He is a prolific publisher in leading academic journals in management and organization theory. He is a Fellow of the Academy of the Social Sciences in Australia and a Distinguished Fellow of the Australian and New Zealand Academy of Management.

Elisabeth S. Clemens is Associate Professor of Sociology at the University of Chicago. Building on organizational theory and political sociology, her research has addressed the role of social movements and voluntary organizations in institutional change. Her first book, *The People's Lobby: Organizational Innovation and the Rise of Interest Group Politics in the United States, 1890–1925* (Chicago, 1997), received awards in both organizational and political sociology. She is also co-editor of *Private Action and the Public Good* (Yale, 1998), *Remaking Modernity: Politics, History, and Sociology* (Duke, 2005), *Politics and Partnerships: Voluntary Associations in America's Past and Present* (Chicago, forthcoming), and the journal *Studies in American Political Development.*

Michael D. Cohen is William D. Hamilton Professor of Complex Systems, Information, and Public Policy at the University of Michigan. He has worked on the 'garbage can' model of organizational choice and other agent-based models of organization. He has studied leadership in higher education organization, models of organizational learning, the complex adaptive dynamics of cooperation, and the psychological foundations of routinized action. He is co-author, with Robert Axelrod, of *Harnessing Complexity.*

Barbara Czarniawska holds a Chair in Management Studies at GRI, School of Business, Economics, and Law at the University of Gothenburg, Sweden. Her recent publications in English are *A Tale of Three Cities* (2002), *Narratives in Social Science Research* (2004), *Shadowing and Other Techniques of Doing Fieldwork* (2007), and *A Theory of Organizing* (2008). She edited *Global Ideas* (with Guje Sevón, 2005), *ANT and Organizing* (with Tor Hernes, 2005), *Organization Theory* (2006), and *Management Education & Humanities* (with Pasquale Gagliardi, 2006).

Gerald F. Davis is the Wilbur K. Pierpont Collegiate Professor of Management at the Ross School of Business and Professor of Sociology at the University of Michigan. Davis's research examines the interactions among financial markets, institutions, and social structure. Recent publications include *Social Movements and Organization Theory* (Cambridge University Press; co-edited with Doug McAdam, W. Richard Scott, and Mayer Zald) and *Organizations and Organizing: Rational, Natural, and Open System Perspectives* (Pearson Prentice Hall; with W. Richard Scott).

Frank Dobbin is Professor of Sociology at Harvard University. He received his Ph.D. from Stanford University. In *Forging Industrial Policy: The United States, Britain, and France in the Railway Age* (Cambridge, 1994) he explores the historical origins of contemporary industrial policy approaches. He traces modern economic sociology to its roots in classical sociological theory in *The New Economic Sociology: An Anthology* (Princeton, 2004) and explores how corporate human resources professionals managed to define what discrimination meant under the Civil Rights Act in *Inventing Equal Opportunity* (Princeton, forthcoming).

Paul du Gay is Professor of Organizational Behaviour at Warwick Business School and Adjunct Professor of Organization Studies at Copenhagen Business School. He was formerly Professor of Sociology and Organization Studies and a Director of the Centre for Citizenship, Identities, and Governance (CCIG) at the Open University. Recent and forthcoming publications include: *The Values of Bureaucracy* (ed. Oxford University Press, 2005), *Organizing Identity: Persons and Organizations 'After Theory'* (Sage, 2007), *Conduct: Sociology and Social Worlds* (ed. with E. McFall and S. Carter, Manchester University Press, 2008), and *Identity in Question* (ed. with A. Elliott, Sage, 2008).

Gary Alan Fine is John Evans Professor of Sociology at Northwestern University. He received his Ph.D. degree from Harvard University in Social Psychology in 1976. He has written on issues of symbolic interaction for over thirty years, including editing a four-volume collection of articles commenting on the work of Erving Goffman and 'The Second Chicago School'. He received the George Herbert Mead Award for lifetime contributions to symbolic interaction.

Peer C. Fiss is Assistant Professor of Strategy at the Marshall School of Business at the University of Southern California. He received his Ph.D. from the Departments of Management & Organization and Sociology at Northwestern University. His current research interests include corporate governance and the diffusion of practices, framing and symbolic management, and the use of set-theoretic methods such as Qualitative Comparative Analysis (QCA) and fuzzy sets in management and the social sciences.

Tim Hallett is Assistant Professor in the Department of Sociology at Indiana University. He received his Ph.D. from Northwestern University in Sociology in 2003. His research lies at the intersections of social psychology, organizations, and culture. In addition to his research on inhabited institutionalism (with Marc Ventresca, *Theory and Society*, 2007), he has published articles on symbolic power and organizational culture (*Social Psychology Quarterly*, 2007 and *Sociological Theory*, 2003), and how emotions 'blow up' in organizations (*The Sociological Quarterly*, 2003). His current work integrates these concerns by examining how the process of 'recoupling' organizations to their institutional environments creates local turmoil.

Gary G. Hamilton is a Professor of Sociology and of International Studies at the University of Washington. He specializes in historical/comparative sociology, economic sociology, and organizational sociology. He also specializes in Asian societies, with particular emphasis on Chinese societies. He is an author of numerous articles and books, including most recently *Emergent Economies, Divergent Paths: Economic Organization and International Trade in South Korea and Taiwan* (with Robert Feenstra, Cambridge University Press, 2006) and *Commerce and Capitalism in Chinese Societies* (Routledge, 2006).

Heather A. Haveman is Professor of Sociology and Business at the University of California, Berkeley. She studies how organizations, industries, and employees' careers evolve. Her published studies have appeared in *Administrative Science Quarterly*, the *American Sociological Review*, the *American Journal of Sociology*, *Poetics*, *Organization Science*, the *Journal of Business Venturing*, and the *Academy of Management Journal*. Her current research involves antebellum American magazines, post-Prohibition US wineries, and twenty-first-century Chinese firms.

Charles Heckscher is a Professor at Rutgers University and Director of the Center for Workplace Transformation. His research focuses on organization change and the changing nature of employee representation. Before coming to Rutgers he worked for the Communications Workers' union and taught Human Resources Management at the Harvard Business School. His books include *The New Unionism*, *White-Collar Blues*, *Agents of Change*, and *The Collaborative Enterprise*.

Shon R. Hiatt is a Ph.D. candidate in organizational behavior at Cornell University. His research looks at the effects of institutional factors on entrepreneurial opportunity creation, discovery, and exploitation. He also investigates the organizational processes, strategy, and networks of firms in mature and emerging economies. Currently, Shon is investigating the effect of environmental elements and firm strategies on US biodiesel adoption and production and the impact of military ties on companies in Latin America.

Paul Hirsch is the James Allen Distinguished Professor of Strategy and Organization at Northwestern University's Kellogg School of Management, where he is also a member of the Sociology and Communication Studies Departments. Hirsch's research spans economic sociology, institutional theory, culture, and communication studies. He has studied the discourse of corporate takeovers, interviewed Studs Terkel, and addressed issues in institutional and organization theory, and mass communication. Hirsch's articles have appeared in *American Journal of Sociology*, *Work and Occupations*, *Theory and Society*, *Administrative Science Quarterly*, and the *New York Times*.

Amanda Hoel-Green is a Masters Degree candidate in Management and Organization at Northwestern University's Kellogg School of Management. She is interested in sociology and public policy issues, and in how attention to classical theories enhances our understanding of both.

Rosabeth Moss Kanter holds the Ernest L. Arbuckle Professorship at Harvard Business School, where she specializes in strategy, innovation, and leadership for change. The former editor of *Harvard Business Review* (1989–1992), Professor Kanter is the author or co-author of seventeen books, which have been translated into seventeen languages. Among her best-known are: *Men & Women of the Corporation*, *When Giants Learn to Dance*, and *The Change Masters*. She chairs a Harvard University group creating an innovative initiative on advanced leadership, to help successful leaders at the top of their professions apply their skills to addressing challenging national and global problems.

Rakesh Khurana is Associate Professor of Organizational Behavior at Harvard Business School. He received his Ph.D. (Organizational Behavior) and A.M. (Sociology) from Harvard University. His research focuses on the sociology of elites, leadership, and governance. He is the author of *From Higher Aims to Hired Hands: The Social Transformation of American Business Schools and the Unfulfilled Promise of Management as a Profession* (Princeton University Press, 2007) and *Searching for a Corporate Savior: The Irrational Question for Charismatic CEOs* (Princeton University Press, 2002). He is currently researching the impact of financial markets on corporate governance and the social structure of global elites.

Thorbjørn Knudsen is Professor at the Strategic Organization Design Unit, Department of Marketing and Management, University of Southern Denmark. His research interests and publications focus on economic evolution and decision making in organizations.

Arik Lifschitz is Assistant Professor of Strategic Management and Organization at the Carlson School of Management, University of Minnesota. He studies the role of institutions and interorganizational networks in the behavior and performance of firms. His co-authored paper with Paul Ingram, 'Kinship in the Shadow of the Corporation: The Interbuilder Network in Clyde River Shipbuilding, 1711–1990', was recently published in the *American Sociological Review*.

Michael Lounsbury is a Professor at the University of Alberta, School of Business. His research focuses on the relationship between organizational and institutional change, entrepreneurial dynamics, and the emergence of new industries and practices. He is currently investigating the co-evolution of nanoscience and nanotechnology. Professor Lounsbury serves on a number of editorial boards and is the series editor of Research in the Sociology of Organizations and co-editor-in-chief of the *Journal of Management Inquiry*.

Richard Marens is an Associate Professor of Management at the California State University, Sacramento. He earned both a J.D. and a Ph.D. from the University of

Washington and has published in a number of management and ethics journals. His research interests include: the emergence of labor unions as innovative financial activists and the evolution of the construct of Corporate Social Responsibility within the context of American social and economic history.

Stella M. Nkomo is a Professor of Business Leadership at the University of South Africa's Graduate School of Business Leadership. Her nationally recognized work on race and gender in organizations, managing diversity, and human resource management appears in numerous journals, edited volumes, and magazines. She is the co-author of *Our Separate Ways: Black and White Women and the Struggle for Professional Identity* (Harvard Business School Press). Professor Nkomo is listed in *Who's Who in the Managerial Sciences.*

Misha Petrovic (Ph.D., Sociology, University of Washington, Seattle, 2005) is Assistant Professor in the Department of Sociology, National University of Singapore, where he teaches classical and contemporary social theory. His primary research interests are in economic sociology, social theory, and globalization, and his most recent research deals with the development of consumer goods markets in China.

Michael Reed is Professor of Organizational Analysis (Human Resource Management Section) and Associate Dean (Research), Cardiff Business School, Cardiff University, Wales. He has published widely in major international journals and book-length monographs in the areas of organization theory and analysis, expert work and knowledge organizations, public services organization and management, and organizational futures. He is a member of several leading international academic associations, such as the American Academy of Management, the European Group for Organization Studies, the British Sociological Association, and the British Academy of Management (Council Member as from 2004). He is one of the founding editors of the international journal *Organization*, published by Sage.

Alan Scott is Professor of Sociology at the University of Innsbruck, Austria. His research and teaching interests cover political and organizational sociology, and social theory. With respect to organization studies, he is editor of a recent collection on universities and their (regional) external environment, *Bright Satanic Mills* (Ashgate, 2007), and is a board member of the International Sociological Association's RC17, Organizational Sociology. With respect to social theory, he has published on Weber, Durkheim, and Karl Polanyi, and is co-editor and co-translator of Georg Simmel's *Rembrandt* (Routledge, 2005).

David Shulman is Associate Professor of Anthropology and Sociology at Lafayette College. He received his Ph.D. degree from Northwestern University in Sociology in 1997. He has published articles on deception, dramaturgy, and symbolic interactionism. He recently published a book analyzing impression management and lying at work entitled *From Hire to Liar: The Role of Deception in the Workplace* (Cornell University Press, 2007).

Richard Swedberg is Professor of Sociology at Cornell University. His two areas of specialization are economic sociology and social theory. His books include: *The Handbook of Economic Sociology* (edited with Neil Smelser, 1994, 2005), *Max Weber and the Idea of Economic Sociology* (1998), and *Principles of Economic Sociology* (2003). He is currently working on a study of Tocqueville and economics.

Patricia H. Thornton is Adjunct Professor and affiliate of the Center for Entrepreneurship and Innovation at Duke University, Fuqua School of Business and Associate Professor visiting at Stanford University, Department of Sociology. She holds a Ph.D. (1993) in Sociology from Stanford University. Her research and teaching interests are in organization theory, economic sociology, and entrepreneurship. Her research focuses on developing and testing theories on the impact of culture, organization structure, and institutional change on entrepreneurial decisions. She is published in the *American Journal of Sociology*, the *Annual Review of Sociology*, the *Academy of Management Journal*, and *Organization Science*. Her book *Markets from Culture* (2004) chronicles her cumulative research program on institutional logics and organization decisions.

Pamela S. Tolbert is Professor and chair of the Department of Organizational Behavior in the School of Industrial Relations at Cornell University. She came to the ILR School after receiving her Ph.D. in sociology from UCLA. She is broadly interested in processes of organizational change, the role of organizations in social stratification, and the impact of occupations on organizational structures. Her current research includes studies of the use of tenure systems by higher education organizations, the effects of social movements on organizational foundings and failures, sources of variations in the organizational features of hedge funds, and the effects of earnings differences within dual-career couples on spousal relationships.

Andrew H. Van de Ven is Vernon H. Heath Professor of Organizational Innovation and Change in the Carlson School of Management of the University of Minnesota. He received his Ph.D. from the University of Wisconsin, Madison in 1972, and taught at the Wharton School of the University of Pennsylvania before his present appointment. He is author of several books including *The Innovation Journey* (1999) and *Engaged Scholarship: A Guide for Organizational and Social Research* (2007). Van de Ven was 2000–2001 President of the Academy of Management.

Ad van Iterson is Associate Professor of Organization Studies at Maastricht University, The Netherlands. He graduated in sociology at the University of Amsterdam, after which he received his Ph.D. with a thesis on the early factory system. Currently, he mainly publishes on micro-sociological processes in organizations, such as gossip and cynicism, as manifestations of wider (de)civilizing trends: e.g. van

Iterson et al. (eds.), *The Civilized Organization: Norbert Elias and the Future of Organization Studies* (2002). He also writes novels and columns.

Mayer N. Zald is Professor of Sociology, Social Work, and Business Administration (emeritus) at the University of Michigan. He has published more than fifty articles and written or edited eighteen books. He has published on many topics, including sociology of social welfare, political sociology, social movements, and complex organizations. In 2005, he edited (with Gerald Davis, W. Richard Scott, and Doug McAdam) a volume of essays on the relationship of social movement theory to organizational theory and research (Cambridge University Press). Currently, he is continuing his work on complex organizations and social movements and is also working on a long-term project to more adequately link social science to the humanities. He is a member of the American Academy of Arts and Sciences and a three-time Fellow of the Center for the Advancement of the Behavioral Sciences.

PART I

THE ROLES OF THE CLASSICS

CHAPTER 1

INTRODUCTION

A SOCIAL SCIENCE WHICH FORGETS ITS FOUNDERS IS LOST

PAUL S. ADLER

Organizations have deep and pervasive effects on our lives at work and beyond. The previous century witnessed a massive transformation of advanced capitalist societies: whereas families and neighborhoods once constituted the basis of society, now large organizations play a pivotal role in every sphere (Perrow 1991). And the most recent decades have witnessed further, equally profound and disconcerting changes in this landscape. The aim of the present volume is to help scholars in organization studies better understand these changes. In particular, we highlight the enduring value of some of the older work in this field.

The field of organization studies has become well established in both sociology departments and professional schools, most notably in business schools. However, in the course of this institutionalization, the field has progressively lost contact with its founding writers. To some, this represents a welcome sign of maturation: they might quote Alfred North Whitehead: 'A science which hesitates to forget its founders is lost' (Whitehead 1916 413). Whitehead, however, was writing about the natural sciences, and the premise of this volume is that the social sciences are in this specific respect quite different, because in our field founders continue to play a crucial role. We have thus reversed Whitehead's warning as the clarion call for this volume.

Without minimizing the potential contribution of more recent scholarship or the value of earlier scholarship that has been less celebrated, we believe that these classics present unusually rich resources for research today. Most notably, these writers all struggled to make sense of the momentous social changes of their times. In contrast, organization studies today focuses too little on the big issues of our own times and too much on the narrower concerns of academic peers. The classics, this volume argues, serve both as a source of specific insights and also as encouragement to lift and broaden our aspirations.

Alongside some thematic chapters, this volume includes contributions on each of several classic authors. Each chapter addresses the author's ideas and his or her context, the impact of these ideas on the field of organization studies so far, and the potential future research these ideas might inspire. The goal is not reverential exegesis, but rather to examine how these classics can enrich and enliven organizational research—how they can help us make better sense of the social changes currently under way, and perhaps equip us to act more intelligently in our efforts to participate in those changes.

This Introduction first explains why organization studies should reconnect with these classics, and then provides a thumbnail sketch of each of the contributions to this Handbook.

Why Read the Classics?

Organization studies is an interdisciplinary field, bringing together sociology, psychology, economics, political science, as well as other disciplines. The present volume focuses on sociology. Sociology was foundational in shaping the field in its earliest years and has continued to be an important influence. The sociological lens affords unusual depth of insight into the technological, economic, cultural, and political forces that shape organizations both from within and without.

Notwithstanding its interdisciplinary constitution, organization studies suffers from increasing intellectual insularity. Research in organization studies refers increasingly to the field's own journals and less and less to journals in sociology or the other contributing disciplines (Augier, March, and Sullivan 2005). Organization studies is increasingly cut off not only from contemporary sociological research but also from sociology's classics. Statistical analysis of the works cited in articles published in the major journals of sociology and organization studies shows that, on the one hand, the absolute number of citations to the classics (specifically, those classic authors addressed in this volume, taken as a group) has continued at much the same level since the 1950s. At the same time, however, there has been an increase in both the average number of articles published each year and the average number of citations per article. The net result is that the number of citations to classics as a proportion of all citations has fallen dramatically—to below 2 percent in the most recent period (Kennedy and Adler 2007). Moreover, many of these citations are merely ceremonial (Lounsbury and Carberry 2005).

This trend bodes badly for the intellectual development of organization studies. As Jeffrey Alexander (1987), Art Stinchcombe (1982), and others have argued, social sciences—as distinct from natural sciences—are considerably enriched by rereadings of their classics. There are, of course, many sociologists who argue that their discipline should take the form of a natural science and forget its founders. This aspiration goes back to some of these very same founders of the discipline: it can be traced from Comte through the work of Weber and Durkheim; it was given particularly sharp form in a famous essay by Merton (1967); and it has continued to inspire the 'positivist' wing of sociology, for whom the progress of sociological knowledge should rely on the accumulation of empirical, factual findings. According to this positivist view, theory should follow from facts, not precede them, and as a result, more recent theory should replace older theories, and there should be as little space for Marx, Weber, and Durkheim in contemporary sociology textbooks as there is for Ptolemy or Copernicus in contemporary astronomy textbooks.

However, this positivism has been increasingly challenged by a cluster of post-positivist ideas inspired by Kuhn's (1970) history of science and a variety of movements in philosophy and social theory. Kuhn and subsequent historical and philosophical research showed that natural sciences too relied on prior non-empirical, theoretical commitments, even if it was only in periods of deep paradigm conflict that these commitments emerged as directly relevant to scientific debate. In the social sciences, unlike the natural sciences, such paradigm conflict is endemic: social sciences cannot escape the perennial value-laden debates over human nature, its role in behavior, and the nature of social order. The nature of their subject matter thus ensures that the social sciences lie somewhere between the natural sciences and the humanities as regards the relative value of the latest research versus the classics (as argued by Alexander 1987, 2001). Classics serve crucial functions for social sciences: as noted by Alexander, they function as signifiers, allowing us to refer parsimoniously to whole world-views articulated in the works of the major classic thinkers; and more substantively, they continue to inspire new theoretical and empirical research because they encapsulate what were and remain unusually deep and compelling insights into human nature and social order.

Some sociologists hesitate to abandon positivism, fearing that this would mean also abandoning any hope of accumulating real knowledge and obliging us to embrace instead some variant of social constructivist relativism. Kuhn too struggled with this challenge in his analysis of the natural sciences, a field where the reality of progress in our understanding is difficult to deny. However, it is not all that difficult to square this circle once we remind ourselves that all the competing paradigms in sociology take as a key goal to make sense of empirical features of the social world. None of them can claim the kind of success in that effort that we sometimes see in the history of natural sciences, where the success of one paradigm relegates the others to the dustbin of defeated doctrines; but competition within and between paradigms revolves largely around claims to greater success in rendering intelligible the empirical world. The competitive fortunes of different paradigms wax and wane; but for the field as a whole, the result of this process is real progress in understanding.

Why Now?

The contributors to this volume share a concern that organization studies reconnect with broader social issues. Since ours is a society of organizations, many of these big issues are directly organizational, as evidenced by the headlines of the daily news: globalization, outsourcing, the pressure of financial markets on industrial firms, new technologies that make obsolete old organizations, the fate of the individual, the possibility of collective agency in the face of massive systemic forces of change, and so on.

The discrepancy between this list and the list of topics in recent organization studies research is both saddening and troubling. Saddening, because it represents a narrowing of scope, ambition, and concern compared to the founders of the field. Troubling, because this narrowing saps the vitality of the field. A field that turns away from relevance when its ostensible subject matter is undergoing such massive turbulence is a field that risks losing any credibility (Walsh, Meyer, and Schoonhoven 2006; Clegg 2006). Moreover, it risks losing its 'franchise', its legitimacy as a key discipline in the broader public's effort to make sense of these changes. Organization studies competes with other disciplines, most notably economics, when various publics and policy makers reach for frameworks that help them make sense of social and economic issues, and it does not bode well for either the cogency of these public debates nor the future of the field if organization studies abandons these policy terrains.

It is striking that the sociology classics so directly addressed so many of the urgent social issues of their day. This real-world relevance surely explains much of their enduring appeal. In contrast, organization studies has moved in recent decades towards 'incremental, footnote-on-footnote research as the norm for the field' (Daft and Lewin 1990). In part, of course, the contrast between the classics and the field's present condition is a function of the increasing 'professionalization' of research. The world of research today is so very different from that of Marx's,

Weber's, or even Parsons's time, with the quasi-universality of employment in universities, standardization and specialization of training, formalized standards for promotion and tenure, and the elevation of the craft of academic journal article writing into an esoteric art. The way forward for our field is not to retreat from professionalism to amateurism; but we do need a richer form of professionalism, one that does not turn its back on academic rigor, but brings this rigor to bear on the burning issues of our time.

What is at stake in the present volume is not the ongoing debate about our immediate audience. Recently, we have heard calls for the 'public sociology' advocated by Burawoy (2004) or the 'engaged scholarship' advocated by Van de Ven (2007). These are very legitimate in our view; but here we address a distinct, underlying concern: whether in our academic scholarship we are engaging the big social changes of our times, even if we do it in our own ways and forums. Our engagement in public debate adds little if it is not informed by rigorous research on appropriately focused research topics.

Daft and Lewin (1990) suggested several ways for organization studies to break out of the 'normal science straitjacket', in particular that we focus on organization design as a practical task, focus on more equivocal problems, and experiment with heretical research methods. To this list, we add another, arguably more fundamental strategy: reread our field's classics. These provide us not only with paradigms for rigorous engagement with big issues but also with powerful concepts for making sense of these kinds of issues.

An Overview

The body of this Handbook aims to give the reader a sense of what might be learned when we take inspiration from these classics. The volume is organized into two main sections—focused respectively on European and American writers—followed by an Afterword. Within each section, chapters have been sequenced so that the classics discussed are in approximately chronological order. The chapters are standalone contributions, and readers should pick their own path among them. The following paragraphs summarize the main ideas in each of the chapters.

In Chapter 2, Patricia Thornton discusses the value of the classics in developing compelling arguments. Thornton returns to Stinchcombe's (1982) six functions of the classics: touchstones, developmental tasks, intellectual small coinage, fundamental ideas, routine science, and rituals. She illustrates these functions with three mini-cases that show the important roles played by the classics in the development of research streams in organization studies. In particular, the mini-cases outline how the theoretical constructs of disruptive technologies, institutional logics, and status-based markets—three wellsprings for vibrant research and teaching communities—descend from the classics. The mini-cases suggest that students should use the classics to guide the development of compelling arguments in the study of contemporary research problems and the systematic accumulation of knowledge.

In Chapter 3, Richard Swedberg presents Tocqueville as one of the first—possibly the very first—social scientists of any stature to be fully aware of organizations. In Tocqueville's work, especially in *Democracy in America*, the reader finds an elaborate analysis of different types of organizations—economic, political, and voluntary. Tocqueville emphasized the implications of the fact that organizations were composed of people coming together for the purpose of realizing some common goal. This fit well with Tocqueville's personal philosophy of freedom, where organizations were a means towards this end.

In Chapter 4, I address the relevance of Marx to organization studies today. This chapter takes the reader back to the core ideas of Marx and discusses the way they have informed an important stream of work in organization studies. The chapter offers a tutorial on Marx's basic theory and highlights the tension between two readings of Marx, an older, almost forgotten reading that I dub 'paleo-Marxist' and a more recent, 'neo-Marxist' reading. While the latter focuses on class struggle as the motor of history, the former argues that the direction of history—and the forms and vectors of class struggle—are determined by a deeper structural contradiction between the trend towards 'socialization' of the forces of production and the persistence of capitalist relations of production that enshrine private ownership of productive resources. This debate offers fruitful resources for making sense of both the endemic conflictuality of capitalist society and the changes within organizations that might facilitate a transition beyond this form of society. The chapter traces the implications of the Marxist view, in both its variants and in contrast with other theories, for several broad domains of organizational research both within the individual organization and in broader organizational fields.

In Chapter 5, Richard Marens offers a second perspective on Marx's influence. First, Marens broadens his scope to include a wider range of scholars who have been inspired by Marx but are less orthodox—Marxians, rather than formally Marxists—and second, he broadens the focus to address several different time horizons in capitalism's development. Marens argues that Marxian political economy offers a powerful remedy to a blindness increasingly acknowledged by contemporary organization scholars: if the 'environment' is so crucial to the structure and function of organizations, organization studies needs (1) a rich characterization of the structure of that environment and its evolution over time, and (2) an account of how organizations can act to transform that environment. Marxian theory, he shows, can enrich several streams of organizational research by addressing these two gaps.

In Chapter 6, Stewart Clegg and Michael Lounsbury lament the limited use of Max Weber's ideas in organization studies. In contrast to the more suffocating conceptualization of culture proffered by leading neoinstitutional scholars promoting an 'iron cage' imagery via Weber, Clegg and Lounsbury argue that a deeper reading of Weber provides a more nuanced understanding of culture, one that appreciates that culture is often contested and impregnated with power and domination. Revisiting Weber's well-known arguments about bureaucracy, they show that he viewed bureaucracies as culturally diverse and as sites of conflict among different forms of rationalities. In this new perspective, the 'iron cage' appears as more porous, opening up opportunities for new lines of inquiry and multilevel analysis, enriching connections to a broader sociological imagination. Clegg and Lounsbury emphasize that this imagery of a 'sintered' iron cage can be especially helpful in understanding new emergent logics of organizing such as those related to post-bureaucratic forms and associated new technologies that increase surveillance and rationalization beyond traditional bureaucratic incarnations.

In Chapter 7, Paul du Gay offers a second perspective on Weber. He highlights a crucial ethical value criterion of Weber's sociology, one that has been largely neglected by scholars of organization: *Lebensführung*, the conduct of life. Du Gay argues that Weber's analysis is marked by concern for the survival of particular forms of 'character' or 'personality' whose life conduct unites practical rationality with ethical seriousness. Against the image of Weber as a grand theorist of the instrumental rationalization of modern life, du Gay cites a growing body of work emanating from the humanities and social sciences, which paints Weber as a historical anthropologist greatly concerned with the ethics of office. In particular, he argues that Weber's analysis remains a key resource for scholars trying to understand contemporary developments in the reformation of organizational life and identity in the public sector, and in the institutions of government. Du Gay underscores the importance of a particular bureaucratic persona to the production of responsible government and highlights the risk that shifts to more flexible, 'post-bureaucratic' organizational forms pose to the practices of responsible government.

In Chapter 8, Pamela Tolbert and Shon Hiatt bring together Robert Michels's classic analysis of power in political parties and Berle and Means's landmark study of the public corporation. Although they focus on very different types of organizations, these works are linked by a common concern with the general problem of organizational leaders' propensity to exploit decision-making power for their own private interests, and thus to govern in ways that are contrary to the stated goals of the organization. This essay explicates the link between Michels's analysis of conditions that give rise to the formation of oligarchies in organizations and the analysis by Berle and Means of problems created by the separation of ownership and control in modern business firms. Reviewing Michels's arguments and synthesizing findings from research based on parties, unions, producer cooperatives, and social movement organizations, Tolbert and Hiatt create a new lens for making sense of some of the contemporary problems of governance in modern corporations.

In Chapter 9, Frank Dobbin discusses Émile Durkheim and focuses on his masterpiece, *The Elementary Forms of Religious Life*. Durkheim's thesis here was that humans are driven to understand the world through collective classification and meaning-making. This idea informed an important current of post-World War II sociologists of knowledge and organizational sociologists, most notably Erving Goffman, Peter Berger and Thomas Luckmann, Mary Douglas, and also influenced James March and Herbert Simon. Since then, Durkheim's influence on organizational sociology has been mainly via neoinstitutionalism and second-generation power theory. This current attacks the rationalist assumption that the modern scientific-rational world is fundamentally different from the spiritual and religious worlds that preceded it: both religious and scientific-rational social systems are collectively constructed. Durkheim is thus an enduring stimulus challenging organizational scholars to step back from the rationalized practices of the modern firm and to ask how we come to believe those practices to be rational. Durkheim noticed that within primitive societies, there were myriad different ways of making sense of the world: the totem could be just about anything. For much of the twentieth century, organizational theorists were expecting organizations, both within and across societies, to converge on a single model. The most advanced organizations seemed to show the way to the future for less advanced organizations, just as, we thought, the most advanced societies showed the way to the future for less advanced societies. But organizational sociologists have come, like Durkheim, to see that organizations can take different forms in different rationalized societies. Durkheim's work is relevant today for our understanding of how rationalized societies arrive at different rationalized forms of organization, which worship different modern totems, whether bureaucracy, the market, the network, the profession, or the business group.

In Chapter 10, Paul Hirsch, Peer Fiss, and Amanda Hoel-Green argue that Émile Durkheim's insights from *The Division of Labor in Society* can be extended to inform our understanding of the current shift from the nation to the globalized economy. While Durkheim emphasized the potential for material and social progress resulting from greater economic differentiation, he also cautioned against the threat of social instability and disorder ('anomie') that would occur in the absence of a meaningful integration in the economic system. This chapter argues that similar issues arise in the expansion of economic and cultural exchanges to a more global scale. After discussing the central concepts of mechanical/organic solidarity and moral/material density that underlie Durkheim's theory of modernization, the authors review Durkheim's influence on organization studies and argue that the fundamental question of social solidarity has disappeared from current research in organization studies. In response, the chapter offers a call for future empirical analyses and suggests five areas in which the role of solidarity might fruitfully be explored, including topics such as the rise of outsourcing and the emergence of international institutions that regulate trade.

In Chapter 11, Barbara Czarniawska discusses the work of Gabriel Tarde—an intellectual rival of Émile Durkheim and, judging from many contemporaneous accounts, the more prominent of the pair. Translated into many languages and well known to earlier generations of scholars in social psychology and sociology of law, his work was forgotten by the early 1970s. However, there has recently been a resurgence of interest in Tarde's work: his ideas seem to fit our postmodern times. In Tarde's view, all human inventions arise in individual minds, and they are then imitated, binding individuals who imitate one another. Invention and imitation are thus the crucial movers of social life. Tarde used Leibniz's ideas to introduce a cosmology of monads equipped with desires and beliefs, which allowed him to explain individuality and sociality without invoking entities such as 'society'. He emphasized difference rather than identity and attributed a central role to the phenomenon of fashion and the processes of communication.

In Chapter 12, Alan Scott discusses the legacy of Georg Simmel. Despite the revival in Simmel's reputation in social theory, he does not enjoy the kind of influence on organization studies of his contemporary Max Weber. So far, Simmel's main presence has been via network sociology's analysis of brokerage and dyadic/triadic relations. Scott, however, argues that Simmel's central concern was freedom rather than advantage. He also argues that the anti-mechanistic and anti-rationalist principles underlying Simmel's social theory can be translated into a cultural approach to organization. The emphasis here is not on rational actions and plans, but upon how the basic principles that underlie a human community (e.g. an organization) unfold in ways that often subvert the actors' aims and, in the longer run, can undermine the community/organization. Scott shows how Simmel's analysis can help us understand why 'high commitment' organizations present a threat to the sociological conditions supporting a liberal society.

In Chapter 13, Rosabeth Moss Kanter and Rakesh Khurana extend the discussion of Simmel, arguing that Georg Simmel could provide more helpful guidance for understanding complex organizations in the new global information society of the future than better-known classic theorists who helped deconstruct the shift to an industrial era a century ago. The strength of Simmel's approach, the authors contend, is that it points to objective forms and structures that shape actions and outcomes independent of the particular personalities in a social situation, while also recognizing the subjective and emotional nature of social life. The size and complexity of social groupings make a meaningful difference in predictable and reliable ways. Kanter and Khurana examine the implications of size in creating differentiation inside organizations, and the implications for coordination, subordinate–superior relations, and solidarity. They argue, for example, that in large organizations, leadership can channel differentiation productively by creating a broader context in which individual interests are directed in ways that lead to more scope for the development of individuality while accomplishing collectively meaningful goals. Finally, the authors highlight Simmel's prescient treatment of roles such as the 'stranger' and behaviors such as 'secrecy' and show how these concepts emerge as factors in the new twenty-first-century information society. At a time when sociology is grasping for concepts and constructs that help make sense of our post-industrial economy, Kanter and Khurana suggest that Simmel offers a fruitful starting point, in both method and concepts.

Chapter 14 by Markus Becker and Thorbjørn Knudsen discusses Schumpeter and in particular the relevance of his early work on entrepreneurship. Schumpeter offered three major ideas on this topic. First, he defined entrepreneurship as creating new combinations of productive factors. This idea not only captures product or process innovation but also the way inputs, products, processes, and market choices are combined to produce an overall system, often referred to as an industry architecture. Elaborating on the principles governing the (in)stability in industry architectures is a promising avenue for contemporary research. Second, he identified behavioral and cognitive characteristics that stimulate individuals to engage in entrepreneurship: these can be inborn or culturally transmitted. This suggests that an organization can adjust its overall capacity for entrepreneurship by its selection policies, its internal structural arrangements, its training and socialization efforts, and its incentives structure. Third, he considered how organizations can stimulate entrepreneurship by structuring the interaction of individuals who have different motivations and triggers for entrepreneurial behavior. Most notably, entrepreneurship can be stimulated by direct interaction among kindred people, as often happens in the R & D department, or by delegating decision rights to lower levels in the organization. In an era such as ours in which entrepreneurship figures so largely in the discourse on growth, Schumpeter's insights are precious indeed.

In Chapter 15, Ad van Iterson assesses the importance of Norbert Elias's theory of the civilizing process. Elias identified a long-term trend in West European societies towards a refinement of social behavior. In his magnum opus, *The Civilizing Process*, he analyzes the formation of the French absolutist state with its concomitant changes in social relations, conduct, and *habitus*. The key vector of change identified by Elias is the psychological internalization of the constraints that accompanied increasing social interdependence: a shift 'from external constraints to self-constraints'. When brought into the context of contemporary work organizations, Elias's approach is rich in implications for the behavioral and emotional aspects of trends towards empowerment, teleworking, the 24-hour working day, despecialization, and multitasking.

The second group of chapters shifts from a European to a North American frame. In Chapter 16, Gary Hamilton and Misha Petrovic discuss Thorstein Veblen. While Veblen is generally recognized today as a founder of and the main influence in the Institutionalist school in American economics, and while his ideas continue to influence the fields of industrial organization and development studies, the reception of Veblen's work in mainstream economics has ranged from hostility to indifference. Hamilton and Petrovic claim that Veblen's work contains important elements for building an institutionalist, historically oriented theory of the contemporary global economy. They argue that Veblen's insights are even more relevant today than in his time, in particular as concerns: (1) the importance of analyzing firms as both producers of goods and services (industrial arts and craftsmanship) and market makers (business strategies and salesmanship), and the continuing organizational tension between these two types of activity; (2) the significance of consumer goods markets for driving contemporary capitalism, of the firms that make and organize those markets, and of the concomitant changes in consumption patterns; and (3) the need to revise economic and sociological theories of capitalism and business enterprise towards Veblen's developmental conception of cumulative causation, and away from approaches that rely on equilibrium or productionist assumptions.

In Chapter 17, Stella Nkomo argues while race has always been present in organizations, it has never been adequately theorized in organization studies. She reviews the classical works of W. E. B. Du Bois on race, mostly ignored by his contemporaries, to provide insights into the sociology of race that will assist organizational scholars in theorizing and interrogating race in organizations at a deeper level within the complex contours of today's global racial context. While rooted in the momentous changes taking place within the post-Civil War Reconstruction period in the United States, Du Bois's work evolved over several decades to illuminate race's inextricable relationship to the economic and social processes of global capitalism. Racially based social structures of inequality and exclusion persist today not only in the United States but globally—despite the sentiment that we are now in a post-race era. Nkomo demonstrates how Du Bois's conceptualization of race debunked essentialist approaches, instead stressing the importance of attending to the structural, political, and historical forces shaping any observed differences in the so-called races. The idea that race cannot be studied outside of the specific historical, geographical, economic, and cultural processes that constitute its meaning is a key idea in Du Bois's work. Nkomo offers an in-depth discussion of Du Boisian concepts and explores their implications for the study of race in organizations.

In Chapter 18, Andrew Abbott discusses the research on organizations conducted by early Chicago sociologists. He argues that these studies make a powerful case against seeing the social world as a world of organizations, and for instead seeing organizations as an epiphenomenon of underlying social processes. Historically, organizations themselves appear as objects of sociological analysis only in a world that assumes the centrality of large, stable bureaucratic structures—a period that Abbott suggests starts about 1925 but ends around 1975. Since then, we have returned to an organizational world of rapid changes in organization boundaries, and these boundaries become increasingly blurred and ambiguous. Our world is now, as it was in the early years of the twentieth century, a world of processes rather than structures. The Chicago School studies of that earlier period provide a starting point for grappling with the nature of this world.

In Chapter 19, Arne Carlsen discusses the legacy of William James, arguing that James's work represents a resource for a radically novel understanding of identity dynamics in organizations. Organizational identity theory has been predominantly focused on what James called the 'self-as-object', and Carlsen suggests that there is much to be gained from following James in a shift towards the agentic 'self-as-subject' conceived as a collective authoring process situated in ongoing experience. Following James's path has the advantage of connecting identity to the dynamics of practice. Locating practice as the site for authoring of identity helps us to see not only the habitual dimension of identity but also the role of jolts in experience and novelty as seeds of human growth. A turn towards agency allows us to see the forward-looking motives at play in identity construction, motives that form the basis for people's engagement in social change.

In Chapter 20, Michael Cohen discusses the contribution of John Dewey and the importance of his emphasis on the human faculties of habit and emotion. These concerns contrast with the emphasis in recent decades on cognitive processes. In contemporary organizational research there has been an increasing interest in recurring action patterns, such as routines and practices. The conceptual difficulties this work has encountered are usefully illuminated by Dewey's view of the primacy of habit and its interplay with emotion and cognition. It has been all too easy for our theoretical discussions to fall into one or more of fours traps: assuming that routines are rigid in their execution, that they are necessarily mundane in content, that they are typically isolated from thought and feeling, and/or that their underlying action patterns are explicitly stored somewhere. Dewey seems to have worked out in the early 1900s a philosophical position grounded in the primacy of learning and habit that (1) makes each one of these presumptions appear quite unnatural, and (2) suggests why we so frequently fall into them. In our own time many organizations find themselves centrally engaged with changing or improving systems of routine. Efforts to increase the agility of manufacturing processes or reduce the accidental death rate of hospital patients confront organizations squarely with the properties of routinized activity and the dynamics of routines that facilitate and resist change. A better understanding of routine—one grounded in Dewey's analysis of habit, emotion, and decision-making—improves our ability to make these vital changes.

In Chapter 21, Christopher Ansell discusses the work of Mary Parker Follett. An early twentieth-century management theorist, social worker, and political scientist, Follett's ideas about power and authority have been widely influential in organization studies. Yet despite her reputation as a 'prophetic' management theorist, the wider significance of her work is often underappreciated. This chapter argues that one way to gain a greater appreciation for Follett's work and its contemporary significance is to analyze its ontological commitments. Ansell points out that Follett was perhaps the most philosophical of our classical organization theorists and she translated this *Weltanschauung* into a systemic approach to organization. Although strongly influenced by German and British idealism, Follett's most significant works sought to reconcile this idealism with American pragmatism. In fact, her work on organization, education, and democracy is often mentioned in conjunction with the work of her contemporary, the pragmatist philosopher John Dewey. Acknowledging the centrality of power and conflict in organizations, Follett used her idealist pragmatism to explore possibilities for fruitful social cooperation. The central concept of her work was integration, which she famously contrasted with compromise. Whether analyzing the conflict between management and labor or the power of a supervisor over a worker, Follett believed that fruitful social cooperation required a creative integration of different perspectives and interests. In exploring the implications of integration for conflict, control, coordination, communication, and command, Follett's idealist pragmatism created a systematic theoretical framework for understanding non-hierarchical organization—an ideal increasingly salient in the contemporary world.

In Chapter 22, Tim Hallett, David Shulman, and Gary Alan Fine examine classical symbolic interactionist thinkers and their relevance for contemporary organizational studies. They assess founding figures, such as George Herbert Mead, the mid-century contributions of Herbert Blumer and Everett Hughes, and conclude with the later contributions of Erving Goffman, Anselm Strauss, and Howard Becker. The interactionist credo emphasizes that organizations are comprised of people, and that their interpretations of work activities matter because people act and pursue organizational goals based on those interpretations. Hallett, Shulman, and Fine argue that the 'peopled' approach of classic interactionism provides an important contrast to the 'metaphysical pathos' that has plagued some strands of organizational studies. Instead of emphasizing disembodied forces, the authors use classic interactionist work to stress that organizations and institutions are inhabited by people doing things together, and these doings suffuse organizations with meaning and significance.

In Chapter 23, Andrew Van de Ven and Arik Lifschitz review the seminal work of John R. Commons, a founder of institutional economics and industrial relations. They identify four main features of his work of relevance to contemporary organization studies. First, Commons introduced a novel and pragmatic theory of institutional design and change that anticipated much later theorizations of the relationships between action and structure at both individual and collective levels. Second, he viewed institutional change as a social movement. His history of labor unionization and monopoly busting showed how institutional rules are created to address disputes and injustices among conflicting parties with unequal power and diverse interests. Third, Commons replaced natural selection with artificial, purposeful selection, providing us with a powerful reason why we should turn contemporary organizational ecology theory on its head. Finally, Commons introduced the collective standard of prudent reasonable behavior, which is a major alternative theory of valuation to those based on individual rational self-interests and random environmental events. Commons emphasized that solutions to conflicts among parties cannot be based on individual standards of rational self-interest, for that would produce unjust solutions favoring the more powerful parties.

In Chapter 24, Elisabeth Clemens discusses an interesting anomaly: the absence of a classic response to the emergence of the large corporation. The rise of the large corporation fundamentally challenged the foundations of liberalism, with its commitment to a world of rights-bearing individuals embedded in a market society of small enterprises. Yet, despite this opportunity to address a major social change, some of the most important works of political economy of this period—notably Karl Polanyi's *The Great Transformation* and Friedrich Hayek's *The Road to Serfdom*—did not see the corporation. Other legal theorists and commentators did recognize the novelty of the large firm, but then sought to reassure readers that these potentially threatening developments would be counterbalanced by the moral qualities of business leaders, the decentralization of power within the firm, and the application of due process to employment relationships. Thus, the tension between the modern corporation and a political theory premised on the rights of natural individuals was not fully explored. The problem of the large organization and liberalism was left as a classic waiting to happen.

In Chapter 25, Micheal Reed discusses post-World War II bureaucratic theory as developed by Selznick, Gouldner, Blau, and Crozier. Reed revisits these modern classics in order to rediscover the strategic sociological, political, and ethical issues that framed the socio-historical context in which they emerged. He identifies the cycle of 'imaginative reformulations' that these modern classics have undergone over recent decades. His main thesis is that these works still inspire new insights into recurring themes or dilemmas such as agency/structure, power/control, and statics/dynamics. He also identifies the theme of changing and contested forms of organizational governance and control as an issue that would come to dominate public, as well as academic, debate in late twentieth- and early twenty-first-century advanced capitalist societies.

In Chapter 26, Heather Haveman offers a second perspective on post-World War II bureaucratic theory, focusing on Robert Merton and his two students, Alvin Gouldner and Peter Blau. The work of Merton and his students was rooted in Weberian ideas about bureaucracy but moved in directions that Weber might not have expected. Rather than focusing on the technical rationality inherent in bureaucracy as celebrated by Weber, these researchers studied the unanticipated consequences of organizational design; in particular, the dysfunctions of bureaucracy that arise from goal displacement. They highlighted conflicts that ensued both within organizations and between organizations and their surroundings. They saw organizations as the crucible of institutionalization: organizations became valued in and of themselves, far beyond the technical merits of the things they do. A close reading of three pieces in this tradition—Merton's essay on bureaucratic dysfunctions, Gouldner's *Patterns of Industrial Bureaucracy*, and Blau's *Dynamics of Bureaucracy*—reveals many insights that can benefit organizational scholars today, notably the reminder that although organizations may be designed as tools, they inevitably take on lives of their own.

In Chapter 27, Charles Heckscher argues that Talcott Parsons's action paradigm remains the most successful analytic framework for understanding fundamental sociological concepts of trust and commitment within a voluntarist perspective. Parsons specifies the various orientations that are needed to sustain successful social systems, especially ones that are highly complex and differentiated and allow individual choice. The chapter tries to show the continuing utility of the model by applying it to the development of complex relations of influence in knowledge-based business firms, which have increasingly moved beyond bureaucratic orientations describe by Weber to more complex collaborative norms. A central example is the problem of articulation of teams based on collegial influence with the hierarchical structures of power. The Parsonian framework enables us to identify systematically a series of problems posed by this development and to understand some of the constraints that shape potential solutions.

In their Afterword, Gerald Davis and Mayer Zald—taking their cue from Stinchcombe's piece on the functions of classics in sociology—comment on the functions of a book *about* the classics of sociology and what scholars can hope to take away from this volume. The canon of 'classics' is contested terrain in sociology and other disciplines, with certain authors (e.g. Marx, Parsons) being included or excluded according to the intellectual, social, and political environment and the approved forms of rhetoric holding sway at the time. For example, Tarde disappeared for many years then reappeared with shifts in interests and tastes; Simmel found a rebirth thanks to the prevalence of network analysis. Davis and Zald further argue that the classics considered in this volume offer particular relevance to contemporary scholars seeking guidance on how to theorize large-scale economic transformation. Many of the authors considered here grappled with the birth of a 'society of organizations' and thus can help our own efforts to understand new forms of globalized post-industrial capitalism.

Why These Classics?

Our selection of classics has been guided above all by the contributors' sense of whom our field might learn most from today. However, as Davis and Zald remind us, any selection of a group of writers as 'classics' is a gesture fraught with symbolic and political weight. Readers of this volume may contest the inclusion of some writers whose contributions to the future of the field seem too slight and whose presence perhaps reflects idiosyncratic, personal, or passing enthusiasms. Conversely, there are no doubt writers of great value whom we have excluded. There are clearly writers—Smith, Spencer, Sorokin, and Schutz, just to focus on four alphabetically related names—who warrant attention but who are not discussed here for merely practical reasons. The small number of women and non-European/American writers reflects in part their exclusion from the field in the past but perhaps also reflects prejudices that still mask their potential contribution. Given these risks, we hesitated to use the term 'classics' in the title of the volume: our intention is not to create a canon, merely to prompt new readings.

References

Alexander, J. C. (1987). 'The Centrality of the Classics', in A. Giddens and J. Turner (eds.), *Social Theory Today*. Stanford, Calif.: Stanford University Press.

—— (2001). 'Editor's Introduction: Canons, Discourses, and Research Programs: Plurality, Progress and Competition in Classical, Modern and Contemporary Sociology', in J. C. Alexander (ed.), *Mainstream and Critical Social Theory: Classical, Modern and Contemporary*. London: Sage.

Augier, M., March, J. G., and Sullivan, B. N. (2005). 'Notes on the Evolution of a Research Community: Organization Studies in Anglophone North America, 1945–2000'. *Organization Science*, 16/1: 85–95.

Burawoy, M. (2004). 'Public Sociologies: Contradictions, Dilemmas and Possibilities'. *Social Forces*, 82/4: 1603–18.

Clegg, S. R. (2006). 'Why is Organization Theory So Ignorant?' *Journal of Management Inquiry*, 15/4: 426–43.

Daft, R. L., and Lewin, A. Y. (1990). 'Can Organization Studies Begin to Break Out of the Normal Science Straitjacket? An Editorial Essay'. *Organization Science*, 1/1: 1–9.

Kennedy, M. T., and Adler, P. S. (2007). 'What Makes a Classic?' Presentation at conference organized to support the present volume, Wharton, 9–10 August.

Kuhn, T. (1970). *The Structure of Scientific Revolutions*. 2nd edn. Chicago: University of Chicago Press.

Lounsbury, M., and Carberry, E. J. (2005). 'From King to Court Jester? Weber's Fall from Grace in Organizational Theory'. *Organization Studies*, 26 (April): 501–25.

Merton, R. K. (1967). 'On the History and Systematics of Sociological Theory', in *Social Theory and Social Structure*. New York: Free Press.

Perrow, C. (1991). 'A Society of Organizations'. *Theory and Society*, 20: 725–62.

Stinchcombe, A. (1982). 'Should Sociologists Forget Their Mothers and Fathers?' *American Sociologist*, 17 (February): 2–11.

Van de Ven, A. H. (2007). *Engaged Scholarship: A Guide for Organizational and Social Research*. New York: Oxford University Press.

Walsh, J. P., Meyer, A. D., and Schoonhoven, C. B. (2006). 'A Future for Organization Theory: Living in and Living with Changing Organizations'. *Organization Science*, 17/5: 657–71.

Whitehead, A. N. (1916). 'The Organization of Thought'. *Science*, 22 (September): 409–19.

CHAPTER 2

THE VALUE OF THE CLASSICS

PATRICIA H. THORNTON

A recent review of organizations research submitted for publication reveals an apparent trend towards problem-driven, rather than theory-driven papers. In a sample of eighty-nine papers published in *Administrative Science Quarterly*, Davis and Marquis (2005) report that a mere 11 percent conformed to a theory-testing model in which the research question stemmed from a theory's logic. Davis and Marquis's findings raise the question of whether organizational researchers will continue to develop theory at the rapid rate they did, for example, in the late 1970s and early 1980s. Why should we care—after all, what is wrong with good problem-focused research? One view is that problem-focused research is unlikely to accumulate knowledge (Berger 1993). Without development and testing of theory, scientific progress is at risk of languishing (Kuhn 1962; Stinchcombe 1982).

Exemplary research begins by identifying an empirical observation and examining extant theories that might best explain the empirical observation. It is possible that there is no extant explanation or theory and so such empirical observations are seeds for the development of new theory. Davis and Marquis (2005) suggest that exemplary research should focus on mechanisms, that is the 'cogs and gears or the agency by which an effect is produced'. Their suggestion bears some similarity to Merton's ([1949] 1968) classic statements that eschewed grand or universal theorizing and instead suggested a focus on developing theories of the middle range to advance social science.

In this chapter, I suggest that whatever form new theorizing will take, a good way to conduct such research and for organization and management studies to remain a vital segment of the social sciences is to examine and consider building on the foundations of the classics. To support this argument, I sketch three mini-cases to illustrate how the classics have been used to develop cumulative research programs (Berger 1993).

The cases represent a select sample of publications. The sample highlights both empirical and theoretical research articles, including Tushman and Anderson's (1986) transposition of Schumpeter to frame how technology innovation changes market structure, Podolny's (1993) integration of Merton (1968) and Simmel (1950) to understand how the status order of firms in a market affects their behavior, and Friedland and Alford's (1991) and Thornton and Ocasio's (1999) explication of Weber to outline how institutional logics shape behavior. These articles have been selected because they have won awards, are widely cited, and are published in highly rated scholarly journals. I develop a line of reasoning about how these exemplary articles and their descendants relied on the classics to develop compelling arguments. This reliance can be usefully understood using Stinchcombe's (1982) classification of the six functions of the classics: touchstones, developmental tasks, intellectual small coinage, fundamental ideas, routine science, and rituals.

2.1. Stinchcombe's Functions of the Classics

Stinchcombe (1982: 2) argues that the classics serve six distinct functions. First, the classics are 'touchstones', meaning that they serve as exemplars of good work. They are 'beautiful and possible' approaches to conducting one's scientific work and represent concrete examples of what good work should look like in order to make a contribution to the discipline.

A second function of the classics is to provide 'developmental tasks'. Stinchcombe associates the classics with knowledge making. He says that the classics prompt graduate students to elevate their thinking beyond a descriptive textbook understanding of their fields. This could lead students to ground-breaking, yet continuous pathways for original research. For example, Barley and Kunda's (1992) historical description and explanation of the eras of managerial discourse that cycle between normative and rational ideologies is based on the thinking of the classic scholars who, in describing the problem of industrialization, juxtaposed two contrasting paradigms of social order. These paradigms are given different names by different scholars: Weber wrote of *communal* and *associative*. Durkheim contrasted *mechanistic* and *organic* solidarity. Tonnies spoke of *Gemeinschaft* and *Gesellschaft*. In addition to these theoretical constructs for the contrasting waves of management discourse, Barley and Kunda drew on economic long-wave theorists to explain the factors that cause one era to rise and another to decline in the historical cycle of cultural antinomies. To make sense of their data without these classics, Barley and Kunda would have only a historical description of managerial discourse. They needed an overarching set of concepts and an explanation for change. Otherwise, 'the odds of publishing a paper in a highly visible journal were low, and why bother if you aren't going to be read?' (Barley 2004: 74).

Third, in referring to citations to the classics as 'intellectual small coinage', Stinchcombe (1982) illustrates how the classics are shorthand communication of the theoretical lens and method of analysis that readers can anticipate. The classics, therefore, signal a collection of beliefs and agreements shared by social scientists on how problems are to be understood and empirical facts gathered and interpreted. They are a cognitive heuristic that helps to establish theoretical order and allows the reader to easily take away a memorable gestalt—they facilitate the organization of a large number of facts and empirical findings that otherwise would be lost. This also implies that the choice of a classic selected by researchers may influence what they are likely to see as salient and how they are likely to interpret empirical phenomena (Martin 1992). That is, the same data and questions can produce different answers if different classics provide the 'intellectual small coinage' for the analysis. In my own research, I have experimented with this idea by holding constant the same data set and variables of interest, but varying the clocks in event history models from organizational age to historical time and find different results. Why would this be the case? One explanation is that my experiments emphasize different theoretical lenses and methods and levels of analysis—population ecology and institutional theories.

Alexander (1989) makes a similar argument to Stinchcombe's idea of intellectual small coinage when referring to the classics as providing a common culture of discourse or point of reference for scholars—a function that is particularly important in social science because of the level of disagreement and problems of mutual misunderstanding. Alexander (1989: 27–8) notes that classics reduce complexity by allowing a very small number of works to symbolize or 'represent a stereotyping or standardizing process.... It is for this reason that if we wish to make a critical analysis of capitalism we will more than likely draw on Marx's work'.

Fourth, the classics are sources of 'fundamental ideas'—in Stinchcombe's vernacular classics are the trunks of the trees of knowledge, not the branches and twigs. His point is that if one spends his or her research hours modifying the trunk rather than pruning the twigs then one in all likelihood will make a significant contribution to knowledge accumulation. In this sense, the trunks, that is the classics, are rich in fundamental concepts that can lead to the creation of new ideas (Merton 1965). For example, Ocasio (1994) makes sense of the mechanical 'cogs and gears' of his empirical findings by using Pareto's (1968) and Michels's (1962) classic theories of the circulation of elites to frame and understand the dynamics of positional power in US industrial corporations in his analysis of CEO succession. In this case, note that Ocasio has command of technology and hence methodology that did not exist in the time of Pareto and Michels. Moreover, Ocasio extends the fundamental ideas of these classics by transposing them into a different institutional context to challenge and legitimate an alternative to the prevailing dominant view of power entrenchment (Pfeffer and Salancik 1978). Not only does this make his findings memorable by association with familiar ideas, but it also creatively reconnects and extends the analysis of those ideas in light of current issues of interest to contemporary scholarly communities.

Fifth, the classics also serve a 'routine science' function, meaning that they provide puzzles with import for a number of different situations and applications, thus motivating continuous scientific work. Homans's 1964 address to the American Sociological Association—published as an essay in the *American Sociological Review*, 'Bringing Men Back In'—is exemplary of a classic that has multiplied routine social science. The address was originally written as a critique of the structural–functional school's reign in sociology because the school never produced a theory (explanation) due to its focus on the 'role' (structure) and not the acting individual (agency). Note how Homans identified his argument with the more general and abstract issue of agency and structure in sociological theory giving his address scope, extra import, and a life of its own (Selznick 1957).

Homans's essay continues to engender lively debate and has been artfully used by researchers to take stands and call attention to wayward directions in the growth of research in various subfields: 'Bringing the Firms Back In' in which Baron and Bielby (1980) argue that stratification and inequality research should include how organizations structure work as distinct from prior studies on the structural effects on individual attainment or covariation among industrial/occupational characteristics; 'Bringing the State Back In', in which Skocpol (1985) argues for analytic strategies that view the state as an actor or an institution in the study of a range of topics; 'Bringing Society Back In', in which Friedland and Alford (1991) argue for a way to bring the content of societal institutions into individuals' and organizations' behavior; 'Bringing Entrepreneurship Back In', in which Thornton (1999) argues for the return of the study of entrepreneurship into sociology and organization theory; and 'Bringing the Workers Back In', in which Barley and Kunda (1992) argue that organization theory's effort to make sense of post-bureaucratic organizing is hampered by a dearth of studies of work. Moreover, note Homans's alignment with the more general argument on agency and structure, which continues in contemporary literature such as Sewell's (1992) theory of structure and agency, Emirbayer and Mische's (1998) definitions of agency, Seo and Creed's (2002) analysis of embedded agency in institutional theory, and Thornton's (2004) partitioning of individual from structural effects.

Last, classics serve a 'ritual function' in the sense that they bind together groups of researchers, telling them that they have a common scholarly identity. For example, have you heard a scholar referred to as an institutional theorist, a Marxist, or a conflict theorist? These labels automatically imply an alignment with classic roots, for example Weber, Marx, and Coser, respectively.

2.2. Three Examples of Classics-Inspired Research Streams

This section outlines three mini-cases of different lines of research that are inspired by the classic scholars Schumpeter, Weber, Merton, and Simmel. The work of these scholars is central in defining the metatheory[1] and community of the scholars working in these three streams. First, I will introduce a classic scholar's work. I will then show how this work inspired the researchers to use it as a basis to examine contemporary problems and to theoretically frame their empirical observations. Note that these examples include work that illustrates theory development and testing as well as qualitative and quantitative methodologies. Table 2.1 summarizes the comparative genealogy and succession of fundamental ideas that stemmed from these classic scholars and resulted in memorable ideas with traction in the literature.

2.2.1. Schumpeter and Destructive Technologies

Schumpeter in his classic 1942 book, *Capitalism, Socialism, and Democracy*, theorized capitalism as an agent and a form of economic change by introducing two central ideas. The first concept distinguished inventions from entrepreneurs' innovations. The entrepreneur drives economic change by innovating, not just by developing inventions. More importantly, the entrepreneur creates new consumers, new goods, new methods of production or transportation, new markets, and new forms of industrial organization. The second insight is that the entrepreneur's innovations lead to gales of 'creative destruction' that cause old inventories, ideas, technologies, skills, and equipment to become obsolete. These insights in a sense were a defense of capitalism because it sparked entrepreneurship—they departed from conventional thinking that the prime movers of the economy were changes in the social and natural environment such as general competition, industrial change, even wars and revolutions.

[1] Metatheory is a set of interlocking rules, principles, or narratives that describe and prescribe what is acceptable and unacceptable as theory; it is the means of conceptual exploration in a scientific discipline (Overton 1998).

Table 2.1. Examples of research streams

Classic theorist	Merton and Simmel	Weber	Schumpeter
Contemporary theorist	Podolny 1993	Friedland and Alford 1991 Haveman and Rao 1997 Thornton and Ocasio 1999	Tushman and Anderson 1986
Theoretical construct/ mechanism	Status-based markets	Institutional logics	Competence-enhancing and competence-destroying technology Disruptive technology
Sub-field/paradigm	Network theory	Institutional/organization theories	Entrepreneurship/strategy
Researchers	Stuart, Hoang, and Hybels 1999	For summary, see Thornton and Ocasio 2008	Christensen 1997
Application	Effects of status on market processes in investment banking, venture capital investment, and IPO underwriting	Effects of institutional logics on selection and organizational behavior	Effects of technology on firm strategy and market structure

At the same time, Schumpeter's ideas were not simply about start-ups. He appreciated that large firms might have a competitive advantage in developing new types of organization, such as a large-scale unit of control. In citing the Aluminum Company of America, he defended the power of large firms to innovate in order to create and retain monopoly in light of the ever-present discipline that the threat of innovation provides in the market, making his ideas relevant to the study of both entrepreneurship and intrapreneurship.

The competition that was important was not the mainstream notion of perfect price competition and static supply and demand models—Schumpeter argued these were not an accurate depiction of the real world of business—but instead the competition that the new technology, the new type of organization, or the new supply line created in the old system. Schumpeter thought that competition aimed at the outputs and profits of existing firms had little relevance; instead what is important is the competition that rocks their very foundations and livelihoods. For Schumpeter, capitalism is not a governance system for administering economic and social structures. Instead, capitalism creates a process of industrial mutation in which it destroys old and creates new structures, resulting in continuous progress and improved standards of living for everyone. Schumpeter's powerful theoretical construct of creative destruction explained the dynamics of industrial change—the evolution from a competitive to a monopolistic market and back again.

The power of Schumpeter's construct, creative destruction, has been significant in guiding subsequent research on entrepreneurship, organizational behavior, and market structure in a number of theoretical and applied subfields. Many scholars who have picked up on Schumpeter's ideas are from Harvard University, where, no doubt, Schumpeter left his imprint. I will only outline several benchmarks that are noteworthy in the development of these research streams. In 1986 Mike Tushman and Phil Anderson, building on Abernathy and Clark (1985) and Schumpeter's insights on creative destruction, published a still-influential article comparing the effects of competence-enhancing and competence-destroying innovations in three industries: cement, airlines, and minicomputer manufacturing. Through their historical longitudinal studies, they showed the effects of new technologies on a firm's performance and on a firm's market environment.

Their data suggest that the gradual pace of technological evolution is interrupted by innovations. These innovations cause a discontinuity that increases uncertainty and munificence. The discontinuity can be competence-destroying or competence-enhancing, meaning that the product class is either opened up or consolidated, respectively.

A key insight in this article lies in identifying two distinct types of innovation, those that enhance firm competence and those that destroy firm competence. The former gives the advantage to incumbent firms, and the latter is akin to Schumpeter's notion of creative destruction in which incumbent firms lose position in a market because of the innovation of entrepreneurs and entrepreneurial firms that are typically outsiders. These two types of innovations also have consequences for changing market structure. Competence-enhancing innovation increases entry barriers and decreases market or industry munificence, whereas competence-destroying innovation lowers entry barriers and increases munificence.

In 1992, the idea of creative destruction motivated Philippe Aghion and Peter Howitt to translate Schumpeter's construct into formal mathematical terms in an article, 'A Model of Growth through Creative Destruction'. In 1995, Richard Nolan and David C. Croson published a book entitled *Creative Destruction: A Six Stage Process for Transforming the Organization*. Borrowing Schumpeter's arguments on creative destruction and the role of large firms in innovation, they argued that corporations should downsize to free up slack resources for innovation to create competitive advantage.

Starting from a teaching case (Bower and Christensen 1995), in 1997, Clayton Christensen produced a best-selling book, *The Innovator's Dilemma*, that built on Schumpeter by coining the term 'disruptive technology', which circulated so fast that one year after publication of the book, practitioners had adopted the term in their common language—sadly, to the point of not knowing its origins. In his sequel in 2003, *The Innovator's Solution*, he replaced the term 'disruptive technology' with the term 'disruptive innovation'. A disruptive technology or innovation is a technological innovation, product, or service that eventually overturns the existing dominant technology in the market. With the replacement, he apparently realized that few technologies are intrinsically disruptive or sustaining in character. Instead, it is the business model or strategy enabled by the technology that creates the disruptive result. This interpretation is consistent with Schumpeter's distinction between invention and innovation and included as the important innovation—the art and science of the business model, i.e. the new method of organization. While advancing Schumpeter's ideas by linking them to firm strategy, such as stratifying the market into lower and upper ends, product improvements may exceed the rate at which customers can adopt new performance. Therefore, staying too close to the customer can prevent the firm from seeing disruptive technologies on the horizon and positioning the firm in the value chain where performance is not yet good enough will capture the profit because disruption steals markets and commoditization steals profits. Christensen further develops the two central ideas apparently first expressed, though not explicitly cited from Tushman and Anderson (1986). That is, Christensen's disruptive and sustaining technologies seem to pair with competence-destroying and competence-enhancing technologies.

Searches on the web and of the popular press literature appear to indicate that the term 'disruptive innovations' has migrated into the common vernacular. Some would argue that this is a sign of success of this research stream, as it indicates no disciplinary boundaries and barriers in its 'small coinage'. However, while anyone with a cursory knowledge of Schumpeter's ideas would recognize they are indeed the wellspring of the fundamental ideas in this contemporary stream of research and teaching materials, the origins of Christensen's central idea is arguably not as explicitly linked back to Schumpeter as might have been most intellectually fruitful.

This raises the question of whether this seeming break in the idea chain may point to a routine science problem (Stinchcombe 1982). As lively debate among participants in our conference indicated, some in the field of organizations studies view this line of work as more descriptive of 'retrospective sense making', than of contributing to theory building with predictive power for organization and market behavior. Perhaps one way to think about this is to return to Stinchcombe's (1982) imagery of the value of focusing on the trunk of the tree of knowledge rather than on the branches and the twigs. Is there a lesson here? That is, linking back to Schumpeter's theory of 'creative destruction' is more likely to direct the researcher to expect to find an underlying universal pattern of how entrepreneurs and entrepreneurial firms use innovations to punctuate, create, or maintain their positions with the twist that powerful incumbents cannot necessarily sustain their positions in the market or market equilibriums. By pattern I mean a general theoretical model, an underlying functional form that can be expressed in mathematical terms like a statistical distribution. Stinchcombe's analysis of the classics would lead us to argue that greater focus on the fundamental idea or the trunk of the tree would make this literature considerably richer to academics and practitioners alike, allowing the ability of firms to recognize and exploit future states of technology change—competence-enhancing and competence-destroying influences in markets and hierarchies. Interestingly, it is this fundamental idea of cycles or 'gales' that has won the attention of policy makers with consequences for corporate governance and other resource environments relevant for new ventures.

Overall, my point in this discussion is to illustrate the growth of organization and management theory that stems from Schumpeter—his fundamental ideas generated many theoretical constructs resulting in a cumulative stream of research that addresses real-world problems.

2.2.2. Weber, the Carnegie School, and Institutional Logics

Weber's ([1904] 2002) classic treatise on the *Protestant Ethic and the Spirit of Capitalism* explained how culture legitimated individualism and capitalistic behavior. By examining the links between the transformation of Protestantism and the origin of Western capitalism, Weber used religion to operationalize cultural differences and to compare, for example, how different institutional–cultural contexts determine who is likely to become an entrepreneur and which nation-state economies are more or less likely to progress. This is a general argument; clearly in particular and historical contexts there are other ways to operationalize culture in today's societies. Subsequently, in the late 1950s and early 1960s, Weber's metatheory inspired formal testing of his ideas, most notably by psychologists at Harvard (McClelland 1961).

In these classic studies, at the macro level, McClelland (1961) found significant differences in economic development between Catholic and Protestant countries; at the micro level, colleagues (Winterbottom 1958) found significant differences in parenting practices between Catholic and Protestant families and associated these differences with higher levels of achievement and independence in Protestant compared to Catholic children. Since then, other scholars—for example, Collins (1997)—have applied a neo-Weberian model in understanding the Asian route to capitalism. These ideas are far from dead; they are now being picked up by economists to enrich human capital theory (Becker and Woessmann 2007). Moreover, Weber's (1904) ideas continue to be vigorously explored after the one-hundredth anniversary of his classic thesis.

Just as Weber ([1922] 1978) used bureaucracy, political communities, and family systems as institutional contexts for his insights in the seminal volumes *Economy and Society*, Friedland and Alford (1991) in their critique of transaction cost, rational choice, and network theories argued that it is impossible for these theories to predict the behavior of individuals and organizations without knowing the particular institutional context in which the behavior is situated.

Thornton and Ocasio (1999) were inspired by Weber's ([1922] 1978) insights on legitimacy and his historically comparative methods and institutionally situated ideal types—control by individual charisma, by tradition, and by legal bureaucracy. They were also inspired by how Weber had comparatively defined cultural context within one institutional sector, religion, with his comparison of Protestantism and Catholicism. However, in searching for a more complex way to contextualize and analyze institutional comparisons, they were intrigued by Friedland and Alford's (1991) notion of situated behavior in an inter-institutional system, for example, religion, family, state, and the market. Thornton and Ocasio also sought the 'cogs and gears' that would explain agency in these different institutional contexts by drawing on ideas about decision making from the Carnegie School (March and Simon 1958) that identified the mechanisms of bounded rationality. With this synthesis from the classics, Thornton and Ocasio (1999: 804–5) extended the institutional contextual arguments of Weber (1904) and Friedland and Alford (1991) with a longitudinal quantitative study showing that institutional change alters the determinants and consequences of power and control in organizations. They compared the influences of family, professions, and market institutional logics, which they labeled the editorial and market logics, on executive succession in the higher education publishing industry. This approach took Weber's views on culture and legitimacy and linked them to a new way to define cultural content by explicating and operationalizing Friedland and Alford's inter-institutional system of societal sectors.

Without the metatheory and comparable methods of analysis stemming from Weber, which led to the explication of ideal-type institutional logics—the family, corporation, professions, market, state, and religions—the Thornton and Ocasio

(1999) article would have been just a description of change in power in corporations. They would not, for example, have known to explore with statistical modeling, sensitivity analyses, and qualitative methods how institutional change affected the meaning of a change in power. Moreover, they needed a theoretical mechanism—in Davis and Marquis's parlance, the 'cogs and gears'—to explain how the influences of culture at the industry level affected individual and organizational behavior. Taking earlier work by Ocasio (1997) on attention that built on the foundations of the Carnegie School (March and Simon 1958) gave them the theoretical mechanism to link these micro and macro influences. In subsequent analyses to the original paper, Thornton (2004) further developed the mechanisms linking the industry and societal sector levels of analysis in a variety of decisions contexts, finding in particular that the individual-level effects were more resistant to historical and institutional change than the organization-level effects. While to some researchers, the Weberian roots are clear, they are not directly stated in Friedland and Alford's (1991) ideas. In my view this would have lent strength and emphasis to their arguments on an inter-institutional system as a metatheory of how societal culture legitimates individual and organization behavior. To carry this point further, one could argue that had the link to Weber been explicit in Friedland and Alford's discussion of the inter-institutional system a solution to the puzzle of embedded agency would have been clearer in the 1991 article. However, it evidently was not clear as is evidenced by the number of articles since that time, which have attempted to resolve this puzzle (Thornton and Ocasio 2008). The citations to Weber's foundational ideas are explicit in subsequent work (see e.g. Thornton 2004: table 3.1, which is derived from Weber's *Economy and Society*).

2.2.3. Merton and Status-Based Markets

Merton (1968), in interviewing Nobel laureates, argued that the world rewards the already esteemed, observing that famous scientists receive disproportionately greater credit for their contributions to science and relatively unknown scientists receive disproportionately little credit for equal contributions. Merton identifies this misallocation of credit for scientific work by coining the term 'the Matthew effect'—taking his inspiration from a passage from the Gospel of St Matthew. 'For unto every one that hath shall be given, and he shall have abundance: but from him that hath not shall be taken away even that which he hath.' Merton (1968) derives from this passage an understanding of how the reward system works for individuals' careers as well as for the implications for the communication system in science: for example, he generates the hypothesis that a scientific contribution will have greater visibility in the community of scientists when it is introduced by a scientist of higher status rather than by one of lower rank.

Taking Merton's fundamental ideas on the Matthew effect and status enhancement and suppression effects in the behavior and communication patterns of scientists and Simmel's (1950) insight that rewards are largely a function of position, Podolny (1993) extends the scope of these fundamental ideas by applying a variant of the distinction between actor and position to market producers. He examines how a producer's position in the market affects the relative opportunities open to the producer in comparison to those available to its competitors. Applying these insights to the contemporary puzzle of pricing dynamics in the primary securities markets, he shows that on average, the higher status banks underbid lower status banks for a given deal in the investment-grade markets. However, for the larger offerings, the latter must underbid the former, and they must do so from a relatively disadvantageous cost structure. As Podolny (1993: 865) notes, 'the result is significant because it illustrates the fact that for the larger, more difficult issues, status is relevant not only to the investor and potential syndicate members but to the issuer's decision as well', teasing out when positive rents derive from status versus cost advantages. In building on these classics, Podolny (1993) explains the mechanisms through which the market is shaped by non-economic factors, shedding light on several economic puzzles: for example, why higher status firms do not dominate the market and why higher status firms pay less for the goods, services, and human and financial capital, and achieve higher profits. These puzzles stemming from Podolny's development of fundamental ideas from the classics created follow-on research in a variety of different contexts—what Stinchcombe (1982) referred to as creating routine science.

Let me give two more examples to illustrate this routine science function—new theoretical variants and substantive applications stemming from Podolny's ideas of how status processes lead to nuanced understandings of market competition. Stuart, Hoang, and Hybels (1999), in investigating how start-up companies' interorganizational networks affect their ability to acquire the resources necessary for survival and growth, found that, in the venture-capital market, biotechnology firms with higher status equity investors and underwriters had a higher rate of initial public offering (IPO) and a higher market capitalization at IPO than did firms with lower status interorganizational relationships. They found that higher status venture-capital firms maintained close relationships with leading investment banks. Thus, start-ups funded by leading venture-capital firms tended to secure prestigious investment banks to syndicate their IPOs. There is a status spillover effect; higher status interorganizational relationships attract other prestigious relations. The status of interorganizational relationships provides investors with attributions of quality when, in the start-up and risk capital venue, quality is quite uncertain.

Rather than focusing on firm performance at exit from venture-capital portfolios, in another example, Shane and Cable (2002) extend the theory of status-based markets to again uncertain and imperfect market conditions in examining the chances of entrepreneurs receiving seed financing. Their findings suggested that the reason network relationships are important in entrepreneurs' garnering resources is that they are primarily mechanisms for information transfer. Most funded business proposals come by referral because the referral provides information in an imperfect market. However, once information is publicly available about the quality and reputation of entrepreneurs, high reputation or status of the entrepreneur is the primary driver through which seed financing is received.

2.3. Discussion and Conclusion

In this chapter, I have argued there is great value in reflecting on how to use the classics in the development of organization studies and more generally social science research. Applying the functions of the classics specified by Stinchcombe (1982), I have illustrated in three mini-cases how the theoretical constructs of disruptive technologies, institutional logics, and status-based markets—theoretical constructs that are the wellspring for vibrant research and teaching communities—are descendants of the fundamental ideas of the classics. Moreover, while these examples are only outlines of streams of research, they suggest that by connecting to the classics to study contemporary research problems researchers can more systematically accumulate knowledge (Berger 1993).

In returning to the question presented in the introduction about problem-driven research, the mini-cases lead me to suggest that a solution to problem-driven research without the use and development of some form of theory will not be as effective in advancing the discipline of sociology and one of its larger sub-disciplines, organization studies. I have presented examples of researchers who have developed compelling arguments in studying real problems with an understanding of their empirical observations through the guidance of the classics and theory.

The classic scholars were different from contemporary scholars. Because classic scholars were not held to the incentives attached to quantitative research so admired in the American university system, they had greater opportunity to be clairvoyant and visionary in their thinking compared to today's scholars. The work of the classic scholars resulted in fundamental ideas and predictions of a future world that often did not exist in their time. Consider, for example, how Schumpeter's work is now most relevant to our entrepreneurial start-up economy of today when in 1942 the institutional infrastructure for such to happen was a good fifty years away. This point has implications for questions of the relevancy of organization theory or any school of thought.

The sea change that occurred in organization theory in the late 1970s and early 1980s to lift it from the grasp of contingency theory, the dominant paradigm, was based on at least two phenomena. First, the world had changed and the problems facing organizations and more generally management and society at large could not be explained by contingency theory. Second, contingency theory had become such an unruly collection of empirical and problem-driven findings that it challenged one's capacity to make overall sense out of it. It became unclear how the findings were in an integrative sense related to theoretical mechanisms and therefore explanations. In the end, contingency theory lacked an essential feature of stickiness: many of the findings could not be explained by a theory. There may be some parallel now with the current state of organization theory and organization studies in that there is a socio-economic sea change in many institutional sectors around the world. Perhaps this signals a good time for organizational scholars to weed the garden and plant new seeds; I have given examples to illustrate that looking to the classics can help grow this endeavor.

I have argued that we need to invest in theory-building research and the classics can point to pathways in this endeavor. In returning to the question of whether theory development has slowed or become irrelevant since the late 1970s and early 1980s—note that the three mini-cases presented the spinning of new theory from the classics in the late 1980s to present.

When Schumpeter wrote in 1942 as a lone voice about the gales of creative destruction in a world of large American corporations, it fell on deaf ears. It is only now, with our vibrant start-up community spreading worldwide, that his metatheory is the current buzz in Washington, DC; the classic theoretical construct, creative destruction, now echoes throughout the hallways from Federal Reserve chief to the antitrust attorneys in the Department of Justice (Rose 2002). Without the classics, one could argue we would not have the theoretical constructs—destructive technologies, institutional logics, and status-based markets. These constructs are the basis of cumulative research programs currently being translated into vibrant theory, practitioner knowledge, and public policy. In general, I am loath to study what we study. However, in writing this essay, it now seems prudent to turn attention to the classics to inspire investigative action that focuses on both theory and empirical observation and progresses to testing those relationships predicted by theory. Otherwise our research communities may risk impoverishment with problem-focused research.

Acknowledgments

I acknowledge the helpful comments of Paul Adler, Elisabeth Clemens, Heather Haveman, Ray Zammuto, and the participants of the Sociology Classics and the Future of Organization Studies Conference, Wharton School of Management, University of Pennsylvania, August 2007.

References

Abernathy, W., and Clark, K. B. (1985). 'Innovation: Mapping the Winds of Creative Destruction'. *Research Policy*, 14: 3–22.

Aghion, P., and Howitt, P. (1992). 'A Model of Growth through Creative Destruction'. *Econometrica*, 60: 323–51.

Alexander, J. (1989). 'Sociology and Discourse: On the Centrality of the Classics', in A. Giddens and J. H. Turner (eds.), *Social Theory Today*. Cambridge: Polity Press.

Barley, S. R. (2004). 'Puddle Jumping as a Career Strategy', in R. Stablien and P. Frost (eds.), *Renewing Research Practice: Lessons from Scholar's Journeys*. Stanford, Calif.: Stanford University Press.

—— and Kunda, G. (1992). 'Design and Devotion: Surges of Rational and Normative Ideologies of Control in Managerial Discourse'. *Administrative Science Quarterly*, 37: 363–99.

Baron, J. M., and Bielby, W. T. (1980). 'Bringing the Firms Back In: Stratification, Segmentation, and the Organization of Work'. *American Sociological Review*, 45: 737–65.

Becker, S. O., and Woessmann, L. (2007). 'Was Weber Wrong? A Human Capital Theory of Protestant Economic History'. CESifo Working Paper No. 1987, Category 4: Labour Markets. www.CESifo-group.de.

Berger, J. and Zeldtich, M. (1993). *Theoretical Research Programs: Studies in the Growth of Theory*. Stanford, Calif.: Stanford University Press.

Bower, J. L., and Christensen, C. M. (1995). 'Disruptive Technologies: Catching the Wave'. *Harvard Business Review*, 73/1: 43–53.

Christensen, C. M. (1997). *The Innovator's Dilemma*. Cambridge, Mass.: Harvard Business School Press.

—— (2003). *The Innovator's Solution*. Cambridge, Mass.: Harvard Business School Press.

Collins, R. (1997). 'An Asian Route to Capitalism: Religious Economy and the Origins of Self-Transforming Growth in Japan'. *American Sociological Review*, 62: 843–65.

Coser, L. (1956). *The Functions of Social Conflict*. New York: Free Press.

Davis, G. F., and Marquis, C. (2005). 'Prospects for Organization Theory in the Early Twenty-First Century: Institutional Fields and Mechanisms'. *Organization Science*, 16/4: 332–43.

Emirbayer, M., and Mische, A. (1998). 'What is Agency?'. *American Journal of Sociology*, 103: 281–317.

Friedland, R., and Alford, R. (1991). 'Bringing Society Back In: Symbols, Practices, and Institutional Contradictions', in W. W. Powell and P. J. DiMaggio (eds.), *The New Institutionalism in Organizational Analysis*. Chicago: University of Chicago Press.

Greenwood, R., Oliver, C., Sahlin-Andersson, K., and Suddaby, R. (eds.) (2008). *Handbook of Organizational Institutionalism*. Thousand Oaks, Calif.: Sage.

Haveman, H. A., and Rao, H. (1997). 'Structuring a Theory of Moral Sentiments: Institutional and Organizational Coevolution in the Early Thrift Industry'. *American Journal of Sociology*, 102/6: 1606–51.

Homans, G. (1964). 'Bringing Men Back In'. *American Sociological Review*, 29: 809–18.

Kuhn, T. (1962). *The Structure of Scientific Revolutions*. Chicago: University of Chicago Press.

McClelland, D. C. (1961). *Achieving Society*. New York: Irvington.

March, J. G., and Simon, H. A. (1958). *Organizations*. New York: Wiley.

Martin, J. M. (1992). *Cultures in Organizations*. New York: Oxford University Press.
Merton, R. K. ([1949] 1968). *Social Theory and Social Structure*. New York: Free Press.
—— (1965). *On the Shoulders of Giants*. Chicago: University of Chicago Press.
—— (1968). 'The Matthew Effect in Science'. *Science*, 159: 56–63.
Michels, R. (1962). *Political Parties*. New York: Free Press.
Nolan, R., and Croson, D. C. (1995). *Creative Destruction: A Six-Stage Process for Transforming the Organization*. Boston: Harvard Business School Press.
Ocasio, W. (1994). 'Political Dynamics and the Circulation of Power: CEO Succession in U.S. Industrial Corporations, 1960–1990'. *Administrative Science Quarterly*, 39/2: 285–312.
—— (1997). 'Toward an Attention-Based View of the Firm'. *Strategic Management Journal*, 18: 187–206.
Overton, W. F. (1998). 'Metatheory and Methodology in Developmental Psychology'. Working paper, Department of Psychology, Temple University.
Pareto, V. (1968). *The Rise and Fall of the Elites*. Totowa, NJ: Bedminster Press.
Pfeffer, J. (1993). 'Barriers to the Advance of Organizational Science: Paradigm Development as a Dependent Variable'. *Academy of Management Journal*, 19/4: 599–620.
—— and Salancik, G. (1978). *The External Control of Organizations*. New York: Harper and Row.
Podolny, J. M. (1993). 'A Status-Based Model of Market Competition'. *American Journal of Sociology*, 98/4: 829–72.
Rose, F. (2002). 'The Father of Creative Destruction: Why Joseph Schumpeter is Suddenly all the Rage in Washington'. *Wired*, issue 10.03.
Schumpeter, J. A. (1942). *Capitalism, Socialism, and Democracy*. New York: Harper and Row.
Selznick, P. (1957). *Leadership in Administration*. Berkeley: University of California Press.
Seo, M. G., and Creed, W. E. D. (2002). 'Institutional Contradictions, Praxis, and Institutional Change: A Dialectical Perspective'. *Academy of Management Review*, 27/2: 222–47.
Sewell, W. H. (1992). 'A Theory of Structure: Duality, Agency, and Transformation'. *American Journal of Sociology*, 98: 1–29.
Shane, S., and Cable, D. (2002). 'Network Ties, Reputation, and the Financing of New Ventures'. *Management Science*, 48/3: 364–81.
Simmel, G. (1950). 'Superordination and Subordination', in K. H. Wold (trans.), *The Sociology of Georg Simmel*. Glencoe, Ill.: Free Press.
Skocpol, T. (1985). 'Bringing the State Back In: Strategies of Analysis in Current Research', in P. B. Evans, D. Rueschemeyer, and T. Skocpol (eds.), *Bringing the State Back In*. Cambridge: Cambridge University Press.
Stinchcombe, A. L. (1982). 'Should Sociologists Forget Their Mothers and Fathers'. *American Sociologist*, 17: 2–11.
—— (1991). 'The Conditions of Fruitfulness of Theorizing about Mechanisms in Social Science'. *Philosophy of the Social Sciences*, 21/3 (September): 367–87.
Strang, D., and Meyer, J. W. (1994). 'Institutional Conditions for Diffusion', in W. R. Scott and J. W. Meyer (eds.), *Institutional Environments and Organizations: Structural Complexity and Individualism*. Thousand Oaks, Calif.: Sage.
Stuart, T. E., Hoang, H., and Hybels, R. C. (1999). 'Interorganizational Endorsements and the Performance of Entrepreneurial Ventures'. *Administrative Science Quarterly*, 44: 315–49.

THORNTON, P. H. (1999). 'The Sociology of Entrepreneurship'. *Annual Review of Sociology*, 25: 19–46.

——(2004). *Markets from Culture: Institutional Logics and Organizational Decisions in Higher Education Publishing*. Stanford, Calif.: Stanford University Press.

——and OCASIO, W. (1999). 'Institutional Logics and the Historical Contingency of Power in Organizations: Executive Succession in the Higher Education Publishing Industry, 1958–1990'. *American Journal of Sociology*, 105/3: 801–43.

————(2008). 'Institutional Logics', in R. Greenwood, C. Oliver, K. Sahlin-Andersson, and R. Suddaby (eds.), *Handbook of Organizational Institutionalism*. Thousand Oaks, Calif.: Sage.

TUSHMAN, M. L., and ANDERSON, P. (1986). 'Technological Discontinuities and Organizational Environments'. *Administrative Science Quarterly*, 31: 439–65.

WEBER, M. ([1904] 2002). *The Protestant Ethic and the Spirit of Capitalism*. New York: Penguin Books.

——([1922] 1978). *Economy and Society: An Outline of Interpretive Sociology*, ed. G. Roth and C. Wittich. Berkeley: University of California Press.

WINTERBOTTOM, M. R. (1958). 'The Relation of Need for Achievement to Learning Experiences in Independence and Mastery', in J. W. Atkinson (ed.), *Motives in Fantasy, Action, and Society*. Princeton, NJ: Van Nostrand.

PART II

EUROPEAN PERSPECTIVES

CHAPTER 3

TOCQUEVILLE AS A PIONEER IN ORGANIZATION THEORY

RICHARD SWEDBERG

If you consult the standard histories of organization theory, there is no discussion or even a mention of the work of Tocqueville (e.g. Pfeffer 1981; Perrow 1986; Scott 1992; Aldrich 1999; Aldrich and Ruef 2006). A quick look through the major journals confirms the impression that Tocqueville is not seen as having any particular relevance for the field of organization.[1] This is somewhat intriguing, since the rest of the social sciences, including sociology (with close links to organization theory), for a long time have acknowledged the stature of Tocqueville and granted him the status of a classic. They have done so, to a large extent, precisely on the basis of what he has written about organizations and administrative matters.

That this is the case in political science can be illustrated with *Making Democracy Work*, in which Robert Putnam states, a propos his thesis that voluntary

[1] A search of the major organization journals, with the help of JSTOR, shows this. A search on 'Tocqueville' in 'title', 'abstract', and 'full-text' gives zero, zero, and eleven hits for *ASQ* (1956–2003), the *Academy of Management Journal* (1963–2001), and the *Academy of Management Review* (1976–2001). For the ups and downs of references to the work of Max Weber in organization studies, see Lounsbury and Carberry (2005). For early references to Tocqueville in organization theory, see the work of Michel Crozier (Mélonio 1998: 201); for more recent references, see e.g. Courpasson and Clegg 2006; Vasi and Strang 2007.

organizations are important for democracy, that 'the most relevant social theorist here remains Alexis de Tocqueville' (Putnam 1993: 89). In sociology it was Raymond Aron, more than anyone else, who launched Tocqueville as a classic. This was done in a famous lecture series at the Sorbonne in the 1960s that later became an often-cited book, *Main Currents in Sociological Thought* (Aron 1968).

Putnam focused on Tocqueville's analysis of voluntary organizations and Aron on his comparative study of government and administration. Both of these are topics that fit straight into organization theory, even if Putnam and Aron looked to Tocqueville for different things. In Putnam's case, it was democracy, the civil sphere, and social capital, while for Aron it was the government–citizen relationship more generally. When contemporary sociologists have referred to Tocqueville, it may be added, it has often been in similar contexts (e.g. Skocpol 1997; Alexander 2006).

The task to establish Tocqueville's contribution to organization theory still remains, in other words. It is not a particularly difficult task, since *Democracy in America* contains a number of pages on organizations, whose originality and importance have been understood for quite some time. The same can be said of the analysis of administration in *The Old Regime and the Revolution* (even if this work is less known in the United States than *Democracy in America*).

That Tocqueville wrote so much about topics that are central to organization theory is perhaps not so peculiar, since he considered 'the science of associations' to be absolutely central to modern society. It is, as he put it, 'the fundamental science [and] progress in all the other sciences depends on progress in this one' (Tocqueville 2004: 599).

But even if one can easily show that Tocqueville for some reason has been passed over in organization theory, it is more difficult to decide what constitutes the best way to show the merits of his case and why he should be regarded as a classic. One possibility is to simply go through Tocqueville's work, extract everything he has to say about organizations, and discuss this. While this is a reasonable (and economic) way of proceeding, it also builds on some silent assumptions, which need to be discussed.

One of these assumptions is that Tocqueville meant the same thing as we do today when he spoke of 'organizations', 'the science of organization', and so on. Another is that the context of Tocqueville was the same as it is today, including the major issues of the day—what Weber called 'the great cultural problems of the time' (Weber 1949: 112). A third assumption is that social science and its division of intellectual labor were roughly the same today as they were in the early to mid-1800s.

Unless these assumptions are openly discussed, Tocqueville's ideas and analyses run the risk of being 'translated' in a much too harsh manner into the way in which we see things today. I will therefore make an attempt both to provide the reader with a straightforward account of which parts of Tocqueville's work are relevant for a discussion of 'Tocqueville as a pioneer in organization theory' and to show what

Tocqueville meant with the terms he used and the problems he addressed. The same goes for paying attention to the general context of his work and the state of social science in Tocqueville's days.

Tocqueville, as I see it, becomes much more interesting—to people in organization theory as well as to people in other areas—if one goes back and forth between a study of Tocqueville's work on organizations from today's perspective, and the way that his work was understood in his own time, especially by himself. The reason for this is that the meanings that words and arguments had in the past are not exactly the same as the meanings they have today. Proceeding in this way, in short, makes us look at old things in a new light; it also reminds us that today's organization theory is a social fact itself, with its own coercive and authoritarian power (as Durkheim would have put it).

This means that what we primarily are after, in Tocqueville's work, as well as in that of the other classics, is the tension between what some author says and what is today taken to be self-evident and well-established scientific findings. Once it is realized that all of the classics need to be approached in this way, one also understands why they need to be read and studied very carefully, and not just referred to in some symbolic fashion (cf. Lounsbury and Carberry 2005). The classics in organization theory are furthermore classics because they have important things to say on core issues, such as: What is an organization? What should organizations be used for? What is their role in society as a whole? Tocqueville addresses these issues, and he also answers them in an original way.

3.1. *Democracy in America*: The First Study of Organizations?

Alexis de Tocqueville (1805–59) is typically seen as the author of two books: *Democracy in America* (1835, 1840) and *The Old Regime and the Revolution* (1856). This is a simplification; not only are Tocqueville's wonderful political memoirs, *Recollections*, not included, but neither are the twenty or so volumes in his *Collected Works* (Tocqueville 1951–). To this may be added a vast secondary literature, mainly in French and English. There exists today a sophisticated body of literature on Tocqueville's work, which especially draws on the contributions by a small number of outstanding scholars (see e.g. Pierson 1938; Drescher 1964; Schleifer 1980; Jardin 1988; Mélonio 1998; Gannett 2003*b*).

Much of this literature is of relevance when Tocqueville as a pioneer in organization theory is discussed. Tocqueville, of course, made no contribution to 'organization theory', since this type of analysis did not come into being till the 1900s. This means that one has to recast Tocqueville's concerns in a new language, if one is to get a handle on his contribution to this field.

As part of the attempt to criticize a simplistic approach to Tocqueville as a pioneer in organization theory, it should also be noted that Tocqueville's first encounter with organizations did not take place in the United States during his visit in 1831–2. Instead it took place in his native France, under the tutelage of the brilliant historian and later politician François Guizot, whose lectures during 1828–30 Tocqueville listened to or read (Gannett 2003*a*). Guizot drew Tocqueville's attention to the role of the communes during the Middle Ages and argued that they had been important incubators for local liberties. Tocqueville was deeply impressed by Guizot's argument, and it prepared him for one of his most important discoveries in the United States: *the role of organizations in modern society*.

When we turn to Tocqueville's famous picture of the United States, it should also be emphasized that we today do not only have access to *Democracy in America* in the early 1800s but also to Tocqueville's notes from his trip and his correspondence (for Tocqueville's notes from the American trip, see Tocqueville 1959; his correspondence from the nine months' trip and the nine years that it took for him to write the work is scattered throughout a number of volumes in his *Collected Works*). It would take too much space to present and discuss everything that is of relevance to organization theory in all of this material—something which is also a reminder that the current neglect of Tocqueville in organization theory is not going to be remedied over night.

Tocqueville was a very ambitious person and what he wanted more than anything else was to be a successful politician and lead his country to glory and prosperity. Many members of his family had served the king, as was common among the nobility. For a number of reasons Tocqueville was thwarted in his efforts to get into politics as a young man, and *Democracy in America* became a replacement of sorts for this. His work was written, among other reasons, to convince the French political elite during the July Monarchy that its author was a person with a brilliant talent for political and literary writings—someone, in short, who would be a good politician.

The general structure of *Democracy in America* is similarly anchored in a problematic that was special to France in the early 1800s. This was the need to realize, according to Tocqueville, that the France that had existed before 1789 could not be brought back, as many members of the nobility wanted. The clock could not be turned back, he insisted; France was in the process of becoming a new type of society in which the aristocracy was to play a minor role, if any at all.

Translated into the key categories of *Democracy in America*, this meant that society was going from what Tocqueville called 'aristocracy' to 'democracy'. By the former, he meant that all resources in society were in the hands of a small elite (economic, political, and ideological resources); and with the term 'democracy', he meant that these resources were increasingly being shared. Today, when 'democracy' has come to mean that the political power is in the hand of the people (through a representative system, based on universal voting rights), Tocqueville's use of the term seems odd. In the early 1800s in France, however, and especially in the circles of intellectuals and politicians that Tocqueville moved in, '*démocratie*' meant a type of society, centered around equality—the meaning, in brief, that it has in *Democracy in America*, and to which Tocqueville also would add a twist of his own (see esp. Rosanvallon 1995).

Democracy in America is about nine hundred pages long and appeared in two installments, one in 1835 and another in 1840. The argument is cast in a terminology that is partly understandable to today's reader and partly not. The United States, Tocqueville suggests, has moved the furthest of all countries in the direction of democracy or equality in terms of basic resources. Its 'social state', as Tocqueville also calls it, is 'democracy' in a relatively pure form.

Organizations play an important role in both volumes of *Democracy in America*. Volume 1 is devoted to 'the physiognomy of politics' or the influence of 'the democratic social state' on 'laws' and 'political mores'. It contains a famous chapter called 'On Political Associations in the United States' (Tocqueville 2004: 215–23). Volume 2 deals in contrast with 'civil society' or the impact of the democratic social state on 'sentiments', 'social relations', and 'opinions'. Also this volume contains well-known chapters on organizations, especially 'On the Use that Americans Make of Associations in Civil Life' (ibid. 595–9; see also 600–609). The focus in volume 2 is on non-political organizations, especially economic organizations and voluntary organizations.

The chapter on political organizations opens with a statement that Americans in their everyday lives have to deal with a number of problems and cannot rely on the authorities to do things for them. As a result, they join forces and create organizations in all areas of life. Tocqueville divides these as follows. Some are 'permanent associations, established by law and known as towns, cities, and counties' (ibid. 215). The others have been created through 'the initiative of individuals' and consist of 'political associations' and 'civil associations'. The latter include 'commercial and industrial associations' as well as a large number of voluntary associations (ibid. 595).

In the chapter on political associations, Tocqueville comes the closest to providing a definition of an organization that he will ever do in *Democracy in America*. 'An association', he says, 'consists solely in the decision of a certain number of individuals to adhere publicly to certain doctrines, and to commit themselves to seek the triumph of those doctrines in a special way' (ibid. 210). A few sentences later, he adds that 'the association links the efforts of divergent minds and vigorously propels them toward a single goal, which it unambiguously designates'.

From what has been said so far, it should be clear that Tocqueville does not use the term 'organization', but '*association*' (the French terms are the same: '*organisation*' and '*association*'). The term 'association' had a slightly different meaning in the early 1800s from what 'organization' has today even if they are roughly synonymous;

Tocqueville also used it in his own way. While 'association' and 'organization' overlap to a large extent, there is a stronger emphasis in 'association' (in French as well as in English) on a number of people combining their efforts towards a common goal.[2] This means, among other things, that there is a closer link between Tocqueville's 'association' and what we today call social movements, than there is between 'organization' and social movements.

The term 'association' suited Tocqueville well with his theory of democracy/equality; and his organizations are typically the independent products of independent people more than the result of powerful individuals or authorities creating organizations for their own goals. Tocqueville also uses 'association' sometimes in the same meaning as when we today refer to a group or a society. All of humanity, we read at one point in *Democracy in America*, is an 'association' and so is the nation (ibid. 725; on Tocqueville's use of the term 'association', see also Wudel 1993).

Political associations, Tocqueville explains in volume 1 of *Democracy in America*, presupposes three types of freedom: the freedom of speech, the freedom of association, and the freedom to elect people to represent them. In the United States, all of these freedoms exist, he says, and to exemplify what this may entail, he describes the Philadelphia Free Trade Convention in 1831. At this point in time delegates from all over the United States came together in Philadelphia to discuss whether there should be tariffs and if Congress had the power to impose tariffs. Tocqueville also notes that organizations are very much used in the United States to counter the tendency of the majority to decide everything ('the tyranny of the majority').

Sometimes, however, the freedom of association is restricted in a country; and while this is never good, Tocqueville says, it can sometimes be necessary. To illustrate the point, he contrasts the situation in Europe to that in the United States; and the result can be called an early example of a comparative organizational analysis. In the United States, Tocqueville explains, political organizations are used for peaceful and legal purposes, while in Europe they are often used 'to make war at the government' (ibid. 221). They are used 'to act, not talk' and 'to fight, not persuade' (ibid. 223). This tends to make them centralized and non-egalitarian. Since European governments do not allow their citizens to vote, Tocqueville continues, the members in this type of political organization also live in the illusion that they represent the will of the people. In the United States, where there are elections that decide who constitutes the majority, these types of illusions do not exist.

[2] For the English use of the terms 'association' and 'organization', see *The Oxford English Dictionary*; and for the French use of '*association*' and '*organisation*', see *Le Trésor de la langue française informatisé* (available on-line). According to one writer, 'when Tocqueville's generation uses the word *s'associer*, the word has a specific meaning—to join together in overcoming the isolation and powerlessness resulting from the atomization of bourgeois society' (Boesche 1983: 291). By Tocqueville's generation is meant the work of people such as Michelet, Fourier, and Saint-Simon. As Zaleski (2000) has argued, one may also want to establish how Tocqueville's use of the term 'association' is related to the legal meaning this term had in nineteenth-century France. When George W. Bush has referred to Tocqueville in his speeches, the emphasis has been on Tocqueville's advocacy that people join together to achieve a higher purpose (Bumiller 2005).

At this point of the analysis, Tocqueville comes close to the kind of analysis that can be found in Phillip Selznick's study of the Bolshevik Party, *The Organizational Weapon* (Selznick 1952). The members in secret and authoritarian organizations, according to Tocqueville (and Selznick), consist of people who want to sacrifice themselves for the cause. They are authoritarian (like 'passive soldiers') and not of the material you need to create a society of free and independent people (ibid. 222).

Of the political organizations that Tocqueville came across in the United States, the one that interested him the most by far was the township in New England (e.g. Gannett 2003*a*; Pierson 1938: 397–416; for Tocqueville on political parties, see ibid. 198–204). The reason for this fascination from Tocqueville's side was that the township came very close to his own political ideal: a local association of persons who decide together how to run their community.

By the time that Tocqueville realized the importance of the township in New England, he did not have time during his trip to examine them personally. While he regretted this, it did not stop him from researching them in other ways. He turned, for example, to historian Jared Sparks and asked him to write a historical account of the township. The reason for choosing Sparks was that it was he who had told Tocqueville about the importance of the township. According to Sparks, New England was the cradle of American democracy. After some nudging Sparks complied with Tocqueville's request; and the famous account of townships in *Democracy in America* rests primarily on Sparks's report (Sparks 1898).

This concludes Tocqueville's analysis of political organizations in volume 1 of *Democracy in America*, and I will now move on to the analysis of non-political organizations in volume 2, which deals with civil society. Some of the civil organizations that Tocqueville came across in the United States initially struck him as odd and even a bit ridiculous. It is also clear that he arrived totally unprepared for what he was going to experience in this respect.

One example of an association that he initially thought was 'more amusing than serious' was when one hundred thousand Americans came together to pledge never to drink alcohol (ibid. 599). Tocqueville also noted that 'if these hundred thousand men had lived in France, each of them would have petitioned the government individually to keep an eye on taverns throughout the realm' (ibid.).

The example of the public pledge against using alcohol as well as the example of the 1831 Free Trade Convention point to the close link that exists between Tocqueville's notion of association and what we today refer to as social movements. The link, in brief, has to do with Tocqueville's emphasis on many people coming together for a common purpose (as opposed to an organization, which is often the result of a single individual).[3]

[3] Would it therefore be more correct to translate Tocqueville's '*association*' as 'social movement' than as 'organization' and also to cast Tocqueville as a pioneer in the study of social movements rather than in organization theory? In my opinion the answer is 'no'; and the reason for this is that when Tocqueville speaks of 'association', he is in most cases referring to what we today would term 'organizations' and not 'social movements'—such as corporations, political parties, and the like.

After some time in the United States, Tocqueville's attitude to voluntary organizations changed from skepticism and ridicule to genuine admiration. This is mirrored in the following iconic passage in *Democracy in America*:

> Americans of all ages, all conditions, and all minds are constantly joining together in groups. In addition to commercial and industrial associations in which everyone takes part, there are associations of a thousand other kinds: some religious, some moral, some grave, some trivial, some quite general and others quite particular, some huge and others tiny. Americans associate to give fêtes, to found seminaries, to build inns, to erect churches, to distribute books, and to send missionaries to the antipodes. This is how they create hospitals, prisons and schools. (ibid. 595)

It is also here that we find Tocqueville's often cited statement about 'the science of association'. This science, to repeat, is 'the fundamental science' and the one on which 'progress in all the other sciences depend' (ibid. 595). A few pages after having made this statement, Tocqueville adds that 'the art of association then becomes, as I said earlier, the fundamental science; everybody studies it and applies it' (ibid. 606).

By 'science' Tocqueville does not mean exactly what we mean today; the term lacks, for example, the positivistic overtones that Comte and others have infused it with. Tocqueville, for example, speaks of a number of sciences in *Democracy in America*, including 'industrial science', 'political science', and 'etiquette [as] a science' (ibid. 7–8, 649–50, 663). Science, then, means something like serious and sustained knowledge to Tocqueville. He also saw it as being close to practice, as the example with his reference to 'the art of association' indicates. 'Art' and 'science' were very close to Tocqueville; and a 'science' that did not result in practical action was of little interest to him.

There is also a need to explain why Tocqueville regarded the science of association as so important that it constitutes 'the fundamental science' in modern society. As things become increasingly equal, and as aristocratic society disappears, Tocqueville argues, the individuals become increasingly free. But being free in this context also means being free from other people; and the individuals in a democratic society constitute a mass of powerless and isolated individuals.

This situation of isolation and powerlessness is dangerous for the individuals, and it is dangerous for society. If individuals in a democratic society do not join together politically, they will lose their freedom. A new type of tyranny will emerge that only exists in democratic society: a soft type of tyranny—'democratic despotism'. Even worse, if the individuals do not join together in other types of activities than politics, civilization itself will come to an end.

This need to organize or vanish did not exist in earlier forms of society, that is, in aristocratic society. Aristocrats could rely on already existing organizations, in the form of secondary or intermediary bodies ('natural associations', ibid. 219). The individual aristocrat was also a powerful individual who could join other aristocrats or command people to do what he wished ('compulsory associations', ibid. 596).

But nothing of this exists in democratic society, and the void after the intermediary associations and the strong individuals must be filled with democratic associations. Organizations have a nearly mystical power to Tocqueville; they make people come together and thereby make society possible. To cite another famous line about the impact of associations from *Democracy in America*, which could have been written by Durkheim: 'feelings and ideas are renewed, the heart expands, and the human spirit develops only through the reciprocal action of human beings on one another' (ibid. 598).

If people do not create any organizations on their own, Tocqueville argues, one consequence may be that the state will intervene and provide people with what they want. To Tocqueville this represents a dangerous development. Not only does it open the road for a political take-over, since people will be passive ('democratic despotism'); it also makes people incompetent and passive in all areas of social life. By letting the state help people out, they lose the capacity to be free and independent.

Another danger, from Tocqueville's perspective, is something he calls 'individualism' (*individualisme*). By this term he does not mean a belief in the individual, as is common today, but the tendency to make money and material concerns into the first priority in life.[4] The result of doing this, he says, is typically that people begin to ignore politics and withdraw into the circle of family and friends. This decision to leave 'the big world' for 'the small world' means that local political associations will eventually die out; it now also becomes easy for ruthless politicians to seize power (Tocqueville 2004: 585).[5]

While Tocqueville describes greed as an instinct and an emotion that has always existed, individualism is in contrast 'reflexive and tranquil', and typical for democratic society (ibid.). To counter individualism, one may use political associations; religion represents another solution. In Tocqueville's opinion, the United States was very materialistic and individualistic, but it also had a strong associational life and people were religious.

Besides the chapter on the use that the Americans make of organizations in all areas of life, volume 2 also contains two other important chapters on related themes. The first of these is called 'On the Relation between Associations and Newspapers'

[4] Tocqueville does not discuss 'individualism' in the chapter called 'On Political Associations in the United States' but elsewhere in *Democracy in America* (see Tocqueville 2004: 585–94, 610–13). The French term '*individualisme*' seems to have made its first appearance in the 1820s and in English about a decade later. Henry Reeve's use of 'individualism' for the translation of Tocqueville's book represents one of its earliest usages in English. According to Alan Kahan (the translator of *The Old Regime*), 'the word individualism appeared in the 1820s, at first among the counterrevolutionaries, then among the socialists to stigmatize the atomization of postrevolutionary society. It entered the dictionary of the Académie Française in 1835' (Tocqueville 1998: 366).

[5] I have translated Tocqueville's terms '*une petite société*' and '*la grande société*' as 'the small world' and 'the big world' instead of following Arthur Goldhammar's translation of *Democracy in America* ('a little society', 'the larger society'). In doing so, I follow the terminology of Swedish sociologist Hans Zetterberg.

and the other, 'Relations between Civil Associations and Political Associations' (ibid. 500–503, 604–9). The former is a reminder that newspapers played a different role in Tocqueville's days in the United States than they do today, and also that Tocqueville does not mean precisely the same with 'associations' as we do with 'organizations'.

According to Tocqueville, a newspaper helps people come together and act on some special issue; and it does this by tying together people who are scattered over a large geographical area and who otherwise would not have been able to communicate. He sums up his argument as follows: 'Newspapers make associations, and associations make newspapers' (ibid. 601).

In contrast to the chapter on the press, the chapter on civil and political organizations is important in that it addresses an issue that is central to modern organization theory. This is how organizations diffuse and, related to this, the issue of social capital. Tocqueville argues that the skill of creating organizations in one area of society tends to spread also to the other. If people, for example, learn to join together in economic enterprises, this gives them the skill to join together in political matters.

Tocqueville especially emphasizes the spill from political organizations to other types of organizations and states in a famous formulation that 'political associations therefore can be looked upon as vast free schools to which all citizens come to learn the general theory of association' (ibid. 606; cf. Whittington 2001). Tocqueville uses economic organizations to illustrate this. People may be unwilling to join an economic organization, he says, because they are afraid they will lose money. Once they have some experience from political organizations, however, this fear may disappear.

More generally, Tocqueville sees the experience that people get from joining together in associations as essential to living in a democratic society. The individual learns to work with other people and to subordinate his or her will to them. These are skills that are necessary to have if society is to work properly.

A few items need to be added to round off the picture of what Tocqueville has to say that is relevant to organization theory in *Democracy in America*. There is, for example, his analysis of the organization of the state. It is often pointed out that according to Tocqueville there was no state in the United States. This, however, is only true for the beginning of his trip. What one finds in *Democracy in America* is instead the argument that the United States has a state, but that its range of activities is limited. It deals in principle only with issues that the individuals at the local level cannot handle on their own ('governmental administration'). And it stays away from those activities that individuals can take care of through their own efforts ('administrative centralization'; ibid. 97–8).

The argument about administrative and governmental centralization is mainly aimed at the US federal state, and Tocqueville had a somewhat different attitude to the local states. This comes out, for example, in a chapter that Tocqueville wrote for *Democracy in America* but in the end decided not to include (e.g. Schleifer 1980: 82). Its title is 'On the Manner in which American Government Acts towards Associations' (Tocqueville 1990: 106–7).

The main argument in this text is that the Americans 'let the state give certain associations a helping hand and even let the state take their part' (ibid. 106). The type of associations that Tocqueville was referring to in this quote had to do with the transportation system, which was in a dynamic stage during his visit. Canals, roads, and railroads were all part of the transport revolution that was going on in Jacksonian America. Tocqueville, in brief, was positive to the fact that the local state took on certain tasks to help the citizens—but only so long, he was careful to add, as it was not forgotten that 'the main goal of a good government is always to increasingly make the citizens be in a situation where they can manage without its help' (ibid. 107).

Tocqueville not only addresses the topic of the general role of the state in *Democracy in America* but also analyzes its administrative machinery. Just as Tocqueville refers positively to 'the science of association', he speaks highly of 'the science of administration' (Tocqueville 2004: 237–8). The picture of US administration that Tocqueville presents in his work is sociological through and through. According to an expert on the topic, 'he [that is, Tocqueville] was perhaps the first investigator to appraise administrative practise in the United States in terms of such concepts as hierarchy, discipline, integration, responsibility, coordination, personnel practice, degree of professionalism, and the like' (Smith 1942: 229).

In *Democracy in America*, to sum up, Tocqueville presents what may well be the first social science analysis of organizations. He views these very much within the context of his general analysis of society; what once was an aristocratic society is

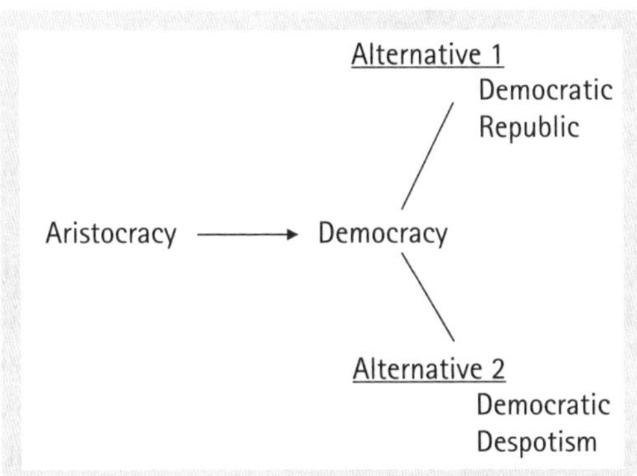

Fig. 3.1. Choices in democratic society, according to *Democracy in America*

Comment: According to *Democracy in America*, society moves from aristocracy to democracy. A democracy can either take the form of a democratic republic or the form of democratic despotism. One important factor in determining the outcome is the existence or absence of political organizations at the local level.

increasingly becoming a democratic or egalitarian society. This development tends to make the individuals rather than estates, classes, and families into the main actors in society. Individuals, however, are isolated and weak, and to build a healthy and strong community they need to come together in organizations. They need to create organizations in all areas of society: political, economic, and voluntary organizations. If they do this, there will be liberty and independence; if not, there will be 'democratic despotism' and 'individualism' (see Fig. 3.1).

3.2. Tocqueville's Less Known Works

Tocqueville, as already noted, wrote much more than *Democracy in America* and *The Old Regime*, and sometimes he touched on issues of importance to organization theory in these other works. To go through the twenty or so volumes of additional writings will not be done in this article, and I will restrict myself to a small sample. The three examples I have selected for brief mention are Tocqueville and Beaumont's prison study, Tocqueville's articles on pauperism, and his writings on administrative issues from his time as a politician.

Tocqueville and Beaumont got the French government to sponsor their trip to the United States in 1831–2 by suggesting that they would study the attempts that were going on at the time in the United States to reform the prison system. The result was a report that appeared in 1833, *On the Penitentiary System in the United States and Its Application in France.* While Beaumont wrote the main text and Tocqueville many of the appendices, both were responsible for the overall analysis.

The Penitentiary System is of interest for Tocqueville as a student of the science of organization mainly in two regards. First, it contains an interesting comparative study of a concrete organization: the prison. In France at the time, many prisoners were locked up in the same room, while the United States was in the process of introducing the single cell system. Tocqueville and Beaumont also analyzed the different ways in which this system could be organized, especially in relation to work. Some of the questions they addressed in their report were the following: Should the prisoners work in isolation or in group? Should the work be contracted out and, if so, should the prisoners get any of the income that came from selling their labor?

The Penitentiary System is also remarkable in that it constitutes the most thoroughly executed case study Tocqueville was ever to produce. He carefully analyzed the administrative structure of the prisons and he worked extra hard to penetrate the budget of every single prison. In one prison, he interviewed sixty-three prisoners, alone in their cells. He did this, it should be noted, nearly a century before the interview started to be regularly used in social science (Platt 2002). Tocqueville, in other words, was a pioneer also in his use of research methods (Swedberg 2009).

While working on *Democracy in America* in the mid-1830s, Tocqueville produced two small articles on pauperism, of which only one was published during his life time (Tocqueville 1968, 1989). Pauperism means assistance to the poor; and Tocqueville's two writings are mainly of interest for what they tell about his attitude to poverty. While Tocqueville mentions poverty in *Democracy in America* and discusses it at some length in the prison study, it is in the articles on pauperism that his fullest analysis is to be found.

Tocqueville draws a sharp line between the kind of poverty one can find in an agricultural setting and the new type of urban poverty that came with industrialization. The latter constituted, to his mind, a grave threat to democratic society. Measures needed to be taken—or there might be a revolution. One organizational innovation that Tocqueville recommended as a possible remedy was that the workers be allowed to own the factories in which they worked. Another was that the French state should create a new kind of savings bank that would facilitate for the workers to save during good times, and then use their savings during bad times (see esp. Tocqueville 1989).

Tocqueville worked as an active politician during the years 1839–51, and he often dealt with administrative issues. In doing so he acquired a thorough knowledge of French administration that would come in very handy for his work on *The Old Regime*. From his various writings from these days it is, for example, clear that he was very critical of the type of civil servants that the French state was producing through schools such as École Polytechnique. If France wanted a proper 'merit system', he argued, it should learn from German administration (Tocqueville 1878: 374–88; Smith 1942: 233).

Tocqueville was also a strong supporter of French colonialism and spent much energy on helping his country in Algeria. France had seized Algiers and some coastal areas in 1830 and eventually decided to take over the whole country. The native population in Algeria resisted the French, who answered by militarizing the country during the 1840s. To Tocqueville, this was not a wise policy, and he instead suggested a number of administrative reforms that would better accomplish the goal of a prosperous French colony (see the texts on Algeria in Tocqueville 2001*b*). He suggested, among other things, that the French follow the English example and create a proper education for civil servants who were going to work in the colonies. Tocqueville, incidentally, admired the English rule in India to the point that he started to write a book on the topic (which was never completed). In his writings on Algeria and India, we see a side of Tocqueville that is less known and less likeable: Tocqueville as a colonialist. In these works Tocqueville used his knowledge of society, including his knowledge of organizations, to undermine and defeat local populations that did not want to be ruled by the French.

3.3. *The Old Regime and the Revolution*: The First Study of Bureaucracy?

In 1851 Tocqueville withdrew from politics in protest against the coup d'état of Louis-Napoleon (later Napoleon III); and it was also around this time that he decided to write a new major study. After a few years of intensive work, *The Old Regime* was published in 1856. Tocqueville's death in 1859 meant that he could not complete the sequel. His notes for the second volume—tentatively entitled *The Revolution*—were published posthumously (Tocqueville 2001*a*).

The Old Regime covers the period in French history leading up to the Revolution of 1789, with an emphasis on the eighteenth century but stretching as far back as the Middle Ages. It contains a huge amount of material on administration, but very little on organizations or associations. One can in particular find a very interesting analysis of bureaucracy in *The Old Regime*, and Tocqueville may well have been the first social scientist of stature to study this phenomenon, which had begun to arouse interest precisely around this time.[6]

Just as in *Democracy in America*, Tocqueville casts his analysis in *The Old Regime* within the conceptual frame of society moving from aristocracy to democracy. The emphasis is naturally on aristocracy, and how this type of society gradually disintegrates as it is transformed in the direction of democracy. The aristocracy gets weaker, while new classes emerge, grow strong, and challenge the aristocracy for its power.

One of the main theses in *The Old Regime* is that the famous administrative machinery of the French state had not been created by the revolutionaries and Napoleon, but had roots far back in French history. Also Tocqueville's main theory of why revolution had broken out just in France and nowhere else, and why it had been so violent, was that the administrative structure of the old regime had been constructed without any contact with the emerging democratic mores of the country. There was a disjunction, in Tocqueville's terminology, between the 'institutions' (roughly laws) of the country and its 'mores' (*moeurs*, meaning norms, attitudes, opinions, and the like). Mores were much more important in shaping a country than its institutions, according to Tocqueville, but both of them had to work in tandem for there to be stability and progress. In the case of France,

[6] According to *Le Trésor de la langue française informatisé*, the first use in French language of the term '*bureaucratie*' (which Tocqueville does not use) dates to the 1840s. The first use of the term 'bureaucracy' in English is somewhat earlier; and it can be found already in 1818, according to *The Oxford English Dictionary*. By the 1830s it could also be found in John Stuart Mill's work as well as in the translation of Tocqueville and Beaumont's prison study (1833). According to Pierson, Francis Lieber (the translator), 'employed a number of new words', including 'bureaucracy' (Pierson 1938: 713 n. 2). For a comparison of Tocqueville and Weber on bureaucracy, see Offe 2005.

institutions and mores were only brought together through force—through the Revolution of 1789.

The centralization that developed before the Revolution, Tocqueville argued, was the result of the state's instinct for power as well as the unintended consequence of many of its acts. The French state moved, for example, towards centralization through its elimination of all competing centers of powers. It also had an enormous need for money, which among other things made it sell offices whenever it could. Old freedoms in the cities and the parishes were destroyed as offices were sold off—with the result that the power of the state increased even more.

After some time of selling offices on a large scale, taking them back, selling them again, and so on, France had acquired such a patchy and inefficient administration that something radical needed to be done. The result was the introduction of a parallel structure of administration, where all power was concentrated. This new system went straight from the king in his Royal Council to each of the main administrative units in France, where the king was represented by an all-powerful functionary called the intendant.

The Royal Council consisted of commoners and was subordinate only to the king. It controlled taxation and the court system, and suggested the laws. At the local level, the intendant had a similar absolute power over legal, political, economic, and social issues. Neither the Royal Council nor the intendant were controlled by any other power.

Centralization in the case of France meant that everything was decided in Paris. It also meant bureaucratization: 'In order to run everything from Paris, and know everything there, it was necessary to invent a thousand new ways of control' (Tocqueville 1998: 138). The officials developed, for example, 'bureaucratic habits' that took a variety of expressions—from the language they used ('colorless, verbose, vague, and flabby') to the need to gather statistics with the help of surveys and more (ibid. 139).

The bureaucracy was becoming a new and powerful elite, to cite an important passage from *The Old Regime*: 'The bureaucracy, almost all bourgeois, already formed a class with its own character, its own traditions, virtues, honor, its own pride. It was the aristocracy of the new society, which was already alive and formed. It was only waiting for the Revolution to make room for it' (ibid. 139). From quotes of this type (and there are many more), it is hard not to draw the conclusion that Tocqueville developed a sociological theory of bureaucracy some fifty years before Max Weber (for a central text in this regard, see 'On Bureaucratic Habits under the Old Regime', Tocqueville 1998: 138–45).

Tocqueville's picture of the bureaucracy was modeled on France and not on Germany, which made it somewhat different in character from Weber's theory of bureaucracy. That Tocqueville was nonetheless sensitive to national differences in his analysis of bureaucracy comes out in his comparison of French to English bureaucracy. This can be illustrated with a quote that also casts an interesting light on how Tocqueville (as opposed to Weber) tried to relate the issue of bureaucratic efficiency to what efficiency meant for the country as a whole:

> Nothing is more superficial than to relate the strength and prosperity of nations solely to the functioning of the administrative machine. One must look not at the perfection of the means of action, but at the internal and central force which makes the machine work.... Even today our administrative system as a mechanism is much simpler, quicker, more rational than that of the English. Look, however, how public life in England today is still more fruitful, more varied, more energetic than among us. The difference comes from the internal source of strength which is the great cause which makes things work and produce. The limbs can be insignificant when the heart is powerful. (ibid. 400)

One result of the centralizing process in pre-Revolutionary France was that all competing powers—including the intermediary powers of the aristocracy—had been eliminated. Much of the aristocracy and the bourgeoisie also lived in the cities, where they could avoid taxation, and had left the peasants behind in the countryside. Through a clever manipulation by the state, again through the system of taxation, all classes had become isolated from one another. Different taxes were imposed on different classes; the way that the taxes were estimated and collected also differed. The isolation of the peasants meant that no one would assist them; and this explains some of the hatred they developed for the aristocrats.

Another effect of the centralization process was, on the one hand, that the government decided everything, and, on the other, that the population learned to be passive and turn to the government whenever it needed something. Tocqueville used the term 'government paternalism' (*tutelle administrative*) for the former tendency (Tocqueville 1998: 124–31). Thanks to this paternalism common people showed no desire to act on their own. They were like newborn birds in a nest, waiting for the mother bird to feed them (Tocqueville 2001*a*: 294).

It is precisely at this point of his argument that Tocqueville raises the issue of associations or organizations in *The Old Regime*. By becoming so reliant on the state, people had forgotten how to form organizations: 'The French sometimes assembled tumultuously to disturb the peace together, but they never came together peaceably for purposes of public interest. They had not only lost the habit of conducting their own affairs together, they had lost the desire to do so and almost the idea' (ibid. 354).

It was not so much that no organizations at all existed in the eighteenth century, but that the ones that did exist had very specific purposes and did not address the basic isolation and helplessness of the people:

> In the eighteenth century many commercial companies were seen, many literary associations were found, but when it came to associations whose purpose was to fill a public need or to concern themselves in common with a public matter, no one [wanted] to speak of it. Although the government was not yet in a position to provide for all public needs,

individuals had already entirely lost the habit and even the idea of helping themselves. Even in times of public disaster people didn't want to make any collective effort. (ibid.)

When the Revolution broke out, people were at first very enthusiastic and fired up by a genuine desire for liberty, according to Tocqueville. They did not, however, know how to translate this desire into free institutions. One reason for this was that they had come to believe that a centralized state was good for society. Another important reason was that they had forgotten how to unite into associations, when something needed to be accomplished. 'When the Revolution happened, one would have searched most of France in vain for ten men who had the habit of acting in common in an orderly way' (ibid. 243).

While the picture that has been presented so far fits most of France, according to Tocqueville, it did not fit all. There was especially one area in the country where things had developed in a very different way; and this case showed to Tocqueville what could have been accomplished if the country had been run in a sensible way.

This area was a province called Languedoc, and it had prospered while most of France had suffered. Languedoc was run by enlightened aristocrats and members of the third estate who had succeeded in keeping as much as possible of the intermediary bodies and the local freedoms intact. Taxation was handled in a much more humane way than elsewhere in the country and so was the forced labor (*corvée*). Tocqueville said that he had included the discussion of Languedoc 'to make clear by example what they [the other provinces in France] could all easily have become' (ibid. 249).

This last remark is an indication that the reason for writing *The Old Regime* was not an academic exercise to Tocqueville. Just as *Democracy in America* had a political purpose, so did his second book. 'I wanted to discover not only what illness killed the patient, but how the patient could have been cured' (ibid. 86).

Before leaving *The Old Regime*, something should also be said about the empirical material that Tocqueville used for his study of the administration and its dealings with the people. For the analysis of organizations in *Democracy in America*, Tocqueville did not use much primary material but relied instead on secondary sources, such as Sparks's report and Kent's *Commentaries*. With *The Old Regime* it was very different, and Tocqueville made a great effort to avoid using anything but primary historical sources.

He especially made an innovative use of two sources. He was probably the first to use a unique primary source on the opinions of the French people just before the Revolution, the so-called *cahiers de doléances* (for this source, see Chaussinand-Nogaret 1985; and for Tocqueville's use of it, see Gannett 2003*b*). Tocqueville also worked his way through a large number of administrative documents from the eighteenth century that he found in an archive at Tours. It was through his work in this archive, for example, that Tocqueville was able to produce his innovative analysis of the role of the intendant.

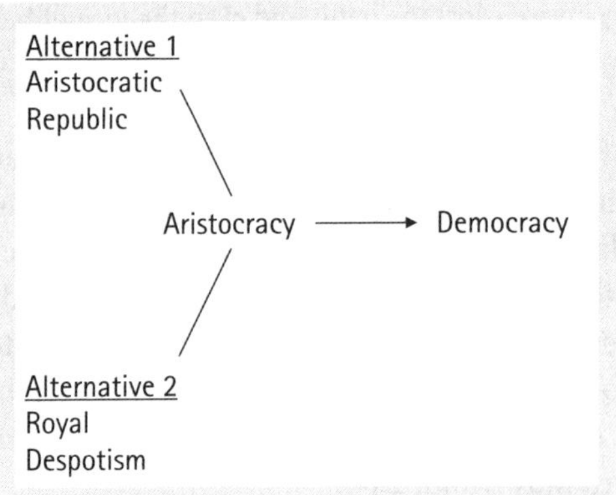

Fig. 3.2. Choices in aristocratic society, according to *The Old Regime and the Revolution*

Comment: According to Tocqueville's scheme in *The Old Regime*, an aristocracy can either take the form of an aristocratic republic or the form of royal despotism. One important factor in determining the outcome is the existence or absence of intermediary bodies of aristocrats.

One may sum up the key features of Tocqueville's analysis in *The Old Regime* as follows. Through its centralizing efforts, the French state had profoundly influenced the character of aristocratic society and, by doing so, made the transition to democracy difficult and violent. All of the revolutions during the nineteenth century, according to Tocqueville, had their origin in the failure of the French state to handle properly the transition to democratic or modern society.

Aristocratic society worked the best, according to Tocqueville, when it took the form of an aristocratic republic. When this was not the case, and when the intermediary bodies of the aristocracy were destroyed, the result was royal despotism (see Fig. 3.2).

3.4. Concluding Remarks

Tocqueville's work, as I hope to have shown in this essay, qualifies him to be regarded as a pioneer in organization theory. His dates (1805–59), as well as the time when *Democracy in America* was published (1835–40), make it natural to raise the question if he should not also be regarded as the founder of organization theory, since he was the first to produce a social science analysis of organizations. It is not, however, possible to give an answer to this question today. The reason for this is that the early history of social science, which roughly covers the period from the end of the eighteenth century to the mid-nineteenth century, is currently little known in organization theory. There is, for example, Saint-Simon (1760–1825), who was active during these years and who made '*organisation*' (and '*industrie*') the center of his work, but whose contribution has received next to no attention in organization theory.

Should one perhaps also look earlier than the late eighteenth century when trying to answer the question of who is the founder of organization theory? The reason for this would be that it has been established that organizations started to appear much earlier, already in the Middle Ages. James Coleman, for example, sets the date for the social invention of the organization to 1243 (Coleman 1993: 3). At this particular date, he explains, the notion that an organization constitutes a reality in its own right was for the first time fully realized. This took place when the notion of legal personality—that an organization can be seen as a person (*persona ficta*)—was invented by Italian jurist Sinibaldi de Fieschi (later known as Pope Innocent IV). Max Weber similarly argues that the early version of the Western firm was invented in the Middle Ages, drawing especially on the organizational form of the family (Weber 2003; for a discussion, see Ford 2007).

Whatever happened between this early date in the Middle Ages and the late eighteenth century is as little explored in modern organization theory as the period when social science was born, during the years from the late eighteenth century to the mid-nineteenth century. But even if this period was researched in a thorough fashion (as it deserves to be), there seems to be something special about the nineteenth century when it comes to modern organizations. My guess is therefore that organization theory, at least in its modern sense, was invented during this period.

This takes us back to Tocqueville and his work. Tocqueville's two most important contributions to organization theory, as I have tried to show, are to be found in his pioneering analysis of organizations in *Democracy in America* and in his pioneering analysis of the bureaucracy in *The Old Regime*. He presents a full picture of organizations in the former work—economic, political, and voluntary organizations—and he suggests what their function is and how they diffuse. In *The Old Regime*, Tocqueville presents the reader with a broad analysis of bureaucracy, which is cultural as well as political and social in nature. Through this picture of bureaucracy in France, we also get a counterpart to Weber's picture of bureaucracy in Germany. Tocqueville has, for example, a very different way of looking at organizational efficiency than Weber.

Much remains to be done before we have explored all that is of interest in Tocqueville's work from the perspective of organization theory. I have already mentioned that one needs to go through all of Tocqueville's work, not just *Democracy in America* and *The Old Regime*. But there is also the fact that Tocqueville was extremely fertile as a thinker, and that his writings are full of sharp observations and analyses, many of which would be enough for a doctoral dissertation today. Everything that Tocqueville encountered, he tried to explain; and the result is a work that brims over with explanations and theories about the way that society

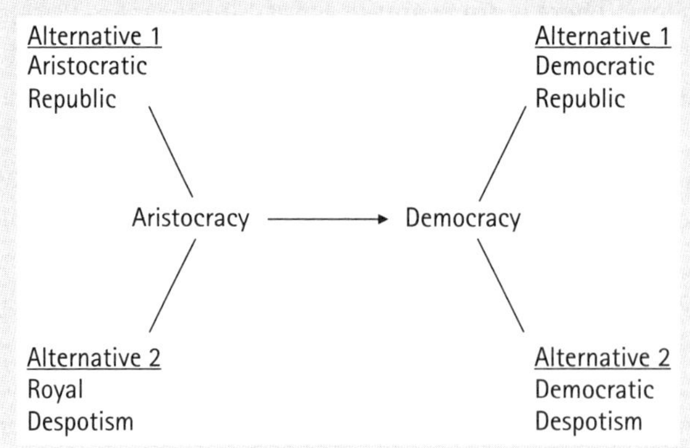

Fig. 3.3. The full conceptual scheme in Tocqueville's work

Comment: There is a distinct symmetry in Tocqueville's scheme of society's development from aristocracy to democracy, in that there are two main options in each social state: either the state takes over everything and creates an authoritarian society or people associate in 'intermediate bodies' (aristocratic society) or in 'associations' (democratic society). In the aristocratic republic, only aristocrats are free, while in a democratic republic all are free. Around each human being, Tocqueville says on the last page of *Democracy in America*, God has traced a *fatal circle* within which he or she is free—but beyond this nothing can be changed (Tocqueville 2004: 834).

works. This is also true, I suggest, for what he has to say about organizations and administration, including bureaucracy.

I have suggested that it would be wrong to squeeze Tocqueville too much into the mold of contemporary organization theory; he had his own agenda, and this agenda was different from the one that is current today. It is in the tension between these two visions, I have suggested, that some of the most interesting ideas can be generated from a study of Tocqueville's work. This can be illustrated by his theory of society moving from aristocracy to democracy. In the part devoted to *Democracy in America* in this chapter, I showed that Tocqueville saw two options for democratic society: either liberty, backed up by people joined in organizations, or democratic despotism, in which the state with its administrative machinery decides what happens (see Fig. 3.1). I then showed how Tocqueville in *The Old Regime* argues that France had two options: the centralized state with its powerful administration or the Languedoc option, in which there exists a set of functioning intermediary bodies (see Fig. 3.2).

The arguments about the two options that exist in *Democracy in America* and *The Old Regime* are symmetrical, something that becomes clear if one unites Fig. 3.1 and Fig. 3.2 into one single figure (see Fig. 3.3). The key argument about organizations and administration in Tocqueville, in brief, is that their main function is not to make administration run smoother and the corporations make money, but to create a society in which individuals can come together in freedom. Once there is freedom, the administration will run smoothly and the economy will do well, according to Tocqueville. But doing well economically is a side-effect; freedom comes first, and one cannot use it in an instrumental fashion to increase in economic well-being (Swedberg 2009).

What one finds in Tocqueville's work is consequently a view of organizations and administration that differs markedly from that of contemporary organization theory, in which organizations are primarily seen as instruments for powerful individuals and institutions, not as *associations* in which people come together as part of their efforts to live in liberty. Tocqueville's vision of associations and their link to freedom is bold—and it is a vision that deserves to be taken seriously in modern organization theory.

References

Adams, H. B. (1898). 'Jared Sparks and Alexis de Tocqueville'. *Johns Hopkins University Studies in History and Political Science*, 16: 7–49.

Aldrich, H. (1999). *Organizations Evolving*. London: Sage.

—— and Ruef, M. (2006). *Organizations Evolving*. 2nd edn. London: Sage.

Alexander, J. (2006). 'Tocqueville's Two Forms of Associations: Interpreting Tocqueville and Debates over Civil Society Today'. *Tocqueville Review*, 27/2: 175–90.

Aron, R. (1968). *Main Currents in Sociological Thought*. 2 vols. New York: Anchor Books.

Beaumont, G. de, and Tocqueville, A. de (1964). *On the Penitentiary System in the United States and Its Application in France*. Carbondale: Southern Illinois University Press.

Boesche, R. (1983). 'Tocqueville and *Le Commerce*: A Newspaper Expressing his Unusual Liberalism'. *Journal of the History of Ideas*, 44/2: 277–92.

Bumiller, E. (2005). 'Bush Finds Affirmation in a Frenchman's Word'. *New York Times*, 14 March, Section A: 15.

Chaussinand-Nogaret, G. (1985). *The French Nobility in the Eighteenth Century: From Feudalism to Enlightenment*. Cambridge: Cambridge University Press.

Coleman, J. (1993). 'The Rational Reconstruction of Society'. *American Sociological Review*, 58: 1–15.

Courpasson, D., and Clegg, S. (2006). 'Dissolving the Iron Cages? Tocqueville, Michels, Bureaucracy and the Perpetuation of Elite Power'. *Organization*, 13/3: 319–43.

Drescher, S. (1964). *Tocqueville and England*. Cambridge, Mass.: Harvard University Press.

Ford, L. (2007). 'Max Weber on Property: An Interpretive Understanding'. Cornell University, Center for the Study of Economy and Society Working Papers # 39.

Galston, W. (2000). 'Civil Society and the "Art of Association"'. *Journal of Democracy*, 11/1: 64–70.

Gannett, R. (2003*a*). 'Bowling Ninepins in Tocqueville's Township'. *American Political Science Review*, 97/1: 1–16.

—— (2003*b*). *Tocqueville Unveiled: The Historian and His Sources for the Old Regime and the Revolution*. Chicago: University of Chicago Press.

Jardin, A. (1988). *Tocqueville: A Biography*. New York: Farrar, Strauss, Giroux.

Lounsbury, M., and Carberry, E. (2005). 'From King to Court Jester? Weber's Fall from Grace in Organizational Theory'. *Organization Studies*, 26/4: 501–25.

Mélonio, F. (1998). *Tocqueville and the French.* Charlottesville: University of Virginia Press.
Offe, C. (2005). *Reflections on America: Tocqueville, Weber and Adorno in the United States.* London: Polity.
Perrow, C. (1986). *Complex Organizations: A Critical Essay.* 3rd edn. New York: McGraw-Hill.
Pfeffer, J. (1981). *Organizations and Organization Theory.* Marshfield, Mass.: Pitman.
Pierson, G. (1938). *Tocqueville and Beaumont in America.* New York: Oxford University Press.
Platt, J. (2002). 'The History of the Interview', in J. Gubrium and J. Holstein (eds.), *Handbook of Interview Research: Context & Method.* London: Sage.
Putnam, R. (1993). *Making Democracy Work: Civic Traditions in Modern Italy.* Princeton: Princeton University Press.
Rosanvallon, P. (1995). 'The History of the Word "Democracy" in France'. *Journal of Democracy*, 6/4: 140–54.
Schleifer, J. (1980). *The Making of Tocqueville's Democracy in America.* Chapel Hill: University of North Carolina Press.
Scott, R. (1992). *Organizations: Rational, Natural and Open Systems.* 3rd edn. Englewood Cliffs, NJ: Prentice Hall.
Selznick, P. (1952). *The Organizational Weapon.* New York: McGraw-Hill.
Skocpol, T. (1997). 'The Tocqueville Problem: Civic Engagement in American Democracy'. *Social Science History*, 21/4: 455–79.
Smith, L. (1942). 'Alexis de Tocqueville and Public Administration'. *Public Administration Review*, 2/3: 221–39.
Sparks, J. (1898). 'On the Government of Towns in New England', in H. B. Adams, 'Jared Sparks and Alexis de Tocqueville', *Johns Hopkins University Studies in History and Political Science*, 16: 7–49.
Swedberg, R. (2009). *Tocqueville's Political Economy.* Princeton: Princeton University Press.
Tocqueville, A. de. (1878). *Études économiques, politiques, et littéraires.* Paris: Calmann Levy.
——(1951–). *Oeuvres complètes.* Paris: Gallimard. This edition (which is still incomplete) represents the major collection of Tocqueville's works.
——(1959). *Journey to America*, ed. J. P. Mayer, trans. G. Lawrence. New Haven: Yale University Press.
——(1968). 'Memoir on Pauperism', in S. Dresher (ed.), *Tocqueville and Beaumont on Social Reform.* New York: Harper & Row.
——(1989). 'Deuxième memoire sur le paupérisme', in *Oeuvres completes.* Paris: Gallimard.
——(1990). *De la démocratie en Amérique.* Première edition historico-critique revue et augmentée par Eduardo Nolla. 2 vols. Paris: Librairie philosophique J. Vrin.
——(1998). *The Old Regime and the Revolution*, trans. A. S. Kahan. Vol. 1. Chicago: University of Chicago Press.
——(2001*a*). *The Old Regime and the Revolution*, trans. A. S. Kahan. Vol. 2. Chicago: University of Chicago Press.
——(2001*b*). *Writings on Empire and Slavery*, ed. J. Pitts. Baltimore: Johns Hopkins University Press.
——(2004). *Democracy in America*, trans. Arthur Goldhammer. New York: Library of America.

Vasi, I. B., and Strang, D. (2007). 'Civil Liberty in America: The Diffusion of Municipal Bill of Rights Resolutions after October 26, 2001'. Unpublished paper.

Weber, M. (1949). *Essays in the Methodology of the Social Sciences*. New York: Free Press.

—— (2003). *The History of Commercial Partnerships in the Middle Ages*. Lanham: Rowman & Littlefield Publishers.

Whittington, K. (2001). 'Revisiting Tocqueville's America: Society, Politics, and Associations in the Nineteenth Century', in B. Edwards, M. W. Foley, and M. Diani (eds.), *Beyond Tocqueville*. Hanover, NH: University Press of New England.

Wudel, D. (1993). 'Tocqueville on Associations and Association', in P. A. Lawler and J. Aulis (eds.), *Tocqueville's Defense of Human Liberty: Current Essays*. New York: Garland Publishing.

Zaleski, P. (2000). 'Tocqueville i spoleczenstwo cywilne: W strone romantycznego postrzegania rzeczywistosci spolecznej' (Tocqueville and Civil Society: Towards a Romantic Vision of the Dichotomic Structure of Society). *Acta Philologica*, 33: 1–7.

CHAPTER 4

MARX AND ORGANIZATION STUDIES TODAY

PAUL S. ADLER

4.1. Introduction

It is hardly obvious that Karl Marx, a philosopher, economist, and revolutionary activist who died a century and a quarter ago, should have much relevance to contemporary organization studies. Surely, the skeptic says, too many important features of contemporary organizations post-date Marx. On further reflection, however, it is obvious that organizations today share many fundamental features with those Marx saw taking shape in his time. In particular, we still live with a basically capitalist form of society and enterprise.

Marx's analysis was not only astute in discerning capitalism's enduring features: it was also deeply critical. He documented and denounced capitalism's dark sides—its enormous human and environmental costs. More controversially, he claimed to have identified some fundamental features of capitalist development that would lead inevitably to capitalism's demise and its replacement by a superior form of society.

This combination of perspicacity, critique, and prediction ensured that over much of the twentieth century Marxist thought was a key reference point for sociology in general and for organization studies in particular—as an explicit premise, or as a foil for contrasting views, or as a source of inspiration that was discreetly left unnamed. In the last decades of the twentieth century, with the weakening of the labor movement in many of the advanced capitalist countries, with the culmination of anti-colonialist struggles in developing countries, and with the demise of the Soviet Union and its allies, Marxist ideas lost some of their traditional impetus. On the other hand, however, Marxist ideas have recently received new impetus from the rise of global justice movements and from growing concerns about capitalism's destructive environmental effects and its unstable financial structure.

Since Marx's time, the general matrix of Marxist theory has not remained fixed in doctrinaire rigidity: numerous variants of the basic theory have emerged (Anderson 1979; Burawoy 1990). This chapter's goal, however, is to show the fruitfulness of Marx's original insights; I therefore address only some particularly important points of debate among Marxists. The following sections discuss, in turn, Marx's basic theory, its main uses in organization studies, and its dialogue with other theories.

4.2. Marxism: Key Ideas

Marx was born in Germany, in 1818, and died in London in 1883. He studied law and philosophy in Bonn and Berlin, where he participated in the iconoclastic, anti-religious 'Young Hegelian' scene. Political activism led him to Paris in 1843 and from there to Brussels, back to Germany, and eventually to Britain in 1849, where he began serious study of political economy. Throughout this period, he was active in revolutionary circles of Europe. He published several major works during his lifetime, and several others appeared posthumously (see a listing in the References below). He was supported financially by Friedrich Engels, who had inherited an ownership share in a textile manufacturing concern in Manchester. Engels was Marx's closest colleague in both writing and political activism. This section summarizes the main themes in Marx's (and Engels's) writing, with an emphasis on those that are most relevant to organization studies.

In *The German Ideology* (originally published in 1845), Marx and Engels mark their distance from Hegel and the Young Hegelians. They advance three main ideas. First, human action is constrained and enabled by its historically specific conditions: generic trans-historical theorizing is therefore a poor foundation for social science. Second, the ideas we work with, including abstract theoretical ones, are conditioned by our own historical context. And finally, because people must produce in order to live, the sphere of production is primary in relation to the sphere of thought and culture.

The *Communist Manifesto* (1848), the preface to the *Contribution to the Critique of Political Economy* (1859), the *Grundrisse* (1857), and *Capital* (1867) articulate Marx's analysis in more detail. The following sections highlight six main themes.

4.2.1. The Class Structure and the Centrality of Class Struggle

If production is primary and if human production is by nature collective rather than individual, then the most basic structure of society is its 'mode of production'. (Concrete societies typically embody residues of earlier modes alongside their dominant mode.) Modes of production are defined by two sets of relations. 'Forces of production' are humanity's relations with the natural world, composed of material 'means of production' (equipment, technology, raw materials) and human productive capacities (skills, etc.). 'Relations of production' define the distribution across social categories ('classes') of rights to ownership and control over these forces of production.

The broad sweep of human history can be understood as the dialectical progression of successively more productive modes of production. In the European region, this progression was from primitive communism, to slavery, to feudalism, and then capitalism. Primitive communism has no class structure *per se* because the forces of production are too primitive to generate enough surplus to support a non-laboring class. Slave relations correspond to a technology of dispersed farming on large estates. Feudal vassalage relations correspond to small-scale agriculture and handicraft tools. And capitalist relations of production—defined by the conjunction of wage-based exploitation within firms and market competition between firms—correspond to machinery and large-scale industry. This progression is dialectical insofar as the emergence of a new structure is the result of the internal contradictions of the old. (On Marx's 'dialectical' approach and the idea that contradictions are to be found in reality rather than only among propositions, see Ilyenkov 1982; Ollman 2003.)

Class struggle between the exploiting and exploited classes is the *motor* of this progression; however, its basic *direction* is set by the vector of advancing forces of production. When the prevailing relations of production are no longer able to assure the further advance of the forces of production, class conflict intensifies and the old class structure is eventually overthrown, allowing a new mode of production to emerge in which human productivity can develop further (see exposition by Cohen 1978). Capitalism is distinctive in this sequence because its characteristic relations of production greatly intensify pressures to further develop the forces of production; in comparison, all previous modes are far less technologically dynamic.

Marxist sociology and organization studies are characterized by their insistence that the relations of production and the resulting class structure constitute the primary axis of social differentiation, determining the broad pattern of economic opportunity, education and health conditions, and political orientations. Marxist theory was for many years the foil against which were elaborated sociological theories of 'the end of ideology', which culminated in 1950s 'functionalism' and the celebration of normative integration of US society. Marxism is one of the family of 'conflict' theories that re-emerged in opposition to this 'apologetic' condition in sociology.

4.2.2. The Specific Form of Capitalist Exploitation

Capitalism as a mode of production is distinguished by the centrality of commodity production (see Foley 1986 for a particularly clear exposition of Marx's theory). A commodity is a product (good or service) produced for sale rather than use—a 'contradictory unity', Marx says, of exchange-value (the commodity's capacity to command other products and money in exchange) and use-value (its capacity to satisfy a need or desire). Capitalism emerges from small-scale commodity production when labor too becomes a commodity. This happens through a process of violent dispossession that deprives workers of alternative ways to access means of consumption or production, and that thus forces workers to exchange their capacity to work for a wage as if this creative capacity too were a commodity.

Marx follows classical political economists such as Ricardo in arguing that supply and demand do not determine the price of a commodity (as argued by neo-classical economics), but only influence its fluctuation around its objectively determined value. This value is determined by the socially necessary labor time invested in the product's production. (Note that, contrary to a popular misconception, this 'labor theory of value' is not a normative theory: Marx is not arguing that value should be based on labor input; he is adamant that use-values typically also require a host of non-labor contributions; his theory aims to explain how capitalist exchange-value actually works.) Under normal conditions, labor power too receives a wage that reflects the socially necessary labor time required to produce it, which is the cost of the daily consumption required for workers and their families as well as of their investment in training and education. (Note that for Marx, the value of labor power has a social and historical component: it is not just a biological minimum as assumed in Malthus's account.) Given the level of advance of the forces of production in the capitalist phase of historical evolution, it only takes a few hours in the working day for workers to produce the equivalent of their wages ('necessary labor-time'); and employers can legally appropriate the value produced in the rest of the working day ('surplus labor' and thus 'surplus value') with which to pay both the non-labor inputs and investors' profit.

When Marxists use an ethically charged term such as 'exploitation' to describe these relations of production, non-Marxists often criticize them for lack of objectivity, since even in Marx's own theory it is assumed that wages normally reflect the value of labor power, and since no economic growth would be possible without some surplus being withheld. Marx, however, understands the need for a surplus; but he argues that surplus labor represents exploitation because workers have no control over the use of that surplus and because their share is depressed by the portion siphoned off for capitalists' private consumption.

Moreover, calling this wage relation 'exploitation' captures nicely its essentially conflictual character. On the one side, under competitive pressure in product and financial markets, employers are pushed to increase surplus labor, regardless of their personal preferences. On the other side, workers struggle to maintain their jobs, their dignity, and their wage levels. Exploitation and class conflict are thus not abnormal conditions created by distortions of the market process: they are a fundamental feature of capitalist production even under hypothetically pure competitive conditions.

To emphasize conflict is not to deny the simultaneous need for cooperation in production. Indeed, the large-scale capitalist enterprise depends crucially on cooperation to coordinate its complex division of labor, and managers play a key productive role in that coordination. Managers' roles are, however, simultaneously productive and exploitative (Carchedi 1977; Wright 1985), and labor–management relations in the capitalist firm embody a contradictory unity of cooperation and conflict, reflecting the basic use-value/exchange-value contradiction of the commodity itself.

4.2.3. The Development of Capitalist Production

Marx identifies two generic strategies for increasing surplus labor. First, capitalists can extend and intensify the working day and can force more members of each family into the labor force: these generate what Marx calls 'absolute surplus-value'. Second, employers can respond to competitive pressures with technological and organizational innovations that reduce necessary labor time: this generates 'relative surplus-value'.

When capitalism first establishes itself, firms usually leave the technology of production unchanged, and exploitation takes the form of increasing absolute surplus-value. The resulting contrast in hours and intensity of work between traditional village life and early factory life has been documented in numerous scholarly and literary accounts (see Thompson 1963). This is what Marx (1976: Appendix) calls the *formal subordination of labor to capital*: it is merely formal because the underlying production process is as yet unchanged. As capitalism consolidates, the negative social externalities of excessive working hours and of child labor prompt political action by both workers and enlightened capitalists, resulting in new laws and regulations. These increase incentives for firms to accelerate technological innovation, and as a result, relative surplus-value becomes progressively more important, and we see the emergence of the *real subordination* of labor to capital as the labor process itself is progressively reshaped.

The contradictions of capitalism do not disappear with this shift from absolute to relative surplus-value and from formal to real subordination—they deepen and mature. Marx sees capitalist development as the unfolding of a real contradiction between, on the one side, the ineluctable tendency towards what he calls the 'socialization' of the forces of production, and on the other side, the maintenance of an increasingly obsolete structure of relations of production based on private property of the means of production. Marx's concept of socialization was more expansive than in current usages: activity is socialized insofar as it comes to embody the capabilities of the larger society rather than only those that emerge from isolated, local contexts (e.g. Marx 1973: 705; 1976: 1024).

The socialization of the forces of production plays out at three levels. First, it appears as the growing mastery of large-scale cooperation in complex organizations. The individual worker is now productive only as part of what Marx calls a 'collective worker'. In this light, techniques of work organization—such as the principles of bureaucracy, scientific management, or lean production—are part of the forces of production. The development of such principles represents steps towards socialization insofar as they allow more rational, conscious planning and management of large-scale, interdependent operations.

Second, on a more global level, the socialization of the forces of production means that increasingly differentiated, specialized branches of activity are conjoined in an increasingly interdependent global economy. Even though this interdependence is coordinated by the invisible hand of the market rather than by conscious planning, society's productivity is increased by the development of universally accessible science, by the latter's embodiment in specialized materials and equipment, and by the ability to access and integrate these capabilities on an increasingly global scale.

Finally, socialization appears on an individual, subjective level. When the effective subject of production is no longer an individual worker but the collective worker, workers' identities change—they are re-socialized. (Marx's analysis is similar here to Elias 2000.) The development of the forces of production pulls workers out of what Marx and Engels call in the *Communist Manifesto* 'rural idiocy'. In *The Poverty of Philosophy* (1955), Marx similarly celebrates the end of 'craft idiocy'. Marx's use of the term 'idiocy' preserves both its colloquial sense and the meaning from the Greek *idiotes*, denoting an asocial individual isolated from the polis. At the opposite end of the spectrum from the *idiotes* is the 'social individual' described by the *Grundrisse*, in the form of the technically sophisticated worker who accesses and deploys society's accumulated scientific and technological knowledge.

Marx argues that these various forms of the socialization of the forces of production are stimulated by the capitalist relations of production and the associated pressures of competition and exploitation; and at the same time, however, these latter pressures distort and limit socialization. Instead of a broadening association of producers progressively mastering their collective future, this socialization appears, at least at first, in the form of intensified coercion by quasi-natural laws of the market over firms and by corporate bureaucracy over workers. Under capitalist conditions, the substance of socialization takes on a form that is exploitative and alienating. Forms of work organization, for example, are means of coordination in the form of means of exploitation. To use a dialectical formulation: the content is in contradiction with its form.

The socialization tendency is, however, difficult to repress, and eventually, the exigencies of production impel the socialization of the relations of production too. The latter appears at first in limited, capitalistic form, as the shift from private to public corporations, the concentration of ownership, and the growing government role in the economy (the 'creeping socialism' denounced by Hayek 1944). These partial steps encourage rather than undercut calls for further socialization: Schumpeter's (1942) account is very faithful to Marx's analysis, even if his regretful tone contrasts with Marx's enthusiasm. Eventually, Marx predicts, we will see a wholesale 'socialist' transformation that reestablishes a correspondence between relations and forces of production at a new, higher level—with socialized production now under socialized ownership and control.

4.2.4. The Social Impact of Commodity Production and Capital Accumulation

In the *Manifesto* and elsewhere, Marx is eloquent on the progressive content of this process of capitalist development. The world market brings humanity together, to huge productivity advantage and freeing us from parochialism and petty nationalism. But Marx is also savage in his critique of the dark side of this historical process.

Consider commodity production. Competition drives technological innovation, prompting the proliferation of new goods and services. On the one hand, there is no denying the use-value of many of these new products. On the other, many of them are frivolous or even dangerous, and the underlying market process has an enormous social cost in employment precariousness and environmental damage. Moreover, capitalism as a system of generalized commodity production engenders *commodity fetishism*: instead of mankind consciously and collectively mastering modern industry's complexity, commodities appear as the active agents, struggling for monetary recognition. Abstract 'laws of the market' impose themselves as an alien, coercive force. The structure of the capitalist economy works to produce an inverted understanding of itself in our minds, as if the market 'decides' while we merely submit. *Alienation* is a structural feature of such an economy.

The commodity form progressively takes over more spheres of activity such as food production and preparation, childcare and education, healthcare, and culture. In this process, traditional forms of community—with both their attractive features and their features inimical to women's freedom and to creative individual flourishing—are swept away, as gift exchange and traditional fealty are replaced by the cash nexus and instrumental association. In place of local markets, a global market emerges for products, labor power, and finance: small-scale commodity producers (the traditional petty bourgeoisie) disappear, and a new middle class of salaried managers and experts is created.

Alongside a general tendency to improvement in average standards of living, capitalist growth continually reproduces unemployment and poverty. Capitalism develops not only endogenously but also through imperialist expansion (see Brewer 1980), and as capitalists based in the more 'advanced' regions exploit the populations of the less advanced regions, average incomes and health conditions improve, but at the cost of considerable inequality, poverty, and misery.

4.2.5. The Limits of Capitalist Development

Capitalism is not the last in the sequence of modes of production; it is not the end of history. As capitalism develops and expands, not only does socialization consolidate the material preconditions for socialism, but the conditions for a revolutionary change in the mode of production progressively ripen.

On the one hand, the system loses its historical legitimacy. In *Capital*, Marx shows that an economy based on competition will necessarily experience periodic crises, and that in the long term, these crises are more likely to worsen than to moderate. Each firm, in order to survive, must attract investment funds and grow faster than its peers; this creates a permanent tendency to overproduction. The dynamic equilibrium of the capitalist economic system relies not on conscious planning but on the spontaneous functioning of the market—plus, since the mid-twentieth century, some very crude instruments of government intervention—and as a result, its homeostatic properties function only poorly and at enormous social cost. As markets expand in geographic scope, crises sweep across ever-larger regions. As the productivity of modern industry grows, the parallel growth of inequality, the persistence of poverty, the periodic crises, the development of negative social and environmental externalities become ever more incongruous, indeed obscene.

On the other hand, the social class capable of doing away with capitalism and creating a new form of society becomes stronger. The working class—broadly construed as those who must sell their capacity to work, whether they be blue- or white-collar, skilled or not, urban or rural—is strengthened by the development of capitalism itself: as the forces of production develop in a socialized direction, they call for an increasingly educated workforce; workers are brought into ever-larger units of production and acquire habits of coordinated activity; communication technologies facilitate workers' collective action; and the everyday experience of class struggle both at work and in the electoral sphere teaches workers how to mobilize. Recent Marxist sociology has paid less attention to the positive effects of capitalist development on working-class capabilities; but it has been constant in highlighting the persistence of crisis tendencies and the wastefulness of the market mechanism.

4.2.6. The Role of Politics, Ideology, and Culture in Class Struggle and Social Change

In Marx's materialist account, ideas, political action, and culture are important causal factors in both the reproduction and the transformation of society; but they are secondary relative to the effects of the structural contradictions characteristic of the capitalist mode of production. The state is basically an instrument of class domination, as are culture and religion. Marx allows that this political-ideological superstructure has a certain autonomy relative to the technological-economic base of society, and that it has real effects on that base. In the broader sweep of history, however, this autonomy is relative and the bidirectional causality is not symmetrical. (In a famous footnote in *Capital* (Marx 1976: 175–6), Marx notes that the base has less direct influence in pre-capitalist societies than in capitalist ones; but he argues that if politics was the dominant factor in ancient Greece, and if religion was the dominant force in the Middle Ages, it is the economic structure of those societies that in turn explains why these superstructural factors were so influential.) Exactly how to conceptualize this asymmetry has been the object of a long debate among Marxists (for an overview, see Jessop 2001). Marxist-inspired sociologists such as Domhoff (1983) highlight the class character of the state. Kolko (1963) and Weinstein (1968) show the dominant role of ruling-class interests even in relatively benign domestic legislation as well as foreign policy.

Revolutionary change would require the political and ideological mobilization of the working class against this domination. The objective contradictions created in the realm of production (the maturation of the productive forces and the acuteness of their contradiction with prevailing relations of production) as well as the conflicts within the political and cultural realms together create more or less propitious circumstances for this mobilization.

4.3. Reasserting Marx

Marxist scholarship faces several challenges in the organization studies field. First, many organizational scholars today are based in business schools, where they labor under the weight of instrumentalist norms, and the Marxist perspective offers little if research is seen as valuable only insofar as it helps managers fulfill a mission of shareholder wealth maximization.

In contrast to this institutional challenge, several of the properly theoretical challenges posed to Marxism reveal strengths of the Marxist approach. First, skeptics wonder what credibility we should accord Marxist theory when the polities that claim inspiration from Marx—notably the former Soviet Union—seem to have failed. However, Marxist theory provides a good starting point for understanding this failure (for a short overview, see Murphy 2007; for a more comprehensive survey, see Liden 2007) and indeed most Marxists at the time of the Bolshevik Revolution were skeptical of prospects for socialism there, since its economy was so backward.

Second, critics argue that the lack of revolutionary activity on the part of the working class belies the *Communist Manifesto*'s argument that capitalism 'produces its own gravediggers' and that socialism is therefore inevitable. However, Marx never predicted any specific life-span for capitalism. While his political writings sometimes express enthusiastic optimism for imminent change, his theory only predicts the form of capitalism's development and the increasingly likelihood of its supercession—not whether capitalism's supercession is years, decades, or centuries away (Desai 2002).

Third, Marx seems focused on factory work, so some might wonder what he has to say about a modern economy based mainly on services. However, Marx's insightful comments on clerical and sales and other services (notably in *Capital*) have provided a platform for fruitful research on service work of various kinds (e.g. Callahan and Thompson 2001). Similarly, skeptics might wonder whether Marx is relevant in an age when knowledge seems increasingly to have replaced capital or simple labor as a source of wealth. This challenge too reveals strengths of Marxist theory. Marx was eloquent on the growing centrality of knowledge as a productive resource (see most notably Marx 1973: 704 ff.). Marxists point out that in reality the vast bulk of knowledge workers can produce nothing without access to capital and without subordination to the wage relation (either directly or as ostensibly independent contractors). And Marxist theory provides fruitful ideas for studying the challenges confronting capitalist firms in assuring the effectiveness of these knowledge workers (see e.g. Adler 2001; Smith 1987).

Finally, skeptics often attack Marxism for its failure to acknowledge real progress under capitalism. Over the past century or so, albeit with ups and downs and great unevenness across regions, capitalist development has brought rising standards of living and education, improved mortality and morbidity, growing capacity to communicate and travel, increased opportunities for individual self-development and expression, and less autocratic forms of organization. This progress is visible in both the capitalist center and in imperialism's effects on the periphery (Warren 1980). But Marxist scholarship is partisan: it is constantly seeking to highlight the problems of capitalism and to show why these problems cannot be satisfactorily resolved without fundamental change in social structure. This partisanship tends to blind Marxists to the progressive effects of capitalist development.

If Marxists often fall into this polemical trap, it is also because they often shy away from the technological determinism implied by Marx's view of the role of the forces of production in historical process, and as a result they reduce Marxism to class struggle (Adler 2007). A small but persistent current within Marxist sociology has attempted to restore a richer version of Marx (see e.g. Hirschhorn 1984; Kenney and Florida 1993; Van der Pijl 1998; Warren 1980). I have called this current 'paleo-Marxist' to signal ironically the contrast with the more recent 'neo-Marxist' interpretations. This paleo-Marxism goes back to Marx's argument that class struggle is itself conditioned by a deeper contradiction—that between the progressive socialization of the productive forces and the persistence of capitalist relations of production. This version of Marx has little difficulty making sense of progress under capitalism without abandoning its radical critique.

4.4. Marxist Organization Studies

This section highlights some key features of Marxist organization studies, reviewing research focused first on the organization level, then on the broader context beyond the organization. Space limitations preclude a detailed review of this literature (in particular, I focus on English-language publications and I do not discuss Marxist analyses of specific forms of organization nor specific categories of workers); but within each subsection we can identify the main arguments and distinguishing features of Marxist versus non-Marxist approaches and of paleo- versus neo-Marxist versions.

4.4.1. Organizations

Marxist research on organizations has focused primarily on the conflictual aspects of the employment relation, and the ramifications for the structure and functioning of organizations. Marxist organization studies are thus counterposed to traditional functionalist, organicist conceptions of organizations and society and to scholarship that obscures the fundamental divergence of interests that shapes organizations. Marxist theory is not alone in its focus on conflict; the distinctive feature of the Marxist approach is in attributing the deep cause of this conflict to exploitation rather than to domination by authority as argued by writers such as Weber and Dahrendorf (see Clegg and Dunkerley 1980; Thompson and McHugh 2002: 365–70). Where the neo-Marxists make this conflictuality foundational, the paleo strand argues that it coexists with cooperation in a contradictory unity. The sections below sketch the main dimensions of this field of research.

4.4.1.1. *Work, Skills, and Learning*

Marx offers a powerful transhistorical ('anthropological') theory of human activity in general and of productive activity in particular. In analyzing capitalist work organizations, Marx adds to this abstract account more 'concrete' layers of determination associated with the specific mode of production; but the anthropological substratum of his theory is fruitful too.

For Marx, the prototypical activity is a practical rather than contemplative engagement with the world around us. Marx's understanding of practical activity is very close to Dewey's (as argued by Hook 2002). In Marx's account, human activity is distinctive in its reliance on tools, both concrete and symbolic. The object of our activity is not a simple brute empirical fact, a mere 'stimulus' to our 'response'; but nor is it merely in our heads. It is a material reality; but our relation to this reality is always mediated by the material tools, abstract concepts and theories, and human desires that we bring to the situation. Productive activity is further distinguished by its collective character, so the individual's relation to the object of activity is further mediated by that individual's relation to the collectivity.

This understanding was developed by the Soviet psychologists (Vygotsky 1962, 1978; Luria 1976; Leont'ev 1978; see also Cole 1996). The resulting Marxist version of 'practice' theory affords useful insights into the nature of work, skills, and learning. Recently these have been developed by Lave (1988) and Wenger (1998), and by a current of research known as cultural-historical activity theory (Engeström 1987, 1990; Engeström, Miettinin, and Punamaki 1999; Sawchuk, Duarte, and Elhammoumi 2006).

This perspective gives us a fruitful way to understand some key changes in workers' skills. In its pre-capitalist form, skill was largely tacit; working knowledge was deeply local; it was learned in intimate apprenticeship as a farmer or artisan. Under advanced capitalist conditions, skill requires the internalization of a much larger universe of accumulated knowledge; but this knowledge has become increasingly scientific and thus far more explicit and less exclusively tacit, making society's accumulated knowledge available to vastly greatly numbers. Skills are therefore no longer formed by intimate apprenticeship, but by more rigorously managed skill-formation processes. On the one hand, as neo-Marxists argue, the real subordination of labor to capital leads to the narrowing of craft workers' skills; on the other hand, as paleo-Marxists argue, skills are deepened and socialized in this process. Innovation is similarly socialized: what was once a highly localized and embedded process relying on tacit knowledge becomes a formalized, globally dispersed process based on a mix of tacit and explicit knowledge—a mix in which the explicit component grows exponentially (Adler 2001; Miettinin 1999; Miettinin and Hasu 2002).

4.4.1.2. Exploitation and Control

Given the key role of exploitation and conflict in Marxist theory, control naturally becomes central to Marxist research on organizations. Control is a central theme in a broad range of studies of work organization; but Marxist theory insists that the transhistorical, generic problems of control that arise in any collective endeavor take on a distinctive form in capitalist enterprise, since control here is in the interest of capitalist exploitation.

Braverman (1974) inaugurated a wave of explicitly Marxist-inspired research on control. Braverman identifies Frederick Taylor as the apostle of the real subordination of labor to capital, and on this foundation draws a compelling portrait of the deskilling and degradation of work in the twentieth century: how modern technology and organizing techniques are deployed as tools of control and exploitation of manual, service, and clerical workers. A considerable body of case studies and ethnographies illustrate Braverman's thesis (see e.g. Zimbalist 1979; Graham 1995). Braverman's work on control also inspired a considerable body of Marxist research on accounting (see Tinker 1991, and various papers in the journal *Critical Perspectives on Accounting*).

Braverman's landmark study has attracted criticism in proportion to its prominence (see e.g. Thompson 1989; Thompson and Warhurst 1998; Wardell, Steiger, and Meiskins 1999; Warhurst, Grugulis, and Keep 2004; Wood 1982). Neo-Marxist criticisms focus on restoring the centrality of ongoing class struggle against capitalist control efforts. Several such critics point out that Braverman ignores workers' resistance, and that managers have an alternative to deskilling in 'responsible autonomy', which is particularly attractive where workers' resistance is strong (Friedman 1977). The outcome is perhaps therefore not a trend towards deskilling and ever-greater managerial control, but instead historically contingent and regionally particular (Edwards 1979; Littler and Salaman 1982; Wood 1982). Other sympathetic critics argue that Braverman's account misleads by ignoring other dimensions of differentiation, such as gender and race, and by ignoring the social construction of skill categories.

Braverman retains Marx's premise that capitalist development—damaging though it may be to workers' well-being—increases social productivity (at least, until the capitalist system reaches its apogee). Other neo-Marxists go further: Marglin (1974) and Stone (1973) argue that, even in the early phases of capitalist development, which saw the replacement of inside contracting with the managerial authority of the wage system, productivity was sacrificed to assure greater social control over the workforce.

The paleo-Marxist critiques of Braverman are somewhat different (Adler 2007). They build on Hyman's (1987) argument that management is caught between contradictory imperatives—needing workers who are simultaneously 'dependable' and 'disposable' (see also Cressey and MacInnes 1980). The paleo strand critiques Braverman's deskilling thesis: it embraces the evidence of a long-term skill upgrading trend in the workforce as a whole, seeing in this trend confirmation that capitalism has continued its historic mission of socializing the (subjective) forces of production. It therefore sees managerial control systems as internally contradictory, functioning both as tools of coordination and means of exploitation.

4.4.1.3. Technology

The field of organization studies has long been interested in the relative influence on work organization of technological factors and social factors. The ideological stakes are, of course, high: the most apologetic of mainstream sociology explains away many obnoxious features of the status quo as inevitable corollaries of modern technology. Contingency theory abstracts from this polemic to erect a general theory. In opposition, neo-Marxists insist that technology choices strengthen capitalist exploitation and control (e.g. Braverman 1974; Levidow and Young 1981). The neo-Marxist diagnosis can be reached in either of two ways. First, it is sometimes argued that the implementation of technology and its effects on social structure are socially determined: technology is typically flexible enough to ensure that capitalist-dominated implementation choices will effectively enhance this class domination. Second, moving upstream, technological design itself can be seen as mainly shaped by the dominant social forces (Mackenzie and Wajcman 1985; Noble 1984): at the limit, some neo-Marxists argue that technology is nothing but the material condensation of the prevailing relations of production.

Where neo-Marxists argue that capitalists adapt technology to the imperatives of control, the paleo approach argues that competition among capitalists deprives individual firms of such strong influence over their technology choices and forces them to adapt to the evolving technology frontier, even where this undermines their control (Hirschhorn 1984: Adler and Borys 1989). Both variants of Marxism argue that the capitalist system under-invests in some technologies that would be socially useful but unprofitable for private firms and over-invests in other technologies that boost private profits but are socially harmful. Marxist research on these themes has been influential not only in studies of manufacturing technologies but also in the Information Systems field (overview in Richardson and Robertson 2007).

4.4.1.4. *Ideology*

Ideology is, in the Marxist view, another key means of control, an instrument of class struggle. It is this anchoring of ideology in material interests that distinguishes the Marxist approach. Left-Weberians such as Bendix (1956) develop a critique of managerial ideology that shares some points with Marx; most Weberians, however, reject Marx's materialism in favor of a more contingent view of the relation between the material and ideational realms. Marxist approaches differ even more sharply from the resolutely culturalist approaches found in Durkheim-inspired neo-institutionalist theory, where 'institutional logics' as disembodied ideas possess world-shaping causal power (see also Levy and Scully 2007). Barley and Kunda's account (1992) is more compatible with a Marxist approach, showing the causal link between the condition of the economy and the predominance of rationalist versus commitment discourses in management literature.

Ideology is also important as a form of control at the organization level (Clegg 1981). Burawoy (1982, 1985) extends the traditional understanding of ideology as a societal-level phenomenon to the organizational level, exploring the ideological mechanisms buttressing class control within the firm and plant. A sizeable Marxist-inspired literature critiques corporate efforts to use participation and teamwork ideologies to undermine worker solidarity and union organization (Barker 1993; Fantasia 1995; Fantasia, Clawson, and Graham 1988; Grenier 1988; Grenier and Hogler 1991; Hales 2000). Research on emotional labor shows how capitalist ideology can reinforce control by shaping deeper aspects of self-consciousness (Hochschild 1965). The paleo-Marxist approach modifies the critique, arguing that practices such as teamwork, participation, and emotional labor have a dual character because they also represents a real advance in the productive forces insofar as workers learn to deploy a broader range of their personal capabilities in production activity and they learn to master the social-interactional and emotional dimensions of work (e.g. Lopez 2006).

4.4.1.5. *Workers' Responses*

Marxist organization studies have naturally devoted considerable attention to workers' responses to control and exploitation. Three responses have garnered most of the attention: alienation, consent, and resistance. I review them in turn.

A large proportion of the references to Marx in the sociology literature are in the context of discussions of *alienation*. In much of this literature, alienation is not strongly tied to Marxist theory, ignoring Marx's point that subjective feelings of alienation are the inevitable counterpart of the workers' objective alienation, expressing the structure of relations of production that deprive workers of control over the ends and means of work activity (Jermier 1985). As much of this sociological literature defines it, alienation can just as easily be the result of inevitable loss of individual autonomy in large-scale organization of any kind, rather than the specifically capitalist kind, or may be the result of an interpersonally inconsiderate style of managerial supervision, or may indeed be an intrinsic feature of any kind of instrumental work as distinct from free activity. Arguably, the real experience of alienation represents the concatenated effects of all of these; but Marxists highlight the different causal roles of each in explaining the observed patterns.

Consent is a second key response to capitalist control and exploitation. Noting the frequency of consent, Burawoy (1982) sees the task of Marxist organization studies as turning managerialist organization-behavior research on its head: instead of asking why workers do not work harder, we should be asking why they work as hard as they do. Burawoy argues that consent is created by ensnaring workers in activities—'games'—that encourage work effort (securing surplus labor) while camouflaging the underlying exploitation (obscuring, mystifying surplus labor). He identifies three main forms of these games: on the shop-floor, games around piecework are partially psychologically fulfilling; in careers, promises of promotion in internal labor markets pit workers in competition against each other; and in collective bargaining, workers have the illusion of negotiating power. In each case, these games provide workers with just enough feeling of choice to ensure their consent.

In understanding these political and ideological processes, Burawoy makes effective use of Gramsci's (1971) concept of hegemony. Hegemony helps explain how consent may signify neither acceptance nor legitimacy: it is not necessarily normative in the sense of strongly internalized values; it is typically a mix of acquiescence, internalized ideology, and coercion (see also Sallach 1974). This acquiescence pacifies the workplace, but does not create solidarity between workers and managers.

Neo-Marxist critics of Burawoy point out that these games often function to workers' real material advantage (Clawson and Fantasia 1983; Gottfried 2001). Conversely, paleo-Marxists are concerned that Burawoy exaggerates the importance of 'obscuring' surplus value. His analysis seems to assume that were it not for these 'games' in the workplace, workers would have long ago seen the truth of capitalism and overthrown it. In contrast, Marx's own analysis emphasizes the role of structures beyond the workplace, most notably the labor market itself, in reproducing labor's subordination.

As for the third basic type of response—*resistance*—the key starting point for Marxist analyses of resistance is the collective nature of the modern labor process (Hyman 1975). Fantasia (1995), for example, shows that wildcat strikes are more common where the labor process requires workers to coordinate closely, on a moment-by-moment basis, and where as a result, it generates strong work-group solidarity. Resistance under these conditions is not a matter of individuals struggling for personal 'recognition' or 'autonomy' (Mumby 2005). However, resistance does not necessarily take a revolutionary form: while unions can more easily find root in this collective labor process than in a dispersed labor process, unions are under great structural pressure to focus on negotiations within capitalism's constraints and not to contest those constraints (Martin 2007).

Unions are, of course, not the only possible vehicle for resistance. Ackroyd and Thompson (1999) discuss a broad range of oppositional misbehavior (see also Jermier, Knights, and Nord 1994). Workers appear to be increasingly oriented to the legal system to express their grievances (Kelly 2005). Whistle-blowing has emerged as a new form of worker resistance (Rothschild and Miethe 1999). Hodson (2001), inspired partly by Marx but taking his distance for the neo-Marxist reading that sees only the conflictual aspect of the employment relation, draws a portrait of workers' efforts to establish 'dignity' at work. Hodson argues that threats to workers' dignity are created by mismanagement and abuse, overwork, illicit constraints on autonomy, and manipulative forms of employee involvement. Workers assert their need for dignity with a mix of resistance behaviors, organizational citizenship, independent meaning systems, and group relations.

4.4.2. Beyond the Organization

Much of mainstream organization studies focuses on the individual organization and sees it purposively adapting to competitive pressure. Relative to this body of work, Marxists advance some of the same critiques as population ecology, neo-institutionalism, and resource-dependence theories, and highlight the broader social forces that act on and through organizations. However, relative to these other approaches, Marxism is distinctive in highlighting the way both the broader environment and the organization are structured by class relations and conflict. This can be seen in research in several fields discussed below.

4.4.2.1. Corporations and Inter-Corporate Ties

One important focus of Marxist research has been the fabric of inter-corporate ties created by ownership and interlocking directorates. 'Organization-centric' studies see these inter-corporate ties as expressing the instrumental rationality of firms. Marxists, on the other hand, are more sensitive to the underlying commonality of class interests that guide these firms, and therefore see these ties as reflecting the internal factional structure of the capitalist class. As such, they are the means by which the capitalist class achieves collective action, even though this achievement is often undermined by competitive rivalries (Useem 1982).

The capitalist class also demonstrates its cohesion without the benefit of formal inter-corporate ties. Several studies have shown the ability of the capitalist class to achieve collective action on political issues that could have split it if capitalists attended only to their individual economic interests (Domhoff 1983; Mizruchi 1989; Ornstein 1984; Palmer and Barber 2001; Whitt 1979). Levy and Egan (2003) use

Gramsci's notion of hegemony to characterize corporations' collective political strategies in the environmental arena.

4.4.2.2. *Production Networks*

Organizational researchers have paid considerable attention over the past couple of decades to the importance of industrial districts and other productive ties among clusters of firms. While some of this work has had Marxist roots (see Raikes, Jensen, and Ponte 2000), other scholars' approaches are explicitly anti-Marxist, in arguing that Marx's prognosis of growing centralization and concentration of capital is belied by the continued vitality and purported resurgence of networks of small firms (e.g. Lazerson 1995; Piore and Sabel 1984). Much of this latter literature is reminiscent of Proudhon's thesis that advanced automation would lead to the reconstitution of craft—which recalls in turn Marx's critique of Proudhon's celebration of craft idiocy. Other research in this area restores Durkheim's insight concerning the importance of the non-contractual elements of contract (e.g. Dore 1983).

By contrast, neo-Marxists point to the domination of these networks by large corporations (Harrison 1994; Sacchetti and Sugden 2003) and the way firms use their make-or-buy decisions to assert power over both 'partner' firms and their own employees (Grimshaw and Rubery 2005). The paleo view highlights the progressive socialization of production implied by the creation of denser networks of collaborative inter-firm ties: notwithstanding their asymmetries, these ties represent the substitution of planned coordination for the anarchy of the market (Adler 2001). Consider, for example, the huge productive efficiencies wrought by Wal-Mart in its supplier network. The bad side is clearly visible in the impoverishment of numerous small-scale, locally focused firms, with negative effects on many communities. On the other hand, the traditional supply chains in this industry were technologically backward, charged exorbitant prices, and offered very variable quality. The concentration wrought by Wal-Mart now offers consumers lower prices and affords social forces an opportunity to push the policies of Wal-Mart and its suppliers in a progressive direction—an opportunity never available when the industry was previously so dispersed (see also Levy 2008). Wal-Mart reminds us of Marx's dictum that history often progresses by its bad side (Marx 1955: 132).

4.4.2.3. *Imperialism/Globalization*

Marxist ideas have played an important role in shaping mainstream research on multinational corporations. This is in large part due to the influence of the work of Hymer (see Cohen *et al.* 1979). Hymer argued that, as Marx predicted, firms would serve as the vectors of imperialist expansion, and in the process these multinational corporations would grow in scale and scope. Subsequent work has nuanced his analysis, showing that the asymmetries of power between the headquarters in the imperialist center and the subsidiaries in the periphery regions have developed along several different paths: the 'global' form assumed by Hymer now coexists with multi-domestic and transnational forms (see review by Tolentino 2002).

On mainstream readings, the transnational model offers the prospect of overcoming the uneven nature of capitalist development, by turning subsidiaries into 'centers of excellence' and thus overcoming the gap between developing and developed economies. Neo-Marxists are skeptical of any perspective that ignores the profound power and wealth asymmetries that persist and the new ones that capitalism engenders. Paleo-Marxists share this skepticism, but are sensitive to the progressive socialization driven by these multinational firms—the productivity benefits, the broadening of people's habitual cognitive frames, the considerable opportunities for women's advancement, and the unprecedented opportunity to exercise social pressure and regulatory controls. Merk (2005), for example, analyzes how the globalization of the athletic footwear production process creates a global collective worker, how this has prompted the emergence of new, globalized forms of struggle, and how this, in turn, has led to new, globalized forms of regulation for the industry.

More broadly, recent Marxist-inspired research in world systems theory has pointed to the likelihood that US global hegemony is in decline, and in this process, is shifting its economic base from production to finance (Arrighi 1994). Marens (2003) points out that this 'financialization' has important implications for the corporate form: the 'nexus of contracts' view of corporate governance becomes a natural way to view the corporation once it leaves the struggle to create exchange-value by producing use-values and enters the world of speculative finance and what Marx called 'fictitious' capital (i.e. paper claims that lacks material collateral) (see also Aglietta and Rebérioux 2005; Harvey 1982).

4.4.2.4. Capitalism and the Environment

Marxism has been influential in the growing community of scholars studying the relations between capitalism and environmental degradation (see various papers in the journal *Organization and Environment*). The essential Marxist insight is that a system predicated on the accumulation of capital has no internal self-control mechanisms that can assure a sustainable 'metabolic interaction' between human beings and the earth (Foster 2000; Burkett 1999). An economic structure predicated on private property relegates environmental concerns to the status of externalities, so only government intervention could restore the balance. However government itself is dominated by capitalist class interests, and even if the long-term collective interests of this class argue for greater environmental responsibility, internal rivalries within that class constantly undermine regulatory efforts. Individual corporations may attempt to win competitive advantage by announcing their commitment to sustainability; but such gestures, even when they are not pure 'greenwashing'

(Jermier, Forbes, Benn, and Orsato 2006), are by nature sporadic and incapable of redirecting the entire pattern of economic growth. So long as environmental threats are only localized, this constitutional deficiency of capitalism is tolerable; but as these threats multiply, capitalism endangers the entire planet, and it becomes increasingly obvious that our survival depends on replacing capitalism with a more evolved mode of production.

4.4.2.5. *Alternatives to Capitalism*

Marxist theory has an ambiguous relation to efforts to specify alternatives to capitalism. On the one hand, Marx's analysis of capitalism as compared to feudalism and other modes of production suggests some specific features of the future higher form of society. These include the subordination of the market to some form of democratic planning at the national and regional levels, and the subordination of corporate bureaucracy to some kind of democratic governance at the enterprise level. On the other hand, Marx argued that efforts to predict the details of such a form of society were futile (since these details would have to be invented through experimentation) and a distraction (since revolutionary mobilization arguably has more to do with anger at past and present injustices than enthusiasm for this or that blueprint for the future).

Marx acknowledged, however, the interest of experiments in cooperatives—even if it was difficult to see how islands of socialism could sustain themselves in a broader sea of capitalism—and Marxist studies of cooperatives have yielded rich insights into the possibilities of a form of organization radically superior to the wage relation (Jossa 2005; Rothschild and Russell 1986; Rothschild-Whitt 1979; Warhurst 1998). Marxist theory has also informed research on work organizations in the socialist bloc (see Burawoy 1985, 1989; Stark 1986) and in the transition from communism to capitalism (Burawoy 2001).

4.5. Marxism in Dialogue with Other Approaches

The most common Marxist criticisms of mainstream organization studies are that they are too often static rather than dynamic; they are functionalist rather than dialectical; they privilege consensus and present conflict as pathological; they take as their unit of analysis individuals, groups, or organizations, and abstract from class. For Marxists eager to show the historical impermanence of the capitalist order, these are important handicaps: these biases encourage us to see the prevailing social order as natural and inevitable (Benson 1977; Burawoy 1982; Goldman and Van Houten 1977; Zeitz 1980). With this general orientation, Marxists have engaged several other theoretical traditions in constructive dialogue. The following paragraphs review these in rapid summary.

Weber rejected Marxism's materialism; but the two traditions are joined in the critique of capitalism's structure of domination, its substantive irrationality, and the alienation implied by the rule of formal rationality (see e.g. Thompson and McHugh 2002: 370–4). The literature on the Marx–Weber relation is already enormous, and that relation continues to provoke valuable research. Like much of Western Marxism, the Frankfurt School (Horkheimer, Adorno, Marcuse, Habermas, etc.) focused on cultural factors to explain the failure of socialist movements to effect systemic change, and to this end, built a fruitful synthesis of elements of Marx and Weber—albeit relinquishing key elements of Marxist theory in the process.

Durkheim has been a powerful influence in organization studies, as visible in the work of Granovetter on the embeddedness of markets, Sabel on development associations, Streeck on associative orders, neo-institutionalists such as Meyer, Powell, and DiMaggio on normative isomorphism's pervasive effects on organizations (as pointed out by Burawoy 2001). Durkheim's earlier work on the division of labor has important convergences with Marx on socialization as interdependence (see Cleghorn 1987; Giddens 1976; Lukes 1973; Stone 1952). His later work rejects Marx's materialism, and Marxists argue that the resulting stream of research affords far too much autonomous causal weight to disembodied values, norms, ideas, and logics. Durkheim-inspired research offers a useful corrective to commodity fetishism in showing how economic relations are typically embedded in social relations; in doing so, however, many contemporary scholars in economic sociology largely accept mainstream economic theory's characterization of economic relations, even if they insist on contextualizing these; Marxists offer a deeper critique of economics, by revealing the contradictory social relations at the heart of economic relations.

Pragmatism has close affinities to Marx's conception of practice as a tool-mediated transaction with the external world. The main difference is that pragmatism has no theory of the broader social context. As pragmatism grew into symbolic interactionism, its proponents increasingly presented this lack as a virtue, and the dialogue with Marxism grew more strained. Convergence is, however, reemerging, as theories of practice and research on the role of artifacts in practice reopen questions about the relations between local activity and the broader social context.

Many feminists, students of race and ethnicity, and other sociologists who study organizations empirically find that identities and projects are more powerful than class structure in explaining change at this level of analysis. They are surely correct to criticize doctrinaire Marxists who refuse to accord non-class dimensions of social structure any relevance; but this leaves entirely open the question of the place of these latter dimensions in the broader, longer term sweep of history. Calás and Smircich (2006) outline a large family of feminist approaches to organization studies that articulate different answers to this question. Their discussion of 'socialist feminism' summarizes some of the key debates and insights associated with the Marxist tradition within feminism. (The earlier literature is reviewed by Thompson 1989; Hartmann 1979.) A key contribution of feminist work to the Marxist project has been to challenge facile partitions erected by theorists between the realms of production and reproduction. Feminists have argued that the production process presupposes a reproduction process, and that differences between women and men in the latter explain differences in the former (see e.g. Acker and Van Houten 1974; Acker 2000; Cockburn 1991; Game and Pringle 1984; Kanter 1977; Reskin and Ross 1992; Smith 2002; Wajcman 1998). Feminist work has also had a fruitful dialogue with Marxism in the study of technology and the organization of both wage work and domestic work (Wajcman 2004). Moreover, feminism has been an arena in which crucial epistemological debates have unfolded. From the Marxist point of view, the most important of these has been around 'standpoint theory' (see Anderson 2003; Harding 2004). Standpoint theory generalizes an argument originally advanced by Marx and later elaborated by Lukács (1971), that all social theory implicitly adopts a social vantage point, and that our theories will be deeper and more useful to an emancipatory project if as theorists we adopt the standpoint of the subaltern.

4.6. To Change the World

Marxism formulates a particularly sharp critique of the aims of much mainstream organization research to inform management action in the service of shareholder wealth. Such a starting point leads researchers to ignore, downplay, or distort the concerns of employees or society at large (Nord 1977). While some of this work is inspired by genuine humanist impulse to reform management, its starting point limits the depth of analysis.

Other mainstream research aims to be value-neutral and takes its distance from the practical needs of any actors. Such approaches too can generate powerful critical insights; but arguably this approach is self-defeating, since no science can in fact be value-neutral, and the aspiration of value-neutrality can easily obscure implicit value positions. Marxists argue that it is more productive to take a stand in favor of the emancipation of the oppressed, and then work to ensure one's research is as rigorous and objective as possible (Adler and Jermier 2005; Frost 1980; Victor and Stephens 1994).

Looking forward, perhaps one of the main opportunities for the development of Marxist organization studies lies in strengthening its public engagements. Burawoy (2004) distinguishes mainstream and critical sociology, and their respective academic and non-academic audiences. Mainstream 'policy sociology' turns 'professional sociology' (mainstream academic research) towards actionable knowledge that can support the technocratic efforts of policy makers. Likewise, Burawoy argues, 'public sociology' can turn 'critical sociology' away from an exclusive focus on internal debates within the field and towards public dialogue in support of struggles for emancipation. Such public dialogue can take more traditional forms (books that stimulate public reflection and opinion columns that address current issues) or more 'organic' forms (see Gramsci 1971) that engage directly with specific communities and social movements. Marxist scholars in many fields have often been engaged in work of this public kind. However, even though organization studies has enormous potential relevance to a range of publics, Marxists in this field have rarely taken up the public sociologist role. With the development of new oppositional movements, opportunities for such engagement seem to be multiplying.

Acknowledgments

This chapter has benefited greatly from comments by Steve Jaros, Craig Prichard, David Levy, Mick Rowlinson, Michael Burawoy, Matt Vidal, Mark Mizruchi, and Paul Thompson, even if there is much with which they still disagree.

References

Marx and Engels: Major Works with Original Publication Dates

Marx

Critique of Hegel's Philosophy of Right (1843), On the Jewish Question (1843), Notes on James Mill (1844), Economic and Philosophical Manuscripts of 1844 (1844), Theses on Feuerbach (1845), The Poverty of Philosophy (1845), Wage-Labor and Capital (1847), The Eighteenth Brumaire of Louis Napoleon (1852), Grundrisse (1857), Preface to A Contribution to the Critique of Political Economy (1859), Theories of Surplus Value, 3 vols. (1862), Value, Price and Profit (1865), Capital, vol. 1 (1867), The Civil War in France (1871), Critique of the Gotha Program (1875), Notes on Wagner (1883)

Marx and Engels

The German Ideology (1845), The Holy Family (1845), Manifesto of the Communist Party (1848), Writings on the US Civil War (1861), Capital, vol. 2 [posthumously, published by Engels] (1885), Capital, vol. 3 [posthumously, published by Engels] (1894)

Engels

The Condition of the Working Class in England in 1844 (1844), The Peasant War in Germany (1850), Revolution and Counter-Revolution in Germany (1852), Anti-Dühring (1878), Dialectics of Nature (1883), The Origin of the Family, Private Property, and the State (1884), Ludwig Feuerbach and the End of Classical German Philosophy (1886)

Other References

ACKER, J. (2000). 'Gendered Contradictions in Organizational Equity Projects'. *Organization*, 7/4: 625–32.

—— and VAN HOUTEN, D. R. (1974). 'Differential Recruitment and Control: The Sex Structuring of Organizations'. *Administrative Science Quarterly*, 19/2: 152–63.

ACKROYD, S., and THOMPSON, P. (1999). *Organizational Misbehaviour*. London: Sage.

ADLER, P. S. (2001). 'Market, Hierarchy, and Trust: The Knowledge Economy and the Future of Capitalism'. *Organization Science*, 12/2: 215–34.

—— (2007). 'The Future of Critical Management Studies: A Paleo-Marxist Critique of Labour Process Theory'. *Organization Studies*, 28/9: 1313–45.

—— and BORYS, B. (1989). 'Automation and Skill: Three Generations of Research on the Machine-Tool Case'. *Politics and Society*, 17/3: 377–412.

—— and JERMIER, J. (2005). 'Developing a Field with More Soul: Standpoint Theory and Public Policy Research for Management Scholars'. *Academy of Management Journal*, 48/6: 941–4.

AGLIETTA, M., and REBÉRIOUX, A. (2005). *Corporate Governance Adrift: A Critique of Shareholder Value*. Cheltenham, UK: Edward Elgar.

ANDERSON, E. (2003). 'Feminist Epistemology and Philosophy of Science' (Stanford Encyclopedia of Philosophy, 2007. Http://Plato.Stanford.edu/Entries/Feminism-Epistemology/).

ANDERSON, P. (1979). *Considerations on Western Marxism*. London: Verso.

ARRIGHI, G. (1994). *The Long Twentieth Century: Money, Power and the Origins of Our Times*. London: Verso.

BARKER, J. (1993). 'Tightening the Iron Cage: Concertive Control in Self-Managing Teams'. *Administrative Science Quarterly*, 38: 408–37.

BARLEY, S. R., and KUNDA, G. (1992). 'Design and Devotion: Surges of Rational and Normative Ideologies of Control in Managerial Discourse'. *Administrative Science Quarterly*, 37/3: 363–99.

BENDIX, R. (1956). *Work and Authority in Industry*. New York: John Wiley & Sons.

BENSON, J. K. (1977). 'Organizations: A Dialectical View'. *Administrative Science Quarterly*, 22/1: 1–21.

BRAVERMAN, H. (1974). *Labor and Monopoly Capital: The Degradation of Work in the Twentieth Century*. New York: Monthly Review Press.

BREWER, A. (1980). *Marxist Theories of Imperialism: A Critical Survey*. London: Routledge & Kegan Paul.

Burawoy, M. (1982). *Manufacturing Consent: Changes in the Labor Process under Monopoly Capitalism*. Chicago: University of Chicago Press.

—— (1985). *The Politics of Production: Factory Regimes under Capitalism and Socialism*. London: Verso.

—— (1989). 'Reflections on the Class Consciousness of Hungarian Steel Workers'. *Politics and Society*, 7/1: 1–34.

—— (1990). 'Marxism as Science: Historical Challenges and Theoretical Growth'. *American Sociological Review*, 55/6: 775–93.

—— (2001). 'Neoclassical Sociology: From the End of Communism to the End of Classes'. *American Journal of Sociology*, 106/4: 1099–1120.

—— (2004). 'Public Sociologies: Contradictions, Dilemmas and Possibilities'. *Social Forces*, 82/4: 1603–18.

Burkett, P. (1999). *Marx and Nature: A Red and Green Perspective*. New York: St Martin's Press.

Calás, M. B., and Smircich, L. (2006). 'From the Woman's Point of View Ten Years Later: Towards a Feminist Organization Studies', in S. R. Clegg *et al.* (eds.), *Sage Handbook of Organization Studies*. 2nd edn. London: Sage.

Callahan, G., and Thompson, P. (2001). 'Edwards Revisited: Technical Control and Call Centers'. *Economic and Industrial Democracy*, 22: 13–37.

Carchedi, G. (1977). *On the Economic Identification of Social Classes*. London: Routledge & Kegan Paul.

Clawson, D., and Fantasia, R. (1983). 'Beyond Burawoy: The Dialectics of Conflict and Consent on the Shop Floor'. *Theory and Society*, 12/5: 671–80.

Clegg, S. R. (1981). 'Organization and Control'. *Administrative Science Quarterly*, 26/4: 545–62.

—— and Dunkerley, D. (1980). *Organization, Class and Control*. London: Routledge & Kegan Paul.

Cleghorn, J. S. (1987). 'Can Workplace Democracy Transform Capitalist Society?: Durkheim and Burawoy Compared'. *Sociological Inquiry*, 57/3: 304–15.

Cockburn, C. (1991). *In the Way of Women: Men's Resistance to Sex Equality in Organizations*. Ithaca, NY: ILR Press.

Cohen, G. A. (1978). *Karl Marx's Theory of History: A Defense*. Princeton: Princeton University Press.

Cohen, R. B., Felton, N., Nkosi, M., and van Liere, J. (eds.) (1979). *Multinational Corporation: A Radical Approach, Papers by Stephen Herbert Hymer*. Cambridge: Cambridge University Press.

Cole, M. (1996). *Cultural Psychology: A Once and Future Discipline*. Cambridge, Mass.: Belknap Press/Harvard University Press.

Cressey, P., and MacInnes, J. (1980). 'Voting for Ford: Industrial Democracy and the Control of Labour'. *Capital and Class*, 11: 5–33.

Desai, M. (2002). *Marx's Revenge*. London: Verso.

Domhoff, G. W. (1983). *Who Rules America Now?* Englewood Cliffs, NJ: Prentice-Hall.

Dore, R. (1983). 'Goodwill and Spirit of Market Capitalism'. *British Journal of Sociology*, 34/4: 459–82.

Edwards, R. (1979). *Contested Terrain: The Transformation of the Workplace in the Twentieth Century*. New York: Basic.

Elias, N. (2000). *The Civilizing Process: Sociogenetic and Psychogenetic Investigations.* Oxford: Blackwell.

Engeström, Y. (1987). *Learning by Expanding: An Activity-theoretical Approach to Developmental Research.* Helsinki: Orienta-Konsultit.

—— (1990). *Learning, Working and Imagining: Twelve Studies in Activity Theory.* Helsinki: Orienta-Konsultit.

—— Miettinin, R., and Punamaki, R.-L. (eds.) (1999). *Perspectives on Activity Theory.* Cambridge: Cambridge University Press.

Fantasia, R. (1995). 'From Class Consciousness to Culture, Action, and Social Organization'. *Annual Review of Sociology*, 21: 269–87.

—— Clawson, D., and Graham, G. (1988). 'A Critical View of Worker Participation in American Industry'. *Work and Occupations*, 15/4: 468–88.

Foley, D. K. (1986). *Understanding Capital: Marx's Economic Theory.* Cambridge, Mass.: Harvard University Press.

Foster, J. B. (2000). *Ecology Against Capitalism.* New York: Monthly Review Press.

Friedman, A. (1977). *Industry and Labour: Class Struggle at Work and Monopoly Capitalism.* London: Macmillan.

Frost, P. (1980). 'Toward a Radical Framework for Practicing Organization Science'. *Academy of Management Review*, 5/4: 501–7.

Game, A., and Pringle, R. (1984). *Gender at Work.* London: Pluto.

Giddens, A. (1976). 'Classical Social Theory and the Origins of Modern Sociology'. *American Journal of Sociology*, 81/4: 703–29.

Goldman, P., and Van Houten, D. R. (1977). 'Managerial Strategies and the Worker: A Marxist Analysis of Bureaucracy'. *Sociological Quarterly*, 18: 108–25.

Gottfried, H. (2001). 'From "Manufacturing Consent" to "Global Ethnography": A Retrospective Examination'. *Contemporary Sociology*, 30/5: 435–8.

Graham, L. (1995). *On the Line at Subaru-Isuzu: The Japanese Model and the American Worker.* Ithaca, NY: Cornell University Press.

Gramsci, A. (1971). *Selections from the Prison Notebooks of Antonio Gramsci.* London: Lawrence and Wishart.

Grenier, G. J. (1988). *Inhuman Relations: Quality Circles and Anti-Unionism in American Industry.* Philadelphia: Temple University Press.

—— and Hogler, R. (1991). 'Labor Law and Managerial Ideology: Employee Participation as a Social Control System'. *Work and Occupations*, 18/3: 313–33.

Grimshaw, D., and Rubery, J. (2005). 'Inter-Capital Relations and the Network Organization: Redefining the Work and Employment Nexus'. *Cambridge Journal of Economics*, 29: 1027–51.

Hales, C. (2000). 'Management and Empowerment Programmes'. *Work, Employment and Society*, 14/3: 501–19.

Harding, S. (2004). *The Feminist Standpoint Reader.* New York: Routledge.

Harrison, B. (1994). *Lean and Mean: The Changing Landscape of Corporate Power in the Age of Flexibility.* Basic Books: New York.

Hartmann, H. I. (1979). 'The Unhappy Marriage of Marxism and Feminism: Towards a More Progressive Union'. *Capital and Class*, 8: 1–33.

Harvey, D. (1982). *The Limits to Capital.* Chicago: University of Chicago Press.

Hayek, F. A. von (1944). *The Road to Serfdom.* Chicago: Chicago University Press.

Hirschhorn, L. (1984). *Beyond Mechanization*. Cambridge, Mass.: MIT Press.
Hochschild, A. R. (1965). *The Managed Heart: Commercialization of Human Feeling*. Berkeley: University of California Press.
Hodson, R. (2001). *Dignity at Work*. New York: Cambridge University Press.
Hook, S. (2002). *Towards the Understanding of Karl Marx: A Revolutionary Interpretation*, expanded edn., ed. Ernest B. Hook. Amherst, NY: Prometheus Books.
Hyman, R. (1975). *Industrial Relations: A Marxist Introduction*. London: Macmillan.
—— (1987). 'Strategy or Structure? Capital, Labour and Control'. *Work, Employment and Society*, 1/1: 25–55.
Ilyenkov, E. V. (1982). *Dialectics of the Abstract and the Concrete in Marx's 'Capital'*, trans. S. Syrovatkin. Moscow: Progress Publishers.
Jermier, J. M. (1985). 'When the Sleeper Wakes: A Short Story Extending Themes in Radical Organization Theory'. *Journal of Management*, 11: 67–80.
—— Knights, D., and Nord, W. (1994). *Resistance and Power in Organizations*. London: Routledge.
—— Forbes, L. C., Benn, S., and Orsato, R. J. (2006). 'The New Corporate Environmentalism and Green Politics', in S. R. Clegg, C. Hardy, T. B. Lawrence, and W. R. Nord (eds.), *The Sage Handbook of Organization Studies*. 2nd edn. London: Sage.
Jessop, B. (2001). 'Bringing the State Back in (Yet Again): Reviews, Revisions, Rejections, and Redirections'. *International Review of Sociology—Revue Internationale De Sociologie*, 11/2: 149–53.
Jossa, B. (2005). 'Marx, Marxism and the Cooperative Movement'. *Cambridge Journal of Economics*, 29/1: 3–18.
Kanter, R. M. (1977). *Men and Women of the Corporation*. New York: Basic.
Kelly, J. (2005). 'Labor Movements and Mobilization', in Stephen Ackroyd *et al.* (eds.), *The Oxford Handbook of Work and Organization*. Oxford: Oxford University Press.
Kenney, M., and Florida, R. (1993). *Beyond Mass Production: The Japanese System and its Transfer to the U.S.* New York: Oxford University Press.
Kolko, G. (1963). *The Triumph of Conservatism*. Chicago: Quadrangle.
Lakatos, I. (1970). 'Falsification and the Methodology of Scientific Research Programmes', in I. Lakatos and A. Musgrave (eds.), *Criticism and the Growth of Knowledge*. Cambridge: Cambridge University Press.
Langton, J. (1984). 'The Ecological Theory of Bureaucracy: The Case of Josiah Wedgwood and the British Pottery Industry'. *Administrative Science Quarterly*, 29/3: 330–54.
Lave, J. (1988). *Cognition in Practice: Mind, Mathematics and Culture in Everyday Life*. Cambridge: Cambridge University Press.
Lazerson, M. (1995). 'A New Phoenix? Modern Putting-Out in the Modena Knitwear Industry'. *Administrative Science Quarterly*, 40/1: 34–59.
Leont'ev, A. N. (1978). *Activity, Consciousness, and Personality*. Englewood Cliffs, NJ: Prentice-Hall.
Levidow, L., and Young, B. (eds.) (1981). *Science, Technology and the Labour Process*. London: CSE Books.
Levy, D. L. (2008). 'Political Contestation and Global Production Networks'. *Academy of Management Review*, 33/4.
—— and Egan, D. (2003). 'A Neo-Gramscian Approach to Corporate Political Strategy: Conflict and Accommodation in the Climate Change Negotiations'. *Journal of Management Studies*, 40/4: 803–29.

—— and Scully, M. (2007). 'The Institutional Entrepreneur as Modern Prince: The Strategic Face of Power in Contested Fields'. *Organization Studies*, 28/7: 971–91.

Liden, M. Van Der (2007). *Western Marxism and the Soviet Union: A Survey of Critical Theories and Debates since 1917*. Leiden: Brill.

Littler, C. R., and Salaman, G. (1982). 'Bravermania and Beyond: Recent Theories of the Labour Process'. *Sociology*, 16/2: 251–69.

Lopez, S. H. (2006). 'Emotional Labor and Organized Emotional Care: Conceptualizing Nursing Home Care Work'. *Work and Occupations*, 33/2: 133–60.

Lukács, G. (1971). *History and Class Consciousness: Studies in Marxist Dialectics*, trans. Rodney Livingstone. Cambridge, Mass.: MIT Press.

Lukes, S. (1973). *Emile Durkheim: His Life and Work. A Historical and Critical Study*. London: Penguin Press.

—— (2005). *Power: A Radical View*. 2nd edn. Basingstoke: Palgrave Macmillan.

Luria, A. R. (1976). *Cognitive Development: Its Cultural and Social Foundations*. Cambridge, Mass.: Harvard University Press.

MacKenzie, D., and Wajcman, J. (eds.) (1985). *The Social Shaping of Technology*. Milton Keynes: Open University Press.

Marens, R. (2003). 'Two, Three, Many Enrons: American Financial Hypertrophy and the End of Economic Hegemony'. *Organization*, 10/3: 588–93.

Marglin, S. (1974). 'What Do Bosses Do? The Origins and Functions of Hierarchy in Capitalist Production'. *Review of Radical Political Economy*, 6: 60–112.

Martin, A. W. (2007). 'Organizational Structure, Authority and Protest: The Case of Union Organizing in the United States, 1990–2001'. *Social Forces*, 3: 1413–35.

Marx, K. (1955). *The Poverty of Philosophy*. Moscow: Progress Publishers.

—— (1973). *Grundrisse*. Harmondsworth: Penguin Books.

—— (1976). *Capital*, Vol. 1. Harmondsworth: Penguin.

Merk, J. (2005). 'Regulating the Global Athletic Footwear Industry: The Collective Worker in the Product Chain', in L. Assassi, D. Wigan, and K. Van Der Pijl (eds.), *Global Regulation: Managing Crises after the Imperial Turn*. London: Palgrave Macmillan.

Miettinin, R. (1999). 'The Riddle of Things: Activity Theory and Actor Network Theory as Approaches of Studying Innovations'. *Mind, Culture, and Activity*, 16/3: 170–95.

—— and Hasu, M. (2002). 'Articulating User Needs in Collaborative Design: Towards an Activity Theoretical Approach'. *Computer Supported Collaborative Work*, 11/1–2: 129–51.

Mizruchi, M. S. (1989). 'Similarity of Political Behavior among Large American Corporations'. *American Journal of Sociology*, 95/2: 401–24.

Mumby, D. K. (2005). 'Theorizing Resistance in Organization Studies: A Dialectical Approach'. *Management Communication Quarterly*, 19/1: 19–44.

Murphy, K. J. (2007). 'Can We Write the History of the Russian Revolution? A Belated Response to Eric Hobsbawm'. *Historical Materialism*, 15/2: 3–19.

Noble, D. F. (1984). *Forces of Production: A Social History of Industrial Automation*. New York: Oxford University Press.

Nord, W. (1977). 'A Marxist Critique of Humanistic Psychology'. *Journal of Humanistic Psychology*, 17/Winter: 75–83.

Offe, C. (1984). *Contradictions of the Welfare State*. Cambridge, Mass.: MIT Press.

Ollman, B. (2003). *Dance of the Dialectic: Steps in Marx's Method*. Champaign, Ill.: University of Illinois Press.

Ornstein, M. (1984). 'Interlocking Directorates in Canada: Intercorporate or Class Alliance?' *Administrative Science Quarterly*, 29/2: 210–31.

Palmer, D., and Barber, B. M. (2001). 'Challengers, Elites, and Owning Families: A Social Class Theory of Corporate Acquisitions in the 1960s'. *Administrative Science Quarterly*, 46/1: 87–120.

Pijl, K. van der (1998). *Transnational Classes and International Relations*. London: Routledge.

Piore, M. J., and Sabel, C. J. (1984). *The Second Industrial Divide: Possibilities for Prosperity*. New York: Basic Books.

Raikes, P., Jensen, M. F., and Ponte, S. (2000). 'Global Commodity Chain Analysis and the French *Filière* Approach: Comparison and Critique'. *Economy and Society*, 29/3: 390–417.

Reskin, B. F., and Ross, C. E. (1992). 'Jobs, Authority, and Earnings among Managers: The Continuing Significance of Sex'. *Work and Occupations*, 19/4: 342–65.

Richardson, H., and Robinson, B. (2007). 'The Mysterious Case of the Missing Paradigm: A Review of Critical Information Systems Research 1991–2001'. *Information Systems Journal*, 17/3: 251–70.

Rothschild, J., and Miethe, T. D. (1999). 'Whistle-Blower Disclosures and Management Retaliation: The Battle to Control Information about Organization Corruption'. *Work and Occupations*, 26/1: 107–28.

—— and Russell, R. (1986). 'Alternatives to Bureaucracy: Democratic Participation in the Economy'. *Annual Review of Sociology*, 12: 307–28.

Rothschild-Whitt, J. (1979). 'The Collectivist Organization: An Alternative to Rational-Bureaucratic Models'. *American Sociological Review*, 44/4: 509–27.

Sacchetti, S., and Sugden, R. (2003). 'The Governance of Networks and Economic Power: The Nature and Impact of Subcontracting Relationship'. *Journal of Economic Surveys*, 17/5: 669–91.

Sallach, D. L. (1974). 'Class Domination and Ideological Hegemony'. *Sociological Quarterly*, 15: 38–50.

Sawchuk, P. H., Duarte, N., and Elhammoumi, M. (eds.) (2006). *Critical Perspectives on Activity: Explorations across Education, Work and Everyday Life*. New York: Cambridge University Press.

Schumpeter, J. A. (1942). *Capitalism, Socialism, and Democracy*. New York: Harper.

Smith, C. (1987). *Technical Workers: Class, Labour and Trade Unionism*. London: Macmillan.

Smith, R. A. (2002). 'Race, Gender, and Authority in the Workplace: Theory and Research'. *Annual Review of Sociology*, 28: 509–42.

Stark, D. (1986). 'Rethinking Internal Labor Markets: New Insights from a Comparative Perspective'. *American Sociological Review*, 51: 492–504.

Stone, K. (1973). 'The Origins of Job Structures in the Steel Industry'. *Radical America*, 7: 17–66.

Stone, R. C. (1952). 'Conflicting Approaches to the Study of Worker–Manager Relations'. *Social Forces*, 31/2: 117–24.

Thompson, E. P. (1963). *The Making of the English Working Class*. London: Victor Gollancz.

Thompson, P. (1989). *The Nature of Work*. 2nd edn. London: Macmillan.

—— and McHugh, D. (2002). *Work Organizations*. 3rd edn. New York: Palgrave.

—— and Warhurst, C. (eds.) (1998). *Workplaces of the Future*. Houndmills: Macmillan.

Tinker, T. (1991). 'The Accountant as Partisan'. *Accounting, Organizations and Society*, 16/3: 297–310.

Tolentino, P. E. (2002). 'Hierarchical Pyramids and Heterarchical Networks: Organisational Strategies and Structures of Multinational Corporations and Its Impact on World Development'. *Contributions to Political Economy*, 21/1: 69–89.

Useem, M. (1982). 'Classwide Rationality in the Politics of Managers and Directors of Large Corporations in the United States and Great Britain'. *Administrative Science Quarterly*, 27/2: 199–226.

Victor, B., and Stephens, C. (1994). 'The Dark Side of the New Organizational Forms: An Editorial Essay'. *Organization Science*, 5/4: 479–82.

Vygotsky, L. S. (1962). *Thought and Language*. Cambridge, Mass.: MIT Press.

—— (1978). *Mind in Society*. Cambridge, Mass.: Harvard University Press.

Wajcman, J. (1998). *Managing Like a Man: Women and Men in Corporate Management*. Cambridge: Polity Press.

—— (2004). *Technofeminism*. Cambridge: Polity Press.

Wardell, M., Steiger, T. L., and Meiskins, P. (eds.) (1999). *Rethinking the Labor Process*. Albany: State University of New York Press.

Warhurst, C. (1998). 'Recognizing the Possible: The Organization and Control of a Socialist Labor Process'. *Administrative Science Quarterly*, 43/2: 470–97.

—— Grugulis, I., and Keep, E. (eds.) (2004). *The Skills That Matter*. London: Palgrave.

Warren, B. (1980). *Imperialism: Pioneer of Capitalism*. London: Verso.

Weinstein, J. (1968). *The Corporate Ideal in the Liberal State*. Boston: Beacon Press.

Wenger, E. (1998). *Communities of Practice: Learning, Meaning, and Identity*. New York: Cambridge University Press.

Whitt, J. A. (1979). 'Toward a Class-Dialectical Model of Power: An Empirical Assessment of Three Competing Models of Political Power'. *American Sociological Review*, 44/1: 81–99.

Wood, S. (ed.) (1982). *The Degradation of Work? Skill, Deskilling and the Labour Process*. London: Hutchinson.

Wright, E. O. (1985). *Classes*. London: Verso.

—— Levine, A., and Sober, E. (1992). *Reconstructing Marxism: Essays on Explanation and the Theory of History*. London: Verso.

Zeitz, G. (1980). 'Interorganizational Dialectics'. *Administrative Science Quarterly*, 25/1: 72–88.

Zimbalist, A. (ed.) (1979). *Case Studies on the Labor Process*. New York: Monthly Review Press.

CHAPTER 5

IT'S NOT JUST FOR COMMUNISTS ANY MORE

MARXIAN POLITICAL ECONOMY AND ORGANIZATIONAL THEORY

RICHARD MARENS

Organizational studies scholars have yet to find theoretically robust and empirically useful ways to analyze the interaction of organizations and their environments. Many organizational theorists acknowledge that environment is an important factor shaping the organization, and at least a few consider how an organization, or set of organizations, will, in turn, influence that environment. Nonetheless, in virtually all organization theories, the structure and transformation of this environment remains largely opaque, effectively a fog shrouding these organizations. Organization scholars will allow that the environment supplies organizations with resources, constrains them with laws, or provides them with models to imitate; but rarely is it acknowledged that the social environment has its own structures, its own unfolding processes of development, and its own internal logic. In most organizational scholarship, the world external to the organization is rarely more than a *deus ex machina*, which unpredictably, almost randomly, buffets organizations about. Researchers might suggest that the 'environment' generates a need for financial expertise among CEOs (Fligstein 1990), or supports a given number of pizza parlors in a given neighborhood (Hannan and Freeman 1989), or imposes a set of laws that coerce insurance companies to adopt very similar organizational structures (DiMaggio and Powell 1983); but this scholarship rarely analyzes when, where, or how, these buffeting and nurturing forces can be expected to appear, let alone how organizations collectively help generate them.

Marxian political economy offers a corrective to this blind spot, a way of shedding light on understanding how the social and economic environment relates to organizations. It can explain a great deal about why, despite ostensibly similar functions, organizations vary over time and space, and conversely, why functionally dissimilar organizations structurally converge in response to broader social pressures. Theorists working in the Marxian political economy tradition do not necessarily agree on all issues, and there are many 'chicken versus egg' disputes within the canon over the priority of various factors, but these disagreements have contributed to the development of a method of analysis that can serve organizational studies well.

Certainly, Marxian political economy is not the only macro-level form of social science analysis that scholars of organizations could usefully employ to broaden the constrained horizons of most organization theory. Marxian political economy, however, is especially well-suited for the study of contemporary organizations, for we live in an era in which market relations are both extending their geographic reach while intensifying within virtually every region of the globe—two tendencies that Marx himself studied with a famously single-minded intensity. Even scholars of non-commercial organizations such as schools, NGOs, and government agencies need to understand the increasingly commercial sea in which these swim. While scholars have applied Marxian political economy to non-capitalist social formations (Anderson 1974; De Ste. Croix 1981), Marx himself spent his last decades attempting to uncover the 'laws of motion' of capitalism, so it is not surprising that capitalist systems are the application for which Marxian political economy is best suited.

Before discussing the elements of this approach, it is worth explaining my choice of the term 'Marxian' rather than 'Marxist'. While there is no bright line distinguishing these two terms, the former is intended to be broader and more inclusive, implying an intellectual approach rather than a formal school that requires fidelity to a specific set of principles and assumptions. While the term 'Marxist' might imply enthusiasm for the revolutionary project of the founder, such fidelity is no more a prerequisite to work within the Marxian tradition than embracing Weber's nationalistic politics is for contemporary Weberians (Ringer 2004). Another distinction between Marxians and Marxists is that the former put less emphasis on the specific analytic formulations of Marx's opus *Capital*, especially with regard to

Marx's labor theory of value. This particular dimension of Marx's work has led to nearly a century and a half of polemical disputes over such correlates as the tendency of the rate of profit to fall, the relationship between so-called 'productive' and 'non-productive' labor, and the 'transformation problem' of relating 'values' to 'prices' (e.g. Moseley 2000). This is not meant to suggest that discussing these and similar issues can never prove to be stimulating or illuminating. However, organizational scholars need not achieve fluency with these disputes in order to understand and apply some of the more general principles of Marxian political economy.

The thesis of this chapter is that organizational theorists could gain a great deal of insight regarding the evolution, structure, and behavior of organizations by better understanding their social, economic, and historical context as analyzed by such Marxian theorists as Aglietta (1979), Arrighi (1994), Brenner (2002), Baran and Sweezy (1966), Gordon, Edwards, and Reich (1982), and Wood (1999). Marxian political economy is particularly useful because of its relative success in understanding the dynamics of capitalism as a largely self-contained system. This starting point obviates the need to rely on unpredictable exogenous shocks to explain changes in the broader social environment of organizations. Despite the failure of regimes supposedly committed to Marxist principles, Marxian analysis 'remains a powerful critique of bourgeois and capitalist society ... still useful in examining the events taking place' (Hoffman 1995: 35). Even politically conservative scholars have acknowledged the explanatory power of a Marxian approach for understanding social and economic change. According to Schumpeter (1942: 40), Marx 'saw industrial change more clearly and he realized its importance more fully than any economist of his time', and Nobel Medal for Economics winner Douglass North does not even qualify his endorsement with the past tense, noting that '[i]n contrast to current neoclassical economists, Marx had an integrated perception of the totality of societal relations. Institutions, the state, and ideology are all part of his analysis. Marx makes clear that if our thinking is to go beyond surface manifestations of an economy, we must explore the integrated relationships of all its parts' (North 1987: 58).

5.1. What Is Marxian Political Economy?

Before we can apply Marxian political economy to organizational studies, it is necessary to lay out the major features of this mode of analysis. Although not always explicitly stated, the starting assumption of all Marxian political economy is that the material elements of a society and the processes and relationships that produce these evolve over time and spread over space through the dialectical interaction of about half a dozen factors. These factors include class struggle, competition, technology, politics, ideology, and to a lesser extent, demographic change and war.

Prevailing material conditions serve as the starting point for two reasons. First, because the social processes that produce food, shelter, and the tools to procure these fundamental requirements of human life are necessarily present in any society, and, therefore, social actors must inevitably work to sustain these in the face of changes within the social and physical environments. Second, even those material conditions that are not strictly necessary to support life contribute to the individual's ability to participate in social activities. Production of material goods is necessary for maintaining the transportation, communication, displays of status, child rearing, and social control that are an integral part of any social organization.

Because the material basis of society is an irreducible foundation in Marxian analysis, class struggle, which is the struggle over the means of producing and acquiring these material products, is the most ubiquitous of the factors employed by Marxian political economists. Class struggle can take many specific forms, ranging from personal disputes between individuals, such as between a supervisor and a subordinate, to planned political battles between collective organizations explicitly mobilized for that purpose. Throughout this range of forms, however, the most crucial struggles are those over the extraction of surpluses of those goods (agricultural as well as industrial) that are the building blocks of the material conditions of social and biological life.

This centrality of class struggle does not imply that other factors such as technological knowledge, political power, or religion cannot be important, even enormously important, in explaining the political economy of a particular time and place. What it does suggest is that these other factors always work within constraints and opportunities generated by the dynamics of class struggle in any particular time and place. Making an analogy with physics, one might think of class struggle as the dimension of time in a physics experiment, since, while time is only one of four dimensions, it is distinguishable from the others as being the only one in which all activity is invariably embedded.

It also needs to be understood that in most versions of Marxian political economy, class struggle is not an independent variable in relation to which the others factors are simply mediating and dependent variables. What the centrality of class struggle does mean is that all the other factors are necessarily constrained by the conflict over shares of the finite supply of those material necessities for physical and social survival. There is, admittedly, a Marxist tradition that began with Engels (1966) that does indeed seek the kind of causal precision associated with physics. Such determinism, however, is no longer influential within Marxian political economy. The dialectical relationship between the major factors is neither deterministic nor linear but rather one of feedback in which these constantly shape and limit one another. As an admiring Schumpeter put it, Marx analyzed the '[a]ctual sequence of those patterns or of the historic process as it goes on, under its own steam, in historic time, producing at every instant that state which will of itself determine the next one' (Schumpeter 1942: 43).

For the purposes of organizational analysis at least, Marxian political economy is more appropriately regarded as not so much a formal theory as what Nelson and Winter (1982: 46) call 'appreciative theory'. It functions less like a testable law from experimental science and rather more like a heuristic that one would find in such field sciences as biology, geology, and paleontology that provides guidance for analyzing complex, evolving phenomena.

Since the concept of 'class struggle' is so central in Marxian political economy, some additional explanation of the distinctive aspects of the Marxian view of class should prove helpful in understanding the value of this approach. In the Marxian tradition, 'class' holds a more specific meaning than its more common usage in mainstream sociology, where it refers to grouping people based on income, type of work, level of skill, or some similar variable. For Marxists and most Marxians, 'class' is defined by one's relation to the means of production. All but the simplest societies are divisible into an exploited class of producers of a surplus that can be seized, taxed, or extorted by an exploiter class, whose power derives from their control over the means of production. This is not to say that Marx was unaware that within, for example, feudal society, there were other occupations and social groupings beside serfs and lords. He certainly understood that feudalism included merchants, craftsmen, entertainers, mercenaries, parish priests, etc., but he argued that these others were supported out of the surplus seized by the lords (including ecclesiastical lords) from the peasantry.

One contemporary implication of this perspective on class is that Marxian political economists tends to reject a long-standing practice among non-Marxians of dividing the economic elite of a capitalist system into separate and fundamentally conflicting classes: a producing class of entrepreneurial owners of private businesses and the top managers of industrial concerns that faces off against a financier class on whom these entrepreneurs depend, but who possess a distinct set of interests. This distinction has its own venerable intellectual tradition that began with Ricardo and assorted populist and 'producerist' political thinkers of the nineteenth century, through Veblen, Weber, Keynes, Berle and Means, up to and including some present-day sociologists (e.g. Davis 1994). In most of the accounts that make this particular class distinction, the entrepreneurs are portrayed more sympathetically as creators of wealth who are hemmed-in and exploited by an implicitly parasitic rentier class.

It is not that Marx and his intellectual successors assume no differences between finance and production, or regard these differences as trivial. Rather, they see these as epiphenomenal, a response to more central class conflicts, much as medieval conflicts between King John and his barons or between the Guelphs and Ghibellines of Central Europe were second-order disputes over the spoils of the exploitation of the peasantry. In the case of capitalism, conflicts between leaders of industry and finance are essentially squabbles over the methods and distribution of the wealth generated by exploitation of those who work for wages. The accuracy of this Marxian assessment is supported by the ease with which corporate executives of industrial firms, after a few years of conflict with the financial world in the 1980s, learned to downsize after initial resistance (Useem 1996) and then became important players themselves in financial transactions, often active participants in many of the resulting scandals (Partnoy 2003).

Another area where Marxian analysis defies conventional wisdom is the importance the latter often places on the service sector within contemporary capitalism. Marxian political economy always places the production of important industrial and agricultural goods in a central role. This 'privileging' of physically tangible products may appear anachronistic in an age when advanced economies are allegedly dominated by computer programming, design and marketing, finance, and business consulting; but three points need to be remembered. First, while more services are now traded across borders than at any time in history, international trade is still dominated in absolute terms by the trade in goods. Moreover, most of the services that are traded today have hardly severed their connection to the production of the material conditions of human life, since most of what these services actually 'service' is the financing, design, production, insuring, or marketing of material goods. Finally, as is discussed in more detail below, the historical record suggests that economies that dominate international trade in services, especially financial services, but no longer dominate with regard to commercial goods are actually economies in the final stages of declining hegemony (Arrighi 1994).

5.2. Marxian Political Economy in Action

Marxian political economy is perhaps best understood with an example. The following brief and highly stylized historical scenario of a twentieth-century industrialized nation demonstrates how this approach can explain and even anticipate how various dimensions of social and economic life interact and influence one another over time. Let us start our account with a relatively advanced industrialized nation, which, after decades of agitation by workers and their spouses, possesses somewhat democratic political institutions. Certain political entrepreneurs, viewing the situation, see an opportunity under these new more democratic circumstances to appeal to these newly enfranchised and politically organized voters by advocating laws protecting and extending unionization. These pro-union laws are eventually enacted during a serious economic downturn, which has left the capitalist ruling class relatively weak and fearful of more radical agitation, perhaps even revolution. These newly legalized unions then successfully bargain to raise the price of labor, a development that prods business leaders to invest in labor-saving technology. Such investments work to increase productivity, which, for a time, raises both wages and profits. Labor and capital can then agree on supporting politically a strong military, convinced this is a way to strengthen this now prosperous national arrangement—an ideological position propagated through the financial support of the 'idea industry' (universities, journalism, think tanks, etc.). Military spending also works to subsidize manufacturing without generating the kind of intense interfirm competition that had reduced profits and wages a half-century earlier, thus creating the appearance of economic stability.

The new technologies that result from military spending generate spin-offs that lead to new products. This at first generates even more demand for labor to produce these new items. Eventually, these manufacturing innovations are copied by lower cost competitors abroad, who, paradoxically, have been economically stimulated by the first country's overseas military spending. Labor, however, in fidelity to the ideology of endless prosperity, continues to demand wage increases under these increasingly less favorable conditions, resulting in inflation. The central bank intervenes on behalf of the ruling class by raising interest rates in order to both increase unemployment and to discourage further investment. As a result, organized labor loses both bargaining power and membership, a process aided by a ruling class that discards even a contingent willingness to cooperate with labor now that the credibility of threats from organized labor has drastically diminished. Consumer demand, however, is still necessary for profitability, so, in place of wage increases, the financial sector extends increasing quantities of credit, which ultimately destabilizes financial markets.

This stylized and simplified sketch of twentieth-century American political economic history illustrates one central aspect of Marxian political economy: the role of crisis in generating change. Compared to conventional economic and organizational theory in which change is implicitly gradual or generated by exogenous shocks, Marxian political economy views structural change as endogenously driven by the resolution of periodic crises. While such crises vary in detail, and no two ever are identical, they tend to cluster around three ideal types. Two of these relate directly to class struggle. In one, capital manages to overexploit labor, and so destroys its own customer base, thus leading to a crisis of underconsumption. In another, if labor wins (or wins back) too high a share of output because of tight labor markets, effective union organization, or its ability to capture and utilize a degree of state power, then investment dries up as capitalists experience lower profitability coupled to the prospect of having to deal with an increasingly powerful and assertive workforce.

Finally, if the balance between labor and capital arrives at what appears to be a balance point in which both profitability and consumer markets are strong, a crisis of overaccumulation will eventually set in. This occurs because too many firms, both incumbents and newcomers, see this 'Goldilocks economy' as a great investment opportunity, and ultimately generate too much capacity and enhanced productivity for the capacity of markets to absorb. Moreover, as firms compete, some are likely to introduce new technology, squeezing those who depend on older fixed capital to generate profits. This heightened competition puts downward pressure on wages, which makes output harder to sell, thus indirectly heightening competitive pressure further (Brenner 2002; Kalecki 1968). Price wars and bankruptcies follow, and these will inevitably upset the fragile balance that existed between capital and labor, which attracted the high levels of investment in the first instance. Extending credit reduces some of these pressures, but at the cost of further increasing economic fragility and financial vulnerability (Minsky 1982).

Moreover, these forms of crises are ideal types, and real-world crises generally include aspects of more than one, perhaps with a different mix in different economic sectors and national economies. The most important point about this short list of varieties of crises is not that a capitalist system simply careens from one type of crisis to another. Marxian theories make a more fundamental point: crisis and crisis resolution are endemic to capitalism, and distinctions between crises types are largely a surface phenomenon reflecting an underlying instability (Fine and Harris 1979). As Marx (1967*a*: 356) himself put it, 'But this constant tendency to equilibrium, of the various spheres of production, is exercised, only in the shape of a reaction against the constant upsetting of this equilibrium.' To take a relatively simple example of how different types of crises can arise simultaneously within a national economy or a more global circuit, imagine trade suddenly expanding between two national economies at different levels of development through a political act such as a free trade agreement. As a result, a nation with a problem of inadequate demand may suddenly mix with one where labor squeezes profits, and, like two bodies of water suddenly connected by a canal, ultimately causing dislocations in both, at least until some new equilibrium is achieved. Marxian political economy, then, does not necessarily postulate a particular pattern or sequence of crises and recoveries, but instead argues that crisis, rather than being an exceptional event punctuating a normal state of equilibrium, is actually the periodic and inevitable product of a fundamentally unstable system.

Another important feature of Marxian political economy visible in these examples is the crucial but contingent role of government. Governments certainly preexisted full-blown capitalist economies, so it would be highly simplistic to dismiss this venerable institution as merely the tool of a capitalist ruling class. Nevertheless, government organs—and these include central bankers, judges, and police as well as elected officials—do indeed tend over time to act in the interests of capitalist ruling classes. As early as the *Communist Manifesto* ([1848] 1977: 223), Marx and Engels referred to the state as 'the executive committee for managing the common affairs of the whole bourgeoisie', arguing that the state acts to preserve the stability and operating efficiency of the system. The history of capitalism is indeed regularly marked by government action to break strikes, bolster business confidence with subsidies and looser regulation, defend investment abroad by diplomacy and arms, raise interest rates to tame demands for higher wages (Galbraith, Giovannoni, and Russo 2007), and sanctify property rights to place them beyond the reach of popular demands.

In part, support of the capitalist class by the state is due to the social, financial, and, sometimes, familial connections between those who govern and those who benefit from the operation of the system (Milliband 1983). Furthermore, even where these personal ties are not strong—when, for example, a populist or pro-labor government wins an election—members of the ruling class, acting in concert, are often in the position to bribe, bully, or threaten a 'capital strike' should they view government as threatening their collective interests (Poulantzas 1973).

However, even within the most capitalistic of societies, governments will on occasion take actions or adopt policies that may earn the disapproval of important segments of the upper class. In some cases, this may be because democratic institutions and popular pressure have enabled part of the state apparatus to act with greater autonomy from ruling class interests. More often, it is because when the state acts in the ruling class's overall interests, it must sometimes act contrary to the prejudices and short-term interests of sizeable segments of the ruling class—in keeping with John Maynard Keynes's famous remark that his role was to save capital from the capitalists. In this manner, states have curbed some of the worse abuses of workers, legislated to raise wage levels, and offered some degree of financial security to employees that the private sector would not or could not supply. Governments also spend money on such items as infrastructure and industrial research, which subsidize both jobs and profits, although, as I discuss below, Marxians view efforts at ameliorating class conflict through spending programs as ultimately generating future conflict and instability (Brenner 2002; Minsky 1982).

It should now be clear why Marxian political economy holds serious implications for encouraging and constraining organizational structure, development, and conflict. Is labor scarce? Must a particular company compete in open markets or can they profit by focusing on government sales? Will taxpayers subsidize research and development? Will innovations be protected by strong intellectual property laws? Is borrowing for investment available? Are cross-border investments and partnerships protected and dependable? Will organized labor be in a position to demand its share of the rents from innovation or monopoly? How interventionist is government likely to prove with regard to safety or financial and environmental risks generated by organizational strategies? And how does the state treat profits and high incomes? All these questions so crucial in organization studies depend for their answers on the political economy of the capitalist system in which the organization is embedded.

5.3. Marxian Political Economy and the Mid-Range Time Horizon

Marx and his disciples are hardly the only theorists who implicitly or explicitly acknowledge the easily observable fact that capitalism changes over time. However, Marxian political economy offers especially rich theoretical explanations of both cyclical and evolutionary change, and Marxian analyses can distinguish between changes that unfold over different periods of time. Marx, himself, explicitly discussed the evolution of capitalism across space and time. In the *Communist Manifesto* (1848), Marx and Engels predicted capitalism's spread throughout the world, and Marx analyzed specific incidents of the spread of capitalism in later writings. Marx was a seminal theorist of the short-term business cycle (Schumpeter 1942), and, as is well-known, he repeatedly predicted that the capitalist system would face increasingly more devastating crises until a revolutionary working class replaced it with socialism. However, neither short nor very long time-frames have proven to be nearly as useful as the mid-range time horizon for understanding organizational structure or change.

While Marx himself did not theorize in any coherent manner the transformation of capitalism within a mid-range time-frame, numerous scholars inspired by his work have sought to fill that gap, and their work is pregnant with implications for organization studies. This mid-range—pegged somewhere between a generation and a century, depending upon the theorist—became a key focus of Marxian research in large part because the substantial organizational changes observed over the decades after Marx's death not only failed to lead to capitalism's eclipse by a new mode of production, but on the contrary, seemed to strengthen the system (Lippit 2006).

It is beyond the scope of this chapter to outline the entire history of these efforts to theorize the mid-range development dynamics of capitalism. It is useful, however, to understand the motivations behind these efforts, which arose out of two phenomena that Marx himself acknowledged in his writings but did not exhaustively theorize. The first is the rise of the large corporation and the ties that this relatively new organizational form was forging with the financial sector. While Marx observed and even analyzed the beginnings of these phenomena in the posthumous third volume of *Capital* (1967*b*, first published in 1894), Rudolf Hilferding's *Finance Capitalism* (1981), originally published in 1910 and tellingly subtitled *The Study of the Latest Phase in Capitalist Development*, became the first widely read attempt to theorize these developments as a full-blown new stage of capitalism. Hilferding had the advantage over Marx of observing the emergence of both the large industrial corporation and this new corporativist pattern of relations between business, banking, and government in Germany, and his book attempted to use Marxism to explain these developments.

Other Marxian theorists of the early decades of the twentieth century focused not so much on new institutions, but on the apparent repetition of certain mid-range patterns of economic behavior within capitalist systems when examined over a sufficiently long time-frame, especially the more dramatic and catastrophic ones such as panics, depressions, euphoric booms, and clusters of technological break-throughs. While Marx recognized the existence of a short-term business cycle, it took inter-war thinkers, most famously Kondratiev and Schumpeter, to argue from empirical data for the existence of longer waves, which they attributed to patterns of investment and technological change.

While few Marxian theorists today accept at face value these early evolutionary and wave theories, more recent scholarship takes inspiration from them by trying to understand the phenomena that inspired them. Some of this work has followed Hilferding in theorizing the interactions of the large industrial and financial concerns, including such influential and revealingly titled works as *Monopoly Capitalism* (Baran and Sweezy 1966), *Late Capitalism* (Mandel 1976), *A Theory of Capitalist Regulation* (Aglietta 1979), *The End of Organized Capitalism* (Lash and Urry 1987), and *The Boom and the Bubble* (Brenner 2002).

To a degree, all contemporary Marxian political economists are evolutionists in that they agree that features of the capitalist system have changed in important ways over time, although not all find the idea of cyclical repetition especially useful or convincing. For organization scholars, however, the distinction between secular and cyclical change over the middle-range is not decisive in understanding, for example, the impact of competitive and unregulated liberalism on organizational structure (Kotz 2003).

Jessop (1997) labels a variety of contemporary efforts to periodicize capitalist development in the medium term as 'regulationism', although the term was originally applied to a specific theory put forward by French political economists (Aglietta 1979). An influential American version of regulationism focuses on the construct of 'social structures of accumulation' (SSA) (Gordon, Edwards, and Reich 1982). An SSA is a set of interlocking and mutually reinforcing institutions within a given capitalist society that work together to promote a degree of economic growth and social stability; new SSAs emerge about every half century, following a period of turbulence, to replace an earlier set of social arrangements that can no longer function to protect order and profitability. Each SSA is eventually discredited not only by its increasing inability to prevent crises that threaten the stability of the system but also by a growing realization that the reforms it originally introduced to remedy the prior period of crisis were partly responsible for generating the current set of contradictions. Thus, for example, using Keynesian stimulation to enliven a weak economy may ultimately sustain uncompetitive businesses too long, protecting investment overseas may strain the tax system, and raising interest rates to reduce employment in order to discipline workers weakens aggregate demand.

Each SSA includes a broad set of institutional arrangements interconnecting political, economic, legal, and organizational practices. These might include labor or property law, the monetary policies of the central bank, the fiscal policies of the legislature, attitudes towards risk in investment, tolerance of unions, government's foreign and military policies, investment and savings practices, the legal and organizational structure of businesses, the strategic orientation of these businesses to different groups of potential consumers (e.g. mass vs. elite marketing), and the regulation of monopoly and other business practices. The point, though, is not to generate an exhaustive list of possible structures, but to understand that they co-evolve to reinforce the strengths and counter the weaknesses of one another.

One relatively recent contribution to Marxian political economy that combines both developmental and cyclical elements while emphasizing the dimension of geographical change has come from Arrighi (1994; see also Arrighi and Silver 1999). It is worth examining in some detail because it is both useful in its own right and because it encompasses many of the insights of other theories. Arrighi builds upon Marx's almost casual insight regarding the movement of the center of the capitalist world over time:

> Thus the villanies of the Venetian thieving system formed one of the secret bases of the capital-wealth of Holland to whom Venice in her decadence lent large sums of money. So also was it with Holland and England. By the beginning of the 18th century the Dutch manufactures were far outstripped. Holland had ceased to be the nation preponderant in commerce and industry. One of its main lines of business, therefore, from 1701–1776, is the lending out of enormous amounts of capital, especially to its great rival England. The same thing is going on to-day between England and the United States. A great deal of capital, which appears to-day in the United States without any certificate of birth, was yesterday, in England, the capitalized blood of children [the last, a reference to English child labor].
>
> (Marx 1967*a*: 754)

Basing his argument on the research of the great French historian Ferdinand Braudel (1981), Arrighi theorizes that each of these successively larger and more technologically advanced states (Venice/Genoa, The Netherlands, England, the United States) initiated and led a century-long wave of capitalist development by dominating the production and manufacturing of the most crucial commodities in international trade of the particular era. Moreover, following Antonio Gramsci (1985), the seminal Marxist theorist of ideology, Arrighi argues that the leading society of each wave leverages its overwhelming financial and industrial power to become hegemonic—dominant because of the acquiescence of the dominated—in the military, cultural, and ideological spheres as well. The rest of the capitalist world not only follows the economic lead of the current hegemon, it also attempts to emulate many other, less material, features of this obviously successful society. As each hegemonic period proceeds, however, the core state inevitably finds that its competitive advantages in producing key commodities is eroded both by the high-cost legacy (a product of successful class struggle) generated by its commercial and industrial successes, as well as the capacity of other regions to imitate and even surpass the hegemon.

As production is increasingly priced out of the core, the capitalist ruling class of the hegemonic economy, on one hand, tries to push down the cost of labor, and on the other, increasingly focuses on financial rent-seeking, an essentially zero-sum process that exploits the reserves of wealth accumulated (often by workers as well as capitalists) during the era of hegemony in commodity production. This process, however, does not lead to the collapse of capitalism as Marx predicted, but rather to the start of a new wave of accumulation based in a new center. The hegemon's ruling class, looking for investment opportunities, provides seed money for the next hegemon. As Marx himself pointed out, Venice (and Genoa) invested in The Netherlands, which eventually invested in England, which in turn invested in the United States, and as the United States appears to be currently doing in China. According to Arrighi, it appears to the hegemon's ruling class that these new investments will leave them in their privileged position. Eventually, however, one of the regions favored by new investment establishes its own leadership in the production of key commodities. Eventually financial hegemony—which is technically easier to imitate, but depends on accumulated wealth—follows as well, and a new hegemonic wave begins.

The implications of this theory for organizational scholarship are twofold. First, it suggests that organizational structures change somewhat cyclically in response to an organization's particular time and place within the particular hegemonic era, whether, for example, the organization is in the core during the upswing or the periphery near the end of an era. Second, organization forms evolve in a secular manner as each new hegemonic society stamps its own comparative advantage on them advantages built upon cultural legacy and historic circumstances. So the firm with a single factory prevalent at the height of British hegemony was eventually eclipsed by the American transcontinental corporations and its imitators elsewhere, and now the East Asian 'networked' form of business appears to have become increasingly dominant and potentially the motor of a new wave of hegemony.

5.4. The Relevance of Marxian Political Economy to Organizational Analysis

Marxian political economy can greatly enrich the study of organizations, especially our understanding of organizational change. Certainly, this theory of large-scale social change can offer richness and insight to explanations of why and when organizations grow and shrink, adopt and discard certain structures, or shift in terms of power relations. Nor need this be an either/or proposition. Marxian political economy can enrich to varying degrees: resource dependency, institutional theory, population ecology, organizational learning, Weberian theory, critical theory, agency theory, and stakeholder theory. These possible applications are discussed below.

5.4.1. Resource Dependency

Marxian political economy provides an excellent explanans for the workings of resource dependency, that is, why one or another so-called 'resource' has become strategically valuable or even essential to an organization. Organizations, for example, operating in an era where capitalists rely on Keynesian demand management will value political connections in their leaders, while another era characterized by cut-throat competition will require marketing skills, and engineering knowledge might be at a premium at a time when military technology is triumphant or wages are set so high as to encourage automation.

Moreover, Marxian political economy can amplify the impact of Pfeffer and Salancik's insight (1978) that those who gain power through control of critical resources can guide an organization to continued dependence upon their specialties. If this process occurs in numerous similarly placed organizations, it should transform the entire society. If the rise of financial interests in the 1980s, for example, led to the increased influence of finance executives within companies (Fligstein 1990), then these same executives would simultaneously use their organizational power to collectively move the society even further down the road towards investor hegemony. They might, for example, form alliances with the financial industry through issuing IPOs, debt packaging, and stock options in order to extract value from outside investors, including the pension funds of ordinary employees.

5.4.2. Institutional Theory

In many ways, institutional theory with its roots in Weber (DiMaggio and Powell 1983) provides the perfect complement to Marxian political economy. If the former tends to be the theory of why organizations converge towards ideal types, Marxian political economy can explain why these powerful tendencies towards inertia and conformity are periodically overcome as organizations finally do change and new organizational forms emerge.

This role for Marxian political economy has actually been suggested by institutional theorists. Acknowledging that a theory anchored in the dynamics of conformity and persistence is ill-suited to account for organizational change, Clemens and Cook endorse Marxian ideas as one way of advancing theory, pointing out that 'in accounts of macro-historical change, the power of internal contradiction is most associated with Marxian dialectics' (1999: 449). Seo and Creed (2002) have taken up the agenda suggested by Clemens and Cook by laying out a series of propositions influenced by Marxian analysis that institutionalists should employ to analyze change. Seo and Creed's suggestions are somewhat abstract, so the following example might illustrate how Marxian political economy might contribute to institutional analysis.

After World War II, most large industrial corporations in the United States accepted the need to accommodate unions, if often grudgingly, and a number of structures and behaviors converged across companies to deal with unions. This convergence was generated by a combination of mimetic, coercive, and normative pressures that arose from institutional arrangements such as the Wagner Act, Master's degree programs in industrial relations, the creation of 'IR' staff positions, pattern bargaining across companies in the same sector, etc. In the 1970s, however, with the rise of international competition, high levels of inflation, and the stagnation of productivity growth, investors and corporate executives funded think tanks that generated and propagated an ideology in which union rent-seeking and inflexibility were condemned as barriers to profitability, productivity, and general prosperity.

This new ideology, coupled to shifts in political contributions by those with the funds to make a difference, altered political behavior, which, in turn, generated a signal of a new norm through the dismissal by President Reagan of striking air traffic controllers in 1981. Coupled with the decline in coercive pressure from a National Labor Relations Board—now dominated by pro-management appointees—the leaders of a handful of entrepreneurial companies (e.g. Greyhound, Phelps Dodge) felt free to generate a new template for overturning unionization, a template that other companies eventually followed in a classic case of mimetic and, ultimately, normative isomorphism.

5.4.3. Population Ecology

Of all the major organization theories, this is perhaps the one for which Marxian political economy is least directly applicable. The theory marginalizes, if not completely eliminates, human agency in the life cycle of organizations (Hannan and Freeman 1977), hardly leaving room for introducing class conflict, a necessary element of any Marxian analysis. Although ironically, this very un-Marxian theory uses the dichotomous terms 'core' and 'periphery' that were first introduced by Marxian dependency theory, albeit with a very different meaning (Frank 1967). Still, the theory makes extensive use of the concept of environmental resources, so the comments regarding resources in the discussion of resource dependency apply equally to the concept of 'environment' as used by population ecologists. If the proliferation of pizza parlors, for example, continues until they fill their particular environmental niche in a particular geographical region, the size and sustainability of that niche is generated by the political and economical factors analyzed by Marxian political economy, such as wage rates, the availability of consumer credit, economic pressure to work long hours necessitating fast food, and the intensity of competition among fast food chains.

5.4.4. Organizational Learning

Tendencies to choose one end or the other of the exploration/exploitation continuum can be explained, at least in part, by Marxian political economy. For example, one could expect that within a political economic environment that includes high wages and relatively autonomous executives, the risk and rewards favor exploration more than they do in a highly competitive economy that features downward pressure on wages and a short-term oriented financial sector disinclined to nurture emerging new technologies for decades, as was the case with television. Moreover, if the business in question experiences high wages as an internal cost, that will create incentives to innovate less labor-intensive production techniques.

Conversely, if a previous crisis ends an era of economic liberalism, and it is replaced with efforts to stabilize and stimulate the economy through a program of military Keynesianism and limiting competition, then the Pentagon can reduce the costs of technological exploration for companies by both subsidizing research and development and purchasing the first commodities generated by new technologies. For example, during the Cold War, American civilian manufacturing 'explored' by using subsidized military technology to move from the production of propeller planes to jets, from leather to plastic football helmets, and from vacuum tube to transistors, and even contributed to automating the manufacturing process itself (Noble 1984).

5.4.5. Weberian theory

The relationship between Marxians and Weberians has been one of ambivalence on both sides as far back as Weber's own effort to confront the ideas of Marx (Ringer 2004). Anderson is typical in his Marxian judgment that for all the extraordinary richness of Weber's work, 'it significantly falls short of any general dynamic or principles of motion' (1984: 87). Many Marxians follow Anderson in viewing Weber as a master 'gap filler': successful at insightfully illuminating the structure of social behavior, but unable to explain how these structures emerge or evolve.

In the case of bureaucracy, its legitimacy and actual performance has fluctuated since the late nineteenth century with the emergence of large industrial corporations in the United States and Europe, and Marxian analysis can help understand why similar bureaucratic tendencies have been viewed as both a boon and a barrier at different times and places (Lash and Urry 1987; Smith 1990). According to the Marxian historical tradition, the development of bureaucracy was not linked to the rise of capitalism, but to the consolidation of 'absolutist' monarchies, which, while based on the expropriation of peasant surpluses like classical feudalism, differed in that it relied on a tax-supported standing army and officialdom for social control and in competition with other absolutist regimes (Anderson 1974; Wood 1999). As capitalism spread from non-absolutist Britain and The Netherlands to other countries with stronger bureaucratic traditions (including the United States with its private railroad bureaucracies), market relations and bureaucratic rationality ultimately fused to a degree. Under some circumstances, private and public bureaucratic organizational forms helped to stabilize capitalism and became part of a particular social structure of accumulation; but, more recently, this stability and predictability has become a cost that cannot be readily borne by businesses under heightened and fluctuating levels of demand and competition (Lash and Urry 1987; Smith 1990). Hence, an important form of organizational structure that once seemed essential to regulate some forms of behavior is increasingly regarded as an unnecessary and costly evil, and this view may well shift again as the world economy confronts future crises and their resolutions.

5.4.6. Critical Organizational Theory

Critical organization theory is a collection of theories and approaches, including more micro-oriented Marxian theories such as Braverman's (1974) theory of deskilling. One defining feature is an effort to link critical analysis of macro-structures with analysis of the subjective experience of domination (Adler, Forbes, and Willmott 2007). Greater clarity in the analysis of political economy could strengthen work in this vein. This point can best be illustrated by considering a prototypical and widely referenced example of critical organizational studies.

James Barker's (1993) 'Tightening the Iron Cage' provides one excellent example. It was published in what is generally regarded as the most prestigious journal in organizational studies, *Administrative Science Quarterly*, won the journal's best paper award for that year, and was the subject of a critical scholars' symposium at an Academy of Management meeting. The article is a field study of employees of a manufacturer of electronic components, which happens to be a spin-off of a large telecommunications company. The workers in this factory were organized during the duration of this study into self-managed teams by a manager who, we are told, sincerely believed in the win–win potential of the new arrangement, and who even eased out or reassigned lower level managers who were uncomfortable with the change. After a period of time, the democratic ebb and flow of team management gave way to heightened levels of monitoring and suspicion among team members, a return to rule making, the exploitation and oppression of temporary employees by permanent team members, and even a partial return to formal hierarchy. Like hierarchy in the play, *The Admirable Crichton*, Weber's iron cage of rationality allegedly returned as the new organizational form settled into a new normality even more repressive than the one it replaced because the employees designed it themselves, thus leading to a higher degree of internalization.

The piece, however, makes little effort to look outside of this factory's gates to explain this evolution, or, perhaps more accurately, devolution of behavior and structure. The neglected larger picture, however, throws additional light on the chronicled events. The employees may understandably have lost some sense of security when their factory was spun-off from a far larger monopolistic firm with a long history of stability. Moreover, in 1991, the year Barker conducted his research, a recession occurred, which undoubtedly increased some people's sense of uncertainty and fear for their future. Furthermore, the previous decade has been rightfully labeled an era of 'deindustrialization' in the United States, which experienced a 17 percent drop in American manufacturing jobs during a period in which the workforce grew by nearly 25 percent (*Economic Report of the President* 2006). While the employees were not economists by training, it is likely that they knew that competition among manufacturing firms had increased and that their jobs were in greater jeopardy than had historically been the case, and they were certainly aware that manufacturing was the best paying sector for individuals without high levels of education or artisanal skills.

Realistic anxiety about the changing economic times could have served as at least a partial explanation for the unpleasant behavior of team members that was depicted in this article. What was indisputably a highly insightful piece with important practical ramifications would have been more of both had the author addressed these issues in observing and interviewing his subjects. It might also have led to interesting questions for further research. Would employees impose concerted control upon themselves if they were represented by a union, or in a growth industry, or in a nation with a stronger safety net for the unemployed? Awareness of Marxian political economy might have led to such follow-up work among the many admirers of this article.

5.4.7. Agency Theory

Surprisingly, in light of its association with the political right, agency theory may hold more in common with Marxian political economy than any other organizational theory. As noted earlier, in the third volume of Marx's *Capital* (1967*b*), Marx made a start on analyzing the financial side of capital, including the joint-stock industrial corporations, which were then just coming into vogue in the most advanced capitalist nations. Marx's own view was that financial capital was the social or collective capital of the capitalist ruling class, and, as such, generally operated, in a manner analogous to government, for the benefit of the ruling class as a whole, sometimes in opposition to the desires or personal interests of individual industrial capitalists. According to Marx, 'money capital emerges, more and more, in so far as it appears on the market, as not represented by the individual capitalist, the proprietor of this or that fraction of the mass of capital on the market, but rather as a concentrated and organized mass, placed under the control of bankers as representatives of the social capital' (1967*b*: 368).

This view of finance is surprisingly close to agency theory, suggesting, only somewhat ironically, that agency theory might be viewed as a form of Marxism that is sympathetic to the interests of the upper class. Certainly, the parallels and overlaps are impressive: where Marxism focuses on management's expropriation of 'surplus value' generated by workers, agency theory accuses this same 'management' of refusing to maximize 'shareholder value' by diverting cash that rightfully belongs to stockholders to 'empire-building projects... bloated staffs, indulgent prerequisites, and organizational inefficiencies' (Jensen 1989: 67). Jensen and other agency theorists also share Marx's advocacy of revolutionary solutions, arguing that ending exploitation of investors might require drastic action led by raiders and shareholder activists who could create 'the crisis atmosphere managers require to slash unsound investment programs, shrink overhead, and dispose of assets' (Jensen 1989: 67).

Strikingly, and in sharp contrast to other mainstream organization theories that are advocated by more 'liberal' academics, agency theorists acknowledge that employees have not shared in the productivity gains generated by the reorganization of American capitalism in the 1980s and 1990s. In a moment of remarkable candor, Jensen and Fagan (1996: A10) admit that for Western workers 'real wages are likely to continue their sluggish growth and some will fall dramatically over the coming two or three decades, perhaps as much as 50% in some sectors'. Not surprisingly, however, given their explicitly stated sympathies for the investing class, they regard these trends as a good thing, although, like many Marxists, they see this trend as the darkest hour before the dawn, the beginning of a process that will generate a new era of economic plenty.

Where Marxian political economy can contribute to agency theory is not in refuting its claims but in pointing out their historical context, and thus their limitations. Despite arguments to the contrary (Friedman 1970), the corporate form was not explicitly created to exclusively benefit shareholders; it was actually promoted in the nineteenth century as a means of fostering broad-based economic prosperity. This egalitarianism was necessitated by the political resistance, especially in the United States, of what Marx termed the petite bourgeoisie: shopkeepers, farmers, and craftsman who saw the benefits of incorporation (limited liability, legal personhood) as a privilege open only to rich and politically connected merchants (Roy 1997). As a result, a purely shareholder-centric view of the corporation was never ideologically hegemonic until the economic crisis of the late 1970s. While the so-called separation of ownership and control within large corporations received comment and even criticism (Berle and Means 1933), it did not seem to discomfit investors very much. Their class interests were still generally promoted by these allegedly autonomous managers, even if managerial focus on investors was diffused, like a butler skimming the house accounts, by managerial self-regard (Sweezy 1953).

However, once American industrial hegemony became less certain because of high wages, aging plant, and increased competition, capital became less patient. Finance was used to extract already accumulated wealth in a largely zero-sum process. As Marx understood, and Jensen and others rediscovered, finance in the form of debt and then through other forms of shareholder pressure served to enforce class solidarity upon an executive stratum that might prove uncooperative for sentimental or selfish reasons. As Useem (1996) notes, executives would soon learn that they would be amply rewarded for looking at their own companies through the eyes of a would-be raider.

After two centuries, wage growth essentially ended in the United States, through union avoidance, layoffs and outsourcing, shifting the tax burden, anti-inflationary monetary policies, and declining real minimum wages (Brenner 2002). To make up the shortfall, employees were offered credit cards, cheap mortgages, and home equity loans, thus transferring more of their income with fees and interest while generating additional pressure to stay on the job to service this increasing level of debt. Furthermore, the risk of this debt, as well as the cost of various other financial instruments, could be passed off, in part, to pension funds, mutual funds, and insurance companies, institutions entrusted with the savings of workers (Partnoy 2003). That financial insiders would also despoil each other as well as the accumulated savings of the working class was a practice that Marx (1967*a*) himself saw in his own age, and if the degree, legitimacy, and sophistication of this practice exploded in recent years, that itself is a rational reflection of the lack of confidence in longer term investment projects, a lack of confidence characteristic of the last decades of a hegemonic era (Arrighi 1994). Thus, finance, formerly a tool of production, becomes for a generation or so, an end in itself. As a result, an agency theory that is informed and enriched by class analysis can explain a great deal about how organizations function and change in the current era.

5.4.8. Stakeholder Theory

While not formally a product of the sociology of organizations, stakeholder theory is definitely an organizational theory, since it focuses on the dynamics of organizations, particularly business organizations. In actuality, stakeholder theory is really at least two theories. There is an ethical theory that asserts that managers should recognize the stakeholders of their organizations, those individuals and groups whose lives are significantly affected by their decisions, and treats them according to certain ethical principles that focus, in Kantian fashion, on the needs and interests of these stakeholders (Evan and Freeman 1993). There is also a more predictive, social scientific version of stakeholder theory, which argues that treating stakeholders according to these same ethical principles tends to generate superior performance, *ceteris paribus* (Jones 1995). Marxian political economy can contribute, albeit critically, to both approaches.

First, Marxian political economy can explain why this particular managerial-centered view of the ethics of corporate behavior took hold when it did. Stakeholder theory first emerged in the 1980s and almost immediately triggered a major shift in the academic discourse on corporate social responsibility. From the 1950s to the 1970s, writers on this topic in the United States mirrored a society in which commodity production was both central to the society and globally hegemonic. As a result, these authors, many trained as Keynesian or labor economists, argued for responsibilities that encouraged productivity while preserving social peace in the American core, primarily union–management cooperation and the sharing of prosperity under the supportive but watchful eye of a pluralistic, independent state to represent the broad public interest. If there was an inherent philosophical justification for this approach, it came from the utilitarian views of John Stuart Mill, the English philosopher who witnessed the similarly hegemonic rise of industrial England in the previous century, with its economic successes and attendant social problems that threatened to generate social upheaval (Marens 2008). Mill himself was an early advocate of both labor–management cooperation and legislation to ameliorate the worst abuses of industrialization, and thus the intellectual predecessor of this first generation of advocates of corporate responsibility.

By the mid-1970s, however, the American economy faced stagflation and a productivity slowdown, which, within a few years, led to the mobilization of financial interests, on one hand, and the repudiation of management's concordat with American Labor, on the other. A new generation of scholars of corporate social responsibility introduced and embraced stakeholder management as a response to the changing political economy of the United States. Consciously or not, they acknowledged the reality of a threatened and increasingly proactive ruling class, and so they appealed instead to what they hoped would prove to be the more enlightened segment of this class. Far more than their intellectual predecessors, they conceded the legitimacy of CEO power and autonomy and refused to advocate constraints through government regulation or the countervailing power of labor unions, two institutional arrangements that these executives were now mobilizing to overturn (Clawson, Neustadtl, and Weller, 1998).

Instead, these new scholars argued against the hegemony of shareholder interests by implicitly harking back to an earlier era characterized by what might be labeled 'the relative autonomy of management'. During most of the twentieth century, American corporate management held both the power and the ideological legitimacy to weigh interests (including, to a degree, their own) alongside those of shareholders. Contemporary stakeholder theorists, however, do not acknowledge that the circumstances that had permitted this relative autonomy have largely eroded. Oblivious to these changed circumstances, they have argued that what remains of managerial autonomy ought to be wielded in a manner consistent with Kantian ideals: that is with respect for each stakeholder's own desired ends and not merely as means or tools for achieving greater profitability and higher stock prices (Evan and Freeman 1993). They argue further that 'high road' competitive advantages would, on average, accrue to those executives who weighed the interests of their stakeholder groups, thus giving them a defensible business justification for resisting pressure from financial interests to directly consider only the interests and expectations of investors (Jones 1995).

The empirical evidence would suggest that this stakeholder model has had little impact upon actual corporate decision making. Almost a generation after stakeholder theory was first introduced in the middle 1980s, there is no evidence that customers or communities have been treated better by American corporations and a great deal of evidence that employees have been treated worse than in previous decades, especially with regard to their sharing in financial gains and their right to organize unions (Marens 2004). From the perspective of Marxian political economy, the problem with stakeholder theory is that it was expecting the nearly impossible under contemporary circumstances, since, given the balance of class forces under contemporary capitalism, the potential, and largely theoretical, rewards from generosity, patience, and sensitivity to stakeholders are simply overwhelmed by the potential profitability from exerting political pressure and limiting the pay and security of all but the most essential employees. In this regard, Immanuel

Kant has proven to be an ironic model of ethical reasoning, given his preference for the enlightened despotism of Frederick II over the uncertainties of democracy (Kant [1784] 1967). Frederick himself had expressed stakeholder management-like sympathy for the plight of the Prussian peasantry, but constrained as he was by the social structure of his absolutist government, he could take no serious action on their behalf as long he depended on their landlords for support in the wars that aggrandized his personal position and sustained his state (Anderson 1974; Kuehn 2001).

Marxian political economy can enrich stakeholder theory by bringing a sense of history and historical alternatives to bear, and thus overcome the intellectual blinders of the field. Such analysis can help stakeholder researchers understand that any pattern of enlightened self-interest practiced in the past by corporate executives was, in part, driven by fear of pressure from mobilized stakeholders and a regulatory state that was more autonomous, and an investing establishment with more confidence in the future. Moreover, Marxian political economy can move beyond the American provincialism that pervades the field and inform it of stakeholder-oriented institutional arrangements in other nations, such as the system of works councils in Germany. What might result is a more realistic perspective for studying stakeholder relations and more practical ways of advocating new forms of stakeholder management.

5.5. Conclusion

Currently, most theorizing and research in organization studies treat specific organizations and organizational types in excessive isolation from the social and economic forces that shape and limit them. At best, organization researchers invoke the idea of an 'environment' to provide the macro context of organizational structure and development. Unfortunately, they rarely attempt to open this environmental black box to better understand how, when, and where it works to effect organizational forms and organizational change. If institutional theory is something of an exception, until recently it has typically addressed only half the story: why organizations look the same.

Marxian political economy can provide this missing macro context because it is concerned primarily with change over time within a capitalist system, the system that increasingly penetrates both private and public organizations around the world. This version of political economy has the advantage of dynamically endogenizing most of the social and economic environment, so it can not only help answer questions regarding organizational change and stability but also explain how these same organizations feed back into the larger system. Furthermore, Marxian political economy does not necessarily require entirely rejecting any of the major organizational theories, but can be used in conjunction with these, lending a new breadth of realism and depth of insight to the study of organizations.

References

Adler, P. S., Forbes, L., and Willmott, H. (2007). 'Critical Management Studies: Premises, Practices, Problems, and Prospects', in J. Walsh and A. Brief (eds.), *Academy of Management Annals*, Vol. 1. London: Taylor & Francis.

Aglietta, M. (1979). *A Theory of Capitalist Regulation: The US Experience*. London: NLB.

Anderson, P. (1974). *Lineages of the Absolutist State*. London: NLB.

—— (1984). *In the Tracks of Historical Materialism*. Chicago: University of Chicago Press.

Arrighi, G. (1994). *The Long Twentieth Century: Money, Power, and the Origins of Our Times*. New York: Verso Books.

—— and Silver, B. J. (1999). *Chaos and Governance in the Modern World System*. Minneapolis: University of Minnesota Press.

Baran, P. A., and Sweezy, P. M. (1966). *Monopoly Capitalism: An Essay on the American Economic and Social Order*. New York: Monthly Review Press.

Barker, J. R. (1993). 'Tightening the Iron Cage: Concertive Control in Self-Managing Teams'. *Administrative Science Quarterly*, 38/3: 408–37.

Berle, A. A., and Means, G. C. (1993). *The Modern Corporation and Private Property*. New York: Macmillan.

Braudel, F. (1981). *The Perspective of the World: Civilization and Capitalism 15th–18th Century*, Vol. 3. Berkeley: University of California Press.

Braverman, H. (1974). *Labor and Monopoly Capital: The Degradation of Work in the Twentieth Century*. New York: Monthly Review Press.

Brenner, R. (2002). *The Boom and the Bubble: The US in the World Economy*. New York: W. W. Norton and Co.

Clawson, D., Neustadtl, A., and Weller, M. (1998). *Dollars and Votes: How Business Campaign Contributions Subvert Democracy*. Philadelphia: Temple University Press.

Clemens, E. S., and Cook, J. M. (1999). 'Politics and Institutionalism: Explaining Durability and Change'. *American Review of Sociology*, 25/3: 441–66.

Davis, G. F. (1994). 'Corporate Elite and the Politics of Corporate Control', in C. Predergast and J. D. Nottnerus (eds.), *Current Perspectives in Sociology*, Supplement I. Greenwich, Conn.: JAI Press.

De Ste. Croix, G. E. M. (1981). *The Class Struggle in the Ancient Greek World: From the Archaic Age to the Arab Conquests*. Ithaca, NY: Cornell University Press.

DiMaggio, P. J., and Powell, W. W. (1983). 'The Iron Cage Revisited: Institutional Isomorphism and Collective Rationality in Organizational Fields'. *American Sociological Review*, 48: 147–60.

Economic Report of the President: Transmitted to Congress (2006). Washington, DC: US Government Printing Office.

Engels, F. (1966). *Herr Eugen Dühring's Revolution in Science*. New York: International Press.

EVAN, W., and FREEMAN, R. (1993). 'A Stakeholder Theory of the Modern Corporation: Kantian Capitalism', in T. Beauchamp and N. Bowie (eds.), *Ethical Theory and Business*. Englewood Cliffs, NJ: Prentice Hall.

FINE, B., and HARRIS, L. (1979). *Rereading Capital*. New York: Columbia University Press.

FLIGSTEIN, N. (1990). *The Transformation of Corporate Control*. Cambridge, Mass.: Harvard University Press.

FRANK, A. G. (1967). *Capitalism and Underdevelopment in Latin America*. New York: Monthly Review Press.

FRIEDMAN, M. (1970). 'The Social Responsibility of Business is to Increase its Profits'. *New York Times*, 13 September, 122–6.

GALBRAITH, J. K., GIOVANNONI, O., and RUSSO, A. J. (2007). 'The Fed's Real Reaction Function'. Working Paper 511, Jerome Levy Institute.

GORDON, D. M., EDWARDS, R., and REICH, M. (1982). *Segmented Work, Divided Workers: The Historical Transformation of Labor in the United States*. New York: Cambridge University Press.

GRAMSCI, A. (1985). *Selections from Cultural Writings*. Cambridge, Mass.: Harvard University Press.

HANNAN, M. T., and FREEMAN, J. (1977). 'The Population Ecology of Organizations'. *American Journal of Sociology*, 82/5: 929–64.

—— —— (1989). *Organizational Ecology*. Cambridge, Mass.: Harvard University Press.

HILFERDING, R. (1981). *Finance Capital: A Study of the Latest Phase of Capitalist Development*. London: Routledge & Kegan Paul.

HOFFMAN, S. (1995). 'Democracy and Society: An Interview with Stanley Hoffman'. *World Policy Journal*, 12/1: 35–9.

JENSEN, M. C. (1989). 'Eclipse of the Public Corporation'. *Harvard Business Review*, 67/5: 61–74.

—— and FAGAN, P. (1996). 'Capitalism Isn't Broken'. *Wall Street Journal*, 29 March, A10.

JESSOP, B. (1997). 'Survey Article: The Regulation Approach'. *Journal of Political Philosophy*, 5/3: 287–326.

JONES, T. M. (1995). 'Instrumental Stakeholder Theory: A Synthesis of Ethics and Economics'. *Academy of Management Review*, 20: 404–37.

KALECKI, M. ([1943] 1971). 'Political Aspects of Full-Employment'. Reprinted in M. Kalecki, *Selected Essays on the Dynamics of the Capitalist Economy*. Cambridge: Cambridge University Press.

—— (1968). 'Trend and Business Cycle Reconsidered'. *Economic Journal*, 78/2: 263–76.

KANT, I. ([1784] 1967). 'The Nature of Enlightenment'. Reprinted in R. Wines (ed.), *Enlightened Despotism: Reform or Reaction?* Boston: Heath Co.

KOTZ, D. M. (2003). 'Neoliberalism and the Social Structure of Accumulation Theory of Long-Run Capital Accumulation'. *Review of Radical Political Economics*, 35/3: 263–70.

KUEHN, M. (2001). *Immanuel Kant: A Biography*. New York: Cambridge University Press.

LASH, S., and URRY, J. (1987). *The End of Organized Capitalism*. Madison: University of Wisconsin Press.

LIPPIT, V. D. (2006). 'Social Structure of Accumulation Theory'. Paper presented at conference on *Growth and Crises: Social Structure of Accumulation Theory and Analysis*, National University of Ireland, Galway, Ireland.

MANDEL, E. (1976). *Late Capitalism*. New York: Schocken Books.

MARENS, R. S. (2004). 'Wobbling on a One-Legged Stool: The Decline of American Pluralism and the Academic Treatment of Corporate Social Responsibility'. *Journal of Academic Ethics*, 2/1: 63–87.

—— (2008). 'Recovering the Past: Reviving the Legacy of the Early Scholars of Corporate Social Responsibility'. *Journal of Management History*, 14/1: 55–72.

MARX, K. (1967*a*). *Capital: A Critique of Political Economy*, Vol. 1. New York: International Publishers.

—— (1967*b*). *Capital: A Critique of Political Economy*, Vol. 3. New York: International Publishers.

—— and ENGELS, F. ([1848] 1977). 'The Communist Manifesto'. Reprinted in David McLellan (ed.), *Karl Marx: Selected Writings*. Oxford: Oxford University Press.

MILLIBAND, R. (1983). *Class Power and State Power*. London: Verso Press.

MINSKY, H. P. (1982). *Can It Happen Again: Essays in Instability and Finance*. Armonk, NY: M. E. Sharpe.

MOSELEY, F. (2000). 'A New Solution to the Transformation Problem: A Sympathetic Critique'. *Review of Radical Political Economics*, 32/2: 282–316.

NELSON, R. R., and WINTER, S. G. (1982). *An Evolutionary Theory of Economic Change*. Cambridge, Mass.: Harvard University Press.

NOBLE, D. F. (1984). *Forces of Production: A Social History of Industrial Automation*. New York: Alfred Knopf.

NORTH, D. C. (1987). 'Is It Worth Making Sense of Marx?' *Inquiry*, 29/1: 57–63.

PARTNOY, F. (2003). *Infectious Greed: How Deceit and Risk Corrupted the Financial Markets*. New York: Henry Holt and Company.

PFEFFER, J., and SALANCIK, G. R. (1978). *The External Control of Organizations: A Resource Dependence Perspective*. New York: Harper and Row.

POULANTZAS, N. (1973). *Political Power and Social Classes*. London: NLB.

RINGER, F. K. (2004). *Max Weber: An Intellectual Biography*. Chicago: University of Chicago Press.

ROY, W. G. (1997). *Socializing Capital: The Rise of the Large Industrial Corporation in America*. Princeton: Princeton University Press.

SCHUMPETER, J. A. (1942). *Capitalism, Socialism, and Democracy*. New York: Harper & Brothers.

SEO, M. G., and CREED, W. E. D. (2002). 'Institutional Contradictions, Praxis, and Institutional Change: A Dialectical Perspective'. *Academy of Management Review*, 27/2: 222–47.

SMITH, V. (1990). *Managing in the Corporate Interest: Control and Resistance in an American Bank*. Berkeley: University of California Press.

SWEEZY, P. (1953). *Present as History*. New York: Monthly Review Press.

USEEM, M. (1996). *Investor Capitalism: How Money Managers are Changing the Face of Corporate America*. New York: Basic Books.

WOOD, E. M. (1999). *Origins of Capitalism*. New York: Monthly Review Press.

CHAPTER 6

WEBER: SINTERING THE IRON CAGE

TRANSLATION, DOMINATION, AND RATIONALITY

STEWART CLEGG
MICHAEL LOUNSBURY

6.1. Introduction

Engagement with Max Weber's corpus of scholarly work has waned since the early Aston studies and efforts to theorize the dynamics of bureaucracy in the 1950s and 1960s. Lounsbury and Carberry (2005) showed that citations to Weber have decreased since that time and that scholars who do cite him often do so in ceremonial ways. In this chapter, we explore Weber's relevance to contemporary organizational theory by revisiting some of his core ideas and highlighting how a deeper engagement with Weber's scholarship can expand the scope of current organizational analysis. In particular, we point to the cultural dimension of Weber's work, an aspect that has been somewhat neglected (see also Clegg 1995; Swedberg 1998).

One of Weber's most pervasive images is the *iron cage* of bureaucracy. Struggling with issues of modernity and rationalization in the late nineteenth and early twentieth centuries, Weber viewed the development of bureaucratic organizations as highly efficient solutions to organizing, but he was quite pessimistic because he believed that they would transform human interaction and behavior into a dreary quasi-mechanization, bereft of sensuality, spirit, and culture. The iron cage is a metaphor more of Parsons's choosing than of Weber's. Actually, the better translation of the German phrase that Weber uses is 'steel-hardened shell or casing', but it has a less poetic ring. The reference to the 'iron cage' resonates with Christian's encounter with the man in the iron cage in Bunyan's *Pilgrim's Progress*: the man who was 'once a fair and flourishing professor' now 'a man of despair ... shut up in it, as in this iron cage'.

While we acknowledge the attractiveness of the iron cage metaphor, Weber's supposed emphasis on efficiency has been vastly overstated. In fact, Weber does not speak of efficiency per se, but of the most formally rational mode of exercising political domination (see Derlien 1999: 64). What is often translated as 'efficiency' in Weber is, in fact, better regarded as 'technical rationality'. In this chapter, we emphasize how Weber's approach to bureaucracy was first and foremost a cultural theory. In addition, we show how the very notion of rationality for Weber was multiplex and culturally embedded (see Clegg 1995; Lounsbury 2007). Conceptualizing organizational environments as comprised of multiple modes of rationality and forms of domination can lead to an understanding of the 'iron cage' as more porous than is traditionally thought, thus opening up new lines of multilevel analysis. This chapter therefore aims to sinter the iron cage. Sintering is a method to make metal porous, and the porosity allows lubricants to flow through the medium of the metal. A sintered 'iron cage' could thus be the container of a far more liquid modernity (Bauman 2000) than one hardened with steel, through which medium nothing could pass either way. To sinter the iron cage is to make it no less tangible but far more porous.

In the next section, we briefly highlight some of Weber's key works and review scholarly developments in organizational theory that have stemmed from his scholarship. We then discuss how some lines of inquiry have been eschewed in favor of others, and how a reengagement with some core foundational ideas can spur new lines of theoretical development.

6.2. Review of Weber in Organization Theory

6.2.1. Weber the Man

Born in Germany in 1864, Max Weber was the eldest son of an aspiring liberal politician whose family had become wealthy in the linen industry. His father was a member of the Prussian House of Deputies (1868–97) and the Reichstag (1872–84), enabling Max to gain exposure to prominent scholars and politicians. Max's mother was raised as a Calvinist, exposing him to strong religious foundations. In 1882, Max began studies at the University of Heidelberg, served in the military in 1884, and then moved back home to Berlin where he continued his intellectual development at the University of Berlin.

While celebrated as one of the founders of sociology, Weber's training was focused on legal and economic history. One of his least discussed works is his dissertation on the *History of Commercial Partnerships* ([1889] 2003), which provided a comparative-historical approach to entrepreneurial activity and Roman and Germanic commercial law. This important work initiated many of the theoretical themes that would be central to Weber's lifetime of work such as rationalization, the historical separation of household and business, and the construction of 'modern' forms of organization and authority that would later culminate in his ideal type of bureaucracy (see Ruef and Lounsbury 2007).

After receiving a temporary position in jurisprudence at the University of Berlin, Weber became a full professor in political economy, first at Freiburg and then at Heidelberg in 1896. Through this period, he was also somewhat active in leftist politics—using his position to make claims about how the Left could advance German society amidst conditions of a weak working class and the continued power of the Junker aristocracy. However, his political activity was muted by his preference for disciplined scholarship. Weber's productivity was interrupted by a nervous breakdown that traumatized him from 1898 until 1903 when his scholarly activity resumed, resulting in his most well-known works such as *The Protestant Ethic and the Spirit of Capitalism*. In this latter period of his life (1903–20), he focused more extensively on developing his ideas about the economy and its relationship to other institutional spheres. For a nice overview of Weber's life and the development of his work, see Swedberg's *Max Weber and the Idea of Economic Sociology* (1998, esp. pp. 180–203); in addition, the Wikipedia entry on Max Weber has details on his 'Life and Career'.

6.2.2. Received Interpretation

Weber's major interest was in the development of the great world civilizations. In this sense, he took up the themes of G. W. F. Hegel's (1998) philosophy of history, especially the specific and peculiar role of rationalism in the development of Western culture. Weber was also concerned with the debate concerning science and history, between interpretive understanding and causal explanation. Weber felt that historical sociology was a cultural enterprise that should be concerned with both individuality and generality (Ritzer 1992: 114).

The philosopher who dominated German philosophical thought during Weber's life was Immanuel Kant, who lived from 1724 to 1804. Kant argued that the methods of the natural sciences as he understood them at that time provided indubitable knowledge about the external phenomenal world as we experience it through our senses. Weber believed that while sociology must be concerned with empirical analysis of society and history, the method of sociology would have to be different from that of the natural sciences because it dealt with the ideational, and thus moral, world. It meant examining social action within a context of social interaction, not just viewing people as objects driven by impersonal forces. Thus, Weber's approach to social analysis led him to reject the overly simplistic formulas of economic base and corresponding cultural superstructure that were so often used in Marxist analysis to account for cultural development. Given his legal training, Weber sought to generalize across cases and developed the method of ideal types to do this.

After English translations of Weber's work were available, mostly in the post-World War II period, the organization scholars who read Weber largely worked outside of contemporary German scholarship. Precursors such as Nietzsche, Hegel, Marx, or contemporaries such as Simmel were not well known, notwithstanding the fact that, as sage commentators such as Martindale (1960) point out, these were key points of scholarly reference for Weber. And, to add a further barrier to the reception of his ideas, while Weber foreshadowed a more critical scholarly approach to the analysis of organizations and economic action, a discourse framed by textbooks and edited collections on management, such as Derek Pugh's (1968) *Organization Theory* or Pugh, Hickson, and Hinings's (1963) *Writers on Organizations*, situated Weber as a classical theorist of administration. Weber came to be seen as a classical scholar of administration, someone whose concern with bureaucracy rounded out the concern with the shop-floor exhibited by F. W. Taylor, and who meshed nicely with other contemporaries, such as the Frenchman Henri Fayol. Weber's inscription as a part of the classical canon by management writers added a touch of class to a rather pedestrian set of concerns. However, Weber was never a conscious part of the classical management canon in any contemporaries' calculations, least of all his own. While Weber (1978) was familiar with the work of Taylor and other scientific management writers they were not familiar with him. While Taylor proposed technologies to exert power, Weber explained them. It would be wholly incorrect to bundle Weber up as a scholar of the 'classical school', akin to F. W. Taylor or to situate his corpus within the narrative of formal management theories. They have very little in common at all. The 'Max Weber' known in most management and organization theory is therefore an exceedingly simplified caricature in which the nuance, depth, and cultural embeddedness of the original texts had been lost.

The translations of Weber's writings on the functions of bureaucracy provided a key catalyst for much of the development of organizational theory post-World War II. A number of studies by Merton and colleagues (1952), and by his students (e.g. Selznick 1949; Gouldner 1954; Blau 1955; Lipset, Trow, and Coleman 1956) provided a solid platform for the emergence of organizational analysis as a distinctive research domain. A good deal of this early work examined the existence of the ideal typical Weberian bureaucracy and subsequently aimed to critique and revise that simple model (e.g. Janowitz and Delany 1956; Etzioni 1959; Simpson 1959; Hage 1965; Thompson 1965; Albrow 1969; for a review, see Lounsbury and Carberry 2005).

A great deal of the early work, fruitful as it was, seems to be premised on a basic misunderstanding of what Weberian ideal types were intended to be. The researchers went out into the field and studied many different organizations, finding that they did not correspond to the ideal type that Weber had proposed. Having found a significant source of variation, they then conceptualized a new ideal type on its basis, thus completing or adding to the Weberian model, or, in some cases, seeking to supplant it. However, the basic conception of the ideal type as something intended to correspond with reality was fundamentally flawed. Weber developed his ideal type in the context of an appreciation of the organizations central to the German state-building process in the nineteenth and early twentieth century. Weber made no claims to have constructed a universal for all places and all times. More effective elaboration of ideal types can be seen in the work of Stinchcombe (1959), Presthus (1961), and Albrow (1969).

Most of these initial empirical studies were of single organizations, but studies of larger organization sets began to be commonplace by the end of the 1960s—especially with the Aston studies (e.g. Pugh *et al.* 1963, 1968, 1969). These studies argued for a contingency perspective that analyzed organizations in terms of key contextual variables such as size, ownership, technology, as well as dependence upon other organizations. They claimed to have rendered the typological method redundant and unnecessary by replacing it with a taxonomic approach that focuses more on inductively deriving categories of difference based on grounded empirical variation rather than a priori theoretical distinctions (Doty and Glick 1994). The shift towards the comparative study of organizations and the taxonomization of the effects of the various contingencies that affected organizational behavior led to a general disengagement with Weber's scholarship as organizational analysis cultivated questions and theories sprung from Weber's fertile soil but separated intellectually from his seed.

The 1970s ushered in an intensive focus on organization–environment relations that expanded the trend initiated by the Aston group (e.g. Hrebiniak1974; Ouchi and Dowling 1974; Lippitt and Mackenzie 1976). This continued through the 1980s as organizational theorists aimed to apply and test emerging perspectives such as population ecology, resource dependency, transaction cost economics, and neo-institutionalism (e.g. Leblebici and Salancik 1982; Hrebiniak and Joyce 1985; Baron and Bielby 1986; Baron, Davis-Blake, and Bielby 1986; Strang 1987). In the 1980s and 1990s, some scholars continued to engage with Weber in a more fundamental way (e.g. Ranson, Hinings, and Greenwood 1980; Clegg 1975, 1981, 1990, 1995; Langton

1984), but these efforts were marginal to the vast machine of large-scale empirical studies that had become dominant by the 1990s. The notion of bureaucracy had virtually vanished from scholarly discourse in favor of the more neutral concept of organizational structure. This was coterminous with the rise of more instrumental approaches to organizations, leading to much less attention paid to authority, power, and culture (Lounsbury and Ventresca 2003).

Among contemporary theories of organization, the neoinstitutional perspective goes furthest in bringing in the broader socio-cultural dynamics that were at the core of Weber's theorizing (see Scott 2001). However, even work in this vein cites Weber in only ceremonious ways (see Hirsch and Lounsbury 1997 and Mizruchi and Fein 1999, for elaborations of this point). To gain new inspiration for organizational theory, it is useful to revisit Weber's notion of the iron cage. In contradistinction to the more instrumental understanding of organizations promulgated by the variable-based analyses of the Aston group, Weber understood rational-legal bureaucracy as an important component of the rise of capitalism and new systems of domination and authority. Weber emphasized how traditional structures of power and domination in social life had been replaced by novel forms emanating from the emergence of bureaucracy and calculable law that supported new capitalistic forms. While there were many elements that gave rise to the new organizational form of bureaucracy, it was first and foremost a cultural process—the development of new ideas/ideologies about how to structure power and authority.

6.2.3. The Politics of Translation

Parsons was somewhat unusual in having read Weber when he did, shortly after Weber's death, for his work was not available in English. As an American visitor to Germany formally attached to the London School of Economics, Parsons visited Heidelberg and learned of Weber's reputation there. In his lifetime the national and international reception of Weber's work was muted. What distinction he enjoyed came almost exclusively from his work on the Protestant ethic (1904), which Parsons translated in 1930, and the printed versions of the lectures on *Wissenschaft als Beruf* ([1919*a*] 1948) and *Politik als Beruf* ([1919*b*] 1948). After Weber's death from influenza in 1920, his widow, Marianne Weber, extended awareness of his work through her success in bringing *Gesammelte Politische Schriften* (Weber 1921), *Gesammelte Aufsätze zur Wissenschaftslehre* (Weber 1922*a*), *Gesammelte Aufsätze zur Sozial- und Wirtschaftsgeschichte* (Weber 1924*a*), and *Gesammelte Aufsätze zur Soziologie und Sozialpolitik* (Weber 1924*b*) to fruition, but none of these succeeded in making Weber well known. Even Weber's (1922*b*) epic *Wirtschaft und Gesellschaft* was not widely distributed. As Kaesler (2004) observes, in a most instructive essay addressing the critical reception of Weber's oeuvre, less than 2,000 copies of this text were sold between its initial publication and its translation into English in 1947.

Weber was not well known outside of certain select circles of scholarship. Parsons (1937) recognized him as a founder of the theory of social action. Schutz (1967), whose work was written in the 1930s in German, and published in 1932 as *Der sinnhafte Aufbau der sozialen Welt: Eine Einleitung in die verstehenden Soziologie* but only published in English in 1967, accorded great centrality to Weber's account of social action as an appropriate point of departure for a phenomenological sociology. In Germany, Weber was perhaps better known as an economist rather than a sociologist concerned with social relations in antiquity and modernity (Swedberg 1998). He was not much read by Anglophone management theorists until after World War II, when his works were widely translated into English (Weber 1946*a*, *b*, 1947, 1949, 1954, 1962, 1965, 1970, 1974, 1976, 1978). However, in a measure of the limited distribution that still pertains, in 1981 Mohr und Siebeck (a German editorial house) announced the publication of an edition of the full work of Weber in thirty-four volumes with approximately 21,000 pages. Such data give us an idea of the still limited knowledge of Weber's work in English at the time that his ideas were being introduced into the language.

In some respects, even if modern management and organization theorists knew much about Weber, it is doubtful that they would be able to make much (out) of him. For one thing, despite being lauded in some (mistaken) quarters as a founder of value-free science, he did not represent himself as anything other than an engaged scholar. The nature of his engagements with certain scholarly and liberal imperatives that were closely related to national values were pre-eminent (see Weber's [1946*a*] two essays on 'vocation') and are barely explicable to post-war American concerns. His attitude to work as a vocation did not resonate with the values of American pragmatism, which saw work as little more than a set of efficient tasks sequentially stitched together, and, in the case of Parsons, lubricated with an ethic of self-regulation in a disinterested concern with the general interest. A calling is an altogether finer thing—it is the will to power made manifest around work as the noblest activity for a person who asserts their mastery through its passion.

For Weber, rational-legal bureaucracy was a main constituent of the new cultural system of domination, and domination was the main constituent of bureaucracy as an organization practice. Main constituent it might have been, but it was cunningly disguised, at least for the first generation of English-language readers. Max Weber's ideas received widespread reception in English, initially due to Talcott Parsons (Weber 1947). Talcott Parsons and A. M. Henderson translated Weber's sociology of domination into a sociology of authority (Weber 1947). From the point of view of the organization theory that claimed Weber as a ceremonial founder, this ensured that there were no awkward questions to be confronted about the legitimacy of organizational domination by various rationalities, such as shareholder value, executive diktat, or management fiat. All of these could be safely glossed as authority.

Parsons became the leading 'functionalist' theorist of the 1950s, whose theory stressed the importance of consensus and a central value system for social order.

Thus, not surprisingly perhaps, Weber's rugged realism, which was most evident in the centrality of *Herrschaft*, or domination, to his scheme of thought, was invariably translated as if it had the qualifier of legitimacy attached to it—thus rendering it as authority, the core notion for functionalist theory. From Parsons's point of view, rendering domination as legitimate per se makes obvious sense, due to functionalism's general concern with stability and endurance. For Parsons, the alternative to authority/domination is not power/conflict but instability/disorder. Given the politics of the Cold War, perhaps it was not seemly to suggest that dominance might be something that liberal society enjoyed when its yoke was so evident in those societies whose economies were dominated not so much by free markets but by strong states. So, from that perspective, it makes sense to gloss 'domination' as 'authority'. Parsons (1964) was then free effectively to render power, or *Macht*, in such a way that it could be analyzed without considering conflict and confrontation between forces and be seen only as a positive system property for getting things done.

Weber's conception of power was in part indebted to German philosophical and literary figures, such as Nietzsche and Goethe (Kent 1983; on the Nietzsche connections, see Fleichmann 1981; Eden 1983; Schroeder 1987; Sica 1988, and Hennis 1988; for the most obvious connection to Goethe, see the new edition of his *Elective Affinities* (2005)). Weber's concept of power, for all of its translation in terms of probability, displays echoes of Nietzsche's concept of the will to power, as a striving to grow, to become predominant, to exercise will. That Weber saw the exercise of this will as power, irrespective of the basis of its probability, is a sure sign of a Nietzschean debt. The basis of power is unimportant because the will always exists, despite however or whatever it manifests itself through. The Nietzchean homage could hardly be clearer.

Initially, through Parsons, *Macht* and *Herrschaft* entered into usage as 'power' and 'authority', respectively. Little controversy surrounds the translation of *Macht* as power (as an active verb rather than a passive noun, although, it should be noted, that 'might' is seen by some scholars as a more appropriate translation). There is considerable dissent surrounding the translation of *Herrschaft* as authority that was initiated by Parsons and Henderson in their edition of the *Theory of Social and Economic Organization* (Weber 1947), as we have seen. Most later translators do not follow Parsons's lead but instead translate *Herrschaft* typically as 'domination', depending on the context of translation. While *Herrschaft* rests on a variable probability of obedience, power or *Macht* does not necessarily do this because it might generate compliance by force. *Herrschaft* is always to some extent legitimate while this is not necessarily true of power, which might involve violence. Hence, while some instances of power may be only episodic (where violence rules), domination has some extension; it is enduring and (more) permanent. In other words, while there might be instances of an illegitimate exercise of power, domination is implicitly both enduring and has the potential to be legitimate.

Weber used the term *Herrschaft* to mean 'the probability that a command with a given specific content will be obeyed by a given group of persons' (Weber 1978: 53). Where obedience occurs, we have an example of legitimate *Herrschaft*, irrespective of the motive for the obedience—whether out of economic interest or a psychological disposition, or whatever. In the case of obedient conduct, Parsons and Henderson appropriately translate *Herrschaft* as authority because to obey is to grant legitimacy to whatever rule is being followed, irrespective of imputed motive. The concept of legitimate *Herrschaft* refers to legitimate, non-coercive rule. Thus, authority is a relationship of legitimate rule, where the meaningfulness of the social relation rests on assumptions accepted without imposition by all parties to that relationship. As Cohen, Hazelrigg, and Pope (1975*a*; 1975*b*) establish, following Gouldner's (1971) tracks, there is every need to 'de-Parsonize' Weber, despite Parsons's (1975) objections to the contrary.

6.3. Weber's Theory of Rationalities and its Relation to Domination

Herrschaft is the central Weberian category: Roth (Weber 1978: lxxxviii) notes that 'the Sociology of Domination is the core of *Economy and Society*'. Domination relies on cultural beliefs that obviate the need for the forceful imposition of power. In turn, these cultural beliefs are importantly related to rationalization processes that operate through four distinct types of rationality: formal, substantive, practical, and theoretical (see Kalberg 1980).

Formal rationality is the extent of quantitative calculation that is technically possible and applied; Weber used the technology of capital accounting in commodity-producing corporations as an illustration of the kind of knowledge and process that facilitates such rationality by enabling the calculation of profit. In contrast to formal rationality, Weber's notion of substantive rationality highlights how behavior can be shaped by ultimate values that are difficult to calculate. The tension between substantive and formal rationality is especially apparent under conditions where aspects of society that are considered sacred are profaned via commensuration (Espeland and Stevens 1998)—by equating their purported value to the price that these 'products' can fetch via commercial exchange in 'markets' (Douglas and Isherwood 1978).

Similar to formal rationality, practical rationality is also concerned with means–end considerations, but is not explicitly enabled by formalized techniques such as accounting. Akin to Bourdieu's (1977) concept of *habitus*, Weber's concept of practical rationality suggests that actors draw on a variety of shared understandings to guide everyday interactions. Where the concepts of formal, substantive, and practical rationality emphasize people's relatively unreflective use of knowledge and value orientations in choosing courses of behavior, the concept of theoretical rationality specifically emphasizes the ability of actors to reflect on their knowledge and to interpret their own and other's actions. Its clearest extensions after Weber are to be found in Schutz (1967) and in Garfinkel (1967), conceptions that, evidentially, display a clear affinity with the concepts of sensemaking (Weick 1995) or rationalization of action (Giddens 1984) where actors reflect on their own actions in order to provide a rationale for previous behaviors and build models for future courses of action.

Even though the iron cage metaphor emphasizes one dominant type of rationality—formal rationality—as having come to play an increasingly important role, Weber was careful to highlight how various kinds of rationality are important for developing a more comprehensive understanding of behavior. Although formal rationality was associated with the rational-legal system of authority (i.e. bureaucracy), traditional and charismatic administrative systems also provided cultural bases for the exercise of authority.

While rational-legal authority is rooted in the idea that laws justify normative rules and those in authority have the right to issue commands under those rules, charismatic authority rests on the heroism or exemplary character of an individual, a view of authority much admired by managerialist writers currying favor with those whom they choose to identify as exemplary CEOs. Of course, Weber himself had faith in charisma, and, as a member of the constitutional committee that founded the Weimar republic, he urged that a strong presidency be designed in order that a charismatic leader might fill the role. Weber advocated a constitution that would put supreme power in the hands of a strong individual leader who would derive his authority from the will of the people. He viewed the legislature primarily as a body to remind the great leader of his need to answer to the people, although the final shape of the Weimar Constitution emerged as a government depending more equally on the separate powers of the President and the Reichstag. Suffice to say that while Hitler may have been a charismatic leader, he was perhaps not the figure that Weber would have hoped for.

In those states that still preserve a monarchy, the basis of authority is frequently rendered as tradition. Traditional authority is supported by long-standing beliefs, customs, and traditions; for instance, while the monarchy may be the most evident example, one could also think of the persistence of traditional domination in patterns of class deference, usually seen at their strongest in rural society, or in the persistence of sexist domination on the basis of gender relations. Like any ideal types, however, it is important to emphasize that different kinds of domination depend on administrative systems and forms of rationality that are often intermingled.

Weber foresaw that ultimate values would be in inexorable decline as modernity (defined in terms of an increasing rationalization of the world through new institutions and a concomitant decline in beliefs in enchantment, magic, and fatalism) developed. In large part, this would be because the 'calculability' contained in the disciplinary rationality of modern management techniques, such as double-entry bookkeeping, would progressively replace values. As techniques increasingly achieved what previously only great value commitments could ensure, then the necessity for these values would diminish. The future would be one in which we strive to work ceaselessly in jobs and organizations that neither serve ultimate values nor adequately fill the space left by the values they purported to replace. The outcome of this process of rationalization, Weber suggests, is the production of a new type of person, the specialist or technical expert, well represented by engineers in the twentieth century (Layton 1986; Veblen 1921). Such experts master reality by means of increasingly precise and abstract concepts. Statistics, for example, began in the nineteenth century as a form of expert codified knowledge of everyday life and death, which could inform public policy (Hacking 1991). The statistician became a paradigm of the new kind of expert, dealing with everyday things but in a way that was far removed from everyday understandings.

Weber sometimes referred to the process whereby all forms of magical, mystical, traditional explanation are stripped away from the world, as disenchantment. The world stripped bare by rational analysis is always open and amenable to the calculations of technical reason under the tutelage of the expert. It holds no mystery. New disciplines colonize it and modern management and organization theory has evidently promulgated many such new disciplines. As a result, attention to power in its various forms has waned. Some theorists suggest that it has waned because of the waxing of the key term of efficiency (Greenwood and Hinings 2002).

Weber did not use the term 'efficiency', preferring instead to write about technical rationality and the formally most rational mode of political domination. Weber understood technical rationality as only one mode of rationality among a wide variety of rationalities. However, he was well aware of its central role in the rationalization of the world. Weber (1978) noted that modern management was a historical 'switching point', a moment when a new rationalized regime of work became possible. For Weber, rationalization meant the ordering of beliefs and action according to specific criteria. Weber's account of contemporary rationalization focused on the imposition of bureaucratic routines on intellectual labor (Berdayes 2002: 37). However, these forms of rationalization, which stressed the relation of means and ends, were not the only ways of being rational.

Weber also listed four forms of social action based upon the principle of rationalization. They are, first, *Zweckrationalität*, making decisions according to planned results. This is a form of decision making in which the social actor chooses both the means and ends of action. In bureaucracy, one effect of this form of rationality is to concentrate control in the hands of managerial elites and legitimate this power on the basis of procedural rules because they define the ends and police the means. Thus, as Berdayes suggests, 'even as it becomes more uniform and pervasive throughout an organization, power is depersonalized, so much so that managerial personnel themselves become subject to impersonal bureaucratic control' (2002: 38).

Second, there is *Wertrationalität*, where one makes decisions according to an absolute value or belief, such as a religious or other ideological commitment, where there is a 'self conscious formulation of the ultimate values governing the actor and the consistently planned orientation of its detailed course to these values' (Weber 1978: 21). In this form of decision making, the actor chooses only the means of his actions because the ends are predestined. Now, it might seem, at first glance, that from the perspective of *Zweckrationalität* action, value rationality will always appear irrational, if only because *Wertrationalität* always orients action to a chosen value or end. However, for one whose sense of calling in their belief in *Zweckrationalität* is unassailable, the inimicality disappears.

Means–ends calculation as a form of life can become an ultimate value; think, for instance, of the reliance of business on sophisticated legal advice concerning the probabilities of adverse action being contingent on a chosen course of action. A faith in the reasoning that creates such probabilistic advice represents an ultimate value. It would be faith in an ultimate value of formal rationality, the pursuit of the most efficient and technically correct, calculable, impersonal, and substantively indifferent choice of means guiding any social action. Weber seems to come close to this with his idea that formal rationality was, in his time, increasingly becoming characterized by abstraction, impersonality, and quantification, to the extent of seeking to quantify even that which seems, essentially, unquantifiable (Gronow 1988).

Third, there is *emotive rationality*, where decisions are made in terms of specific emotional states of the action, which is usually interpreted in terms of affectual action. Finally, there is *traditional rationality*, when people make decisions according to an orientation to a specific tradition; producing traditional action. It is evident that these are idealized modes of rationality that are premised on what is actually empirically possible; analytically it would be wholly inept to privilege one or other of these as in some sense 'more rational' than the others. What is constituted as being rational is a result of the actions of actors embedded in their own constitutions of rationality.

The forms of rational behavior most common to modernity are *Zweckrationalität* and *Wertrationalität*. Weber claimed that industrial civilization is characterized by the rational search by some people for the optimum means to a given end, where that search is shaped by rules, regulations, and larger social structures (Ritzer 1993).

6.3.1. Rationality and Forms of Domination

The institutionalization of formal rationality depends on a will to power becoming material. In organizations this is the structure of dominancy, an order 'regarded by the actor as in some way obligatory or exemplary' governing the organization (Weber 1978: 31). In a later parlance, the structure of dominancy might be thought of as an obligatory passage point (Clegg 1989), something that is decisive in framing how a phenomenon unfolds.

> Without exception every sphere of social action is profoundly influenced by structures of dominancy. In a great number of cases the emergence of a rational association from amorphous social action has been due to domination and the way in which it has been exercised. Even where this is not the case, the structure of dominancy and its unfolding is decisive in determining the form of social action and its orientation towards a 'goal'. Indeed, domination has played the decisive role in the economically most important social structures of the past and present. Viz, the manor on the one hand, and the large scale capitalistic enterprise on the other. (Weber 1978: 941)

The formal structures of dominancy will be experienced as differing substantive types of rule, within which it is probable that there will be willing obedience. Any bureaucracy is an example of a structure of dominancy, although they might vary in their substantive particulars; should it be the case that values infuse its members, binding them with commitments to its rule, then the structure of dominancy may be transformed into a structure of authority, perhaps where the rule is infused with an ultimate value such as the hierarchy of the Roman Catholic Church or is taken for granted and accepted as a legally rational basis for constraining action, as in most commercial and business bureaucracies.

In modern organizations, Weber argues, formal rationality would be best institutionalized, and domination most complete, when rationality is accepted as legitimate in its own terms. Such a state of affairs would be what Weber defined as 'authority'. Thus, authority is legitimated domination. They are not qualitatively different from each other. The differences between them are ones of degree, not of kind. In this regard, power and authority are opposed to violence as a cultural mode of dominance and are themselves specific forms of dominance. For Weber, social relations of power often involve coercion when dominance is not legitimated and social action that seeks to intervene in social relations is enacted, whether proactively, or reactively, as resistance. To speak of authority, however, presumes that legitimacy is present.

In history, domination rarely is as one-dimensional as the Weberian ideal type deliberately represents it in order to provide an accentuated and heightened model of a real phenomenon in order to aid its recognition and analysis in empirical cases. For example, as Bendix (1977) notes, following Weber (1954), fully consistent charismatic leadership is inimical to both rules and tradition but disciples who wish not to see their discipleship lose meaning seek to routinize charisma, usually through either instilling a system of lineage based on sanguinity or rule by rules. The charisma is reconstituted on another basis of rule.

Somewhat confusingly, although Weber defines four types of rationality, he only defines three types of domination, and it is not entirely clear what the relation is between them. It is evident that *Zweckrationalität* corresponds pretty closely to rational-legal domination, and that traditional rationality, as elaborated, corresponds to traditional domination, while his third type, charismatic domination, where obedience is given because of a belief in the extraordinary grace and powers of the person deferred to, which, as we have seen above, also seems close to the type of emotive rationality. The absence of a specific category for *Wertrationalität* might suggest that as a category, it is almost indivisible from the others. For instance, one could make decisions according to an absolute value or belief, such as a religious or other ideological commitment that is traditional, or they could be based on a belief that the absolute value is manifest in a particular charismatic individual or, as Adler (2001) argues, that he saw it as infeasible for anything beyond small-scale collectivities. Or, it might suggest that Weber thought that value-based authority would not be of significance in the modern world. Like all sociologists of his time, he underestimated nationalism and religious fundamentalism, which are paradigmatic instances of this type of authority (see Haugaard 2002). More recently sociologists such as Waters (1989, 1993) and Satow (1975) would nominate professions as candidates for this missing category—although there may be an element of idealization of what it is that professions actually do in this categorization.

From the perspective of a strict *Zweckrationalität*, where values have been effectively held at bay, value-rational action will always appear irrational, since *Wertrationalität* orients action to a chosen value or end, without regard for consequences. However, there is another possibility related to the missing value-based rationality; one could imagine the categories of *Wertrationalität* and *Zweckrationalität* becoming so fused and intertwined, in a situation where rational-legal authority is so institutionalized, that obedience to it becomes an absolute commitment, or as Weber (1947) termed it, a 'vocation'. On such occasions, as Weber stated, 'The fate of an epoch which has eaten of the tree of knowledge is that it must know that we cannot learn the meaning of the world from the results of its analysis, be it ever so perfect; it must rather be in a position to create this meaning itself' (1949: 57). Where *Wertrationalität*-produced meaning surrounds, embeds, and saturates the meaning of organization and its work as a call to duty, an obligation to some sense of a greater purpose than just doing the work itself, then this will surely be the case. Value-rational action, or *Wertrationalität*, is the 'self-conscious formulation of the ultimate values governing the actor and the consistently planned orientation of its detailed course to these values'.

Although Weber is commonly construed as a theorist of authority, in terms of the three types of *Herrschaft* that Weber refers to, they are, in fact, types of domination. Authority is a social relation that stands at the outer limits of a more probable range of social relations of domination. These relations constitute the normalcy of organization—where there is a probability of resistance—which only shades into authority when, for reasons of tradition, charisma, *Zweckrationalität*, or *Wertrationalität*, the subject owes an allegiance that enables them to legitimate their subjection to an external source of domination. It should be evident that authority derives its legitimacy from the ruled not those ruling. Hence, organizational politics, premised on the necessity of acts of power by putative authorities to counter resistance to their imposition of their will, is something to be expected as normal. It will usually be the case that, despite charisma, tradition, discipline, or vocation, situations ensue where there is resistance by some to the will of some other (e.g. Fleming and Spicer 2007; Marquis and Lounsbury 2007).

6.4. Recapitulating the Themes

According to Weber, the modern world increasingly narrows the range of means and ends that an individual can choose from—especially with regard to organization and the proliferation of bureaucracy. In modernity, institutions rationalize and organize affairs, cutting down on individual choices, replacing them with standardized procedures and rules. Rational calculation becomes a monstrous discipline. Everything and everyone seemingly had to be put through a calculus, irrespective of other values or pleasures. It was a necessary and unavoidable feature of organizing in the modern world.

Weber greatly admired the achievements of bureaucracy, as he saw them. In many respects, these achievements were quite limited. Early twentieth-century bureaucracy (that specifically modern form of organization that Weber saw) never achieved its full realization. We are confronting at the beginning of the twenty-first century its full realization in what has been named paradoxically 'post-bureaucracy', a more flexible and subtle form of organization that embodies bureaucracy in technological devices such as computers, cell phones, PDAs, etc. (see Block 1990). In other words, Weber saw an initial version of bureaucracy but not its full realization in modernity as the expression of the iron cage made social and technological (see Barker 1993 and Sewell 1998, respectively).

Weber was pessimistic about the long-term impact of bureaucracy. On the one hand, bureaucracies would free people from arbitrary rule by powerful patrimonial leaders, those who personally owned the instruments and offices of rule. They would do this because they were based on rational legality as the rule of law contained in the files that defined practice in the bureau. On the other hand, they would create an 'iron cage of bondage'. The frame was fashioned from the 'care for external goods' (Weber 1976: 181), by which Weber meant if these goods were to come into one's grasp in a market economy, then one could gain them only by mortgaging one's life to a career in a hierarchy of offices that interlocked and intermeshed, through whose intricacies one might seek to move, with the best hope for one's future being that one would shift from being a small cog in the machine to one that was slightly bigger, in a slow but steady progression.

The iron cage would be fabricated increasingly from the materialization of abstract nouns such as calculability, predictability, and control, to which one must bend one's will. For Weber, economically oriented social action based on the best technically possible practice of quantitative calculation or accounting would be the most formally rational display of the form of rationality. By contrast, any form of substantive rationality must denote concepts of goal-oriented action that are infused with contextually specific values. Where an individual has so internalized commitment to a rational institution, such as the Civil Service, or Science, or Academia, that the commitment shapes their dispositions in such a way that little or no resistance to formal rationality occurs, this represents obedience to an institutionalized will to power. Organizational power, at its most powerful, forms relations that institute themselves in the psyche of the individual. Increasing self-discipline, meshing with intensified bureaucratization, rationalization, and individualization, marked modernity in the social world. External constraint (sovereign power, traditional power) increasingly is replaced by internalization of constraint (disciplinary power, rational domination), assisted by new cultural logics, disciplinary technologies and means.

6.5. Discussion: Sintering the Discipline of Organization

Organization theory has effectively neutered the breadth of Weber's concerns. The main constituents of Weber's thought have been watered down. That this is the case also applies even to those strong accounts of organizations that have emerged with contemporary scholars such as DiMaggio and Powell (1983), who pay homage to the main constituent, *Herrschaft*, weakly refracted through the notion of an institutional constraint. The concerns that have been grafted on to the Weberian corpus have grown such that the core concern with domination has been lost almost completely. Parsons's translation strategy was clearly a key switching device; the rise of institutional theory has merely muddied the waters further. What has been lost is the essential core of organization as a theater of power, an arena of domination, and a place of contested rationalities. In its place we have gained a weak institutional theory, barely able to address the central themes pioneered by its ostensible fountainhead.

However, there is hope that some contemporary developments may help redirect some aspects of organizational theory towards some of Weber's core concerns, reconnecting with earlier scholarship such as Gouldner (1954), Perrow (1986), and Mouzelis (1967). Several directions recommend themselves. First, there is the fusion of Weber's classical concerns with domination and more contemporary scholarship that we find in the work of Clegg, Courpasson, and Phillips (2006), Courpasson (2005), and Gordon (2007). In these works we find a reconnection with Weber as both a political and a cultural theorist and a rethinking of organizations as essentially political and discursive formations in flux. Second, within institutional theory, there have been a variety of calls to reintroduce agency, politics, and contestation (e.g. DiMaggio 1988; Greenwood and Hinings 1996; Hirsch and Lounsbury 1997). In an effort to respond to these concerns, some scholars have begun to integrate social movements theory into institutional analysis; this has led to a broadening of existing imageries of institutional processes and actors to include contestation, collective action, framing and self-conscious mobilization around alternatives to conceptual repertoires of legitimation, diffusion, isomorphism, and self-reproducing systems of taken-for-granted practices as central institutional mechanisms (Davis *et al.* 2005; Schneiberg and Lounsbury, forthcoming). Institutional environments emerge as more fragmented and contested (Schneiberg 2007; Schneiberg and Soule 2005), influenced by multiple, competing logics (Friedland and Alford 1991) or competing modes of rationality, as Clegg (1975) defined them (see also Thornton 2004 for a discussion of institutional logics). Fiss and Zajac (2004) examine how different orientations towards corporate governance—corporatist and shareholder value—have led to dramatic shifts in the practices of German corporations towards Western-style governance but variation in the extent to which the shareholder-value approach is implemented: dominant institutional values—as competing modes of rationality—are variably distributed empirically (see also Lounsbury 2007).

A focus on multiple logics and practices linked to spatial and temporal flows can also open up new kinds of research that reunites the contemporary emphasis on organizational environments with older research emphases on intraorganizational dynamics, bringing together early Weberian traditions focused on the workings of bureaucracy with broader cultural sources of influence on organizational decision making. While institutional analysts have stressed the role of broader cognitive, normative, and regulative beliefs that make practices understandable and appropriate (see Suchman 1995), intraorganizational researchers have drawn on social psychological approaches to emphasize how legitimacy enables authority to be maintained and reinforced within organizational settings (Johnson, Dowd, and Ridgeway 2006). Little effort has been made to bridge the study of legitimacy within organizational settings with broader environmental dynamics (Greenwood and Hinings 1996). Lounsbury's (2001) study of the spread of recycling programs shows how the legitimacy of substantively meaningful college and university recycling programs was dependent upon intraorganizational student social movements that translated growing cultural pressures to be ecologically sensitive into pragmatic organizational responses. Such work can be usefully expanded by engaging more deeply with older concerns regarding struggles over authority and the intraorganizational dynamics of various occupational and professional groups (e.g. Abbott 1988; Barley 1986).

Weber, in his prescience, provided such an opening for us with his conclusion—over a hundred years old—to *The Protestant Ethic and the Spirit of Capitalism*, when he speaks of the working out of the dominant rationality of capitalism until the last ton of fossil fuel is exhausted. Contemporary issues of sustainability and global warming open up a crucial gap that Weber was at least aware of and this gap provides a key opening for those interested in revisiting Weber and developing more comprehensive approaches to organizational life that take multiple forms of power, domination, conflict, and rationality seriously. By moving in such directions, organizations are seen less as constraining iron cages and more as potential sites of conflict, as porous media interpenetrated by other organizations and actors, lubricated by politics. One writer who indicates another direction by which politics might flow is Castells in his work on *The Network Society*. He pays direct homage to Weber in *The Rise of the Network Society* (2000) and is clearly working with similar methods and ambitions. Another space exists in the role of cities. A large portion of *Economy and Society* is devoted to the study of cities, and the idea that they harbor 'non-legitimate domination'. Cities, as socio-economic sites of contest and jostling forms of domination, may be an important area for Weberian-infused organization studies.

Finally, there are linkages that remain to be developed between Foucault and Weber (Clegg 1995). Foucault, as the pre-eminent Nietzschean-influenced scholar of the late twentieth century has some evident points of connection with Weber as a Nietzschean-influenced scholar of the early twentieth century, even though these connections were not explored in Foucault's work (Clegg 1995). How might we use Foucault and link him to Weber? We shall suggest some applications developed from human geography, namely, the idea of life-paths as developed by Hannah (1997) from the work of Hägerstrand (1970) to show how Foucauldian ideas might operate outside the confines of institutions, and in more open organizations. The life-path is a way of representing and understanding how people ordinarily move through time and space (a method that has been elaborated by Pred (1977), but which we need only address in its fundamentals in this context).

Some life-paths are almost entirely confined and visible, such as the prisoner in a high-security jail with closed-circuit TV surveillance of the cell, for instance. Such a person may move only through a very limited and very visible set of spaces, from cell to dining hall to exercise yard and back. Most life-paths are not like this but have many moments of invisibility and a lack of confinement, as we move and mingle with others from one arena of action to another. We may be confined (in the classroom, the office, the factory floor) for intervals in these trajectories, and we may be more or less visible during some of them, but in other areas (at home, in the cinema, on the subway) we are largely invisible as a specific object of any surveillance or inspectorial gaze, even though, in a generalized sense we may be captured in the lens of multiple electronic panopticons, albeit that they are not explicitly focused on us as individuals, as would be the case in a prison. The electronic eyes are both more numerous and aimed at much more generalized bodies, and we are aware of their existence in creating a normative environment, but it becomes a matter of choice as to whether we choose them to target us specifically. Our deviance defines their acuity. In total institutions their acuity defines our deviance. The everyday life that is confined differs dramatically from that which can, apparently, wander free. The extent of wandering free, however, is often more of an illusion than a reality.

Nonetheless, no one is entirely free to be whomsoever he or she chooses to be—from the discourses of choice available—because we do share some features with the confined. We are not fixed permanently by confinement in space, but we are often confined at prescribed times of the day and subject to more or less systematic surveillance either in real time (CCTV, computer monitoring, key pad entry and exit, etc.) or in audit time, retrospectively (tax returns, standards, legal notices, etc.). Moreover, we are confined through the many data traces we leave in the world, including our permanent address, tax file number, passport, driving license, credit cards, bank accounts, etc. These devices, which Rose (1999) and Power (1997) argue are the modern liberal technologies of regulation, make us partially visible, not always in real-time but sufficiently so that our life-paths, or critical incidents in them, can be made accountable. Not only that, but we are aware, constantly, of the threat of observation by the authorities—the tax audit, the speed trap, and so on—as well as being found out for not passing adequately as a member of those communities of practice in which we claim membership (see Garfinkel's (1967) discussion of Agnes's strategies for passing as a female).

As Hannah (1997: 352) says, 'despite only imperfect success', there are authorities to whose power we are, in principle, held accountable. They govern our idea of ourselves as people who take risks with speed limits or who always observe the letter of the law; we are likely to park where and when we should not or only where and when we should, and so on. 'For the average "free" citizen the life-path of information traces is full of gaps, but retains its unity through the matchability of names, permanent addresses, social security numbers, etc.' (Hannah 1997: 352). Moreover, there are those internal governors of the soul, shaping the sense of self that we seek others to have of our self through the presentations that we make of it (Goffman 1956), just as much as Protestantism was for Weber's analysis. The responsibility for the judgments we make lies entirely with us; as Foucault put it in his later work, we have 'a care for the self' (Foucault 1988)—we are responsible subjects—but we are responsible not only to our sense of our self but also to governmental norms that will have variable salience for us, depending not only on who we think we are but also where and when we think we are. To be able to conduct one's self implies some degree of consciousness and reflexive capacity.

We face a variety of normalizing, imperfectly coordinated, partial regimens of authority and power of sanction. These will be vertically and horizontally fragmented organizationally. Vertical fragmentation means that the three moments of normalization (receipt of information traces, judgment, and enforcement of normality) may all take place in uncoordinated and distinct arenas with only imperfect communication between them. Horizontal fragmentation occurs when the individual leaves traces across different organizational arenas, in which these organizations, for reasons of law, technology, or ignorance are unable to exchange and match information regarding different activities. Omniscience recedes dramatically in possibility as the walls of the total institutions are breached and the citizen moves in everyday life; nonetheless, some citizens have greater freedom of unsupervised movement than others, in various organizational arenas, and are subject to more or less coordinated authorities. Additionally, we 'have some leeway to protest, appeal, and complain about the exercise of normalizing authority. We may demand a certain degree of balance between our visibility and that of the vigilant authorities' (Hannah 1997: 353). Of course, crises such as 9/11 may lead the authorities to step-up their attempts at coordination and we may become less inscrutable in more places in consequence.

A life-path is a metaphor. It suggests a journey. Now, that journey may be temporally extended or restricted, such that we might consider a path through a day at work, a week at work, or months at work. For many people it would hardly matter; their discretion is so limited that repetition of the same routines is the order of the day; think of one of those jobs designed by F. W. Taylor. For others, however, there may be little repetition of routines even though the life-path remains tightly constrained physically.

Clearly the life-path is insufficient in itself as a mapping device because, while life-paths through organizations may be represented and analyzed, they also require the addition of Elliot Jacques's (1964) ideas on the time-span of discretion. The difference in span and duration of the time-span of discretion denotes differential responsibilities; the life-paths show the limits to those freedoms enjoyed organizationally. Indeed, as Ibarra(2001: 361) shows, for academics especially, these limits are particularly evident in terms of the CV, and periodic reports on performativity (how many papers published in which journals?) make the university a particularly clear case of the state steering a neo-liberal course from a distance. Although academic work is often creative, always producing new results, we are also prisoners of our own careers, institutions, routines, schedules, etc. We are inscribed as academics, as 'subjects' of the structures that modulate our careers and trajectories. If we want to be successful, we need to represent properly our role as researchers and scholars, appropriately interpreting and following the rules to win a privileged position. In this sense we are, as routinized workers, prisoners of our own existence, always institutionally modulated. And, in the end, maybe we are happy and content with our own conditions of life, like a contented cow chewing on its cud as it surveys the rich pastures around it, ripe for grazing and fresh for milking.

We can compare the life-paths of individuals through organizations. We can analyze the visibility and accountability of organization members in terms of different regimens of authority, as well as in terms of the different members' time-span of discretion (Jacques 1964). As a general rule, we may hypothesize that the greater the individual members' time-span of discretion:

- the less the surveillance of their organizational life-path,
- the less that the subjects correspond to the 'usual suspects' thrown up by bio-power analysis, and
- the less subject they will be to disciplinary power.

Organizationally, the majority of those who are outside total institutions live under the conditions of an imperfect panopticism and regimes of governmentality that are never perfectly socialized; deviance is always possible and is likely to occur from time to time. Of course, deviance is hardly a governmental surprise. Specific segments of the population can be targeted for renewed governmental focus through the mechanism of bio-power, as the authorities learn to anticipate their deviance statistically on a probabilistic basis. One can predict accurately on past probabilities that drivers under 25 years of age are more prone to break the speed limits and be involved in accidents or that supporters of a particular football team are more likely to be 'soccer hooligans' than those who support some other teams.

Through using life-path analysis in conjunction with an account of the responsibilities of members' time-spans of discretion, we can make comparisons between the power relations to which different categories of organizational members are subject. While power is exercised in specific episodes (for instance, of domination, authority, seduction, coercion, and manipulation), it has some presence as a capacity that retains potential effectiveness even when it is not being used; something which life-path analysis can illuminate. Organizations, we may say, are theaters for the constitution of power and all its attendant dramas, as so many life-paths traverse them.

To say that power is constitutive does not mean that it should be seen as constitutive of nearly anything and everything, as being ubiquitous. Power can be woven through different media, through domination, authority, seduction, manipulation, and coercion, for instance. Moreover, rather like the character from the evocative song of ceaseless travel that Dylan (1974) conjured, the effects of power are always 'tangled' up in the rhythms and routines of everyday life. And everyday life is always lived in specific places. Drawing on Dylan (1974) one thinks of the East Coast, out West, New Orleans, outside of Delacroix, a topless place, or Montague Street, part of a topological landscape through which we move here-and-now, there-and-then, in the present, the recollected and imagined pasts as well as those futures we aspire to. And as we move we seek to conjure up the powers we wish to exercise and vanish those we wish to avoid, seeking to stabilize interaction rituals associated with specific places; these can place people in terms of markers of their identity, they can be displaced, they can be contained in specific places or may spill over into other places, be recognized, mocked, disdained, subverted, or copied. In short, we seek to stabilize our causal powers; the fact that others will also be doing this, and doing so on life-paths and projects opposed to those we pursue is a sufficient reason to always keep a certain indeterminacy, a certain contingency, even randomness, in play. Hence the possibilities of transformation can never be eliminated because of all the intentional agents who intermingle, act at a distance, and often produce only unintended effects, as well as those non-intentional agents, such as viruses, natural disasters, and technologies that lay waste to life-paths and projects (Clegg 1989: ch. 9).

Something strange happened to Weber as he was transported and translated from old Europe to the New World—he was sucked into an organization theory that sank issues of power and domination as metaphorically as the Bermuda Triangle sank ships.[1] It is long past time to drag him out of the depths to which he has been sunk. The persistence of the cosmopolitan in a globalized world, the resilience of regions and the creative space of cities, as well as the work of cultural geographers on life-paths, offer fruitful possibilities for re-engaging with Weberian themes. Organization theory has nothing to lose but a discredited rendering of an old but by no means exhausted canon. Organization theory can reclaim Weber as a scholar of domination for a discourse whose translations of Weber—in every sense of this word—are more useful and usable.[2] Given the present-day state of the dead zone to which his work has been consigned, whether by functionalist or institutional theory—between which, in fact, much of the time there barely seems a discernible difference—the time is more than ripe.

References

Abbott, A. (1988). *The System of Professions*. Chicago: University of Chicago Press.

Adler, P. (2001). 'Market, Hierarchy, and Trust: The Knowledge Economy and the Future of Capitalism'. *Organization Science*, 12: 214–34.

—— and Borys, B. (1996). 'Two Types of Bureaucracy: Enabling and Coercive'. *Administrative Science Quarterly*, 41/1: 61–89.

1 Thanks to Ad van Iterson for the metaphor of the Bermuda Triangle.

2 We have in mind the sociology of translation: see Callon's (1986) classic article.

Albrow, M. (1969). *Bureaucracy.* London: Pall Mall Press.
Barker, J. R. (1993). 'Tightening the Iron Cage: Concertive Control in Self-Managing Teams'. *Administrative Science Quarterly*, 38: 408–37.
Barley, S. R. (1986). 'Technology as an Occasion for Structuring: Evidence from Observations of CT Scanners and the Social Order of Radiology Departments'. *Administrative Science Quarterly*, 31: 78–108.
Baron, J. N., and Bielby, W. T. (1986). 'The Proliferation of Job Titles in Organizations'. *Administrative Science Quarterly*, 31: 561–86.
—— Davis-Blake, A., and Bielby, W. T. (1986). 'The Structure of Opportunity: How Promotion Ladders Vary within and among Organizations'. *Administrative Science Quarterly*, 31/2: 248–73.
Bauman, Z. (2000). *Liquid Modernity.* Oxford: Polity.
Bendix, R. (1977). *Max Weber: An Intellectual Portrait.* Berkeley: University of California Press.
Berdayes, V. (2002). 'Traditional Management Theory as Panoptic Discourse: Language and the Constitution of Somatic Flows'. *Culture and Organization*, 8/1: 35–49.
Blau, P. (1955). *The Dynamics of Bureaucracy.* Chicago: University of Chicago Press.
Block, F. (1990). *Postindustrial Possibilities: A Critique of Economic Discourse.* Berkeley: University of California Press.
Bourdieu, P. (1977). *Outline of a Theory of Practice.* Cambridge: Cambridge University Press.
Callon, M. (1986). 'Some Elements of a Sociology of Translation: Domestication of the Scallops and the Fishermen of St Brieuc Bay', in J. Law (ed.), *Power, Action and Belief.* London: Routledge.
Castells, M. (2000). *The Information Age: Economy, Society, and Culture*, Vol. I., *The Rise of Network Society* (1996 revised edition). London: Blackwell.
Clegg, S. R. (1975). *Power, Rule and Domination: A Critical and Empirical Understanding of Power in Sociological Theory and Organizational Life.* London: Routledge.
—— (1981). 'Organization and Control'. *Administrative Science Quarterly*, 26/4: 545–62.
—— (1989). *Frameworks of Power.* London: Sage.
—— (1990). *Modern Organizations: Organization Studies in the Postmodern World.* London: Sage.
—— (1995). 'Weber and Foucault: Social Theory for the Study of Organizations'. *Organization*, 1/1: 149–78.
—— Courpasson, D., and Phillips, N. (2006). *Power and Organizations.* Thousand Oaks, Calif.: Sage.
Cohen, J., Hazelrigg, L., and Pope, W. (1975*a*). 'De-Parsonizing Weber: A Critique of Parsons' Interpretation of Weber's Sociology'. *American Sociological Review*, 40/S: 229–41.
—— —— —— (1975*b*). 'Reply to Parsons'. *American Sociological Review*, 40/S: 670–4.
Courpasson, D. (2005). *Soft Constraint: Liberal Organizations and Domination.* Copenhagen: Copenhagen Business Press/Liber.
Davis, J., McAdam, D., Scott, W. R., and Zald, M. (eds.) (2005). *Social Movements and Organization Theory.* Oxford: Oxford University Press.
Derlien, H. U. (1999). 'On the Selective Interpretation of Max Weber's Concept of Bureaucracy in Organization Theory and Administrative Science', in P. Ahonen and K. Palonen (eds.), *Dis-Embalming Max Weber.* Jyväskylä, Finland: SoPhi.

DiMaggio, P. J. (1988). 'Interest and Agency in Institutional Theory', in L. Zucker (ed.), *Institutional Patterns and Organizations*. Cambridge, Mass.: Ballinger.

—— and Powell, W. W. (1983). 'The Iron Cage Revisited: Institutional Isomorphism and Collective Rationality in Organizational Fields'. *American Sociological Review*, 48: 147–60.

Doty, D. H., and Glick, W. H. (1994). 'Typologies as a Unique Form of Theory Building: Toward Improved Understanding and Modeling'. *Academy of Management Review*, 19: 230–51.

Douglas, M., and Isherwood, B. (1978). *The World of Goods: Towards an Anthropology of Consumption*. London: Penguin Books.

Dylan, B. (1974). 'Tangled up in Blue', from the CBS album *Blood on the Tracks*. New York: Ram's Hom Music.

Eden, R. (1983). *Political Leadership and Nihilism: A Study of Weber and Nietzsche*. Tampa: University of South Florida Press.

Espeland, W. N., and Stevens, M. L. (1998). 'Commensuration as a Social Process'. *Annual Review of Sociology*, 24: 313–43.

Etzioni, A. (1959). 'Authority Structure and Organizational Effectiveness'. *Administrative Science Quarterly*, 4/1: 43–67.

Fiss, P. C., and Zajac, E. J. (2004). 'The Diffusion of Ideas over Contested Terrain: The (non)Adoption of a Shareholder Value Orientation among German Firms'. *Administrative Science Quarterly*, 49: 501–34.

Fleichmann, E. (1981). 'Max Weber, die Juden und das Ressentiment', in W. Schluchter, *Max Webers studie über das antike Judentum*. Frankfurt am Main: Suhrkamp.

Fleming, P., and Spicer, A. (2007). *Contesting the Corporation: Struggle, Power and Resistance in Organizations*. Cambridge: Cambridge University Press.

Foucault, M. (1988). 'The Care of the Self as a Practice of Freedom', in J. Berbauer and D. Rasmussen (eds.), *The Final Foucault*. Cambridge, Mass.: MIT Press.

Friedland, R., and Alford, R. R. (1991). 'Bringing Society Back in: Symbols, Practices, and Institutional Contradictions', in W. W. Powell and P. J. DiMaggio (eds.), *The New Institutionalism in Organizational Analysis*. Chicago: University of Chicago Press.

Garfinkel, H. (1967). *Studies in Ethnomethodology*. Englewood Cliffs, NJ: Prentice-Hall.

Giddens, A. (1984). *The Constitution of Society*. Cambridge: Polity.

Goethe, J. W. von (2005). *Elective Affinities* (trans. J. Hollingdale). Harmondsworth: Penguin.

Goffman, E. (1956). *The Presentation of Self in Everyday Life*. Harmondsworth: Penguin.

Gordon, R. (2007). *Power, Knowledge and Domination*. Oslo/Copenhagen: Liber/CBS Press.

Gouldner, A. (1954). *Patterns of Industrial Bureaucracy*. New York: Free Press.

—— (1971). *The Coming Crisis of Western Sociology*. London: Heinemann.

Greenwood, R., and Hinings, C. R. (1996). 'Understanding Radical Organizational Change: Bringing Together the Old and the New Institutionalism'. *Academy of Management Review*, 21: 1022–54.

—— —— (2002). 'Disconnects and Consequences in Organization Theory'. *Administrative Science Quarterly*, 47: 411–21.

Gronow, J. (1988) 'The Element of Irrationality: Max Weber's Diagnosis of Modern Culture'. *Acta Sociologica*, 31: 327–9.

HACKING, I. (1991). 'How Should We Do the History of Statistics?' in G. Burchell, C. Gordon, and P. Miller (eds.), *The Foucault Effect: Studies in Governmentality*. London: University of Chicago Press.

HAGE, J. (1965). 'An Axiomatic Theory of Organizations'. *Administrative Science Quarterly*, 10/3: 289–320.

HÄGERSTRAND, T. (1970). 'What about People in Regional Science?' *Regional Science Association Papers*, 24: 7–21.

HANNAH, M. (1997). 'Imperfect Panopticism: Envisioning the Construction of Perfect Lives', in G. Benko and U. Stohmayer (eds.), *Space and Social Theory: Interpreting Modernity and Postmodernity*. Oxford: Blackwell.

HAUGAARD, M. (2002). 'Nationalism and Modernity', in S. Maleševi and M. Haugaard (eds.), *Making Sense of Collectivity: Ethnicity, Nationalism and Globalism*. London: Pluto.

HEGEL, G. W. F. (1998). 'Philosophy of History' and 'History of Philosophy', in S. Houlgate (ed.), *The Hegel Reader*. Oxford: Blackwell.

HENNIS, W. (1988). 'The Traces of Nietzsche in the Work of Max Weber' (trans. K. Tribe), in *Max Weber: Essays in Reconstruction*. London: Allen & Unwin.

HIRSCH, P. M., and LOUNSBURY, M. (1997). 'Ending the Family Quarrel: Towards a Reconciliation of "Old" and "New" Institutionalism'. *American Behavioral Scientist*, 40: 406–18.

HREBINIAK, L. G. (1974). 'Job Technology, Supervision, and Work-Group Structure'. *Administrative Science Quarterly*, 19/3: 395–410.

HREBINIAK, L. G., and JOYCE., W. F. (1985). 'Organizational Adaptation: Strategic Choice and Environmental Determinism'. *Administrative Science Quarterly*, 30/3: 336–49.

IBARRA-COLADO, E. (2001). 'Considering "New Formulas" for a "Renewed University": The Mexican Experience'. *Organization*, 8/2: 203–17.

JACQUES, E. (1964). *Time-Span Handbook: The Use of Time-Span of Discretion to Measure the Level of Work in Employment Roles and to Arrange an Equitable Payment Structure*. London: Heinemann.

JANOWITZ, M., and DELANY, W. (1956). 'The Bureaucrat and the Public: A Study of Informational Perspectives'. *Administrative Science Quarterly*, 2/2: 141–62.

JOHNSON, C., DOWD, T. J., and RIDGEWAY, C. L. (2006). 'Legitimacy as a Social Process'. *Annual Review of Sociology*, 32: 53–78.

KAESLER, D. (2004). 'From Academic Outsider to Sociological Mastermind: The Fashioning of the Sociological "Classic" Max Weber'. *Bangladesh e-Journal of Sociology*, 1/January: 4–13.

KALBERG, S. (1980). 'Max Weber's Types of Rationality: Cornerstones for the Analysis of Rationalization Processes in History'. *American Journal of Sociology*, 85: 1145–79.

KENT, S. A. (1983). 'Weber, Goethe, and the Nietzschean Allusion: Capturing the Source of the "Iron Cage" Metaphor'. *Sociological Analysis*, 44: 297–320.

LAKOFF, G., and JOHNSON, M. (1999). *Philosophy in the Flesh: The Embodied Mind and its Challenge in Western Thought*. New York: Basic.

LANGTON, J. (1984). 'The Ecological Theory of Bureaucracy: The Case of Josiah Wedgwood and the British Pottery Industry'. *Administrative Science Quarterly*, 29/3: 330–54.

LAYTON, E. T. (1986). *The Revolt of the Engineers: Social Responsibility and the American Engineering Profession*. 2nd edn. Baltimore: Johns Hopkins University Press.

LEBLEBICI, H., and SALANCIK, G. (1982). 'Stability in Interorganizational Exchange: Rulemaking Processes of the Chicago Board of Trade'. *Administrative Science Quarterly*, 27/2: 227–42.

Lippitt, M., and Mackenzie, K. (1976). 'Authority-Task Problems'. *Administrative Science Quarterly*, 21/4: 643–60.

Lipset, S. M., Trow, M. A., and Coleman, J. S. (1956). *Union Democracy: The Internal Politics of the International Typographical Union*. Glencoe, Ill.: Free Press.

Lounsbury, M. (2001). 'Institutional Sources of Practice Variation: Staffing College and University Recycling Programs'. *Administrative Science Quarterly*, 46/1: 29–58.

—— (2007). 'A Tale of Two Cities: Competing Logics and Practice Variation in the Professionalizing of Mutual Funds'. *Academy of Management Journal*, 50: 289–307.

—— and Carberry, E. (2005). 'From King to Court Jester? Weber's Fall from Grace in Organizational Theory'. *Organization Studies*, 26: 501–25.

—— and Ventresca, M. (2003). 'The New Structuralism in Organizational Theory'. *Organization*, 10: 457–80.

—— —— and Hirsch, P. (2003). 'Social Movements, Field Frames and Industry Emergence: A Cultural-Political Perspective of U.S. Recycling'. *Socio-Economic Review*, 1/1: 71–104.

Marquis, C., and Lounsbury, M. (2007). 'Vive la Résistance: Competing Logics in the Consolidation of Community Banking'. *Academy of Management Journal*, 50: 799–820.

Martindale, D. (1960). *The Nature and Types of Sociological Theory*. London: Routledge & Kegan Paul.

Merton, R. K. (1952). *Reader in Bureaucracy*. New York: Free Press.

Mizruchi, M., and Fein, L. (1999). 'The Social Construction of Organizational Knowledge: A Study of the Uses of Coercive, Mimetic, and Normative Isomorphism'. *Administrative Science Quarterly*, 44/4: 653–83.

Mouzelis, N. (1967). *Organisation and Bureaucracy: An Analysis of Modern Theories*. London: Routledge and Kegan Paul.

Ouchi, W., and Dowling, J. (1974). 'Defining the Span of Control'. *Administrative Science Quarterly*, 19/3: 357–65.

Parsons, T. (1937). *The Structure of Social Action: A Study in Social Theory with Special Reference to a Group of Recent European Writers*. New York: Free Press.

—— (1964). *Essays in Sociological Theory*. New York: Free Press of Glencoe.

—— (1975). 'On "de-Parsonizing" Weber (comment on Cohen et al.)'. *American Sociological Review*, 40/5: 666–70.

Perrow, C. (1986). *Complex Organizations: A Critical Essay*. Glenview, Ill.: Scott, Foresman.

Power, M. (1997). *The Audit Society: Rituals of Verification*. Oxford: Oxford University Press.

Pred, A. (1977). 'The Choreography of Existence: Comments on Hagerstrand's Time Geography and its Usefulness'. *Economic Geography*, 53: 207–21.

Presthus, R. (1961). 'Weberian v. Welfare Bureaucracy in Traditional Society'. *Administrative Science Quarterly*, 6/1: 1–24.

Pugh, D. S. (ed.) (1968). *Organization Theory*, Harmondsworth: Penguin.

—— Hickson, D. J., and Hinings, C. R. (1963). *Writers on Organizations*. Henley: Administrative Staff College.

—— —— —— Macdonald, K. M., Turner, C., and Lupton, T. (1963). 'A Conceptual Scheme for Organizational Analysis'. *Administrative Science Quarterly*, 8/3: 289–315.

—— —— —— and Turner, C. (1968). 'Dimensions of Organizational Structure'. *Administrative Science Quarterly*, 13: 65–105.

———— (1969). 'The Context of Organization Structures'. *Administrative Science Quarterly*, 14/1: 91–114.

RANSON, S., HININGS, B., and GREENWOOD, R. (1980). 'The Structuring of Organizational Structures'. *Administrative Science Quarterly*, 25/1: 1–17.

RITZER, G. (1992). *Sociological Theory*. New York: McGraw-Hill.

—— (1993). *The McDonaldization of Society*. Thousand Oaks, Calif.: Pine Forge.

ROSE, N. (1999). *Powers of Freedom*. Cambridge: Cambridge University Press.

RUEF, M., and LOUNSBURY, M. (2007). 'The Sociology of Entrepreneurship'. *Research in the Sociology of Organizations*, 25: 1–29.

SATOW, R. L. (1975). 'Value-Rational Authority and Professional Organizations: Weber's Missing Type'. *Administrative Science Quarterly*, 20: 526–31.

SCHNEIBERG, M. (2007). 'What's on the Path? Path Dependence, Organizational Diversity and the Problem of Institutional Change in the US Economy, 1900–1950'. *Socio-Economic Review*, 5: 47–80.

—— and LOUNSBURY, M. (2008). 'Social Movements and Neo-institutional Theory: Analyzing Path Creation and Change', in R. Greenwood, C. Oliver, S. Sahlin-Andersson, and R. Suddaby (eds.), *Handbook of Institutional Theory*. Thousand Oaks, Calif.: Sage.

—— —— (2008). 'Social Movements and Institutional Analysis', in R. Greenwood, C. Oliver, K. Sahlin, and R. Suddaby (eds.), *Handbook of Organizational Institutionalism*. London: Sage Publications.

—— and SOULE, S. A. (2005). 'Institutionalization as a Contested, Multilevel Process: The Case of Rate Regulation in American Fire Insurance', in G. F. Davis, D. McAdam, W. R. Scott, and M. N. Zald (eds.), *Social Movements and Organization Theory*. Cambridge: Cambridge University Press.

SCHROEDER, R. (1987). 'Nietzsche and Weber: Two "Prophets" of the Modern World', in S. Lash and S. Whimster (eds.), *Max Weber, Rationality and Modernity*. London: Allen & Unwin.

SCHUTZ, A. (1932). *Der sinnhafte Aufbau der sozialen Welt: Eine Einleitung in die verstehenden Soziologie*. Vienna: Springer.

—— (1967). *The Phenomenology of the Social World*. Evanston, Ill.: Northwestern University Press.

SCOTT, W. R. (2001). *Institutions and Organizations*. 2nd edn. Newbury Park, Calif.: Sage.

SELZNICK, P. (1949). *TVA and the Grass Roots*. Berkeley: University of California Press.

SEWELL, G. (1998). 'The Discipline of Teams: The Control of Team-Based Industrial Work through Electronic and Peer Surveillance'. *Administrative Science Quarterly*, 43: 397–428.

SICA, A. (1988). *Weber, Irrationality, and Social Order*. Berkeley: University of California Press.

SIMPSON, R. (1959). 'Vertical and Horizontal Communication in Formal Organizations'. *Administrative Science Quarterly*, 4/2: 188–96.

STINCHCOMBE, A. (1959). 'Bureaucratic and Craft Administration of Production: A Comparative Study'. *Administrative Science Quarterly*, 3/4: 509–25.

STRANG, D. (1987). 'The Administrative Transformation of American Education: School District Consolidation, 1938–1980'. *Administrative Science Quarterly*, 32/3: 352–66.

SUCHMAN, M. C. (1995). 'Managing Legitimacy: Strategic and Institutional Approaches'. *Academy of Management Review*, 20: 571–610.

SWEDBERG, R. (1998). *Max Weber and the Idea of Economic Sociology*. Princeton: Princeton University Press.

THOMPSON, V. (1965). 'Bureaucracy and Innovation'. *Administrative Science Quarterly*, 10/1: 1–20.

THORNTON, P. H. (2004). *Markets from Culture: Institutional Logics and Organizational Decisions in Higher Education Publishing*. Stanford, Calif.: Stanford University Press.

USDIKEN, B., and PASADEOS, Y. (1995). 'Organizational Analysis in North America and Europe: A Comparison of Co-citation Networks'. *Organization Studies*, 16/3: 503–26.

VEBLEN, T. (1921). *The Engineers and the Price System*. London: Transaction Books.

WATERS, M. (1989). 'Collegiality, Bureaucratization and Professionalization: A Weberian Analysis'. *American Journal of Sociology*, 94/5: 945–72.

—— (1993). 'Alternative Organizational Formations: A Neo-Weberian Typology of Polycratic Administrative Systems'. *Sociological Review*, 54–81.

WEBER, M. ([1889] 2003). *The History of Commercial Partnerships in the Middle Ages* (trans. by L. Kaelber). Lanham, Md.: Rowman and Littlefield.

—— ([1919*a*] 1948). *Wissenschaft als Beruf*. Berlin: Duncker & Humblot.

—— ([1919*b*] 1948). *Politik als Beruf*. http://www.mynetcologne.de/~nc-clasenhe/soz/lk/beruf.htm.

—— (1921). *Gesammelte Politische Schriften*. München: Duncker & Humblot.

—— (1922*a*). *Gesammelte Aufsätze zur Wissenschaftslehre*. Tübingen: Mohr.

—— (1922*b*). *Wirtschaft und Gesellschaft: Grundriß der Verstehenden Soziologie Studienausgabe*. Köln/Berlin: Kiepenheuer & Witsch.

—— (1924*a*). *Gesammelte Aufsätze zur Sozial- und Wirtschaftsgeschichte*. Tübingen: Mohr.

—— (1924*b*). *Gesammelte Aufsätze zur Soziologie und Sozialpolitik*. Tübingen: Mohr.

—— (1930). *The Protestant Ethic and the Spirit of Capitalism* (trans. T. Parsons). London: Allen & Unwin.

—— (1946*a*) *From Max Weber: Essays in Sociology* (trans. and ed. by H. H. Gerth and C. W. Mills). New York: Oxford University Press.

—— (1946*b*). *The Theory of Economic and Social Organization* (ed. and trans. by A. M. Henderson and T. Parsons). New York: Oxford University Press.

—— (1947). *The Theory of Social and Economic Organization* (trans. A. M. Henderson and T. Parsons). New York: Harper & Row.

—— (1949). *The Methodology of the Social Sciences*. New York: Free Press.

—— (1951). *The Religion of China: Confucianism and Taoism*. Glencoe, Ill.: Free Press.

—— (1952). *Ancient Judaism*. Glencoe, Ill.: Free Press.

—— (1954). *Max Weber on Law in Economy and Society*. Cambridge, Mass.: Harvard University Press.

—— (1958). *The Religion of India: The Sociology of Hinduism and Buddhism*. Glencoe, Ill.: Free Press.

—— (1962). *Basic Concepts in Sociology*. Secaucus, NJ: Citadel.

—— (1965). *The Sociology of Religion*. London: Methuen.

—— (1970). *Max Weber: The Interpretation of Social Reality*. London: Joseph.

—— (1974). *Max Weber on Universities: The Power of the State and the Dignity of the Academic Calling in Imperial Germany*. Chicago: University of Chicago Press.

—— (1976). *The Protestant Ethic and the Spirit of Capitalism*. 2nd edn. London: Allen & Unwin.

—— (1978). *Economy and Society: An Outline of Interpretive Sociology*. Berkeley: University of California Press.

WEICK, K. E. (1995). *Sensemaking in Organizations*. Thousand Oaks, Calif.: Sage.

CHAPTER 7

MAX WEBER AND THE ETHICS OF OFFICE

PAUL DU GAY

It is indeed hard to take on the study of Weber in a collection such as this without being immediately overwhelmed—not only by the need to justify the endeavor in and of itself but also by the sheer quantity and variety of what has already been written on the topic of Weber, as well as in the name of Weberian research, in the fields of organization studies and the sociology of economic life. In this chapter, I seek to treat the work of Max Weber less as a topic in and of itself, and more as an enduring resource that speaks as vitally to the political and organizational concerns of the contemporary world as it did to those of the world in which Weber wrote. After all, much of Weber's work, not least, perhaps, the essays and lectures on politics, possesses a dual character (Lassman and Speirs 1994: xi). Occasioned by current events and problems, they nonetheless point beyond their immediate context towards much wider considerations. Weber's discussion of the fate of politics in Germany—in 'Parliament and Government in Germany under a New Political Order' and 'The Profession and Vocation of Politics', for example—however intense its immediate engagement, always has implications for the ways in which we are to understand the organization and politics of the modern western state, and how we are to consider the possibilities of ethical action open to persons 'placed into various life spheres [*Lebensordnung*], each of which is governed by different laws' (Weber 1994*b*: 362).

It is a particular approach to, and understanding of, some of these wider considerations that will dominate my discussion of Weber's work in this chapter. Without engaging in the sort of total 'reconstruction' of Weber that has become quite fashionable,[1] I nonetheless wish to highlight a crucial—some have argued the crucial—ethical value criterion of Weber's sociology, one that has been largely neglected by scholars of organization. That is *Lebensführung*, the conduct of life, and Weber's concern for the survival of a particular 'character' or 'personality' whose life conduct unites practical rationality with ethical seriousness.

The chapter is organized along the following lines. In the first section, I seek to show how a particular image of Weber as a grand theorist of the instrumental rationalization of modern life, an image that has haunted organizations studies as much as it has sociology, has been challenged by a range of work emanating from the humanities and social sciences. Although diverse and far from constituting a mutually agreed line, these interpretations have all sought to paint a rather different picture of Weber as a sort of historical anthropologist whose polymath interests are linked by a set of ethical-cultural concerns. I will argue that these ethical-cultural concerns locate Weber as a late but prodigious practitioner in a tradition of the ethics of office, particularly as the latter becomes a defensive doctrine. In the second section, I seek to explore the vocabulary of office in more detail, to indicate its crucial place within Weber's work—in 'The Profession and Vocation of Politics' and the discussion of bureaucracy in *Economy and Society*, for example—and to highlight its importance for understanding the cultural and ethical constitution of a variety of organizational personae. In the final section, I show how a Weberian ethics of office remains a key resource for scholars of organization, particularly when it comes to understanding and engaging with contemporary developments in the reformation of organizational life and identity in the public sector, and in the institutions of government.

7.1. Persons and Life Orders: Rationalization and *Lebensführung*

References to Weber in recent literature within social theory and the sociology of organizations have tended to focus on the theme of rationality and rationalization (Ritzer 2004). Weber's key theme, it is frequently suggested, concerns the

[1] Such as that proposed by Wolfgang Schluchter (1981), who reads Weber's various comparisons between different forms and instances of rationalization as instalments towards an integrated developmental sociology of world history.

rationalization and objectification of all aspects of human conduct, and the ethical and emotional disfigurements this process produces. However, it does not take much familiarity with Weber's work to see that Max Weber is innocent of the so-called Weberianism that adopts a uniform, monolithic conception of the historical phenomena of rationalization. As Weber argued, on a number of occasions, rationalism can mean many different things. In *The Protestant Ethic and the Spirit of Capitalism*, for instance, he warns that

> The history of rationalism shows a development which by no means follows parallel lines in the various departments of life.... In fact, one may—this simple proposition should be placed at the beginning of every study which essays to deal with rationalism—rationalise life from fundamentally different basic points of view and in very different directions. Rationalism is a historical concept which covers a whole world of different things.
>
> (Weber 1930: 77–78)

Many sociologists and scholars of organization studies who comment on his work often appear to imagine that the distinctions suggested by Weber are, so far as Weber's own studies are concerned, flattened out by the modern advance of that dead hand of instrumental rationality—bureaucracy. Yet, it is relatively easy to point to the vital importance that Weber attaches to the lasting and intrinsic differences between, for instance, the style of rationality appropriate to the bureaucrat, and those of the entrepreneur and the politician, for example (Gordon 1987: 294; du Gay 2000).

This still leaves open the question of whether, and in what ways, rationalization determines the overall themes and purposes of Weber's oeuvre. As I indicated above, one response to this question has been provided by Wolfgang Schluchter (1981), who sees the varieties of rationalization that Weber's studies deal with as ultimately staging posts on the road to a complete theory of rationalization. Perhaps one of the most problematic aspects of this proposal is Weber's own stated doubts concerning the extent to which the different historical 'problem-spaces within which questions about rationalisation come to be posed can usefully be merged together under the auspices of a single overarching theory' (Gordon 1987: 294).

If, as Weber argued, we need 'to remind ourselves that rationalism may mean very different things', then to represent Weber as involved in a project of tracing 'a universal-historical process of rationalization' (à la Schluchter) is somewhat misleading, if not misplaced. The problem of rationalization is more diverse and context-specific than such a grand narrative allows for or appreciates. Rather, Weber's work points to the ways in which different 'orders of life' (*Lebensordnungen*) exhibit their own distinctive and non-reducible forms of 'organized rationality'. These have to be described and understood in their own terms, rather than being 'co-ordinated' into a metatheory of rationalization (Mommsen 1987: 42–3). As Wilhelm Hennis (1988: 94) puts it, the process of rationalization for Weber has 'to be related to each life order if we are to perceive the significance it has in his work'. Not only this, the tensions between these forms of organized rationality need to be outlined and appreciated. They do not follow the same path, towards the same end. Rather, they have non-uniform trajectories, not entirely unrelated to their rather differing purposes and the ethos framing them. Here, then, there are in principle a plurality of competing rationalizations, each of which 'is dependent upon a different value position, and these value positions are, in their turn, in constant conflict with one another' (Mommsen 1987: 44).

As Weber (1994*b*: 357) famously put it, and this point should also be well taken by those seeking the 'universal point of view' when it comes to rationalism and rationalization, 'Is it in fact true that any ethic in the world could establish substantively identical commandments applicable to all relationships, whether erotic, business, family or official, to one's relations with one's wife, greengrocer, son, competitor, with a friend or an accused man?'

In contrast to those commentators seeking to find in Weber's work, or more likely, imprint upon that work, the tracing of a uniform, unilinear, and monolithic process of rationalization, recent interpretations of the Weberian *oeuvre* have stressed the importance of a more contextually specific focus on the organized forms of rationality that must be confronted by all those who become involved in particular 'life orders'. Here the central focus is upon *Lebensführung*: the conduct of life and the various forms of rationalization in specific life orders (Hennis 1988, 2000; Saunders 1997; Turner 1992).

In 'Science as a Vocation', Weber encourages his audience to be 'polytheistic', and to take on the persona specific to the life order within which they are engaged. In the absence of a universal moral norm, or a conclusive victory for one form of organized rationality over all others, Weber asks, how are individuals to develop 'character' or 'personality' (*persönlichkeit*)? In considering the future of modern societies, and the individuals existing within them, Weber's deepest concern is the cultivation of individuals with 'personality': those willing and able to live up to the ethical demands placed upon them by their location within particular life orders, whose life conduct within those distinctive orders and powers—the public bureau, the firm, the parliament—can combine practical rationality with ethical seriousness (Hennis 1988).

In 'Science as a Vocation', Weber's answer to this problem is clear and direct: 'Ladies and gentlemen: Personality is possessed in science by the man [*sic*] who serves only the needs of his subject, and this is true not only in science' (1989: 11). The individual with 'personality' is one who is capable of personal dedication to a cause (*Sache*), or the instituted purposes of a given life order, in a manner that 'transcends individuality' (Hennis 1988: 88). It is in this sense that it is possible, for example, for bureaucrats to be 'personally' committed to the ethos and purposes of their distinctive office even though that ethos lies outside of their own personal (i.e. individual) moral predilections or principles.

Weber's focus upon the milieu specificity of 'personality' cautions against the siren calls of those political romantics—socialists, anarchists, the littérateurs—seeking to hold onto, or re-establish, the idea of the 'complete' human being: an ultimate, supra-regional persona that could function as the normative benchmark of all others.

Hennis argues passionately, and with a wealth of documentary evidence, that at the heart of Weber's work lies a moral anthropology at profound variance with both the positivistic tendencies and Kantian philosophical assumptions of the human sciences in the present and previous century. In his view, Weber's work belongs, rather, to the late history of a rather different practical science of mankind (*menschentum*) and to a distinctive ethical tradition: the ethics of office. Seen in this way, Max Weber's work provides a classic account of the ways in which a distinctive and important role for an ethics of office can be maintained in an increasingly alien environment, through, for example, his theorization of bureaucracy as *officium* and politics as a vocation (Hennis 1988: 104; Condren 2006*a*: 347). It is to this ethical tradition and its place at the heart of Weber's work that attention is now turned.

7.2. The Ethics of Office

Notions of persona and 'role playing' have enjoyed considerable usage in sociological and social theoretical discourse, being deployed to provide organizational and explanatory models for understanding diverse aspects of social existence (Burkitt 1992). What is meant by the term 'persona', though, has varied quite dramatically. At one extreme, as Conal Condren (2006*b*: 67) has suggested, 'it is little more than a performed role and presupposes an inner but ultimately accessible moral and decision-making agent who decides when to adopt a persona and when to put it aside. The inner "self" is thus the postulated *explanans* for conduct'. At another extreme, however, is the idea of the persona as a manifestation and representative of an office, an embodiment of moral economy. It is this sense of persona that Ernst Kantorowicz (1958) famously explored in his study of medieval kingship. Here, office denotes an assemblage of duties, responsibilities, rights of action for their fulfilment, necessary attributes, skills, and a register of virtues, vices, and failures. The determinants of office include its purposes and its limits: assertions as to end and limit thus operate as axes 'for the definition of particular sort of persona, and the qualities that best fitted the purposes and recognized the limits of office' (Condren 2006*b*: 67).

Thus, a presupposition of office was the expectation that people must behave according to the requirements of their respective offices. Because different patterns of moral quality and skill helped to distinguish one office from another, the ethics of office was not therefore exhausted by any posited global pattern of virtue. Different offices embodied and expressed differing purposes. They could not therefore be reduced to one over-arching 'office' that could stand in for all of the others, no matter how expansive its vocabulary might be. Because the display of differing intellectual, moral, and political competences and attributes was a function of office, offices were distinctive and non-reducible, even if their purposes and the boundaries separating them one from another could shift and blur over time (Geuss 2001: 10–12).

Not only this, people in office were seen exclusively as personae—as bundles of instituted rights and duties—and not as integrated selves. Thus, liberties and rights pertained to personae tied to duties, these being limited in distribution and scope by the purposes of the office to which they were attached (Hunter 2001; Condren 2006*a*, *b*).

The possibility that different personae attached to different offices represent distinctive ethical comportments, irreducible to common underlying principles, is quite foreign to contemporary, predominantly 'personalist', 'individualist', or 'subject-centered' modes of ethical reflection. In the latter, a common form of ethical judgment is assumed to reside in the capacities of the self-reflective person, whether, as with certain forms of liberal theory, these capacities are identified with the figure of the rational, autonomous individual or, as with certain forms of communitarianism, these capacities are projected onto 'radical' social movements or an integrated 'public sphere'. It is, however, as I suggested earlier, a crucial component of Max Weber's analysis of *Lebensführungen* (instituted conducts of ethical life). The ends of value-rational action are multiple and specific to particular spheres of life: military, religious, aesthetic, political, economic, and so on. And it is for this reason that Hennis's representation of Weber as something akin to a prestigious late practitioner of an ethics of office seems eminently plausible. Indeed, in his descriptive theorizations of bureaucracy and politics as office-based vocations, Weber provides clear and pressing examples of the ways in which the ethics of office offers an appropriate vocabulary through which to frame and evaluate the organized conduct of specific sorts of instituted personae. It is to those two examples that attention will now be turned.

7.2.1. Bureaucrat and Politician: Two Styles of Ethical Life

Despite its evident usefulness as an organizational device for the conduct of any number of activities, bureaucracy somehow remains morally suspect and indefensible (Parker 1993; Wilson 2000; Goodsell 2004; du Gay 2005). Critics of bureaucracy routinely castigate it for offences ranging from the ostensibly banal (procrastination, obfuscation, circumlocution, and other products of a typical 'red tape' mentality) to the truly appalling (genocide, totalitarianism, and despotism). Bureaucracy has been the object of sustained denunciation for as long as it has existed but over the last three decades criticism of the bureau has reached new heights. In the fields of sociology, social theory, and organization studies, the work of Weber has been deployed to back up and legitimate this renewed bureau critique. The 'Max Weber' in evidence in these attacks is one presumed to be most interested in delineating something called 'modernity' and the pre-eminent role of processes of rationalization in its constitution and development. Here a privileged role is attributed to bureaucracy in disenchanting 'the life-world', not least by spreading its disciplinary nexus into every nook and cranny of existence, with often inhuman consequences, including most obviously the domination of formal or instrumental rationality over more substantive values and thus the undermining of the possibility of morality (Habermas 1986; Bauman 1989; Clegg 1994).

For radical critical sociologists of rationalization, bureaucracy is viewed not as a particular form of ethical life, but rather as something destined to dissolve the possibility of meaningful moral action. Despite the limited space that Weber actually devotes to bureaucracy in his *oeuvre* (mainly in the incomplete and posthumously published *Economy and Society* and in the essays on politics, most especially 'The Profession and Vocation of Politics' and 'Parliament and Government in Germany under a New Political Order'), the overall impression generated is not one of essential negativity (du Gay 2000; Höpfl 2006). Rather, in Weber's account the impersonal, expert, procedural, and hierarchical character of bureaucratic rationality and conduct is definitely not treated as a symptom of moral deficiency. What is distinctive about bureaucratic rationality in Weber's analysis is not its lack of authentic ends but rather the kinds of ends that it pursues and the manner in which it pursues them. In other words, in these texts, Weber is not simply or primarily concerned with critiquing bureaucracy but rather with outlining the ethic framing of the office of the bureaucratic persona, most notably in relation to its neighboring office, that of the persona of the professional politician.

It is a mistake therefore—à la Bauman (1989) or Habermas (1986), for instance—to approach bureaucracy as the merely 'instrumental' side of an integrated moral personality, or 'public sphere'. On the contrary, as Weber was at pains to point out, the bureau is a 'life order' or 'office' comprising the technical and 'spiritual' (ethical-cultural) conditions of a distinctive and independent organization of a persona. Among the most important of these are (1) that access to office is dependent upon lengthy training in a relevant form of expertise, usually certified by some form of public examination; and (2) that the office itself constitutes a 'vocation' (*Beruf*), a focus of ethical commitment and duty, autonomous of, and superior to, the bureaucrat's extra-official ties to kith, kin, class, conscience, or community.

Legally and actually, office holding is not considered ownership of a source of income, to be exploited for rents or emoluments in exchange for the rendering of certain services, as was normally the case during the Middle Ages... nor is office holding considered a common exchange of services, as in the case of free employment contracts. Rather entrance into an office... is considered an acceptance of a specific duty of fealty to the purpose of the office [*Amstreue*] in return for the grant of a secure existence. It is decisive for the modern loyalty to an office that, in the pure type, it does not establish a relationship to a *person*, like the vassal's or disciple's faith under feudal or patrimonial authority, but rather is devoted to impersonal and functional purposes.... The political official—at least in the fully developed modern state—is not considered the personal servant of a ruler. (Weber 1978: ii. 959)

In Weber's account, these conditions mark the bureau out as a distinctive life order, and they provide the bureaucrat with a distinctive ethical bearing or status conduct. The ethical attributes of the good bureaucrat—strict adherence to procedure, acceptance of subordination and superordination, *esprit de corps*, abnegation of personal moral enthusiasms, commitment to the purposes of the office—are not some incompetent subtraction from a complete (self-concerned and self-realizing) comportment of the person. Quite the opposite, in fact; they represent a positive moral achievement requiring the mastery of a difficult ethical milieu and practice (Hunter 1994*a*). They are the product of definite ethical techniques and routines—declaring one's personal interest, subordinating one's ego to the dictates of procedural decision making, and so on and so forth—through which individuals develop the disposition and ability to conduct themselves according to the ethos of bureaucratic office. No less than that of the knight, the monk, or the puritan, the ethical attributes of the bureaucrat are the contingent and often fragile achievements of a particular organized sphere of moral existence (Hunter 1994*a*).

In 'Parliament and Government in Germany under a New Political Order' and 'The Profession and Vocation of Politics', Weber explicitly addresses the different kinds of responsibility that bureaucrats and politicians have for their actions. For Weber, the institutional and moral responsibility of these different official personae is to be understood in terms of the quite distinct duties attached to their particular responsibilities of office. By framing his analysis in terms of an ethics of office, Weber is insisting on the irreducibility of different spheres of ethical life and the consequent necessity of applying different ethical protocols to them:

An official who receives an order which, in his view is wrong can—and should—raise objections. If his superior then insists on the instruction it is not merely the duty of the official it is also a point of *honour* for him to carry out that instruction as if it corresponded to his own inner most conviction, thereby demonstrating that his sense of duty to his office overrides his individual wilfulness.... This is what is demanded by the spirit of [bureaucratic] *office*. A political leader who behaved like this would deserve our *contempt*. He will often be obliged to make compromises, which means sacrificing something of less importance to something of greater importance.... The official should stand 'above the parties', which in truth means that he must remain outside the struggle for power of his own. The *struggle* for personal power and the acceptance of *full personal responsibility for one's cause* (*Sache*) which is the consequence of such power—this is the very element in which the politician and the entrepreneur live and breathe (1994*a*:160–1; original emphasis)

According to Weber (1978: ii. 958 ff.), then, the bureaucrat or administrative official, on the one hand, and the politician or ruler, on the other, have very different purposes and forms of responsibility. Such differences are not to be deduced from the relative 'interest' or 'complexity' of the tasks each performs, nor from a mechanistic distinction between policy and administration, but rather from the demands made upon them by the distinctive offices they occupy.

Officials too are expected to make independent decisions and show organizational ability and initiative, not only on countless individual cases but also on larger issues. It is typical of littérateurs and of a country lacking any insight into its own affairs or into the achievement of its officials, even to imagine that the work of an official amounts to no more than the subaltern performance of routine duties, while the leader alone is expected to carry out the 'interesting' tasks which make special intellectual demands. This is not so. The difference lies, rather, in the kind of responsibility borne by each of them, and this is largely what determines the demands made on their particular abilities. (Weber 1994*a*: 160)

Weber is clearly referring to 'responsibility' in a very specific sense. The term as he deploys it does not pertain to a simple division of organizational labor, in which bureaucratic officials are allocated the sole responsibility for administration, and politicians the sole responsibility for policy. Rather, 'responsibility' refers to a division of ethical labor in which both official and political leader are subject to specific imperatives and points of honor and develop quite different capacities and comportments as a result of the demands of their respective 'offices'.[2]

Forged in the party system and tempered by the organized adversarialism of the parliament, the politician belongs to an order of life quite unlike that of the bureaucrat. The party leader possesses the political abilities and ethical demeanor required by the unremitting struggle to win and regain power (Hunter 1994*a*). As Weber (1994*a*, *b*) makes clear, it is this, and not the trained expertise and impersonal dedication of the bureaucratic official, that equips the politician to pursue the worldly interests of the state in the face of a hostile and unpredictable political and economic environment. The honor of 'the political leader, that is, the leading statesman', consists for Weber (1994*b*: 331; original emphasis), 'precisely in taking exclusive *personal* responsibility for what he does, responsibility which he cannot and may not refuse or unload onto others'. By contrast, as we have seen, the crucial point of honor for the bureaucrats is to guard their impartiality and to act impersonally—not to allow their extra-official ties or enthusiasms to determine the manner in which they perform their official duties. The bureaucrat 'takes pride in preserving his impartiality, overcoming his own inclinations and opinions, so

2 This plurality of obligation and comportment also occurs within, as well as between, institutional milieux—such as that characterizing modern government—where life orders intersect.

as to execute in a conscientious and meaningful way what is required of him by the general definition of his duties or by some particular instruction, even—and particularly—when they do not coincide with his own political views' (1994*a*: 160).

In particular, Weber (1978: ii. 983 ff.) stresses the ways in which the ethos of bureaucratic office holding constitutes an important political resource because it serves to divorce the administration of public life from private moral absolutisms. Without the historical emergence of the ethos and persona of bureaucratic office holding, Weber argues, the construction of a buffer between civic comportment and personal principles—a crucial feature of liberal government—would never have been possible. Indeed, without the 'art of separation' (Walzer 1984) that the bureau effected and continues to effect, many of the qualitative features of government that are regularly taken for granted—for instance, reliability and procedural fairness in the treatment of cases—would not exist. As Weber (1994*b*: 331) puts it, without this 'supremely ethical discipline and self-denial', the whole apparatus of government, and state, would disintegrate.

Seen in this light, modern systems of government appear as irrevocably hybrid institutional milieux housing quite different and distinct personae (Orren and Skowronek 1994; March and Olsen 2004). Here, as Weber argues, the persona of the bureaucratic official is and needs to be very different from the persona of the professional politician, not because the former 'administers' and the latter 'makes policy', for instance, but precisely because they are subject to different demands as a result of the purposes of the respective offices they occupy. For Weber, the blurring of official personae can create political and organizational dangers.

Writing in the last years of World War I, Weber's key interests were in the survival of the German state. The central point for Weber was how to prevent the elimination of genuine political activity and leadership by the bureaucratic practice of 'rule by officials'. This placed the question of the role and nature of parliament at the top of the agenda: '*How is parliament to be made capable of assuming power?* Anything else is a side issue' (1994*a*: 190).

For Weber, bureaucratic 'Officialdom has passed every test brilliantly wherever it was required to demonstrate its sense of duty, its objectivity and its ability to master organisational problems in relation to strictly circumscribed, official tasks of a specialised nature. Anyone who comes from a family of officials, as I do, will be the last to permit any stain on his shield' (1994*b*: 177). The problem, though, was not whether bureaucrats were good officials *per se*, but in the absence of a body of political leaders, whether they were capable and competent to act as a certain sort of public official: namely, as a political leader. Weber's answer was clear, precise, and in line with his thinking as an ethicist of office.

> But what concerns us here are political achievements rather than those of 'service', and the facts themselves proclaim loudly something which no lover of truth can conceal, namely that rule by officials has failed utterly whenever it has dealt with political questions. This has not

happened by chance. Indeed, to put it the other way round, it would be quite astonishing if abilities which are inwardly so disparate were to coincide within one and the same political formation. As we have said, it is not the task of an official to join in political conflict on the basis of his own convictions, and thus, in this sense of the word, 'engage in politics', which always means fighting. (1994*a*:177–8)

He reiterates this point in 'The Profession and Vocation of Politics'. Practicing bureaucrats are not ideal professional politicians. Their respective offices differ, the competences, deportment, and capabilities are quite distinct. To make one function in lieu of the other is asking for trouble:

> Precisely those who are officials by nature and who, in this regard, are of high moral stature, are bad and, particularly in the political meaning of the word, irresponsible politicians, and thus of low moral stature in this sense—men of the kind we Germans, to our cost, have had in positions of leadership time after time. This is what we call 'rule by officials'. Let me make it clear that I imply no stain on the honour of our officials by exposing the political deficiency of this system, when evaluated from the standpoint of success. (1994*b*: 331)

For Weber, claims to representational totality made by and on behalf of the state bureaucracy in early twentieth-century Germany were politically (and organizationally) dangerous because they required bureaucrats to assume an office they were signally ill-equipped so to do: to become professional politicians. The political stability and social dynamism he viewed as resting in part upon the separation and co-existence of these two distinct life orders were threatened by a lack of role differentiation that seemed destined to produce a system of administration without government. It was this particular concern with the implications of the lack of differentiation between offices and official personae that underlies one of Weber's most famous and dramatic epithets.

As he makes clear in 'The Profession and Vocation of Politics' and 'Parliament and Government in Germany under a New Political Order', the extensions of bureaucratic administration demanded, for example, by the romantic socialism of 'naïve littérateurs', and already evidenced in the practice of 'rule by officials', were 'in the process of manufacturing the housing of future serfdom, to which, perhaps, men will have to submit powerlessly... *if they consider that the ultimate and only value by which the conduct of their affairs is to be decided is good administration and provision of their needs by officials (that is "good" in the purely technical sense of rational administration)*' (1994*a*: 158; my italics). With bureaucrats being allowed or encouraged to take direct responsibility for the actions of the state, it appeared to Weber that an ethic of administration was fast freeing itself from its proper moorings and was set to efface government as a political process.

Rather than signaling an inherent antipathy toward bureaucracy *per se*, Weber is indicating that offices have limits. There is nothing here to suggest a universal or objectivist point of view, or an evolutionary or teleological trajectory, such that the essential trait of bureaucracy is to produce a 'shell of servility' or an 'iron cage'.

Instead, Weber indicates a specific instance, which, if it is not countered, could become a trend in the domain of the political, as well as in other orders of life. As Mommsen (1987: 41) has argued in this respect, 'These statements were intended to mobilize counter forces in order to arrest those trends.'

For Weber then, there are indeed limits to bureaucracy and bureaucratic conduct. These limits are not, however, the general and principled limits envisaged by humanist critics such as Bauman (1989) and Habermas (1986), who demand that bureaucrats take individual moral responsibility for otherwise 'technicist' decision making; that is, when they imagine bureaucratic conduct as an incomplete fragment of an ideally integrated rational and moral personality. The sorts of action specific to the office of the bureaucrat are not signs of a moral vacuum that must be filled by individual moral conscience before we can have a just polity. On the contrary, as Weber points out, bureaucratic conduct requires a specific kind of ethical work and competence that is formed and maintained in the ethical life order of the bureau. The bureaucratic office thus constituted what Weber describes as a particular department of existence. It is, of course, not the only one. We have already noted that political leadership possesses its own office and exhibits its own specific form of organized rationality. The same can be said of the sort of humanist critique practiced by intellectuals such as Habermas and Bauman (Hunter 1994*b*), not to mention the diverse forms of ethical life characteristic of religious sects, armies, families, and legal systems, for example. The limits to bureaucracy and bureaucratic action are not therefore set by its place in a larger moral and ethical whole, but by the fact that no such 'whole' exists. The bureau is simply one among a plurality of organized forms of rationality. Its limits emerge—and must be described—in a non-principled manner, as the outcome of its purely contingent historical interactions with other orders of life.[3]

7.3. Reinstating an Ethic of Office

The idea of Max Weber as a moral theorist is not one that has held a great deal of appeal for the sociology of economic and organizational life or for organization studies. Rather, it has been left to those working in adjacent disciplines to fully explore Weber's status as a moral theorist of office and to register the ethical implications of his theorizing of bureaucracy as *officium* and of politics as a vocation (Hennis 1988, 2000; Hunter 1994*a*, *b*; Condren 1997, 2006*a*, *b*).

[3] Weber's position here has clear connections with the ideas advanced by Orren and Skowronek (1994) on 'institutional intercurrence'.

One area in which this work has been developed is in relationship to exploring the ethical implications of organizational reforms of state bureaucracies conducted in a range of political contexts under the auspices of the New Public Management (NPM) (du Gay 1994, 2000, 2007; Minson 1993, 1998). Indeed, in recent years there has a been a considerable upsurge of interest in the ethics of 'office' within the social sciences as well as among scholars of public law and public administration, in large part kindled by the growing ethical uncertainties attendant upon these ongoing managerial reforms of a wide range of public institutions (Dobel 1999; Loughlin 2004; Uhr 1999, 2001).

7.3.1. New Public Management and the Ethics of Office

By the mid-1980s tolerably similar problematizations of public bureaucracies, and the main ingredients for their reform, had emerged from a variety of sources—public choice theory, the burgeoning privatization literature, and contemporary management theory. These problematizations and prescriptions came to be known collectively as the New Public Management (NPM), or in a more politically populist nomenclature, 'entrepreneurial governance'. According to the authors commonly acknowledged with formulating the latter term, reforms of public bureaucracy were necessary because 'government was broken' and bureaucratic practices were in large part to blame for this. 'Re-invention' was not only necessary but urgently required, and the ten essential principles of 'entrepreneurial governance' constituted the recipe for salvation.

> Entrepreneurial governments promote *competition* between service providers. They *empower* citizens by pushing control out of the bureaucracy and into the community. They measure the performance of their agencies, focusing not on inputs but on *outcomes*. They are driven by their goals—their *missions*—not by their rules and regulations. They redefine their clients as *customers* and offer them choices—between schools, between training programs, between housing options. They *prevent* problems before they emerge, rather than simply offering services afterward. They put their energies into *earning* money, not simply spending it. They *decentralize* authority and embrace participatory management. They prefer *market* mechanisms to bureaucratic mechanisms. And they focus not simply on providing public services but on *catalyzing* all sectors—public, private, and voluntary—into action to solve their community's problems. (Osborne and Gaebler 1992: 19–20)

These ten elements or principles have comprised something like a shopping list for those seeking to modernize their public sectors in OECD countries. Even when allowing for real and significant differences between countries, most reform efforts have involved the simultaneous deployment of a number of these key elements. At the very least, it seems obvious that the principles so succinctly articulated by Osborne and Gaebler, and the mechanisms used to operationalize them, do interact quite strongly. So, for example, the separation of purchasing from provision is a prerequisite for the introduction of market-type mechanisms, which are, in turn, a crucial means of disaggregating traditional bureaucracies. Similarly, the setting of performance targets is a useful precursor to moving the terms of employment for public bureaucrats towards fixed-term contracts and performance-related pay schemes (Pollitt 1995). In other words, there do seem to be good reasons for regarding these ten elements or principles as something like an intersecting set or system, as Osborne and Gaebler suggested they were, rather than seeing each element separately as if it were simply a distinct project or program of its own. As the Australian Department of Finance indicated: 'the various strands of reform are no accident of history. They are mutually supportive and their integrated nature is crucial to the overall success of the reforms' (quoted in du Gay 2000: 6).

If the NPM, or 'entrepreneurial governance', has had one overarching target—that which it most explicitly defines itself against—then it is the impersonal, hierarchical, and procedural organization of the traditional (Weberian) bureaucracy. The rise of the NPM has been accompanied by what Herbert Kaufman (1981) once described as 'a raging pandemic' of anti-bureaucratic sentiment. For the last three decades, the organizational and ethical form, or 'life order'—of which Max Weber is the acknowledged supreme analyst—has been in retreat as wave after wave of reform has been directed at dismantling many of its defining institutional and ethical characteristics. Put simply, bureaucracy is represented as the 'paradigm that failed', in large part because the forms of organizational and personal conduct it gave rise to and fostered are regarded as out of step with, or otherwise unsuited to, the exigencies of the contemporary economic, political, and social environment (Moe 1994). The latter is characterized as subject to constant and profound change. Here, for instance, the image of the well-ordered national economy providing resources for the national state and society is replaced by the image of the extravagant, un-enterprising 'big' government state and society undermining national economic performance (Hindess 1998).

> In this environment bureaucratic institutions ...—public and private—increasingly fail us. Today's environment demands institutions that are extremely flexible and adaptable. It demands institutions that deliver high-quality goods and services, squeezing ever-more bang out of every buck. It demands institutions that are responsive to their customers, offering choices of non-standardized services; that lead by persuasion and incentives rather than commands; that give their employees a sense of meaning and control, even ownership.
>
> (Osborne and Gaebler 1992: 15)

As Osborne and Gaebler's *cri de cœur* illustrates, the rhetoric and imagery of contemporary business discourse has been a crucial constituent of the New Public Management movement, and its deployment has had a profound effect on the ways in which state bureaux are conceptualized and their purposes and performances assessed (Rohr 1998; Wilson 2000; Goodsell 2004). For over a century, it has been customary for politicians and state bureaucrats to speak fondly and freely of running government on a businesslike basis. By this, though, little more has normally been meant than the salutary aspiration that state bureaux should work more effectively. Recent enthusiasms for NPM have had a rather different intent. Here we see the ideal of 'being like a business' given a much more literal spin, one in which differences between administration as governance, and management as delivering services to customers, are elided. The conduct of government in all of its manifestations is represented first and foremost as a particular sort of managerial enterprise. Here, the statist or governmental dimensions of the work of public officials outlined by Weber disappear from view. This contemporary managerial ideal has a number of components, but three in particular, stand out. We might label them: market creation, entrepreneurial conduct, and performance measurement (see Goodsell 2004: 150–61).

7.3.2. Market Creation

A key feature of recent reforms of state bureaux has been the use of market-type mechanisms to reform working practices and ethics, and to create competition within government itself. Internal markets, agencification, contracting out, market testing, and private finance initiatives are but some of the techniques deployed by government to make the provision of public services more businesslike. Each, in their particular ways, involves the establishment of a system for the delivery of public services modeled on a conception of market relations (what we might term an 'imagined' or 'virtual' market), and thus has (in no matter how artificial a manner) the production of profit as one of its basic organizing principles (Scott 1996).

Justifications for contracting out or 'outsourcing', for instance, frequently begin by invoking the purported failures of in-house systems of provision based on hierarchies of public offices. In assuming that office holders are self-interested and opportunistic, public choice theories of bureaucracy, for example, on which much of the justification for contracting is based, turned traditional virtues of office-based governance into their opposites: permanency was an invitation to complacency; the combination of 'purchaser' and 'provider' roles was regarded as being inevitably accompanied by inefficiency and ineffectiveness as incentives to perform were absent, and so on and so forth. One obvious remedy, given the assumption of inherent 'economic' self-interest and opportunism, was to harness these capacities more productively through the use of competitive tendering and contracting out, or the development of internal markets again based on a contractualist logic (Le Grand 2003). Not only would contracting reduce costs, due to downward pressure on prices from competitive tendering, it would result in continuous quality improvement as providers sought to outdo each other in meeting service specifications.

However, it is clear that when the language of office holding is replaced by that of market creation, in the form of contracting and competitive tendering, a number of profound consequences can flow for the structural and institutional integrity of public administrative activity, and the ability of public officials to live up to the demands of their office. First, in the name of (a distinctive understanding of) economy, efficiency, and delivery, public offices and officials in many areas of activity have been replaced by contracted private agencies or businesses. Thus, public officials begin to lose many intrinsic aspects of their role, not the least of which being their status as 'authorities'. As government contracts out more and more of its activities, its constituent office holders really do begin to lose competence in the areas covered by contractors, areas within which until now public office holders have had unrivalled expertise. As Crouch (2004: 100) has argued, 'As they become mere brokers between public principals and private agents, so professional and technical knowledge passes to the latter. Before long it will become a serious argument in favour of private contractors that only they have the relevant expertise.' Attempts by public officials to write codes of ethics that both defend traditional public service conduct and celebrate market-mimicking conduct, clearly testify to the nature of the choices that contractualization brings in its wake (Painter 2000). Attempts by contract managers to adapt contracts to incorporate the more complex dimensions of public office-holding responsibilities, for instance, highlight both the difficulties of attempting to have your cake and eat it, and perhaps, more importantly, the inappropriateness of such instruments to the tasks in question. These tensions are made evident in the manner in which traditional forms of political accountability are mostly bypassed or supplanted by narrow, one-dimensional mechanisms of contract enforcement and service delivery (Plant 2003).

In sum, the replacement of the generic, comprehensive forms of supervision, accountability, regulation, and teamwork inherent in a system of state service based on a structure of interrelated public offices, by the particularistic, task-specific, and often privatized forms inherent in the contract represents 'a threat to the basis of ethical conduct in the management and delivery of public services' (Painter 2000: 181). This threat refers, primarily, to the ways in which the expert tasks, powers, and responsibilities of government in a sovereign state—that forgotten 'core' business of public administration—are irreducible to business terms alone, much as they are to democratic terms. Such reductionism is often attractive—particularly to partisan reform enthusiasts—and clearly not impossible, but its costs are apt to be quite high, as Weber's (1994*a*) work indicates. Weber's point was that there are limits; limits, that is, to the extent to which the complex oscillations and balances between different ethical capacities within a given bureaucratic life order can be pushed in one direction towards any single vision of ordering without significant, perhaps pyrrhic, costs attaching to such an endeavor. In Weber's work on early twentieth-century Germany, his focus was upon the usurpation of political leadership by the state bureaucracy, and the political and ethical problems developing from 'rule by officials'. In the case of contracting out, the focus is rather different. It is the diminution of bureaucratic authority and expertise that needs addressing. Here the costs include not only a loss of public expertise and authority (a diminution of office-based competence) but vastly increased scope for patronage and private influence, as well as enhanced opportunities for and temptations to corruption—the blurring of office and self, and the re-emergence in suitably modern guise of office as a tradable good (Doig and Wilson 1998; Chapman 2004; Crouch 2004).

7.3.3. Entrepreneurial Conduct

A second central feature of the business management discourse framing NPM reforms is the role allotted to enterprise and entrepreneurialism when discussing the changing ethics required of 'new' public managers as opposed to that of public officials. Much like the discussion of 'markets', the enterprise evoked and praised in new public management discourses is of a hybrid or 'virtual' sort. It has little to do with business start-ups or the model *habitus* of successful entrepreneurs. Rather, the signifier 'Enterprise' functions here as a rhetorical move in a political polemic, 'sexing up' the content of what was, until comparatively recently, a largely non-emotive subject matter: namely public administration. Thus, the category of entrepreneur, when applied to public management, functions itself as an umbrella term for a range of measures deemed necessary to making state bureaux more businesslike. 'Leadership', 'innovation', 'creativity', 'risk taking', 'experimenting', and so on are all attached to the signifier to evoke new ideals of conduct to be embodied and expressed in the activities of public officials.

In recent years, the issue of 'executive leadership' has emerged as a hot topic within the field of public management. The British 'New' Labour Government's White Paper *Modernising Government* (Cabinet Office 1999*a*) and its related policy documents (Cabinet Office 1999*b*), for instance, placed considerable emphasis upon the capacity of executive leadership to help change the culture of 'risk aversion' that it considers endemic to the British Civil Service. Thus, the White Paper stated that officials must 'move away from the risk-averse culture inherent in government' and that this was to be achieved through removing 'unnecessary bureaucracy which prevents public servants from experimenting, innovating and delivering a better product'. As with a previous attempt to inculcate 'real qualities of leadership' among senior civil servants, the *Next Steps Report* (Efficiency Unit 1988: para. 35) paved the way for agencification in the British Civil Service, quite what this means in the British constitutional context where ministerial accountability is still assumed to be a crucial constitutional convention is not at all clear. After all, the business of a government department must, inevitably, be scrutinized in a different way than shareholders of a public company judge the operations of a firm. As Bogdanor (2001: 298) has argued:

In the latter case, the net financial outcome of all the firm's operations over a period of time will be evaluated at the annual meeting of shareholders. Parliament, however, may scrutinise any single operation varied out by government at any time, and may do so some considerable time after the operation in question has occurred. This has obvious implications for record-taking and for the avoidance of risk. It makes it difficult for civil servants to be 'creative', or to display the 'leadership' so beloved of the management consultants—indeed, it might be argued that under ... [this] constitution it is for politicians and not for civil servants to display leadership.

Seen in this light, the creativity and innovation demanded of public officials looks like an invitation to set aside the constitutional obligations of their office. Creativity is represented as something that is blocked by bureaucratic constraint and therefore bureaucracy must bow to its demands. The cases of WorldCom and Enron from the private sector come to mind, where creativity was exhibited precisely by acting 'outside of office', and supplanting or subverting bureaucratic procedure (Armbrüster 2005).

Public accountability also looks like one of the victims of this managerial demand. By encouraging all senior civil servants to become leaders and to take individual responsibility for their decision making, the managerialist impulse seems determined to turn them into politicians or even entrepreneurs. This puts them at odds with Weber's (1994*a*: 160–1) description of the ethos of bureaucratic office as one in which the official should stand 'above the parties', remaining outside the struggle for power 'of his own'(*sic*). The struggle for personal power and the acceptance of personal responsibility for one's cause, Weber continued, was not an appropriate logic of action for the bureaucrat to follow. For the persona of the professional politician and that of the entrepreneur, however, it constituted the 'very element' in which they 'live and breathe'.

In this way, by blurring the responsibilities of office, public accountability enforcement becomes more difficult. With so many people being 'leaders' in the system, where and with whom does the buck stop, exactly? In practice, in the United Kingdom, as elsewhere, the NPM demand for 'entrepreneurial conduct' among governmental officials presupposes a degree of freedom on the part of civil servants that the constitution just does not tolerate, and whose practical effects most ministers would in reality be most unlikely to condone. As Page (quoted in Amann 2006: 348) observes in the UK context, 'If officials followed the advice of Michael Barber, Head of the Prime Minister's Delivery Unit, and really did "imagine six impossible things before breakfast ... and then do some of them by tea time", there is a good chance they would be out on their ear by supper.'

Similarly, the demand for entrepreneurial styles of conduct among public bureaucrats can also encourage, *contra* Weber, individuals to identify the goals of office with their own sense of self. The appointment to official civil service positions of people with known prior policy enthusiasms to act as 'committed champions' of government policy can lead to the development of what Dobel (1999: 131) calls 'zealous sleaze': a process whereby individuals come to see public office as an extension of their own will and ideological commitments. Here the importance of entrepreneurial 'innovation' and 'risk taking' in the name of 'delivery' is held to override the office-specific obligations of a civil servant's given institutional milieu. Once again, though, while bureaucratic ethics involves discretion, judgment, and choice as to right action, those choices are not the individual's own, but official ones: choices or judgments facing him or her in their official persona as a professional public servant. Here a singular and committed focus on 'delivery' is not acceptable if one's official role requires one to a balance a range of competing values or demands in the name of public interest.

7.3.4. Performance and Performativity

A third key feature of the business discourse framing NPM is the issue of performance and performance evaluation. In Britain, the current Labour government's obsession with 'delivery', combined with none-too-subtle distaste for the traditions of state bureaucrats led it quickly to demand changes in the 'ethos' governing the conduct of civil servants. As a former Home Secretary put it in 2002, 'What I think we'd benefit from is a more effective managerial quality at the top, and I'd say put the "just do it" ethic in, is the change that's needed' (Charles Clarke on BBC Radio 4, 25 July 2002). Once again, the civil servant as part of an institutional 'gyroscope of state' and bulwark against what Walt Whitman once called, 'the never ending audacity of elected persons', was to be reconfigured as a something akin to an energetic and entrepreneurial 'yes person'. In order to be able to 'just do it', though, the variety of duties and obligations that bureaucrats were traditionally expected to fulfill had to be transmuted into, or reduced to, the more modest activities of generic management.

In order for managers to 'really' be able to manage, a space had to be created permitting freedom from day to day supervision. This distance could not be total, however, only partial and this is where targets, audits, and the other paraphernalia of 'responsibilization' come into play. The increased use of devolved budgets, targets, performance evaluation, and audit attest to managerial independence at the same time as channeling managerial freedom and shaping managerial action in increasingly narrow directions (Power 1997; Rose 1999; Strathern 2001).

One of the main features of the contemporary passion for 'performance' is its distinctive reductionism. The language of performance requires relatively simple, mainly quantitative measures to be created so that evaluation of success or failure can be unambiguously reached. But what if certain, perhaps crucial, aspects of a complex and contingent office-based role are simply not amenable to calculation in these terms? What happens to these in the performance mix? According to Power (1997) and Paton (2003), for instance, that which is not amenable to performance 'verification' ('performativity') is simply white noise: at best an irritation, at worst an irrelevance. As Paton (2003: 29) puts it:

> The problem is that the language of performance takes no prisoners. Through its lenses, the world is straightforward, situations are or should be controlled, the issues are clear, the criteria unambiguous—and results have either been achieved or they have not. Uncertainty, patchiness, ambiguity, riders and qualifications—all these can be read as excuses, signs of weakness. 'Performance' is categorical—that is precisely its attraction.

And, some might argue, precisely its weakness. As suggested earlier, office-based obligations tend to be plural rather than singular. A senior civil servant working in the institutional milieu of British Central Government, for instance, has, traditionally at least, needed to be, *inter alia*, something of an expert in the ways of the constitution, a stickler for procedure, and a stoic able to accept disappointments with equanimity (Chapman 1988; Bogdanor 2001). As an institution of government, the public administration in Britain therefore reflects and performs not simply bureaucracy but also politics, diplomacy, and indeed certain forms of enterprise (clearly, an institution that in the immediate aftermath of World War II, under extraordinarily difficult circumstances, succeeded in establishing a National Health Service, a new social security system, the expansion of education at all levels, and the nationalization of the major public utilities could hardly be considered to lack the qualities of managerial initiative and enterprise). However, reduction to any one of these various ethical capacities and comportments alone would undoubtedly damage the purposes the public administrator is charged with fulfilling. It would, in other words, have a significant impact upon their ability to live up to the obligations of their office. Such reductionism is not impossible but, as I argued earlier, its costs are apt to be high.

In his classic text, *Bureaucracy in Modern Society*, Peter Blau (1956) indicated what would happen if performance targets are allotted too much weight in framing the conduct of bureaucratic office. The lessons he outlined appear not to have been learnt. In their text *Re-Inventing Government*, Osborne and Gaebler (1992: 157) commended Arkansas and Florida state administrations for removing funding from adult education programs if 70 percent of its graduates fail to get jobs. Blau's argument was that organizations would respond by accepting recruits to the program on a selective basis. His assumption is born out in the experience of professionals working throughout the public sector, where, as Power (1997) and Miller (2005) for instance, have shown, meeting narrowly defined targets has had a profound impact on the ability of officials to live up to the plural obligations consequent upon their occupation of a given office. In the 1990s, for instance, the

British Government's Child Support Agency was held to have found it easier to meet certain financial targets by attempting to gain increased sums from fathers who lived apart from their children but who were already making a contribution to their upbringing, rather than to seek new fathers who were absent and gave no assistance (Jordan 1994: 27).

Because a system of government requires bureaucratic officials to act as custodians of the constitutional values it embodies, it cannot frame their official role or persona solely in terms of performance, responsiveness, and meeting targets. The pursuit of more 'businesslike' management in government, no matter how important it may be in and of itself, has to recognize the constitutional and political limits to which it is subject (Johnson 1993: 194).

The New Public Management is undoubtedly a multifaceted rather than monochromatic creation. It is probably best not to overstate its singleness of purpose or its technical homogeneity. Likewise, it would be foolish to dismiss all of the techniques and practices associated with it out of hand. It may well be that some of its concerns are far from unhelpful in making public administration more effective. Nonetheless, the transparency it demands in all its manifestations is more troubling than it might at first appear. It is certainly possible to view constructs such as 'customer satisfaction'—in both their managerialist and populist democratic manifestations—as relatively banal devices for increasing the efficiency and effectiveness of governmental departments and agencies by ensuring that officials include new calculations in the performance of their role. However, the language of the 'customer', as part and parcel of a distinctive way of conceiving of the activity of state service—that of a commercial enterprise—not only has clear limits in the public administrative context but also has clear and present dangers for the Weberian ethos of bureaucratic office traditionally conceived. For the languages of NPM, with its explicit distinctions—between policy and management, and autonomy and authority, for instance—overrides and thus, in a sense, occludes many of the virtues of bureaucratic office, as outlined by Max Weber, because the latter simply cannot be registered in the language NPM insists on using. As John Rohr (1998: xi), for instance, has argued, this is a 'forest and trees problem of the first order... and underscores one of the most fundamental problems with the public management movement', namely its diminution of the statist and constitutional character of public bureaucratic office through the substitution of a language of political administration by a managerialist lexicon. As Rohr (2000: 203) continues, echoing Weber, managerial innovations cannot change the fact that public administration is governance. Many other things it may well be, but it remains crucially a form of governance. In this respect, then, the consequences of the NPM redefinition of administration as management cannot be overstated. In seeking to 're-imagine' public bureaucrats as first and foremost managers, the NPM is in danger of engaging in the sort of supra-regional unification of 'offices' or life orders criticized by Max Weber.

7.4. Concluding Comments

Clearly political circumstances change and so should the machinery of government. After all, too narrow a focus on the inviolability of a set of pre-existing commitments can be just as problematic, politically and administratively, as too passionate a fixation on the imperatives of change and modernization. Institutions must be allowed to adapt from their original purposes if the circumstances in which they operate have changed. This, though, raises a very large question. Have political or organizational circumstances changed so much that we can do away with office-based conceptions of ethical agency?

To judge by the comments of some advocates of entrepreneurial government, for example, many of the problems the state evolved to address have been solved; the only issues left to deal with concern better management of contracts, or how to make decision making more 'deliberative' or 'participative'. These may be the 'parish pump' concerns of what has been epochally characterized as a fundamentally 'anti-statist' age (Mulgan 1998; Gamble and Wright 2004), but are such assumptions warranted? Has the state and its hierarchically structured domain of offices been transcended?

We have been here before. Early in the twentieth century, we find Max Weber railing against the various political romanticisms—anarchists, socialists, armchair litterateurs—who would do away with bureaucracy, law, and other detritus of the liberal state in pursuit of their own radical 'visions'. Weber was quite clear that the ethos of bureaucratic office constituted a virtue that a liberal regime, with a parliamentary democracy and market economy, could not do without. As we saw earlier, he was adamant that 'without this supremely ethical discipline and self-denial the whole apparatus would disintegrate' (1994*b*: 331).

It is not simply public or state bureaux to which this injunction would still apply. After many years in which bureaucracy and office-based ethical constraints more generally have been represented in private sector management literature precisely as stumbling blocks to those wishing to display initiative and exercise autonomy at work, even the fulsomely anti-bureaucratic *Economist* magazine noted evidence of a 'return to values that we thought were gone forever' (2002: 118). These included a new found respect for hierarchy, attention to detail, and the importance of people acting within the confines of their office, so as to be on their guard against temptations to impetuosity and other heartfelt enthusiasms—the very passions that management gurus such as Tom Peters had built a career urging organizations to let loose (ibid.).

The recent obsession with individual creativity and autonomy, 'break-though thinking', and expressivism in both public and private sector management literature, and the currently commanding position occupied by the concept of moral autonomy in contemporary Western ethical culture, are probably not entirely unrelated. The concept of moral autonomy involves the supposition, common to all the leading moral theories, that people should only be subject to moral constraints that they could have rationally or consensually formulated for themselves. On this assumption, authentic moral deliberation requires detachment from institutionally given obligations—bureaucratic roles are often a paradigm instance in both philosophical and management literatures—in order to 'think for themselves' about right conduct. Within such a framework, the ethics of office finds little or no place.[4]

It was precisely such supra-regional obsessions with moral autonomy and expressivism that Weber's work was concerned to negate. His theorization and description of bureaucracy as *officium* and of science and politics as vocations offer an alternative to these obsessions, indicating instead the importance and indeed indispensability of office-specific conceptions of moral agency and ethical substance. It is this that leads us to locate Weber as a late practitioner of the ethics of office as this becomes a defensive doctrine—defensive, that is, in the context of the overwhelming dominance of moral autonomy as a value criterion.

Yet, we do not have to rely only upon Weber's work to evidence the continuing significance, practically, normatively, and intellectually, of office-specific concepts of moral agency. Organizational cases as diverse as the Enron scandal and the official enquiries on both sides of the Atlantic into events surrounding the decision to go to war with Iraq have shown what happens when office-specific rights, duties, and obligations are overridden, whether in the pursuit of private policies by stealth, or, in the governmental context, as part and parcel of a demand from the central executive for more 'responsive' forms of management conduct, or from a desire to create an 'all on one team' mentality.[5]

Nor is Weber's work the only resource that might inform a reinvigorated concern in the sociological study of institutional and organizational life with what we have been describing as an ethics of office. In historical sociology, for instance, Norbert Elias's monumental two-volume, *The Civilising Process* (1978 and 1982), as well as his related *The Court Society* (1983) has much to teach about the ways in which official personae were practically assembled and for what purposes (see Van Iterson, in this volume); in the history of philosophy and political thought,

[4] It is interesting to note that for Weber, as for his early modern predecessors such as Hobbes and Pufendorf, the terms 'officious' and 'officiousness' do not carry any pejorative meaning. Quite the opposite, in fact; they commend the proper use of authority (Condren 2006*a*: 24).

[5] As the former high-ranking British civil servant Sir Michael Quinlan (2004: 128) observed, in relation to its conduct in making the case for war against Iraq, the British government exhibited

> Little interest in, or tolerance for, distinctions of function and responsibility between different categories of actor within the Government machine (except perhaps when political defences needed to be erected, as over the purported 'ownership' of the September, 2002 dossier).... [T]here was a sense of all participants—ministers, civil servants, special policy advisers, public relations handlers—being treated as part of an undifferentiated resource for the support of the central executive.

scholars such as Condren (1997, 2006*a*, *b*), Hunter (2001), and Minson (1993) have shown the importance of the ethics of office to early modern state formation, and to the conduct of the personae of the governed as well as the governing; similarly, new institutional historians such as Orren (1994, 2000), Orren and Skowronek (1994), and Novak (1996) have 'rediscovered' the discourse of office in their analyses of the role of institutions in American political development; public policy based scholars such as Chapman (1988), Rohr (1998), and Uhr (1999, 2001) have highlighted the importance of role and status-specific ethics in the realm of governmental administration; political scientists such as Dobel (1999), Sabl (2002), and Thompson (1987) have explored the political ethics of a variety of public offices; and in organization studies, new institutional theorists such as March and Olsen (1989, 2004) and those following in the footsteps of Friedland and Alford (1991) have focused, via the respective notions of the 'logic of appropriateness' and 'institutional logics', upon the ways in which role-specific forms of human action are driven by rules of exemplary behavior organized into institutions.

While it is clear that existing research in this area of office, role, or status-specific ethics is segmented and specialized, often being conducted in disciplinary or subdisciplinary 'silos', it is possible nonetheless, to suggest that there are some important general lessons to be drawn from this work for those interested in institutional and personal ethics. For instance, it is evident that both historical and contemporary analyses of office-specific ethics put into question several received assumptions of contemporary moral and management theory concerning the nature of 'the person'. As I have already indicated, an ethics of office means breaking with the habit of thinking that one among the several personae that any individual may happen to occupy in their passage through social institutions must be the fundamental form of personhood, the point of unity. Moral expressivists—whether they be philosophers like Alasdair MacIntyre (1981) or management 'gurus' such as Tom Peters (1992)—require institutions to express certain moral ideals, such as an all-pervading spirit of community or an inalienable right to personal autonomy. In making such demands, they fail to appreciate that different institutions heed different priorities, and that these differing purposes and priorities are routinely formatted into the personal dispositions and competences required of the office holders charged with fulfilling them. Given their 'regional', as opposed to supra-regional character, these personae, and their definite but limited settings, should not be left under-described. If they are, we will fail to see that each has its own history and distribution, and is directed by its own techniques and to its own ends or purposes. Conversely, it is only under-description that enables normative generalizations about 'the person' to have any (ideological) purchase—whether this is invested in the ideal of the self-directing, autonomous individual, or that of the moral community. As Weber's work indicates, to treat the plurality of modern personae as only partial realizations of an as yet to be fully realized supra-regional person is but the first step on the road to intellectual fundamentalism.

References

Amann, R. (2006). 'The Circumlocution Office: A Snapshot of Civil Service Reform'. *Political Quarterly*, 77/3: 334–59.

Armbrüster, T. (2005). 'Bureaucracy and the Controversy between Liberal Interventionism and Non-Interventionism', in P. du Gay (ed.), *The Values of Bureaucracy*. Oxford: Oxford University Press.

Bauman, Z. (1989). *Modernity and the Holocaust*. Cambridge: Polity Press.

BBC Radio 4. *Analysis* 'Miraculous Mandarins'. Broadcast Date, 25 July 2002.

Blau, P. (1956). *Bureaucracy in Modern Society*. New York: Random House.

Bogdanor, V. (2001). 'Civil Service Reform: A Critique'. *Political Quarterly*, 72/3: 291–9.

Burkitt, I. (1992). *Social Selves*. London: Sage Publications.

Cabinet Office (1999*a*). *Modernising Government*. Cm 4310. London: HMSO.

—— (1999*b*). *Vision and Values*. London: Cabinet Office.

Chapman, R. (1988). *Ethics in the British Civil Service*. London: Routledge.

—— (2004). *The Civil Service Commission 1855–1991: A Bureau Biography*. London: Taylor Francis Routledge.

Clegg, S. (1994). 'Max Weber and Contemporary Sociology of Organizations', in L. Ray and M. Reed (eds.), *Organizing Modernity*. London: Routledge.

Condren, C. (1997). 'Liberty of Office and its Defence in Seventeenth Century Political Argument'. *History of Political Thought*, 18/3: 460–82.

—— (2006*a*). *Argument and Authority in Early Modern England: The Presupposition of Oaths and Offices*. Oxford: Oxford University Press.

—— (2006*b*). 'Persona and Office in Early Modern England', in C. Condren, S. Gaukroger, and I. Hunter (eds.), *The Philosopher in Early Modern Europe: The Nature of a Contested Identity*. Cambridge: Cambridge University Press.

Crouch, C. (2004). *Post-Democracy*. Cambridge: Polity Press.

Dobel, P. (1999). *Public Integrity*. Baltimore: Johns Hopkins University Press.

Doig, A., and Wilson, R. (1998). 'What Price New Public Management?' *Political Quarterly*, 69/3: 267–76.

du Gay, P. (1994). 'Making Up Managers: Bureaucracy, Enterprise, and the Liberal Art of Separation'. *British Journal of Sociology*, 45/4: 655–74.

—— (2000). *In Praise of Bureaucracy*. London: Sage Publications.

—— (2005). 'Bureaucracy and Liberty: State, Authority and Freedom', in P. du Gay (ed.), *The Values of Bureaucracy*. Oxford: Oxford University Press.

—— (2007). *Organizing Identity: Persons and Organizations after Theory*. London: Sage Publications.

The Economist (2002). *The World in 2003*. London: *The Economist*.

Efficiency Unit (1988). *Improving Management in Government: The Next Steps*. London: HMSO.

Elias, N. (1978). *The Civilizing Process*, vol. i., *The History of Manners*. Oxford: Basil Blackwell.

—— (1982). *The Civilizing Process*, vol. ii., *State Formation and Civilization*. Oxford: Basil Blackwell.

—— (1983). *The Court Society*. Oxford: Basil Blackwell.

Friedland, R., and Alford, R. (1991). 'Bringing Society Back In: Symbols, Practices, and Institutional Contradictions', in W. W. Powell and P. DiMaggio (eds.), *The New Institutionalism in Organizational Analysis*. Chicago: Chicago University Press.

Gamble, A., and Wright, T. (eds.) (2004). *Restating the State*. Oxford: Blackwell.

Geuss, R. (2001). *History and Illusion in Politics*. Cambridge: Cambridge University Press.

Goodsell, C. (2004). *The Case for Bureaucracy*. 4th edn. Washington, DC: CQ Press.

Gordon, C. (1987). 'The Soul of the Citizen: Max Weber and Michel Foucault on Rationality and Government', in S. Whimster and S. Lash (eds.), *Max Weber, Rationality and Modernity*. London: Allen & Unwin.

Habermas, J. (1986). *The Philosophical Discourse of Modernity*. Cambridge: Polity Press.

Hennis, W. (1988). *Max Weber: Essays in Reconstruction*. London: Allen & Unwin.

—— (2000). *Max Weber's Science of Man*. Newbury: Threshold Press.

Hindess, B. (1998). 'Neo-Liberalism and National Economy', in B. Hindess and M. Dean (eds.), *Governing Australia*. Sydney: Cambridge University Press.

Höpfl, H. (2006). 'Post-Bureaucracy and Weber's "Modern" Bureaucrat'. *Journal of Organizational Change Management*, 19/1: 8–21.

Hunter, I. (1993). 'Subjectivity and Government'. *Economy & Society*, 22/1: 123–34.

—— (1994*a*). *Re-Thinking the School*. Sydney: Allen & Unwin.

—— (1994*b*). 'Metaphysics as a Way of Life'. *Economy & Society*, 23/1: 93–117.

—— (2001). *Rival Enlightenments*. Cambridge: Cambridge University Press.

Johnson, N. (1993). 'Management in Government', in M. J. Earl (ed.), *Perspectives on Management*. Oxford: Oxford University Press.

Jordan, G. (1994). 'Re-Inventing Government: But Will It Work?' *Public Administration*, 72: 21–35.

Kantorowicz, E. (1958). *The King's Two Bodies: A Study in Medieval Political Theology*. Cambridge: Cambridge University Press.

Kaufman, H. (1981). 'Fear of Bureaucracy: A Raging Pandemic?' *Public Administration Review*, 41/1: 1–9.

Lassman, P., and Speirs, R. (1994). 'Introduction', in P. Lassman and R. Speirs (eds.), *Weber: Political Writings*. Cambridge: Cambridge University Press.

Le Grand, J. (2003). *Motivation, Agency, and Public Policy*. Oxford: Oxford University Press.

Loughlin, M. (2004). *The Idea of Public Law*. Oxford: Oxford University Press.

MacIntyre, A. (1981). *After Virtue*. London: Duckworth.

March, J., and Olsen, J. (1989). *Rediscovering Institutions: The Organizational Basis of Politics*. New York: Free Press.

—— —— (2004). 'The Logic of Appropriateness'. Oslo: ARENA Working Papers WP 04/09.

Miller, D. (2005). 'What Is Best Value? Bureaucracy, Virtualism, and Local Governance', in P. du Gay (ed.), *The Values of Bureaucracy*. Oxford: Oxford University Press.

Minson, J. (1993). *Questions of Conduct*. Basingstoke: Macmillan.

—— (1998). 'Ethics in the Service of the State', in M. Dean and B. Hindess (eds.), *Governing Australia*. Sydney: Cambridge University Press.

Moe, R. (1994). 'The "Re-Inventing Government" Exercise: Misinterpreting the Problem, Misjudging the Consequences'. *Public Administration Review*, 54/2: 111–22.

Mommsen, W. (1987). 'Personal Conduct and Societal Change', in S. Whimster and S. Lash (eds.), *Max Weber, Rationality and Modernity*. London: Allen & Unwin.

Mulgan, G. (1998). *Connexity*. London: Vintage.

Novak, W. (1996). *The People's Welfare: Law and Regulation in Nineteenth Century America*. Chapel Hill: University of North Carolina Press.

Orren, K. (1994). 'The Work of Government: Rediscovering the Discourse of Office in Marbury v. Madison'. *Studies in American Political Development*, 8/1: 60–80.

—— (2000). 'Officer's Rights: Towards a Unified Field Theory of American Constitutional Development'. *Law & Society Review*, 34/4: 873–909.

—— and Skowronek, S. (1994). 'Beyond the Iconography of Order: Notes for a "New" Institutionalism', in L. Dodd and C. Jillson (eds.), *The Dynamics of American Politics: Approaches and Interpretations*. Boulder, Colo.: Westview.

Osborne, D., and Gaebler, T. (1992). *Re-Inventing Government*. Reading, Mass.: Addison-Wesley.

Painter, M. (2000). 'Contracting, the Enterprise Culture and Public Sector Ethics', in R. A. Chapman (ed.), *Ethics in Public Service for the New Millennium*. Aldershot: Ashgate.

Parker, R. (1993). *The Administrative Vocation*. Sydney: Hale and Iremonger.

Paton, R. (2003). *Managing and Measuring Social Enterprises*. London: Sage.

Peters, T. (1992). *Liberation Management*. Basingstoke: Macmillan.

Plant, R. (2003). 'A Public Service Ethic and Political Accountability'. *Parliamentary Affairs*, 56: 560–79.

Pollitt, C. (1995). 'Justification by Works or by Faith? Evaluating the New Public Management'. *Evaluation: The International Journal of Theory, Practice and Research*, 1/2: 133–54.

Power, M. (1997). *The Audit Society*. Oxford: Oxford University Press.

Quinlan, M. (2004). 'Lessons for Governmental Process', in W. G. Runciman (ed.), *Hutton and Butler: Lifting the Lid on the Workings of Power*. Oxford: British Academy/Oxford University Press.

Ritzer, G. (2004). *The MacDonaldization of Society*. Thousand Oaks, Calif.: Pine Forge Press.

Rohr, J. (1998). *Public Service, Ethics and Constitutional Practice*. Lawrence: University of Kansas Press.

—— (2000). 'Ethics, Governance and Constitutions: The Case of Baron Haussman', in R. A. Chapman (ed.), *Ethics in Public Service for the New Millennium*. Aldershot: Ashgate.

Rose, N. (1999). *Powers of Freedom*. Cambridge: Cambridge University Press.

Sabl, A. (2002). *Ruling Passions*. Princeton: Princeton University Press.

Saunders, D. (1997). *The Anti-Lawyers*. London: Routledge.

Schluchter, W. (1981). *The Rise of Western Rationalism: Weber's Developmental History*. Berkeley: University of California Press.

Scott, A. (1996). 'Bureaucratic Revolutions and Free Market Utopias'. *Economy & Society*, 25/1: 89–110.

Smart, B. (1985). *Michel Foucault*. London: Ellis Horwood/Tavistock.

Strathern, M. (2001). *Audit Cultures*. London: Routledge.

Thompson, D. (1987). *Political Ethics and Public Office*. Cambridge, Mass.: Harvard University Press.

Turner, C. (1992). *Modernity and Politics in the Work of Max Weber*. London: Routledge.

UHR, J. (1999). 'Institutions of Integrity'. *Public Integrity*, Winter: 94–106.
—— (2001). 'Public Service Ethics in Australia', in T. L. Cooper (ed.), *Handbook of Administrative Ethics*. New York: Marcel Dekker.
WALZER, M. (1984). 'Liberalism and the Art of Separation'. *Political Theory*, 12/3: 315–30.
WEBER, M. (1930). *The Protestant Ethic and the Spirit of Capitalism*. London: Harper Collins.
—— (1978). *Economy & Society*, vols. i–ii. Berkeley: University of California Press.
—— (1989). 'Science as a Vocation', in P. Lassman and I. Velody (eds.), *Max Weber's Science as a Vocation*. London: Unwin, Hyman.
—— (1994*a*). 'Parliament and Government in Germany under a New Political Order', in P. Lassman and R. Speirs (eds.), *Weber: Political Writings*. Cambridge: Cambridge University Press.
—— (1994*b*). 'The Profession and Vocation of Politics', in P. Lassman and R. Speirs (eds.), *Weber: Political Writings*. Cambridge: Cambridge University Press.
WILSON, J. Q. (2000). *Bureaucracy: What Government Agencies Do and Why They Do It*. New York: Basic Books.

CHAPTER 8

ON ORGANIZATIONS AND OLIGARCHIES

MICHELS IN THE TWENTY-FIRST CENTURY

PAMELA S. TOLBERT

SHON R. HIATT

8.1. Introduction

A central problem for those interested in studying and explaining the actions of organizations is how to conceptualize these social phenomena. In particular, because organizations are constituted by individuals, each of whom may seek to achieve his or her interests through the organization, questions of how decisions are made in organizations and whose preferences drive those decisions are critical to explaining organizational actions. Although early organizational scholars spent much time wrestling with these questions (e.g. Barnard 1938; Simon 1947; Parsons 1956; March and Simon 1958), more recent work in organizational studies has tended to elide them, adopting an implicit view of organizations as unitary actors, much like individuals, and in particular, like individuals who operate with a coherent utility function that they seek to maximize (e.g. Porter 1985; Baum *et al.* 2005; Casciaro and Piskorski 2005; Mezias and

Boyle 2005; Jensen 2006). Thus, organizational behavior is seen as reflecting efforts to achieve a specific goal, which is, presumably, that of enhancing the organization's interests.

While this may be the dominant conceptualization underlying much contemporary research, other work sharply questions the validity and usefulness of this approach to organizational analysis (March and Simon 1958; Cohen, March, and Olsen 1972; Jackall 1988). Studies in this tradition suggest that it is more appropriate in most instances to conceive of organizations as battlefields, constituted by shifting factions with differing interests that vie for control of the organization; hence, organizational actions should be viewed as reflecting the preferences of a victorious coalition at a given point in time. We suspect that, although most people's experience in organizations may make them sympathetic to the coalitional view and skeptical of the unitary actor view, the continuing predilection for the latter stems at least in part from problems of deriving systematic predictions of organizational behavior from a more chaotic, coalitional kaleidoscope perspective.

A different model of organizations is represented in the work of Robert Michels (1876–1936), who, nearly a century ago, offered his now-famous, pithy summary of the fundamental nature of organizations ([1911] 1962: 365): 'Who says organization, says oligarchy.' Drawing on his own experiences with early twentieth-century German political party organizations, Michels presented the drift to oligarchy as an 'iron law', inevitably resulting in the division of even the most expressly democratic organizations into two parts: a small stable set of elites and all the other members. His analysis offered a catalog of the processes and forces that produced such a division, and he postulated that the directives of the elite, while nominally reflecting the set of interests shared by all members, in actuality are driven by their own personal interests in the organization. His provocative (and very pessimistic) arguments have served as the basis for many studies over the years, particularly of organizations specifically formed to represent the interests of groups seeking to promote change in political arenas. Much of this work has been focused on assessing the purported inevitability of the emergence of oligarchies and defining the conditions of the iron law—i.e. those that affect the realization (or suppression) of oligarchic tendencies.

In this chapter, we argue that Michels's core arguments about the nature of oligarchies in organizations, and research generated in response to his work, are not only relevant to understanding the dynamics of political organizations but can be extended as a useful framework for thinking about important aspects of contemporary economic corporations as well. In making this argument, we highlight the parallels between Berle and Means's analysis (1932) of modern, publicly held corporations and that of Michels. Both analyses address the general organizational problem of ensuring representation of members' interests. In political organizations, it is the rank-and-file members' interests that leaders are charged with representing; in publicly held organizations, leaders are primarily responsible for representing the interests of stockholders, as the nominal 'owners' of the firm. In this context, we consider evidence and research on problematic corporate behavior to show how Michels's work provides a useful framework for understanding these problems and for formulating ways of addressing them.

8.2. Where Do Oligarchies Come From?

Michels's interest in the problems of oligarchy stemmed directly from his own experiences in the left-wing German Social Democratic party, which he joined as a university student and served in various administrative roles for several years. Michels became progressively disenchanted with the party, and particularly with the leaders, whom he viewed as cynically building a highly undemocratic political machine while mobilizing members based on a platform of increasing social equality and democracy. This ultimately led him to dissolve his relationship with the party, but his prior affiliation took a toll on his career prospects as a faculty member in the conservative circles of early twentieth-century German academia. Despite the sponsorship of Max Weber, his friend and intellectual mentor, he was unable to obtain a position in Germany and was forced to take a position at the University of Turin in Italy (Gerth and Mills 1946: 19). Convinced of the impossibility of sustaining truly democratic organizations, he eventually became a supporter of Benito Mussolini, on the grounds that strong leaders were most effective (Collins and Makowsky 2005).

His analysis of oligarchy in organizations clearly reflects his own experience in political and academic organizations. Ironically, he argued, it is the very success of organizations that sets in motion the evolutionary forces towards oligarchy. As organizations grow, the ability of members to participate directly in decision-making becomes progressively more constrained for a variety of reasons. At the most fundamental level, problems of finding times and places for all members to assemble for discussion of issues and decision making increase exponentially as the number of participants increases. In addition, his description of decision making in large groups foreshadows the sorts of social-psychological dynamics later elaborated by Janis's (1971) discussion of groupthink: 'It is a fact of everyday experience that enormous public meetings commonly carry resolutions by acclamation or by general assent, whilst these same assemblies, if divided into small assemblies... would be much more guarded in their assent' (Michels 1962: 64).

Organizational growth eventually requires delegating responsibility for most decision making to a small subset of members. Michels notes that such delegation is often done with great reluctance and the freedom of the delegates to make decisions without general membership approval may be sharply curtailed. Such restrictions, however, typically negate the advantages of delegation. Coleman (1974: 38–9) describes this problem well in the following extended discussion:

> When men join together to create a corporate actor, whether it is an industrial corporation, a trade union, a neighbourhood association, or a political party, they find themselves confronted with a dilemma: to gain the benefits of organization, they must give over the use of certain rights, resources or power to the corporate body.... But each person, in turning over these rights, thereby loses a large measure of control over them. For the corporate actor may well act in a direction that he opposes.... There is one apparent remedy for this: to create a constitution such that the corporate resources can be committed only when *all* corporators favour the action. This gives each person a veto power over corporate action. The defect of this solution, of course, is that the corporate actor is emasculated: it can do nothing in the absence of unanimity of the members.

In consequence, efforts to assert effective membership control typically are abandoned, and the delegates are increasingly empowered to set agendas with little input from members, to offer recommendations for action with only brief expositions of rationales, and to make decisions on behalf of all members.

Moreover, organizational growth almost always induces increased complexity—the creation of separate, specialized positions and offices to carry out different tasks—and this leads to a need for in-depth, hard-to-gain knowledge of the organization in order to carry out administrative functions (Blau, Heydebrand, and Stauffer 1966; Hall, Johnson, and Haas 1967; Pugh *et al.* 1968.) Increased complexity, in turn, gives rise to problems of coordination among task-interdependent subunits, which often lead to the development of formal rules and other more tacit integrative procedures (Lawrence and Lorsch 1967; Donaldson 1996; Sine, Mitsuhashi, and Kirsch 2006). Because mastery of these formal and informal rules, on which the day-to-day running of the organization rests, requires skills and experience that are not readily available among the rank-and-file members, the leaders of the organization gain additional power over the latter and increased freedom to direct the organization as they see fit. Control of such 'administrative secrets' makes it difficult for members to question, let alone effectively challenge, decisions made by the leaders. Since this knowledge accumulates with tenure, the longer the tenure of the leaders, the more costly and difficult it is to replace them. Formal responsibility for managing communications within the organization, as well as those involving the representation of the organization to the outside world, further enhances leaders' power vis-à-vis other members. As a result of these combined sources of power, Michels notes (1962: 70), 'Thus the leaders, who were at first no more than the executive organs of the collective will, soon emancipate themselves from the mass and become independent of its control.'

As leaders acquire more specialized, insider knowledge of the organization, they are also likely to acquire vested interests in maintaining their positions within the organization. Michels underscored the importance of leaders' material interests in motivating their behavior (1962: 207): '[T]hey hold firmly to their positions for economic reasons, coming to regard the functions they exercise as theirs by inalienable right...loss of their positions would be a financial disaster'. Thus, rather than making administrative decisions aimed at maximizing the nominal goals of the organization (those identified with the interests of the rank-and-file members), the leaders are inclined to govern in a way that ensures a flow of benefits specifically to themselves. And as their economic fortunes become tied to the survival of the organization, they become progressively disinclined to take actions that could lead to state or general social sanctioning, and to the ultimate disbanding of the organization. Sociologists have often referred to this (rather euphemistically) as a problem of 'goal displacement' or 'goal transformation' (Selznick 1943; Zald and Ash 1966; Jenkins 1977; Osterman 2006).[1]

Recognizing common interests in maintaining their positions, leaders begin to exhibit social solidarity, protecting each other against any and all efforts by lower level members to dislodge or discipline them. Serious challenges to the power and perpetuation of leaders in office that are led by insurgent members, if not readily suppressed, are typically dealt with through a process of cooptation: the heads of the insurgency are brought into the inner leadership circle. The larger membership, deprived of its own independent leaders, is thus effectively hobbled in its resistance to the established leadership.

In line with this, Michels (1962: 127) postulated the development of a sharp psychological as well as social division between the leaders and members. There is a clear connection in this part of Michels's analysis to Marx's and Weber's notion of class-based social action (with organizational leaders as a *klasse für sich*). Organizations are portrayed as inevitably divided into an elite group and others, with the elites having material interests that are distinct from, and at least partially opposed to, those of the others. The activities of the larger membership are directed and exploited by the elite for the latter's benefit. Thus, Michels's analysis points to the use of a class-based model in explaining and analyzing organizational behavior (see Hinings and Tolbert 2008 for a discussion of such models within an institutional theoretic approach).

[1] While the defining features of oligarchies, in Michels's sense, have been subject to some dispute, several authors have argued that the concentration of resources in the hands of a small subset of a group, and the use of the resources specifically for the subset's benefit, is a critical element (see Cassinelli 1953; Acemoglu and Robinson 2007).

8.3. Are Oligarchies Inevitable? Evidence from Political Organizations

Over the years, this model has served as a key point of departure for scholars interested in studying various forms of democratically oriented organizations, from trade unions to economic cooperatives to social movements. Much of this work has aimed at identifying the limits to the iron law—that is, the conditions that may mitigate the drift towards oligarchic control.

8.3.1. Research on Unions

One of the best-known works in this tradition (perhaps *the* best known) is the historical analysis of the International Typographical Union (ITU), conducted by Lipset, Trow, and Coleman (1956) in the decade following World War II. Based on the claim that the ITU represented a rare, but clear exception to Michels's postulate of the inevitability of oligarchy (as evidenced by the maintenance of two distinct opposing political factions within the union, relatively frequent turnover in the union's key offices, and active participation and interest by members in union politics), the authors sought to identify aspects of the organization that had contributed to its exceptionalism. Their answer locates the maintenance of the organization's democratic functioning in unique events in the union's historical development, which gave rise to a culture in which contention was legitimate; this culture was maintained by certain structural features of the organization and by occupationally based informal social relations.

Structural features of the organization that supported the culture of democratic conflict included members' right to use referenda to bring issues to a vote (preventing leaders from complete agenda-setting control), minimal differences in the salaries of union officials and members (reducing leaders' economic interests in continued office-holding), and direct election of union leaders (versus selection of leaders by a smaller subset of representatives, whose votes could be more easily corralled). In addition, the union was characterized by very dense interpersonal ties and patterns of interactions among the members, due in part to the odd working hours and conditions of printers' work that fostered social relations with other occupational members. Such relations prompted frequent informal discussions of union politics, thus contributing to members' ongoing interest and participation.

Although the analysis of the ITU offers intriguing insights into conditions that may help check tendencies towards oligarchic drift, it is impossible to disentangle the relative contributions of the different countervailing factors. It is worth noting, however, that work on producer cooperatives points to some of the same organizational factors as counter valences to oligarchic tendencies as union studies. We turn next to this literature.

8.3.2. Research on Producer Cooperatives

Based on research on a variety of collectivist organizations (those that are employee-owned and dedicated to the maintenance of members' democratic control), Rothschild-Whitt (1979) proposed an ideal type of such organizations, defined by core characteristics. The most elemental of these is the refusal to take the initial step that Michels identified as the foundation of oligarchy: delegation of authority. In enduring collectivist organizations, she argued, all key decisions are made collectively and require consensual agreement of all members (1979: 512). Many of the other characteristics in her model flow from this fundamental property, including: minimal formal rules, selection of members with similar, homogeneous values, and a minimum of specialization and division of labor.

While severely limiting the delegation of authority may be feasible only in a very small set of organizations, other characteristics linked to membership control in her proposed model are similar to those suggested by the ITU study. For example, she suggested that the minimization of reward differentials among the membership, and lack of opportunities for individual career advancement contributed to a focus on collective interests. This parallels Lipset *et al.*'s observations of the beneficial effects of limiting the differences in the compensation of the union leaders and the rank and file. An additional characteristic of collectivist organizations identified in her analysis, one that is relevant to Michels's arguments about 'administrative secrets' enhancing leaders' power, is the demystification of expertise through the rotation of jobs among members and through a culture that encouraged the sharing of special knowledge possessed by individual members. This relates to a key debate within the literature on social movement organizations (SMOs), concerning the impact of professional leadership on SMOs' change efforts.

8.3.3. Research on Social Movement Organizations

Clearly reflecting the influence of Michels's legacy, a handful of early studies of social movements focused specifically on the transformation of movements into bureaucratic organizations and the accompanying transformation of movement goals. One exemplar of this tradition is a study of The March of Dimes, a movement begun in the 1930s, which mobilized thousands of volunteers over a twenty-year period to obtain support for medical research on polio (Sills 1957). The study documented the way in which the discovery of a vaccine in the 1950s for the disease led to a crisis within the organization, which by that time had developed a full-time administrative staff, entered into long-term contracts for facilities, and gained considerable expertise in managing volunteer employees. Rather than disbanding with the achievement of its objective, the organization redefined its goals as raising funds to combat birth defects, a much broader and presumably less easily achieved goal (see also Messinger 1955; Zald and Denton 1963 for similar case studies of the transformation of social movements into organizations, and the accompanying transformation in mission).

Although rarely made explicit in these analyses, the suggestion that, at base, such transformations are probably driven largely by the leaders' own interests in perpetuating the organization lurks very close to the surface. But specific concern with the exploitation of the rank and file by the leaders as a part of such transformation, made clear in Michels's analysis, is much less evident. This is also true of more contemporary work in this tradition, which has centered on a debate over the relative advantages and costs of professional, more centralized leadership in social movement organizations.

This debate has its roots in the emergence of the theoretical tradition of resource mobilization in the 1970s, which drew attention to a largely neglected issue in the literature—the organizational properties of effective movements (Gamson 1975; McCarthy and Zald 1977; Tilly 1978). Within this context, researchers renewed attention to the question raised in earlier work of the conditions that fostered a more participatory form of movement organization (versus a more professionalized, oligarchic form) and opened a debate on the relative costs and benefits of these different forms.

In the first flush of the anti-corporate, anti-bureaucratic ideology that blossomed in the 1960s and early 1970s, many new movements in the United States sought to maintain membership control through consciously minimizing formal organization and hierarchical delegation of authority in particular. Some soon rediscovered the validity of Michels's suggestion that high levels of participatory control can pose severe constraints on collective action (Freeman 1972) and came to view often ineffective participatory arrangements as part of a cultural identity that they shunned (Polleta 2002; Clemens and Minkoff 2004).[2] Perhaps partly in response to this (and certainly in line with it), the professionalization of social movements—the development of a group of essentially freelance administrators with experience both in organizing protest activities and fund-raising for political causes—emerged as a distinctive trend by the mid-1970s (McCarthy and Zald 1977; Jenkins 1977; Gelb and Palley 1982), one that was easily identified with potential problems of oligarchy.

In this context, researchers soon became embroiled in a debate over the relative merits and costs of more professionalized control of social movements, with some research suggesting that this resulted in the cooptation and de-radicalization

[2] Despite this perception, Clemens's (1993) research provides persuasive evidence that participatory forms are not necessarily ineffective, but may require that participants have sufficient personal and social resources needed for non-hierarchical coordination of actions.

of movements in terms of both tactics and goals (e.g. Piven and Cloward 1977; McAdam 1983), and others arguing that such conservative effects were far from inevitable (Jenkins 1977; Ruecht 1999), and that even when professionalization did lead to greater conservatism, it also helped to prevent the movement's complete dissolution (Staggenborg 1988). Unfortunately, this debate has been cast largely in oppositional terms—that is, the guiding question has been whether the professionalization of movement leadership generally has a positive or negative effect on the maintenance and achievement of the initial movement goals. Consequently, it provides few insights into the conditions that may mitigate or exacerbate professionalization's impact on these outcomes or on leadership entrenchment. One exception to this is provided by a study by Osterman (2006, which examined the mechanisms that allowed a social change-oriented non-government organization (NGO) with a highly bureaucratized, oligarchically structured leadership to maintain high levels of involvement by the volunteer workers in the organization. His analysis suggests that this was the result of training provided to volunteers that encouraged and facilitated their participation, and thus gave rise to a culture in which discussion of (and dissension from) established policies was valued and accepted.

As noted, though, the literature on social movement organizations has shown a surprising lack of concern with a key issue raised by Michels, leaders' propensity to exploit the organization specifically for their own gain. This issue has been engaged, however, in a very different context, an analysis of changes in economic organizations that was first laid out in the early 1930s.

8.4. Extending Michels to Economic Organizations

As suggested at the outset of this chapter, a Michelsian view of the nature of organizations is in many respects quite consistent with the analysis of Adolf Berle and Gardiner Means, a lawyer and an economist, respectively, whose classic work, *The Modern Corporation and Private Property* (1932), addressed some of the implications of the replacement of owner-directed firms by managerially directed firms as dominant organizational forms in the American economy.[3] We now turn to consider Berle and Means's basic thesis, along with analyses that have sought to address their arguments, offered primarily by economists under the banner of agency theory.

[3] Roy (1997) provides a very provocative and compelling account of the historical processes that enabled large publicly held corporations to dominate the US economy by the time Berle and Means offered their analysis.

Writing in the early throes of the economy-shaking depression of the 1930s, Berle and Means focused on two major trends that distinguished the economic landscape of the period from earlier eras. The first was the increasing flow of capital into a smaller and smaller set of firms that were, necessarily, becoming clearly distinguished in both size and economic power from other firms. The second was the dispersal of ownership of these firms through the purchase of shares by larger and larger numbers of individuals; as a consequence, most stockholders held only a small fraction of a company's total shares, and their exercise of stockholder power (e.g. through selling off their shares) generally had no discernible effect on the functioning of the organization.

As a result, they argued, top-level managers of these organizations were no longer constrained to follow the wishes of stockholders, the nominal owners of the firm, and were empowered to run it in ways that they saw fit—which were likely to entail enhancement of their own positions, either through continuing organizational growth (allowing them to derive both greater status and compensation from their positions) or through siphoning off resources from the firm via various corporate perks for managers (represented as part of normal, if perhaps not absolutely necessary, business operations) or both. In their words:

> In its new aspect the corporation is a means whereby the wealth of innumerable individuals has been concentrated into huge aggregates and whereby control over this wealth has been surrendered to a unified direction. The power attendant upon such concentration has brought forth princes of industry, whose position in the community is yet to be defined... The direction of industry by persons other than those who have ventured their wealth has raised the question of the motive force back of such direction and the effective distribution of the returns from business enterprise. ([1932] 1991: 4)

Much of their discussion of the nature of stockholders' loss of control over the firm's direction focused on the way in which managers are elected by stockholders. This typically entails ratification of a slate of candidates chosen by the board of directors—who are themselves originally selected by top managers—through proxy votes. As they note, the slate (unsurprisingly) is usually composed of existing management members. In the absence of social connections and organization among stockholders, it is virtually impossible for any significant voting block to emerge to change the selection process, resulting in a 'self-perpetuating oligarchy' (Mizruchi 2004: 581). The similarity of this depiction to Michels's discussion of the machinations of leadership groups to preserve the illusion of democracy while perpetuating themselves in office is noteworthy.

In addition to their role in selecting the board of directors, Berle and Means also alluded to the ability of managers to control information about and communications within organizations as an element of their autonomy from stockholder control. They observe that management 'may issue financial statements of a misleading character or distribute informal news items which further its own market manipulations' ([1932] 1991: 115). Although not elaborated, this observation offers a parallel to Michels's arguments about control of information as a source of leadership power.

Also like Michels, Berle and Means suggest that the interests of the management (leaders) commonly diverge from those of the stockholder owners (rank and file). They catalog some of the ways in which such diverging interests may be manifested, a catalog that is particularly interesting in light of some of the organizational debacles of the early twenty-first century:

> Profits may be shifted from a parent corporation to a subsidiary in which the controlling group has a large interest. Particularly profitable business may be diverted to a second corporation largely owned by the controlling group.... When it comes to the questions of distributing such profits as are made, self-seeking control may strive to divert profit from one class of stock to another, if, as frequently occurs, it holds interests in the latter issue. In market operations, such control may use 'inside information' to buy low from present stockholders and sell high to future stockholders. ([1932] 1991: 115)

Although they made a prima facie case for the existence of diverging interests between managers and owners, and outlined the mechanisms that could allow this divergence to be enacted, Berle and Means offered little in the way of empirical support for such. Despite voluminous documentation for other main points of their argument, such as the concentration of resources in key organizations and the dispersion of stock ownership, the only evidence provided for a divergence in the interests of owners and control (managers) consisted of a list of railroads sent into receivership as a result of financial mismanagement during a fifteen-year period around the turn of the twentieth century (see [1932]1991: 115 n. 2). Later, more systematic research on this issue, based on the comparison of the economic performance of management-controlled and owner-controlled firms, turned up mixed evidence. While several studies found that profits and productivity were positively related to the concentration of stockholding (Monsen, Chiu, and Cooley 1968; Holl 1977; Hill and Snell 1989), others failed to turn up such a relation (Kamerschen 1968; Demsetz and Lehn 1985).

The latter results are consistent with one line of work, known as agency theory, whose main tenets were initially proposed by economists in response to Berle and Means's arguments. Classic work in this tradition acknowledges the potential divergence in the interests of stockholding owners (principals) and managers (agents of the principals), and focuses on identifying mechanisms that ensure agents do in fact run the firm in ways that are in concert with the principals' interests (Jensen and Meckling 1976; Fama and Jensen 1983; see also Davis 2005). Such mechanisms include designing managerial incentives to align their behavior with the interests of principals (e.g. through the provision of stockownership to managers) and removing managers whose firms are underperforming, either through direct dismissal by the board of directors or as a result of takeovers by other firms and investors. As

Mizruchi (2004: 586) notes, however, these mechanisms have some noticeable costs from the standpoint of stockholders (see also Davis and Thompson 1994), and there is a fair amount of evidence, from a variety of sources, that suggests that they may be less than effective, for some of the reasons suggested by Michels.

8.5. Are Managers' Interests Aligned with Stockholders' Interests? Symptoms of Oligarchic Problems in Modern Businesses

The faltering performance of many US firms in the face of increasing global competition in the 1980s created a context in which agency theorists' recommendations for increasing managerial stockholding as a means of dealing with problems of the separation of ownership and control were well received. Firms' relatively poor economic showing was often attributed to managers' lack of incentives to maximize shareholder value. In response, many firms undertook significant revisions in their managerial compensation practices, and in particular, increased stockholding as a component of executive pay. In larger companies today, salary represents a little less than 10 percent of CEOs' total compensation on average; the bulk of compensation is derived from bonuses and the exercise of stock options (Simon 2007; see also Gerhart and Rynes 2003; Murphy 1999).[4]

8.5.1. Effects of Stock Options and Ownership

Despite efforts to align managers' and shareholders' interests through managerial stock ownership and stock options, one does not need to look far to find examples of apparently significant misalignment. One part of the explanation for this is that top managers differ from average shareholders in one very key respect: the possession of specific, private information about the firm's plans and functioning—or 'administrative secrets' in Michels's terms. While the use of such knowledge in making decisions about selling or buying company stock is technically illegal, as insider trading, this is often hard to regulate, although there are some notable recent

[4] Stock options refer to the right to purchase a fixed amount of a company's stock at a given price (the strike price, or exercise price). Executives may profit from stock options by purchasing and then selling stocks when the current value exceeds the strike price (see Gerhart and Rynes 2003 for a useful discussion of stock options as an element of compensation).

cases of top management prosecution for such activities. One example is provided by the case of Joseph Nacchio, former CEO of Qwest Communications, who is scheduled to go on trial (at the time of this writing) for forty-two counts of insider trading. In 2001 Nacchio sold $100.8 million in shares, knowing that the company's financial woes were mounting and while presiding over an accounting scandal that led to a restated loss of $2.48 billion in revenue for 2000 and 2001 (Lattman and Searcey 2007). Likewise, in the infamous debacle of the Enron Corporation, CEO Kenneth Lay and other top managers began selling off their company stock months before the firm's downward performance spiral became public knowledge, while its value was still high. Lay was later prosecuted for insider trading, in addition to conspiracy and fraud (McLean and Elkind 2004; US Securities and Exchange Commission 2004).

Moreover, the decision-making power of top managers enables them to take actions that other stockholders cannot, in ways that can adversely affect the others. This issue is reflected in the current controversy swirling around the issue of backdating stock options.[5] This practice, apparently widespread before the passage of the Sarbane-Oxley Act in 2002 (Lie 2005), has resulted in serious economic fallouts in a variety of firms. An example is provided by KB Homes, a homebuilding company whose CEO, Bruce Karatz, was ranked among the top five in Forbes' yearly CEO Compensation Ranking for several years. Karatz became the target of a criminal probe by the Securities and Exchange Commission (SEC) for allegedly backdating his options to increase his pay by $41 million. In response to protests by KB's shareholders to this alleged abuse, Karatz resigned and agreed to forfeit approximately $13 million in options (Corkery and Forelle 2007). (It is worth noting, however, that he also began collecting a $175 million exit package. The widespread provision of exit packages to executives is discussed below.) Research in Motion, Ltd. (RIM), the maker of Blackberry hand-held devices, offers another example. The company announced in early 2007 that stock-options backdating going back to the 1990s would lead to a financial restatement showing earnings reduced by $250 million. The co-CEOs of RIM both agreed to pay about $4.25 million of the amount back to 'to assist RIM in defraying costs' while two board members on the compensation committee resigned without public comment (Vascellaro 2007). And in a third, especially spectacular case, the top managers of Comverse Technology reportedly created fictitious employee names to generate hundreds of thousands of backdated options and then stashed them in a secret slush fund entitled I. M. Fanton (after *Phantom of the Opera*)(Bray 2007).

[5] Backdating of stock options involves granting an employee stock option with a date that is prior to the time the option was actually granted—typically a date on which the price of the stock was relatively very low. This right to purchase stocks, with knowledge of their actual future profitability, is clearly something that average stockholders lack, although it is not necessarily illegal. Backdating may require earnings restatements which can cause a company's stock values to plunge.

Evidence indicates that these are far from isolated cases. By May 2007, the *Wall Street Journal* reported that over 160 companies were under accounting investigation by the SEC involving financial restatements totaling billions of dollars (Hughes 2007), leaving thousands of shareholders with plummeting revenues and asset values. More than a dozen executives have been indicted for illegal backdating, although only a handful have been actually convicted.

Thus, whether compensation that emphasizes the allocation of stock ownership and stock options to managers effectively aligns their interests with those of other stockholders, as agency theorists have argued, seems open to question. While a number of studies have found an overall positive relation between rates of managerial stockholding and firm performance (e.g. Morck, Shleifer, and Vishny 1988; McConnell and Servaes 1990; Mehran 1995), this research also suggests puzzling non-linear effects that are inconsistent with agency theorists' predictions. Other research has found changes in managerial ownership to have very little effect on firm performance (Himmelberg, Hubbard, and Palia 1999). The link between the size of managerial stock options and firm performance is even more equivocal (Kole 1997; Hall and Liebman 1998; Hall and Murphy 2000). Since there is reason to expect the effects of stock options to differ from actual stock ownership, the relatively weak effects of options on firm performance are not altogether surprising (Sanders 2001).

8.5.2. Effects of Market and Board Discipline

Similarly, a second mechanism posited to mitigate the effects of the separation of ownership and control, the 'market for corporate control' (the removal of top managers of a poorly performing firm following its acquisition by another firm), has been greatly blunted by the widespread adoption of 'poison pills' and 'golden parachutes' among large companies. Poison pills are stock-issuing arrangements that substantially increase the costs of taking over a firm; these require acquiring firms to pay inflated dividends to the takeover target's current stockholders. Poison pills were initially put in place by some firms in response to the wave of corporate raiding in the early 1980s; by the 1990s, the majority of large companies had adopted this defensive strategy (Davis 1991; Davis and Greve 1997). Golden parachutes are less directly aimed at preventing takeovers, but they serve to protect managers from adverse economic consequences if they are terminated or quit because of unanticipated events (including takeovers) by providing lucrative severance pay and other benefits. Interestingly, one of the justifications for such arrangements parallels Michels's observation that top-level elites seek to perpetuate themselves in office because of the financial benefits they derive. It is argued that golden parachutes discourage top managers from blocking takeovers that are in the interests of other stockholders just to preserve their own jobs (West Publishing Company 1998).

However, it appears that these arrangements often entail significant costs to stockholders—and in today's corporate environment these costs may be higher than those associated with managerial resistance to takeovers. Big awards paid out to exiting executives, notwithstanding poor performance, have infuriated investors. Despite the fact that Pfizer's stock declined nearly 37 percent during his five-year tenure, CEO Henry McKinnell was still awarded an exit package of over $200 million in 2006 (Thurm and Lublin 2006). That same year, Robert Nardelli received a $210 million severance package upon being fired from his head post at Home Depot. Nardelli received an annual compensation of over $127 million, yet Home Depot's stock price failed to increase at all during his seven-year tenure (Mui 2007).

Such revelations have inspired grass-roots movements among shareholders to increase executive accountability. From August 2006 to May 2007, over sixty companies voted on shareholder proposals that would give investors a nonbinding vote at the board level on executive compensation packages, although these 'say-on-pay' proposals have so far won the majority of shareholder votes in only two companies. It is doubtful that many companies will voluntarily adopt such proposals (Whitehouse 2007). However, in April 2007, the House began debating a bill that would give shareholders a nonbinding vote on the pay packages of senior executives as well as a right to vote on any golden parachute compensation plans (Labaton 2007).

Both the grass-roots and legislative efforts to address problems of apparent divergence in the interests of management and other stockholders would be unnecessary if the third mechanism, oversight of management by the boards of directors, were more effective. Although directors are legally charged with representing shareholders' interests by monitoring executive decisions and actions, academic research, as well as reporting by the popular press, suggest that efforts by boards to exercise real discipline over management are normally quite limited.

Research highlights a number of factors that are especially likely to enhance the power of organizational executives and limit board control.[6] CEO duality, the assignment of CEO and board chairman responsibilities to the same individual, is perhaps the most notorious of these factors. Duality enables the organizational leader to command greater authority over board members by reducing the monitoring effectiveness of outside board members (Harrison, Torres, and Kukalis 1988; Wade, O'Reilly, and Chandratat 1990; Finkelstein 1992) and by making it more difficult for inside board members to act independently of the CEO (Westphal and Zajac 1995). As Jensen (1993: 36) noted, 'The function of the chairman is to run board

[6] To say that there is a vast literature on boards of directors and the distribution of power within corporations is to understate the case significantly. We consider only a relatively small part of this literature, just to provide a sense of why board control may be problematic.

meetings and oversee the process of hiring, firing, evaluating and compensating the CEO. Clearly the CEO cannot perform this function apart from his or her personal interest. Without the direction of an independent leader, it is much more difficult for the board to perform its critical function.'

Studies have linked duality to the questionable practice of re-pricing options that are 'underwater', where the strike price is greater than the stock's current value (Pollock, Fischer, and Wade 2002), to higher levels of executive compensation overall (Westphal and Zajac 1995), to greater incidences of fraudulent financial reporting (O'Connor *et al.* 2006), and to a greater likelihood of white-collar crime (Schnatterly 2003). In a similar way, CEOs are also likely to have greater power vis-à-vis the board when they are organizational incumbents, i.e. have risen through the ranks of the company to their position. Incumbency enables CEOs to form strong coalitions with other company executives as well as social ties with board members. In line with Michels's notion of the unification of elites, research has shown that CEOs have a significantly lower probability of being dismissed under these conditions (Shen and Cannella 2002).

Some evidence suggests that boards whose members are demographically similar to the CEO are more likely to take actions that enhance the CEO's position. For example, a study by Westphal and Zajac (1997) indicated that the more board members share key demographic characteristics with the CEO, the less likely they are to put contingent compensation practices in place for the CEO. Along similar lines, research by Hallock (1997) showed that demographic similarity between board members and the CEO was associated with significantly higher levels of CEO pay. These advantages may be a key reason that more powerful CEOs are more likely to replace board members with ones who are similar to themselves than less powerful CEOs (Westphal and Zajac 1995; Zajac and Westphal 1996; see also Duguid 2006).

Finally, a number of studies have found a positive impact of executive tenure on CEO power (Wade, O'Reilly, and Chandratat 1990; Ocasio 1994). Again, in line with Michels's arguments, it appears that as length in office increases, CEOs acquire expert power through an increased familiarity with the firm's resources (Zald 1969) and personal power by appointing boards with supporters (Finkelstein and Hambrick 1989). Research suggests that longer CEO tenure empowers top managers to secure larger compensation packages, participate less in contingent compensation practices (Westphal and Zajac 1994; Westphal and Zajac 1995), and avoid being dismissed (Ocasio 1994) and replaced by inside succession (Shen and Cannella 2002).

Thus, there is clearly reason to question the extent to which existing interest-aligning mechanisms succeed in minimizing the divergence of managers' and stockholders' interests in contemporary business organizations, and preclude the occurrence of the kinds of problems of oligarchic control and leadership exploitation suggested by Michels's model of organizations. In the following section, we consider the implications of this model for further research on firms and for policy.

8.6. Michels's Legacy: Implications for Studying and Managing Contemporary Business Organizations

The preceding summary of the various problems that often have been identified with contemporary corporate management is intended to provide some graphic illustrations of the kinds of phenomena to which Michels's concepts and arguments might be applied. To make use of his analysis more systematically, however, there are a number of conceptual issues that will require further development. One primary issue for research involves the construction of both theoretical and operational definitions of oligarchy. A second issue entails thinking through the implications for policy and ongoing efforts at corporate reform. At this juncture, we can only identify some of the issues that seem most critical to us on each of these fronts and offer some initial thoughts on handling them.

8.6.1. Research Implications

At first blush, both theoretical and operational definitions of the phenomenon to which Michels draws attention would seem to involve a categorical state: either an organization is characterized by oligarchy or it is not. However, we suspect that, in the long run, it will be more useful to work on definitions and related measures that are continuous—that is, to treat oligarchy as a matter of degree. Although Michels does not define the concept specifically, his analysis suggests a number of different dimensions that are relevant.

One is, obviously, concentration of decision-making power in the hands of a relatively small subset of organizational members, or a high level of centralization, in the parlance of organizational theory. Thus, the degree of centralization would be one component of a definition of the degree of oligarchy. Unfortunately, while there is a long and venerable tradition of research on this aspect of structure (see Hall and Tolbert 2004; Scott and Davis 2007), this has not led to significant agreement on how best to measure it, and this issue merits more attention from organizational researchers.

A second dimension involves the entrenchment of a leadership group, or the stability of this group (i.e. longer average tenure would serve as a component indicator of a higher degree of oligarchy). Although much work on managerial entrenchment has focused simply on CEO tenure (e.g. Wade, O'Reilly, and Chandratat 1990; Westphal and Zajac 1995), we argue that using information on the top management team is preferable, since it is possible that turnover among CEOs as a result of scapegoating (Boeker 1992) may obscure the amount of stability that actually exists in the leadership group. In empirical studies, the degree of stability is apt to be partly a function of the parameters used to define this group.

In general, more objective criteria seem preferable to us, as well as ones that produce groups of a fairly consistent size. One pragmatic (albeit admittedly arbitrary) approach would be to use the top five managers, since standard archival resources often contain information on these (e.g. Hoover's *Complete Guide to U.S. Public Companies*), including length of tenure. An alternative—or additional—component of the operationalization of entrenchment might be the frequency of inside succession to the CEO position, based on the assumption that inside succession signals a more entrenched leadership group.

Yet a third dimension suggested by Michels is the degree to which leaders are insulated from control by the rank and file. In the context of contemporary economic organizations, this is most likely to involve relations between top managers and the board of directors, since by law, managers are charged with acting in the fiduciary interests of stockholders, and the board is charged with ensuring such.[7] It is common to use the proportion of outsiders on the board (those not employed by an organization) as a reverse indicator of leadership insulation (Westphal and Zajac 1997: 512), based on the assumption that such directors will be more likely to question a CEO's decisions. Indeed, one of the key recommendations for corporate reform has been to require more outside directors (Fama and Jensen 1983), though the evidence on whether such directors actually ensure CEOs' and managers' commitment to stockholder interests is equivocal (see e.g. Wade, O'Reilly, and Chandratat 1990; Duguid 2006). Alternative indicators might include CEO duality, or the appointment of the current CEO as board chair, and/or the proportion of board members appointed by the current CEO.

Although individual dimensions (and even single measures) could serve as indicators of oligarchy in empirical studies, the development of a multidimensional measure is conceptually more defensible for examining the validity of Michels's arguments. Such examinations could focus on the relationship between the measure of oligarchy and an array of outcomes suggested in the preceding review of corporate problems, including firms' adoption of arrangements that often benefit

[7] Note that Berle and Means considered the board to be part of the management structure: 'direction of the activities of the corporation is exercised through the board of directors' (quoted in Mizruchi 2004: 591). Although we appreciate the logic of this argument, we think it is more useful to conceptualize the board as representatives of stockholders—that is its legal function.

managers but provide questionable value to shareholders (such as poison pills and golden parachutes), the frequency of backdating of stock options by managerial members, increasing executive compensation in the face of declining firm performance, and so forth. In this context, an interesting potential agenda for future research that, as far as we know, has not been examined at all is linking more objective indicators of oligarchy in a firm to managers' attitudes towards a stewardship role in the firm, and indicators of firms' orientation towards social corporate responsibility.

8.6.2. Policy Implications

A Michelsian view of organizations not only provides a framework for addressing a variety of research problems, extant research that has been generated by Michels's arguments also contains potentially useful insights for policy involving corporate reform. Looking across the studies from unions, economic cooperatives, and social movement organizations described above, we can identify a number of forces or arrangements that may minimize oligarchic abuses in business organizations.

One important factor, suggested by the ITU study, is the division of organizational elites—and here, we are thinking primarily of the board of directors—into self-consciously differing factions. Some small groups research suggests that formally assigning different expert roles to individuals can serve as an antidote to groupthink (Stasser and Titus 1985); by the same token, selecting or assigning directors to represent different factions of stockholders—employee stockholders, institutional investors, etc.—might provide impetus for fuller discussion of issues and enhance decision making within the organization.[8]

A second factor, pointed up in work on unions, collectives, and social movement organizations, is sharing knowledge of administrative expertise, thus diluting power based on the possession of 'administrative secrets'. Again, focusing on the board as the embodiment of stockholders' and non-managers' interests, one way to achieve this might be ensuring regular rotation of board chairmanships (and would entail eliminating CEO duality), and also setting term limits for board members. We recognize the trade-off here: shorter tenures for chairs and board members could also work against the acquisition of relevant knowledge of firm operations, thus weakening the effective power of the board by making it more difficult for members to challenge the rationales offered by managers for given action (see Lipset 1950). Hence, careful thought would have to be given to the details of such

[8] The same idea is embodied in the use of employee and labor director positions on the boards of German corporations, and in the representation of a wide range of stakeholders (including company employees, ex-government officials, trading partners, and bank officials) on the boards of Japanese corporations (Ahmadjian 2001).

arrangements (e.g. the best length of term limits for effective participation by board members).

A third factor, also underscored in studies of unions and collectives, involves creating better mechanisms for input by stockholders (the corporate analog of the rank and file). Lipset, Trow, and Coleman (1956) provide persuasive documentation of the role of member-generated referenda as a means of countering union leaders' ability to control which issues were placed on the public decision-making agenda. The development of such mechanisms in economic corporations have, for many years, been thwarted by SEC rules, including ones that limited any communications among stockholders aimed at influencing stockholder votes (Black 1990). If more than ten stockholders were to be contacted, this was defined as an interest group, and if the group owned more than 5 percent of company stock, then the SEC required examination and approval of the communications in advance. Presumably such rules reflected a populist ideology, that is, the protection of the interests of smaller and unorganized investors, but in practice, these often enhanced managerial autonomy, as suggested by the fact that members of the Business Roundtable fought changes in these rules, changes that were finally implemented in 1992 and helped to set off a wave of institutional investor activism (Davis and Thompson 1994). While previous restrictions have been lifted, more systematic encouragement of input from investors could serve to ensure fuller consideration of different viewpoints in both board and day-to-day management decisions. Such arrangements have already been implemented in the United Kingdom, Australia, The Netherlands, and Sweden, where stockholders have been given advisory votes on annual decisions concerning executive compensation (Ossinger 2006; White and Patrick 2007).

Finally, as noted, recent work on social movement organizations suggests that organizational conservatism and managerial self-enhancement are not inevitable outcomes of conditions that are associated with oligarchic control; this is also affected by the culture of organizational leaders. In particular, Osterman's (2006) study suggests that a culture in which challenges to managerial decisions are accepted and valued can be cultivated by relevant training of both managers and subordinates (see also Postmes, Spears, and Cihangir 2001). Unfortunately, it is not clear that the current business training that most managers (and board members) have received encourages this. In fact, several studies suggest that greater exposure to economic theory, which predominates in business education, encourages individuals to give greater attention and weight to self-interests in making decisions, even decisions involving collective goods (Frank, Gilovich, and Regan 1993, 1996; Marwell and Ames 1981). How to change this influence in management education is clearly a thorny issue (a bit like trying to move a graveyard, to borrow Woodrow Wilson's famous phrase), but one that, certainly from a Michelsian vantage point on organizations, warrants much more consideration by management scholars and educators.

References

Acemoglu, D., and Robinson, J. A. (2007). 'On the Economic Origins of Democracy'. *Daedalus*, 136/1: 160–1.

Ahmadjian, C. (2001). 'Changing Japanese Corporate Governance'. Working paper, Center on Japanese Economy and Business, Columbia University.

Andreas, J. (2007). 'The Structure of Charismatic Mobilization: A Case Study of Rebellion during the Chinese Cultural Revolution'. *American Sociological Review*, 72: 434–58.

Barnard, C. I. (1938). *Functions of the Executive*. Cambridge, Mass.: Harvard University Press.

Baum, J., Rowley, T. J., Shipilov, A. V., and Chuang, Y.-T. (2005). 'Dancing with Strangers: Aspiration Performance and the Search for Underwriting Syndicate Partners'. *Administrative Science Quarterly*, 50/4: 536–75.

Berle, A. A., and Means, G. C. ([1932] 1991). *The Modern Corporation and Private Property*. New Brunswick, NJ: Transaction, New York: Harcourt, Brace and World.

Black, B. S. (1990). 'Shareholder Passivity Reexamined'. *Michigan Law Review*, 89/3: 520–608.

Blau, P. M., Heydebrand, W., and Stauffer, R. E. (1966). 'The Structure of Small Bureaucracies'. *American Sociological Review*, 31/2: 179–91.

Boeker, W. (1992). 'Power and Managerial Dismissal: Scapegoating at the Top'. *Administrative Science Quarterly*, 37/4: 400–421.

Bray, C. (2007). 'Former Comverse Officials Receive Prison Term in Options Case'. *Wall Street Journal*, May 11: A6.

Casciaro, T., and Piskorski, M. J. (2005). 'Power Imbalance, Mutual Dependence and Constraint Absorption: A Closer Look at Resource Dependence Theory'. *Administrative Science Quarterly*, 50/2: 167–99.

Cassinelli, C. W. (1953). 'The Law of Oligarchy'. *American Political Science Review*, 47/3: 773–84.

Clemens, E. S. (1993). 'Organizational Repertoires and Institutional Change: Women's Groups and the Transformation of U.S. Politics, 1890–1920'. *American Journal of Sociology*, 98/4: 755–98.

—— and Minkoff, D. C. (2004). 'Beyond the Iron Law: Rethinking the Place of Organizations in Social Movement Research', in D. A. Snow, S. A. Soule, and H. Kriesi (eds.), *The Blackwell Companion to Social Movements*. Maldwell, Mass.: Blackwell Publishing.

Cohen, M. D., March, J. G., and Olsen, J. P. (1972). 'Garbage Can Model of Organizational Choice'. *Administrative Science Quarterly*, 17/1: 1–25.

Coleman, J. S. (1974). *Power and the Structure of Society*. New York: W. W. Norton.

Collins, R., and Makowsky, M. (2005). *The Discovery of Society*. Boston: McGraw Hill.

Corkery, C., and Forelle, M. (2007). 'Former KB Officials Face U.S. Backdating Probe'. *Wall Street Journal*, February 24: A4.

Davis, G. F. (1991). 'Agents without Principles: The Spread of the Poison Pill through the Intercorporate Network'. *Administrative Science Quarterly*, 36/4: 583–613.

—— (2005). 'New Directions in Corporate Governance'. *Annual Review of Sociology*, 31/1: 143–62.

—— and Greve, H. R. (1997). 'Corporate Elite Networks and Governance Changes in the 1980s'. *American Journal of Sociology*, 103/1: 1–37.

—— and THOMPSON, T. A. (1994). 'A Social Movement Perspective on Corporate Control'. *Administrative Science Quarterly*, 39/2: 141–73.

DEMSETZ, H., and LEHN, K. (1985). 'The Structure of Corporate Ownership: Causes and Consequences'. *Journal of Political Economy*, 93/6: 1155–77.

DONALDSON, L. (1996). 'The Normal Science of Structural Contingency Theory', in S. Clegg, C. Hardy, and W. Nord (eds.), *Handbook of Organization Studies*. London: Sage.

DUGUID, M. M. (2006). 'Board Diversity and Corporate Financial Performance'. Master's thesis, Cornell University.

ETZIONI, A. (1958). 'The Functional Differentiation of Elites in the Kibbutz'. *American Journal of Sociology*, 64/3: 476–87.

FAMA, E. F., and JENSEN, M. C. (1983). 'Separation of Ownership and Control'. *Journal of Law and Economics*, 26/2: 301–25.

FINKELSTEIN, S. (1992). 'Power in Top Management Teams: Dimensions, Measurement and Validation'. *Academy of Management Journal*, 35/8: 505–38.

—— and HAMBRICK, D. C. (1989). 'Chief Executive Compensation: A Study of the Intersection of Markets and Political Processes'. *Strategic Management Journal*, 10/3: 121–34.

FRANK, R. H., GILOVICH, T., and REGAN, D. T. (1993). 'Does Studying Economics Inhibit Cooperation?' *Journal of Economic Perspectives*, 7/2: 159–71.

—— —— —— (1996). 'Do Economists Make Bad Citizens?' *Journal of Economic Perspectives*, 10/1: 187–92.

FREEMAN, J. (1972). 'The Tyranny of Structurelessness'. *Ms.* 2/1: 76–8, 86–9.

GAMSON, W. A. (1975). *The Strategy of Social Protest*. Homewood, Ill.: Dorsey Press.

GELB, J., and PALLEY, M. L. (1982). *Women and Public Policy*. Princeton: Princeton University Press.

GERHART, B., and RYNES, S. L. (2003). *Compensation: Theory, Evidence and Strategic Implications*. Thousand Oaks, Calif.: Sage.

GERTH, H., and MILLS, C. W. (1946). *From Max Weber: Essays in Sociology*. New York: Oxford University Press.

HALL, B. J., and LIEBMAN, J. B. (1998). 'Are CEOs Really Paid Like Bureaucrats?' *Quarterly Journal of Economics*, 113/3: 653–92.

—— and MURPHY, K. J. (2000). 'Optimal Exercise Prices for Executive Stock Options'. *American Economic Review*, 90/2: 209–14.

HALL, R. H., and TOLBERT, P. S. (2004). *Organizations: Structures, Processes and Outcomes*. Upper Saddle River, NJ: Prentice Hall.

—— JOHNSON, N. J., and HAAS, J. E. (1967). 'Organizational Size, Complexity and Formalization'. *American Sociological Review*, 32/6: 903–12.

HALLOCK, K. F. (1997). 'Reciprocally Interlocking Boards of Directors and Executive Compensation'. *Journal of Financial and Quantitative Analysis*, 32/3: 331–44.

HARRISON, J. R., TORRES, D. L., and KUKALIS, S. (1988). 'The Changing of the Guard: Turnover and Structure Change in Top-Management Positions'. *Administrative Science Quarterly*, 33/2: 211–32.

HILL, C. W. L., and SNELL, S. A. (1989). 'Effects of Ownership Structure and Control on Corporate Productivity'. *Academy of Management Journal*, 32/1: 25–46.

HIMMELBERG, C. P., HUBBARD, R. G., and PALIA, D. (1999). 'Understanding the Determinants of Managerial Ownership and the Link between Ownership and Performance'. *Journal of Financial Economics*, 53/3: 353–84.

HININGS, C. R., and TOLBERT, P. S. (2008). 'Organizational Institutionalism and Sociology: A Reflection', in R. Greenwood, C. Oliver, K. Sahlin-Andersson, and R. Suddaby (eds.), *Handbook of Organizational Institutionalism*. New York: Sage.

HOLL, P. (1977). 'Control Type and the Market for Corporate Control in Large U.S. Corporations'. *Journal of Industrial Economics*, 25/4: 259–73.

Hoover's (2007). *Hoover's Billion Dollar Directory: The Complete Guide to U.S. Public Companies*. Austin, Tex.: Hoover's Business Press.

HUGHES, S. (2007). 'SEC Says It's "Looking at Subprime"'. *Wall Street Journal*, March 20.

JACKALL, R. (1988). *Moral Mazes: The World of Corporate Managers*. New York: Oxford University Press.

JANIS, I. L. (1971). 'Groupthink'. *Psychology Today*, 5/6: 43–4, 46, 73–4.

JENKINS, J. C. (1977). 'Radical Transformation of Organizational Goals'. *Administrative Science Quarterly*, 22/4: 568–85.

JENSEN, M. (2006). 'Should We Stay or Should We Go? Accountability, Status Anxiety and Client Defections'. *Administrative Science Quarterly*, 51/1: 97–128.

JENSEN, M. C. (1993). 'The Modern Industrial Revolution, Exit and the Failure of Internal Control Systems'. *Journal of Finance*, 48/3: 831–80.

—— and MECKLING, W. H. (1976). 'Theory of the Firm: Managerial Behavior, Agency Costs and Ownership Structure'. *Journal of Financial Economics*, 3/4: 306–60.

KAMERSCHEN, D. R. (1968). 'The Influence of Ownership and Control on Profit Rates'. *American Economic Review*, 58/3: 432–47.

KOLE, S. R. (1997). 'The Complexity of Compensation Contracts'. *Journal of Financial Economics*, 43/1: 79–104.

LABATON, S. (2007). 'Democrats Seek Shareholder Voting on Executive Pay'. *New York Times*, April 19.

LATTMAN, D., and SEARCEY, P. (2007). 'Secret Signals: Ex-Telecom CEO Fields "Black Box" Trial Defense'. *Wall Street Journal*, March 16: A1.

LAWRENCE, P. R., and LORSCH, J. W. (1967). *Organization and Environment: Managing Differentiation and Integration*. Boston: Graduate School of Business Administration, Harvard University.

LIE, E. (2005). 'On the Timing of CEO Stock Option Awards'. *Management Science*, 51/5: 805–12.

LIPSET, S. M. (1950). *Agrarian Socialism*. Berkeley: University of California Press.

—— TROW, M., and COLEMAN, J. (1956). *Union Democracy*. New York: Free Press.

MCADAM, D. (1983). 'Tactical Innovation and the Pace of Insurgency'. *American Sociological Review*, 48/6: 735–54.

MCCARTHY, J. D., and ZALD, M. N. (1977). 'Resource Mobilization and Social Movements'. *American Journal of Sociology*, 82/6: 1212–41.

MCCONNELL, J. J., and SERVAES, H. (1990). 'Additional Evidence on Equity Ownership and Corporate Value'. *Journal of Financial Economics*, 27/2: 595–612.

MCLEAN, B., and ELKIND, D. (2004). *The Smartest Guys in the Room: The Amazing Rise and Scandalous Fall of Enron*. New York: Portfolio Books.

MARCH, J. G., and SIMON, H. A. (1958). *Organizations*. New York: Wiley.

MARWELL, G., and AMES, R. (1981). 'Economists Free-Ride, Does Anyone Else? Experiments in the Provision of Public Goods, IV'. *Journal of Public Economics*, 15/3: 295–310.

MEHRAN, H. (1995). 'Executive Compensation Structure, Ownership, and Firm Performance'. *Journal of Financial Economics*, 38/2: 163–84.

Messinger, S. (1955). 'Organizational Transformation: A Case Study of a Declining Social Movement'. *American Sociological Review*, 20/1: 3–10.

Mezias, S. J., and Boyle, E. (2005). 'Blind Trust: Market Control, Legal Environments and the Dynamics of Competitive Intensity in the Early American Film Industry, 1893–1920'. *Administrative Science Quarterly*, 50/1: 1–34.

Michels, R. ([1911] 1962). *Political Parties: A Sociological Study of the Oligarchical Tendencies of Modern Democracy*. New York: Collier Books.

Mizruchi, M. S. (2004). 'Berle and Means Revisited: The Governance and Power of Large U.S. Corporations'. *Theory and Society*, 33/3: 579–617.

Monsen, R. J., Chiu, J. S., and Cooley, D. E. (1968). 'The Effect of Separation of Ownership and Control on the Performance of the Large Firm'. *Quarterly Journal of Economics*, 82/3: 435–51.

Morck, R., Shleifer, A., and Vishny, R. W. (1988). 'Management Ownership and Market Valuations: An Empirical Analysis'. *Journal of Financial Economics*, 20/1: 293–316.

Mui, Y. Q. (2007). 'Seeing Red over a Gold Parachute: Home Depot's CEO Resigns and his Hefty Payout Raises Ire'. *Washington Post*, January 4: D01.

Murphy, K. J. (1999). 'Executive Compensation', in O. Ashenfelter and D. Card (eds.), *Handbook of Labor Economics*. Amsterdam: North Holland.

Ocasio, W. (1994). 'Political Dynamics and the Circulation of Power: CEO Succession in U.S. Industrial Corporations, 1960–1990'. *Administrative Science Quarterly*, 39/6: 285–312.

O'Connor, J. P., Priem, R. L., Coombs, J. E., and Gilley, K. M. (2006). 'Do CEO Stock Options Prevent or Promote Fraudulent Financial Reporting?' *Academy of Management Journal*, 49/6: 483–500.

Ossinger, J. L. (2006). 'CEO Compensation Survey (A Special Report)'. *Wall Street Journal*, April 10: R6.

Osterman, P. (2006). 'Overcoming Oligarchy: Culture and Agency in Social Movement Organizations'. *Administrative Science Quarterly*, 51/4: 622–49.

Parsons, T. (1956). 'Suggestions for a Sociological Approach to a Theory of Organizations, I'. *Administrative Science Quarterly*, 1/1: 63–85.

Piven, F. F., and Cloward, R. A. (1977). *Poor People's Movements*. New York: Vintage Books.

Polleta, F. (2002). *Freedom Is an Endless Meeting: Democracy in American Social Movements*. Chicago: University of Chicago.

Pollock, T. G., Fischer, H. M., and Wade, J. B. (2002). 'The Role of Power and Politics in the Repricing of Executive Options'. *Academy of Management Journal*, 45/ 12: 2273–83.

Porter, M. E. (1985). *Competitive Advantage: Creating and Sustaining Superior Performance*. New York: Free Press.

Postmes, T., Spears, R., and Cihangir, S. (2001). 'Quality of Group Decision Making and Group Norms'. *Journal of Personality and Social Psychology*, 80/6: 918–30.

Pugh, D. S., Hickson, D. J., Hinings, C. R., and Turner, C. (1968). 'Dimensions of Organizational Structure'. *Administrative Science Quarterly*, 13/1: 65–115.

Rothschild-Whitt, J. (1979). 'The Collectivist Organization: An Alternative to Rational-Bureaucratic Models'. *American Sociological Review*, 44/4: 509–27.

Roy, W. G. (1997). *Socializing Capital: The Rise of the Large Industrial Corporation in America*. Princeton: Princeton University Press.

Ruecht, D. (1999). 'Linking Organization and Mobilization: Michels' Iron Law of Oligarchy Reconsidered'. *Mobilization*, 4/2: 151–69.

Sanders, W. G. (2001). 'Behavioral Responses of CEOs to Stock Ownership and Stock Option Pay'. *Academy of Management Journal*, 44/3: 477–92.
Schnatterly, K. (2003). 'Increasing Firm Value through Detection and Prevention of White-Collar Crime'. *Strategic Management Journal*, 24/7: 587–614.
Scott, W. R., and Davis, G. F. (2007). *Organizations and Organizing: Rational, Natural and Open System Perspectives.* Upper Saddle River, NJ: Prentice Hall.
Selznick, P. (1943). 'An Approach to a Theory of Bureaucracy'. *American Sociological Review*, 8/1: 47–54.
Shen, W., and Cannella, A. A., Jr. (2002). 'Power Dynamics within Top Management and their Impacts on CEO Dismissal Followed by Inside Succession'. *Academy of Management Journal*, 45/12: 1195–1206.
Sills, D. (1957). *The Volunteers: Means and Ends in a National Organization.* Glencoe, Ill.: Free Press.
Simon, E. (2007). 'CEOs with $1 Salary Still Make Millions'. Associated Press, June 11.
Simon, H. A. (1947). *Administrative Behavior.* New York: Macmillan.
Sine, W. D., Mitsuhashi, H., and Kirsch, D. A. (2006). 'Revisiting Burns and Stalker: Formal Structure and New Venture Performance in Emerging Economic Sectors'. *Academy of Management Review*, 49/1: 121–32.
Staggenborg, S. (1988). 'The Consequences of Professionalization and Formalization in the Pro-choice Movement'. *American Sociological Review*, 53/4: 585–605.
Stasser, G., and Titus, W. (1985). 'Pooling of Unshared Information in Group Decision Making: Bias Information Sampling during Discussion'. *Journal of Personality and Social Psychology*, 48/6: 1467–78.
Thurm, J., and Lublin, S. S. (2006). 'Money Rules: Behind Soaring Executive Pay, Decades of Failed Restraints'. *Wall Street Journal*, October 12: A1.
Tilly, C. (1978). *From Mobilization to Revolution.* Reading, Mass.: Addison-Wesley.
Turner, J. H., and Beeghley, L. (1981). *The Emergence of Sociological Theory.* Homewood, Ill.: Dorsey Press.
US Securities and Exchange Commission (2004). SEC Charges Kenneth L. Lay, Enron's Former Chairman and Chief Executive Officer, with Fraud and Insider Trading. Report # 2004–94. Washington, DC.
Vascellaro, J. E. (2007). 'RIM Sets Restatement, Shake-up on Board in Backdating Fallout'. *Wall Street Journal*, March 6: A3.
Wade, J. B., O'Reilly, C. A., and Chandratat, I. (1990). 'Golden Parachutes, CEOs and the Exercise of Social Influence'. *Administrative Science Quarterly*, 35/4: 587–603.
Westphal, J. D., and Zajac, E. J. (1994). 'Substance and Symbolism in CEOs' Long-Term Incentive Plans'. *Administrative Science Quarterly*, 39/3: 367–90.
—— —— (1995). 'Who Shall Govern? CEO/Board Power, Demographic Similarity and New Director Selection'. *Administrative Science Quarterly*, 40/1: 60–83.
—— —— (1997). 'Defections from the Inner Circle: Social Exchange, Reciprocity and the Diffusion of Board Independence in U.S. Corporations'. *Administrative Science Quarterly*, 42/1: 161–83.
West Publishing Company (1998). *West's Encyclopedia of American Law.* Minneapolis: West Group.
White, E., and Patrick, A. O. (2007). 'Shareholders Push for Vote on Executive Pay'. *Wall Street Journal*, February 26: B6.
Whitehouse, K. (2007). 'Pros: Give Holders a Say on Pay'. *Wall Street Journal*, April 4.

ZAJAC, E. J., and WESTPHAL, J. D. (1996). 'Director Reputation, CEO-Board Power and the Dynamics of Board Interlocks'. *Administrative Science Quarterly*, 41/3: 507–29.

ZALD, M. N. (1969). 'The Power and Functions of Boards of Directors: A Theoretical Synthesis'. *American Journal of Sociology*, 75/1: 97–111.

—— and ASH, R. (1966). 'Social Movement Organizations: Growth, Decay and Change'. *Social Forces*, 44/3: 327–44.

—— and DENTON, P. (1963). 'From Evangelism to General Service: The Transformation of the YMCA'. *Administrative Science Quarterly*, 8/2: 214–34.

CHAPTER 9

HOW DURKHEIM'S THEORY OF MEANING-MAKING INFLUENCED ORGANIZATIONAL SOCIOLOGY

FRANK DOBBIN

9.1. Introduction

Émile Durkheim's *Division of Labor* has palpably influenced students of organizations, occupations, and stratification. Chapter 10, by Paul Hirsch, Peer Fiss, and Amanda Hoel-Green, documents Durkheim's influence by exploring his contribution to our understanding of the global division of labor. In this chapter I examine the influence of Durkheim's theory of meaning on organizational sociology, which has taken a cultural turn since the late 1970s with the rise of the new institutional theory (Meyer and Rowan 1977; DiMaggio and Powell 1983) and organizational culture theory (Barley and Kunda 1992; Schein 1996). As the founder of the cultural approach in sociology, Durkheim might well have won credit for the cultural turn in organizational analysis. But while he is frequently cited for his influence on symbolic interactionists, such as Erving Goffman (1974) and Karl Weick (1995), Durkheim is rarely cited by social constructionists who study organizations (but see Dobbin 2004).

Perhaps Durkheim has not often been credited with influencing cultural approaches to organizations because his ideas about culture have been absorbed and have been refracted through the influence of cultural anthropology on sociology (Lévi-Strauss 1978; Douglas 1966; Geertz 1983). Or perhaps it is because certain themes in Durkheim's work were appropriated by Talcott Parsons, and Parsons's structural functionalism was the paradigm that culturalists fought against (Lincoln and Guillot 2005). In other words, Durkheim may have posthumously sided with the enemy of cultural theorists of organizations.

Yet Durkheim's ideas about the social underpinnings of cognition, and about our inclination to act collectively to make sense of the world by classifying things and attaching meaning to them, inform much of the cultural work in organizational sociology. In his early work on the division of labor and suicide, Durkheim tackled the issue of social attachment to the group from a structural and normative perspective by asking how societal cohesion could work in the context of occupational divisions (*Division of Labor*) or in religions with weak normative control systems (*Suicide*). His later anthropological work on tribes was also concerned with social attachment to the group, but there his focus was cultural rather than structural or normative. In *The Elementary Forms of the Religious Life* ([1912] 1961), Durkheim outlined a micro theory of behavior that was more collectivist than the theories that Marx or Weber had outlined and more focused on meaning-making (as opposed to self-interest) (Swedberg 2003; Lukes 1985). Durkheim emphasized that even the basic categories of meaning—time and space—could only be produced collectively and that the drive to make meaning is fundamental, in much the way that Karl Marx or Adam Smith saw self-interest as fundamental.

In *Elementary Forms*, Durkheim showed that tribes collectively make sense of the world through categorization. They categorize entities from the plant and animal worlds, making connections between human communities and totems, between individuals and their personal totems. Their explanations of how things are grouped together are mystified, rather than scientistic (our own explanations would begin with species and genus, for instance, and so a frog totem and spiritual leader would not be grouped together), and so the connections between things are understood in terms of a spirit system—the link between the totem and fertility, for instance. Their myths locate the origins of social practices outside of social life, in an external world of spirits. These 'elementary forms' of religious life are early drafts of modern religious systems and contain all of the elements of spirituality, ritual, sacred and profane. Thus, the meaning-making found in totemic systems, which involves categorizing animate and inanimate things in the surrounding world as well as social conventions, underlies modern religious systems as well.

Social constructionists have built on these insights to argue that the rationalization of the modern world parallels the mystification of the pre-modern world. Human groups identify an external source of social customs, whether that source be transcendental spirits, under animism, or transcendental economic laws, under contemporary norms of scientific rationality. In organizational theory, social constructionists depict the evolution of modern laws of efficiency and rationality as a process paralleling that which Durkheim described in totemic societies. Meyer and Rowan (1977) famously describe organizational practices as myth and ceremony, taking a page from Durkheim's work on totemic societies to characterize rationalized meaning systems. Durkheim himself had seen this connection between different sorts of worldviews, not only in describing totemism as an 'elementary form of religious life' in the title of his 1912 book but also in describing modern economic theory as akin to metaphysics, in that it establishes an extra-societal force (economic laws) that drives worldly behavior.

In this chapter, I sketch Durkheim's contribution in *Elementary Forms* and, in particular, his idea that humans are driven to understand the world through collective classification and meaning-making. Then I show how that idea informed postwar sociologists of knowledge and organizational sociologists: Erving Goffman, Peter Berger and Thomas Luckmann, and James March and Herbert Simon. Finally, I describe Durkheim's influence on organizational sociology since the late 1970s, particularly on the new institutionalism and second-generation power theory. To begin with, I discuss how his work on meaning evolved from his early work on social structure.

9.2. Durkheim's Early Work on Social Structure

Émile Durkheim was born in 1858 in the province of Lorraine to a family of three generations of rabbis. His dissertation, *The Division of Labor in Society* ([1893] 1933), and books on the sociological method ([1895] 1966) and suicide ([1897] 1966), provided a new model for the study of society, a model that was scientific rather than humanistic, with a focus on social structure and social solidarity. In *Division of Labor*, Durkheim asked how social solidarity was maintained in agricultural and industrialized societies, and he showed that different social structures corresponded to different forms of solidarity. Under feudalism, solidarity emerged from the fact that people shared a common situation in the social structure and common life experiences. Mechanical solidarity in agricultural systems was a result of shared experience. But with industrialization, the division of labor undermined common life experience as a form of solidarity. Now people had very different life experiences depending on their places in the occupational structure. Industrialization had challenged the classical form of social solidarity. What emerged in its place was organic solidarity, in which solidarity was a function of each person's dependence on others in the social system. The butcher depended on the baker, the mason on the lumberjack. Within occupations and professions, however, bonds of solidarity still emerged based on shared experiences and circumstances.

In *Suicide*, Durkheim built on this understanding of social attachment to the group to analyze suicide rates across different societies and regions, finding that suicide rates rise in settings where people become anomic, or detached from the group. In Protestant regions people are more detached than in Catholic regions because the Protestant denominations exert less social control than the Catholic Church. Normative social control, then, is a key mechanism attaching the individual to the social group. But there is an ideal level of normative control, and suicide rates rise again in settings with too much social integration, where social control becomes oppressive. *Suicide* not only treated the issue of group attachment from a social control perspective but also showcased the scientific approach Durkheim had set out in *Rules of Sociological Method*, where he argued that, to establish causality, social scientists must compare societies, or groups, to establish causal patterns. He compared statistics from different countries, and from different regions within countries, to garner evidence that suicide rates indeed vary with social integration. Following his precepts in *Rules of Sociological Method*, he amassed evidence from diverse sources to show the generality of the relationship between anomie and suicide. In *Rules of Sociological Method*, Durkheim had sketched a general method for studying social phenomena, emphasizing the need to treat social facts as phenomena worthy of scientific study, and the importance of making comparisons across individuals and groups to accumulate evidence for a theory.

Elementary Forms represented a break in Durkheim's oeuvre, in a sense, in that he turned from modern societies to pre-modern tribes and moved from Europe to Australia, China, and the Sioux. But it represented continuity on two important fronts. First, Durkheim continued to be interested in social solidarity and cohesion, and in *Elementary Forms* he sought to understand the religious and cultural forces that produce cohesion and collective consciousness. He was fascinated by the 'collective effervescence' in religious rituals that made tribal members, and modern worshippers, believe in a force beyond society. The turn to tribal societies was deliberate, for Durkheim sought to trace the modern religious forces that produce social cohesion to their originals in tribal spirituality. In *Elementary Forms*, moreover, Durkheim continued to insist on the importance of social facts. At the time, some economists had been arguing that all social phenomena could be traced to the individual (pursuing methodological individualism), and it was in that context that Durkheim insisted that social facts themselves shape subsequent social phenomena. In the tribes he studied, the tribe's belief system was a social fact that palpably shaped future beliefs and behaviors. For Stephen Lukes (1985), Durkheim at times reified society in this work, in the process of arguing that tribal members deified their own society in inventing a spirit world that reflected it.

The second way in which *Elementary Forms* represented continuity with Durkheim's earlier work is that it applied the methodological dictates from *Rules of Sociological Method*. Rather than focusing on a single tribe, which had been the modus operandi in anthropology, Durkheim conducted a systematic comparison of ethnographic materials from tribes in Australia, China, and North America to understand the most fundamental patterns of meaning-making. He drew lessons from the patterns these tribes shared, not from their idiosyncrasies.

9.3. Durkheim's Theory of Meaning

The view of culture that emerges in *Elementary Forms* can be seen in Durkheim's earliest work. He saw culture as a product of social processes, but as a consequential product that influences social phenomena. In *Suicide*, he wrote that once cultural representations are in place, 'they are, by that very fact, realities *sui generis*, autonomous and capable of producing new phenomena' (Durkheim [1897] 1966: 130). Or as Lincoln and Guillot (2005: 97) describe Durkheim's view of culture: 'Culture may originate with social structure, but people experience structure through cultural frames and filters.' Cultural meanings are social facts just as social structures are social facts, facts which sociologists should endeavor to explain and should use in explaining other social phenomena.

Durkheim's ideas about cognition and categorization were first set out in 1902, a decade before *Elementary Forms* appeared, in an essay titled 'Primitive Classification' (Durkheim and Mauss [1902] 1963), which appeared as 'De Quelques Formes de Primitives de Classification' in *Année Sociologique*. 'Primitive Classification', which Durkheim wrote in collaboration with his nephew Marcel Mauss, set out ideas that would be developed by structural anthropologists in France. Evidence from Australian tribes, the Zuni and Sioux, and China provided the empirical foundation for the argument that classification systems originate in social organization—that symbolic systems derive from the organization of social life.

In *Elementary Forms*, which appeared in French in 1912 and in English translation in 1915, Durkheim built on that collaborative effort to understand the emergence of tribal sacred systems. Whereas others before him had seen these belief systems as arising from a need to understand the mysteries of the real or dream worlds—from psychological phenomena—Durkheim saw sacred totemic systems as originating in the need to understand the power of the social group over the individual. Here, as in *Division of Labor* and *Suicide*, he is fascinated by individual attachment to the group. He identifies a sort of cognitive dissonance in Australian tribes, whose members wonder how particular people and groups can exert such influence over them. They explain this power with reference to a sacred world beyond direct observation. The totem represents what is transcendental in social life. This insight represents a major break with anthropologists of the time, and in a sense it underlies the social constructionist theory of cognition that informs cultural approaches in organizational theory.

For Durkheim, the human mind is programmed not to maximize self-interest so much as to develop categories, causal frameworks, and maps of the world as a means of sense-making. We do this collectively. Australian tribes categorized the world in ways alien to Durkheim, lumping the tribe with the totem, animals with plants, and so on. Their categories were based on affinities tribe members believed had been established by the spirit world, which gave power to certain objects and social roles. Sacred objects (an animal or plant totem) give meaning to the social group and confer sacred powers, often through direct physical contact. Thus, the totem is inscribed on arrows to bring its powers to the hunt. In Durkheim's view, the spiritual world is an abstraction and reflection of the social world, which, being a social fact, acts back upon the social world.

The world is given intersubjective meaning through social processes, where categories, maps, frames, and causal models become part of a collective language. Social categorization confers the status of sacred or profane on everything the tribe experiences. Tribes locate socially produced conventions and meanings not merely outside of the individual, but outside of the social world itself in a system of spirits.

By comparing the religious systems of different tribes, Durkheim saw that individual consciousness comes to reflect social conventions and the collective consciousness (shared understanding) that develops to make sense of conventions. Conventions themselves take many different forms, largely as a result of happenstance. Tribes elevate the lizard or frog or anteater as their totem as a result of historical accident, without any larger rhyme or reason. Durkheim insisted at the end of *Elementary Forms* that modern religious systems were built on the same foundations as totemic systems, meaning, on the one hand, that they were likewise organized around spirituality, ritual, the sacred and profane, and, on the other hand, that their particular forms were consequences of history and happenstance.

Durkheim challenged classical economists' view of the individual as driven by narrow self-interest. He also challenged economists' methodological individualism, or the idea that social patterns must be based in human nature. The commitment to self-interest and methodological individualism was at the base not only of neoclassical economics but also of the political philosophy of Thomas Hobbes (1982) and John Locke (1965), who depicted modern social and economic institutions as built up from the interactions of individuals pursuing their interests. The consequence of free individual exchange was the spot market, and market and political institutions followed from this free exchange. Because pursuit of self-interest is natural, the theory goes, social and economic institutions that allow free exchange are merely a reflection of the human soul (Somers 2001). Durkheim challenged this view in describing collective consciousness as emerging from the interaction of group members rather than from the qualities of the individual. While he described society as the individual mind writ large, which might be read as compatible with the view of classical economics, Mary Douglas (1986: 45) argues that Durkheim was pointing out the correspondence between mind and society, and that it is more in the spirit of his work 'to think of the individual mind furnished as society writ small'.

Like Durkheim, Marx and Weber saw the human psyche as shaped quite fundamentally by social institutions; however, the process of collective meaning-making was much more fundamental to Durkheim than it was for either Marx or Weber. Like Durkheim, Marx and Weber saw the human psyche as shaped quite fundamentally by social institutions; however, the process of collective meaning-making was much more fundamental to Durkheim than it was for either Marx or Weber. Weber (1978: 4) turned the observation that meaning varies from society to society into a methodological dictum, arguing that, to understand social action, one must understand its meaning to the actor. In *The Eighteenth Brumaire*, Marx ([1852] 1963: 1) famously wrote, 'Men make their own history, but they do not make it as they please; they do not make it under self-selected circumstances, but under circumstances existing already, given and transmitted from the past.' History leaves not only material relations but also a framework that shapes consciousness. Yet Marx saw class interests underlying frameworks of meaning and described those interests as key and frameworks as only 'superstructure'. For Marx ([1859] 1968: 181), forms of consciousness emerge to support the 'real foundation' of society, 'the economic structure... on which arises a legal and political superstructure and to which correspond definite forms of consciousness'. While there is scholarly debate over whether Marx saw consciousness as merely epiphenomenal, as this passage implies, there is little debate that Durkheim gave it greater primacy of place in his work. For Marx, genuine material relations can be obscured by group consciousness and what mattered most were those material relations. For Durkheim, collective consciousness could not be wrong, for it was a gloss on experience, and could not be merely epiphenomenal, because collective consciousness is a social fact with concrete effects.

9.4. Durkheim's Influence on Post-War Sociologists of Knowledge

Durkheim's thinking shaped much of the work of post-war American social constructionists and symbolic interactionists. Erving Goffman (1974) drew on Durkheim's notion of how meaning is created in social groups, building on

Durkheim's notion that the individual in the modern world 'is allotted a kind of sacredness that is displayed and confirmed by symbolic acts' and arguing that 'a version of Durkheim's social psychology can be effective in modern dress' (Goffman [1967] 2005: 47). Societies offer different 'frames' for understanding the world that are situated in individual consciousness, but that are shared among groups of people exposed to common institutions. In French organizational sociology, the convention school expanded on this idea to suggest that people are exposed to a multitude of different frames—market efficiency, democracy, economic justice—and depict action in terms of one such frame or another (Boltanski and Thevenot 1991). Randall Collins (2004) takes Durkheim's work on ritual as a starting point for expanding on Goffman's interactionism, building social institutions up from dyadic interactions.

While Peter Berger and Thomas Luckmann build explicitly on Alfred Schutz's *The Phenomenology of the Social World* ([1932] 1967) to sketch a social constructionist view of human cognition, their approach can be seen as an extension of Durkheim's project in *Elementary Forms*, for they seek to understand how social understandings of the world come about not only in tribal and religious systems, but in philosophical and scientific-rational systems. Berger and Luckmann (1966: 20) say that their task is to grasp 'the objectivations of subjective processes (and meanings) by which the *inter*subjective commonsense world is constructed'. How is it, in other words, that our subjective 'knowledge' of the world comes to have the feel of an objective reality? The fact that those around us share that subjective knowledge helps to give it the feel of objective fact, and so we do not see the socially constructed reality around us as a social product.

For Berger and Luckmann, the inclination to assign objective status to intersubjective reality is characteristic of human society. In mystified, religious, philosophical, and rationalized social systems alike, individuals make causal connections on the basis of the wider system of meaning institutionalized in concrete customs. That was one of Durkheim's points about totemic and modern religious systems alike. Compare quotes juxtaposed by Finn Collin (1997: 4) from *Elementary Forms* and *The Social Construction of Reality*. In the first, Durkheim makes clear (as he did in *The Rules of Sociological Method* ([1895] 1966) that ideas about reality are what we know of reality: 'There is one division of society where the formula of idealism is applicable almost to the letter: this is the social kingdom. Here more than anywhere else the idea is the reality' (Durkheim [1912] 1961: 228). In the second, Berger and Luckmann make the same point, and then underscore how people participate in sustaining ideas about reality: 'Knowledge about society is thus a realization in the double sense of the word, in the sense of apprehending the objectivated reality, and in the sense of ongoingly producing this reality. ... The sociology of knowledge understands human reality as socially constructed reality' (Berger and Luckmann 1966: 210–11).

For Berger and Luckmann, as for Durkheim, modern societies are not so different from tribal societies, in that they trace social conventions to something outside of society, in the modern case to natural laws (laws of the market, laws of 'human nature') that are unvarying across time and space. For them, human cognition is a reflection of the surrounding social order. We are rational actors, but only because we live in a universe governed by imagined scientific laws. In a universe governed by ancestors, our cognitive structures would reflect the imagined world of ancestors. Moreover, rationalized cognitive systems come in as many flavors as mystified cognitive systems because the laws of rationality are social inventions. Through objectivation, we come to see the social construction of the universe we know, mystified or rationalized or whatever, as natural and true rather than as a social product.

Berger and Luckmann used slightly different language to describe the process by which societies categorize objects to make sense of them (1967: 4), but as Bryan Turner (1997: 378) writes, their arguments owe homage both to Marx and to Durkheim: 'These Propositions can be seen as a summary of the theories of alienation and anomie, of Marx's claim in *The Eighteenth Brumaire of Louis Bonaparte* that "Men make their own history, but they do not make it just as they please" and of the theory of the *conscience collective* in Durkheim.'

This view of the modern psyche as, like the tribal psyche, a social product rather than a realization of human nature continues to fuel debate in the social sciences. Avner Greif (1993) has argued that rational self-interested behavior was found in the trading patterns of antiquity, with the corollary that self-interest and the inclination to truck and barter in modern form are hard-wired. Yet Albert Hirschman's *The Passions and the Interests* (1977) challenges that view, tracing the historical rise of interest as a framework for understanding human behavior. That framework replaced a view of human behavior as driven by such innate passions as greed and lust. Sociologists from Max Weber (1978) to Richard Swedberg (2003) have seen nascent elements of self-interest in early modern Europe, but Neil Smelser's (1995) review of anthropological evidence suggests that, in aboriginal societies, members did not view self-interest as underlying their own behavior and did not create incipient modern markets. It is more in keeping with Durkheim's view to see economic theory as a social fact than as an extra-social fact, and hence to explore how humans made up this theory as a way to explain the world of experience.

9.5. Durkheim's Influence on Organizational Sociology

Beyond Goffman's idea of frames, and Berger and Luckmann's work on the social construction of reality, many others in sociology have built on Durkheim's ideas about the correspondence between social structure and psyche, and on the social creation of the psyche. Pierre Bourdieu's *habitus* describes the class-based schemas for seeing the world that come from the social world. Ann Swidler (1986) uses 'cultural tool-kit' to describe the shared cultural elements that people use to interpret the world and act upon it. Luc Boltanski and Laurent Thevenot (1991) use the term 'justification' to refer to the menu of standard culturally constructed ways of understanding social action. Societies produce broadly different sorts of cognitive orientations—maps of reality—and modern societies create multiple, overlapping, maps.

In organizational sociology, March and Simon (1958) and organizational culture theorists describe the social construction of reality found within each organization (Schein 1996; see Pedersen and Dobbin 2006). At the other end of the micro–macro continuum, cultural psychologists characterize broad national differences in those maps. Cross-national studies of the human psyche confirm that societies produce different models of social order. Experiments have shown that people in different countries describe the same picture in very different ways, Americans focusing on the subject and Japanese focusing on the context (Nisbett *et al.* 2001). Hence Americans are more likely to attribute the behavior of others to character, while Japanese are more likely to attribute it to context. Recent work in infant cognition seems to challenge some of Durkheim's basic assumptions by suggesting that certain categories of cognition are hard wired (see Bergesen 2004), but this comparative work in psychology shows consistent societal patterns suggesting that context shapes some quite fundamental categories (see DiMaggio 1997).

Next I trace Durkheim's influence on several lines of thought important to organizational sociology. James March and Herbert Simon's 'Cognitive Limits on Rationality' sketches how members of organizations develop rationalized routines for solving problems, and how they come to apply these routines as rationalized rituals to solve problems. The psychologist Karl Weick explores cognitive sense-making within organizations, showing how people explain their own behavior post hoc, to themselves and to others, in socially meaningful terms. We invent meaningful rationales for action after we have acted, simultaneously reinforcing existing rationales and justifying our own behavior. New organizational institutionalists depict the interorganizational construction of rational myths and rituals, which spread through the network of organizations. Second-generation power theorists have built on the social constructionist insights that Durkheim first sketched to explain how we come to accept institutions that reinforce power differentials.

9.5.1. Cognition in Organizational Tribes: Bounded Rationality

James March and Herbert Simon's classic *Organizations* (1958) sketches how habits and routines reproduce themselves in today's organizational tribes. Within an organization, customary problem-solving strategies influence how people respond to new problems, following habits rather than engaging in fully rational search processes for optimal solutions. Organizational members use habitual solutions to solve new problems, identifying characteristics of the new problem that correspond with characteristics of an earlier problem, and applying the solution applied in that situation. Thus, what the organizational tribe has done in the past shapes how current members behave.

March and Simon focus on the limits of human cognitive capacity in rational decision making. Managers are seldom able to identify the optimal means to a particular end because of the difficulty of assessing the costs and benefits of each imaginable strategy. They act out of habit and adapt existing customs to new problems. They typically settle on solutions that meet minimal criteria for achieving a goal rather than searching for the ideal solution, 'satisficing' rather than optimizing. Rather than fully exploring all options, people begin the search process by thinking of an analogous problem from the past. They apply a solution similar to that applied in the analogous case, expanding beyond off-the-shelf remedies only when they can think of no analogous situation. What March and Simon describe is almost indistinguishable from what Durkheim describes in the tribe, where members inscribe the tribe's totem on every tool crafted for the hunt. In both cases they enact the tribe's customs without much thought about what they are doing.

Organizations, like tribes, offer different menus of past solutions to choose from. They develop precise problem-solving routines for dealing with common and predictable functions and general routines for dealing with rare and unpredictable functions. The routines exist as organizational culture at the level of the firm and as cognitive problem-solving scenarios in the minds of individuals. March and Simon argue that customs and cognitive frameworks are really two sides of the same coin, for cognitive frameworks reflect the customs individuals encounter in their work organizations. That is very much the model of the social world that Durkheim described for totemic and modern religious systems alike.

March and Simon's idea of bounded rationality, in which the way we see the world is influenced by the social constructions in our environment, is certainly compatible with Durkheim's view of collective consciousness. In both models the collectivity develops an interpretive framework that shapes the behavior of members—their understandings are not their own, neither devised autonomously nor a consequence of the way the brain is wired ('human nature').

Simon's interest in routine can be traced to John Dewey. Durkheim as well had been influenced by Dewey and the pragmatists, and while he critiqued the approach, it was a proximate critique of intellectual differentiation not a distant critique of intellectual rejection (see Michael D. Cohen, 'Reading Dewey: Some Implications for the Study of Routine', in this volume). In his 'transactional' pragmatism, Dewey treated knowledge as a socially produced system, expressed in language, that was constantly open to amendment and reinterpretation. Durkheim's own view of knowledge, produced in society as collective consciousness, was quite similar, and his belief in using the scientific method to refine knowledge about society in particular overlaps with Dewey's view (Joas 1993; Dewey 1998). Dewey was, not surprisingly then, Durkheim's favorite philosopher (Martin 2002).

Cultural sociologists have shown that conventions vary across nations, but March and Simon point to how they vary in important ways even across work organizations in the same nation and industry, shaping workers' cognitive frameworks and problem-solving toolkits. For March and Simon, people in modern work organizations pursue rationalized solutions to problems, but those solutions are determined by organizational culture. Rationality, then, takes different cultural forms in different organizations just as totemism, for Durkheim, takes different forms in different tribes. Sociologists have expanded on this observation to show that across countries, the repertoire of rationalized management practices varies widely (e.g., Hofstede 1980; Whitley 1992). 'National character' used to be thought to explain these differences, and character was thought to be passed down from parents to children. But scholars have increasingly treated national differences as consequences of the social construction of national institutions (e.g., Whitley and Kristensen 1996). Thus, the institution of lifetime employment for managers in Japan (Dore 2000) or getting ahead by moving around in the United States shapes collective consciousness. It is not that one system is rational and the other prerational, but that different rationalized rituals, and worldviews, emerge in different settings.

9.5.2. Seeing Action through the Tribe's Kaleidoscope

In exploring the relationship between social structure and individual cognition, Durkheim's followers argue that human customs are framed as driven by forces outside of society. The rationalized organizational customs March and Simon describe are tied to universal principles of rationality (formalism, bureaucracy, professionalization). The sense-making approach to organizations builds on these ideas, returning the focus to the individual and his or her interaction with the existing meaning system. In *Sensemaking in Organizations* (1995), Karl Weick examines how frames for understanding the world are activated and manipulated by individuals. Weick does not see the meaning of an action as tightly wedded to the action itself, but instead sees individuals as operating with a range of interpretive frames. People make sense of much of their behavior retrospectively, using these interpretive frames. Weick illustrates with Garfinkel's study of jury decisions, which shows that jury members tend to select a punishment first, and then make sense of the evidence so that the crime fits the punishment. For Weick, organizational behavior tends to follow the same pattern. People act first, and later develop rationales for that action based in existing, socially accepted, frameworks.

Weick's innovation is the idea that action shapes cognition—that we make cognitive sense of even our own actions after they have occurred—within the limits of socially constructed reality. Decisions and actions are often spontaneous, but we interpret them with customary frameworks. People's accounts of a single action, then, may vary, but their accounts conform to one or another of the collective interpretive frameworks currently in use. Because people's cognitive frameworks are shaped by experience with social customs, each of us is equipped with a range of frameworks for interpreting behavior.

9.5.3. The Institutionalization of Rational Myths

John Meyer and Brian Rowan's 'Institutionalized Organizations: Formal Structure as Myth and Ceremony' (1977) shook up the world of organizational sociology by proposing a constructionist approach to understanding organizational practices and routines. Meyer and Rowan describe modern organizations as adopting structures that symbolize rationality and fairness, and describe those structures as 'myth and ceremony'. At the time, the prevailing view of the firm was that economic laws determined 'best practices' and that those 'best practices' would come to the surface everywhere. If organizations looked alike, it was because they were subjected to the same economic pressures. If they had accounting departments and strategic planning teams and performance evaluations, it was because each organization had found each one of those practices to be efficient.

Meyer and Rowan's revolutionary article described rationalized organizational practices as symbolic and ritualized, even though those practices often symbolize rationality. Organizations adopt practices that embody myths of rationality both to trumpet their commitment to efficiency and to achieve it. Not only within organizations (as March and Simon point out) but also across organizations, we socially construct reality by classifying behavior patterns, norms, and rules and linking them to myths of rationality. Meaningful 'institutions' thus shape behavior in organizations: 'Institutionalized rules are classifications built into society as reciprocated typifications or interpretations' (Meyer and Rowan 1977: 341).

It is not tribal elders who invent new organizational rituals, for institutionalists, but entrepreneurs who devise new rituals and promote them directly as rational problem-solving devices to members of their networks, and to the wider management audience through cover stories in *Fortune* or *Harvard Business Review*. New practices—quality circles, empowerment, high-performance work practices—became 'institutionalized' (taken for granted) as this process proceeds. Those practices must conform to the wider understanding of what is rational, and so it is easier to sell certain kinds of practices in Marseilles than in Minneapolis. In Meyer and Rowan's world, firms come to look alike because they jump on the same bandwagons and not, *pace* functionalist organizational theorists, because each figures out the single best way to organize.

In 1983, Paul DiMaggio and Walter Powell built on this idea, sketching the networks through which new rational customs diffuse among organizations—political networks, professional networks, and networks of firms. Schools were coming to look more like one another, and so were hospitals, auto factories, and charities. A growing body of standard practices could be found in each field. Like Meyer and Rowan, DiMaggio and Powell described the driving force behind institutionalization as social. Auto plants do not resemble one another because their managers independently invent the same business practices, but because they copy from the same sources.

Each new practice comes fully equipped with a story about why it is efficient, just as, in Durkheim's tribes, each ritual comes with a story about why the spirit world requires it. The spread of rituals across organizations usually follows one of three patterns. Sometimes public policy encourages organizations to adopt new conventions ('coercive isomorphism'). For instance, federal regulations dictate that schools must meet certain standards or give certain tests (Meyer and Scott 1983). Sometimes professional networks that span organizations promote new conventions with native, usually untested, theories of their efficacy ('normative isomorphism'). For instance, finance managers promoted the portfolio approach to corporate diversification (Fligstein 1990). Sometimes managers copy practices of successful organizations without a clear theory of how the new innovation works ('mimetic isomorphism'). For instance, American automakers copied Japanese production strategies willy-nilly after Japan made inroads into America's auto market. Mimetic isomorphism can have the character of a cargo cult, in which the tribe builds a wooden replica of a cargo plane in the hope that the replica will bear the same fruit as the real plane.

Key business strategies often spread through mimetic isomorphism, and as Heather Haveman (1993) shows in a paper titled 'Follow the Leader', firms that are defined as industry leaders due to high growth or sheer size are more likely than others to be copied by their peers. Among savings and loans, when industry leaders diversify into real estate or into commercial loans, other firms follow their lead. The very definition of a savings and loan is changed in the process.

Diffusion of management myths made sectors quite internally homogeneous in the post-war period, and diffusion across sectors has in recent decades made organizational practices homogeneous across sectors (Meyer 1994). With the rise of a generic, non-sectoral, model of organizing, social service agencies increasingly appoint CEOs and hospitals increasingly write mission statements—innovations that first appeared in the for-profit world.

Meyer and Rowan and DiMaggio and Powell describe how myth and ceremony contribute to the spread of rational conventions through the forest of organizations. The quality management movement, for example, turned the tide against the earlier movements of Taylorism and Fordism to encourage production workers to help design the production process (Cole 1989). The movement spread the idea that worker participation in job design could be more efficient than a strict division of labor between those who design assembly lines and those who work on them. To call the new theory of empowerment a rational myth is not to say that there is nothing to it. It is to suggest that such ideas are the myth, and that related practices are the ceremony, around which rationalized organizational cultures are constructed.

9.6. Second-Wave Power Theorists and Cognitive Classification

Mid-twentieth-century American theories of power, exemplified by C. Wright Mills (1956), focused on the elite and their capacity to control corporations and institutions. Since the rise of institutional theory, students of capitalist firms have imported social constructionist insights to build a constructionist theory of power. Neil Fligstein's *The Transformation of Corporate Control* (1990) brings insights from the social constructionist paradigm that Durkheim inspired to the study of strategy among America's largest corporations.

Fligstein's work on corporate management is framed as the antithesis of *The Visible Hand* (1977), by America's pre-eminent business historian, Alfred DuPont Chandler, who told the story of the evolution of corporate control from the perspective of business efficiency. Early firms were run by managers with backgrounds in production. Later, sales and marketing managers took over, as the axis of firm competition shifted from production to marketing. Later still, finance managers took over, as firms shifted focus from sales and marketing to diversification. Chandler treats these changes as part of the natural progression of the modern firm, from a perspective that was more evolutionary than sociological.

Fligstein finds that these changes were the result of a series of power struggles among management factions. Each group succeeded in taking control of the large corporation by convincing investors that its management specialty held the key to corporate efficacy. Under each equilibrium, people came to understand the world in terms of the business customs and institutions they faced. These equilibriums constitute social constructions of reality, or 'conceptions of control' in Fligstein's terms. Each equilibrium was disrupted by an external shift that required business leaders to search for a new model of behavior, and a new theory of the firm or 'conception of control'.

The shift from sales to finance management was kicked off in 1950 when Congress passed the Celer-Kefauver Act, which made it difficult for firms to acquire others in related businesses. Finance managers responded with a new business model, later reinforced by portfolio theory in financial economics, in which the large firm should not act like a marketing machine growing in a single sector, but like an investor with a diversified portfolio. Finance managers now argued before corporate boards and investors that the diversified conglomerate was the way of the future and that they, finance managers, were best qualified to manage conglomerates. They thereby came to displace experts in sales at the helms of the biggest corporations.

Under Fligstein's political-cultural approach, business customs and institutions are held in place by beliefs. Belief in the rationality of existing customs and institutions comes from experience with them (as does belief in the totem in Durkheim's Australian tribes), and from rational theorization by consultants, economists, and management theorists (the equivalent of witch-doctors and tribal elders). When an external shock—a recession, a policy shift—destabilizes one broad business strategy, entrepreneurial consultants and managers promote new practices and theories to go along with them. The powerful are most likely to be able to put their preferred alternatives into place. Once in place, the new business strategy is held in place by a theory that makes sense within the existing social construction of reality. The conglomerate model of the firm, then, was shaken by policy and economic shifts circa 1980, and institutional entrepreneurs successfully promoted a new model rooted in ideas about 'core competence' in management (Davis, Diekmann, and Tinsley 1994; Fligstein and Markowitz 1993). In Durkheim's terms, the collective consciousness changes when the social rituals of the corporation change.

Fligstein's second-wave power theory, then, builds directly on the insights that Meyer and Rowan developed in their institutional approach to explain how culture and legitimacy reinforce particular organizational strategies, across the organizational field. One of Fligstein's innovations is to explore how power shapes what emergent strategies will look like. Like Durkheim, Fligstein emphasizes that the collective constructions of rituals is what keeps them in place and emphasizes that this construction is a social rather than an individual process.

William Roy, in *Socializing Capital: The Rise of the Large Industrial Corporation in America* (1997), sketches a somewhat different theory of the role of power under modern capitalism, but one which also owes a debt to Durkheim and the social constructionists. Under his theory, the social construction of efficiency keeps particular policy regimes, and corporate strategies, in place. Public and organizational policies that are put in place because they support the interests of particular groups become legitimated through rhetorical strategies and economic theories, and institutional power differentials thus become obscured. The power of groups that put new policies in place is thus sustained through the cultural legitimacy gained by those policies.

Roy seeks to explain a wave of mergers at the beginning of the twentieth century that produced huge industrial enterprises and a business model based on economies of scale. For Roy, the initial enforcement of antitrust in 1897 had an unanticipated effect on the balance of power between large and small firms. It was not only economies of scale that gave big firms an edge and spawned a merger wave, as Alfred Chandler (1977) contends, because firms merged even in industries that could not benefit from economies of scale. Roy argues that, when antitrust prevented firms from joining together to set prices, large firms demanded that smaller competitors sell out or face certain death in price wars. The huge concentrated firm was born of an unanticipated coincidence of public policy and private power. Public policy fostered price competition, and large firms forced their smaller competitors to sell out.

One result is that the theory of economies of scale received a boost, and Americans came to see the large corporation as inevitable because of its superior efficiency. Public policy was increasingly tolerant of large firms, and growth in size was seen less as an effort to extinguish competition (as it had been seen circa 1890) and more as a move towards efficiency. Americans soon came to take the huge industrial enterprise for granted, and to presume that large firms are large because they enjoy economies of scale. For Roy, once this pattern was established, it became self-reinforcing, largely because people make sense of the world around them by attributing rationality to practices, explaining surviving economic solutions teleologically, as a consequence of evolution and natural selection. This collective process of making sense of rituals, and giving social practices meaning in the process, closely parallels Durkheim's discussion of tribal religions.

For Roy, the successful theorization of new organizational practices means that they no longer have to be actively supported by the powerful. They become taken for granted, and advantages to certain groups (in the United States, owners of large corporations) become institutionalized.

This pattern of making sense of the social customs of the world collectively, and doing so iteratively and interactively, is very much what Durkheim described in his study of primitive classifications, and in *Elementary Forms*. For Roy and Fligstein alike, organizational rituals are given meaning through collective social construction, as for Durkheim, and then they are held in place by that meaning. They become ritualized as they are connected to a totem, or an economic or social law, that rules society from without.

9.7. Conclusion

In totemic societies, Durkheim found the same broad form of meaning-making that he had seen in modern religious societies. In both settings, people categorized things to make sense of the world. In both, they traced physical and social patterns to forces outside of society—to a spirit world or to a religious world with a single deity. For Durkheim, it is human nature to make sense of the world collectively and to assign to things in the world meaning, most simply as sacred or profane. For Durkheim, social processes produce our mental categories—our ideas—and those mental categories have real effects in the world (Rawls 1996; Emirbayer 1996).

I began by arguing that Durkheim's influence on the organizational sociologists who have championed a cultural approach has largely been neglected. Durkheim was the first to recognize the mechanisms by which totemic tribes make sense of the world. They categorized the objects and customs and beings in the world around them, drawing connections between things as a way of making collective sense of them. Modern religious systems, and rationalized systems, made sense of the world in much the same way. That may be the key insight underlying social constructionist approaches to the modern organization, namely, that the human inclination to try to make sense of the world as it is given to us leads us to develop shared mental maps of the world, categorizing things and people and theories and then projecting those categorizations onto a force that is exogenous to society itself.

Those mental maps of the world, which Durkheim described as collective consciousness, are what keep modern organizational practices in place. It is because we attach meaning to the chain of command, the job ladder, or the disciplinary procedure that we sustain those organizational practices, day in and day out. It is because we share a broad, socially produced, system of meaning that we understand the logic of organizational innovations, recognizing that they operate under a theory of professional expertise, or of empowerment, or of the division of labor itself.

In the last generation, organizational sociology has undergone a revolution. The classic studies in the field had been designed to divine the universal social laws that governed efficiency in social organization. Frederick Taylor's (1911) *Scientific Management* purported to identify the optimal work patterns on the shop floor, and later the assembly line, and the optimal division of labor between workers and managers. More than half a century later, Peter Blau (1970) and Joan Woodward ([1958] 1984) were still seeking to understand the universal social laws that determined the optimal span of supervisory control in the factory, or the optimal number of layers of bureaucracy. In the meantime, March and Simon (1958), Roethlisberger and Dickson ([1939] 1981), Selznick (1957), and Zald and Denton (1963) had sought to understand the irrational, human side of organizational behavior. But their studies had not challenged the central view of organizational sociologists, that organizational practices were driven by universal laws of efficiency. Instead, they challenged the view that real people in real organizations can operate according to precepts of rationality.

The hyper-rationalist studies depended on a view of the organization that came from within the scientific-rational worldview. Under that view, the modern scientific-rational world is fundamentally different from the spiritual and religious worlds that preceded it because it is not based on myth and ceremony, but on an accurate comprehension of the nature of reality. In place of superstition and hocus pocus, we now have a scientific approach to understanding the world around us that will eventually yield truth, even if there are some missteps along the way. Observable organizational practices in this system reflect universal laws of efficiency, or they will eventually come to reflect those laws, even if there are some false starts in the process and even if such cognitive constraints as bounded rationality get in the way.

While they were developed in the context of totemic systems, Durkheim's observations about the collective creation of meaning provide a lens for viewing religious and scientific-rational social systems as collectively constructed. Since the late 1970s, organizational scholars have stepped back from the rationalized practices of the modern firm, asking how we came to believe those practices to be rational rather than what the transcendental laws of rationality underlying those laws are. One reason for this revolution was growing awareness of organizational systems outside of the United States that operated differently. Those systems—in countries such as Japan, France, and Germany—made organizational scholars realize that if laws of organizational efficiency existed, they seemed to be local rather than transcendental. And so organizational scholars began to do just what Durkheim did. Durkheim had compared tribal societies to understand the mechanisms by which they collectively construct spiritual systems, and organizational scholars began to compare national organizational systems to understand the mechanisms by which they collectively construct rational systems (and laws of organizational efficiency) (Hofstede 1980; Whitley 1992).

Most of the social constructionist organizational studies that build on Durkheim's insights have taken a single country as their focus and have charted change over time in the social construction of organizational efficiency (Fligstein 1990; Roy 1997). This project has now pinned down a number of insights concerning how new organizational paradigms diffuse through social networks, how institutional entrepreneurs convince others of the efficacy of the programs they promote, and how power relations come into play in the rise of new conceptions of how to organize firms. But the project is new, and there is much work to do to further pin down how these mechanisms work. That work is typically broad in scope, involving hundreds of organizations observed over time, and sometimes across continents.

As most of the constructionist work to date has focused on organizational fields, there are three important areas of research at different levels of analysis that require further research. First, we understand poorly the mechanisms by which organizational innovations diffuse across nations and are changed in the process of diffusion (but see Guillén 1994; Djelic 1998; Czarniawska-Joerges and Sevon 1996). How are new social constructions of efficiency put into place in countries that have no experience with them or with the building blocks from which they are assembled? Second, what goes on within the firm is largely a black box, for most studies focus on the diffusion of new rituals without asking how they are implemented in individual firms. We little understand the organizational mechanisms by which new innovations are brought into the firm, put into place, and made sense of locally (but see Lounsbury and Glynn 2001; Pedersen and Dobbin 2006). Third, we understand poorly how new organizational rituals and native theories of organizing emerge through interaction, perhaps in what Randall Collins (2004), following Durkheim and Goffman, dubs 'interaction ritual chains'. How do organizational innovations first bubble up through interaction rituals? These are all questions that would have been at the top of Durkheim's own to-do list.

Acknowledgments

Thanks to Paul Adler, Michael Cohen, Anne Fleischer, Mark Kennedy, and Steve Mezias for comments and Lynn Childress for expert editing.

References

Barley, S. R., and Kunda, G. (1992). 'Design and Devotion: Surges of Rational and Normative Ideologies of Control in Managerial Discourse'. *Administrative Science Quarterly*, 37: 363–400.

Berger, P. L. (1967). *The Sacred Canopy*. Garden City, NY: Doubleday.

—— and Luckmann, T. (1966). *The Social Construction of Reality: A Treatise in the Sociology of Knowledge*. Garden City, NY: Doubleday.

Bergesen, A. J. (2004). 'Durkheim's Theory of Mental Categories: A Review of the Evidence'. *Annual Review of Sociology*, 30: 395–408.

Blau, P. M. (1970). 'A Formal Theory of Differentiation in Organizations'. *American Sociological Review*, 35: 201–18.

Boltanski, L., and Thevenot, L. (1991). *De la justification: Les Economies de la grandeur*. Paris: Gallimard.

Chandler, A. D., Jr. (1977). *The Visible Hand: The Managerial Revolution in American Business*. Cambridge, Mass.: Belknap.

Cole, R. E. (1989). *Strategies for Learning: Small-Group Activities in American, Japanese, and Swedish Industry*. Berkeley: University of California Press.

Collin, F. (1997). *Social Reality*. London: Routledge.

Collins, R. (2004). *Interaction Ritual Chains*. Princeton: Princeton University Press.

Czarniawska-Joerges, B., and Sevon, G. (eds.) (1996). *Translating Organizational Change*. Berlin: de Gruyter.

Davis, G. F., Diekmann, K. A., and Tinsley, C. H. (1994). 'The Decline and Fall of the Conglomerate Firm in the 1980s: The Deinstitutionalization of an Organizational Form'. *American Sociological Review*, 59: 547–70.

Dewey, J. (ed.) (1998). *The Essential Dewey*, vols. 1 and 2. Bloomington: Indiana University Press.

DiMaggio, P. J. (1997). 'Culture and Cognition'. *Annual Review of Sociology*, 23: 263–87.

—— and Powell, W. W. (1983). 'The Iron Cage Revisited—Institutional Isomorphism and Collective Rationality in Organizational Fields'. *American Sociological Review*, 48: 147–60.

Djelic, M.-L. (1998). *Exporting the American Model: The Postwar Transformation of European Business.* New York: Oxford University Press.

Dobbin, F. (2004). 'The Sociological View of the Economy', in F. Dobbin (ed.), *The New Economic Sociology: A Reader.* Princeton: Princeton University Press.

Dore, R. (2000). *Stock Market Capitalism: Welfare Capitalism—Japan and Germany Versus the Anglo-Saxons.* New York: Oxford University Press.

Douglas, M. (1966). *Purity and Danger: An Analysis of Concepts of Pollution and Taboo.* London: Routledge.

—— (1986). *How Institutions Think.* Syracuse, NY: Syracuse University Press.

Durkheim, É. ([1893] 1933). *The Division of Labor in Society.* New York: Free Press.

—— ([1895] 1966). *The Rules of Sociological Method.* Glencoe, Ill.: Free Press.

—— ([1897] 1966). *Suicide: A Study in Sociology.* New York: Free Press.

—— ([1912] 1961). *The Elementary Forms of the Religious Life.* New York: Collier.

—— and Mauss, M. ([1902] 1963). *Primitive Classification.* London: Cohen and West.

Emirbayer, M. (1996). 'Useful Durkheim'. *Sociological Theory*, 14: 109–30.

Fligstein, N. (1990). *The Transformation of Corporate Control.* Cambridge, Mass.: Harvard University Press.

—— and Markowitz, L. (1993). 'Financial Reorganization of American Corporations in the 1980s', in W. J. Wilson (ed.), *Sociology and the Public Agenda.* Beverly Hills: Sage Publications.

Geertz, C. (1983). *Local Knowledge: Further Essays in Interpretive Anthropology.* New York: Basic.

Goffman, E. ([1967] 2005). *Interaction Ritual: Essays in Face to Face Behavior.* New Brunswick, NJ: Aldine Transaction.

—— (1974). *Frame Analysis.* Cambridge, Mass.: Harvard University Press.

Greif, A. (1993). 'Contract Enforceability and Economic Institutions in Early Trade: The Maghriibi Traders' Coalition'. *American Economic Review*, 83: 525–48.

Guillén, M. F. (1994). *Models of Management: Work Authority and Organization in a Comparative Perspective.* Chicago: University of Chicago Press.

Haveman, H. A. (1993). 'Follow the Leader: Mimetic Isomorphism and Entry into New Markets'. *Administrative Science Quarterly*, 38: 593–627.

Hirschman, A. O. (1977). *The Passions and the Interests: Political Arguments for Capitalism before its Triumph.* Princeton: Princeton University Press.

Hobbes, T. (1982). *Leviathan.* London: Penguin.

Hofstede, G. (1980). *Culture's Consequences: International Differences in Work Values.* Beverly Hills, Calif.: Sage.

Joas, H. (1993). *Pragmatism and Social Theory.* Chicago: University of Chicago Press.

Lévi-Strauss, C. (1978). *Myth and Meaning.* London: Routledge and Kegan Paul.

Lincoln, J., and Guillot, D. (2005). *A Durkheimian View of Organizational Culture.* Oxford: Oxford University Press.

Locke, J. (1965). *Two Treatises of Government.* New York: Mentor.

LOUNSBURY, M., and GLYNN, M. A. (2001). 'Cultural Entrepreneurship: Stories, Legitimacy and the Acquisition of Resources'. *Strategic Management Journal*, 22: 545–64.

LUKES, S. (1985). *Émile Durkheim: His Life and Work, a Historical and Critical Study.* Stanford, Calif.: Stanford University Press.

MARCH, J. G., and SIMON, H. A. (1958). *Organizations.* New York: Wiley.

MARTIN, J. (2002). *The Education of John Dewey: A Biography.* New York: Columbia University Press.

MARX, K. ([1852] 1963). *The Eighteenth Brumaire of Louis Bonaparte.* New York: International.

——([1859] 1968). Preface to a Contribution to the Critique of Political Economy, in K. Marx and F. Engels (eds.), *Selected Works.* London: Lawrence & Wishart.

MEYER, J. W. (1994). 'Rationalized Environments', in W. R. Scott and J. W. Meyer (eds.), *Institutional Environments and Organizations: Structural Complexity and Individualism.* Thousand Oaks, Calif.: Sage.

—— and ROWAN, B. (1977). 'Institutionalized Organizations: Formal Structure as Myth and Ceremony'. *American Journal of Sociology*, 83: 340–63.

—— and SCOTT, W. R. (1983). *Organizational Environments: Ritual and Rationality.* Beverly Hills, Calif.: Sage.

MILLS, C. W. (1956). *The Power Elite.* New York: Oxford University Press.

NISBETT, R. E., PENG, K., CHOI, I., and NORENZAYAN, A. (2001). 'Culture and Systems of Thought: Holistic Versus Analytic Cognition'. *Psychological Review*, 108: 291–310.

PEDERSEN, J. S., and DOBBIN, F. (2006). 'In Search of Identity and Legitimation: Organizational Culture and Neoinstitutionalism'. *American Behavioral Scientist*, 49: 897–907.

RAWLS, A. W. (1996). 'Durkheim's Epistemology: The Neglected Argument'. *American Journal of Sociology*, 102: 430–82.

ROETHLISBERGER, F. J., and DICKSON, W. J. ([1939] 1981). 'Human Relations', in O. Grusky and G. A. Miller (eds.), *The Sociology of Organizations: Basic Studies*, 2nd edn. New York: Free Press.

ROY, W. (1997). *Socializing Capital: The Rise of the Large Industrial Corporation in America.* Princeton: Princeton University Press.

SCHEIN, E. H. (1996). 'Culture: The Missing Concept in Organization Studies'. *Administrative Science Quarterly*, 41: 229–40.

SCHUTZ, A. ([1932] 1967). *The Phenomenology of the Social World.* Evanston, Ill.: Northwestern University Press.

SELZNICK, P. (1957). *Leadership in Administration: A Sociological Interpretation.* New York: Harper and Row.

SMELSER, N. J. (1995). 'Economic Rationality as a Religious System', in R. Wuthnow (ed.), *Rethinking Materialism: Perspectives on the Spiritual Dimension of Economic Behavior.* Grand Rapids, Mich.: William B. Eerdmans.

SOMERS, M. M. (2001). 'Romancing the Market, Reviling the State: Historicizing Liberalism, Privatization, and the Competing Claims to Civil Society', in C. Crouch, K. Eder, and D. Tambini (eds.), *Citizenship, Markets, and the State.* New York: Oxford University Press.

SWEDBERG, R. (2003). *Principles of Economic Sociology.* Princeton: Princeton University Press.

SWIDLER, A. (1986). 'Culture in Action: Symbols and Strategies'. *American Sociological Review*, 51: 273–86.

TAYLOR, F. W. (1911). *Scientific Management.* New York: Harper.

Turner, B. S. (1997). *The Absent Body in Structuration Theory.* London: Routledge.

Weber, M. (1978). *Economy and Society.* Berkeley: University of California Press.

Weick, K. E. (1995). *Sensemaking in Organizations.* Thousand Oaks, Calif.: Sage.

Whitley, R. (1992). *Business Systems in East Asia: Firms, Markets, and Societies.* London: Sage.

—— and Kristensen, P. H. (eds.) (1996). *The Changing European Firm: Limits to Convergence.* London: Routledge.

Woodward, J. ([1958] 1984). 'Management and Technology', in D. S. Pugh (ed.), *Organization Theory: Selected Readings*, 2nd edn. New York: Penguin.

Zald, M. N., and Denton, P. (1963). 'From Evangelism to General Service: The Transformation of the YMCA'. *Administrative Science Quarterly*, 8: 214–34.

CHAPTER 10

A DURKHEIMIAN APPROACH TO GLOBALIZATION

PAUL HIRSCH

PEER C. FISS

AMANDA HOEL-GREEN

10.1. Introduction

The work of Émile Durkheim, and particularly his theory of the division of labor, occupies a somewhat peculiar place in the pantheon of classical sociologists. On the one hand, Durkheim is rightly recognized as one of the founding fathers of the discipline, and *The Division of Labor in Society* (hereafter referred to as *Division*), first published in 1893, remains not only 'one of the peak contributions of modern sociology' (Merton 1934: 328), but may even be considered 'sociology's *first* classic' (Tiryakian 1994: 4). Yet, on the other hand, *Division* has been critiqued on a variety of grounds. Later authors have suggested that 'its conclusions are too sweeping,... its methods at times faulty' (Merton 1934: 328) and that Durkheim's attempt to distinguish the two major concepts of his book—mechanical and organic solidarity—introduces theoretical problems that are extremely difficult to disentangle (Pope and Johnson 1983). In fact, Durkheim himself rarely used the mechanical–organic distinction after *Division* and modified it somewhat in his preface to the second edition. In terms of its importance for theory building, mechanical and organic solidarity were arguably overshadowed by Durkheim's later works (cf. Nisbet 1966: 86; Pope and Johnson 1983: 690).

Several attempts have been made to rescue *Division* from becoming a merely reverential classic with little relevance to our understanding of current conditions. For instance, a number of authors have aimed to bring greater rigor to Durkheim's thought by trying to organize his arguments into a tighter nomological network, offering a formal restatement with interconnected principles and propositions (e.g. Gibbs 2003; Turner 1981). Furthermore, at least one attempt has been made to empirically examine the relationship between the division of labor, the level of technological development, and the degree of urbanization in societies (Gibbs and Martin 1962). However, *Division* has clearly not initiated a robust research program aiming to test Durkheim's model of what it is that holds societies together and how levels of social interaction are connected to differentiation of the production system.

Why, then, is it useful to revisit this old work and see how it might help our understanding of a current social phenomenon, namely the higher levels of international connectedness usually referred to as 'globalization'? We rarely see *Division* invoked in current theorizing, and instead much of the recent work drawing on Durkheim focuses on the collective conscience as the more attractive theoretical concept. Yet, there are good reasons, we believe, to apply Durkheim's thinking to the issue of globalization. Others have made the case for the relevance of the classics in an eloquent way (e.g. Alexander 1989; Collins 1997), and we will not revisit their arguments here although we do agree with most of them. There is one argument, however, that we do want to point out. In his essay on the functions of the classics in a discipline, Stinchcombe (1982) suggested that they serve as 'routine science', or more specifically, as a quarry of ideas for the sociologists who come after them and develop new research agendas by applying some of the classics' assumptions to other fields. In a half-serious way, Stinchcombe further suggested that to prove especially fruitful for further research, it might be useful to build some small mistake into a grand theory. This could then stimulate generations of other researchers to try to refute the theory, and thereby come across new insights and eventually enlarge our understanding of the whole complex (Stinchcombe 1982: 3).

It is in this spirit that we believe the application of a work such as *Division* can be most usefully conceived: to see how applying it—with all its faults—can nevertheless help us better understand what we are currently facing and what theoretical and empirical tools are needed to develop and push beyond our current appreciation of the phenomena at hand; here, the idea of 'globalization'. Durkheim's legacy centers on his analysis and concerns about the societal transformations of his day and their impacts on individuals' psyches. These provide obvious parallels to today's era of increasing global transformation and concerns over its contributions and consequences (e.g. Guillén 2001*a*; Fiss and Hirsch 2005; Giddens 1990).

In this chapter, we extend Durkheim's analysis of Europe's transformations in the early twentieth century to suggest how his theoretical apparatus might be used to interpret subsequent developments in the twenty-first. In particular, we suggest that Durkheim's concern with solidarity—a key theme of his work—has been largely neglected in the current field of organization studies, which might be reinvigorated by a greater concern for issues of inequality in the global arena.

10.2. Durkheim's Theory of Social Change and Solidarity

Durkheim has been accused of having no theory of social change (Parsons 1937). Yet, as Harms (1981) and others have argued, a deep concern for the 'moral crisis' of Europe in general and France in particular pervades most if not all of his major works, from *Division* to *Suicide* and the *Elementary Forms of Religion*. Nevertheless, if one considers how the economic and social spheres are connected in the transformation of societies, one might argue that *Division*, despite its title, has rather little to say about how a society might best organize its production system or about how the separation of tasks might improve productivity and efficiency. Durkheim largely bypasses the concerns a modern economist would focus on and instead examines how the differentiation of occupational groups affects patterns of social interaction, and in turn, social consciousness. Several features of Durkheim's work in this regard are noteworthy. *Division* was not only written at a time of economic and social upheaval but it also carried a strong normative component, that is, a clear notion of what a healthy society looks like, what pathologies are, and how to rectify them. Durkheim ascribed a high value to the integrative function of social relations as well as a deep concern about the shortcomings of modernizing society, which he attributed not so much to the division of labor itself but rather to pathologies arising from an 'unnatural' state of affairs. This brings up a second issue; Durkheim's theory is marked by a belief that a 'good' society has some kind of natural order among its members and that regulation is needed to maintain this order (Inglis and Robertson 2004; Pickering 1984). Absent this order and its regulation, unhappiness, chaos, and anomie arise. The need for regulation as a tool to increase the overall amount of human happiness clearly pervades Durkheim's writing and thinking about how societies should organize.

Concerns about the transformation of society thus very much lie at the center of *Division*, which was likewise true of the new field of study named sociology. As a discipline, sociology emerged as a response to and an analysis of modernity and the large-scale social changes that marked the entrance of the twentieth century.

The 1890s were a time of advanced industrialism, which ruthlessly transformed the Western societies. It was a time of 'unbridled economic individualism' (Tiryakian 1994: 7) with relatively little regulation of the dominant economic classes and the establishment of new ventures. It was also a time that witnessed a series of economic scandals in the later 1880s and 1890s 'wherein greed brought on financial crises and panics' (Tiryakian 1994: 7). In both regards, we see intriguing parallels between Durkheim's time and the current period of neo-liberal market orientation and the series of financial scandals that have shaken up investor confidence in the early twenty-first century.

The goal of our chapter is to suggest that the theoretical tools of *Division* can be usefully applied to globalization and the role that organizations in particular play in it. However, before we can explore this argument in more detail, it is necessary to briefly discuss the concepts of mechanical and organic solidarity that lie at the center of *Division*. For Durkheim, mechanical solidarity, or solidarity through likeness, is marked by uniform beliefs and practices to which the individual must submit. It is commonly found in pre-industrial societies where the collective conscience holds a powerful grip on the individual and where we observe relatively little differentiation of work tasks. Furthermore, because these societies are segmentary, there is little interdependence between the respective segments, since most individuals can still perform almost all tasks necessary for survival. Accordingly, the social bonds between individuals tend to be weak, necessitating powerful shared symbolic orders with repressive sanctions and little individual freedom.

In contrast, organic solidarity is characterized by advanced division of labor and social differentiation. It is characteristic of developed, industrialized societies, which consist of a system of functionally different 'organs', each of which has to fulfill a special task. The morphological comparison is somewhat less than fortunate but is meant to underscore the importance of interdependence in modern societies where the collective conscience is less strongly developed and no longer by itself holds society together. Instead, it is really the division of labor that integrates the individuals into society: having to work together day by day, individuals realize their interdependence, and this results in a strengthening of the social bonds between them. Accordingly, organic solidarity is marked by restitutive rather than repressive sanctions and leaves considerably greater freedom for the individual as status tends to be determined by occupation rather than kinship ties.

Durkheim's argument was clearly developmental in nature, with mechanical solidarity being gradually replaced by organic solidarity in modern societies. Naturally, this opens up the question of what factors lead to this gradual disappearance of segmentary societies and their eventual replacement with advanced and highly differentiated ones. To explain this transition, Durkheim introduced the twin concepts of moral (sometimes also referred to as dynamic) and material density. Durkheim viewed moral density as a function of the number of social relations within a society, with 'individuals sufficiently in contact to be able to act and react upon one another' (Durkheim 1964: 257). This level of interaction between the individuals and the resulting level of connectivity in a society, however, is dependent on material factors. From Durkheim's discussion, one can collect a list of factors that affect this material density. The one that has received the most attention in subsequent research is population size, a function of birth and death rates in combination with immigration. Beyond mere population increases, material density is also a driven by what may be called ecological concentration, this being a function of (a) the extent of constrictive geographical boundaries that increase interactions, (b) the degree of political centralization, and (c) the degree of consensus over cultural symbols (Turner 1981: 383). Increases in material density and thus in each of these factors lead to increases in competition among the members of any given society. Specialization due to greater division of labor thus offers a way out of this increased struggle to survive and prosper. According to Durkheim, 'if society effectively includes more members at the same time as they are more closely in relation to each other, the [competitive] struggle is still more acute and the resulting specialization more rapid and complete' (Durkheim 1964: 269). The division of labor is thus first and foremost, a result of 'struggle for existence' (Durkheim 1964: 270), and it offers a remedy that allows former rivals to coexist and avoid selection pressures. Durkheim's argument about the transition from segmented to highly differentiated societies is thus quite functional in nature, as the greater division of labor ameliorates competitive pressures.

In introducing competition between similar competitors as the driver of differentiation, Durkheim follows the lead of Herbert Spencer's theory of social competition. In competition, both moral and material density are connected. As Durkheim points out regarding the nature of human interaction, 'this moral drawing together cannot produce its effect unless the actual distance among individuals has itself diminished in some way. Moral density cannot grow unless material density grows at the same time, and the latter can be used to measure the former' (1964: 257). However, it is important to note that the causality that Durkheim implies here runs both ways: moral and material density constitute each other and it would therefore be 'useless to try to find out which has determined the other; they are inseparable' (1964: 257). It is thus clear that Durkheim's explanation is not one of material determinism. It is not merely that moral density increases as population density intensifies, but on the contrary, population density itself only becomes possible given moral density. In this sense, 'the social relationships among the members of a society are what caused them to concentrate in an area in the first place' (Schmaus 1995: 68). Indeed, Durkheim takes pains to point out that 'we do not mean to say that the development of density results from economic changes. The two facts mutually condition each other, and the presence of one proves the other's' (Durkheim 1964: 258 n. 4). His point, then, is the mutual constitution of the material and the social, finding a middle way between Marxist determinism and Hegelian idealism.

10.3. Durkheim's Influence on Organization Studies

Durkheim's thinking on the transition from mechanical to organic solidarity and the interconnectedness of human life has informed subsequent work in the field of organizations in numerous ways. Despite the fact that the distinction between both forms of solidarity became less central over time, Durkheim's ideas regarding solidarity laid the groundwork for a number of organizational theorists' later works. For instance, the human relations school (Mayo 1945) built on Durkheim in developing its understanding of unity in small groups. Specifically, the human relations school focused on the ways in which a new form of moral order could arise from belonging to a work group, a force that could counter the anomic aspects of industrial organization and the division of labor (Starkey 1992). While these ideas again disappeared during the functionalist period of organization studies, they reemerged during the early 1980s in the field of organizational culture (Dandridge, Mitroff, and Joyce 1980; Deal and Kennedy 1982; Peters and Waterman 1982; Smirich 1983). From its early stages, organizational culture—and its close relative organizational symbolism—conceived itself as running counter to traditional organization research with its focus on rationality and technology that manifested itself in an almost dogmatic functionalism and pervasive 'number crunching'. The proponents of organizational culture emphasized the 'irrational' aspects of organizational life, which included the realm of metaphors, myths, rituals, emotions, and perhaps most importantly, the role of symbols. What resonates in this stream of work is a strong concern with fostering a sense of integration (Barnard 1938), a theme that has its roots both in Durkheim's focus on the role of solidarity and in his work on symbols and the collective conscience (Lincoln and Guillot 2005; Starkey 1992, 1998). This research stream, though less prominent recently, has produced significant insights into how Durkheimian thinking can enlighten life within organizations, including how micro-situational consciousness is connected to a Marxian concern with macro-societal issues (Brown 1978).

While Durkheim has been most influential regarding the role of organizational culture and collective memory, his work has also affected organization studies more broadly. Durkheim's thinking on competition as an engine of differentiation in particular has influenced population ecology (e.g. Hannan and Freeman 1977: 940), which likewise sees competitive mechanisms at the heart of patterns of social organization (e.g. Swaminathan and Delacroix 1991). Similarly, studies of organizational control mechanisms have drawn on Durkheim's concepts of mechanical and organic solidarity to explain how the sharing of common values and objectives can lead to integration in the modern work organization (Ouchi 1980; Ouchi and Johnson 1978). Ironically, even those that criticized Durkheim, such as Parsons

(1937) and Merton (1934), formed their own ideas to a considerable extent based on what they felt were errors in Durkheim's thinking.

However, there are also significant aspects in Durkheim's thinking that have largely been neglected, particularly due to a waning interest in the concept of solidarity within the field of organization studies. We believe that the study of globalization in particular offers an opportunity to revive this interest.

10.4. Globalization: A Durkheimian Reading

There are few concepts in recent years that rival globalization in its effect on the social sciences. Since it began its dramatic rise in the early 1980s, the discourse on globalization has steadily grown both in size and intensity. While there can be little denying that globalization is a term whose time had come by the end of the 1990s, there is nevertheless little agreement on the nature of globalization or even on its proper definition (Held *et al.* 1999; Fiss and Hirsch 2005). As it has been used in the media, globalization may be understood as 'the inexorable integration of markets, nation-states and technologies to a degree never witnessed before—in a way that is enabling individuals, corporations and nation-states to reach around the world faster, deeper and cheaper than ever before' (Friedman 1999: 7). While globalization thus denotes 'a process fueled by, and resulting in, increasing cross border flows of goods, services, money, people, information, and culture' (Held *et al.* 1999: 16), this definition raises the question as to when globalization actually began. Indeed, the start of globalization is a contested issue, with historians (Mazlish 1993) and world-systems theorists (Wallerstein 1974; Waters 1995) generally pointing to an earlier beginning around the sixteenth century, while economic historians tend to locate globalization as beginning with the sharp increase in international trade and investment that occurred after the 1880s (Robertson 1992; Williamson 1996). Even more contested are the effects of globalization, which have been variously defined as either positive, negative, or grossly overstated.[1]

What these discussions of globalization share is an attempt to link globalization to specific events or changes in international trade and governance regimes. There is thus a common concern for the 'true' nature of globalization and whether the term refers to real or imagined process. However, to limit the discussion on globalization to the changes in the structure of the international economy is to miss the point of

[1] For overviews of this debate, see e.g. Fiss and Hirsch 2005; Guillén 2001*b*; Sklair 1999.

globalization as a socially constructed issue. Precisely because globalization involves high levels of uncertainty and is not easily measured, it is subjected to substantial interpretive work. Globalization has to be named, explained, elaborated, placed in context, and generally situated within the larger universe of economic and social relations. This process of giving meaning to globalization more often resembles myth making than scientific enquiry (Spich 1995) and takes places largely within the realm of public discourse (Fiss and Hirsch 2005).

As we have noted earlier, the 1890s—when Durkheim wrote *Division*—were a time of fundamental societal transformation from an agricultural, small-town way of life to a more urban, industrial economy. In a similar manner, the large-scale social transformation commonly labeled as globalization that we are currently witnessing offers sociology and organization scholars the opportunity to again interpret the emerging new world society. Table 10.1 provides a comparison of the transformations experienced in European society at the end of the nineteenth century with the more recent changes experienced at the end of the twentieth century. While each dimension may have expanded at the end of the nineteenth century, advances in technology and social organization greatly increased the scale of cross-border exchanges at the end of the twentieth century in all of them. Specifically, during the century since *Division*'s publication, organizations have grown enormously in size, scale, and assets, both domestically and internationally (Perrow 2004). On nearly all the social dimensions in Table 10.1, the activities moved across nations, and the formats in which they appear became increasingly standardized, although this is not necessarily true of the content and underlying social relations.

As the table illustrates, technological advances enabled the expansion of transportation, travel, and communication, across such areas as education (study abroad programs, standardized tests taken internationally), business practice (locations and outsourcing), and popular culture and social interaction (international hits in movies and TV programs; internet websites). Across nations, we have also seen the emergence of expanded suffrage and voting rights and greater attention to aiding disaster victims in far-away nations. Much as employees are encouraged to look forward to 'boundaryless careers' with multiple employers (Hirsch and Shanley 1996), organizations are more committed to being located and operating in more than one nation. These transformations indicate that along many dimensions the interconnectedness between industrialized nations in particular is unprecedented in terms of broadness.

In addition to 'boundarylessness' in terms of voting and disaster relief, patterns of corporate governance and investors' expectations now also exert global pressures (Fiss and Zajac 2004). For example, managers in multinational and multicultural settings may develop a new form of 'corporate' identity and solidarity, more global and less national in its commitment and perspective. At the same time, managers in multinational firms, though geographically dispersed, can communicate increasingly freely as the cost of long-distance telephony decreases, and as

Table 10.1. Dimensions of transformation at the end of the nineteenth and twentieth centuries

	Late 1800s to early 1900s Local to national communities	Modern day National to global communities
Education	Small schoolhouses; slowly expanding; education is exclusive, but opening over time to others	Shift to 'studying abroad'; learning different languages; standardized testing across countries; education is for all social classes
Organization	Local to national	Multiple physical locations; national to multinational
Business practices	Social networks based on family–community relations breaking down	Increasing use of outsourcing, consulting; emergence of network forms of corporations
Corporate identity	Mostly family-owned; rural to city	Mobile, flexible boundaries; national to global
Communication	Shift from letters to telephone	Shift from telephone to email and instant messaging
Religion	Increase in secularity as people move towards cities, but life still revolves much around religion, the main socializing source	Mega-churches, television evangelist broadcasts worldwide
Mass media	Growing number of newspapers; radio stations and papers are locally owned	Unified formats, particularly global news; centralized ownership
Criminal justice	Diversified systems begin to converge, but still more methods of punishment and death sentences than today	Converging systems with most countries banning or limiting death sentence
Entertainment	Shift from reading and storytelling towards radio	Blockbuster movies grossing millions, social life on internet
Warfare	Fought by troops; with technological advances just entering	Fought by troops and increasingly by technology
Politics	Fewer voters; efforts required to research candidates	More voters; mass media political endorsements
Charity	Affiliated with one's own community/society, broadening to national charity	Corporate philanthropy; increasingly cross-national charity efforts

wireless and internet technologies are more accessible. Thus, as Friedman (2005) argues, worldwide communication and solidarities, within and outside the work realm, increase without the need for geographical proximity. New solidarities and social networks emerge as a result of communication technology (Podolny and Baron 1997; Burt 1997). This suggests that embeddedness may also become less local.

Collectively, the table shows that the shift in focus from national to global has greatly increased since Durkheim's era. Nevertheless, we believe his theories pertaining to shifts in solidarity are as relevant today as they were then. As we have seen, Durkheim identified several factors that correlate with greater moral and material density. Leaving aside for the moment factors relating to greater population size, those factors are (a) the extent of constrictive geographical boundaries, (b) the degree of political centralization, and (c) the degree of consensus over cultural symbols. To this list, we can add (d) communication and transportation technology, since their development contributes to 'increasing the density of society' (Durkheim 1964: 259–60). Interestingly, all of these factors have been argued to play a key role in current accounts of globalization:

1. *Geographical boundaries.* Current accounts of globalization frequently argue that geographical borders have lost their relevance in a globalized world (Friedman 2005). As communication and transportation technologies have rapidly advanced, physical barriers become less of an issue. However, this does not imply that the level of competition decreases, but rather the opposite: a lack of geographical restrictions and thus increased factor mobility puts actors everywhere around the world in competition with each other. Naturally, we are nowhere near such a state of affairs yet and local monopolies are likely to remain for indefinite periods of time, but as a general tendency the increased levels of competition due to globalization (or conversely increased globalization due to greater international competition) seem hard to deny.
2. *Political centralization.* Similarly, the role of the polity has arguably been weakened in a globalized world. A number of authors have argued that the state is becoming increasingly less meaningful as firms and business move fluidly across state boundaries (Cox 1996; Kobrin 1997). Indeed, states may compete with each other in providing the most economically attractive climate in order to attract these highly mobile corporations, leading to a world where state actors become less and less important, eventually leading to the establishment of transnational organizations and communities (e.g. Djelic and Quack 2003; Djelic and Sahlin-Andersson 2006). As the weakening of the state would lead to less interaction at the national level, it is replaced by interaction beyond the state's jurisdiction, suggesting that levels of interaction will remain at least as high if not higher.
3. *Consensus over cultural symbols.* This is perhaps the most intriguing aspect of globalization. The question of whether globalization leads to an increase or decrease in the consensus over cultural symbols has been at the focus of a considerable debate. While some authors have argued for globalization leading to increased cultural homogeneity (Hamelink 1994; Latouche 1995), others have pointed to the persistence and even increases in diversity (e.g. Featherstone, Lash, and Robertson 1995). We do not subscribe to the notion

that globalization will eventually lead to a universally shared culture. However, the global spread of certain cultural forms facilitates the levels of interaction due to shared values and vocabularies indicating, again, higher levels of competition as facilitated by cultural 'compatibility'.

4. *Communication and transportation technology.* There can be little doubt that advances in communication and transportation technology are among the key drivers of globalization (Castells 1998). Both factors lie at the heart of a sophisticated division of labor, which in turn is a precondition for what Gibbs and Martin call a 'high degree of external dispersion', or the average distance between the points of origin of raw materials and the points at which these materials are being consumed (Gibbs and Martin 1962: 673). This high degree of dispersion is marked by ever longer interaction chains including chains of exchange.

10.5. Solidarity in a Globalized World

The dual nature of globalization parallels Durkheim's model of social interactions, where structural aspects of human interaction such as the material and moral density are paralleled by symbolic aspects such as collective conscience and consensus over cultural symbols. However, while in many ways the current move towards globalization echoes Durkheim's thoughts on social transformation at the turn of the twentieth century, we are currently witnessing a development that runs counter to the overall movement from segmentary to differentiated societies, notably the return of mechanical solidarity in various forms (cf. Tiryakian 1994). Rather than interdependence based on a division of labor, a common response to globalization appears to be the reemergence of mobilization based on shared identity, and particularly religious and national identity. Yet, this return of mechanical solidarity may not only be negative. The emergence of collective identities based for instance on ethnic identity can—in an age where the means of communication have been radically democratized and become available to people dispersed around the globe—give voice to those who are being marginalized (Tiryakian 1994).

While the re-emergence of mechanical solidarity would appear to run counter to a movement from mechanical to organic solidarity as originally suggested in *Division*, it is important to note that such a phenomenon is in fact already foreshadowed in Durkheim's own thinking. In the preface to the second edition, Durkheim to a considerable extent revised his original view of solidarity to argue that both forms—mechanical and organic—are necessary, and that the challenge of the modern age is indeed an insufficiency of mechanical solidarity. He particularly pointed to intermediary occupational groups and associations[2] as the settings, or mechanism, helping to fill the gap between the individual and the state. He considered their health critical to the formation of the attitudes and actions taken by their members, as they are the primary place in which the members of an occupational group can create a shared moral system of rules (1964: 5).

Beyond this, there is another important condition that needs to be met for the division of labor to be the effective glue that holds society together. Specifically, social groups of (world) society need to be able to participate in a meaningful way in the economic sphere. Durkheim himself noted that a lack of regulation of individuals by norms and a situation where inequalities are considered illegitimate and not corresponding to the distribution of talents ('forced distribution of labor') is likely to lead to a breakdown of organic solidarity. To achieve solidarity, Durkheim considered the fair treatment of participants as necessary at all levels in economic and other transactions. Specifically, he argued that excessive disparities need to be avoided, and that preventing them is the proper task of political authorities. A concern for morality and fairness thus becomes a necessary condition for the division of labor to unfold successfully, to get citizens, workers, and managers to willingly work towards and contribute to the success of society as a whole. These deliberations indicate that Durkheim would likely find problematic contemporary employment relationships which are at-will, subject to severance at any time, likely to be temporary, lacking fringe benefits, and are on the verge of being outsourced. In such employment relations, it is difficult for individuals to develop the sense of community and shared interdependence that Durkheim thought essential for solidarity to emerge.

Indeed, there is little doubt that what is currently labeled 'globalization' comes along with high levels of economic marginalization. Most increases in trade and investment flows have been between Europe, North America, Australia, and Asia, but Africa and parts of Asia have been marginalized with little hope of participating in the newly emerging economic world order. Suggestions that such countries should focus on their natural resources or cheap labor ring hollow in the face of increasing economic inequality and the ability of advanced economies to appropriate much of the rents generated in the value chain that stretches, for instance, from the beans harvested in Colombia to the cup of Starbucks coffee sold to the North American customer. A Durkheimian analysis suggests that the residents of the Brazilian *favelas*, who exist essentially outside the social, legal, and economic boundaries of world society, are not likely to share the same values and aspirations. The marginalization and effective exclusion of such populations, as well as countries, is likely to lead to a breakdown of moral solidarity. Durkheim himself was quite cautious regarding the realization of greater solidarity as part of a world

[2] Durkheim himself used the term 'corporations' or 'occupational group' to refer, for example, to professional associations that would include both employees and employers.

society and viewed the division of labor as a necessary though not sufficient condition in stating that 'the ideal of human fraternity can be realized only in proportion to the progress of the division of labor' (1964: 403).

10.6. Durkheim and Globalization: An Empirical Agenda

It has become clear from our discussion that a Durkheimian analysis of the effects of globalization on solidarity would note two related yet separate aspects: (a) a concern about the breaking of existing moral and communal bonds, with the ensuing possibility of anomic disintegration, and (b) a concern for whether and how moral unity could be reconstituted, particularly at the international level—that is, by an international moral order backed by an international legal system. These considerations open up a considerable amount of research opportunities to organizational researchers. Some of the most promising ones include:

1. *Comparative studies of the effects of global deregulation on organizations.* Deregulation—the institution of market principles for other principles of organization and distribution—carries strong implications for the emergence of anomic conditions marked by a self-interest not reined in by moral sentiment. Such studies might focus on the impacts of the privatization of public goods, diminishing fringe benefits, and the decline of smaller business firms along the value chain (e.g. Henisz, Zelner, and Guillén 2005).
2. *The redefinition of employment and work in nations that shift from socialist to market economies* (e.g. Stark 1996). These situations are particularly interesting as they are examples of the dissolution of prior moral orders of economic exchange and the creation of new ones with a focus on efficiency and competition. The ensuing redefinitions of interdependencies, particularly in nations where 'unemployment' was not normal in the labor force, raise significant 'moral density' questions.
3. *The rise of outsourcing and decline in the countervailing power of unions and professional associations.* Both developments present challenges to workers' and managers' sense of belonging by revising the power-dependence aspects of the employment relationship. As we noted, Durkheim placed particular importance on the role of occupational groups as intermediate entities between the state and the individual. However, it appears now evident that transnational epistemic communities of experts and practitioners are among the most powerful agents of dissemination of policy and management models (Adler and

Haas 1992; Fourcade 2006). Such communities can successfully diffuse policies leading to uniform standards, thus creating a shared cultural and cognitive sphere (Meyer *et al.* 1997). Epistemic communities frame debate and define what issues are 'important' in reference to globalization, and their role thus appears central in a Durkheimian account of globalization, with Durkheim himself pointing to the importance of such intermediate actors between the state and society.

4. *The emergence of international institutions that regulate trade.* We are already seeing an emerging interest in the study of transnational governance (e.g. Djelic and Sahlin-Andersson 2006). In particular, trade agreements that promote economic globalization yet lack provisions for worker protection and human rights issues would run counter to a Durkheimian emphasis on the integrative function of the division of labor. The potential negative implications of such agreements seem clear, as they are likely to negatively affect the fairness of how rents are distributed, leading to higher levels of anomie both at the individual and organizational level. Durkheim himself was quite aware of the need for transnational regimes, noting that 'intersocial conflicts [can] be regulated only by a society which comprises in its scope all others' (1964: 405). Transnational governance thus offers intriguing opportunities to examine the integrative function of economic interdependence.
5. *The perception of globalization by occupational groups in organizational settings and its effect on local working orders and solidarity.* For instance, there is a greater need for qualitative case studies on the pros and cons of the reshaping of employment by large companies like Wal-Mart and professional organizations in the service sector, such as health maintenance organizations (Lincoln and Guillot 2005). Such studies could directly assess the ways in which globalization affects both mechanical and organic solidarity, and how organic solidarity might further become the core organizing principle of the firm as a collaborative community (Adler and Heckscher 2006).

All of these research topics share as their underlying theme Durkheim's concern that for the division of labor to progress and his vision of the organic society to unfold, solidarity needs to be fostered and regulations in place to avoid unfettered opportunism. It would follow from these concerns that there is too little attention provided to developing leaders, programs, and policies that contribute to solidarity across firms' constituencies. In particular, it seems to us that a Durkheimian analysis of rent distribution would find problematic a greater focus on firms' financial performance and 'shareholder value' while neglecting how wealth generated might be more widely shared with other stakeholder groups that likewise have an important part to play for the proper functioning of society. In a related fashion, such an analysis would have to problematize the view that an organization is a bundle of contracts and that 'self-interest seeking with guile' is the basic assumption of economic behavior (Williamson 1985: 47). Where no firm or leader will sacrifice for the common good, then all will suffer when the value and benefits of the commons are exhausted. There are considerable warning signs that globalization may not currently be associated with higher levels of organic solidarity, as evidenced by rising inequality in the workforce of the more 'advanced' industrial nations, with some combination of overwork and anomie suggested by the widespread use of (legal) tranquilizer drugs among their populations.

Our considerations have so far not taken into account how one might actually test the relationship between material and moral density, the division of labor, and levels of solidarity. Durkheim's espoused relationship between such increasing interdependencies and greater social interactions stemming from the expanded division of labor have rarely been examined empirically. An unusual exception here is the work of Gibbs and Martin (1962), who examine the relationship between urbanization, the division of labor, and the dispersion of consumption. Gibbs and Martin defined 'urbanization' as the exchange or mass movement of raw materials and other resources outside the boundaries of one's own society. While the term 'globalization' had not yet appeared, for Gibbs and Martin this process was tightly coupled with the division of labor. Their study classified societies via the dispersion of consumable products, both internal and external:

> The degree of 'internal dispersion' in a society refers to the average distance between the points of origin of raw materials and the points at which the materials are consumed, with both points being within the society's boundaries. The degree of 'external dispersion,' on the other hand, is the average distance between the points when the origin is outside the society. (Gibbs and Martin 1962: 669)

For a society to have a high degree of external dispersion, a highly sophisticated division of labor had to reside within that specific economy. Occupational diversification within and across societies constituted this division of labor. Technology facilitated a nation's division of labor: 'Just as it is necessary for the populations of large cities to draw objects of consumption from great distances so is it equally necessary for them to have a high degree of division of labor and technological development to accomplish the task' (Gibbs and Martin 1962: 674).

The work of Gibbs and Martin has intriguing implications for empirically examining the relationship between the division of labor and moral density. To measure the division of labor, Gibbs and Martin used data on the diversification of industries. The argument here is that lower levels of industry differentiation will go along with little diversity, while greater division of labor will indicate higher levels of diversity as measured by the Herfindahl index, a widely used measure of concentration. The index ranges from 1/N to 1, where N is the number of industries and is usually reverse-coded for ease of interpretation. For instance, if all individuals were employed in only one industry (such as 'hunting and gathering'), the index of industry differentiation would be close to zero, whereas if all individuals were equally distributed across many industries, the index would eventually approach 1.

To measure the internationalization of the division of labor across countries, one might similarly employ data on the diversification of inputs and outputs across countries. While some empirical work in this regard has been done in the world-systems literature (e.g. Krempel and Plümper 1999), much remains to be done to develop our understanding of how organizations in general, and business corporations in particular, enact the creation of a new global division of labor (Schwartzman 2006). While the weakening of the state would decrease interaction at the national level, it is replaced by interaction beyond the state's jurisdiction, suggesting that levels of interaction will remain at least as high if not higher. Similarly, one might consider using Durkheim's own measure of organic solidarity—the move from punitive to restitutive law—to examine how, for instance, international law might reflect the emergence of a different order based on increasing division of labor.

With greater globalization we should see considerably higher levels of material and moral density. However, a Durkheimian approach also implies a different reading of the concept of globalization, which becomes not only the result of intensified flows of goods, services, money, people, and so forth, but instead is constituted by a greater social need to be connected. Globalization, in this sense, is not only the effect, but the cause of higher material and moral density. Such an understanding points our attention to issues surrounding the discursive construction of globalization (e.g. Fiss and Hirsch 2005), and how the need for and effects of greater global connectedness may be translated into policy that then brings about the very changes it means to address.

Until now, we have largely focused on direct interactions between organizations and the globalized world. The view of globalization that underlies these considerations is one of making nation states largely irrelevant in the economic processes as organizations are connected directly with each other around the globe. This vision of globalization is perhaps best expressed by Longworth, who views globalization as 'a revolution that enables any entrepreneur to raise money anywhere in the world and, with that money, to use technology, communications, management, and labor located anywhere the entrepreneur finds them to make things anywhere he or she wants and sell them anywhere there are customers' (Longworth 1998: 7). Here, factor markets are accessible across the globe, as are customers, mostly due to decreases in transportation and communication costs.

However, there is a different view of globalization that also connects to Durkheim's arguments of competitive struggles leading to increased levels of differentiation. In particular, a number of authors have argued that in a globalized world, countries can achieve competitive advantages due to their specific capital, such as location, natural resources, nature of the labor force, wage levels, and so forth. The argument goes back to the work of economist David Ricardo, who famously argued that 'under a system of perfectly free commerce, each country naturally devotes its capital and labour to such employments as are most beneficial to each'(Ricardo 1937: 80). This, of course, is the division of labor writ large on a global level, where there is growing functional interdependence based on specialization (e.g. Münch 2005). Much as Durkheim pioneered taking social facts and collective levels of analysis for his frames of reference, the contemporary analogue would be to frame the nation as based on mechanical solidarity and the global system of markets and alliances as based on organic solidarity.

One might believe that this kind of an international division of labor will likewise lead to greater levels of connectedness and eventually solidarity. However, a closer examination reveals that this is not necessarily the case. First, note that differences in nation-specific capital have to be complementary in order for organic solidarity to emerge in the new global division of labor. If, instead, countries begin to compete with each other in the global marketplace—for instance based on low wages and less restrictive labor regulation—then one would expect fierce competition and a 'race to the bottom' rather than increased solidarity. Furthermore, for solidarity to emerge, it is necessary for the actors involved to recognize each other and their interdependence. However, it is unclear whether the majority of individuals within any given country will indeed experience such a common social bond in any meaningful way. If outputs are traded on global markets with prices set according to market mechanisms, the potential for interaction with other actors seems to diminish. Furthermore, increasing homogeneity in industrial sectors due to specialization at the country level may lead to higher levels of the division of labor at the international level, but it may do so at the cost of the division of labor at the national level. Finally, note also that globalization introduces a new quality to this social solidarity. Previously, 'if the bonds of social solidarity are too weak... people may simply emigrate instead of specialize' (Schmaus 1995: 70). At the level of globalization, emigration is of course no longer an option, leading to the need to cooperate or move the struggle to more destructive forms such as conflict or suicide.

10.7. Concluding Thoughts

The division of labor implies a division of responsibility; an arrangement that can have potentially harmful consequences. Particularly in highly developed and tightly coupled technological systems that are prone to 'normal accidents' (Perrow 1984), dividing tasks carries the potential for creating disconnections that result in catastrophic outcomes. Similarly, vested interests as the result of the division of labor can negate any increased solidarity, as will the non-participation in the labor force of considerable segments of society (Catton 1985).

In contrast to the emphasis that his contemporary Tönnies laid on the cultural and spiritual losses incurred by a shift from traditional to modern society, Durkheim pioneered the counter (and counterintuitive) arguments that: (1) the resulting division of labor would increase productivity; (2) improve life chances for all in this new world of opportunity and excitement; and (3) promote social solidarity and shared values among its participants. This unity would be enhanced when crimes were committed, for such deviance—if properly punished—would help show the line between right and wrong, and bring the citizens of this expanded world closer together. Yet, Durkheim was also painfully aware of the constant threat of anomie encountered by a minority not benefiting from these societal changes, whose problems would manifest themselves in social disorder, or worse yet, suicide.

Max Weber noted some of the same apprehensions. Regarding the rise of rational bureaucracies compatible with society, he voiced concern that 'the great question is not how can we promote and hasten [rationality and efficiency] but what can we do to oppose this machinery in order to keep a portion of mankind free of this parceling out of the soul, from this supreme mastery of the bureaucratic way of life' (Weber 1958: 212). For Weber, one can argue the transformation from the ideal type of *Gemeinschaft* to *Gesellschaft* would signify the occurrence of a change in the master served by subordinates, and to whom they are accountable. He prophesied resistance to the efficiency and increased productivity that such modernity represents: 'Wherever modern capitalism has begun its work of increasing the productivity of human labour by increasing its intensity, it has encountered immensely stubborn resistance [from] pre-capitalistic labour' (Weber [1904] 1930). If solidarity is spurred by such resistance, it can work counter to what Durkheim may have anticipated. We suspect Weber would be less shocked, for example, by the solidarity of Islamic radicals, and the success of their administrative apparatus in mobilizing support towards the goal of destroying Western icons. He and Durkheim shared the concern that a lack of constructive solidarity and unification could hold back a society. Were Durkheim alive today, one would expect him to be gravely concerned by a lack of moral accord at the international level, which leaves the way open to anomic and egoistic distortions of globalization, and one would expect him to argue vehemently for the value of a globally binding morality. Yet, it would appear that currently the scope of moral unity and the scope of economic unity are going in different directions, which in his view must certainly lead to crisis.

In the twenty-first century, we are currently witnessing vigorous debates about whether the spread of common symbols and cultures across nations contributes to their unification and solidarity or to the loss and isolation of particular regions', nations' and ethnicities' distinctive identities. The growing universality of media formats, including TV news and entertainments, restaurant specialties, and clothing styles support the view that people across nations participate in an increasingly global popular culture. Are the artisans and other representatives of local traditions being eclipsed and downgraded by these developments? Or is the common appreciation of the same music, movies, and other global icons uniting people across cultures, promoting solidarity, and reducing anomie? In his study of national response to globalization and organizational change in Argentina, South Korea, and Spain, Guillén affirms the coexistence of both trends, concluding that nations can 'use their unique economic, political, and social advantages as leverage in the global marketplace' (2001*a*: 3). If that is the case, then it may be to the advantage of these nations to increase their value to the local marketplace by putting forward their best idiosyncratic cultural capital.

Another cautionary voice regarding the solidarity of capital, of course, was Marx, whose expectation was for a conflict between the international solidarity of capital lined up against that of its workers. Durkheim's thinking, however, runs counter to Marx's anticipation of a revolution preceded by increased inequality, as well as a view of globalization as the triumph of the market and withering away of the state. As an educator in France, Durkheim foresaw a definite role for the state, favored government regulation, and the continuation of economic relationships and alliances embedded in social ties and trust. While he advocated a more cosmopolitan than provincial framework for society to move towards, Durkheim also set out concerns over a resulting decline in common values and proposed ways to counter the potential increase in anomie. He saw the division of labor as increasing solidarity, but envisioned a social solidarity between individuals as well as economic solidarity between states. Durkheim believed the state guaranteed individual rights and held society together. He defended the state when he said, 'We might say that in the State we have the prime mover. It is the State that has rescued the child from patriarchal domination and from family tyranny; it is the State that has freed the citizen from feudal groups and later from communal groups; it is the State that has liberated the craftsmen and his master from guild tyranny' (Durkheim 1957: 64). Nevertheless, the state worked secondarily to the religion in terms of fostering a unified society.

Durkheim's emphasis on the contribution of religions to the social order stemmed from his great respect for their 'grounding' and providing a moral compass for individuals to better relate to their social surroundings. He opposed 'egoism'—an excessive focus on the interests of the individual over those of society. Durkheim's focus on a grounding in collective values is very counter to the more economic presumption of commensuration, that prices can be put on anything, hence nothing is sacred (Becker 1976; Espeland 1998). Such secularization and economizing of utility functions encourages a different, more individualistic focus, with fewer comfort zones and spiritual safe harbors that individuals may rely on. In America, the spate of recent attacks on strangers or co-workers, colloquially described as 'going postal', may be seen as an indicator of Durkheim's concern over individuals 'losing it', both literally and figuratively.

It thus appears whereas Durkheim held high hopes for the division of labor and the transition from mechanical to organic solidarity, he specified a series of moral, practical, and analytical concerns that resonate well with contemporary discussions of the promise of globalization, combined with what potential social ills we need to avoid as it unfolds.

Acknowledgments

We thank Charles Heckscher, Ed Carberry, Paul Adler, and participants at the Sociology Classics and the Future of Organization Studies Conference, Wharton School of Management, University of Pennsylvania, August 2007, for their insightful comments on the ideas expressed here.

References

Adler, E., and Haas, P. (1992). 'Epistemic Communities, World Order, and the Creation of a Reflective Research Program'. *International Organization*, 46: 367–90.

Adler, P. S., and Heckscher, C. (2006). 'Towards Collaborative Community', in C. Heckscher and P. S. Adler (eds.), *The Firm as a Collaborative Community: Reconstructing Trust in the Knowledge Economy*. Oxford: Oxford University Press.

Alexander, J. (1989). 'The Centrality of the Classics', in A. Giddens and J. H. Turner (eds.), *Social Theory Today*. Cambridge: Polity Press.

Barnard, C. I. (1938). *Functions of the Executive*. Cambridge, Mass.: Harvard University Press.

Becker, G. (1976). *The Economic Approach to Human Behavior*. Chicago: University of Chicago Press.

Brown, R. H. (1978). 'Bureaucracy as Praxis: Toward a Political Phenomenology of Formal Organizations'. *Administrative Science Quarterly*, 23: 365–82.

Burt, R. (1997). 'The Contingent Value of Social Capital'. *Administrative Science Quarterly*, 42: 339–65.

Castells, M. (1998). *The Information Age: Economy, Society, and Culture. End of Millennium*. Oxford: Blackwell.

Catton, W. R. (1985). 'Emile Who and the Division of What?' *Sociological Perspectives*, 28/3 (July): 251–80.

Collins, R. (1997). 'A Sociological Guilt Trip: Comment on Connell'. *American Journal of Sociology*, 102: 1558–64.

Cox, R. W. (1996). 'A Perspective on Globalization', in J. H. Mittelman (ed.), *Globalization: Critical Reflections*. Boulder, Colo.: Lynne Rienner.

Dandridge, T. C., Mitroff, I., and Joyce, W. F. (1980). 'Organizational Symbolism: A Topic to Expand Organizational Analysis'. *Academy of Management Review*, 5: 77–82.
Deal, T., and Kennedy, A. (1982). *Corporate Cultures: The Rites and Rituals of Corporate Life*. Reading, Mass.: Addison Wesley.
Djelic, M., and Quack, S. (2003). *Globalization and Institutions: Redefining the Rules of the Economic Game*. Cheltenham: Edward Elgar.
—— and Sahlin-Andersson, K. (2006). *Transnational Governance*. Cambridge: Cambridge University Press.
Durkheim, É. (1957). *Professional Ethics and Civil Morals*. London: Routledge.
—— (1964). *The Division of Labor in Society*, trans. G. Simpson. New York: Free Press.
Espeland, W. (1998). *The Struggle for Water*. Chicago: University of Chicago Press.
Featherstone, M., Lash, S., and Robertson, R. (1995). *Global Modernities*. London: Sage Publications.
Fiss, P. C., and Hirsch, P. M. (2005). 'The Discourse of Globalization: Framing and Sensemaking of an Emerging Concept'. *American Sociological Review*, 70: 29–52.
—— and Zajac, E. J. (2004). 'The Diffusion of Ideas over Contested Terrain: The (Non)adoption of a Shareholder Value Orientation among German Firms'. *Administrative Science Quarterly*, 49: 501–34.
Fourcade, M. (2006). 'The Construction of a Global Profession: The Transnationalization of Economics'. *American Journal of Sociology*, 112: 145–94.
Friedman, T. L. (1999). *The Lexus and the Olive Tree: Understanding Globalization*. New York: Farrar, Straus, and Giroux.
—— (2005). *The World is Flat: A Brief History of the Twenty-First Century*. New York: Farrar, Straus, and Giroux.
Gibbs, J. P. (2003). 'A Formal Restatement of Durkheim's "Division of Labor" Theory'. *Sociological Theory*, 21/2: 103–27.
—— and Martin, W. T. (1962). 'Urbanization, Technology, and the Division of Labor: International Patterns'. *American Sociological Review*, 27/5: 667–77.
Giddens, A. (1990). *The Consequences of Modernity*. Cambridge: Polity in Association with Blackwell.
Guillén, M. (2001*a*). *The Limits of Convergence*. Princeton: Princeton University Press.
—— (2001*b*). 'Is Globalization Civilizing, Destructive or Feeble? A Critique of Five Debates in the Social Science Literature'. *Annual Review of Sociology*, 27: 235–60.
Hamelink, C. J. (1994). *The Politics of World Communication: A Human Rights Perspective*. London: Sage.
Hannan, M. T., and Freeman, J. (1977). 'The Population Ecology of Organizations'. *American Journal of Sociology*, 82: 929–64.
Harms, J. B. (1981). 'Reason and Social Change in Durkheim's Thought: The Changing Relationship between Individuals and Society'. *Pacific Sociological Review*, 24/4: 393–410.
Held, D., McGrew, A., Goldblatt, D., and Perraton, J. (1999). *Global Transformations: Politics, Economics and Culture*. Cambridge: Polity Press.
Henisz, W. J., Zelner, B. A., and Guillén, M. F. (2005). 'The Worldwide Diffusion of Market-Oriented Infrastructure Reform, 1977–1999'. *American Sociological Review*, 70: 871–97.
Hirsch, P., and Shanley, M. (1996). 'The Rhetoric of Boundaryless—Or How the Newly Empowered Managerial Class Bought into Its Own Marginalisation', in M. B. Arthur and

D. Rousseau (eds.), *The Boundaryless Career: A New Employment Principle for a New Organizational Era*. Oxford: Oxford University Press.

Inglis, D., and Robertson, R. (2004). 'Beyond the Gates of the Polis: Reconfiguring Sociology's Ancient Inheritance'. *Journal of Classical Sociology*, 4/2: 165–89.

Kobrin, S. J. (1997). 'The Architecture of Globalization: State Sovereignty in a Networked Global Economy', in J. H. Dunning (ed.), *Governments, Globalization, and International Business*. Oxford: Oxford University Press.

Krempel, L., and Plümper, T. (1999). 'International Division of Labor and Global Economic Processes: An Analysis of International Trade in Automobiles'. *Journal of World-Systems Research*, 3: 487–98.

Latouche, D. (1995). 'Democratie et nationalisme a l'heure de la mondialisation'. *Cahiers de Recherche Sociologique*, 25: 59–78.

Lincoln, J., and Guillot, D. (2005). 'A Durkheimian View of Organizational Culture', in M. Korczynski, R. Hodson, and P. K. Edwards (eds.), *Social Theory at Work*. Oxford: Oxford University Press.

Longworth, R. C. (1998). *Global Squeeze*. Chicago: Contemporary Books.

Mayo, E. (1945). *The Social Problems of an Industrial Civilization*. Boston: Harvard Graduate School of Business Administration.

Mazlish, B. (1993). 'An Introduction to Global History', in B. Mazlish and R. Buultjens (eds.), *Conceptualizing Global History*. Boulder, Colo.: Westview.

Merton, R. K. (1934). 'Durkheim's "Division of Labor in Society"'. *American Journal of Sociology*, 40: 319–28.

Meyer, J. W., Boli, J., Thomas, G., and Ramirez, F. O. (1997). 'World Society and the Nation State'. *American Journal of Sociology*, 103/1 (July): 144–81.

Münch, R. (2005). 'Die Konstruktion des Welthandels als legitime Ordnung der Weltgesellschaft' (The Construction of World Trade as Legitimate Order of World Society). *Zeitschrift für Soziologie*, Sonderheft Weltgesellschaft: 290–313.

Nisbet, R. A. (1966). *The Sociological Tradition*. New York: Basic Books.

Ouchi, W. G. (1980). 'Markets, Bureaucracies, and Clans'. *Administrative Science Quarterly*, 25: 129–41.

—— and Johnson, J. B. (1978). 'Types of Organizational Control and Their Relationship to Emotional Well Being'. *Administrative Science Quarterly*, 23: 293–317.

Parsons, T. (1937). *The Structure of Social Action*. Glencoe, Ill.: Free Press.

Perrow, C. (1984). *Normal Accidents: Living with High-Risk Technologies*. New York: Basic Books.

—— (2004). 'A Society of Organizations'. *Theory and Society*, 20/6: 725–62.

Peters, T., and Waterman, R. (1982). *In Search of Excellence*. New York: Harper and Row.

Pickering, W. S. F. (1984). *Durkheim's Sociology of Religion: Themes and Theories*. London: Routledge.

Podolny, J. M., and Baron, J. N. (1997). 'Resources and Relationships: Social Networks and Mobility in the Workplace'. *American Sociological Review*, 62/5: 673–93.

Pope, W., and Johnson, B. D. (1983). 'Inside Organic Solidarity'. *American Sociological Review*, 48/5: 681–92.

Ricardo, D. (1937). *The Principles of Political Economy and Taxation*. London: J. M. Dent and Sons.

Robertson R. (1992). *Globalization: Social Theory and Global Culture*. London: Sage.

SCHMAUS, W. (1995). 'Explanation and Essence in "The Rules of Sociological Method" and "The Division of Labor in Society"'. *Sociological Perspectives*, 38/1: 57–75.

SCHWARTZMAN, K. C. (2006). 'Globalization from a World-Systems Perspective: A New Phase in the Core—a New Destiny for Brazil and the Semiperiphery?' *Journal of World-Systems Research*, 2: 265–307.

SKLAIR, L. (1999). 'Competing Conceptions of Globalization'. *Journal of World-Systems Research*, 5: 143–63.

SMIRICH, L. (1983). 'Concepts of Culture and Organizational Analysis'. *Administrative Science Quarterly*, 28: 339–58.

SPICH, R. S. (1995). 'Globalization Folklore: Problems of Myth and Ideology in the Discourse on Globalization'. *Journal of Organizational Change*, 8: 6–29.

STARK, D. (1996). 'Recombinant Property in East European Capitalism'. *American Journal of Sociology*, 101: 993–1027.

STARKEY, K. (1992). 'Durkheim and Organizational Analysis: Two Legacies'. *Organization Studies*, 13: 627–42.

—— (1998). 'Durkheim and the Limits of Corporate Culture: Whose Culture? Which Durkheim?' *Journal of Management Studies*, 35: 125–36.

STINCHCOMBE, A. L. (1982). 'Should Sociologists Forget Their Mothers and Fathers?' *American Sociologist*, 17: 2–11.

SWAMINATHAN, A., and DELACROIX, J. (1991). 'Differentiation within an Organizational Population: Additional Evidence from the Wine Industry'. *Academy of Management Journal*, 34: 679–92.

TIRYAKIAN, E. A. (1994). 'Revisiting Sociology's First Classic: "The Division of Labor in Society" and Its Actuality'. *Sociological Forum*, 9/1: 3–16.

TURNER, J. H. (1981). 'Emile Durkheim's Theory of Integration in Differentiated Social Systems'. *Pacific Sociological Review*, 24/4: 379–91.

WALLERSTEIN, I. (1974). *The Modern World-System*. New York: Academic Press.

WATERS, M. (1995). *Globalization*. New York: Routledge.

WEBER, M. ([1904] 1930). *The Protestant Ethic and the Spirit of Capitalism*, trans. Talcott Parsons. New York: Charles Scribner's Sons.

—— (1958). *From Max Weber*, trans. and ed. H. H. Gerth and C. Wright Mills. New York: Galaxy.

WILLIAMSON, J. G. (1996). 'Globalization, Convergence, History'. *Journal of Economic History*, 56: 277–306.

WILLIAMSON, O. E. (1985). *The Economic Institutions of Capitalism*. New York: Free Press.

CHAPTER 11

GABRIEL TARDE AND ORGANIZATION THEORY

BARBARA CZARNIAWSKA

In his lifetime, Gabriel Tarde (1843–1904) was a competitor of Émile Durkheim and, judging from many contemporary accounts, a victorious one. Although his works were translated into many languages and were well-known in social psychology and the sociology of law, they were forgotten by the early 1970s. At present, there is a strong renewed interest in Tarde's work, to the point of some critics talking of a 'Tardomania'. This wave has not yet reached organization studies; however, in this chapter I shall claim that it should. In the text, I first offer differing interpretations of Tarde's work that might explain the changing fate of his reputation. In what follows I scrutinize several Tardean concepts, illustrating their potential relevance for understanding organizations.

11.1. Prologue: An Intellectual Duel AD 1903

In December 1903, the École pratique des hautes études in Paris[1] hosted two lecturers: Mr. Émile Durkheim and Mr. Gabriel Tarde. René Worms, the editor of the

[1] http://www.ephe.sorbonne.fr

first-ever sociological journal, *Revue Internationale de Sociologie*, took notes and printed summaries of the lectures and the discussion that followed in his journal. In the discussion, Mr. Tarde asked:

> Does Mr. Durkheim think that social reality is anything other than individuals or individual acts or facts? 'If you believe that,' said Mr. Tarde, 'I understand your method, which is pure ontology. Between us is the debate between nominalism and scholastic realism. I am a nominalist. There can only be individual actions and interactions. The rest is only a metaphysical entity, mysticism.'[2] Mr. Durkheim thought that Mr. Tarde was confusing two different questions, and declined to say anything about a problem that he had not touched upon and, he maintained, had nothing to do with the discussion. (Tarde [1904] 1969: 140)

Who was that daredevil who challenged the pillar of modern sociology, obviously putting him into some discomfort, a contemporary reader may ask? A reader in 1903 might have possibly asked, who was that newcomer who was considered important enough to discuss with Mr. Tarde? Tarde was at first a magistrate in the provincial town of Sarlat, who indulged in writing and publishing on criminology; then he was appointed Director of Criminal Statistics at the Ministry of Justice in Paris (Durkheim's data on suicide came from this office); subsequently he was given, together with Henri Bergson, a chair in modern philosophy at the Collége de France (he asked the title to be changed to sociology, but was refused; he was given permission to teach what he wanted, though). 'In December, 1900, when he was elected to the Académie des Sciences Morales et Politiques, Tarde held virtually every leading position open to a French social scientist outside the university system'[3] (Clark 1969: 7).

Nor was he unknown in English-speaking communities. His *Laws of Imitation* from 1890, translated by anthropologist Elsie Clews Parsons, was published by Henry Holt in 1903 and reprinted in 1962 and his *Social Laws: An Outline of Sociology* from 1897 was published by Macmillan in 1899 and reprinted in 1974. The editor's (J. Mark Baldwin) preface to the latter begins: 'It goes without saying that no introduction of M. Tarde is necessary to English and American readers who are versed in current sociological discussions' (p. vii). Robert E. Park and Ernest W. Burghess quoted Tarde forty times in their *Introduction to the Science of Sociology* from 1922, which places him, together with Darwin, Simmel, and Spencer, among the most quoted authors in that book (Hughes 1961: 554). Hughes (1961) wrote about *Psychologie économique* as 'an unknown classic by a forgotten sociologist'. Rogers (1962: 41) was convinced that Tarde's appreciation would be growing from the 1960s on because of 'an invisible college of American scholars' who 'coalesced around Tarde's "laws of imitation"'. Instead, Terry N. Clark's lovingly compiled selection *Gabriel Tarde on Communication and Social Influence* (1969) appeared to be the last of the English translations.

[2] Some translations render it as 'ontological phantasmagorias' (Alliez 2004).

[3] i.e. not a 'Normalien' and without formal education in philosophy.

Afterwards, it was only Gilles Deleuze and Niklas Luhmann who continued to read Tarde. Some students could learn in their introductory courses that Tarde was the founder of the sociology of law, of social psychology, and the pioneer of the use of statistics in sociology. Otherwise, almost thirty years of silence followed, and then, in the late 1990s, a 'Tardomania' occurred (Mucchielli 2000) with reprints of original works, articles, books, and special issues—at least in France, Italy, Germany, Denmark, and Sweden. How can one explain these vicissitudes of Gabriel Tarde's role in social sciences? Before I move on to consider the elements of Tarde's thought in the context of organization theory, I shall try to answer this question by quoting the prevailing opinions of the time: of Tarde's contemporaries, of social scientists in the 1970s, and our own contemporaries.

11.2. The Rise, Fall, and Return of Gabriel Tarde

11.2.1. Tarde in his Time

According to the historian of sociology Roger Geiger (1972), the sociologists and would-be sociologists in France at the end of the nineteenth century shared three main assumptions: (1) they assumed society (or norms and rules) to be prior to individuals; (2) they saw sociology as the road to resolving current problems of their own country; and (3) they believed in science as a guarantee of progress. Before his death, Tarde was generally acknowledged as the leading sociologist in France, with Durkheim's fame rising. Yet Tarde believed that society arises from groupings of individuals and that science is not a guarantor of progress; he also did not suggest any improvement programs.[4]

In Geiger's highly critical view of Tarde, he has become a renowned sociologist because sociology was not yet formed; his forays into more established psychology, economics, history, and statistics were ignored as too radical. But his fame is beyond doubt: 'the short run success of Gabriel Tarde, the *sociologue*, was spectacular. In the last fifteen years of his life he published an astonishing total of fifteen volumes and nearly one hundred articles' (Geiger 1972: 123). How was it possible? Geiger points out that Tarde was a highly skilled literary stylist; that he had fresh ideas; that his contemporaries constantly praised his intelligence, his imagination, and his acute insights. To these belong his cosmology of monads, equipped with desires and beliefs, that allowed him to explain individuality and sociality without added

[4] However, at least in Everett Hughes's reading, Tarde 'was preoccupied in a sensitive and rather prophetic way with the trends and issues of his time' (1961: 558).

entities such as 'society'; his emphasis on difference in place of identity; and the centrality he attributed to the phenomena of invention and imitation, fashion and communication. Why did all these cease to enchant the readers?[5]

11.2.2. Tarde as Seen in the 1970s: A Tardean Anti-Tarde Analysis

This section is based mostly on Roger L. Geiger's doctoral dissertation 'The Development of French Sociology 1871–1905' (1972), as this is both a thorough historical work and also a work that in evaluative modality reflects the attitudes of its time in the Anglo-American community.[6] Thus, it needs to be added that if I oppose Geiger's statements, this opposition is also reflecting the attitudes of my time; it is up to the reader to decide whose opinion to follow.

As I read it, there were two main criticisms directed against Tarde's work: its elitism and its non-scientific character.[7]

First, let us consider the charge of elitism. It springs from Tarde's suggestion that invention is more important than imitation, and that invention is typical of elites. However, the accusation of elitism is tied, at least in Geiger's rendition, to two indices. One is that Tarde fought for restoration of 'de' to his family name, which reveals his aristocratic ambitions. While indeed such restoration took place, Tarde never used 'de' in his writing (Clark 1969). The other is Tarde's statement that, in earlier epochs, imitation went from the court down, while in Tarde's times it was the big city that hosted most inventions and from which imitation spread. It seems to me that Tarde was simply evoking the Spencerian notion of 'reverential imitation' (Spencer 1880: 206), with the demurrer that it was not the court but the city that had become the center of fashion. The current interpretations may be two: one elitist in the style of Richard Florida (e.g. Florida 2005), who located 'creative elites' in the cities; the other in tune with many theorists of fashion who posited that much of fashion in modern times is born in the city, it surfaces in its marginal population, percolates up to the upper classes, and then trickles down again to the middle classes (Partington 1992).

Further, Geiger spoke critically of Tarde's eulogy of leisure (combined with a critique of economists who emphasized the importance of work), but there, although differing from Veblen, Tarde was in agreement with Marx, if leisure is

[5] Ending reasoning in questions was one of Tarde's habits severely criticized by Geiger as a rhetorical device unworthy of a scientist.

[6] The only text that presented the whole work of Gabriel Tarde, Jean Milet's dissertation 'Gabriel Tarde et la philosophie de l'historie' appeared in France in 1970 (Alliez 2004).

[7] The latter was the main reason for Tarde's oblivion in the eyes of Mucchielli (2000), who deeply deplores the present 'Tardomania'.

defined as freedom from commercial labor.[8] This seems to be especially visible in Tarde's utopian fantasy called *Fragment d'histoire future* ([1896] 2003), in which, in a completely egalitarian society, people are free of needs and develop an intense 'interspiritual' life, consisting of the circulation of ideas—all barriers to conversation gone (Hughes 1961: 555). And here is Hughes, saying that 'although Tarde was ahead of his time in defining the problems of industrial work and fatigue, he was even more so on those latest concerns of sociologists, consumption and the use of leisure' (Hughes 1961: 553).

It needs to be added that *Fragment* is strongly satirical, and sometimes today's reader may have problems in deciding what Tarde is ridiculing and what he is extolling. The elements of the latter type are discernible, however, by their parallels in Tarde's 'serious' writings. He indeed extols genius, but he sees it as a common property, and bearing fruit only through a collective endeavor. A 'mother-idea', born in a genial mind, must be developed by thousands of 'auxiliary geniuses' ([1896] 2003: 25). The originator of the first idea might become a temporary leader, but is of no importance for future developments, which are determined by the followers. Struck by the 'global cooling', *Fragment*'s people of the future repair to the inside of the globe, which was the idea of a genius. This genius, however, later on chooses to follow a wrong idea and meets an early end, permitting the people to venerate him without the disturbance of his actual existence.

As to the second criticism, that of the non-scientific character of Tarde's work, it had to do with the fact that he did not believe in laws determining development of society. Tarde belonged to the school of thought called Spontaneity—a movement to be found both on the political right and on the political left; the opposite of the Cartesianism of Durkheimians (Clark 1969). He also espoused the doctrine of the Possible (Geiger 1972: 104), according to which the universe that exists is a particular case of an infinite number of possible cases (neither for the first nor for the last time, the coincidence of Tarde's doctrines with present theories is truly surprising).

Furthermore, in contrast to many of his contemporaries, Tarde did not look for certainty in science and postulated that it needs to be closely related to philosophy and art. For him, the basis of science did not lie in the chains of causes and effects, but in resemblance and repetition (thus the title of Deleuze's famous book, *Difference and Repetition* [1968] 1997). Also, Tarde saw no point in social sciences imitating natural sciences: people know most about the human condition, so it is natural sciences that should be imitating social sciences. Thus, the idea of *diffusion*, taken up by Rogers (1962) did not suggest that ideas spread like particles, but that particles possibly spread like ideas. Whereas such a postulate might seemed shocking in the 1970s, the last thirty years or so of studies of science and technology reveal that natural sciences, when observed from the outside rather than self-represented, indeed are very similar to social sciences in their procedures.

[8] Marx is the most quoted economist in *Psychologie économique*.

Tarde's concepts of *monads* that are different from one another because separate, but are imitating one another and therefore similar, struck Geiger as 'queer'; this is in tune with Avishai Margalit's recent (2007) opinion that Leibniz's idea of monads was 'weird'. Perhaps Leibniz meant monads literally; Tarde meant it as a metaphor, and it is indeed so that metaphors that do not catch on seem weird, whereas metaphors that become popular turn into proper names. Some current examples may be Richard Dawkins's 'memes' and Douglas Hofstadter's 'simms'.

Tarde's lectures at the Collége de France became the basis for the two volumes of *Psychologie économique* ([1901] 2007), known in English only from the praise by Hughes (1961) and the fragments included by Clark (Tarde [1888] 1969). Geiger quoted Tarde as saying in those volumes that the value of money 'is purely fictitious and conventional' (Geiger 1972: 113), exactly what economic sociology is saying nowadays. Tarde also proposed another Marx-like utopia, where the value of things would be based in buyers' and sellers' desires and beliefs ('what is this worth to you?'). Perhaps impracticable, this seems to be a suggestion concerning a betterment of society, contrary to Geiger's earlier critique.

A skillful statistician, Tarde tried also to

> lay to rest another chimera of the statisticians: namely, the idea that at some future date, when all social phenomena have been reduced to mathematical formulae, future social conditions will become as predictable as future planetary positions. Such a hope is founded on error, because statistics must confine itself to imitation alone while the future will be shaped by unknown and unpredictable inventions. (Geiger 1972: 115)

Although Deirdre McCloskey does not quote Tarde, she seems to be taking an identical position in her critique of the use of statistics in economics (e.g. McCloskey 2001).

When discussing reasons for Tarde's subsequent disappearance from the social sciences, Geiger produced something that can be seen as a Tardean analysis. All the criticisms above are what Tarde would have called 'logical reasons' for the fading of Tarde's fame. As to 'extra-logical', Geiger pointed out that Tarde's observations were so alien to the thought structure that was gaining dominance in France at that time that they could not be assimilated.[9] Tarde had no imitators; he did not care to create a school of disciples, and he was too stylistically eccentric to be imitated at a distance. Durkheim, on the other hand, 'developed a strategic constituency within the government, the universities and among the liberal intelligentsia' (Geiger 1972: 251).

Rogers (1962) also suggested that Tarde's contemporaries did not have the appropriate methodological tools to follow in practice the s-curve of diffusion he postulated. One could add that they did not have digital tools, either.

[9] This is sometimes seen as the basic tenet of Tarde's theory (see Clark 1968).

11.2.3. Tardomania of the 1990s

Imagine that Karl Marx has published *Capital* and that nobody paid any attention to it. The book becomes rediscovered and the readers remain stupefied in the face of the audacity and plenitude of the ideas contained in this isolated and forgotten work that did not have any effect on science, politics, or society; a work that did not have either followers or exegetes; that did not inspire any more or less unfortunate applications. How different would the history of the 20th century be if it were Tarde's *Psychologie économique*, 1902, and not Marx's book, that became the breviary of the people of action!

(Latour and Lépinay 2007: 1, my translation)

A hyperbole? Perhaps. It all depends on whether one believes that ideas circulate because of their innate qualities (a non-Tardean view) or because of the contingencies of their emergence. At any rate, this preface to a republishing of a shortened version of Tarde's book (two volumes around 400 pages each) indicates the eagerness accompanying the rediscovery of Tarde. Why was he rediscovered right now? Several great and some smaller contingencies can be mentioned in explanation.

The first is that, if we accept that social sciences thrive on sensitizing concepts (Blumer 1954), then satiation of meaning (Wertheimer and Gillis 1958) inevitably occurs: after a long while they are not sensitizing anymore. If Durkheim, Weber, and Marx explained everything convincingly, sociology could close shop, or else try to apply its concepts to new phenomena, a somewhat anachronistic exercise.[10] In fact, both sociology and organization theory look constantly for new concepts, and rediscoveries offer many attractive candidates (see e.g. Thomas Kuhn's and Mary Douglas's rediscovery of Ludwik Fleck).

Why Tarde? Because, as could be seen already from my short review above, his work resonates well with much of contemporary thinking. Nobody is scandalized at the idea of re-joining sciences to philosophy and arts anymore, as it is constantly done; it is taken for granted that knowledge increases ignorance (Luhmann 2002); and Tarde is seen as offering new ways of analyzing contemporary capitalism (Lazzarato 2003). His work antecedes concepts of network and cultural capital, culture industry, and knowledge economics (Irenius 2002). Irenius noticed also that the contemporary reader might feel that Tarde was actually speaking of IT and virtual reality (2002: 27).

It could also be that Tarde's voice fits better the present times of darkness, whereas Durkheim's positive thinking reverberated with the optimism of the 1970s. Consider one of the proofs of Tarde's anti-liberalism in Geiger's eyes: Tarde 'implied that elected assemblies, far from embodying the intelligence and volition of the social

[10] According to Hughes, older texts should be sources of inspiration, not of hypotheses to be tested: 'A great deal of time has... been wasted in taking the specific hypothesis of Durkheim on suicide, or some of those of Weber on protestantism or of Park on the marginal man or the race-relations cycle, and going through the exercise of proving those men wrong—as one obviously can' (1961: 558–9).

organism, were selected capriciously and operated arbitrarily' (1972: 230). Who would disagree with that description AD 2008?

It is also relevant to recall that Deleuze's book from 1968 was translated into English in 1997, and Tarde has been rediscovered partly because Deleuze became highly fashionable in the Anglo-American community. While Tarde is not yet highly popular in organization theory, the 'laws'[11] of imitation predict that it is only a question of time.

11.3. Would Organization Theory Be Different with Tarde?

11.3.1. People and Organizations: On Monads, Desires, and Beliefs

As mentioned before, Tarde borrowed the concept of 'monads' from Leibniz, but gave it a personal twist: 'the world outside me is composed of souls other than mine, but similar to mine' (Tarde [1893] 1999).[12] Tarde was not fond of notions denoting additional entities bigger than their parts if these parts can be conceived as individuals. 'Monads' was his metaphor for individuals (human and non-human), entities equipped with belief (apperception in Leibniz[13]) and desire (appetite).[14] Monads remain separated, but are never lonely; they imitate the desires and beliefs of other monads.

As mentioned before, one of the fields that rediscovered Tarde were the studies of science and technology (SST) (Latour 2002). The tenet of Tarde's thought that was attractive to SST was his abolition of the micro–macro dimension in claiming that 'macro' is but a multiple repetition of 'micro' actions, and that each monad is bigger than the apparently large association to which it may lend one aspect of itself. Indeed, for a reader of both Tarde and actor-network theory, the similarities are many: their view on power (Tarde said that certain monads dominate other

[11] Tarde used the term 'laws' in a metaphorical sense, which earned him criticism for a lack of coherence, as he opposed the idea of social sciences formulating law-like propositions (Geiger 1972).

[12] 'tout l'univers extérieur est composé d'âmes autres que la mienne, mais au fond semblables à la mienne' ([1893] 1999: 44).

[13] For a short introduction to Leibniz's monadology that inspired Tarde, see Audi 1995: 425–9 and 358–9. Alliez (1999) pointed out that Leibniz's monads were basically points of view, reconciled by Harmony created by God. Tarde gave them materiality, making them capable of action, subsequently replacing harmony with imitation.

[14] The notion of imitation of desire was adopted by René Girard (1977). For the application of Girard's thought to the phenomenon of organizational imitation, see Sevón 1996.

monads, but that they all originally started from the same state, power being an effect of actions and not their cause); their idea of representation as giving one monad a voice; the idea that the social and not society is the clue to sociality.

The same traits should be attractive to organization theory. Tarde managed to render a world that was populated with individuals—human and not—who were associated: no loners and no aggregates. 'Monads' equipped with beliefs and desires might be a better metaphor for those who organize than 'cogs in a wheel'. Monads may be pushy in following their desires but not always successful in that endeavor; and they continue to watch other monads, as this enables them to imitate.

The humanists in our midst, baffled by too much attention paid to machines, might feel appeased by the idea that each monad is bigger than any large association to which it lends some aspect of itself. In the parlance of organization theory, one could say that each person employed in a company is much bigger and much more complex than the company itself, the latter being a collection of a repetition of one or a few properties of its employees and machines. In his debate with Durkheim, Tarde postulated that there were two categories of social things to study: '(1) groups of people acting inter-mentally[15] (families, classes, nations); (2) groups of actions (languages, customs, institutions)' (Tarde [1904] 1969: 139). Indeed, is not that what we do—some of us studying 'organizations' (the first category) and others studying 'organizing' (the second)?

Other scholars see a much more ambitious use for the idea of associated monads suggested by Tarde. The French-Italian sociologist and philosopher Maurizio Lazzarato (2003) pointed out that for Tarde the source of wealth lay not in land, labor, capital, or utility, but in invention and cooperation. In Tarde's eyes, political economy did not deal with 'production' but with 'reproduction'; that is, with repetition and not with invention. Even Schumpeter, Lazzarato pointed out, left invention out of the economic model; it was 'external' to economy. This happened because the desire to know, the curiosity, has been omitted from the list of—mostly material—needs. If this omission is rectified, consumption, too, can be divided into a passive, repetitive consumption and an active consumption that invents new desires and new beliefs. 'Truth value' and 'beauty value' need to be added to 'utility value' for portraying the economy adequately.

The distinction between invention and repetition does not correspond to the hand–mind dichotomy. To begin with, both invention and repetition require body and mind. It is not a dichotomy at all, but a dimension, with 'the work of an automaton', on the one extreme, and 'the work of the genius', on the other. Everything inbetween—which is infinite—depends on the 'intercerebral cooperation'. If there needs be any organic metaphor for society (Tarde opposed Spencerian organicism), it would be that of a brain, a corporeal mind. Even the production of knowledge is not limited to an intellectual, cognitive, or linguistic activity, because

[15] 'Intersubjectively' would be an obvious contemporary translation.

it involves a production of public opinion as well as a production of safety and trust (Tarde foresaw the emergence of the 'risk society' and production of information). Seen from a Tardean perspective, the development of a communication industry (the media), a culture industry, an entertainment industry, etc. is not a result of the crisis of Fordism, but a development that started hand in hand with modernity.

Far from proposing a hierarchical society, Tarde wished for an egalitarian one, but steered away both from the norms of 'state socialism' and from the 'trivial individualism' of liberal theories. Workers, in his eyes, associated not on the basis of common interests, but on the basis of common desires and beliefs. His ideal society would be based on a 'polytheism' of beliefs and desires, organized according to a differentiation spawned by associations. Even his futuristic fantasy acknowledged, however, that such a differentiation could never be perfected, as any 'ideal' society is also a static, lifeless society.

11.3.2. Alterity Rescued from Identity

While difference and repetition may be seen as building blocks for the new theory of capitalism, I suggest their more modest application to organization theory. I wish to recruit them in opposing the all-encompassing idea of 'identity', a colonial heritage that social scientists help to keep alive. After all, as Tarde pointed out:

> To exist is to differ; difference, in a sense, is the substantial side of things, is what they have only to themselves and what they have most in common. One has to start the explanation from here, including the explanation of identity, taken often, mistakenly, for a starting point. Identity is but a *minimal* difference, and hence a type of difference, and a very rare type at that, in the same way as rest is a type of movement and circle a peculiar type of ellipse.
>
> (Tarde [1893] 1999: 72–3, my translation)

As this quote indicates, the concept of identity was already beginning to overshadow the crucial role of differences at the turn of the previous century; by now the eclipse has become total. Peter Brooks (2005) called this phenomenon an emergence of an *identity paradigm*.

Two trends were at the center of attention in the nineteenth century, especially the attention of the young nation states. One was urbanization: the enormous movement from the countryside to the city. The bourgeois became frightened; criminality was on the rise, and it was taking new, sophisticated forms. As Brooks pointed out, the picturesque figure of a 'master criminal' in a variety of disguises was not only a figment of the vivid imaginations of novelists, but existed in reality, to the exasperation of police forces. Another nineteenth-century problem had to do with the exigencies of running the colonies. How to tell the natives from one another if they all look alike to the eye of the colonialists? Also, how to tell working-class people from one another, if they not only wear the same clothes but also imitate the bourgeois (or the other way around)? The problem, therefore, was too many differences and too few differences. A search for various technologies of identification was activated during this period: physiognomy, phrenology, and then photography and fingerprinting were put at the service of the police and the colonial authorities.

Whereas the issues of identity were born in relation to persons, they were transferred, by analogy, to the realm of abstract entities, such as legal persons (corporations; Lamoreaux 2003) and nation states. Thus, the emergence of the identity paradigm in the nineteenth century was also most likely connected to the rise of nationalism (Anderson [1983] 1991). People grouped within the new borders desperately needed to know what they had in common, as the tendency was for them to see too many differences. This attempt was so successful that, in the opinion of Ian Buruma, 'identity' is behind most of the present world troubles:

> Identity is a bloody business. Religion, nationality or race may not be the primary causes of war and mass murder. These are more likely to be tyranny, or the greed for territory, wealth and power. But 'identity' is what gets the blood boiling, what makes people do unspeakable things to their neighbors. (Buruma 2002: 12)

The situation in organizations might not be as drastic. Nevertheless, organization theory does not deviate from the current public discourse, with its focus on the phenomenon of *identity construction* (see e.g. Whetten and Godfrey 1998; Schultz, Hatch, and Larsen 2000; Hatch and Schultz 2003). What about difference, or, as it should be symmetrically called, alterity?

> **alterity**
> Term used in postmodern writings for the 'otherness' of others, or sometimes the otherness of the self.
>
> (*The Oxford Dictionary of Philosophy*)

Being different is hardly a postmodern invention, so why is it that 'alterity' is reserved for esoteric writings, and even there only 'sometimes' related to the self? Both identity and alterity do appear in social studies—but usually in two versions, which can be situated at the two extremes of the exclusion–inclusion dimension (Czarniawska 2007).

One version, typical for cultural studies, originates in writings by Michel Foucault, who said that 'the forceful exclusion and exorcism of what is Other is an act of identity formation' (Corbey and Leerssen 1991: xii).[16] The other, post-Hegelian version postulates the interplay between identity and alterity as a dialectical move, resulting in 'increasing expansion and incorporation, assimilating or at least harmonizing all otherness in terms of expanding identity' (ibid. xi). Thus, in the discourse of and on identity, alterity is either *attributed* to other people ('they

[16] The anthology edited by Corbey and Leerssen, *Alterity, Identity, Image: Selves and Others in Society and Scholarship*, is an excellent example of this school of thought.

are different and therefore not us') or *incorporated* in the self-definition ('they are actually very much like us'). The third possibility, the *affirmation of difference* ('*we* are different'), is ignored, with the exception of the work of Gilles Deleuze, who continued the Tardean tradition.

Deleuze's anti-Hegelian project introduced the notion of the identity continuum, constituted by the Same, the Similar, the Analogous, and the Opposed ([1968] 1997: 265). The last instance, the Opposed, negates a given identity ('we are not like this') but it must be distinguished from affirmation of difference ('this is how we are different from them' or 'from everybody else'). The alterity dimension is separate, and non-continuous. It contains a declaration of uniqueness, as well as an affirmation of a partial difference, but even a claim of minimal difference, which amounts to an identity admission.

Although the Same can be seen as an ideal on the identity continuum, it is not so. It is only 'the primitive Other' who returns to the Same, and therefore does not progress (de Certeau [1975] 1988). The primitive Other imitates; the moderns only emulate (do whatever they imitate better than the model). The primitive Others are therefore located at the extremes of both dimensions: they repeat themselves and they are unlike anybody else. The moderns, on the other hand, can move freely between the two dimensions, engaging identity and alterity in an interplay.

The observation of actual practices shows that, with moderns or non-moderns, the negotiation of the selves (Czarniawska, n.d.) requires an interplay of identity and alterity, even if current fashion might prefer some modes and some types of interplay. The primitive Other is but an invention, a prop to be used in the interplay.

The analogy with corporations and 'corporate citizenship' is obvious. Actors and observers constantly produce and reproduce organizational images, which are used to control the employees and the investors, to legitimate, and to attract attention (Czarniawska 2002). Corporate leadership tries to convince employees that they have much in common and convince customers that the other corporations are different. The 'unsophisticated' organizations are either impossible to tell apart, or are unique and therefore irrelevant. But while practitioners construct images playing on both identity (whom are we like? and how?) and alterity (how are we different? and from whom?), organization scholars tend to concentrate only on the former part of this process.

Although the simultaneous presence of exclusion–inclusion movements has been acknowledged before (Höpfl 1992), the simultaneous construction of identity and alterity of such collective images as 'an organization' or 'management practice' requires attention. The dominant conceptualization of 'identity free of alterity' supported in the notion of 'identity work' has caused a significant semantic gliding in organization studies. At one time merely denoting a relation (identity, like an alterity, is a judgment resulting from a comparison), identity has become an attribute—something that an organization or a person can have or lack. A *relational* view of the identity/alterity interplay in organizational and individual image construction promises a more nuanced understanding of these complex phenomena (Czarniawska 2002, 2007).

The 'interplay of alterity and identity' is my vocabulary; Latour (1993) chose to speak of acts of differentiation and identification, but the underlying idea is the same. Tarde visualized the process of individuation through the metaphor of a wave in the sea. The wave—an individual brain—is a fold caused by the movement of the sea, this space of associated brains. The wave folds in and returns to the sea, but the movement continues. Thus, it does not make sense to speak of the sea as 'influencing' or 'determining' the waves, but it does make sense to speak of waves as forming the sea, and of the sea as forming the waves.

11.3.3. Invention and Imitation

> [C]ertain social realities ... once formed ... impose themselves upon the individual, sometimes, though rarely, with constraint, oftener by persuasion or suggestion or the curious pleasure that we experience, from childhood up, in saturating ourselves with the examples of our myriad surrounding models. (Tarde [1899] 1974: 184)

Imitation, claimed Tarde, is the main mechanism of sociality, the main mode of binding people (and things) to one another. The post-Tardean social scientists were, of course, aware of the phenomenon of imitation. In a Durkheimian mode, however, imitation, together with 'primitive classification' (Durkheim and Mauss [1903] 1963) were judged to be 'premodern', and, as such, were properly attributed to children and to equally childlike 'premodern people'. The moderns 'adopted' (Rogers 1962); they did not imitate.[17]

In contemporary organization theory, dominated by new institutionalism, 'isomorphism' regained a central place in a critique of rational choice theories.[18] However, its conceptualization and explanation followed the Durkheimian way of conceiving social action (DiMaggio and Powell [1984] 1991). DiMaggio and Powell distinguished among coercive, normative, and mimetic isomorphism within the homogenizing tendency observable in forms of organizing within the same organization field.

As Tarde pointed out, there is sometimes an element of constraint in imitation, but its proportion to a voluntary, and frequently unconscious, imitation is negligible. There can also be an element of coercion at times in the introduction of organizational forms and practices, particularly of the legal kind; but, again,

[17] The 'adoption' idea used by many diffusionists was originally only the last step of the diffusion process, which consisted of (1) knowledge, (2) information collection, (3) evaluation, (4) trial, (5) adoption (Clark 1968).

[18] I say 'regain' because there existed an earlier concept—that of 'conformism', the Latin synonym of the Greek 'isomorphism'—which, however, in the light of modernist science, could only have a negative meaning. Tarde himself was speaking of 'psychomorphism'.

coercion as the main force behind imitation is rarely observed in non-totalitarian societies.

Norms, especially professional norms, are playing an important role in the circulation of organizing practices in contemporary societies, which DiMaggio and Powell called normative isomorphism. Here it can be clearly seen that, on the one hand, the differences between Durkheim and Tarde were not very dramatic, as they concerned, above all, the direction of influences; on the other hand, this directional difference leads to radically different consequences. As pointed out by Clark (1969: 17–18), Durkheim wished to explain micro events by macro laws, whereas Tarde postulated that macro patterns can be explained by micro events. Similarly, whereas, for Durkheim, rules were the causes of social action; for Tarde, they were the effects of social action. The ambiguity of the term 'norm' captures this difference well: a norm is that which 'normates', which tells people what to do, but also that which people 'normally' do. Professional norms exist because professionals willingly imitate one another, not the other way around.

A mimetic isomorphism, in the case of organizations, was to DiMaggio and Powell a 'simple' case of imitation resulting from spatial or ideological proximity. They introduced the notion of organization fields, akin to that of a branch in industry or sector in public administration: organizations that are legitimately considered to be 'in the same business', whether private or public, form an 'organization field'. Such organizations watch, and often imitate, one another, even in the absence of official regulations or professional norms. DiMaggio and Powell claimed, however, that mimetic isomorphism is a sign of uncertainty: people imitate only when they do not know how to conduct themselves. Considering the fact that uncertainty is the human condition, this explanation certainly underestimates the pervasiveness of *mimesis*. This is where the insights of Gabriel Tarde are of great importance. Imitation is not a residual category, but a pivotal explanatory concept for those who try to understand the phenomena of the contemporary world of organizations. Also, in a virtual space, proximity is a matter of decision, and therefore proximity that counts is ideological (imitation of desire, Sevón 1996).

The similarity among forms of organizing—across time, but especially across space—has often been explained by various theories, from diffusionism to evolutionism in anthropology, from convergence (a modern version of diffusionism) in political science to contingency (a modern version of evolutionism) in management theory. As John Meyer pointed out, contemporary 'societies vary by factors of one hundred to one in resources, and enormously in their own traditions. But they adopt surprisingly similar forms of modernity' (Meyer 1999: 5). Is this an expression of a universal human nature that evolved (from premodern to modern) and finds its expression in similar ways? Are these reactions to similar conditions prevalent in an era called modernity? The two deterministic explanations look for causes, as used to be the custom, outside the phenomenon of interest. It was Tarde who attracted attention to the dynamics of the phenomenon itself, pointing out that '[o]ur social life includes a thick network of [imitative] radiations ... with countless mutual interferences' (Tarde [1899] 1974: 101).[19] Consequently, he did not share Meyer's surprise. Yes, modernity is a great homogenizing force, and yes, with each of its moves it re-creates myriads of local differences (Tarde [1893] 1999: 71).

Why has the imitation not yet led to a complete homogeneity—of people and peoples, of countries and organizations? New inventions emerge because of 'the necessary weakening of that which is imitated ... new inventions or entirely fresh sources for imitation are therefore necessary for the timely reanimation of expiring social energy' (Tarde [1890] 1903: 210). Ideas, practices, or objects that became widely spread are not fashionable anymore; an established fashion becomes its opposite—a custom or an institution.

11.3.4. Customs and Fashions

> [W]hy, given one hundred different innovations conceived of at the same time ... ten will spread abroad, while ninety will be forgotten? (Tarde [1888] 1969: 177)

In other words, which inventions are imitated?

Those imitated are allegedly superior, on the grounds of their perceived qualities (Tarde called these 'logical reasons'; I called them pragmatic, Czarniawska 2004), or on the grounds of their provenience in time and place (Tarde's 'extra-logical' reasons; I called them power-symbolic, ibid.). The third type of superiority, according to Tarde, characterizes ideas that have many allies in other ideas—ideas that are well anchored or that do not threaten the institutionalized thought structure. This 'power of associations' has been pointed out both by the 'old' institutionalists like Clark (1968) and Warren (Warren, Rose, and Bergunder 1974), and by the actor-network theorists (Latour 1986).

Thus, an invention in organizing happens at one place, becomes known, and is marketed by the inventors themselves and by consultants, journalists, and researchers. Although in principle an invention can crop up anywhere, in practice the cities are watching those who are considered to be the fashion leaders—certain big cities but also, at present, big corporations. The translation, necessarily occurring with each displacement, makes that which was imitated into something else: same form, different content; same content, different form. Translation is a vehicle, imitation its motor, and fashion sits at the wheel (Czarniawska and Sevón 2005).

[19] Tarde is often seen as a 'diffusionary evolutionist', as he differs from diffusionists pointing out the variation inherent in each displacement, and from evolutionists pointing out the role of action, i.e. imitation. Thus, he spoke of 'evolution by association' ([1893] 1999: 41) à la Stephen Jay Gould, or 'diffusion by transformation'.

Tarde wrote, '[I]n our European societies ... the extraordinary progress of fashion in all its forms, in dress, food and housing, in wants and ideas, in institutions and in arts, is making a single type of European based upon several hundreds of millions of examples' ([1890] 1903: 16). Tarde claimed that fashion was already a strong force in antiquity, although he admitted, and contemporary scholars of fashion from Braudel on agreed (Wilson 1985), that it was the eighteenth century that 'inaugurated the reign of fashion on a large scale' (Tarde [1890] 1903: 293 n. 2). He contrasted fashion with custom; but he did not discuss fashion separately, as it inevitably accompanied imitation in his writings, to the point that it was often joined by a hyphen: fashion-imitation, as contrasted with custom-imitation. Two younger social scientists, Veblen and Simmel,[20] took up the topic of fashion and examined it in great detail. Because of their mode of referencing, or rather non-referencing, it is impossible to know whether they were aware of Tarde's work. But, whereas, for Veblen fashion was a negative phenomenon at the service of conspicuous consumption ([1899] 1994), Simmel seemed to continue along Tarde's train of thought: 'Fashion is the imitation of a given example and satisfies the demand for social adaptation.... At the same time, it satisfies in no less degree the need of differentiation, the tendency for dissimilarity, the desire for change and contrast' (Simmel [1904] 1971: 296).

Herbert Blumer quoted Simmel rather than Tarde to postulate that fashion is a competition mechanism that influences the market and distorts the demand and supply curves, both using and serving the economic competition (Blumer 1969). Its important element is a *collective choice* among tastes, things, and ideas; it is oriented towards finding but also towards creating what is typical of a given time. One could add that fashion operates at institutional fringes. On the one hand, its variety is limited by the 'iron cage' of existing institutions, which fashion actually reproduces; on the other hand, fashion is engaged in a constant subversion of the existing institutional order, gnawing at its bars. This is the first paradox connected to fashion: its simultaneous unimportance and saliency.

Another paradox, created by observation that fashion is created even as it is followed, can be understood with help of the notion of translation, borrowed from Michel Serres, developed by Bruno Latour, and transplanted to organization studies (Czarniawska and Sevón 1996). It is the subsequent translations that simultaneously produce and reproduce variations in fashion: repetition creates and re-creates difference. Hence, yet another paradox: fashion followers act differently as a result of their attempt to act in the same way: fashion encompasses and feeds on the identity/alterity interplay. Tarde has pointed out that this concept need not be treated as a contradiction, merely as a difficulty: a difficulty consisting of discovering an original idea within an already dominating style (Tarde [1902] 1969: 157). This is why Lyotard ([1979] 1987) insisted on differentiating between an invention and an

[20] Veblen was fourteen years younger and Simmel fifteen years younger than Tarde.

innovation (Tarde, or at least his translators, treat them as synonymous): whereas an innovation remains within the already prevailing style, an invention changes such style.

This observation can be directly applied to managers. Fashion is for them an expression of what is modern, of what the community to which they belong—that is, their organization field—recently chose as the most valuable or exciting thing. For people in high organizational positions who perceive their mission to be that of bringing progress to organizations, to follow what is modern often feels like a duty. However, this obligation is only part of their mission. Their duty is, equally, to protect organizations from what might be a passing fad. One of their tasks is to keep a distance from 'mere' fashion, or to be more precise, to detect fads.

Fashion stands for change. But as fashion is also repetitive, in a long-range perspective it stands for tradition, as well. Indeed, as pointed out by Agnes Brook Young, fashion is not related to progress (although it stands for modernity):

> In a real sense, fashion is evolution without destination. The world generally considers that progress in material things consists in changes that make them more useful, or better looking, or less expensive. In the long run fashion never attains these objectives. [It] is slow, continuous change, unhampered by the restrictions of either aesthetics or practicality. (Young [1937] 1973: 109)

Young's notion of 'evolution without destination' is close in spirit to Tarde's 'evolutionary diffusionism', although she, too, quoted only Simmel. Fashion operates through dramatized 'revolutions', but 'in a real sense, fashion is evolution' (ibid.). Tarde would agree: in his view, fashion first opposes custom, and then, if successful, becomes a custom itself, only to be opposed by the next fashion.

Tarde also noted that, due to the peculiarities of a modernization that both homogenizes and heterogenizes, differences in space became smaller than differences in time (Tarde [1893] 1999: 70). Fashion means that many people do the same thing at the same time across space, but fashions mean that they will be doing something else soon.

Nor is the notion of a 'fashionable city' a new one, although undoubtedly a modern one (Czarniawska 2002). Tarde quoted an author who studied cities of the old regime in France as noting that it was 'fashionable' in the eighteenth century to use secret ballots in municipal elections. Moreover, the city of Angers adopted this mode of voting as early as the sixteenth century, justifying it by the example of Venice, Genoa, Milan, and Rome (Tarde [1890] 1903: 293).

Big cities, especially capitals, are indeed laboratories of fashion (to be condemned or admired in the provinces, but always imitated). Big cities set examples, but they also collect experiences from their region or country and re-present it in further contacts. An innovation can either start in a capital or, initiated somewhere else, find its most extreme expression there. The duty of modernization resides in big cities, were it to be seen as the work of 'urban elites' or, to the contrary, of the 'urban fringe'.

11.4. Is It Too Late to Learn from Tarde?

Niklas Luhmann ([1992] 1998: 98) pointed out that Tarde's notion of imitation offers a unique explanation of how order can exist without knowledge. As the platitudes about the 'knowledge society' seem to be reaching the point of exhaustion, it is perhaps time to start thinking of alternatives, and Tarde may be a valuable source of inspiration. The main attraction of Tarde's thought for organization theory is the capacity of its metaphors to capture paradoxes typical for all organizing. It may help to conceptualize organizations as both bigger and smaller than their members; fashion-following as a desire for conformity and uniqueness, and organizational images as constructed with the help of both repetition and difference. That which disqualified Tarde in the eyes of his critics—his tolerance of paradoxes—can at present be seen as the strength of his thought.

Perhaps the influence of Tarde is already felt, albeit unacknowledged. He suggested a need to invent 'a *gloriometer* to measure notoriety and admiration' (Hughes 1961: 557). A closer look at the description of such an instrument reveals that the gloriometer already exists in several variations, for example, the Web of Science or the Google Scholar. Perhaps the main reason for the neglect of Tardean ideas was that computers were not yet invented in his time.

Counting glory was not the only suggestion offered by Tarde as an aid to quantitative research. From the perspective of today, it can be said that he both explained the currently observable phenomena and suggested ways of changing their shape. The obsession with quantification will never cease, he reasoned, because people want to compare desires that are incomparable by nature. During the American Sociological Association meeting in New York City in August 2007, Naomi Klein suggested that it is important to know if Donald Rumsfeld's desire for oil is bigger or smaller than the sociologists' desire for better world. She was applauded. The problem is, said Tarde, that introducing one measure for all desires—money—leads nowhere, because it confuses the measure with the measured. The solution is to look for fitting measures and measurements for different kinds of desires and beliefs. Here is an interesting challenge for organization scholars: find relevant things to count!

In sum, Tarde's work seems to me eminently suitable as an inspiration for contemporary organization theory. His texts combine relativism with pragmatism to a point that Richard Rorty could have authored some of them. His emphasis on services and consumption rather than on production only; his appreciation of the power of public opinion and the role of the media; his understanding of the role of communication, knowledge, and esthetics in economy—all seem to fit our times better than his own.

Acknowledgments

My profound thanks go to all my commentators: Paul Adler, Peter Bryant, Michal Frenkel, Roger Geiger (who rose above our differences and gave me generous advice), and Bruno Latour.

References

Alliez, É. (1999). 'Présentation. Tarde et le probléme de la constitution', in Gabriel Tarde, *Monadologie et sociologie*. Paris: Institut Synthélabo.

—— (2004). 'The Difference and Repetition of Gabriel Tarde'. *Distinktion*, 9: 49–54.

Anderson, B. ([1983] 1991). *Imagined Communities*. Chicago: University of Chicago Press.

Audi, R. (ed.) (1995). *The Cambridge Dictionary of Philosophy*. Cambridge: Cambridge University Press.

Blumer, H. G. (1954). 'What Is Wrong with Social Theory'. *American Sociological Review*, 18: 3–10.

—— (1969). 'Fashion: From Class Differentiation to Collective Selection'. *Sociological Quarterly*, 10: 275–91.

Brooks, P. (2005). 'The Identity Paradigm'. A talk at the Center for Cultural Sociology Spring Conference, 6–9 May, Yale University, Yale, Conn.

Buruma, I. (2002). 'The Blood Lust of Identity'. *New York Review of Books*, 49/6 (11 April): 12–14.

Certeau, M. de ([1975] 1988). *The Writing of History*. New York: Columbia University Press.

Clark, T. N. (1968). 'Institutionalization of Innovations in Higher Education: Four Models'. *Administrative Science Quarterly*, 13/1: 1–25.

—— (1969). 'Introduction', in Terry N. Clark (ed.), *Gabriel Tarde on Communication and Social Influence*. Chicago: University of Chicago Press.

Corbey, R., and Leerssen, J. (1991). 'Studying Alterity: Backgrounds and Perspectives', in Raymond Corbey and Joep Leerssen (eds.), *Alterity, Identity, Image: Selves and Others in Society and Scholarship*. Amsterdam: Rodopi.

Czarniawska, B. (2002). *A Tale of Three Cities, or the Glocalization of City Management*. Oxford: Oxford University Press.

—— (2004). 'Gabriel Tarde and Big City Management'. *Distinktion*, 9: 81–95.
—— (2007). 'Alterity/Identity Interplay in the Organizational Image Construction', in Daved Barry and Hans Hansen (eds.), *The Sage Handbook of New Approaches to Organization Studies*. London: Sage.
—— (n.d.). 'Negotiating Selves: Gender'.
—— and SEVÓN, G. (1996). 'Introduction', in Barbara Czarniawska and Guje Sevón (eds.), *Translating Organizational Change*. Berlin: de Gruyter.
—— —— (2005). 'Translation Is a Vehicle, Imitation Its Motor, and Fashion Sits at the Heel', in Barbara Czarniawska and Guje Sevón (eds.), *Global Ideas: How Ideas, Objects and Practices Travel in the Global Economy*. Malmö/Copenhagen: Liber/CBS Press.
DELEUZE, G. ([1968] 1997). *Difference & Repetition*. London: Athlone.
DIMAGGIO, P. J. (1983). 'State Expansion in Organizational Fields', in Richard H. Hall and Robert E. Quinn (eds.), *Organizational Theory and Public Policy*. Beverly Hills, Calif.: Sage.
—— and POWELL, W. W. ([1984] 1991). 'The Iron Cage Revisited: Institutional Isomorphism and Collective Rationality', in Walter W. Powell and Paul J. DiMaggio (eds.), *The New Institutionalism in Organizational Analysis*. Chicago: University of Chicago Press.
DURKHEIM, É., and MAUSS, M. ([1903] 1963). *Primitive Classification*. Chicago: University of Chicago Press.
FLORIDA, R. (2005). *Cities and the Creative Class*. New York: Routledge.
GEIGER, R. L. (1972). 'The Development of French Sociology 1871–1905'. Ph.D. diss. (University of Michigan).
GIRARD, R. (1977). *Violence and the Sacred*. Baltimore: Johns Hopkins University Press.
HATCH, M. JO, and SCHULTZ, M. (eds.) (2003). *Organizational Identity: A Reader*. Oxford: Oxford University Press.
HÖPFL, H. (1992). 'The Making of the Corporate Acolyte'. *Journal of Management Studies*, 29/1: 23–34.
HUGHES, E. C. (1961). 'Tarde's *Psychologie Économique*: An Unknown Classic by a Forgotten Sociologist'. *American Journal of Sociology*, 66/6: 553–9.
IRENIUS, L. (2002). 'Samhället består av sömngångare som imiterar varandra'. *Axess*, March: 26–7.
LAMOREAUX, N. (2003). 'Partnerships, Corporations, and the Limits on Contractual Freedom in U.S. History', in Kenneth Lipartito and David B. Sicilia (eds.), *Constructing Corporate America*. New York: Oxford University Press.
LATOUR, B. (1986). 'The Powers of Association', in John Law (ed.), *Power, Action and Belief*. London: Routledge and Kegan Paul.
—— (1993). *We Have Never Been Modern*. Cambridge, Mass.: Harvard University Press.
—— (2002). 'Gabriel Tarde and the End of the Social', in Patrick Joyce (ed.), *The Social in Question*. London: Routledge.
—— and LÉPINAY, V. (2007). 'L'économie, science des intérêts pasionnés'. Préface à la republication partielle de *Psychologie èconomique*. Paris: Les Empêcheurs.
LAZZARATO, M. (2003). 'Invenzione e lavoro nella cooperazione tra cervelli'. *Materiali resistenti*, 17 August. http://materialiresistenti.blog.dada.net/archivi/2003-08-01_5.html #20030817
LUHMANN, N. ([1992] 1998). *Observations on Modernity*. Stanford, Calif.: Stanford University Press.

—— (2002). *Theories of Description: Redescribing the Definitions of Modernity*. Stanford, Calif.: Stanford University Press.

Lyotard, J.-F. ([1979] 1987). *The Postmodern Condition: A Report on Knowledge*. Manchester: Manchester University Press.

McCloskey, D. N. (2001). *Measurement and Meaning in Economics*. Northampton, Mass.: Edward Elgar.

Margalit, A. (2007). 'The Lessons of Spinoza'. *New York Review of Books*, 12 April: 71–4.

Meyer, J. (1999). 'Globalization: Sources, and Effects on National States and Societies'. Paper presented at the conference 'Globalizations: Dimensions, Trajectories, Prospects', Stockholm, August 1998.

Mucchielli, L. (2000). 'Tardomania? Réflexions sur les usages contemporains de Tarde'. *Revue d'histoire des sciences humaines*, 3: 161–84.

Partington, A. (1992). 'Popular Fashion and Working-Class Affluence', in Juliet Ash and Elizabeth Wilson (eds.), *Chic Thrills: A Fashion Reader*. Berkeley: University of California Press.

Rogers, E. (1962). *Diffusion of Innovation*. New York: Free Press.

Schultz, M., Hatch, M. Jo, and Larsen, M. H. (eds.) (2000). *The Expressive Organization: Linking Identity, Reputation and the Corporate Brand*. Oxford: Oxford University Press.

Sevón, G. (1996). 'Organizational Imitation in Identity Transformation', in Barbara Czarniawska and Guje Sevón (eds.), *Translating Organizational Change*. Berlin: de Gruyter.

Simmel, G. ([1904] 1971). 'Fashion', in Donald N. Levine (ed.), *Georg Simmel on Individuality and Social Forms*. Chicago: University of Chicago Press.

Spencer, H. (1880). *Principles of Sociology*, iv. *Ceremonial Institutions*. New York: D. Appleton and Company.

Tarde, G. ([1888] 1969). 'Logical Laws of Imitation', in Terry N. Clark (ed.), *Gabriel Tarde on Communication and Social Influence*. Chicago: University of Chicago Press.

—— ([1890] 1903). *The Laws of Imitation*. New York: Henry Holt.

—— ([1893] 1999). *Monadologie et sociologie*. Paris: Institut Synthélabo.

—— ([1896] 2003). *Fragment d'histoire future*. Electronic edition by Jean-Marie Tremblay, University of Chicoutimi, Quebec, Canada, www.uqac.ca/class/classiques/tarde_gabriel/fragment_histoire_future/fragment.html

—— ([1899] 1974). *Social Laws: An Outline of Sociology*. New York: Arno Press.

—— ([1901] 2007). *Psychologie économique*. Paris: Les Empêcheurs.

—— ([1902] 1969). 'Invention', in Terry N. Clark (ed.), *Gabriel Tarde on Communication and Social Influence*. Chicago: University of Chicago Press.

—— ([1904] 1969). 'A Debate with Émile Durkheim', in Terry N. Clark (ed.), *Gabriel Tarde on Communication and Social Influence*. Chicago: University of Chicago Press.

Veblen, T. ([1899] 1994). *The Theory of the Leisure Class*. New York: Dover Publications.

Warren, R. L., Rose, S. M., and Bergunder, A. F. (1974). *The Structure of Urban Reform: Community Decision Organizations in Stability and Change*. Lexington, Mass.: Lexington Books.

Wertheimer, M., and Gillis, W. M. (1958). 'Satiation and the Rate of Lapse of Verbal Meaning'. *Journal of General Psychology*, 59: 79–85.

Whetten, D. A., and Godfrey, P. C. (1998). *Identity in Organizations: Building Theory through Conversations*. Thousand Oaks, Calif.: Sage.

Young, A. B. ([1937] 1973). 'Recurring Cycles of Fashion', in Gordon Wills and David Midgley (eds.), *Fashion Marketing*. London: Allen & Unwin.

Wilson, E. (1985). *Adorned in Dreams: Fashion and Modernity*. Berkeley: University of California Press.

CHAPTER 12

GEORG SIMMEL

THE INDIVIDUAL AND THE ORGANIZATION

ALAN SCOTT

12.1. Introduction: Simmel in Organization Studies

While the previously ubiquitous influence of Max Weber on organizational analysis is arguably waning (Lounsbury and Carberry 2005), that of his contemporary, Georg Simmel, seems increasingly robust. This follows a long-term revival of Simmel's reputation in sociology and social theory; a revival largely due to the efforts of translators, editors, and commentators on both sides of the Atlantic. But we may be dealing with more than the belated entry of an intellectual fashion into organization studies? The type of organization of which Weber is the supreme analyst, namely bureaucracy, has been the object of sustained intellectual and political attack over the last quarter of a century or so. The rise of new public management (NPM) and its influence upon both corporate and political decision makers has not only undermined the claim of bureaucracy to technical superiority but also has been accompanied by massive efforts to dismantle state and private bureaucracies and replace them with more flexible, customer-friendly, flatter, and, last but not least, cheaper organizational forms. Weber's influence may thus be declining with the fortunes of the organizational type that he considered to be the ultimate expression of modern instrumental rationality, leaving those who refer to him with the choice of joining the game of bureaucracy-bashing by emphasizing the critical and/or ambivalent side of his analysis (e.g. Bauman 1989) or defending bureaucracy with classically Weberian arguments concerning proceduralism, equality of treatment, and rule of law (*Rechtsstaatlichkeit*) (e.g. du Gay 2000).

In contrast, Simmel's social theory suddenly seems more contemporary to an age that seeks to understand itself via categories such as networks, flows, and scapes. The dominance of mechanical metaphors in classical social thought (see Scott 1997)[1] has, at least temporarily, given way to such notions as 'network society' (Castells 1998: 350) and 'liquid modernity' (Bauman 2000). Simmel's growing importance to social theory generally has not gone unnoticed in organization studies. Nevertheless, we must be careful not to exaggerate Simmel's influence here. Mark Granovetter's famous article 'The Strength of Weak Ties' (1973) is generally taken to be the key moment in development of network theory, and in this literature Simmel is generally referred to, if at all, as someone who earlier, though less systematically, proposed an analysis of social circles that was a precursor of current more elaborated and formalized models. Deconstructionist or post-structuralist organizational thinkers draw their inspiration largely from French philosophers, notably from Jacques Derrida and from Gilles Deleuze and Félix Guattari. Again, Simmel is largely ritualistically referred to as someone whose ideas have an affinity with current thought, at least if he is appropriately 'postmodernized' (Weinstein and Weinstein 1993).

There are some exceptions; cases where his social theory has been used to support or modify theories of networks (Diani 2000)[2] or trust (Möllering 2001). At a more metatheoretical level, Simmel has also been evoked by deconstructionist organizational theorists in their efforts to effect a move away from static social-scientific categories—individual, organization, society—and towards more dynamic and relational ones (see e.g. Cooper 2005). However, these isolated exceptions alone would not be enough to place Simmel at the center of debates in organization studies. The view might be of him as someone whose influence was mediated by others—e.g. by Erving Goffman's famous analysis of 'total institutions' (Goffman 1961)—and/or as a reference for early social network theorists (e.g. Breiger 1974; Alba and Kadushin 1976).

However, there is one other exception that is significantly influential to potentially move Simmel from a somewhat marginal position into the center of

[1] Weber characterized the modern organization as a 'a living machine' (*lebende Maschine*) in contrast to Marx's dead machines: the loom, the forge, etc., and as 'congealed spirit' (*geronnener Geist*) (Weber 1918: 158).

[2] Strictly speaking, Diani's analysis is directed more towards social movement analysis than to organization studies.

organization studies debates, namely Ronald Burt's theory of structural holes and of brokerage (see Burt 1992 and 2005, respectively). Burt and those who have engaged with him (e.g. David Krackhardt's (1998, 1999) work on 'Simmelian ties') make a very direct appeal to Simmel as the inspiration behind their analyses. In particular, they refer to his 'formal sociology' and, more specifically, to his analysis of the dyad and triad (Simmel 1950: pt. 2, chs. 3–4; original: Simmel 1908). For this line of analysis, Simmel's key insight was into the qualitative difference between dyadic (two-party) and triadic (three-party) relationships.[3] The use of Simmel in this influential literature is ingenious. If social theory is not to become ancestor worship, then the classics have to be made to work their passage. However, this analysis uses a relatively narrow selection from Simmel's work and arguments. Here I shall seek to construct Simmel with reference to a wider range of his texts and arguments. This is less for scholarly reasons than because I shall suggest that there are potential uses to which organization studies can put Simmel that go beyond brokerage and Simmelian ties.

This chapter then has two basic tasks: (1) to extract from Simmel's sociology those strands of potential significance for the analysis of organizations; and (2) to locate those elements within, and identify their significance for, his wider analysis. These are potentially conflicting aims. The former treats Simmel as a resource for contemporary analysis; the latter seeks to relocate those arguments in the context of authorial intentions (cf. Skinner 1969). While the former risks the danger of presentism, the latter can lead to undue deference towards the texts. I shall seek to avoid either extreme. In order to avoid presentism—i.e. foreshortening historical interpretation by picking out only those aspects thought to be of contemporary relevance—we need to note in the first place that it was not Simmel's intention to contribute to, or assist the emergence of, the (sub- or trans-)discipline we now call organization studies. Anything in his work of relevance to understanding organizations is the by-product of an analysis with wider, or at least other, aims, namely understanding types of 'sociation' (*Vergesellschafung*).

The discussion will be organized under the following headings: (1) Simmel's analysis of sociation: intersecting social circles (*Kreuzung soziale Kreise*),[4] life/form, and the individual law; (2) towards a cultural theory of organization: the case of the secret society; and (3) contemporary relevance: the organizational imperatives of 'fast capitalism' and the 'high commitment' organization.

[3] Readers interested in these debates can follow up these references. See also Dekker 2006 and Fernandez-Mateo 2007 for further development of this line of analysis.

[4] This is usually translated as the 'intersection of social spheres'. Reinhard Bendix (Simmel 1955: 124 n. 1) claims that the literal translation—the intersecting of social circles—is 'almost meaningless' and prefers 'the web of group affiliations'. This is a highly evocative image but may be misleading: one can get caught in a web, whereas Simmel's main point is that multiple membership of diverse social circles is potentially liberating for the individual.

12.2. Simmel's Analysis of Sociation: Intersecting Social Circles and the Life/Form Distinction

In his influential account of individualism, Steven Lukes (1973) distinguishes a number of types: political, religious, ethical, methodological, etc. Nowhere does he mention possible sociological forms of individualism. Indeed, a sociological individualism is an apparent oxymoron. The subject of sociology—*homo sociologicus*—is so caught in the game of social life as to appear the antithesis of the autonomous and sovereign individual. But Lukes draws a useful distinction between the pluralist and the sociological critique of individualism that may help us locate Simmel:

> For the pluralist, society is ... to be seen as a basically harmonious network of groups, organizations and associations, which both influence and compete for the loyalties of individuals. Individuals move in the interstices of these overlapping groupings, which provide them with a plurality of role-definitions and attachments, while serving to prevent both a tyrannical domination of the individual by the state and the growth of an overriding and all-embracing conflict within society. A sociological perspective differs from the individualistic picture in revealing all the manifold ways in which individuals are dependent on, indeed *constituted by*, the operation of social forces. (Lukes 1973: 85–6)

While this account of pluralism does not quite capture Simmel's position—the emphasis upon harmony is not necessary to him and his subjects move within and across rather than in the interstices between social groups—clearly he is not a 'sociological' critic of individualism in the above sense. Lukes is, of course, here equating the sociological critique of individualism with determinism and 'sociologism'. It might, however, be more useful to view pluralism and the social forces argument as competing forms of the sociological account of the subject and to locate Simmel somewhere between the 'sociological' and pluralist positions. Furthermore, as already indicated, I shall argue that Simmel seeks not to criticize individualism at all, but rather to find ways of making individualism compatible with sociology, at least in its more pluralistic guise. Simmel's account of intersecting social circles seeks to socialize Kant's autonomous subject without thereby vitiating that autonomy, rather as Habermas, in his discourse ethics, was later to attempt to socialize Kantian ethics without giving in to moral relativism (Habermas 1990).

Simmel's socialization of the autonomous subject requires both a sociological and historical analysis. The notion of intersecting social circles provides the sociological part of the story. Pre-modern societies are like concentric circles in which an individual's location within any one ring fixes his or her position vis-à-vis all the others. Group membership not individuality; ascription not election fix identity. With increasing social differentiation, concentric circles come to be replaced by intersecting circles across which the individual can migrate opening up an element of choice: 'it was the free association that first made the will of the affiliated individuals the basis for its unity' (Simmel 1908: 460; trans. 1955: 132).[5] Furthermore, the individual does not play the same role nor have the same rank in all the groups of which he or she is a member. Multiple membership also brings multiple and diverse benefits, whether for socializing or for competition. Under such conditions

> on the one hand the individual finds a community for each of his inclinations and efforts making their satisfaction easier, offering each of his activities a suitably tested form and the advantages of group membership. On the other hand, that which is specific to his individuality will be secured through the *combination* of circles that can certainly be diverse. Thus, one can say: from individuals emerges society, and from society the individual.
>
> (ibid. 485; trans. 1955: 163)

The point becomes clearer if we look at one of the examples Simmel uses: women's solidarity. In modern conditions, the gender-specific aspects of an individual's role are no longer coterminous with the entire person. This means that women are no longer subject to subordination to a given individual man—e.g. father or husband—in all aspects of their lives: 'the woman is here in fact released from the sole tie via which she was completely determined by her subordination to the man or by the absolute differences between her activities and his' (ibid. 501; trans. 1955: 182).[6] It is this partial liberation—e.g. the possibility of a life outside the home and family—that is a necessary sociological condition for women to form purposive associations (e.g. social movements) through which the demands for a fuller emancipation can be made. Simmel's argument here is not that modernity emancipates women, but rather that in partially doing so it (1) creates the conditions under which full emancipation becomes thinkable at all and (2) enables women to register that demand collectively.

Simmel's account of intersecting social circles as a sociological condition of modern freedom builds upon a historical account of the emergence of that condition. This is particularly evident in the *Philosophy of Money*:

> By thus eliminating the pressure of irrevocable dependence upon a particular individual master, the worker is already on the way to personal freedom despite his objective bondage. That this emergent freedom has little continuous influence upon the material situation of the worker should not prevent us from appreciating it. (Simmel [1900] 1990: 300)

Given that Simmel asserts no correspondence between freedom and the material well-being of the worker—i.e. that he concedes Marx's point that 'objective

[5] I have sometime, as here, adjusted the English translation. I have therefore usually given the reference to both the German original and to the most widely available English translation.

[6] Amartya Sen (1999) makes a very similar case with respect to women's paid employment. Sen's argument, that markets typically increase human capabilities ('agency', in more sociological parlances) because they weaken older forms of personal and cultural subordination, is strikingly close to Simmel's view.

bondage' remains—what does this freedom amount to? First, it amounts to the principle or legal possibility of leaving any given master. Second, in the labor contract only a part of the personality of the worker—namely that part relevant to the task—is under control and surveillance. In pre-capitalist society, the former was for most not even a theoretical possibility; the whole personality and much of the life of the serf was under the master's control. Thus, the attempt to debunk the notion of freedom by demonstrating an asymmetry between formal (legal/political) and substantive (social/economic) freedom (Marx) fails to appreciate the subjective significance of formal freedoms for those who lack them, or have a memory of lacking them.

Simmel's assertion of the equation of the wage contract and money with personal freedom stems from his general characterization of the dual nature of modern social relations within the money economy: on the one hand, there is an unprecedented level of mutual dependency but, on the other, an equally unprecedented level of personal autonomy:

> The currents of modern culture flow in two apparently opposite directions: in one direction towards levelling out, equalization; the production of ever more inclusive social circles via the subsumption of the most remote elements under the same conditions; in the other direction towards emphasizing individual traits, the independence of the person, the autonomy of its formation. Both directions are borne by the money economy which makes possible, on the one hand, general, and in all places similarly functioning, interests, means of association and communication; on the other, intellectual reserve, individualization, and freedom. (Simmel 1896: 83)

As David Frisby (1990) has shown, Simmel's analysis both extends and critiques the Marxist view of money as the objectification or reification of human relations,[7] in which 'the connection between persons is transformed into a social relation between things' (Marx [1857–8] 1973: 157). Simmel shares Marx's understanding of money as an indifferent medium in which social relations are reified, but inverts the conclusions drawn from this. Whereas for Marx the fact that with money we carry our social relations around in our pockets is an expression of our objectification (*Verdinglichung* or *Versachlichung*)—of the power of the object over the subject who created it—for Simmel, it is precisely the indifference of the medium towards the subject that is the source of our new-found freedom. Our increasing dependence on all within the market economy is compensated for and only bearable because we are indifferent towards each other: 'we are compensated for the great quantity of our dependence by the indifference towards the respective persons and by our liberty to change them at will' ([1900] 1990: 298). Money is the medium of this indifference. Correspondingly, money 'makes possible relationships between people but leaves

[7] A view developed at length in the 'Chapter on Money' in the *Grundrisse*, written around 1857–8 but not published until the late 1930s/early 1940s in Moscow and in 1953 in Germany, and thus unknown to Simmel.

them personally undisturbed' ([1900] 1990: 303). Roberta Sassatelli has summed up this aspect of Simmel's position as follows:

His perspective is opposed to the notion that the growth of market objectivity goes hand in hand with the dissolution of the individual and with the fall of his or her signification space. On the contrary, subjectivism is heightened insofar as individuals' capacities to sustain difference is vital to social, objective exchange. (Sassatelli 2000: 212)[8]

For Simmel, the psychological counterpart to the indifference of the medium is the indifference of the subjects towards each other; their increasing '*Blasiertheit*' (blasé attitude) (Simmel 1903). No less important, however, is that this individual subjective dimension has in its turn an intellectual counterpart in individualism. The choice made by those who flee personal domination is not freedom as such, but one specific form or conception of freedom, namely personal or negative freedom: 'the emancipation of the labourer has to be paid for, as it were, by the emancipation of the employer, that is, by the loss of welfare that bonded labourers enjoyed' (Simmel [1900] 1990: 300). Positive freedoms (e.g. protection from the effects of the market) are sacrificed for the sake of negative freedom: the right to non-interference and to self-determination. Individualism in this view is not some *post factum* ideological reflex, nor is it imposed from above. Rather, it is implicit in the millions of original acts that have contributed to bringing the modern money economy into being. Simmel's modern subjects occupy a *habitus* in which they are disposed to *Blasiertheit* at the level of personality and to individualism at the level of ideas. The new urbanite and the emigrant are not individualists merely because of the nature of the urban or emigrant experience but also by dint of the fact that in many cases they have chosen personal freedom over security. Thus, individualism—the modern ideology for Simmel—has its origins in and gains its continued subjective power from the context of the struggle against personal subordination:

The ideal of freedom and equality, which animated the eighteenth century ... expresses most vividly the unavoidable reaction against the dominant constitution of society. It was a time in which the individual forces were seen to be in the most painful opposition to their social and historical bonds and forms. The privileges of the dominant classes appeared as obsolete and degenerate; as slave chains which constricted one's very breath. Among those privileges were the despotic control of trade and traffic [*Handel und Wandel*], the still powerful vestiges of guild constitutions as well as the intolerant coercion of the church, the peasant population's tithes [*Fronpflichten*], political disenfranchisement [*Bevormundung*] in the sphere of the state, and the restrictions on municipal constitutions. Out of the oppressiveness of such institutions—which had lost all inner justification—grew the ideal of the pure freedom of the individual [*bloßer Freiheit des Individuums*]. (Simmel 1904: 273–4)

Simmel's concern with the tensions between social constraint and individual autonomy and creativity are just as evident in his methodological reflections as

[8] Sassatelli argues that Simmel is able to reach this conclusion because he, in contrast to Marx, has a relativist theory of value with Kantian roots.

they are in his substantive sociology, particularly where he is concerned with the irreducibility of life as creative motion and form as the deposits life leaves—i.e. as that which in more conventional sociology one might call 'norms', 'structures', 'systems', etc. 'Life', for Simmel, is flow or movement and cannot be captured in the static language of sociology whose concern is exclusively with 'form'—i.e. with structure and material culture (e.g. money or artifacts). Sociology and psychology are, however, plagued by the confusion of life and form and suffer from the mechanistic and reductionist illusion that their analytical tools and research methods can capture life's movement and explain the individual. In contrast, for Simmel, the relationship between life and form is an antagonistic one analogous to Marx's distinction between the forces and relations of production (see Nedelmann 1991: 172). In each case, the latter seeks to channel, and thus constrains, the former. Life and form are both mutually antagonistic and mutually interdependent. The distinction drawn between life and form, and the notion of the individual law that he developed relatively late and under the influence of *Lebensphilosophie*, enabled Simmel to distance himself from a mechanistic sociology and to articulate his commitment to a type of social analysis that abstains from evoking collective entities and avoids reification:

> The more we go into details, the more we find traits that we also encounter in others. Perhaps not continuously, but in many respects going into details and individualization are mutually exclusive. If this conceptual differentiation appears surprising, then this is because of our mechanistic habit.... If, however, a mental existence is grasped from within—not as the sum of its individual qualities, but as a living thing whose unity produces or determines all those details, or whose dissected parts are these details—so such an existence is there from the outset as a full individuality. (Simmel [1916] 2005: 46)

Failing to recognize this, mechanistic sociology and psychology seek to grasp the individual by piling one secondary characteristic upon another; a scientific practice based upon a conceptual error that inevitably leads us back to the general. Simmel makes the point by contrasting the tradition of the Renaissance portrait, where the subject is a type on stage for a public, with Rembrandt's portraits and self-portraits, which capture the trajectory of a life in its full, unique individuality: as movement, as life.[9] The former corresponds to the habits of mechanistic sociology and psychology; the latter to the inner life that cannot be categorically fixed. The notion of the individual law, which emphasizes the uniqueness of individual experience and of a person's life, gives even greater emphasis to the ways in which life eludes form: 'This is the same error as when one identifies the law within the field of morality with the general law, not thinking that an individual reality may perhaps also correspond to an individual law: an ideal that may be valid only for this existence in its totality and

[9] A recurrent theme in Simmel's work is the difference between Southern and Northern European culture, where the former embodies this social being-for-others with its emphasis upon appearance and the latter inwardness (*Innerlichkeit*).

particularity' (ibid. 49). On Simmel's individual law, life eludes not merely form but thereby also categorization and generalization.

In these theoretical and methodological writings, Simmel is posing a problem that is not as unfamiliar within organizational theory and practice as it may at first seem, and to which we shall return later. Organization is form in Simmel's sense and this raises the issue of individuality and individual creativity vs. constraint that is a subset of the more general tensions he identifies between cultural (or social) processes and systems (see Nedelmann 1991). Furthermore, in the final section, I shall consider the possibility that systems of control and evaluation within contemporary organizations reproduce the kinds of conceptual errors that Simmel identifies in a mechanistic sociology: the confusion of life and form. Before that, however, we examine how the approach outlined above may be applied to a type of sociation that approximates what we commonly think of as an organization.

12.3. Towards a Cultural Theory of Organization: The Case of the Secret Society

How does Simmel's socialized individualism pan out in an analysis of organizations? Fortunately, Simmel has made the task of answering this question easier by doing so himself, above all in his analysis of the secret and the secret society that forms chapter 5 of his *Soziologie* (Simmel 1908 and translated in Kurt Wolff's selection, 1950: pt. 4). This section will focus closely on this piece of organizational analysis.

The secret is a particular kind of social relationship—one based upon reciprocal confidence—which, once internalized into a group as its chief organizing principle, shapes the course of that group's development. The process is not exclusively one of the unfolding of the inner logic of the secret itself (its 'germ' [*Keim*] to use a common Simmelian metaphor) but also through interaction with the wider social environment. The secret—the attempt to make oneself invisible—is the most radical form of protection; one not available to an individual, but to a group. It is a protective measure typically adopted under hostile political conditions, notably despotism, to protect a developing (or declining) group and to create a space of freedom for its members outside normal surveillance and control; something like Foucault's 'heterotopian' spaces. Secret societies provide protection against what Simmel dramatically characterizes as the 'the coercive pressure of central powers' (*vergewaltigenden Druck zentrale Mächte*) (1908: 424), but in order to do so they make high demands upon their members, above all the ability to keep silent (*das Schweigen-Können*), which is itself a specific, and very fragile, form of trust. As Mark Granovetter was much later to argue, trust is a condition for malfeasance and 'clever institutions' have to find ways of making malfeasance 'too costly to engage in' (Granovetter 1985: 489). The vulnerability of the secret, which can be betrayed at any moment, poses the malfeasance problem in a particularly stark form,[10] and the secret society has to be especially clever in devising ways of retaining members' commitment to the secret. Complex techniques are required to assure this, making the secret society a highly effective 'schooling in moral solidarity' (Simmel 1908: 425; trans. 1950: 348). In this way, Simmel is using the secret society as a kind of living ideal type[11] in which general features of sociation—e.g. trust and betrayal—become transparent. But the secret society is also atypical in one key respect: its necessary cleverness means that it is somewhat artificial and self-conscious. Its development lacks the organic or more spontaneous quality of looser forms of human sociation. For example, it demands strict self-discipline and displays a 'stylised purity of life' into which the novice has to be initiated (with accompanying rituals and rites of passage) over an extended period (ibid. 427; trans. 1950: 350). Such an order (*Bund*) once more takes the form of concentric circles with those closest to the center (normally those with the longest membership) having greater access to the order's secret(s). The thickest walls, however, are those to the outside. Where the group is formed with the aim of keeping a specific secret, that secret must not get through (*durchdringen*) to the multitude, or the crowd (*die Menge*) (ibid. 433; trans. 1950: 355). The secret society is therefore both internally and externally hierarchical; it has a necessarily 'aristocratic' character. The organization and its members understand themselves as something better than the rest. Thus, the organization not only seeks to make malfeasance 'too costly' but also offers psychological rewards to its members: keeping the secret promises status both within the organization and vis-à-vis the wider community.[12]

So far we have seen how Simmel thinks the secret society works; how it creates and sustains itself in the face of a hostile, and possibly dangerous, environment and on the precarious basis of the secret. But the analysis is no less concerned with the ways in which the secret society fails both in reproducing itself ad infinitum and for its members. Secret societies have much in common with what the late Mary Douglas called 'enclaves' (e.g. Douglas and Mars 2003).[13] Enclaves build 'walls of virtue'

[10] Simmel formulates the malfeasance problems rather nicely: one 'gives' trust (*schenkt Vertrauen*) but cannot demand it. In other words, trust is a gift. It therefore requires a 'positive nefariousness' (*positive Schlechtigkeit*) to break it (Simmel 1908: 425).

[11] Simmel has been identified as a key source of Weber's methodology, including the concept of the ideal type. See e.g. Ringer 1997: 50–1.

[12] Vis-à-vis the wider community, but not necessarily within it. Insofar as the order's secrets have got through to the multitude, they may appear vaguely ridiculous to the latter.

[13] In terms of her well-known grid-group model (where 'grid' is the degree of rule-boundedness and 'group' the degree of solidarity), enclaves are simple groups based upon strong group but weak

around themselves and work with an extreme form of friend–enemy schemata. While, Douglas argues, this makes them appear very strong, in fact, it makes them fragile. Within the walls, the logic of the friend–enemy schema keeps on working with members competing to outdo each other in virtue, to recruit followers, and to condemn peers. Enclaves are thus vulnerable to internal dissension and factionalism unless under direct attack by an external enemy.[14] Simmel's analysis follows a similar course in tracing how the very measures that the group adopts to protect itself and maintain its boundaries have implications for its inner life that are, in the longer term, destructive. Here again, what makes such orders strong also makes them vulnerable. The secret society lays claim to the whole person, which leads to a loss of individuality (*Entindividualisierung*) and self-erasure (*Entselbstung*). Thus, paradoxically, the secret society eventually destroys those very freedoms that it initially created in the face of political despotism. In time it takes on some of the characteristics that Erving Goffman later ascribed to the asylum (Goffman 1961). It becomes a kind of 'total institution' laying claim to the entire personality. Both total institutions and secret societies are highly ritualistic and have high walls—whether physical or symbolic, or both—to the outside.[15] Furthermore, walls, as Susanne Lohmann (2004: 82) notes of the lines between academic disciplines, 'keep right on protecting' after the society has become obsolete or its original purpose lost. Thus, the secret society (like the types of organizations of which it is a close to ideal type) is prone to drift and is ultimately antithetical to the principle of intersecting social circles, which is, for Simmel, the sociological *conditio sine qua non* of the personal freedom and of the individual autonomy that modern societies uniquely allow their members.

By comparing Simmel's account of the secret society to Mary Douglas's account of terrorist (and other) enclaves, I am implying something I shall now make explicit: if there is a general theory of organization lurking in Simmel's social theory, then is it a cultural account not dissimilar in key respects to the Douglas-inspired Cultural Theory of organization. This is a perspective that does not marginalize or deny

grid. They are thus egalitarian. Simmel's secret societies, however, are, in Douglas's terms, strong on both dimensions. They are 'complex groups', like regiments or monasteries, which fall into the 'hierarchical' or 'positional' box within the Douglas model. To make matters somewhat more complex, Simmel also gives an example of a secret society, the late nineteenth-century radical Czech 'Omladina', with a cell and network structure (1908: 434–5; trans. 1950: 357). In contrast to the common current practice of contrasting networks and hierarchies, he emphasizes the compatibility of a network form and hierarchy.

[14] Douglas and Mars are addressing the issues of entrenched religious communities and of terrorism, and there are clear policy implications: do not resolve these groups' key internal organization dilemma for them by declaring war on them.

[15] I do not mean to imply that Goffman's and Simmel's analyses are identical. Individuals are 'committed' to the secret society and to the asylum in ways that correspond to the two distinct senses of that term and, in the former, there is no direct equivalent of the staff–inmate divide so central to Goffman's account.

the role of advantage-seeking, but rather explicitly locates it as one of a number of possible orientations for and within human communities. The focus of such a cultural approach shifts attention away from rationality, intentionality, strategy, and planning towards the inherent logic at work within the community; a logic that works behind the actors' backs, often against their expressed aims, and without their knowledge. The interest here is not so much in how plans unfold but rather in the many ways actions misfire. In culturalist approaches, there are few heroic—or even 'good news'—stories of the kind commonly found in populist management literature and no recipes.

In order to develop the point that a Simmelian approach to organization is a cultural theory in this sense, it is worthwhile trying to deduce some general principles for understanding organizations from his analysis of the secret society as a living ideal type. These basic principles are as follows:

1. First, identify the type of social relationship—idea, germ (*Keim*)—that provides the organizing principle underlying the organization;
2. Then identify the type of society or community against which the organization is a reaction and vis-à-vis which it defines itself and its boundaries;
3. Trace the ways in which the logic of the basic idea/relationship unfolds and the interactions with the group–external environment in order to understand the inner life and internal development of the group or organization;
4. Finally, identify the ways in which this basic idea/relationship plays itself out in a way that can potentially (a) systematically undermine the original aim and (b) weaken the organization and/or lead to its decay.

These principles are close to the approach adopted by organizational analysts influenced by Mary Douglas's Cultural Theory; not only Douglas herself (1986) but also Christopher Hood's brilliant adaptation in his *The Art of the State* (1998). What Cultural Theory adds to Simmel is a systematic breakdown of the possible types of human community into four basic forms along two axes: (1) the degree of solidarity within the community (group); and (2) the degree of its rule boundedness (grid). But beyond this systematization, the Cultural Theory of organization follows very closely the principles that I have just ascribed to Simmel. Hood (1998) perhaps provides the best example here. From Douglas's four community types (isolates [strong grid/weak group]; hierarchies [strong group/strong grid]; opportunists [weak grid/weak group], and enclavists [strong group/ weak grid]), Hood deduces four corresponding types of management: fatalists, hierarchists, individualists, and (elite or sequestrated) egalitarians. What Hood then does for each management/organizational type closely resembles Simmel's analysis of the secret society and roughly follows the order of Simmel's approach as set out above. The affinities become clear if we likewise break Hood's analysis down into a series of steps:

1. Each of these managerial/organizational types is characterized by a set of simple basic principles;
2. Because they define themselves vis-à-vis their opposites (e.g. egalitarians define themselves against heartless neo-liberal individualists; individualists reject the sentimental solidarity of chaotic egalitarians, etc.), each community is prone to move towards its purest or ideal form;
3. In this process, the inherent, and likewise contrasting, risks of each managerial type become increasingly evident, and the initial organizing principles decay (e.g. solidaristic egalitarians end up as 'co-existing' isolated individuals);
4. The unfolding of this logic produces a reaction in which disappointed and/or frustrated subgroups seek to overturn the initial basic principles and install a regime that is as far removed from the current order as possible, i.e. there is a swing to another corner within the grid–group model.

Hood's analysis is a great deal more subtle than this sketch, but with it I seek to make two points. First, there is a contemporary form of organizational analysis that is not merely partially influenced or inspired by Simmel or with which it might be said to have an elective affinity (which one might identify even in Foucault), but one in which the basic principles and moves of Simmel's approach are carried forward.[16] Second, the Cultural Theory of organization might in turn be strengthened by a more explicit reference to Simmel. Ironically, or perhaps unfortunately for my argument, it is not Simmel, but Durkheim who is the social theorist informing the Cultural Theory of organization.

12.4. Contemporary Relevance: The Organizational Imperatives of 'Fast Capitalism' and the 'High Commitment' Organization

I have thus far sought to relocate Simmel's views on organizations within his broader intellectual project in order to counter the tendency to cherry pick those ideas that seem most appealing to contemporary organizational analysts. I have also

[16] It is, of course, a different matter to identify Simmel as the direct source. Hood makes no reference to Simmel here or, as far as I am aware, elsewhere. We can assume that Douglas was fully aware of Simmel's work, but Durkheim was her chief inspiration and *How Institutions Think* likewise makes no reference to him.

given an exposition of a case where Simmel applied his approach to a body—society or order (*Bund*)—that closely approximates an organization. My general claim has been that a Simmelian approach to understanding organizations is broadly cultural. It emphasizes the unintentional unfolding of a logic inherent within a community of whose working actors are largely unaware. Such an approach is both anti-mechanistic and anti-rationalist. With respect to the latter, culturalist approaches tend to be skeptical or, as in Hood's case, somewhat ironic ways of observing the workings of organizations. It is now time to conclude by connecting this approach with contemporary concerns within organization studies. What do these hundred-year-old arguments still have to say to us?

Here I will consider the possible relevance of Simmel's social theory for the critique of contemporary—allegedly post-bureaucratic—organizational forms. Weber has already been deployed to this end and has been used to criticize the loss of an ethic of office and procedural propriety in the types of state and corporate organizations that, under the influence of NPM, have displaced the classical bureaucracy (for a discussion, see du Gay, in this volume). My argument will be that a Simmelian critique of these organizational forms would have a different, but complementary, emphasis, namely on the loss of individuality and the tightening of the grip of form over life. If we want to defend the principles of political liberalism against contemporary styles of organizational governance, then one part of the story (the Weberian) must be about *Rechtsstaatlichkeit*, but the other (the Simmelian) must be about individual autonomy.

The continuing relevance of Simmel's arguments can be seen if we relate them to debates within Critical Management Studies (CMS) and Critical Accounting concerning those organizational forms that have emerged from policies influenced by New Public Management, i.e. so-called 'post-bureaucratic' or 'flatter' organizations. Weber feared that bureaucratization might re-establish the pre-modern forms of personal subjugation that capitalism destroyed, particularly if personal welfare services, whether provided by the state or the company, were to become tied to occupational status (Weber [1918] 1994: 158–9). This leaves Weber asking 'how is it *at all possible* to salvage any remnants of "individual freedom" of movement *in any sense*, given this all-powerful trend towards bureaucratization?' (ibid. 159). From a Simmelian perspective, we might ask the same question about the so-called 'post-bureaucratic' organizations of the current stage of capitalist development; however we choose to label the latter: 'late', 'fast', 'turbo', or whatever. In other words, the threat to individual freedom may not stem exclusively from state or private bureaucracies, as Weber appears to believe, but also from those organizational forms that seek to supplant bureaucracy. The problem becomes evident if we return to the idea of intersecting social circles.

A circle has a circumference, a radius, and a diameter. It is a bounded space. But what constitutes the boundaries of social circles? The latter can be bounded in a variety of ways, some of which are set out in Table 12.1:

Table 12.1. The boundaries of social circles

	Type of social circle	Bounded	Implications for individual freedom
Pre-modern	concentric	spatially	unfree: tied to place and to a particular master or masters
Modern	intersecting	spatially and temporally (over short runs)	freedom of movement across social circles despite continuing 'objective bondage' within the employment relation, the family, etc.
Total/carceral institutions	single and separated	spatially and frequently, but not necessarily, temporal (usually over long runs)	unfree: tied to a particular spatially bounded institution for an extended, often indeterminate and sometimes indefinite, period of time
Contemporary work/ organizational forms	expanding/ contract-ing	increasingly spatially and temporally 'unbounded'	freedom of movement but increasingly accessible at any time and place; the unfreedom of being 'on call'

The key question here is how does this final category differ from the modern one with respect to: (1) organizational boundaries; (2) expectations; and (3) performance evaluation?

(1) *The blurring of boundaries between organizational and extra-organizational life.* While the early proletariat frequently lived in close proximity to the factory, often in housing built by the employer and sometimes—as in Berlin's Siemensstadt—the result of corporate paternalism, the fundamental principle of industrial labor was the separation of the work and private spheres. Work takes place in a workplace and during working hours; it is both spatially and temporally bounded. Both white-collar and blue-collar workers were working when they were at work. In this sense, the bureaucratic subject and the manual worker had much in common. Furthermore, as Weber notes, with respect to the latter, office and person (*Amt* and *Person*) are strictly separated. These are the conditions that, for Simmel, allow both movement across circles and multiple identities. No matter how central work or professional identity is, it is not coextensive with the person. There is now, however, a growing CMS literature, both theoretical and empirical, that emphasizes the increased blurring of the work/non-work and organizational/extra-organizational life divide (e.g. Casey 1995; Thrift 2000, 2006; Fleming and Spicer 2004). The issue here is not merely one of the increasing compression of space and time (Harvey 1989), but of the, at least partial, suspension of spatial and temporal limitations on work made possible by mobile information technology and

encouraged by 'cultural management' (Kunda 1992). For example, in their study of a call center—Iocus—Fleming and Spicer note not only the ways in which employees are encouraged to take the home into the workplace and work into the home but also how this management ethic becomes inscribed into the physical arrangement of the office itself, which 'folds transit spaces and workspaces onto one another to create buildings where the division between the inside and the outside of work and organization are unclear' (Fleming and Spicer 2004: 88).

Whereas Simmel's social circles are porous in the sense that they can be crossed by individual subjects but bounded in spatial and temporal terms, the organizational type described in much CMS literature is porous with respect to its spatial-temporal boundaries, making a clear passage across those boundaries increasingly difficult. If one is encouraged to drink alcohol at work and, conversely, sexual harassment rules apply in the pub after work (both are the case with Iocus on Fleming's and Spicer's account), then the rituals that accompany the transitions between work and non-work—organizational and extra-organizational life—have largely lost their marker functions.

Summary: From a Simmelian perspective, one sociological condition for individual freedom (the mix of bounded circles and freedom of movement) is weakened. As the boundaries of organizations dissolve and work insinuates itself into every aspect of life, the individual will find it increasingly difficult to construct a bounded and independent non-work identity and defend his or her autonomy.

(2) *Organizational expectations.* Weber argued that the modern organization—whether a bureaucracy or a factory—rests upon and demands obedience. Indeed, he defined these organizations in terms of the relations of domination (*Herrschaftverhältnisse*) and of obedience (*Gehorsamsverhältnisse*). Obedience relies on rational discipline, which has its roots in military drill and monastic asceticism, but it is also behavioral, external. One can obey without believing. Weber in fact thinks that it is the particular virtue of civil servants that they can carry out an order as though it issued from their own will whatever their actual views on the matter. The modern organization thus leaves at least enough room for dissemblance. The force that is deployed is factual: the force of circumstances, the most important being our non-ownership of the means of production (the worker), administration (the civil servant), warfare (the soldier), or research (the university assistant). Furthermore, for Weber, it is the bureaucratic revolution that changes us from without, not the charismatic revolution that seeks to alter our core convictions (*Gesinnung*) that accompanies the rationalization process (see Scott and Weiskopf 2008).

In contrast, from a Critical Management Studies' perspective, the contemporary—'high commitment'—organization demands not (merely) conformity or instrumentally motivated loyalty, but conviction: identification with the organization, its products, and its aims. This is particularly the case with so-called cultural management: 'It is not just their behaviors and activities that are specified, evaluated, rewarded or punished. Rather they are driven by internal commitment, strong identification with the company goal, intrinsic satisfaction from work. These are elicited by a variety of managerial appeals, exhortations, and actions' (Kunda 1992: 11).

Just how far this new organizational demand is thought to delve into the subject's identity is clear in Nigel Thrift's assertion that contemporary capitalism is 'attempting to use the huge reservoir of non-cognitive processes, of *forethought*, for its own industrial ends in a much more open-ended way' (2006: 285). Such 'creative' labor is often organized in the form of temporary project work rather than through the standard employment relation (see Boltanski and Chiapello 2006) or taps into the commitment of user groups who constitute a free resource for the company in which 'the market is no longer outside the value chain' (Thrift 2006: 290). In this way, the consumer is co-opted into the innovation and production process, erasing the boundary yet further between social circles, notably that between the subject as producer and as consumer; a distinction central to Simmel's account of modernity. For Thrift, it is not only the walls between the work organization and the external world that are becoming increasingly porous but also those within the organization. The office or bureau—the key building blocks of the Weberian bureaucracy—is undermined by permanent reform, staff churn, and team building (ibid. 294). Thrift's account takes us very far from Simmel's intersecting social circles: 'No longer can the value form be restricted to labour at work. It encompasses life, with consumers trained from an early age to participate in the invention of more invention by using all their capabilities and producers increasingly able to find means of harvesting their potential' (ibid. 295).

Whereas the potential threat to individual freedom for Simmel typically stems from political despotism, for Thrift, and many similar commentators, it is now the all-pervasive market that allows no hiding place. Thrift here invokes Sheldon Wolin's notion of 'inverted totalitarianism' to identify the market, rather than the state, as the chief threat to individual autonomy. Not bureaucratic domination, as for Weber, but market domination feeds the imagination of critics of current work organizations.

Summary: The co-optation of the consumer into the innovation and production process erases the boundaries between social circles yet further, notably the line between the subject as producer and as consumer. The mobilization of human capacities beyond those normally engaged in the work processes makes the kinds of total claims on the person that Simmel associates with the pre-modern rather than the modern.

(3) *Audit, surveillance, and assessment.* We should not forget that these attempts to invoke and tap creativity have been accompanied by mechanisms of a more recognizably bureaucratic type, albeit in an ever more refined and, in Weber's sense, rationalized form, namely audit. The now well-established critique of auditing, of which Michael Power's *The Audit Society* is the best known example, points to a problem that Simmel's life/form distinction can illuminate. Power argues that performance is ultimately immeasurable precisely in those cases—e.g. intellectual

labor and services—where its measurability would be particularly valued. In the light of this, it becomes necessary to search for an ersatz that can be 'made auditable'. Power follows the logic of this process through to its somewhat absurd conclusion: it is the quality of the measures and policies introduced to receive the auditing processes and not the performance itself that comes to be assessed. The source of this logical absurdity is a possible conceptual confusion: the attempt to transfer forms of quality control and measurement from the field of engineering into human, and particularly intellectual, labor. In Simmel's terms, we seek to audit life when we can only audit form; spirit merely as 'congealed spirit' (*geronnener Geist*). Power's distinction between performance and auditing systems, and his argument that high-quality systems are not evidence of high-quality performance (indeed, that they may mask the latter's failings) is a specific example of the problem Simmel identifies in mechanical sociology and psychology: the more we go into detail by collecting yet further secondary characteristics, the more life (read: performance) eludes us. This, in part, explains the insatiable nature of audit and quality assurance. Not only do these undermine trust in and within the organization, thus creating a demand for more audit (O'Neill 2002) but also some of the questions that auditing seeks to answer cannot be answered. Paradoxically, this too (as with mechanical sociology and psychology) only intensifies the search.[17]

Whether based upon conceptual confusion or not, the increasing emphasis upon quality and evaluation has real effects. Trained to perform to specified criteria, and under semi-permanent evaluation, the room for individual autonomy and for personality is constricted. In Simmel's terms, these are conditions that can lead to a loss of a sense of self and to deindividualization. Where, as is often the case, those criteria are ill-defined or shifting, anxiety and mutual blaming may result. Like the increasing dissolution of the barriers between the organization and extra-organizational life, persistent, and sometimes 360 degree, assessment increasingly restricts individual autonomy and, to use Simmel's term, 'levels out' (*nivelliert*) personality and difference.[18] Auditing and quality management are further refinements of organizational method, which, as Sheldon Wolin neatly puts it, 'by simplifying and routinizing procedures, eliminates the need of surpassing talent. It [organization] is predicated on "average human beings"' (Wolin [1960] 2004: 343).

Summary: Simmel's life/form distinction and his critique of mechanical social science are potential sources of argumentation for the kinds of Critical Accounting in which Power and others are engaged.

[17] The parallels between organizational steering and social science may not be coincidental. Sheldon Wolin ([1960] 2004), for example, has argued that both are grounded in a faith in method, not least as a way of improving levels of rationality and compensating for human weakness.

[18] We should not, however, underestimate the degree to which actors are able both to distance themselves from these conditions by developing what Simmel (1903) would call a 'protective organ' (*Schutzorgan*)—here perhaps cynicism rather than the urbanite's blasé attitude—and subvert managerial intentions.

The restrictions emerging from these three features of current organizations are neither a return to the concentric circles of pre-modernity nor are they the rigid walls of the total or carceral institution: freedom of movement—capitalism's original promise—is respected. In Simmelian terms, the image that emerges from much recent analysis of the work organization is of a circle that can at any time expand to draw in the subject, irrespective of where—within which other social circles—he or she happens to be. Like Carl Schmitt's sovereign, the organization can declare the emergency anytime, anywhere. Resisting this requires increasingly difficult and conscious decisions: not bringing, or turning off, the laptop, BlackBerry, or mobile phone; not checking emails; consistently not answering the phone; not installing a home office; seeking places beyond wireless reach or which are screened. These options are not open to all and are difficult for many. Particularly for those within what Boltanski and Chiapello (2006) call the 'project polity', voluntarily putting yourself out of the loop is often a luxury that the project worker simply cannot afford, while those in more standard employment relations are subject to pressures to remain accessible outside 'office hours' and to an increasing range of clients and stakeholders.

The proximity of concerns about the reach of contemporary organizations into the lives of their members and of the effects of increasing evaluation and monitoring to Simmel's critique of the secret society becomes clearer through a simple thought experiment. Substitute contemporary/high commitment/fast organization for 'secret society' in the following passage:

> Where the society does not have the interests of its individual [members] as its immediate aim, but rather, so to speak, steps outside itself by using them as a means [towards ends] extraneous to their own aims and actions, there the secret society demonstrates an exaggerated measure of self-erasure (*Entselbstung*); of the levelling out (*Nivellierung*) of individuality. (Simmel 1908: 451; trans. 1950: 372–3)

Current CMS demonstrates both continuity and breaks with Simmel's ethical critique of the kinds of closed communities of which the secret society is an example. Like such communities, the modern organization is said to restrict individual freedom and flatten or level out difference. Rather than the exaggerated subjectivism that Simmel feared was the price to be paid for modernity, objectification, and instrumentalization remain sources of concern in CMS. Furthermore, it is not the incarcerating nature of contemporary organizations that is said to threaten a liberal order, but their reach and their increasing claim on our entire life.

If Simmel is right that individualism requires specific sociological conditions and that those conditions include the ability to cross social circles that are relatively spatially and temporally bounded, and if the current critics of high commitment organizations are right that organizations increasingly approximate expanding circles, then organization does indeed threaten the kinds of freedoms that Simmel believed to be modernity's key achievement. The worry here is that contemporary organizations seek to claw back some of the concessions the modern market economy made: freedom of movement and personal freedom outside the 'sphere of necessity'. However, there is also a warning in Simmel not to view these developments one-sidedly. As noted earlier, he argues that 'the currents of modern culture flow in two apparently opposite directions': both 'towards levelling out' and 'towards emphasizing individual traits' (Simmel [1886] 1983: 83). This sense of the duality of social development is something occasionally missing from contemporary critical organizational analysis. Perhaps here Simmel could be used to greater effect: both as a source of argument and as a counterweight to unilinear analysis, whether pessimistic or optimistic.

Acknowledgments

For comments on an earlier draft, I wish to thank Paul Adler and his team of respondents: Isabel Fernandez-Mateo, Candace Jones, and Andy Van de Ven. Maksim Kokushkin and Roberta Sassatelli made further very helpful suggestions. For some useful pointers to social network analysis and the Simmel connection, thanks are due to Nick Crossley and John Scott.

References

Alba, R., and Kadushin, C. (1976). 'The Intersection of Social Circles'. *Sociological Research Methods*, 5: 77–102.

Bauman, Z. (1989). *Modernity and the Holocaust*. Cambridge: Polity Press.

—— (2000). *Liquid Modernity*. Cambridge: Polity Press.

Boltanski, L., and Chiapello, È. (2006). 'The New Spirit of Capitalism'. *International Journal of Politics, Culture and Society*, 18: 161–88.

Breiger, R. (1974). 'The Duality of Persons and Groups'. *Social Forces*, 53/2: 181–90.

Burt, R. (1992). *Structural Holes*. Cambridge, Mass.: Harvard University Press.

—— (2005). *Brokerage and Closure*. Oxford: Oxford University Press.

Casey (1995). *Work, Self and Society: After Industrialism*. London: Sage.

Castells, M. (1998). *The End of Millennium*, iii. *The Information Age: Economy, Society and Culture*. Oxford: Blackwell.

Cooper, R. (2005). 'Peripheral Vision: Relationality'. *Organization Studies*, 26/11: 1689–1710.

Dekker, D. (2006). 'Measures of Simmelian Tie Strength, Simmelian Brokerage, and, the Simmelianly Brokered'. *Journal of Social Structures*, 7: http://www.cmu.edu/joss/content/articles/volume7/dekker_simmbrok3b.pdf.

Diani, M. (2000). 'Simmel to Rokkan and Beyond: Towards a Network Theory of (New) Social Movements'. *European Journal of Social Theory*, 3/4: 387–406.
Douglas, M. (1986). *How Institutions Think*. Syracuse, NY: Syracuse University Press.
—— and Mars, G. (2003). 'Terrorism: A Positive Feedback Game'. *Human Relations*, 56/7: 763–86.
du Gay, P. (2000). *In Praise of Bureaucracy*. London: Sage.
Fernandez-Mateo, I. (2007). 'Who Pays the Price of Brokerage? Transferring Constraint through Price Setting in the Staffing Sector'. *American Sociological Review*, 72: 291–317.
Fleming, P., and Spicer, A. (2004). '"You Can Checkout Anytime, But You Can Never Leave": Spatial Boundaries in a High Commitment Organization'. *Human Relations*, 57/1: 75–94.
Frisby, D. (1990). 'Introduction to the Translation', in Georg Simmel, *The Philosophy of Money*. London: Routledge.
Goffman, E. (1961). *Asylums*. New York: Doubleday.
Granovetter, M. (1973). 'The Strength of Weak Ties'. *American Journal of Sociology*, 78: 1360–80.
—— (1985). 'Economic Action and Social Structure: The Problem of Embeddedness'. *American Journal of Sociology*, 91/3: 481–510.
Habermas, J. (1990). *Moral Consciousness and Communicative Action*, trans. C. Lenhardt and S. Weber Nicholsen. Cambridge: Polity Press.
Harvey, D. (1989). *The Condition of Postmodernity*. Oxford: Blackwell.
Hood, C. (1998). *The Art of the State*. Oxford: Oxford University Press.
Krackhardt, D. (1998). 'Simmelian Ties: Super Strong and Sticky', in R. Kramer and M. Neale (eds.), *Power and Influence in Organizations*. Thousand Oaks, Calif.: Sage.
—— (1999). 'Ties That Torture: Simmelian Ties in Organizations'. *Research in the Sociology of Organizations*, 16: 183–210.
Kunda, G. (1992). *Engineering Culture: Control and Commitment in a High Technology Cooperation*. Philadelphia: Temple University Press.
Levine, D. N. (1997). 'Simmel Reappraised: Old Images, New Scholarship', in C. Camic (ed.), *Reclaiming the Sociological Classics*. Oxford: Blackwell.
Lohmann, S. (2004). 'Darwinian Medicine for the University', in R. G. Ehrenberg (ed.), *Governing Academia*. Ithaca, NY: Cornell University Press.
Lounsbury, M., and Catberry, E. J. (2005). 'From King to Jester? Weber's Fall from Grace in Organizational Theory'. *Organization Studies*, 26/4: 501–25.
Lukes, S. (1973). *Individualism*. Oxford: Blackwell.
Marx, K. ([1857–8] 1973). *Grundrisse*, trans. M. Nicolas. London: Penguin Books.
Möllering, G. (2001). 'The Nature of Trust: From Georg Simmel to a Theory of Expectation, Interpretation and Suspension'. *Sociology*, 35/2: 403–20.
Nedelmann, B. (1991). 'Individualization, Exaggeration and Paralysation: Simmel's Three Problems of Culture'. *Theory, Culture and Society*, 8/3: 169–94.
O'Neill, O. (2002). *A Question of Trust*. Cambridge: Cambridge University Press.
Power, M. (1997). *The Audit Society: Rituals of Verification*. Oxford: Oxford University Press.
Ringer, F. (1997). *Max Weber's Methodology: The Unification of the Cultural and Social Sciences*. Cambridge, Mass.: Harvard University Press.

Sassatelli, R. (2000). 'From Value to Consumption: A Socio-theoretical Perspective on Simmel's *Philosophie des Geldes*'. *Acta Sociologica*, 43: 207–18.

Scott, A. (1997). 'Modernity's Machine Metaphor'. *British Journal of Sociology*, 48/4: 561–75.

—— and Weiskopf, R. (2008). 'Freedom and Constraint under the "Neo-Liberal" Regime of Choice', in C. Cooper and S. Clegg (eds.), *Handbook of Macro-Organizational Behaviour*. London: Sage.

Sen, A. (1999). *Development as Freedom*. Oxford: Oxford University Press.

Simmel, G. ([1886] 1983). 'Das Geld in der modernen Kultur', in *Georg Simmel: Schriften zur Soziologie*, ed. H.-J. Dahme and O. Rammstedt. Frankfurt am Main: Suhrkamp.

—— ([1900] 1990). *Philosophy of Money*, 2nd enlarged edn., ed. D. Frisby and trans. T. B. Bottomore and D. Frisby. London: Routledge.

—— ([1903] 1995). 'Die Großstädte und das Geistesleben', in *Georg Simmel: Aufsätze und Abhandlungen 1901–1908*, i/7. *Georg Simmel Gesamtausgabe*, ed. R. Kramme, A. Rammstedt, and O. Rammstedt. Frankfurt am Main: Suhrkamp Verlag. Translated as 'The Metropolis and Mental Life' in Simmel 1950.

—— ([1904] 1995). 'Kant und der Individualismus', in *Georg Simmel: Aufsätze und Abhandlungen 1901–1908*, i/7. *Georg Simmel Gesamtausgabe*, ed. R. Kramme, A. Rammstedt, and O. Rammstedt. Frankfurt am Main: Suhrkamp.

—— ([1908] 1992). *Soziologie: Untersuchungenen über die Formen der Vergesellschaftung*, xi. *Georg Simmel Gesamtausgabe*, ed. O. Rammstedt. Frankfurt am Main: Suhrkamp.

—— ([1916] 2005). *Rembrandt: An Essay in the Philosophy of Art*, ed. and trans. A. Scott and H. Staubmann. London and New York: Routledge.

—— (1950). *The Sociology of Georg Simmel*, trans. and ed. K. H. Wolff. New York: Free Press.

—— (1955). *Conflict and the Web of Group-Affiliations*, trans. K. H. Wolff and R. Bendix. New York: Free Press.

Skinner, Q. (1969). 'Meaning and Understanding in the History of Ideas'. *History and Theory*, 8: 3–53.

Thrift, N. (2000). 'Performing Cultures in the New Economy'. *Annals of the Association of American Geographers*, 90/4: 674–92.

—— (2006). 'Re-Inventing Invention: New Tendencies in Capitalist Commodification'. *Economy and Society*, 35/2: 279–306.

Weber, M. ([1918] 1994). 'Parliament and Government in Germany under a New Political Order', in P. Lassman and R. Speirs (eds.), *Weber: Political Writings*. Cambridge: Cambridge University Press.

Weinstein, D., and Weinstein M. A. (1993). *PostModern(ized) Simmel*. London: Routledge.

Wolin, S. S. ([1960] 2004). *Politics and Vision*, extended and revised edn. Princeton: Princeton University Press.

CHAPTER 13

TYPES AND POSITIONS

THE SIGNIFICANCE OF GEORG SIMMEL'S STRUCTURAL THEORIES FOR ORGANIZATIONAL BEHAVIOR

ROSABETH MOSS KANTER
RAKESH KHURANA

13.1. Introduction

Georg Simmel's contributions to sociology are undisputed. Most introductory graduate syllabi assign at least some of Simmel's writings. Several books about the history of sociological thought devote at least one chapter or section to Simmel's contributions to early twentieth-century German sociology (Collins 1994: 10; Coser 1977; Nisbet 1970).[1] In recent decades, sociologists working in business schools have

[1] Coser regarded Simmel's contributions to modern sociology as highly positive and foundational, whereas Collins was more ambivalent about Simmel's work, suggesting that his illustrative examples were sometimes coarse and over-generalized.

applied some of Simmel's ideas to organizational scholarship (Burt 1992; Kanter 1977). Yet, within the field of organizational studies, Simmel is mostly neglected. Indeed, Simmel's writings rarely appear on graduate syllabi in organizational theory and organizational behavior. Is there a place for Georg Simmel in twenty-first-century organizational scholarship?

Our aim in this chapter is to make a case for using Simmel's ideas to illuminate features of organizational life that connect individuals, groups, organizations, and society. We first summarize three related aspects of Simmel's approach to social action that are relevant to organizational research: his method of using 'pure types' for describing social roles; positions for locating social actors in relation to each other; and structure for describing recurring social relationships. We then examine Simmel's applications of these ideas to social groupings of increasing complexity beginning with simple social interactions consisting of a monad, dyad, and triad; pyramidal hierarchies of dominant and subordinate relations; and finally, overlapping and interacting affiliations. Throughout this section, we will continually draw parallels between Simmel's conceptual ideas and how they relate to critical topics in organizational behavior—e.g. leadership, cohesion, and questions of the relationship between the individual and society—and to the larger social context—e.g. tensions between cosmopolitans and locals in the backlash against globalization or the growing importance of religion in what had been assumed by other theorists of modernization to be a society following a straight-line secular trend. We conclude this chapter by suggesting that Simmel may be even more relevant to a post-industrial age than he was to the machine age in which bureaucracy dominated, which might account for his relative neglect in the past and—we hope—re-emergence today.

13.2. Simmel's Overall Perspective: Pure Types, Positions, and Structure

Simmel construed sociology as a science of human relationships (Simmel 1950: 9). Unlike contemporaries such as Tönnies (1988), who focused on the master trends of modern society such as the ascendance of the industrial order, or Weber, whose predominant interest was in the larger institutionalized structures of society such as bureaucracy, Simmel began with relationships among individuals and explained larger entities in terms of their constituent relationships—a distinctively micro approach. He dealt with how relationships in groups are structured and with the emotional consequences of occupying particular positions within these structures, whether these are defined formally (as in large organizations) or arise informally (as in crowds). For Simmel, the interaction between structure (positions) and individual psychology (emotion) produces social action. 'Sociology', Simmel wrote, 'asks what happens to men and by what rules they behave, not insofar as they unfold their understandable individual existences in their totalities, but insofar as they form groups and are determined by their group existence because of interaction' (Simmel 1950: 11).

Simmel began to develop a science of society by creating a rich taxonomy of 'pure types' of social relations and positions. Pure types are similar in many ways to Weber's ideal types. Not readily observable in everyday behavior, they are conceptual constructs meant to illustrate a social form so 'as to bring out configurations and relations which underlie reality but are not factually actualized in it' (Wolff 1959: 84). Simmel's formal taxonomy of pure types begins with the positional elements of group life. Individual motivations, goals, and action, Simmel argued, are largely catalyzed by where one is positioned in a group and the number of other similarly placed individuals. Position determines the possibilities for action by influencing the range of choices available to a person. In any social grouping, some people are dependent, while others are relatively independent. Some are strategically located and can communicate with or influence other groups, while others operate on the margins, having limited access to other groups.

Simmel's descriptions of 'pure types' was tempered and informed by psychology. He recognized that individuals as the atoms of social life are characterized by intention and emotion (which he tended to equate), and that positions in social structures tend to give rise to emotions that might push back at the structures. Without incorporating emotions into its theoretical apparatus, sociology would be incomplete (Arditi 1996). For Simmel, the distinction between cognition and emotion is theoretically problematic.[2] His theories are not static views of structures and forms. Relationships involve human interactions, and human psychology influences the reactions people have to the positions they are in, thereby creating a dynamic force that shapes action.

Through their emotions, people attempt to express the moral and human meaning of the roles they find themselves in. Emotions, however, can create instability because they may evoke conflicting responses to social roles. Every social relationship contains seemingly paradoxical elements. Children do not flourish without believing in the authority of their parents. Yet, in adult life, an over-dependence on the parental authority can create emotions that inhibit individual development. Similarly, a group of friends can foster a sense of connection and solidarity but can also provoke in-group and out-group responses about who belongs. Isolated individuals are unconstrained but can also experience feelings of anomie.

[2] Simmel's essay *On Love* ([1921–2] 1984) is but one example of an emotional phenomenon that resists a separation between cognition and emotion. Love, Simmel states, is something that exists 'in complete independence from all practical and theoretical considerations, and from all judgments of real value as well' ([1921–2] 1984: 158). Simmel makes similar observations in his essays on respect, which he calls a 'general quality of worthiness' and feelings of 'alienation'. For a detailed discussion on Simmel's focus on non-rational behaviors, see Arditi (1996).

Structures become dynamic as a result of the emotions that people bring to their positions. As much as people are willing to submit to authority or to a higher principle, they are also distressed by this submission. Social superiority or inferiority in the objective sense of position is experienced as personal superiority or inferiority. But what begins as individual emotional reactions can persist as an aspect of group identity—as in conflicts between groups that are maintained by physical separations long after anyone remains who directly experienced the original impetus for conflict. At the same time, as we shall see later in this chapter, being in a variety of positions in a variety of groups can override this tendency, so that identity is not so dependent on any one position. In fact, the more social circles to which a person belongs, the more he or she becomes a distinct individual.

Overall, Simmel's unit of analysis is the social relationship itself. This is important to his work and what distinguishes his contribution from that of his contemporaries. That is, he was preoccupied with the impact of how individuals stand in relation to one another, whether in very small or very large entities. He sought to develop a kind of physics of social relationships, echoing the growing physical science of his day, to identify and define the mechanisms of attraction and repulsion among elements that accounts for patterns of social organization. He wanted to explain differentiation and integration: how individuals come to cohere in groups, how groups divide into particular roles, and how differentiated groups are reintegrated in society, albeit in complex patterns in which individuals might belong to more than one group.

Thus, at the simplest level, Simmel argued that structures derive from certain physical properties of social relationships: the numbers of people in a relationship and their spatial locations. At a second, somewhat more complex level, he posited the pyramid as a default form of social organization, and that human groups are characterized by relationships of domination and subordination. Finally, at the most complex level, as groups grow in size, individuals gain freedom from domination or definition by a group, and social organization becomes defined by overlapping social circles (which today would be called networks). Table 13.1 summarizes the link between three types of relations of increasing complexity, Simmel's core concepts, and links to organizational phenomena. We will explore each of these levels in turn.

13.3. Simple Forms: Numbers and Locations

Simmel's theory of the quantitative determination of social interactions is one of his best-known contributions. He argued that there are only four significant numbers

Table 13.1. Three types of relations

Structures	Simple	Intermediate	Complex
Descriptive characteristics	One, two, three, many	Group	Multiple affiliations
Key concepts	*Tertius gaudens, divide et impera*, mediator	Domination, subordination, authority	Cosmopolitanism, differentiation, stranger, secrecy
Relevance to organizational phenomena	Social networks, interpersonal dynamics	Leadership, motivation	Diversity, knowledge work, conflict

in social life—that is, only four that matter in creating social forms: *one*, *two*, *three*, and *many*.

The 'monad', or single individual, is not only an atom; it is the simplest social molecule. A 'single' is still a social relationship because the person stands apart as an individual only by reference to those with whom he or she is not joined (Simmel 1950: 118–22). Some groups permit individuals to be isolated—a negation of social interactions in their emotional connection to others. Individuals can gain freedom through an absence of social restraint or self-assertion of a position of strength with respect to others. This understanding is echoed in Simmel's well-known writing about the role of the stranger: the member of a group who sits on the boundary, not quite part of the group, able to observe it independently and carry messages among groups. The stranger is a phenomenon at the boundary of groups and between groups. Traders were the classic strangers whose positions give them connectivity across fields. Among other sociologically significant effects, the stranger is an important mechanism of social change. Strangers can destabilize a group merely by their presence. The stranger confronts the group with another reality, thereby forcing a group to examine its boundaries and taken-for-granted assumptions. Because they are not entrenched by 'habit, piety, and precedent', strangers can introduce new techniques and ideas to a group (Simmel 1950: 405). As transitive social actors, strangers can sometimes be more influential than entrenched social actors. They can be more objective and are also likely to be accepted as a confidant by other members of the group.

The dyad is the second important social form: two people constitute a pair. Pairs have unique properties. Unlike larger groups, which, Simmel argued, can experience a division of roles and also take on a life beyond the individuals constituting them, pairs exist only as long as each party decides to remain connected (although Simmel pointed to institutionalized pairs, such as business partnerships and marriages, as exceptions in which society adds constraints to reduce the tendency for pairs to split) (Simmel 1950: 122–32). A member of a dyad depends on only one other person, with each having to take responsibility for all collective action. This helps explain the difficulty organizations have in establishing buddy systems or mentoring relationships (Murrell, Crosby, and Ely 1999). Because a pairing is voluntary and can become overly consuming, it can easily dissolve if not surrounded by legal and institutional mechanisms that require the relationship to endure (Simmel 1950: 128–9).

The triad, or threesome, begins to define complex social relationships and contains within it most of the power relationships examined by political theorists. Simmel identified at least three social configurations that can arise in a triad (Simmel 1950: 145–69). One individual can become the mediator, the non-partisan arbitrator, who helps the relationship cohere. Or two of the three can form an alliance to dominate the third: two against one. Or one can emerge to divide and conquer. Position, Simmel recognized, is also an instrument for control. In social network research, Burt's (1992) well-known description of the strategy open to a social actor who is positioned between two other disconnected actors rests on Simmel's insight about triads, the simplest structure in which the tensions between opportunity and constraint emerge (see Scott, this volume). A third party, Burt noted, can opportunistically act as a *tertius gaudens* (the third who benefits) by taking advantage of the disconnect between two social actors or *divide et impera* (divide and conquer) by splitting two actors in order to further the third party's gains. Simmel's discussion of the third party as a mediator or *tertius jungens* vis-à-vis two other actors has been applied to explain the role of certain market actors, such as executive search firms, labor mediators, and market makers, who benefit by aligning the interests of the other two actors (Friedman and Podolny 1992; Khurana 2002; Zuckerman 1997; Obstfeld 2005).

After one, two, or three comes 'many'. Here, Simmel's focus was on the relative size of a group and its impact on group cohesion and action. Small groups, Simmel argued, demand more from each member. In order to sustain themselves, small groups require greater participation by individual members than do larger groups, absorb a larger part of their personalities, create boundaries that are more clearly and sharply separated from other groups, and are more likely to be self-policed by norms. In contrast, larger groups need special institutional structures and formal efforts to foster the relationships among individuals. Like Durkheim, Simmel recognized that the division of labor allowed large groups to become organized into subgroups. If left unorganized, Simmel contended, large groups turn into crowds in which social order breaks down. Crowds are literally unruly. They can be either magnanimous or mercilessly cruel. Because they are unrestrained by direct interpersonal exercise of authority, individuals easily surrender their individuality to the crowd, as happened in lynch mobs in America. (Like other European social theorists of his time, Simmel was fascinated with the relatively new nation across the Atlantic and drew many of his examples from the American Civil War and afterwards.)

13.4. Intermediate Forms: Group Cohesion or Conflict, Domination and Subordination, Leadership and Authority

Given the tendency of large groups to fissure, Simmel asked what keeps groups together as they expand in size and diversity. Here, he turned to the structure of domination and subordination. Social order, he argued, requires the acceptance of leadership and subordination to authority. He posited the pyramid as the ultimate form that emerges from most social relationships and further argued that monarchy (surely an anachronism in the twenty-first century) is the archetype. Common subordination to a single individual can unify a group, whether in solidarity or in shared opposition to the controlling power of the head.

Simmel also recognized, however, that coercion or dependence is rarely enough for group purpose to be realized. Groups would be unstable units if it were not for authority. Social organization, however, derives from both vertical relationships and horizontal ties among individuals who decide to join under a single head. Authority enables group integration.

Simmel sees two aspects of authority as particularly important for group stability. The first general feature of authority, as Simmel approaches it, is its link with legitimacy. Simmel argues that people will not obey those whom they think are illegitimate. Authority, he notes, is thus interactive and often voluntary. It 'presupposes in a much higher degree than is usually recognized a freedom on the part of the person subjected to authority. Even where authority seems to "crush" him, it is based not *only* on coercion or compulsion to yield to it' (Simmel 1950: 183). Seeing authority as legitimate is critical not only for the ruled but for the rulers. No individual, Simmel contends, 'wishes that his influence completely determine the other individual. He rather wants this influence, this determination of the other, to act back on *him*. Even the abstract will-to-dominate, therefore, is a case of interaction' (Simmel 1950: 181).[3]

[3] Trained originally as a philosopher (he wrote his dissertation on Immanuel Kant), Simmel's notions about the tragedy of the individual in modern life bears more than passing resemblance to Nietzsche's position about societal constraint as inhibiting the development of the full person, Kant's notions of the infinite striving of the individual, and the romanticism of Goethe's Faust. It would prove to be an explosive mix, with many of these intellectuals, including Georg Simmel, celebrating and encouraging Imperial Germany's nationalistic ambitions and celebrating its entry into World War I. At the start of World War I, Simmel (like Weber, Tönnies, and others) uncharacteristically became an enthusiastic supporter of the war. 'I love Germany,' he wrote, 'and therefore want it to live—to hell with all "objective justification of this will in terms of culture, ethics, history or God knows what else."' One interpretation is that this was Simmel's attempt, as a Jew who faced enormous anti-Semitism

The second feature of authority, in Simmel's conception, is that it is socially constructed. Authority is not a thing, though it may be experienced as such. It is an interpretative process that seeks for itself the legitimacy of consensus that gives authority the character of a thing. Simmel believed that people think about power in a number of ways, but only certain kinds of emotions will lead them to conceive of the powerful as authorities, and these thoughts are determined by the kinds of controls the powerful exercise.

According to Simmel, there are two means by which leaders acquire authority over a group (Hunt 1984). First, leaders acquire their dominance over a group by virtue of outstanding qualities such that 'a group comes to place its faith and trust in their abilities'. Or, second, because formal roles in social institutions, such as a university, church, government department, or the military, may provide individuals with 'a reputation, a dignity, a power of ultimate decision, which would never flow from his individuality' (Simmel 1950: 183). In the former case, which resembles Weber's concept of charismatic leadership in obvious respects, the leader's authority is derived from *ascribed* qualities that exert influence on the followers. In the second case, it is conferred by the *achieved* quality of a leader's place within a hierarchy (Hunt 1984; Khurana 2005). This conception of leaders gaining authority through the prestige of the institutions with which they are associated clearly identifies this authority as a social product rather than something conceived as emerging from the personal qualities of the leader.

For Simmel, as for Weber, since it is impossible to base authority solely on coercion, the leader and led have an interactive relationship. Thus, the led always have the option of following or not following. Yet in his discussion of leadership and how followers experience its various forms, Simmel uncovers an interesting irony that, once again, distinguishes his thinking from Weber's. For Simmel says that those under the sway of institutionally based leadership may feel themselves (like the followers of Weber's charismatic leader) to be following the leader in a spontaneous fashion, and thus may experience their act of devotion as a liberation from the institutionalized authority that the prestige leader actually embodies even as they reaffirm that authority (Hunt 1984). Moreover, those who recognize authority in an appointed office rather than in the person of a leader may feel themselves to be more 'free' than those who become enchanted by a hero or a prophet. Thus, we might conclude, it is fallacious to assume that a particular type of leadership necessarily elicits a particular kind of response from the followers. It may also then be true that charisma can be a constricting, conservative force as well as the disruptive one that Weber described.

In any event, Simmel views leaders as subject to the response of their followers and describes them as often leading a group in the group's own direction, 'the slave of his slaves' (Simmel 1950: 185). The leader is conceptualized as the 'unitary

in his academic career, to 'fit in' with the dominant culture he had always been somewhat alienated from.

expression' of the group's will rather than as a solution to bringing together division within it. He or she is seen as critical to the coherence of the group. Simmel's conception of leadership points to the possibility of leadership as something aligned with, rather than opposed to, institutionalization and rationalization.

Simmel noted that people could subordinate themselves to ideals and principles, not merely to other individuals or groups. Like Weber, he speculated about the differences in reaction to authority exercised through impersonal or personal relationships. For example, he raised the question of whether it is better for an individual to be subordinate to a collective entity such as a bureaucracy or to another individual, such as the owner of a family-owned firm. Much of Simmel's writing seems to suggest that the 'highest' (that is, least personally discomfiting) form of subordination is impersonal—thus to institutions rather than persons, but even better, to ideas or ideals that also serve as sources of identity. For example, Simmel argued that individuals separated in space can remain a group because of a mental bond, an emotional tie that is meaningful and helps people make sense of their place in the world.

Even within clearly defined structures of authority, Simmel's conceptions of the interactional nature of superior–subordinate relations finds room for individual action and emotions. For example, he notes that even the subordinate enjoys power by skillfully using the formula of obsequious deference appropriate to his status. Ingratiating and respectful means of engaging others without arousing anxiety in them are his only tools for manipulating the interpersonal situation. They are methods of social control. What is more, by doing his part in permitting the superior–subordinate relation to continue, the subordinate, to some extent, constrains the actions of the superior, even from his inferior position. Even a boss can tire of the boss-worshipping, uber-obsequious subordinate, 'Please stop agreeing with everything I say.' It is a protest against being manipulated by an overly constrictive social definition of one's identity. As Simmel recognized, sometimes in society, one is too easily put in another's box.

13.5. Complex Forms: Multiple Groups, Inter-Group Relationships, Individuation, Networks, Organizations, and Modern Society

Part of what moderates the absolute exercise of authority in modern industrial and post-industrial society, and requires bosses to turn into interactive leaders, is the fact that no single group encompasses all of a person, providing degrees of freedom for voluntarily chosen identities and affiliations. Even authority figures themselves exist in nested structures. They can be in a commanding position within a hierarchy and a servant to constituencies outside. Individual freedom, Simmel appeared to propose, means that meaning becomes even more important as a motivator of behavior, even as the tools of coercion increase.

As we read Simmel's work as a whole, we see that the defining feature of modern society is not just the division of labor, as Durkheim had it, but the fact that specialization gives rise to many groups in close contact with one another (some formalized, some informal) whose members overlap—in a word, pluralism.

Simmel attempted to create a taxonomy of affiliations or social circles that define a person's identity in a pluralistic society, including interest groups (associations), acquaintance, friendship, and love. Participation in work organizations, which forms the centerpiece of organizational behavior studies, is only one affiliation defining a person, and perhaps a weak one at that, in Simmel's terms. Groups in which members have more psychological empathy for one another exhibit greater strength. Moreover, groups in which cohesion is facilitated by monetary exchange are often impersonal, which to Simmel meant that they create weaker, more temporary affiliations remote from a person's identity or source of meaning and less likely to command loyalty or serve as the basis for social solidarity.[4]

Furthermore, according to Simmel, the more social circles that exist, the greater the likelihood that individuals participate in more groups, and the more differentiated individuals become (Simmel 1950: 409–24). Simmel equates multiple group affiliations with freedom of choice. Some social circles are concentric, so that the original relationship with primary groups (such as the family) remains even as the number of groups with which an individual is affiliated expands; those concentric circles help integrate the differentiated individuals. But associations such as work organizations are not necessarily a means of reintegrating society because family members, friends, neighbors, etc., might all have different ranges of associations. To paraphrase Simmel:

> the more different social classes and groupings there are, the more is the individual sociologically determined by his membership in these classes. The groups or circles to which an individual belongs form a system of sociological coordinates. Each new circle added to the ones in which he participates determines more fully his place in the sociological structure. The more associations he participates in, the less chance there is that there exists for another individual a fully identical system of co-ordinates. (Spykman and Frisby 2004: 184)

[4] In her fascinating book *The Purchase of Intimacy* (2005), Viviana A. Rotman Zelizer challenges Simmel's thesis on the commoditization effects of money, identifying processes by which interpersonal and social meaning can be infused into monetary transactions.

Thus, being different one from another is a condition of modern urban life—a condition described by Putnam in his analysis of creating social capital in a diverse society (Putnam 2007).

Simmel proposed a related sociological corollary: that as individuals become more differentiated with an increase in social circles (or networks), the groups that constitute society become more similar. Simmel thus anticipated the concepts of normative and mimetic isomorphism used in institutional theory (Powell and DiMaggio 1983). Competition requires that individuals be specialized, but in a complex society with a large number of ways in which individuals are differentiated, new groups increasingly look like existing ones because there are only a small number of sociological forms. Simmel reasoned as follows: in small groups, individuals are more likely to lose their distinctiveness and to identify with the group, but the group itself can be highly differentiated from other groups. As groups expand and extend themselves, individuals have more opportunities to experience and express their uniqueness, with the result that the distinctive social characteristics that make any particular group appealing quickly diffuse. Simmel used an example from pre-Civil War America. He contrasted small townships in the northern United States that regulated the lives of individuals but had a distinct character of their own through voluntary associations, capitalist exchange, and democratic participation with the more amorphous social organization of southern towns in which groupings rarely overlapped, the social character remained essentially parochial and feudal, and a social context in which individual differences across groups were strong but communities were weak. He also distinguished personal life, in which individuals are aware of their differences from other members of their group, with group life, in which individuals are aware of their similarity to their own group and differentiation from others. He argued for a fixed quantum of differentiation and conformity that would play out in different configurations depending on other aspects of structure.

As the number of ever-widening social circles and groups in contact with one another increases, people are also more likely to have contacts across groups and to form networks that span types of groups, which diminish their loyalty to any one group. Simmel also indicated that when groups become composed of specialized individuals and engage in exchanges with other groups, a further differentiation occurs. Widening contact can produce greater feeling about more people or else cause direct personal contact to disappear and leave individuals to pursue ruthless egoism; impersonal relations leave only material or financial gain as a motivation. Simmel, indeed, wrote a great deal about money as increasing personal liberty, albeit at the risk of social cohesion. Thus, Simmel anticipated social issues of the global economy: the rise of a large class of cosmopolitans and their tensions with locals (Kanter 1995). He also foreshadowed the question of whether cosmopolitans will become philanthropists or greedy pillagers; so far, the debate over corporate social responsibility indicates that they will be some of both (Reich

2007). Three other issues flow from Simmel's discussions about ever-widening social circles and intersecting groups that are perhaps even more important in our present Information Age society than they were when Simmel was writing in the industrial era.

The first issue echoes our earlier discussion of the growing importance of leadership that produces meaning. Simmel argued that when people have multiple social circles (or networks in our modern parlance), their loyalty goes to the smallest or the largest entities but not to intermediate ones. In short, they might sacrifice themselves for family or country but not for a corporation! In order to deserve loyalty and commitment, organizations must provide meaning, a sense of purpose that is grand in scope. In fact, a few vanguard global corporations have recently rewritten their statement of values to include the largest level: making a difference in the world as a whole (Kanter 2008).

The second issue is the recognition of increased friction stemming from increased diversity, implying increased contact among differentiated individuals and groups. Simmel anticipated that without overarching ideals to unite people, intolerance would grow. He said:

> If differentiated elements or elements which are apt to differentiate are combined in an inclusive social circle, there often result increased intolerance and friction and repulsion. The large common framework, which requires on the one hand a certain amount of differentiation among the elements as a condition of its existence, induces on the other hand an increased friction and opposition among these elements. . . . The attempted and partially realized synthesis [of empire or of attempts to create overarching unity] create[s] and stimulate[s] the individualism which finally destroyed it.
>
> (Spykman and Frisby 2004: 207)

Simmel could have been foretelling the fact that a scientific/technological era has been characterized by the rise of religious zealotry, and that greater devotion by believers has been accompanied by what some call a potential 'clash of civilizations' between the Christian West and the Muslim world (Huntington 1996).

The third issue is secrecy. Modern life makes it possible to have not only a differentiated identity but also to possess secrets, Simmel wrote. Between individuals or groups, the question of secrecy—whether to reveal or conceal, and how much—characterizes every social relationship. The privacy of mental life means that even in the most homogeneous of groups or committed of relationships there is an individuation of mind that makes it possible to have private knowledge, ideas no one else can see unless one chooses to communicate (see Scott, in this volume). This takes on added significance in the twenty-first century with the rise of knowledge workers whose work process and product are not subject to viewing by others, as well as for those who contribute time and energy to collective projects, such as open-source software, with little to gain except a sense of individual accomplishment or the admiration of virtual peers (O'Mahoney and Ferraro 2007; O'Mahoney 2007).

Simmel also proposed that the tension between concealing and revealing is one of the main choices people make in shaping their relationships. 'The secret produces an immense enlargement of life; numerous contents of life cannot even emerge in the presence of full publicity. The secret offers, so to speak, the possibility of a second world alongside the manifest world; the latter is decisively influenced by the former' (Wolff 1959: 330). It is striking that he wrote that before anyone imagined there would be information technology that would make it easy to create a new life and a second self via the Internet (Turkle 1995; Kanter 2001).

Because secrets exclude, there is an assumption that whatever is concealed must have special value. As a result, the possessor of secrets then has a specialized form of power, the power of surprises, destruction, even self-destruction. The selective use of information for advantage anticipates Kanter's argument that every person in an organization possesses veto power, the power to withhold. Finally, the secret puts a barrier between individuals but can also be a source of connection. When relationships are characterized by secrets, there is also a temptation to break through, which is manifested in gossip and confession. Secrets also make possible secret societies characterized by trust that other members will not reveal the secret (see Scott, in this volume). Societies, such as fraternities and sororities, use initiation rites, the powers of exclusion and inclusion, and debasing methods to cohere their groups.

What follows from Simmel's analysis is the proposition that cults, cabals, and secret societies will always exist on the fringe of modern life. Certainly, the interior nature of the mind is a continuing factor; no technology yet exists to 'read minds'. But there is more to it than that. The complexity of social circles and multiple organizations with people experiencing overlapping relationships makes many people search for meaning, identity, and an anchor in informal, even underground, groups that provide that identity through exclusion, secret knowledge, and unpredictable actions. Though it would be a stretch to say that Simmel anticipated modern terrorist cells, it is striking that researchers studying terrorist groups close at hand (Stern 2003), turned to sociology of group commitment for explanations (Kanter 1972). Simmel's contribution is to help scholars understand why secrecy might persist despite all the tools of surveillance available today—why the structure of society facilitates the emergence of secrets in both democratic and authoritarian regimes, and why people might seek to have secrets. This is a classic example of the interplay between structural position and emotion. By adding human psychology to structural sociology, Simmel was able to provide unique insights into the problematic nature of social order.

13.6. Conclusion: The Significance of Simmel

While our essay can be read as an appreciative study of a social scientist whose work has contributed many important concepts to sociology, our goal is somewhat more ambitious. We believe that Georg Simmel's work needs to be rediscovered. Few social scientists have explored so many subjects or demonstrated such a restless desire to get at the essence of the society.

Writing at the turn of the twentieth century, Simmel, like other sociologists, was concerned about the impact of modernity on society. He recognized that individuals were increasingly finding themselves in larger and cross-cutting groups with diverse membership. Whereas individual life in traditional society was characterized by membership in a primary community (what Cooley described as the 'nurseries of human nature'), modern life was increasingly characterized by cross-cutting group affiliations. However, unlike Weber or Tönnies, who had pessimistic visions of modern society that saw the loss of tradition as the root of many symptoms of social and personal disorganization, Simmel was more optimistic, believing that there were alternative means by which social cohesion could be achieved, in particular membership in diverse groups. Stated somewhat differently, where modern society for scholars such as Weber seemed barren and a source of disenchantment, Simmel saw it as an opportunity for creation. Rationality, which many sociologists regarded as a permanent form of domination from which no one was exempt, was seen by Simmel as a momentous separation to break free from rigid traditions. Simmel may have been too far ahead of his time. His view that modernity presented an opportunity for a new discourse of manners, morals, and the mission of society itself, creating a moment in which individuals could finally break free of a taken-for-granted view of the world into one which the individual could be more self-defining, is perhaps better suited to the Information Age than it was for the industrial one.

Simmel's work provides scholars with a set of insights that can help explain social and organizational phenomena that continued to emerge after his time, as we have seen. From these insights, researchers can derive testable propositions about organizational behavior because Simmel's work points them to unique phenomena and perspectives as he focused on the relationship as a unit of analysis in organizational behavior.

Simmel also educates us about how to think more profoundly and deeply about social order and how its components are constituted: individuals, groups, organizations, and society. He joins formal sociology with observed psychology, providing a dynamism to relationships that is sometimes missing in correlational studies. He searches for the underlying form that an observed phenomenon represents, and he puts that form in context. Deep deconstruction of the context can improve studies that otherwise connect variables in isolation. We should read and thank Simmel for offering a distinctive and important intellectual approach to understanding social life.

References

Arditi, J. (1996). 'Simmel's Theory of Alienation and the Decline of the Nonrational'. *Sociological Theory*, 14/2: 93–108.

Burt, R. S. (1992). *Structural Holes: The Social Structure of Competition*. Cambridge, Mass.: Harvard University Press.

Collins, R. (1994). *Four Sociological Traditions*. New York: Oxford University Press.

Coser, L. A. (1977). *Masters of Sociological Thought: Ideas in Historical and Social Context*. 2nd edn. New York: Harcourt Brace Jovanovich.

Friedman, R. A., and Podolny, Joel (1992). 'Differentiation of Boundary Spanning Roles: Labor Negotiations and Implications for Role Conflict'. *Administrative Science Quarterly*, 37/1: 28–48.

Hunt, S. (1984). 'The Role of Leadership in the Construction of Reality', in Barbara Kellerman (ed.), *Leadership: Multidisciplinary Perspectives*. Englewood Cliffs, NJ: Prentice-Hall.

Huntington, S. P. (1996). *The Clash of Civilizations and the Remaking of World Order*. New York: Simon & Schuster.

Kanter, R. M. (1972). *Commitment and Community: Communes and Utopias in Sociological Perspective*. Cambridge, Mass.: Harvard University Press.

—— (1977). *Men and Women of the Corporation*. New York: Basic Books.

—— (1995). *World Class: Thriving Locally in the Global Economy*. New York: Simon & Schuster.

—— (2001). *Evolve! Succeeding in the Digital Culture of Tomorrow*. Boston: Harvard Business School Press.

—— (2008). 'Transforming Giants: What Kind of Company Makes it its Business to Make the World a Better Place?' *Harvard Business Review*, forthcoming.

Khurana, R. (2002). *Searching for a Corporate Savior: The Irrational Quest for Charismatic CEOs*. Princeton: Princeton University Press.

—— (2005). 'Leadership and the Social Construction of Charisma', in J. Doh and S. Strumpf (eds.), *Leadership and Governance in Global Business*. London: Edward Elgar, Inc.

Murrell, A. J., Crosby, F. J., and Ely, R. J. (1999). *Mentoring Dilemmas: Developmental Relationships within Multicultural Organizations*. Applied Social Research. Mahwah, NJ: L. Erlbaum Associates.

Nisbet, R. A. (1970). *The Sociological Tradition*. London: Heinemann Educational.

Obstfeld, D. (2005). 'Social Networks, the Tertius Iungens Orientation, and Involvement in Innovation'. *Administrative Science Quarterly*, 50/1: 100–130.

O'Mahoney, S. (2007). 'What Does it Mean to be Community Managed'. *Journal of Management and Governance*, 11/2: 139–50.

O'Mahoney, S., and Ferraro, F. (2007). 'Governance in Collective Production Communities'. *Academy of Management Journal*, 50/5: 1079–1106.

Powell, W. W., and DiMaggio, P. J. (1983). *The New Institutionalism of Organizational Analysis.* Chicago: University of Chicago Press.

Putnam, R. D. (2000). *Bowling Alone: The Collapse and Revival of American Community.* New York: Simon & Schuster.

—— (2007). '*E Pluribus Unum*: Diversity and Community in the Twenty-First Century. The 2006 Johan Skytte Prize Lecture'. *Scandinavian Political Studies*, 30/2: 137–74.

Reich, R. B. (2007). *Supercapitalism: The Transformation of Business, Democracy, and Everyday Life.* New York: Alfred A. Knopf.

Simmel, G. ([1921–2] 1984). *On Women, Sexuality, and Love.* New Haven: Yale University Press.

—— (1950). *The Sociology of Georg Simmel*, trans. Kurt H. Wolff. Glencoe, Ill.: Free Press.

Spykman, N. J., and Frisby, D. (2004). *The Social Theory of Georg Simmel.* New Brunswick, NJ: Transaction Publishers.

Stern, J. (2003). *Terror in the Name of God: Why Religious Militants Kill.* New York: Ecco.

Tönnies, F. (1988). *Community & Society.* New Brunswick, NJ: Transaction Books.

Turkle, S. (1995). *Life on the Screen.* New York: Simon & Schuster.

Wolff, K. H. (1959). *Georg Simmel, 1858–1918: A Collection of Essays, with Translations and a Bibliography.* Columbus: Ohio State University Press.

Zelizer, V. A. R. (2005). *The Purchase of Intimacy.* Princeton: Princeton University Press.

Zuckerman, E. (1997). 'Focusing the Corporate Product: Securities Analysts and the Scope of the Firm'. Working Paper, Stanford University Graduate School of Business.

CHAPTER 14

SCHUMPETER AND THE ORGANIZATION OF ENTREPRENEURSHIP

MARKUS C. BECKER

THORBJØRN KNUDSEN

14.1. Introduction

The young Schumpeter was far ahead of his times. By the age of 30, he had completed three books that would each attain landmark status: an elaborate treatise on economics (Schumpeter 1908), a foundation for an evolutionary theory of economic change (Schumpeter 1911), and a history of economic thought (Schumpeter 1914). Each work made a huge impression. His book on the foundations of economics (Schumpeter 1908) was a catalyst for the mathematical turn of economics in continental Europe, his *Theory of Economic Development* (1911)[1] stimulated the evolution of evolutionary economics (Winter [1968] 2006; Nelson and Winter 1982), and his history of economic thought led to important work on doctrinal history.

[1] The second German edition (Schumpeter 1926) was translated as *Theory of Economic Development* (Schumpeter 1934).

Yet, to many of his contemporary colleagues and students, the mature Schumpeter appeared strangely out of touch with the times. As a professor at Harvard, his students perceived him as a gentleman perpetuating an odd lifestyle from an empire (the Austro-Hungarian Empire) that had outlived its place in history and disappeared. His colleagues increasingly found him out of touch; Schumpeter's star waned as he was unable to fulfill the promises of mathematical theorizing he himself had inspired.[2] He was increasingly seen as lacking in *gravitas* and with a progressively more outmoded and somewhat tragic patina to his work and personal ways.[3] More than a century after he first put pen to paper, Schumpeter the man might well be regarded as a romantic image from an oil painting decorating an imperial hall in Vienna. (An Appendix gives a detailed chronology of the main events in Schumpeter's life.)

In contrast to the man, however, Schumpeter's works have become classics, and indeed pillars of our conceptual inventory. They are an important part of our intellectual heritage. Yet, as often befalls the classics, Schumpeter is more cited than he is read. This chapter invites a closer look at his works because they contain as yet unmined ideas that could provide powerful stimuli for future research. In particular, we elucidate a set of immediate implications for entrepreneurship studies, which is a topic of great contemporary interest. Our choice of perspective is not to imply that Schumpeter's writings are limited to entrepreneurship, but to illustrate how Schumpeter's works still have something to say to contemporary research.

While Schumpeter is widely known for his stimulation of entrepreneurship studies, it may be surprising to learn that some of his most important works on that topic are not yet available in English.[4] Because Schumpeter's scholarship had a distinct Continental prelude to its expression in an Anglo-American context, much of the work completed in his formative years has never been translated from German into English. Among this are works that elucidate entrepreneurship and its implications for the economy, which is the central theme running through all of Schumpeter's works. This material adds a fresh view on Schumpeter's contribution to entrepreneurship that we wish to share with the reader.

The chapter is structured as follows. We start by briefly introducing Schumpeter, the issues he tackled in his work, and the contributions he is best known for (section 14.2). We then offer a concise guide to Schumpeter's works and the

[2] Young Schumpeter had stimulated the mathematical turn in economics and been instrumental in founding *Econometrica*, the most prestigious outlet of formal work in economics. It was up to mathematically trained economists, such as Schumpeter's star student Paul Samuelson, to advance the mathematical foundations of economic analysis.

[3] Interview with Paul A. Samuelson, December 2005, conducted by Markus C. Becker.

[4] Some of the important early works have recently become available in English. For example, Schumpeter's 1928 essay 'Entrepreneur' has recently been translated from the German. It is a relatively short essay that contains most of the central ideas Schumpeter developed in his later works (Becker and Knudsen 2003*a*; Choi 2003).

secondary literature (section 14.3) and discuss the evolving pattern of citations to Schumpeter's work in the social sciences (section 14.4). We then provide a comprehensive assessment of Schumpeter's works on entrepreneurship in order to identify insights of practical and theoretical relevance to contemporary research (section 14.5). We draw on sources that are little known, rarely referenced, and in most cases only published in German, in order to distill Schumpeter's insights on entrepreneurship. We conclude with an assessment of why, even today, Schumpeter's insights can help to further our understanding of entrepreneurship and its organization.

14.2. Schumpeter the Man and his Best Known Ideas

Schumpeter had a remarkable career. Having studied economics at Vienna University, Schumpeter became the youngest *Privatdozent* (a teaching position) in the Austro-Hungarian Empire in 1909, the youngest associate professor of economics[5] in the very same year, and full professor[6] in 1911, at a mere 28 years of age. In this first phase of his career, he participated in an extraordinarily fertile intellectual world populated by Carl Menger, Friedrich von Wieser, Eugen Böhm-Bawerk, and other members of the Austrian School.

After nine years as a university professor, Schumpeter left for a stint in politics. He was appointed to the German Coal Socialization Commission in 1918 and in 1919 as the Austrian State Secretary of Finance. He was forced to leave the position after seven months. He returned briefly to academia to serve two semesters at the University of Graz in 1920 (Shionoya 1997), and then ventured into the business world as president of the Biedermann Bank in Vienna. The bank failed in 1924, leaving him with heavy personal debts. After these disappointing 'real-world' experiences, Schumpeter re-entered academia for good in 1925. By this time, the Austro-Hungarian Empire had disintegrated. He found a position in the Economics Department at the University of Bonn, where he was at the University of Bonn hired to teach public finance. Thus, inter-war Germany provided a new academic context for Schumpeter's academic efforts. During his time at Bonn, Schumpeter turned

[5] In 1909, at the age of 26, while working on *Theorie*, Schumpeter achieved his first academic appointment at the University of Czernowitz (Bukowina) located in the eastern borderland of the Austro-Hungarian Empire (now in the Ukraine) (Swedberg 1991*a*). Note that Schumpeter himself says that many of the ideas in *Theorie* go back as far as 1907 and that all of them had been worked out by 1909 (Schumpeter 1934: ix).

[6] In 1911, approaching 29, i.e. just before the publication of *Theorie*, Schumpeter became full professor at the University of Graz.

his attention to a detailed examination of entrepreneurship, elaborating on what he had said on this topic in *Theory of Economic Development* in 1911. (In this period Schumpeter wrote some pieces on entrepreneurship that we will consider in detail below.)

Having been a visiting professor at Harvard during the Bonn period, it was not surprising that Schumpeter accepted an appointment as professor of Economics at Harvard in 1932. He would remain in this position for the rest of his life. Among his colleagues there were luminaries such as Wassily Leontief, Paul Samuelson, and Talcott Parsons.

Schumpeter's career thus unfolded in academia, politics, and business, three very different environments. He relocated, physically, from one side of the *Methodenstreit* (Menger in Vienna) to the other (Schmoller in Berlin), and then from the German-speaking to the English-speaking academic world. Nevertheless, in all these different settings, Schumpeter pursued one big question: the nature of social and economic change. Why and how did society at large change? Why and how did the economy change? What was the origin of novelty in the economy and in society more generally? Schumpeter started by analyzing the economic theory of his time—the early versions of marginalist, equilibrium theory that is still the dominant paradigm of our time—and quickly arrived at the conclusion that it was limited to static analysis, i.e. a world where there was a stable 'circular flow' with no fundamental change. By its very constitution, such a theory could not, he argued, ever provide an explanation for economic change and for the evolution of new firms and industries. Schumpeter aimed at a theory that was sufficiently broad to explain phenomena such as technological change or changes in the political or institutional systems.

Schumpeter was looking for causes from within the economic system. In the theory he developed, these causes are found in the process of innovation, famously defined as 'new combinations'.[7] According to Schumpeter's typology of innovation, shown in Figure 14.1, an innovation could be a new combination of inputs, products, processes, or ways of reaching the market. Whenever one of these components of the economic system changed, there would obviously be an overall change in the way the entire system works, from extraction of raw materials to consumer demand. Therefore, Schumpeter added, as a fifth form of innovation, the idea of carrying out new ways of organizing the entire economic system or a subset thereof, such as the value chain or industry architecture.

New combinations introduce novelty into the economic system, forcing firms to change, or, in the case of firms that were unable to adjust in the face of changing

[7] Schumpeter was haunted by the rigor of scientific explanation in the face of indeterminism and novelty (see, in particular, Schumpeter 2005). His definition of innovation as a matter of new combinations seems very fortuitous in that regard. Combinations of interdependent elements in a huge space will appear as novel phenomena at higher levels of analysis. Even though the elements to combine from eventually must be explained, Schumpeter's combinatorial perspective goes a long way to avoid *de novo* (*ex nihilo*) creativity.

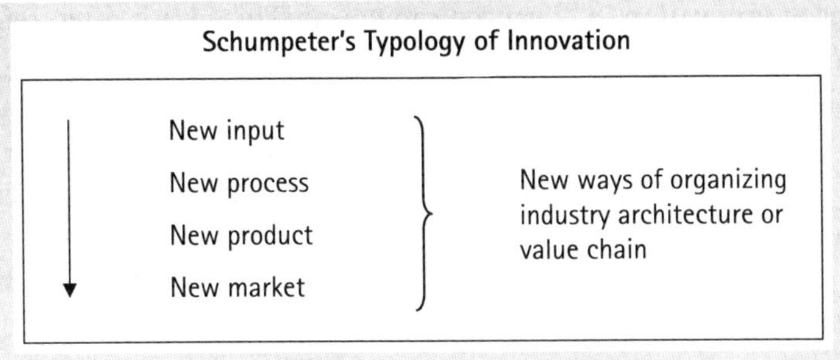

Fig. 14.1. Schumpeter's typology of innovation. An innovation is a new way of combining components of the value chain of an industry (or industry architecture)

demands from the business environment, forcing them to terminate their businesses. The old is destroyed by the joint forces of innovation and competition. A competitive race among innovators sometimes resolves itself in a major transition from an old economic order to a new one (see Knudsen and Swedberg 2007). Well-known examples include the transition from horse carriages to the railway and, more recently, from analogue to digital cameras. This Schumpeter described as *creative destruction*.

But what, then, causes innovation? What causal mechanism brings about the new combinations, the creative destruction, and the economic change? In short, what is the cause of novelty in the social and economic domain? Schumpeter located the cause of novelty in the actions of the entrepreneur. In contrast to individuals who merely adapt to changing circumstances, the energetic entrepreneur identifies new combinations and 'pushes them through'. The will required to push innovation through against all resistance defines the entrepreneur. It sets the entrepreneur apart from those who discover new combinations but are unable to carry them through.[8]

In the 1934 version of *Theory*, which is the most familiar to English-speaking readers, innovation is no longer attributed to a distinctive character trait in the entrepreneur. Rather, it originates in a depersonalized function of 'carrying out new combinations', a function anyone can fulfill, which indeed can be the consequence of a sequence of operations within the firm conducted by different people. This shift reflects Schumpeter's interest in the new combinations generated in large corporations rather than by independent entrepreneurs. He considered large corporations (which increasingly were equipping themselves with R & D laboratories dedicated to invention and innovation) as the dominant locus of entrepreneurship and the

[8] Schumpeter then considered whether such an explanation would suffice to explain the generation of novelty, a question he struggled with throughout his career without reaching a clear answer (Becker, Knudsen, and March 2006).

main driver of innovation in advanced capitalism. This idea is often referred to as the 'Schumpeterian Hypothesis'.

While his later works are often cited in relation to the observation that innovations tend to originate in large corporations, it is generally not perceived that he had much to say on the organization of entrepreneurship and its influence on the identification and carrying out of new combinations. Before we turn to his work on these topics, we provide a little more context, with a quick overview of Schumpeter's main works and their place in academic scholarship.

14.3. A Concise Guide to Schumpeter's Work

Schumpeter's writings are vast. As entry points, we would recommend to the English-speaking reader three books, which are regarded classics. *Theory of Economic Development* published in 1911 contains the basis of Schumpeter's thinking on economic change and development, including the role of the entrepreneur as a source of innovation. In *Capitalism, Socialism, and Democracy* from 1942, Schumpeter elaborates this thinking to include his much-cited idea of creative destruction and his famous prediction of the demise of capitalism through its own success. *History of Economic Analysis*, which was published posthumously in 1954, is the third of our recommendations. It is a *tour de force* of the history of economic thought and highly recommended to readers with a serious interest in the history of ideas.

It should be mentioned that Schumpeter also wrote a monumental two-volume book on *Business Cycles* (Schumpeter 1939). This book is essentially an empirical elaboration of the ideas in *Theory of Economic Development*. Even though *Business Cycles* never caught on and quickly faded into oblivion, it contains important material: chapters 3 and 4 on economic evolution are highly recommended. *Business Cycles* is an ambitious attempt to characterize the overall evolutionary dynamics of the economy as a wavelike phenomena that in the aggregate comprises the actions of entrepreneurs and other economic agents. It is not entirely successful in that regard, but it helped inspire an agenda that is better suited to derive the evolutionary dynamics of the economy from a realistic characterization of individual behavior (see, in particular, Nelson and Winter 1982).

A number of Schumpeter anthologies have been published. Of particular interest to readers in organization studies is one entitled *The Economics and Sociology of Capitalism*, which contains most of Schumpeter's works in sociology (Swedberg

1991*b*). There is also a classic anthology edited by Richard V. Clemens (1951) that contains an excellent introduction to the major themes in Schumpeter's work.

The secondary literature on Schumpeter is enormous. For readers interested in the biographical details of Schumpeter's life, we would point to Richard Swedberg (1991*a*), who provides a concise and easily accessible biography of Schumpeter that should serve most readers well, and Robert Loring Allen's (1991) two volumes, which are an authoritative biography and contain extensive details relating to Schumpeter's life. Yuichi Shionoya (1997) provides a nice complementary treatment of Schumpeter's ideas and their relation to a sociological perspective. More recently, Thomas McCraw (2007) has written a fine Schumpeter biography, *Prophet of Innovation*, that adds to prior works in a number of ways. Finally, Massimo M. Augello (1990) has written a comprehensive reference guide to Schumpeter's works, including a useful overview of Schumpeter's writings in sociology. As regards websites, we recommend www.Schumpeter.info maintained by Ulrich Hedtke.

14.4. The Enduring Influence of Schumpeter's Works in the Social Sciences

We can trace the evolution of Schumpeter's influence on later scholarship by examining the references to his work in the top five economics journals, the top three sociology journals, and the top five organization theory journals.[9] We conducted a search of the JSTOR database, based on inclusion of the word 'Schumpeter' in the text. The search covered a period of 100 years, from 1898 to 1998. For each five-year period, we recorded the number of references to Schumpeter's work in economics, sociology, and organization theory. As to any possible obsolescence of Schumpeter's work, the citation analysis shows that his influence has

[9] The journals include: Economics: *The American Economic Review* first published in 1886, *Econometrica* first published in 1933, *The Economic Journal* first published in 1891, *Journal of Political Economy* first published in 1892, and *The Quarterly Journal of Economics* first published in 1886; Sociology: *American Journal of Sociology* first published in 1895, *American Sociological Review* first published in 1936, and *Social Forces* first published in 1922; Organization Studies: *Academy of Management Journal* first published in 1958, *Academy of Management Review* first published in 1976, *Administrative Science Quarterly* first published in 1956, *Organization Science* first published in 1980, and the *Strategic Management Journal* first published in 1990.

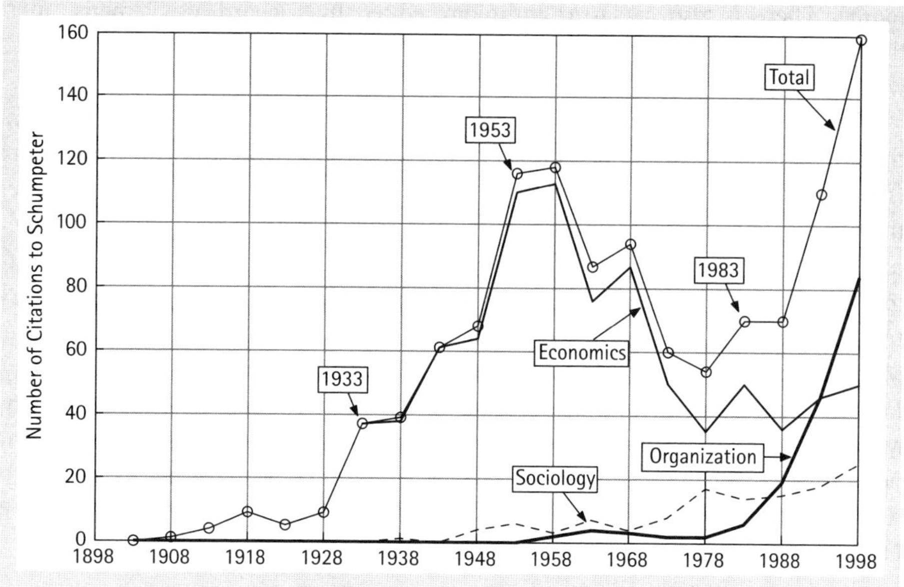

Fig. 14.2. The number of references to Schumpeter's work in the top economics, sociology, and organization theory journals

increased over the last century. As measured by number of references, Schumpeter continues to be an inspiration for research published in the top journals in the social sciences, and his influence has continued to grow during the most recent decades. Indeed, the highest number of references to Schumpeter's works in the entire period was recorded in the last period of 1994 to 1998. In this five-year period, a total of 159 articles mentioned Schumpeter, an impressive 31.8 references per year.

The growing number of references in the latest of the periods examined here (1994–8) is solely due to the effect of the references in organization theory. This literature discovered Schumpeter in the mid-1980s, since when Schumpeter's influence has increased dramatically. Around that time, organization and management scholars latched onto Schumpeter and began to draw inspiration from his works for issues such as the organization of entrepreneurship. In the 1980s, for a variety of reasons, entrepreneurship studies became all the rage (Swedberg 2000). Also, Nelson and Winter's (1982) evolutionary theory of economic change acted as a stimulant to Schumpeter's influence on management and organization studies. Winter's reading of two chapters of Schumpeter's *Theory of Economic Development* a few years earlier had inspired a brilliant and pioneering paper on a neo-Schumpeterian theory of the firm (Winter [1968] 2006) that was carried over into the classic work with Richard R. Nelson.

14.5. Unmined Contributions to Entrepreneurship Studies

Several factors stimulated the growth of interest in entrepreneurial studies in the 1980s, including the revival of small business, the emergence and rapid diffusion of a pro-market ideology, the emergence of the global economy, and a concern with the economic performance of countries in a global economy (Swedberg 2000). The advent of powerful, cheap computers and communication systems and the fall of communism further energized the pro-market ideology.[10] Western economies were thriving and the dot-com businesses became the epitome of entrepreneurship (Aldrich 2004). The time was ripe for exploring innovations in practice, and the organization literature was quick to relate to the phenomenon.

Schumpeter's classic works on entrepreneurship turned out to be of great relevance to this endeavor; however, Schumpeter has more to contribute to this research than has so far been taken up. The most frequently cited of Schumpeter's works in the *Academy of Management Journal* and the *Academy of Management Review* in the period 1961 to 1997 is *Theory of Economic Development*.[11] The second most cited work is *Capitalism, Socialism, and Democracy*.[12] In the Academy journals and the three other leading organization theory journals, the citation frequency for any other writings by Schumpeter is very low.

Some of this sidelined material contains important elements of Schumpeter's theory of entrepreneurship that do not appear in the more cited works. In the following, we draw insights from this neglected material. In particular, we consider a number of important articles written in Schumpeter's German period (1908–32) that substantially add to his better-known works.[13]

[10] There is a further possible reason for the increased interest in entrepreneurship in the economics literature during recent decades. From roughly the 1930s to the 1970s, equilibrium theory was the main interest in economics, and there is no place for the entrepreneurial function in equilibrium. With the increasing prominence of theories of technical change and economic evolution during the 1980s, the entrepreneurial function regained its important explanatory role.

[11] We found twenty-five references to *Theory of Economic Development*. In most cases, the edition cited is the English edition (Schumpeter 1934), a translation of the 2nd German edition (Schumpeter 1926).

[12] We found sixteen references to *Capitalism, Socialism, and Democracy*.

[13] 'Unternehmerfunktion und Arbeiterinteresse' (1927*a*), 'Unternehmer' (1928), 'Der Unternehmer in der Volkswirtschaft von heute' (1929*a*), 'Ökonomie und Psychologie des Unternehmers' (1929*b*), 'Development' (2005). A translation of 'Unternehmer' is available (Becker and Knudsen 2003*b*). Hartmann (1959) is one of the rare articles that cites some of these works in the original. Schumpeter's work on entrepreneurship also includes a few articles published in the late 1940s as well as some passages of *Capitalism, Socialism, and Democracy* (1942), but none of these, nor the earlier ones listed above, equals 'Entrepreneur' or *Theory* in scope or detail.

Table 14.1. Schumpeter's typology of entrepreneurial motivation

Type of entrepreneur	Motivation	Origin of motivation
The factory owner and merchant	Care of the family, duty	Socially transmitted
The modern captain of industry	Will to win, exercise power	Inborn personality trait
The manager who actually carries out the entrepreneurial function	Applause of colleagues, recognition from others	Socially transmitted
The 'founder' (promoter)	Urge to action, seeking and carrying out new possibilities	Inborn personality trait

14.5.1. Individual-Level Entrepreneurship

In an effort to systematize the many descriptions of entrepreneurship available at the time,[14] Schumpeter developed a typology (Schumpeter 1928: 483–5).[15] Considering that several modern authors have developed typologies of entrepreneurs (Webster 1976, 1977; Smith and Miner 1983; Gartner 1985; Cooper and Dunkelberg 1986; D'Amboise and Muldowney 1988), and there has been broad recognition of Schumpeter's crucial role in laying the foundations for the study of entrepreneurship (Baumol 2003), it is surprising that no one has referred to Schumpeter's typology. Furthermore, Schumpeter's typology provides some reinforcement of the Mintzbergian interpretation of managerial roles, which has been widely taken up by the management and organization literatures (Mintzberg 1977; Miner 1977; Koontz 1980; Mintzberg and Waters 1982; Carroll and Gillen 1987). Schumpeter's typology of entrepreneurial motivation, reproduced in Table 14.1, distinguishes four types of modern entrepreneurship.

The terminology for describing the four types is perhaps specific to Schumpeter's time; but the basic distinctions are still very pertinent. The most striking characteristic of the *factory owner and merchant* is autocratic behavior in considering the firm to be 'his' establishment. Having inherited his firm, he is 'family minded', and his efforts are oriented towards the benefit of the family. He lives in a bourgeois universe and holds a social position akin to that of a 'capitalist' (Schumpeter's term for an investor). As an autocrat who owns and leads a firm, he fulfills many different management functions himself (control, finance, marketing, etc.). Amongst these duties, the entrepreneurial function—carrying out new combinations—at times assumes a peripheral role or may be completely absent.

[14] The reference list in Schumpeter (1928) gives an idea of the literature on entrepreneurship at the time Schumpeter wrote.

[15] The English translation of this entry is available as Becker and Knudsen (2003*b*). An accompanying article describes the background to the entry and how Schumpeter delayed the publication of the Handbook by being last to submit (Becker and Knudsen 2003*a*).

A very different kind of entrepreneur, the *modern captain of industry*, is a much 'purer' type. He does not take on the numerous heterogeneous tasks necessary for the running of an enterprise. Rather, he holds a senior managerial position and focuses on strategic decision making in risky and ambiguous situations.[16] Because the social recognition of the entrepreneur is closely linked to the capacity to dispose of the means of production (i.e. is closely linked to the position of capitalist), the modern captain of industry is recognized as an entrepreneur (only) to the extent that he controls the major shareholders. His motivation starkly contrasts with that of the factory owner and merchant: it derives not from profit, but from the exercise of power, the attainment of performance, and the salience of the will to win and the urge to action.

What both these types of entrepreneurs have in common is that they either change slowly (personality traits) or belong to a family that has accrued large financial means; the third type of entrepreneur is very different. As the label implies, *the manager who actually carries out the entrepreneurial function* is a corporate actor. He is an entrepreneur by virtue of his activity—carrying out the entrepreneurial function of identifying and pushing through new combinations. He is the type of entrepreneur that is the least conspicuous and most easy to overlook. His achievement and career resemble those of a public servant (he is employed and promoted by others); he is not concerned with influencing the capitalist shareholders of the firm and often lacks the means to do so; he is motivated by recognition from others (something not specific to entrepreneurs); and he is not acknowledged as an entrepreneur. This type of entrepreneur generally appears as nothing more than an ordinary (middle) manager, even less an entrepreneur. Yet, those applying Schumpeter's analytical lens would think otherwise. The carrying out of the entrepreneurial function is key to the manager's performance.

The *'founder' (promoter)* is also commonly not considered to be an entrepreneur, although for completely different reasons. The most striking characteristic of the founder is his almost exclusive focus on seeking and carrying out new possibilities. This does not entail any power over the means of production though, something often considered a defining characteristic of entrepreneurship. From Schumpeter's point of view, however, the founder is the purest expression of the entrepreneur.

In the last column of this typology, Schumpeter classifies the four types of entrepreneurs in terms of whether their motivations are inborn or culturally transmitted. Schumpeter was concerned with describing entrepreneurs and identifying the sources of entrepreneurial behavior.[17] He offered two possible explanations for entrepreneurial behavior at the individual human actor level: they can be inborn (this is the avenue explored in the first edition of *Theorie der wirtschaftlichen*

[16] Note that innovations are often surrounded by such situations.

[17] See particularly the first German edition of *Theorie der wirtschaftlichen Entwicklung* (Schumpeter 1911; for an English translation, see Becker and Knudsen 2002).

Entwicklung, 1911) or they can be handed down in families and other social groups (explored in Schumpeter 1927*a*, *b*; 1929*a*). The captain of industry and the founder are examples of entrepreneurs whose behavior can be explained by inborn characteristics such as the 'will to win' and 'the urge to action' (Schumpeter 1928: 484–5); whereas the factory owner, the merchant, and the manager are entrepreneurial types that are driven by characteristics such as 'care of the family' and 'applause of colleagues' that are socially transmitted expressions of self-interest and are social in nature because they are oriented towards others.

The motivations of the captain of industry and the founder are to a large extent inborn—a matter of biological inheritance. Modern evolutionary biology provides a widely accepted explanation of biological inheritance, but in Schumpeter's time the detailed mechanisms of inheritance were not completely known. Even so, Schumpeter had a good working knowledge of the ideas relating to genetic inheritance.[18]

Less clear is the origin of the motivation of entrepreneurial types such as the 'factory owner and merchant' and 'the manager who actually carries out the entrepreneurial function'. Motivations such as 'care of the family' and 'applause of colleagues' are social in nature. Such motivation is clearly generated by social expectations, norms, taboos, etc. It aims at achievement of high social status in the individual's social group. The explanation of personality traits of the entrepreneur is therefore a cultural one: the behavior of individuals is influenced to a large extent by cultural traits handed down in families and other social groups.

In 'Social Classes in an Ethnically Homogenous Environment' (Schumpeter 1927*b*), Schumpeter attempts to develop a sociological explanation of how cultural traits are transmitted. The family, but also wider social groups such as classes, plays a central role in this process (see also Schumpeter 1927*a*, 1928). Schumpeter provides a theoretical foundation here, pointing to how role models influence entrepreneurial behavior, the relation between role models and the nature of the family, and the importance of the wider cultural inheritance and the broad socio-economic background identified by authors such as Aldrich and Fiol (1994), Hambrick and Mason (1984), Cooper and Dunkelberg (1986), and Gimeno *et al.* (1997).

This observation has important implications for contemporary research on the organization of entrepreneurship. If the motivations for entrepreneurial behavior are mainly inborn, then adjustment of the mixture of entrepreneurial traits in an organization becomes the obvious focus for managing entrepreneurship. Thus, hiring and firing would be the instrument of primary interest for the management and organization of entrepreneurship. By contrast, if entrepreneurial behavior is mainly driven by culturally transmitted motives, then training and cultural transmission must be emphasized.

[18] As Schumpeter's (2005) recently published article 'Development' shows. See also Schumpeter (1927*a*).

Schumpeter's ideas invite us to think of organizations as means to produce mixtures of different motivations or to adapt such mixtures to what circumstances demand. Whether the adjustment of the tendency (and ability) to engage in entrepreneurship is best achieved by selection of personnel (implying a relatively high turnover) or by training employees to engage in entrepreneurship when it is needed (implying a stable workforce) is an open question even today.

14.5.2. Corporate Entrepreneurship

In his later works, Schumpeter shifted the focus towards corporate entrepreneurship, placing a stronger emphasis on the *organization* of the entrepreneurial function than on the individual entrepreneur.[19] Having specified the components (the individuals) to his satisfaction, he turned to specifying how their composition and interaction mattered. His contribution to the discussion of dispersed entrepreneurship was in defining entrepreneurship as a *function*, whose 'essence ... lies in recognizing and carrying out new possibilities in the economic sphere' (Schumpeter 1928: 483). According to this definition, *if and when* a person carries out new combinations, this person has assumed the role of an entrepreneur on this occasion.

In Schumpeter's later works, entrepreneurship is a function, which, in principle, anybody can fulfill. Schumpeter also likened the entrepreneur to a middleman, who acts as buyer in the market of the means of production and as a supplier in the market of consumption goods (Schumpeter 1928). On those occasions when the middleman introduces new combinations, he is acting as an entrepreneur (Schumpeter 1928). Recognizing the entrepreneurial function as a special case in the middleman function allowed Schumpeter to overcome the strong contrast between new combinations (instances of entrepreneurship) and the recurrent use of existing combinations (the circular flow). A consequence of this position is that entrepreneurship becomes the motor of an under-determined, emergent, evolutionary process of change in economic relations. It therefore becomes important to understand whether or not the middleman will combine factors in a new way. What are the determinants of the propensity to engage in entrepreneurship? Are they based on personal experience, socially transmitted, or both? What is the role of organization in stimulating the expression of entrepreneurship?

In a modern economy, organizations and their structure have an important influence on the expression of entrepreneurship.[20] The focus therefore shifts from the personality of the individual entrepreneur to organization structures and practices

[19] The shift in Schumpeter's thinking occurred with the 1926 revision *Theorie der wirtschaftlichen Entwicklung*.

[20] In 'The Sociology of Imperialisms' (Schumpeter 1919), Schumpeter explores a different aspect of the question, in a context that is not focused on the economy.

that influence who enacts the entrepreneurial function and what the conditions are for carrying it out. These questions are the very essence of organization theory. Against this background, Schumpeter contributes a perspective for linking organizations to entrepreneurship studies. In two speeches delivered in 1927, Schumpeter made the point that one of the most important factors in determining who becomes an entrepreneur in an organization is the way in which the leaders (top managers) are selected. Such leaders can themselves act as entrepreneurs when and if they produce new combinations (this is the type of entrepreneur Schumpeter calls 'the manager who actually carries out the entrepreneurial function' in his typology). They can also, however, have an impact on corporate entrepreneurship by making policy choices that influence the propensity of other agents in the organization to engage in entrepreneurship. Schumpeter suggests studying the selection of leaders in organizations from the point of view of how such selections influence corporate entrepreneurship (Schumpeter 1927*a*, 1929*a*). In Schumpeter's time, just as today, a variety of mechanisms were used to select leaders (and human resources more generally): election, examination, appointment, etc. (Schumpeter 1929*a*). Applying a different mechanism and/or different selection criteria would produce different leaders and therefore different propensities for, and types of, entrepreneurship. Identifying the mechanisms used to select leaders, the biases associated with these mechanisms (Kahnemann, Slovic, and Tversky 1982), and the sources of systematic error in selection (Reason 1990) can thus contribute to an explanation of corporate entrepreneurship.

So, to briefly sum up Schumpeter's contribution to understanding corporate entrepreneurship, he identified several possible ways that the composition of individuals in an organization can influence entrepreneurship. For instance, organizations influence who enacts the entrepreneurial function, set the conditions for doing so, and thus trigger the creation of new (rather than existing) combinations.

14.6. Discussion and Conclusion: How Schumpeter's Insights can Deepen our Understanding of the Organization of Entrepreneurship Today

Schumpeter combined three major ideas within one framework. The first idea was to consider individuals as components of organizations and to examine how individuals interact in organizations, i.e. how organizations structure a collectivity of individuals and their interactions. Second, Schumpeter described each of these parts, the components and their composition, in a realistic but stylized manner. Regarding the individuals, Schumpeter took seriously the heterogeneity of agents. He characterized individual entrepreneurs in detail and developed a typology that identified different drivers of entrepreneurial behavior. Third, entrepreneurship is a function in which productive factors are combined in new combinations (rather than previously existing ones).[21] This idea allows us to avoid the one-sided explanations of organizational entrepreneurship that either rely on individual-level characteristics (of the founder, of a group of 'entrepreneurial' employees) or that see it simply as the fruit of standard operating procedures for the innovation process, or an innovation bureaucracy.

Schumpeter puts emphasis on two aspects: (1) the selection mechanisms for appointing leaders and (2) social interaction. Selection mechanisms trigger agents with different motivations to display entrepreneurial behavior (produce new combinations). An interesting open issue relating to this idea concerns the extent to which entrepreneurship can be replicated. If it can, would the quest for identification of personality traits that correlate positively with entrepreneurship crowd out unique personality traits that are at least as important for the expression of entrepreneurship? As we use book-knowledge to educate and select people that engage in entrepreneurship, we might lose the raw talent that has great success in following instinct or 'gut feeling'. Social interaction too can be a source of new combinations. Through his analysis of this aspect, Schumpeter develops an explanation of novelty that is neither over- nor under-socialized, to use Granovetter's (1985) terms. Both structure and individual will and motivation play a role in Schumpeter's explanation, and the main weight of explaining combinations is borne by processes of social interaction (Goss 2005).

Schumpeter does not provide us with a complete theory of entrepreneurship; but he does suggest a framework that can guide a broad program of research. The notion of combinations provides the cornerstone of such a program. In particular if it is applied to the economic process and the economic system as a whole (Knudsen and Swedberg 2007), it is the perhaps most fundamental notion one can draw on to approach the question. From there, several lines of inquiry can be developed. First, characterizing the kind of social interaction that produces new, rather than existing, combinations from existing elements. Second, identifying regularities in the way the elements of the economy become stable and lend themselves to be combined. The quest along this road of inquiry would be for something like Mendel's laws in biology (Becker, Knudsen, and March 2006). A third issue that Schumpeter hints at is to identify social rules that have an impact on combinations by providing an error threshold that facilitates the reliable reproduction of combinations (ibid.). Schumpeter sketches such social rules in his typology of entrepreneurs. Finally,

[21] As with all innovation, the perimeter of what 'new' refers to obviously has to be specified (e.g. new to the world, to the industry, to the firm, etc.).

another line of inquiry that can be unfolded on the basis of the notion of combinations is to ask what role organizations have in creating certain combinations rather than others (Miner, Ciuchta, and Gong 2008).

Finally, it should be remembered that this framework is capable of resolving the apparent paradox of the Schumpeterian hypothesis by proposing research questions about which organizational mechanisms are used to trigger entrepreneurial behavior or which entrepreneurial type best promotes innovation. How to best organize innovation in large organizations continues to be a much-debated issue. Thus, by mining Schumpeter's classic works, scholars can further advance current research agendas in entrepreneurship, innovation, and organization research.

Acknowledgments

For valuable comments, the authors thank Paul Adler, Richard Swedberg, Renee Rottner, Wes Sine, Laura Singleton, Jerry Davis, David Musson, Russel Schutt, Andy Van de Ven, Peer Fiss, Maksim Kokushkin, and other participants of the conference on Sociology Classics and the Future of Organization Studies, 9–10 August 2007, Wharton, Philadelphia. We also thank Nils Stieglitz for useful comments. Support from the Agence Nationale de Recherche (ANR), France, is gratefully acknowledged ('Jeunes Chercheuses et Jeunes Chercheurs' program, grant no. JC05_44029).

References

Aldrich, H. E. (2004). 'Entrepreneurship', in N. Smelser and R. Swedberg (eds.), *Handbook of Economic Sociology*. Princeton: Princeton University Press.

—— and Fiol, C. M. (1994). 'Fools Rush in? The Institutional Context of Industry Creation'. *Academy of Management Review*, 19/4: 645–70.

Allen, R. L. (1991). *Opening Doors: The Life and Work of Joseph Schumpeter*. 2 vols. New Brunswick, NJ: Transaction Publishers.

Augello, M. M. (1990). *Joseph Alois Schumpeter: A Reference Guide*. Berlin: Springer-Verlag.

Baumol, W. (2003). *The Free-Market Innovation Machine*. Princeton: Princeton University Press.

Becker, M. C., and Knudsen, T. (2002). 'Joseph A. Schumpeter: Theorie der wirtschaftlichen Entwicklung'. Translation of excerpts from chapters 2 and 7. *American Journal of Economics and Sociology*, 61/2: 405–37.

—— —— (2003*a*). 'The Entrepreneur at a Crucial Juncture in Schumpeter's Work: Schumpeter's 1928 Handbook Entry *Entrepreneur*'. *Advances in Austrian Economics*, 6: 199–234.

—— —— (2003*b*). 'Joseph A. Schumpeter: Unternehmer (1928)'. *Advances in Austrian Economics*, 6: 235–66.

—— —— and March, J. G. (2006). 'Schumpeter, Winter, and the Sources of Novelty'. *Industrial and Corporate Change*, 15/2: 353–71.

CARROLL, S. J., and GILLEN, D. J. (1987). 'Are the Classical Management Functions Useful in Describing Managerial Work?' *Academy of Management Review*, 12/1: 38–51.

CHOI, Y. B. (2003). 'Schumpeter on Entrepreneurship'. *Advances in Austrian Economics*, 6: 275–8.

CLEMENS, R. V. (1951). *Essays on Entrepreneurs, Innovations, Business Cycles and the Evolution of Capitalism—Joseph A. Schumpeter*. Cambridge, Mass.: Addison Wesley Press, Inc.

COOPER, A. C., and DUNKELBERG, W. C. (1986). 'Entrepreneurship and Paths to Business Ownership'. *Strategic Management Journal*, 7/1: 53–68.

D'AMBOISE, G., and MULDOWNEY, M. (1988). 'Management Theory for Small Business: Attempts and Requirements'. *Academy of Management Review*, 13/2: 226–40.

GARTNER, W. B. (1985). 'A Conceptual Framework for Describing the Phenomenon of New Venture Creation'. *Academy of Management Review*, 10/4: 696–706.

GIMENO, J., FOLTA, T. B., COOPER, A. C., and WOO, C. Y. (1997). 'Survival of the Fittest? Entrepreneurial Human Capital and the Persistence of Underperforming Firms'. *Administrative Science Quarterly*, 42/4: 750–83.

GOSS, D. (2005). 'Schumpeter's Legacy? Interaction and Emotions in the Sociology of Entrepreneurship'. *Entrepreneurship Theory & Practice*, 29/2: 205–18.

GRANOVETTER, M. (1985). 'Economic Action and Social Structure: The Problem of Embeddedness'. *American Journal of Sociology*, 9/3: 481–510.

HAMBRICK, D. C., and MASON, P. A. (1984). 'Upper Echelons: The Organization as a Reflection of Its Top Managers'. *Academy of Management Review*, 9/2: 193–206.

HARTMANN, H. (1959). 'Managers and Entrepreneurs: A Useful Distinction?' *Administrative Science Quarterly*, 3/4: 429–51.

KAHNEMANN, D., SLOVIC, P., and TVERSKY, A. (1982). *Judgment under Uncertainty: Heuristics and Biases*. Cambridge: Cambridge University Press.

KNUDSEN, T., and SWEDBERG, R. (2007). 'Capitalist Entrepreneurship: Making Profit through the Unmaking'. Paper presented at the Conference on Capitalism and Entrepreneurship, Center for the Study of Economy and Society, Cornell University, 28–29 September 2007.

KOONTZ, H. (1980). 'The Management Theory Jungle Revisited'. *Academy of Management Review*, 5/2: 175–87.

MCCRAW, T. (2007). *Prophet of Innovation: Joseph Schumpeter and Creative Destruction*. Cambridge, Mass.: Belknap Press of Harvard University Press.

MINER, A. S., CIUCHTA, M., and GONG, Y. (2008). 'Organizational Routines and Organizational Learning', in M. C. Becker (ed.), *Handbook of Organizational Routines*. Cheltenham: Edward Elgar.

MINER, J. B. (1977). 'Implications of Managerial Talent Projections for Management Education'. *Academy of Management Review*, 2/3: 412–20.

MINTZBERG, H. (1977). 'Policy as a Field of Management Theory'. *Academy of Management Review*, 2/1: 88–103.

—— and WATERS, J. A. (1982). 'Tracking Strategy in an Entrepreneurial Firm'. *Academy of Management Journal*, 25/3: 465–99.

NELSON, R., and WINTER, S. G. (1982). *An Evolutionary Theory of Economic Change*. Cambridge, Mass.: Belknap Press of Harvard University Press.

REASON, J. (1990). *Human Error*. Cambridge: Cambridge University Press.

SCHUMPETER, J. A. (1908). *Das Wesen und der Hauptinhalt der theoretischen Nationalökonomie*. Leipzig: Duncker & Humblot.

—— (1911). *Theorie der wirtschaftlichen Entwicklung*. 1st edn. Leipzig: Duncker & Humblot.

—— (1914). 'Epochen der Dogmen- und Methodengeschichte', in M. Weber (ed.), *Grundriss der Sozialökonomik*, 1. Abteilung: 'Wirtschaft und Wirtschaftswissenschaft'. Tübingen: Mohr.

—— (1919). 'Zur Soziologie der Imperialismen'. *Archiv für Sozialwissenschaften und Sozialpolitik*, 46: 1–39 and 275–310. Reprinted in E. Schneider and A. Spiethoff (eds.) (1953), *Aufsätze zur Soziologie*. Tübingen: Mohr.

—— (1926). *Theorie der wirtschaftlichen Entwicklung*. 2nd edn. Leipzig: Duncker & Humblot.

—— (1927*a*). 'Unternehmerfunktion und Arbeiterinteresse'. *Der Arbeitgeber*, 17: 166–70. Reprinted in W. F. Stolper and C. Seidl (eds.) (1985), *Aufsätze zur Wirtschaftspolitik*. Tübingen: Mohr.

—— (1927*b*). 'Die sozialen Klassen im ethnisch homogenen Milieu'. *Archiv für Sozialwissenschaften und Sozialpolitik*, 57: 1–67. Reprinted in E. Schneider and A. Spiethoff (eds.) (1953), *Aufsätze zur Soziologie*. Tübingen: Mohr.

—— (1928). 'Unternehmer', in *Handwörterbuch der Staatswissenschaften*, 4th edn., viii. 476–87. Jena: Verlag von G. Fischer.

—— (1929*a*). 'Der Unternehmer in der Volkswirtschaft von heute', in B. Harms (ed.), *Strukturwandlungen der Deutschen Volkswirtschaft*, 2nd edn., i. 303–26. Berlin: Verlag von Reimar Hobbing. Reprinted in W. F. Stolper and C. Seidl (eds.) (1985), *Aufsätze zur Wirtschaftspolitik*. Tübingen: Mohr.

—— (1929*b*). 'Ökonomie und Psychologie des Unternehmers'. Vortrag vor der 10. Ordentlichen Mitgliederversammlung des Zentralverbandes der deutschen Metallwalzwerkes- und Hütten-Industrie e.V. am 22. Mai 1929 in München. Leipzig: Haberland. Reprinted in W. F. Stolper and C. Seidl. (eds.) (1993), *Aufsätze zur Tagespolitik*. Tübingen: Mohr.

—— (1934). *The Theory of Economic Development: An Inquiry into Profits, Capital, Credit, Interest, and the Business Cycle*. Cambridge, Mass.: Harvard University Press.

—— (1939). *Business Cycles*. New York: McGraw-Hill Books Co.

—— (1942). *Capitalism, Socialism, and Democracy*. New York: Harper & Brothers.

—— (1954). *History of Economic Analysis*. New York: Oxford University Press.

—— (2005). 'Development'. *Journal of Economic Literature*, 43 (March): 108–20. With an introduction by M. C. Becker, H. U. Eβlinger, U. Hedtke, and T. Knudsen. Translated by M. C. Becker and T. Knudsen.

Shionoya, Y. (1997). *Schumpeter and the Idea of Social Science: A Metatheoretical Study*. Cambridge: Cambridge University Press.

Smith, N. R., and Miner, J. B. (1983). 'Type of Entrepreneur, Type of Firm, and Managerial Motivation: Implications for Organizational Life Cycle Theory'. *Strategic Management Journal*, 4/4: 325–40.

Swedberg, R. (1991*a*). *Joseph A. Schumpeter: His Life and Thought*. Oxford: Polity Press.

—— (1991*b*). *Joseph A. Schumpeter: The Economics and Sociology of Capitalism*. Princeton: Princeton University Press.

—— (2000). *Entrepreneurship: The Social Science View*. Oxford: Oxford University Press.

Webster, F. A. (1976). 'A Model for New Venture Initiation: A Discourse on Rapacity and the Independent Entrepreneur'. *Academy of Management Review*, 1/1: 26–37.

—— (1977). 'Entrepreneurs and Ventures: An Attempt at Classification and Clarification'. *Academy of Management Review*, 2/1: 54–61.

Winter, S. G. ([1968] 2006). 'Toward a Neo-Schumpeterian Theory of the Firm'. *Industrial and Corporate Change*, 15/1: 125–41.

Appendix: Chronology of Schumpeter's Life

1883	Joseph Alois Schumpeter is born on 8 February in Triesch, located on the southern edge of the border between Moravia and Bohemia. He is the son of manufacturer Josef A. K. Schumpeter and Johanna M. Schumpeter, a physician's daughter.
1887–8	His father dies suddenly at age 32. Schumpeter's mother is 26. Schumpeter and his mother move to Graz, about 150 miles south of Vienna.
1888–93	Graz elementary school.
1893	Schumpeter's mother marries the retired Lieutenant Field Marshal Sigmund von Kéler, and the family moves to Vienna.
1893–1901	Attends elite grammar school at the Maria Theresa Academy of Knights (Theresianum) located at Favoritenstrasse 15 in Vienna.
1901–5	Enrolled at the Faculty of Law at the University of Vienna. In 1903 Schumpeter begins to discover economics.
1906	Earns the degree of Doctor Utruisque Juris (doctor of both Roman and canonical law).
1906–7	Research education at the University of Berlin and London School of Economics.
1907–20	Marriage with Gladys Ricarde Seaver, a daughter of an official of the Church of England.
1907–8	Employed as lawyer in a law firm in Cairo, Egypt.
1908	*Das Wesen und der Hauptinhalt der theoretischen Nationalökonomie.*
1909	Return to Vienna and Habilitation in economics on the basis of his 1908 book (*Wesen*). The Habilitation made him eligible to become a professor and to teach at universities.
1909–11	Extraordinary Professor at the University of Czernowitz about 100 miles away from Vienna.
1911	*Theorie der wirtschaftlichen Entwicklung.* This book was reissued in a revised edition in 1926 and then translated into English in 1934.
1911–21	Professor at the University of Graz in Austria.
1914	'Epochen der Dogmen- und Methodengeschichte'.
1919	State Secretary of Finance.
1921–5	President of Biedermann Bank in Vienna.
1925–32	Professor at the University of Bonn (in Germany).
1926	Schumpeter's mother dies.
1925–6	Marriage with Anna Josefina Reisinger, who dies on 3 August 1926 after giving birth to a son. The unnamed son also dies a few hours after his birth.
1926	*Theorie der wirtschaftlichen Entwicklung,* revised edition.
1930	Sixteen economists, in a meeting chaired by Schumpeter, founded the *Econometric Society,* a term coined by Ragnar Frisch.
1932–50	Professor at the Department of Economics of Harvard University.
1934	*Theory of Economic Development* is published as a revised translation of the 1926 edition of *Theorie der wirtschaftlichen Entwicklung.*
1937–50	Marriage with Elizabeth Boody Firuski.
1939	*Business Cycles: A Theoretical, Historical, and Statistical Analysis of the Capitalist Process.*
1940–1	President of the Econometric Society.

1942	*Capitalism, Socialism, and Democracy.*
1948	President of the American Economic Association.
1950	Dies on 8 January in Taconic, Connecticut, USA.
1954	*History of Economic Analysis*, edited from manuscript by Elizabeth Boody Schumpeter.
1968	Sidney G. Winter publishes a *Neo-Schumpeterian Theory of the Firm* (this article was made available to a broad audience in a special issue of ICC published in 2006).
1982	Richard R. Nelson and Sidney G. Winter publish *An Evolutionary Theory of Economic Change*, which elaborates and formalizes the idea of Schumpeterian competition in a capitalist economy.
1986	International Schumpeter Society (ISS) founded at the initiative of Wolfgang F. Stolper and Horst Hanusch.
1983	Centenary of Schumpeter's birth.

CHAPTER 15

NORBERT ELIAS'S IMPACT ON ORGANIZATION STUDIES

AD VAN ITERSON

15.1. Introduction

The impact of Norbert Elias's sociological writings on organization studies is still small. To date, his approach has been largely neglected by the field. In contrast, his influence on other sociological sub-disciplines is much larger, e.g. the sociology of sports, teaching, health and illness, knowledge, and of the welfare state. Arguably, his impact is strongest on general theoretical sociology (for discussions of his work and approach, see e.g. Rojek 1986; Goudsblom 1987; Fletcher 1997; Mennell 1998; Van Krieken 1998; Kilminster 1998, 2007). This may not come as a surprise. Although his magnum opus *The Civilizing Process* ([1939] 2000) provides a rich historical account of state formation and changing manners, morality, and *habitus* among secular upper classes in late medieval and *Ancien Régime* (Old Order) France, it can best be read as primarily a critique of what Elias saw as the major flaws of contemporary sociological theorizing.

In this chapter, I will attempt to show how Elias's ideas might open some new avenues of research for organization studies. I will rely almost exclusively on *The Civilizing Process*, to the neglect of other important, but later works such as *The*

Established and the Outsiders ([1965] 1994; co-authored with John L. Scotson), *What is Sociology?* (1970), *Involvement and Detachment* (1987*a*), *The Symbol Theory* (1991*b*), *Time: An Essay* (1991*c*), and *The Germans* (1996).

15.2. Biography

Norbert Elias (1897–1990), the son of a textile trader, was born in the present Polish city of Wroclaw (for a fascinating account of his extraordinary life and times, see his autobiographical *Reflections on a Life*, 1994). He served in the German forces in World War I. On demobilization he enrolled at Breslau University both in philosophy and medicine. After a disagreement with his neo-Kantian supervisor, Elias switched to sociology. At Heidelberg, Alfred Weber accepted him as a candidate for Habilitation, a senior post-doctoral qualification. Elias came in contact with another leading sociologist, Karl Mannheim. In 1929, Mannheim was offered the chair of sociology at Frankfurt, and Elias followed him as his academic assistant. When the National Socialists came to power, in 1933, Mannheim was among the first university teachers to be cast out. Elias's Habilitation was rushed through. The thesis—*Die höfische Gesellschaft* [The Court Society, 1983]—was not published until thirty-six years later.

After nearly two years in Paris, where he began to write the first volume of *Über den Prozess der Zivilization* [The Civilizing Process], Elias moved to London. On a grant from a Jewish refugee organization, he completed the two volumes of his most recognized study, spending numerous hours in the British Museum Library. It was published in Basel, Switzerland, in 1939—unfortunate timing, indeed. Being the work of a German on the issue of civilization, the book understandably must have raised eyebrows. It was hardly reviewed. Moreover, those who did notice the study characterized it as a work of cultural history rather than as a sociological study. Elias's extensive use of etiquette manuals as historical evidence together with the fact that at first only volume one was published may account for this misunderstanding. Only in the concluding section of the second volume was Elias's theory of the civilizing process laid out in its full sociological implication.

The neglect of Elias's study lasted for thirty years. Imagine the drama. Having written a book that at any time earlier than the late 1930s would have given him high recognition in the field and surely also a professorship, Norbert Elias now had to wait seemingly endlessly for the first signs of approval.

His parents died during the war, his mother Sophie in the Nazi death camp Auschwitz. It was the major trauma of his life: 'I'll never get over it' (1994: 52). Elias remained in the United Kingdom, living on the fringes of academia, for instance working in an adult-education organization. He suffered from what seems a long-lasting writer's block, perhaps related to the feeling of guilt over not being able to get his mother out of the concentration camp before she was killed, as he wrote to his friend Cas Wouters (Israëls, Komen, and De Swaan 1993: 10). Being an early adopter of psychoanalytical thought, which he incorporated in his civilizing process theory, he co-founded the Group Analytic Society in London. Group analysis seeks to build social relations into psychoanalytical practice, and Elias worked indeed for some time as a group therapist. Only in 1954, at the age of 57, did he obtain an official university post, at Leicester, in the East Midlands of the United Kingdom. With Ilya Neustadt, he built up a successful department of sociology, where prominent academics such as Anthony Giddens and John Goldthorpe were educated.

From 1965 on, when *The Established and the Outsiders* (a community study of in-group/out-group relations, co-authored with John L. Scotson) appeared, Elias's reputation slowly rose. The decisive event was the republication in 1969 of the original German text of *The Civilizing Process.* Widespread recognition had finally come—not so much in the Anglo-American world,[1] but rather on the European continent. By his seventies, Elias had become a scholarly celebrity, although remaining very much an outsider. Also, a period of renewed writing vigor had been set off. Fame energized Elias, as the historian Gordon (2002) observed in a somewhat sarcastic vein.

Elias died in 1990, still working, in Amsterdam. *The Society of Individuals* (1991*a*), *The Symbol Theory* (1991*b*), *Time: An Essay* (1991*c*), *Mozart: Portrait of a Genius* (1993), and *Reflections on a Life* (1994) have been published posthumously. By 1993, Elias was one of the best-selling authors at the leading German publishing house Suhrkamp. In a 1998 opinion survey, organized by the International Sociological Association among its members, as to which sociological work from the twentieth century has been most influential, *The Civilizing Process* reached the seventh position, with 6.6 percent of the votes. Because this book was initially published in 1939, Elias may be considered as essentially a pre-World War II sociologist. Indeed, it seems right to identify him as the last of the classical sociologists.

15.3. The Civilizing Process Theory

The Civilizing Process identifies a long-term trend in Western European societies towards a refinement of social behavior. More precisely, Elias analyzes the

[1] A reader of essential Elias texts primarily aimed at the North American market was only published in the late 1990s (Elias 1998*b*). The publication of Mennell's study of the American civilizing process (2007) will probably contribute to more recognition of the Eliasian approach (see also Goudsblom 2000).

formation of the French absolutist state up until the end of the *Ancien Régime* (1792) with its concomitant changes in social relations, conduct, and *habitus*. From the twelfth century onwards, a number of princely courts in the fragmented region, now called 'France', succeeded in acquiring ever larger territories. Their supremacy was built on a monopoly of the means of violence and of the levy of taxes. The ensuing absolutist state, ruled by the victorious Capetian house of Bourbon, exerted these two monopolies with unprecedented power. The defeated, 'pacified' nobility was accommodated in the monarchic royal court. In this 'semi-ritualized setting', marked by ongoing political and status struggles, new standards of manners and morality were articulated. Elias has selected this *casus*, which he contrasts with the German and English roads to nation formation, because he considered the French court society as the focal stage of the Western civilizing process (for a critique, see Gordon 1994, 2002, who claims that Elias ignored the liberal and democratic dynamism that also mark the epoch, e.g. the critical Enlightenment, see also Duindam 1995). Elias goes on to argue that the behavioral codes, essential for pacified interaction at the Versailles court, were later intentionally or unintentionally imitated by bourgeois elites, including the early capitalistic entrepreneurs, and subsequently diffused down the social ladder. This extension of civilized behavior was central to the development of the *habitus* characteristic of the modern era: an ingrained disposition to act, think, and feel (cf. Bourdieu and Passeron 1990) in ways that are characterized by greater individuation and more empathy, and which are emotionally controlled, curbed, and refined, better capable of postponing immediate gratifications.

In Elias's civilizing process theory, three levels of analysis can be distinguished:

1. state formation, monopolization of violence and taxation, growing social differentiation and interdependence;
2. changing standards of manners and morality; and
3. emotional controls and *habitus* formation.

But it should already be clear that such a distinction only serves heuristic purposes. Elias tries to demonstrate that macro-structural developments (he uses the word: *sociogenesis*) and behavioral and mental changes at the micro-individual level (*psychogenesis*) are strongly interrelated and can only be fully understood in that interrelation. By applying both a multileveled and a historical (i.e. 'process') perspective covering centuries, Elias aims to bridge the gap between macro and micro levels of explanation in sociology—one of the most persistent problems in sociological theory.

In linking the three levels, the highest level concepts of 'power inequalities', 'social differentiation', and 'social interdependencies' seem to be the most crucial.[2] They

[2] Elias has focused on such structural determinants as power, differentiation, and interdependence. Strikingly, he disregarded values, norms, and common understandings as 'independent variables'. At best, these served as 'mediating variables' in explaining changes in *habitus*.

take the lead, as it were, in the civilizing process. In late medieval Western Europe, Elias finds evidence of quite impulsive behavior amongst noblemen at the local courts. Outbursts of ferocity could occur at any moment (for a different interpretation of medieval behavior and emotions, see Rosenwein 2006). Elias demonstrates that this 'wild', 'animal-like' behavior was gradually tempered as authority was centralized at the victorious court and a growing number of people became mutually dependent while simultaneously more socially differentiated.

In the subsequent centuries, characterized by further concentration of power and increasing differentiation and interdependency, the pattern of controls over individual behavior changed dramatically. Whereas behavioral and emotional restraints of humans initially arose from marked power imbalances (as we saw in the formation of absolutism), later on restraints were induced by the more impersonal, less visible coercions of yet closer interdependencies as typified by the latter years of the *Ancien Régime* court. Concurrent with the progressive diminution of power disparities between groups (as an outcome of further advancing human interdependence and differentiation[3]), desired behavior was more and more produced by individuals on their own accord. Elias labels this change as a shift from external constraints (*Fremdzwänge* in German) to self-restraints (*Selbstzwänge*).

The increasing constraints have led to fundamental changes in the psychological make-up of humans. When the external constraints were still dominant, one could witness what Elias calls the advance of the threshold of shame and repugnance. This advance meant that 'more and more spheres of action became social "danger zones" in which one could lapse into gestures or expressions that were liable to give cause to shame' (Goudsblom 2007). When self-restraints became more prominent, feelings of shame yielded to a more 'advanced' stage of self-consciousness: a quasi-automatic self-discipline and foresight regardless of whether one was observed or not. This self-discipline was also patently more differentiated, more all-round, and more stable. In addition, self-discipline and foresight were more effective. Urges and impulses came to be more effectively subordinated to the requirements of increasingly intricate social relationships that resulted from lengthening interdependency chains. Notice Elias's use of the adjective 'advanced' here. His main intellectual contender Michel Foucault (1975) saw the trend towards internalization of the disciplinary power of the observing eye of panopticism in a much less favorable light (see also Burkitt 1993, on Elias vs. Foucault).

Elias summarizes the psychological concomitants of power centralization, increasing interdependencies, and stricter codes of self-restraint as follows: 'If in this or that region, the power of central authority grows, if over a larger or smaller area people are forced to live at peace with one another, the molding of affects and the standards of the economy of instincts are very gradually changed as well'

[3] Elias argues that shifts in power balances at the court are explicable in terms of social processes in French society at large, especially the increasing capacity of bourgeois and professional groups to get their own way—a token of growing differentiation.

(2000: 169). Here we see at work Elias's main line of reasoning from macro to micro. Although Elias warned repeatedly against the dangers of reification—collectivities such as the court or the state are not actors themselves and in the end consist only of multiple human individuals—agency is given but little room.

Elias's introduction of his central concept of 'figuration', some decades after publication of *The Civilizing Process*, was intended to help eliminate the antithesis immanent in the customary use of the words 'society' and 'individual' (1970). A figuration is a structure of mutually oriented and dependent people, with shifting asymmetrical power balances—in short, a nexus of human interdependencies. The dynamics of such networks of interdependent humans must be understood in terms of individual preferences and actions. But Elias almost immediately submerges these voluntaristic manifestations in the 'blindness' of figurational processes. Elias over and again points at the unplanned and unforeseen nature of long-term developments taking place in human figurations. Instead of 'unintended consequences' (Robert K. Merton), Elias uses the concept of 'relative autonomy' (1970). Social structures develop relatively autonomous from the intentions of the initiating or partaking individuals. The autonomy is only relative because, once more, in the end social action is the sum of individual actions. But the emphasis is unmistakably on autonomy.

In sociological analysis, Elias argues, there is too much stress on the functions for individuals of, say, Weber's 'protestant work ethos', to the detriment of this ethos being a function of the wider human figuration(s) in which it emerged. The twofold use of the word function, in this respect, is telling. Although he later became an unwavering opponent of Parsonian thinking, Elias was, for all intents and purposes, something of a structural-functionalist (cf. Mouzelis 1995: 149). Despite the blindness of processes at large and in the long run, when one zooms in it appears that everything in the world is in service of something else—in particular control, rationality, and realism. The more civilized humans become, the better they can control themselves in a detached, rational manner, which enables them to do away with obscuring and dangerous 'myths' and embrace the a-metaphysical reality of human existence. Note that, in Elias's perspective, more control does not lead to an entrapment in a Weberian iron cage, but is the means by which individuality can develop and thrive (see also Elias 1987*a*).

Despite his functionalist tendency, Elias's fame is to some extent based on his promise that his approach offers a break away from mainstream mid-twentieth-century sociology. In Elias's view, expressed in many glosses on *The Civilizing Process* and in other works, Parsonian sociology had become a static rather than a dynamic discourse. As one outcome of its exclusive focus on the status quo or 'retreat of sociologists in the present' (Elias 1987*b*), Parsonian sociology had come to promote a strict dichotomy between 'society' and 'individual'. This dichotomy is characteristic of the *homo clausus* self-experience of present-day Western humans. For the individual as *homo clausus*, there exists a sort of a small world inside herself or himself. This world is totally independent of the world outside, as if the two are separated by an invisible wall. Inevitably, every other human being is equally seen as a *homo clausus* living in her or his private world to which no one has full access.

Elias's project is to develop a sociology that is free from both the flaws of reification (regarding an abstraction such as 'society' as a material or concrete entity) and presentism (today-centered thinking) in the human sciences. The question remains whether he succeeds in overcoming the flaws of structuralism and functionalism.

Nevertheless, it is now broadly acknowledged that Elias has been a pioneer in that he proposed a paradigm shift for sociology in three ways: (1) from the static analysis of social systems to the long-term study of evolutionary social processes; (2) from a focus on individual action to figurations of humans where action is always conceived with regard to the actor's position in a network of relationships; and (3) from an (ever more strict) working division between sociology, psychology, history, etc. to a synthesized, genuine 'human science' (*Menschenwissenschaft* in German). Such claims were not easily reconciled with much of the thinking that dominated the social sciences for a major part of Elias's lifespan, and this has certainly contributed to his marginal position.

In conclusion to this section: *The Civilizing Process* Theory may have the ring of a universal evolutionist theory à la Herbert Spencer. Elias objected fiercely when confronted with such allegations. His thesis was certainly not intended to be teleological. Elias did not believe in an overall purpose. The civilizing process may have an endpoint, Elias speculates on the final page of *The Civilizing Process*, but for the time being it is still in a state of becoming, to put it paradoxically. Nevertheless, there is still debate about Elias's universalistic ambitions, which he, arguably, cherished to the extent that he seemed to regard the Western civilization process as a template that will be taken on in other parts of the world (e.g. Barraclough 1982; Duerr 1988, 1990, 1993, 1997, 2002; Goody 2006). Some 'Eliasians' deny this; others try to reassure critics that, admittedly, non-Western civilizing processes will follow suit, but with different itineraries (for a summary of the disagreement, see Mennell 1998: 228–34).

15.4. The Civilizing Process Theory and Organization Studies: Basic Concepts and Counter Concepts

Let us turn now to the possible contribution to organization studies of a number of core elements of *The Civilizing Process*, together with supplementary or competing concepts. To apply Elias's perspective to organization studies, it would make sense to draw on the three-level approach ('authority structures', 'codes of conduct', '*habitus* formation'), with the central concepts of power balances and interdependencies at the front, as outlined in the previous section. Such an approach could sensitize organization studies students to the interconnectedness of the following themes:

1. the emergence and possible demise of productive organizations based on subordination, spatial and temporal concentration, and labor division;
2. the enforcement and internalization of various codes of 'proper' behavior related to work (e.g. managing, cooperation); and
3. the development of managerial, professional, craft, and worker *habituses*, and of shaming and humiliation practices in organizations.

Aside from collective undertakings such as the mobilization of armies and the building of pyramids, which obviously required considerable organizing effort, it was only since the emergence of the factory system (e.g. Pollard 1965), starting in late eighteenth-century England, that all the conditions of productive organizations were met. These conditions are: subordination, spatial and temporal concentration, and extensive labor division. For the first time in history, work was organized and controlled under one roof, at fixed working hours, by 'organizational members' with specialized tasks and limited discretion. Similar to the (French) court, the early factory system was characterized by a new scale of human interdependencies (Newton 1999). The problems of ever-broadening interdependencies in the early decades of industrialization were dealt with by (1) coercing the workers in line through orders, rules, and sanctions (the Eliasian external constraints) and (2) stimulating their discipline and motivation (self-constraints) (cf. Bendix 1956). As we have already seen, on both the factory floor and in the administrative offices, people increasingly realized that they had to learn to live together in peace and order (cf. Kieser 1998), which required considerable self-constraint, e.g. *in sexualis*.

Like the (courtier) manners books analyzed in Elias's *The Civilizing Process* and in *The Court Society*, factory rule books may prove to be informative.[4] *The Potters Instructions* and the *Common Place Book*, developed by the eighteenth-century English factory master Josiah Wedgwood, offer evocative examples of such disciplinary rules that aimed to fight 'waste', 'inefficiency', 'arbitrariness', and 'idleness'. The following sanctions clearly indicate severe external constraints: 'Any workman conveying Ale or Licquor into the manufactory in working hours forfits 2s.', 'Any workman strikeing or otherwise abuseing an overlooker to lose his place' (McKendrick 1961: 45). At the same time, these documents instructed overseers how to show 'marks of approbation' to the punctual and skillful. This may already point in the direction of self-control enhancing efforts. Indeed, when it comes to modern

[4] Elias's use of etiquette and manners books has been objected to. Often these texts were in fact propaganda and should thus not be naively used as evidence. Despite the critique on Elias's use of literary sources, his approach may serve as an example of linking the social sciences and the humanities, which is currently supported (e.g. Zald 1996).

times, the factory seems to provide a model nexus for studying civilizing processes. Regrettably, to date the Eliasian approach has been little applied to factory work figurations. A number of exceptions will be mentioned in the next section.

Subordination, spatial and temporal concentration, and extensive labor division have been enduring features of modern bureaucratic organizations. Only since the advent of post-bureaucratic (or postmodern) organizations do these four basic characteristics seem to begin to fade. Recent phenomena such as empowerment, teleworking, the 24-hour working day, home–work spillover flows, despecialization, and multitasking suggest that long-standing trends may be beginning to operate in reverse. Virtual organizations—another fashionable concept—are defined as 'electronically networked organizations that transcend conventional organizational boundaries with information technology-enabled linkages both within and between organizations' (McAuley, Duberley, and Johnson 2007: 211). Obviously, virtuality reduces the need for physical and temporal concentration. People no longer need to work together in one location, obeying time schedules.

What will the possible demise of productive organizations based on subordination, spatial and temporal concentration, and labor division entail for organizational members' *habitus*? One may question whether empowerment and other forms of decentralization really reverse subordination. Although it seems that overt displays of authority have given way to a more negotiated order, implying a greater role for give-and-take in a 'civilized' manner, some argue that these new arrangements are but 'soft domination': a subtle mechanism through which obedience is produced. This mechanism has the appearance of equality among peers, but in reality it is characterized by a pervasive system of controls (Courpasson 2002). Thus, the concentration of decision power may in essence not have diminished in post-bureaucratic organizations. However, spatial and temporal dispersion, as well as despecialization of labor, are trends that can hardly be denied. *The Civilizing Process* theory with its focus on the balancing aspects of external constraints and self-constraints may offer a fruitful framework for studying current and impending organizational changes. How will organizational members' constraints and expressions alter in reaction to the liquefying boundaries of place, time, and work activities?

One hypothesis would be that growing work complexity and dissolving organizational boundaries necessitate more self-restraint. Both trends imply more teamwork and more intra- and interorganizational linkages. So, organizations represent ever more complex webs of interdependency, requiring people to take each other more into consideration. Following Elias, such complex and lengthy interdependency chains are likely to imply a further shift towards self-restraint.

The alternative hypothesis would be that the blurring of work responsibilities (which accompanies the despecialization of tasks) and loosening of the demand for spatial and temporal proximity of organizational members on one site (which accompanies teleworking, the 24-hour working day, and virtuality in general) will lead to less civilized behavior. First, competition over (challenging) work tasks might become harsher. The battle for better jobs will get nastier in postmodern societies. Second, since many working contacts will disappear or occur only electronically, restraints will be weakened. Why bother about people whom you never see? In both cases, people will experience shame and repugnance less easily. Growing concerns about internet use by employees and attempts to develop corporate netiquettes (rules for online etiquette) may be early reactions to a trend towards the loosening of behavioral restraints.

15.4.1. Interdependency and Proximity

Elias gives much weight to the lengthening of chains of interdependencies over time as a 'driver' of increasingly restrained behavior. The first of the two hypotheses above is informed by that notion. Mouzelis (1995) has argued that the idea of interdependency chains increasing in length makes or breaks *The Civilizing Process* theory. In relation to that, the second hypothesis of the previous paragraph becomes very relevant. The hypothesis draws attention to physical proximity of members as a vital aspect of modern productive organizations. If one regards the fact that Elias empirically studied civilizing processes in such spatially confined contexts as the battlefield, the castle, and the court, one is tempted to give priority to the alternative explanatory notion of physical proximity. Admittedly, if one has to take into account the preferences and sensitivities of more and more humans, as is the case when interdependencies extend, one is inclined to higher restraint. But the effect of being visible may well be considerably stronger (cf. the Foucauldian gaze, which also stimulates self-control). Unseen and unknown fellow humans will always stay to some extent an abstraction, it can be argued. 'Proximity'—the immediate presence of others—may drive civilizing processes much more rapidly and broadly than 'interdependency' per se. This is also in line with Duerr's (1988, 1990, 1993, 1997, 2002) argument that humans who lived in the late Middle Ages were more restrained in their behavior than humans in early modern and modern eras just because they lived so close to each other and everyone could see what the other was doing. There was hardly any chance to escape the social control of the castle, village, or town. Moreover, as Durkheim (1947) has forcefully argued, social differentiation, and the reduced human closeness that goes with it, promotes anomie. This is a far cry from refined and relaxed civilized behavior.

Giving primacy to 'proximity' would also call for stricter contextualization of the study of civilizing processes. Under which structural conditions and boundaries do agents enact more versus less civilized behavior? More case studies are needed when applying the Eliasian approach. Modern and postmodern organizations proffer fertile and relevant research ground. Their specific structure–agency dialectics, in larger institutional contexts, have to be taken seriously when studying trends towards more or less civilized behavior. Put differently, *The Civilizing Process* approach is not a one-size-fits-all method, based on and leading to 'quasi-universal generalizations between growing social interdependence and self-discipline' (Mouzelis 1995: 150).

15.4.2. Discipline and Informalization

The Civilizing Process theory, developed in the harsh 1930s, found new impetus some thirty years ago through the argument, articulated by Elias and some of his followers, that self-restraint has become both more subtle and skilled since the end of the nineteenth century, again particularly in the West. Wouters (1977, 1986, 1990) refers to this trend as *informalization.* He claims that informalization gained momentum in the 1960s and 1970s, with the 1920s as a sort of forerunner. The net effect of this 'refinement' might give the impression that the necessity of 'mastering' one's emotions is loosening, since this sophistication implies less rigidity and more relaxed or 'natural' behavior. But informalization has not been accompanied by a lapse in self-discipline. Informalization does not simply involve a linear loosening of morals, marked by permissiveness. Following Elias and Dunning (1986: 44), Wouters uses the not very elegant notion of 'controlled decontrolling of emotional controls' (for a critical discussion of Wouters's contribution, see Newton 1997). This controlled decontrolling implies *more differentiation in manners expressing control and distinction* rather than sheer moral decline, as an observational visit to a nudist beach may confirm.

The element of *differentiation* (or variation) in defining informalization also allows for new sensibilities that require new self-restraints. For instance, expressions of superiority and of inferiority feelings are no longer tolerated in the age of informalization. These need to be repressed, although in an easygoing, unforced way. Tactics to distinguish oneself from others need to be even more sophisticated than at the French court. In short, at present there can be more variation in expression, while stark differences in behavior within individuals and between groups have been reduced. Elias summarizes this trend with the law-like principle: 'diminishing contrasts, increasing varieties' (Elias 1998*b*). One might say that the civilizing process in developed countries has opened up a wide spectrum of grey tones at the cost of pure black and pure white.

In organizational settings, informalization may be seen at work in such trends as lowered acceptance of status differences and feelings of superiority, less ceremony in meetings and other formal events, increasingly relaxed interaction between organizational members of different age, gender, tenure, and position. Other evidence of informalization may be the growing tolerance for informal clothing, the use of first names and colloquial speech, confessing private feelings and expressing emotions, engaging in romantic relations on the work floor, and in general the blurring of the boundaries between work life and private life. But, again, all this apparent 'decontrolling' goes hand in hand with an increase or broadening of skillfulness: such is the argument.

On the other hand, one might wonder whether informalization is really so new a trend. Mastenbroek (2000) claims that the germs of the behavioral norms of informalization can already be found in the Italian city-states of the early sixteenth century. Manners books by Gracián, focusing on tactical refinement (1994), and Castiglione, advocating flexible and pleasant conduct (1991) seem to support Mastenbroek's argument. Castiglione regards discipline highly, but the 'true courtier' behaves above all in an unaffected, flexible, and natural manner. This also includes humor, irony, and verbal dexterity, all of which demand considerable flexibility. Initially intended for courtiers, the Renaissance manners books gained popularity among other elites; by the eighteenth and nineteenth centuries, they had reached the bourgeois who were active in trading and manufacturing, in the civil services, and the professions (for an analysis of the continuities between the courtly society and bourgeois life, see Elias 1983).

Following Mastenbroek's view, Van Iterson, Mastenbroek, and Soeters (2001) argue that *The Civilizing Process* theory overemphasizes increasing self-restraint of the suppressive kind, because it overlooks the trends since the fifteenth century towards the simultaneous development of both formalization and informalization. The notion of a balance between discipline and informality to which Castiglione seems to refer provides an alternative way to explain changing patterns of emotion management among occidental elites. Although Castiglione advocates a natural ease, he seems aware that the decontrolling of formality proves difficult. The balance between formality and informality requires delicacy: 'That is why I feel that casualness, which if taken too far, as when someone lets his cloak slip off, degenerates into artificial carelessness, is no lesser fault than dignity, also in itself praiseworthy, which goes so far that someone keeps his head motionless for fear of getting his hair tangled' (Castiglione 1991: 55).

The balance between formality and informality is a precarious one. More discipline inflames the desire to unleash, to phrase it in a psychodynamic idiom. On the other hand, 'free and easy conduct' presupposes and cultivates adherence to the rules of law or the discipline of mutual consent. Research on civilizing processes typified by a tension between discipline and informalization, and on their effect on *habitus*, may contribute to a better understanding of behavior and emotion in current organizations (cf. Fineman 1996). Again, the potential seems particularly strong with regard to trends such as empowerment, teleworking, the 24-hour working day, despecialization, and multitasking. The blurring of the boundaries of place, time, and organizational domain may bestow on organizational members both more freedom and more restraint. Discretion increases because of the larger distance from direct supervision, standardization, and peer control. Limitations increase as an outcome of despecialization and the like. Multiskilled work implies more consideration of others' sensitivities, expertise, and identity. Despecialized or dedifferentiated workers (cf. Clegg 1990) have to be more proficient 'network players', just like the courtiers at Versailles (cf. Kuzmics 1991). And since postmodern workers are often equally dedifferentiated and less—literally—overseen, they have to juggle the balls of anxious, disciplined behavior and relaxed, informal behavior. How this tension will affect organizational members' *habitus* is an intriguing issue for further study. Mastenbroek (2000) sees the possibility of an advancing tolerance for the tension between autonomy and interdependence.

15.4.3. Shame and Shaming

The concept of the 'threshold of shame and embarrassment', as Elias calls it, is central to the third and 'lowest' level of analysis in the civilizing theory: emotional controls and *habitus* formation. As indicated in the discussion of the second level of analysis, Elias sees a trend towards increasing control over individual behavior in late medieval and early modern Western Europe. These increasing constraints and their shift in form from external to internal have led to fundamental changes in people's *habitus*. These can be summarized by the notion of advancing shame and embarrassment: a greater sensibility, characterized by strong emotional pain, for social disgrace that may follow from a failure to control bodily functions such as blushing, sweating, trembling, breaking wind, or from being caught in sexual activities. Being a typical social emotion, shame results from any kind of transgression against the rules and codes—above all those relating to the body—of the groups to which humans belong or with which they identify. Especially in the first volume of *The Civilizing Process*, shame is a leading Eliasian concept. Social constraints brought about 'a veritable explosion of shame', in Scheff's words (2000: 89). Elias argues that shame denotes a crisis emotion: it is an emotion 'to be avoided and, if that is not possible, ignored', while on the other hand it is an emotion that is almost impossible to evade or disregard (see also Elias 1998*a*). With the advance of self-constraints and its associated self-awareness, the disgust of the natural functions of the body—particularly one's own—is also moving forward. In turn, the embarrassment of the body encourages humans to increasingly repress their sexuality and aggression—in a word, to constrain themselves. As Smith (2000*a*: 149) says: 'civilization is rooted in shame, shame is, in turn, rooted in the body'.

In this constraint–shame dynamic, however, one essential variable is missing: humiliation, shame's 'half-sister' (Smith 2001*a*). In *The Civilizing Process*, Elias argues that courtly etiquette, which developed in part as a way of managing shame feelings pertaining to the body, was furthermore used to debase those who did not know their place. But Smith argues that Elias fails to treat the humiliating aspect systematically enough: 'humiliation and shame are two of the best-kept secrets in modern societies and modern organisations' (in Van Iterson *et al.* 2002: 41). Shame may have the effect of both disciplining and integrating an 'offender' within an organizational group. Humiliation has the capacity to undermine the identity of its victims and expel them from collectivities and positions. Smith shows how shame and humiliation may vary in relation to power balances, established-outsiders dynamics, the type and degree of informalization, and whether or not human rights are recognized within the organizations. This seems a promising avenue for further research.

Without denying the prevalence of humiliation in organizational arenas, *shaming* seems the more fundamental concept. It can also comprise softer, more familiar forms of degradation. For sure, making individuals or groups bow their head is the outcome of power display. Whether the intent of shaming people is to discipline and (re)integrate organizational members or to undermine their identity, possibly via expulsion, it cannot be successful without asymmetric power balances in the organization. And shame can only be acknowledged by the shamed when the power display by superiors or peers is accepted. If the correction or degradation remains unacknowledged, e.g. because it is felt as being too painful, hidden shame may cause anger at the individual level (Scheff and Retzinger 1991), and perhaps organizations become neurotic (cf. Kets de Vries and Miller 1984).

When shaming becomes sheer humiliation, the civilizing process turns into its opposite. Such trends are labeled as decivilizing processes (for a general discussion, see Mennell 1990). These processes are visible in total institutions such as mental asylums, prisons, and ultimately the concentration camp that aim at bringing about 'group disgrace', of which genocide is the most extreme form (Elias 1996, 1998*a*). The civilizing process is thus potentially caustic; it contains the possibility of turning into its opposite. The notion of the 'civilizing offensive' (e.g. Mitzman 1987), used to denote organized efforts by classes and interest groups to accelerate the civilizing process, may express this inherent ambiguity. Making humans more civilized by assaulting them via an 'offensive' is surely a hazardous venture.

De Swaan (2001) tries to avoid interpreting decivilizing processes as total regression or 'a breakdown of civilization' or, as some postmodern thinkers would have it, as a manifestation of modernity, or even its very essence. At the core of the civilizing process an opposite current may manifest itself, De Swaan argues. This allows extreme violence and destruction on a mass scale to be perpetrated towards specific categories of people, while civilized relations and modes of expression are maintained in other sections of society. Identification with one group can concur with disidentification with another group. De Swaan proposes to denote this compartmentalization of behavior with the notion of *dys*civilizing processes. This *habitus* differentiation is often illustrated with the case in point of the 'servant of death' who chases concentration camp prisoners into the gas chambers, whereas, in the evening, enjoys the company of his wife and children, and listens to Schubert songs. Dyscivilizing processes, however, may also be observed in less dramatic forms, in more peaceful organizations such as the ones we usually study.

15.5. Discussion

This chapter began with the observation that Elias's sociology has hardly received attention in organizational studies. There are a few exceptions. These include Dopson 1997, 2001, 2005; Newton 1999, 2001; Smith 2001*b*; Van Iterson, Mastenbroek, and Soeters 2001; Van Iterson *et al.* 2002; and Stacey 2005, some of which already have been referred to above. A number of these studies lean largely on post-war work of Elias, particularly *What is Sociology?* (1970). For instance, Dopson (2005) seeks to explore the relevance of Elias's 'figurational, or process sociological approach' to the study of managing change in the medical profession. She particularly takes in Elias's concept of 'figurations' and his understanding of 'longer term unplanned processes'. Aspects of external and self-constraints are not contained in the discussion. The same, 'pure' figurational and processural approach marks her previous studies in the health industry (1997, 2001). Stacey (2005) calls upon Elias's essay on involvement and detachment (1987*a*), originally published in 1956, to affirm that mainstream organizational literature and development programs are still promoting 'magico-mythical thinking'. To talk about culture 'as a system that someone can design and move about' confers an 'illusion of control' and is thus a far cry from a rational, detached mode of thinking. Stacey also engages with Elias's *The Civilizing Process*—again, not so much with regard to changes in constrained behavior, but more to illustrate that Elias, with his incessant macro–micro linking, too has dealt with 'global patterns' and 'local interaction', which are Stacey's central organizational concerns in this volume. For Stacey, *The Civilizing Process* serves thus mainly as a source of methodological inspiration.

An important contribution is provided by Newton's 2001 *Organization* article on the relevance and limitations of Elias in organizational studies. Newton examines the relationship between interdependency, power, and subjectivity. An Eliasian approach to (our sense of) subjectivity in organizations would be to see it as a 'product of generations of interwoven interdependency networks'. Only then one can overcome regarding subjectivity on the work floor as 'self-evident' and detached from the experience of others, which is what people tend to do. In his plea for a long-term perspective to grasp networked agency, Newton summarizes *The Civilizing Process* theory to assert how the 'subjectivity' of knights, chieftains, and courtiers was interwoven with 'figurational change' (2001: 470). The article goes on to outline Elias's potentiality for a more informed understanding of strategy, change, knowledge, emotions, violence, and so on in current organizations. Newton admits that the presented ideas are in need of further development. The same may be said of the essays in Van Iterson *et al.* (2002). They call attention to organizational topics such as meeting behavior, gossip, privacy, and also corporate governance—all in an Eliasian glow. However, more empirical research in these topics seems warranted. Part three of this edited volume is labeled 'Crossing Cultures'. It contains a comparative study of organizational coordination in France and Germany, as well as case studies on the development of Chinese management and of business education in India. To apply Elias's perspective to cross-cultural research in management and organization is an outstandingly promising avenue for further study.

Norbert Elias was—and still is—much of an outsider in sociology. No doubt, he has been marginalized by the established in the field. But one also has the impression that he treasured this position, which would be quite at odds with his fundamental notion of human interdependency. For one thing, Elias typically did not acknowledge fellow sociologists (e.g. Pels 1991: 179). This is regrettable. Elias owed a lot to Marx (and Engels) in that he followed the famous sixth thesis on Feuerbach, which maintains that 'the human essence is no abstraction inherent in each single individual. In its reality it is the ensemble of the social relations' (Marx and Engels 1970: 122; cf. Van Krieken 1998). Why did Elias accept the primacy of social structure, but hardly give (capitalistic) relations of production a place in his writings? Other remarkable discrepancies with classical sociologists remain unresolved as well. Above, I have, in passing, referred to Durkheim's and Weber's position regarding topics that are also central to Elias. Durkheim's fear of anomie resulting from social differentiation and Weber's apprehension of the 'iron cage' of rationalization stand in stark contrast to Elias's optimism regarding the two developments. What grounds did Elias have not to follow Durkheim and Weber in their worried analysis of modernity? Unfortunately, Elias has not opted for an explicit dialogue with his predecessors.[5]

In a book review, Zygmunt Bauman (1979: 123) stated that Elias was 'perhaps the last representative of classical sociology, someone striving after the great synthesis'. This compliment annoyed Elias. He 'would rather be the first one to open up a new path' (Elias 1994: 75). Former pupil—but not follower—Anthony Giddens (1992: 389) has described Elias's work as 'an extraordinary achievement, anticipating issues which came to be generally explored in social theory only at a much later date'. Indeed, as the last of the classical sociologists, Elias has particularly fulfilled the role of precursor. On account of his relentless attention to the power inequalities characteristic of human interdependencies, which lead to disciplining and self-regulation of all involved, Elias may be regarded as the forerunner of Michel Foucault, that most uncompromising observer of the making of the 'modern soul'.

Of paramount significance in the Eliasian approach, it is argued above, are (1) the explicit long-term study of social processes stretching far into the pre-industrial

[5] Another case in point is Elias's neglect of other classical sociological work on civilization. For instance, in their famous 'Note on the Notion of Civilization', Durkheim and Mauss ([1913] 1998) define 'civilizational processes' as 'those symbolic cultural processes common to two or more societies sharing geographical proximity'. Their approach to civilization—and, of course, Max Weber's work on various civilizations—has not only been taken up by many sociologists but also is echoed in the literatures of contemporary comparative cultural analysts such as Inglehart (1997). It would be interesting to link Elias's work on French civilization to these studies.

era, (2) the persistent attempt to show the intricate connection between macro-level societal developments and micro-level changes in behavior and *habitus*, (3) the focus on figurations (or networks) of humans instead of on individuals responding to 'their' group, organization, or environment at large, and (4) the plea to come to an integrated 'human science'. These four ambitions may be a source of inspiration for organizational studies. On average, organizational scholars do not transcend the industrial era when trying to capture the emergence of organizations and their specific features (e.g. Kieser 1994).[6] Also, many are still inclined to separate micro from macro, individual from organization, and sociology from psychology.

But these are mainly methodological issues. We do not need the core content of *The Civilizing Process* theory to learn these lessons. What can we gain from the civilizing thesis as such? In the previous section, I explored some essential Eliasian concepts (increasing constraints, interdependencies, shame) and some complementary and counter concepts, advanced by Elias himself or others (informalization, proximity, and shaming). I have tried to link these basic ideas to the study of organizations by proposing domains and issues to which *The Civilizing Process* theory may shed light. These were but modest suggestions that require much more systematic elaboration.

The overall discussion may suggest that Elias's main work is beset with theoretical and ethical problems. This is indeed a position taken by various critics. However, it would be pitiful to do away with *The Civilizing Process* altogether. How can this work be 'saved'? This question has been brought forward by Mouzelis (1995) in his appeal to return to the achievements made by 1950s' and early 1960s' sociologists.

Mouzelis points out that civilizing processes in one area (say, table manners) do not rule out decivilizing processes in another (say, violence surrounding sporting events). When one can agree on that, Mouzelis concludes rather bluntly, *The Civilizing Process* theory boils down to the hypothesis that an increase in differentiation and interdependence does lead to growing self-regulation and refined behavior in some instances, but in other instances it does not. But it would be too simple to conclude that *The Civilizing Process* theory therefore has no explanatory value. Its apparent weakness could be turned into strength. The question then is: where does it happen and where not? To 'save' Eliasian analysis, universalistic pretensions should be brought to light and more 'modest' case studies should be undertaken. Where, when, and under what conditions do we witness accelerations of civilizing, decivilizing, and dyscivilizing trends? One should look at spurts in civilizing or decivilizing direction in specific settings and indicate as precisely as one's sociological imagination allows the impact of (1) institutional constraints and (2) actors' enactments.

[6] One exception is provided by the population-ecology perspective in organization studies. A comparison with Elias's work might be instructive, especially when the concept of 'indeterminacy' (of outcomes of evolutionary processes) (e.g. Aldrich and Rueff 2006: 32–3) is included in the assessment. The ecological approach stays far away of teleological thinking, which Elias also aspires to do.

Elias's civilizing process theory has been developed in a specific setting—the places where Occidental elites lived—but then the findings have been too widely extrapolated. Above we have also noticed that Elias's sensitivity for actors' enactments (agency) has remained quite modest, despite his recognition that the dynamics of human figurations are triggered by individual preferences and actions. With regard to institutional constraints, Mouzelis comes to a similar conclusion. Elias's notion of figuration as an umbrella concept for all human collectivities has obscured the distinctiveness of institutions in relation to, for example, a courtiers' circle, a football team, or a working-class neighborhood. Therefore, Eliasian analysis could gain from introducing the impact of institutions on (de)civilizing spurts. Arguably, institutional (de)civilizing will produce more rapidly changes in *habitus*, given the stronger power basis of institutions vis-à-vis 'normal' groups. Also in organizational analysis, the study of (de)civilizing spurts within and between specific institutional spheres seems particularly promising. Comparative analysis of processes of civilizing, decivilizing, and dyscivilizing behavior in organizations and their various stakeholding institutions would be a case in point.

To recapitulate, a stricter contextualization of the study of civilizing processes, as called for above, is warranted. Indirectly, De Swaan's notion of compartmentalization, see above, may be taken on. Decivilizing trends in corporate boardrooms may well concur with civilizing trends on the work floor and vice versa.

Furthermore, more critical attention should be given to the pitfalls of naïve interpretation of texts and talk. It is imperative to ask critical questions such as: where, when and under what organizational conditions are things written or said, or not written or said, by whom and with which intentions? Eliasian analysis can learn from postmodernist sophistication, in this respect.

Let us return once more to the ethicality of the Eliasian project. *The Civilizing Process* still is subject to fierce disputes between sociologists, historians, psychologists, and anthropologists. The most severe criticism is that Elias has been charged with ethnocentrism (for a summary of the disagreement, see Mennell 1998: 228–34). For instance, Goody (2006) makes a strong point in demonstrating that *The Civilizing Process* theory suggests a kind of universalism, putting Western civilization on top of a process that apparently is only at a lower stage of development elsewhere in the world. In this respect, Duerr (1993: 12) accuses Elias of attributing to the military and technical dominance of Western Europe 'superiority in the modeling of drive structure'. Others (e.g. Mennell 1998; Burkitt 1996) have defended Elias's project against such disapproval. Indeed, it can be argued that the choice of Western Europe as a study object must be seen in terms of feasibility: researchers' time and energy are limited and the point has to be made somewhere.

Another line of protective reasoning goes like this: Elias's perspective has always been 'humanity as a whole'; charges of ethnocentrism are therefore beside the point. Studying processes of organizing in a great variety of institutional contexts using the Eliasian approach could contribute to this debate on the universalistic pretensions—or alleged pretensions—of *The Civilizing Process* theory. The application of Elias's sociology to organizational studies therefore not only is beneficial to our understanding of organizational structures and behavior but would also enhance the impact and depth of Elias's wider theorizing. The benefit may go in both directions.

Acknowledgments

The author would like to thank Peter Berends, Peer Fiss, Maksim Kokushkin, Mark F. Peterson, Robert R. Roe, and all the participants to the workshop *The Relevance of the Classics for Organization Theory* in Philadelphia, 8–10 August 2007, for their comments on the first draft.

References

Aldrich, H., and Rueff, M. (2006). *Organizations Evolving*. London: Sage.

Barraclough, G. (1982). 'Clockwork History'. *New York Review of Books*, 21 October.

Bauman, Z. (1979). 'The Phenomenon of Norbert Elias'. *Sociology*, 13: 117–25.

Bendix, R. (1956). *Work and Authority in Industry*. New York: Wiley.

Bourdieu, P., and Passeron, J.-C. (1990). *Reproduction in Education, Society, and Culture*. 2nd edn. London: Sage.

Burkitt, I. (1993). 'Overcoming Metaphysics: Elias and Foucault on Power and Freedom'. *Philosophy of the Social Sciences*, 23/1: 50–72.

—— (1996). 'Civilization and Ambivalence'. *British Journal of Sociology*, 47/1: 135–50.

Castiglione, B. (1991). *The Book of the Courtier*. Harmondsworth: Penguin.

Clegg, S. R. (1990). *Modern Organizations: Organization Studies in a Postmodern World*. London: Sage.

Courpasson, D. (2000). 'Managerial Strategies of Domination: Power in Soft Bureaucracies'. *Organization Studies*, 21/1: 141–61.

De Swaan, A. (2001). 'Dyscivilization, Mass Extermination and the State'. *Theory, Culture and Society*, 18/2–3: 265–76.

Dopson, S. (1997). *Managing Ambiguity and Change: The Case of the NHS*. Basingstoke: Macmillan.

—— (2001). 'Applying an Eliasian Approach to Organizational Analysis'. *Organization*, 8/3: 515–35.

—— (2005). 'The Diffusion of Medical Innovations: Can Figurational Sociology Contribute?' *Organization Studies*, 26/8: 1125–44.

Duerr, H. P. (1988). *Der Mythos vom Zivilisationsprozess: Nacktheit und Scham*. Frankfurt a/M: Suhrkamp.

Duerr, H. P. (1990). *Der Mythos vom Zivilisationsprozess: Intimität*. Frankfurt a/M: Suhrkamp.
—— (1993). *Der Mythos vom Zivilisationsprozess: Obszönität und Gewalt*. Frankfurt a/M: Suhrkamp.
—— (1997). *Der Mythos vom Zivilisationsprozess: Der erotische Leib*. Frankfurt a/M: Suhrkamp.
—— (2002). *Der Mythos vom Zivilisationsprozess: Die Tatsachen des Lebens*. Frankfurt a/M: Suhrkamp.
Duindam, J. (1995). *Myths of Power: Norbert Elias and the Early-Modern Court*. Amsterdam: Amsterdam University Press.
Durkheim, É. (1947). *The Division of Labor in Society*. New York: Free Press.
—— and Mauss, M. ([1913] 1998). 'Note on the Notion of Civilization', in J. Rundell and S. Mennell (eds.), *Classical Readings in Culture and Civilization*. London: Routledge.
Elias, N. ([1939] 2000). *The Civilizing Process: Sociogenetic and Psychogenetic Investigations*. Oxford: Blackwell.
—— (1970). *What is Sociology?* New York: Columbia University Press.
—— (1983). *The Court Society*. Oxford: Basil Blackwell.
—— (1987*a*). *Involvement and Detachment: Contributions to the Sociology of Knowledge*. Oxford: Blackwell.
—— (1987*b*). 'The Retreat of Sociologists into the Present'. *Theory, Culture and Society*, 4/2–3: 223–47.
—— (1991*a*). *The Society of Individuals*. Oxford: Blackwell.
—— (1991*b*). *The Symbol Theory*. London: Sage.
—— (1991*c*). *Time: An Essay*. Oxford: Basil Blackwell.
—— (1993). *Mozart: Portrait of a Genius*. Cambridge: Polity.
—— (1994). *Reflections on a Life*. Cambridge: Polity Press.
—— (1996). *The Germans: Power Struggles and the Development of Habitus in the Nineteenth and Twentieth Centuries*. Cambridge: Polity Press.
—— (1998*a*). 'Group Charisma and Group Disgrace', in J. Goudsblom and S. Mennell (eds.), *The Norbert Elias Reader*. Oxford: Blackwell.
—— (1998*b*). *Norbert Elias: On Civilisation, Power and Knowledge*, ed. J. Goudsblom and S. Mennell. Chicago: Chicago University Press.
—— and Dunning, E. (1986). *Quest for Excitement: Sport and Leisure in the Civilizing Process*. Oxford: Basil Blackwell.
—— and Scotson, J. L. ([1965] 1994). *The Established and the Outsiders*. London: Frank Cass.
Fineman, S. (1996). 'Emotion and Organizing', in S. R. Clegg, C. Hardy, and W. Nord (eds.), *Handbook of Organization Studies*. London: Sage.
Fletcher, J. (1997). *Violence and Civilization: An Introduction to the Work of Norbert Elias*. Cambridge: Polity.
Foucault, M. (1975). *Discipline and Punish: The Birth of the Prison*. New York: Pantheon Books.
Giddens, A. (1992). 'Review of "The Society of Individuals"'. *American Journal of Sociology*, 98/2: 388–9.
Goody, J. (2006). *The Theft of History*. Cambridge: Cambridge University Press.
Gordon, D. (1994). *Citizens Without Sovereignty: Equality and Sociability in French Thought, 1670–1789*. Princeton: Princeton University Press.

—— (2002). 'The Canonization of Norbert Elias in France: A Critical Perspective'. *French Politics, Culture, and Society*, 20/1: 68–94.

Goudsblom, J. (1977). *Sociology in the Balance*. Oxford: Basil Blackwell.

—— (1987). 'The Sociology of Norbert Elias: Its Resonance and Significance'. *Theory, Culture and Society*, 4/2–3: 323–37.

—— (2000). 'Norbert Elias and American Sociology'. *Sociologia Internationalis*, 38/2: 173–80.

—— (2007). 'Shame as Social Pain'. Elias forum on the internet, http://elias-i.nfshost.com, retrieved 23 May 2007.

Gracián, B. (1994). *The Art of Worldly Wisdom: A Pocket Oracle*. London: Mandarin.

Inglehart, R. (1997). *Modernization and Postmodernization: Cultural, Economic and Political Change in 43 Societies*. Princeton: Princeton University Press.

Israëls, H., Komen, M., and De Swaan, A. (1993). *Over Elias*. Amsterdam: Het Spinhuis.

Kets de Vries, M., and Miller, D. (1984). *The Neurotic Organization: Diagnosing and Changing Counterproductive Styles of Management*. San Francisco: Jossey-Bass.

Kieser, A. (1994). 'Why Organization Theory Needs Historical Analysis—and How This should be Performed'. *Organization Science*, 5: 608–20.

—— (1998). 'From Freemasons to Industrious Patriots: Organizing and Disciplining in 18th Century Germany'. *Organization Studies*, 19/1: 47–71.

Kilminster, R. (1998). *The Sociological Revolution: From the Enlightenment to the Global Age*. London: Routledge.

—— (2007). *Norbert Elias: Post-Philosophical Sociology*. London: Routledge.

Kuzmics, H. (1991). 'Embarrassment and Civilization: On Some Similarities and Differences in the Work of Goffman and Elias'. *Theory, Culture, and Society*, 8: 1–30.

McAuley, J., Duberley, J., and Johnson, P. (2007). *Organization Theory*. Harlow: Prentice Hall.

McKendrick, N. (1961). 'Josiah Wedgwood and Factory Discipline'. *Historical Journal*, 4/1: 30–55.

Marx, K., and Engels, F. (1970). *The German Ideology*. New York: International Publishers.

Mastenbroek, W. (2000). 'Organizational Behavior as Emotion Management', in N. Ashkanasy, C. Härtel, and W. Zerbe (eds.), *Emotions in the Workplace: Research, Theory, and Practice*. Westport, Conn.: Quorum Books.

Mennell, S. (1990). 'Decivilizing Processes: Theoretical Significance and Some Lines of Research'. *International Sociology*, 5: 205–23.

—— (1998). *Norbert Elias: An Introduction*. Dublin: University College Dublin Press.

—— (2007). *The American Civilizing Process*. Cambridge: Polity.

Mitzman, A. (1987). 'The Civilizing Offensive: Mentalities, High Culture and Individual Psyches'. *Journal of Social History*, 20/4: 663–87.

Mouzelis, N. (1995). *Sociological Theory: What Went Wrong? Diagnosis and Remedies*. London: Routledge.

Newton, T. (1997). 'An Historical Sociology of Emotion?' in G. Bendelow and S. Williams (eds.), *Emotions in Social Life: Social Theories and Contemporary Issues*. London: Sage.

—— (1999). 'Power, Subjectivity and British Industrial and Organizational Sociology: The Relevance of the Work of Norbert Elias'. *Sociology*, 33/2: 411–40.

—— (2001). 'Organization: The Relevance and the Limitations of Elias'. *Organization*, 8/3: 467–95.

Pels, D. (1991). 'Elias and the Politics of Theory'. *Theory, Culture, and Society*, 8: 177–83.

Pollard, S. (1965). *The Genesis of Modern Management.* Cambridge, Mass.: Harvard University Press.

Rojek, C. (1986). 'Problems of Involvement and Detachment in the Writings of Norbert Elias'. *British Journal of Sociology,* 37/4: 584–96.

Rosenwein, B. (2006). *Emotional Communities in the Early Middle Ages.* Ithaca, NY: Cornell University Press.

Scheff, T. J. (2000). 'Shame and the Social Bond: A Sociological Theory'. *Sociological Theory,* 18: 86–99.

—— and Retzinger, S. M. (1991). *Emotions and Violence: Shame and Rage in Destructive Conflicts.* Lexington, Mass.: Lexington Books.

Smith, D. (2001*a*). *Norbert Elias & Modern Social Theory.* London: Sage.

—— (2001*b*). 'Organizations and Humiliation: Looking Beyond Elias'. *Organization,* 8/3: 537–60.

Stacey, R. (2005). *Experiencing Emergence in Organizations.* London: Routledge.

Van Iterson, A., Mastenbroek, W., and Soeters, J. (2001). 'Civilising and Informalising: Organizations in an Eliasian Context'. *Organization,* 8/3: 497–514.

—— —— Newton, T., and Smith, D. (2002). *The Civilized Organisation: Norbert Elias and the Future of Organisation Studies.* Amsterdam: Benjamins.

Van Krieken, R. (1998). *Norbert Elias: Key Sociologist.* London: Routledge.

Wouters, C. (1977). 'Informalization and the Civilizing Process', in P. Gleichmann, J. Goudsblom, and H. Korte (eds.), *Human Figurations: Essays for Norbert Elias.* Amsterdam: Amsterdams Sociologisch Tijdschrift.

—— (1986). 'Formalization and Informalization: Changing Tension Balances in Civilizing Processes'. *Theory, Culture, and Society,* 3/2: 1–18.

—— (1990). 'Social Stratification and Informalization in Global Perspective'. *Theory, Culture, and Society,* 7: 69–90.

Zald, M. N. (1996). 'More Fragmentation? Unfinished Business in Linking the Social Sciences and the Humanities'. *Administrative Science Quarterly,* 41/2: 251–61.

PART III

AMERICAN PERSPECTIVES

CHAPTER 16

THORSTEIN VEBLEN AND THE ORGANIZATION OF THE CAPITALIST ECONOMY

GARY G. HAMILTON

MISHA PETROVIC

16.1. Introduction

Among those economists whose writings straddle the nineteenth and twentieth centuries, only Max Weber (1864–1920) and Thorstein Veblen (1857–1929) continue to influence how sociologists, writing a century later, understand the rise and success of industrial capitalism. Weber's influence on latter-day sociologists is, of course, great; so immense, in fact, that sociologists have selectively forgotten Weber's disavowal of sociology (Schluchter 1989: 3–4) and his continuing involvement in the methodological struggles within the economics of his time (Ringer 1997). Disregarding history, sociologists have canonized Weber as one of the founders of their discipline. In contrast to Weber, Veblen's influence among sociologists, while substantial before the 1950s, is now very modest and is mostly confined to one item in Veblen's oeuvre. That one piece, *The Theory of the Leisure Class*, published in 1899, was Veblen's first book. It is rightly regarded as a classic, but a rather curious one, known mainly for Veblen's acerbic wit skewering upper-class Americans. In today's sociology, the book is primarily mined for one of its key concepts, 'conspicuous consumption'. This term remains on a relatively short list of sociological concepts coined in the nineteenth century that continue to be used today and that are still attached to the persons who originally coined them. Other than this one work, and other than this one key concept with which it is associated, sociologists coming of age in the 1970s or later remember very little about Thorstein Veblen.[1]

Veblen's legacy, if not his current influence, has fared much better in economics than in sociology. Unlike Weber, whom economists rarely cite as one of their own, Veblen remains an economist to economists and sociologists alike. Practitioners of both disciplines acknowledge him, along with Commons and Mitchell, as one, and arguably the most important, of the founders of the institutional school in American economics.[2] From its beginnings in the late 1890s through World War II, institutionalism was an extremely influential school of thought among American economists, social reformers, and New Deal planners (Yonay 1998), and Veblen himself was widely read and much admired (Gruchy 1958).

For example, Veblen is widely credited with developing, in *The Theory of Business Enterprise* (1904), an account of organized capitalism that Edward Chamberlin later expanded in his path-breaking *Theory of Monopolistic Competition* ([1933] 1962). This work, together with the work of Joan Robinson, laid the foundation for 'industrial organization', a subfield in the discipline of economics. Berle and Means (1933) explicitly drew on Veblen's last book, *Absentee Ownership and the Business Enterprise in Recent Times* (1923), to develop their famous theory of America's managerial revolution based on the separation of ownership and management in modern corporations. Veblen's book on *Imperial Germany and the Industrial Revolution* (1915) describes the advantages of latecomers long before Gerschenkron (1962) made the same, and now better known, observation (Ozawa 2004). Foss (1998) convincingly argues that, with his persistent and acute analysis of the roles of engineers and workmanship in modern industrial firms, Veblen was the first to fashion a 'competence-based approach' to understand modern firms, an approach that Penrose (1959), Chandler (1977, 1990), and others later elaborated and that has become standard fare in the business-school approach to modern corporations. Finally, as we will describe in more detail below, Veblen's major influence on economists today comes

[1] This failure of the collective memory for sociologists is true not only for Veblen but also for all the other scholars writing during the renaissance of American social science, an era named after the philosophy of the day: pragmatism.

[2] Oliver Williamson (1994) pushed these earlier economists aside when he categorized their writings collectively as the 'old institutionalism', in contrast to the 'new institutionalism' that he and his colleagues were building up from the writings of Ronald Coase.

from his being an advocate of economics as an evolutionary science and, linked to this advocacy, from his thorough critique of the mainstream economics of his time.

Veblen (1899–1900) coined the term 'neoclassical economics' to refer to the marginalists, particularly the school of thought gathering around Alfred Marshall, whose *Principles of Economics* (1890) was then (and continued to be later) the most influential book in economics (Aspromourgos 1986). Veblen used the term 'neoclassical' to show that the preconceptions underlying the classical economics of Adam Smith carried forward to the work of Marshall and others who cast economics in non-evolutionary terms. We will discuss Veblen's critique later in this chapter, but it is important to note here that the institutionalists' main rival for the 'soul' of American economics, the neoclassical marginalists led by John Bates Clark (Yonay 1998), did not find Veblen's work to be interesting or scientific enough, a statement that applies to orthodox economists both then and now.

Some years later, Ronald Coase (1984: 230; cited by Williamson 1994: 78), whose work established the 'new institutionalist' school, an extension of the neoclassical approach to the analysis of formal organizations and legal norms, wrote that the 'old' institutionalism, including Veblen's work, comprised a 'mass of descriptive material waiting for a theory, or a fire'. Similarly, writing from the point of view of orthodox economics, Blaug observes:

> As we read [Veblen], we have the feeling that something is being 'explained.' Yet what are we really to make of it all? Although Veblen's books 'appear to be about economic theory... 'they are actually *interpretations of values and beliefs of the 'captains of industry.'* ... [H]e is continually hinting that *a description is a theory, or, worse, that the more penetrating is the description, the better is the theory.* (1985: 709–10, our emphasis)

Blaug concludes, 'in the final analysis, institutional economics did not fulfill its promise to supply a viable alternative to neoclassical economics and for that reason... it gradually faded away. The moral of the story is simply this: it takes a new theory, and not just the destructive exposure of assumptions or the collections of new facts, to beat an old theory' (ibid. 710).

True as this statement about theory may be in general, it misrepresents the range of possible theories and equates the meaning of theory with a very narrow conception of what theory signifies in neoclassical economics. Moreover, this criticism notwithstanding, Veblen and the old institutionalism did not fade away. They are back. With the supremacy of the Chicago School of neoclassical economics in the closing decades of the twentieth century, it appeared momentarily that Veblen's works were destined to become a footnote, and institutionalism, a brief interlude in the history of economics. In the last twenty years, however, the theoretical base of economics has undergone a 'fundamental shift... away from neoclassical economics' (Colander, Holt, and Rosser 2004: 485). Economists are now finding that the formerly heterodox schools of economics, including the 'old institutionalists,' are now useful to those working 'on the edge of economics' because 'these schools can play an important role in developing new critiques of the orthodoxy' (ibid. 492).

It is in this context that Veblen, the acute observer of American organized capitalism in its formative years, provides both sociologists and economists working a century later with the 'penetrating descriptions' they could use to develop theories of contemporary capitalism. The intervening century between the time when Veblen wrote and the state of the capitalism today is the period needed to 'test' Veblen's descriptions, to turn those meeting the test into descriptions of contemporary capitalism, and perhaps even to realize Veblen's ambition to make economics (and economic sociology as well) into an evolutionary science, a science based on what Veblen (1898*c*) called 'cumulative causation'.

We divide our discussion of Veblen's work into two parts. In the first part of the chapter, we emphasize three of Veblen's most important observations about early twentieth-century capitalism: (1) an interpretation of economic development as the evolution of economic institutions; (2) the importance of consumption, and of factors that drive consumption, for capitalist growth; and (3) the recurring organizational (and ideological) tension between 'industrial arts and craftsmanship', on the one hand, and 'business strategies and salesmanship', on the other hand. In the second part of the chapter, we show how Veblen's insights of a century ago are, if anything, more useful today than they were when he first wrote them. Here we stress, in reverse order: (1) the importance of analyzing firms as both producers of goods and services (industrial arts and craftsmanship) and market makers (business strategies and salesmanship); (2) the significance of consumer goods markets for driving contemporary capitalism; and (3) the need to revise economic and sociological theories of capitalism and business enterprise towards Veblen's developmental conception of cumulative causation and away from approaches having equilibrium or productionist biases.

16.2. Veblen's Description of American Capitalism

16.2.1. Veblen as a Theorist

Locked into their own narrow conceptions of theory, the neoclassical critics of Veblen got it wrong. Veblen was a theorist through and through, and his books and articles should be read that way. Veblen's descriptions of early twentieth-century American capitalism are never mere descriptions. Veblen did not conduct interviews, run surveys, or use historical documents systematically. Very much a person of his times, Veblen dabbled in empirical analysis. Every now and then, he used government reports and statistics, newspaper accounts, and personal observations, but generally he did not document his observations. His frequent footnotes do not provide documentary evidence for what is in the text, but rather extend his analyses by offering additional ideas. Veblen (1898*c*: 375) claimed his approach was inductive, a 'realistic' approach that 'deal[s] with the facts'. His intent, however, was not to list the facts, but rather to go behind the facts and theorize the dynamic processes of capitalism, the processes of cumulative causation.

Veblen's theoretical stance was the result of a continuous process of positioning himself relative to other social scientists. Much is made of Veblen's early life and of the fact that he was an outsider and an iconoclast throughout his entire life.[3] These aspects of Veblen's personal life are apparent in his writings and certainly important, but in terms of Veblen's stature as a theorist, two aspects of his life stand out.

First, Veblen's doctorate was not in economics, but rather in philosophy.[4] With great sophistication, he repeatedly critiqued economists from the vantage point of the philosophic foundations of their theories, and he honed his own position with careful awareness of its philosophical implications. Moreover, Veblen was fully cognizant of the pragmatist movement in American philosophy that was in full swing at the turn of the century. Although he critiqued some of the utilitarian directions that pragmatism began to take with regard to science, Veblen accepted many of the philosophic tenets of the movement, especially, as we will explain below, the idea of the reflexive self.

Second, Veblen was a voracious reader of the economics of his time, especially of the economics coming out of Europe. While at the University of Chicago, during the formative part of his career, he was a prolific reviewer for the *Journal of Political Economy*, a journal that he helped to edit.[5] During this period between

[3] The sixth child of twelve, Veblen grew up in the rural outback of Minnesota and Wisconsin. His first language was Norwegian. He received no formal education until he attended Carleton College when he was seventeen. After graduating from Carleton, he followed his elder brother to Johns Hopkins University, where Thorstein had planned to study philosophy. Although he stayed at Johns Hopkins for less than a year, he did manage to take a course in logic from Charles Peirce, who coined the term 'pragmatism' and who was a friend and former colleague of William James. Johns Hopkins did not offer the philosophy courses that Veblen desired, so he moved on to Yale.

[4] Veblen's Ph.D. degree was earned, in 1884, at Yale University, where Veblen wrote his dissertation on an aspect of Kant's and Spencer's philosophies with the title of 'The Ethical Grounds of a Doctrine of Retribution'. Unable to get an academic job after finishing his degree, Veblen and his wife spent the rest of the decade living off his relatives and reading widely on many topics. His training in economics began in 1891, when he enrolled in Cornell University and studied with J. Laurence Laughlin, one of the leading conservative economists in the United States at the time. A year later, Laughlin moved to the newly founded University of Chicago, taking Veblen with him, to establish the Department of Economics.

[5] After he moved to the University of Chicago, J. Laurence Laughlin founded and was first editor of the *Journal of Political Economy*.

1892 and 1906, he wrote no less than forty-one book reviews under his name, and, according to his biographer (Dorfman 1934), he wrote many other reviews anonymously. The signed reviews covered works by such noted social thinkers as Sombart, Schmoller, Kautsky, Patten, Turgot, Tarde, Hobson, Ward, and Marx. A noted polyglot, Veblen frequently reviewed works written in German (12) and French (11) that were unfamiliar to his American contemporaries. During the same period, he also wrote long articles about the economics of noted theorists, including Böhm-Bawerk (1892), Adam Smith, his predecessors and followers (1899–1900), Schmoller (1901), Clark (1906*b*), and Marx and his followers (1906–7). As we describe below, Veblen knew exactly where he stood with regard to these thinkers.

16.2.2. Economics as an Evolutionary Science: Against the Equilibrium Bias

First and foremost, Veblen wanted economics to be an evolutionary science. Veblen's most important theoretical statements come early in his career, during roughly the same time that he was writing *The Theory of the Leisure Class* (1899*b*). Starting in 1898, Veblen (1898*b*, *c*; 1899–1900) published a series of articles that surveyed the mainstream economics of his time and its 'philosophical preconceptions'. In these works, he critiqued classical and neoclassical economics and laid the foundation for his own position. The most important and perhaps the most enduring element of this critique is the failure of mainstream economics to recognize and account for evolutionary change in economic institutions.

In 'Why Is Economics Not an Evolutionary Science?' (1898*c*), Veblen observed that economics, unlike other social sciences of his day, 'fell short of being an evolutionary science'. Both classical and neoclassical economics developed economics as a taxonomic science. Classical economists derived their taxonomies from their belief in 'natural laws'. 'With Adam Smith,' observed Veblen, 'the ultimate ground of economic reality is the design of God, the teleological order; and his utilitarian generalizations, as well as the hedonistic character of his economic man, are but methods of the working-out of this natural order' (1948: 258). In this characterization of human nature, hedonism is a consequence of the natural order and not its cause.

Neoclassical economists, observed Veblen, reversed the direction of causation. First, they thoroughly disliked the metaphysical natural law foundation of Smith, but they embraced the hedonistic conception of human nature, making hedonism the cause, rather than the consequence, of economic action. 'The hedonistic conception of man is that of a lightning calculator of pleasure and pains, who oscillates like a homogeneous globule of desire of happiness under the impulse of stimuli that shift him about the area, but leave him intact' (Veblen 1919*c*: 73).

Starting with this conception of human nature, the neoclassical economists used the 'deductive method' to establish 'a body of logically consistent propositions concerning the normal relations of things'. Underlying these propositions is the assumption that human action moves towards 'an equilibrium at the normal'. Veblen observes that an economics so construed is only a taxonomic science, a science lacking a theoretical framework capable of interpreting genuine long-term economic changes, evolutionary changes.

To Veblen, evolutionary economic change is not a historical progression of economic facts. 'Realism,' he notes, 'does not make an evolutionary science' (1919*c*: 58). In fact, the most realistic, fact-filled school of economics, the German Historical School, is, according to Veblen, the school of thought furthest removed from being an evolutionary science, from being a science at all. The practitioners of this school 'have contented themselves with the enumeration of data and a narrative account of industrial development, and have not presumed to offer a theory of anything or to elaborate their results into a consistent body of knowledge' (ibid.).

By contrast, an evolutionary science is 'a close-knit body of theory' (ibid.). To develop such a conception of economics, the most fundamental step is to reject the idea of an unchanging human nature and develop a conception of human action as changing and co-evolving with social institutions. Drawing on developments in the psychology of his day, Veblen outlined two distinct aspects of such a conception. First, individuals are knowing actors, ever engaged in the process of self-realization. '[I]t is the characteristic of man', wrote Veblen, 'to do something, not simply to suffer pleasure and pains through the impact of suitable forces. He is not simply a bundle of desires that are to be saturated by being placed in the path of the forces of the environment, but rather a coherent structure of propensities and habits which seeks realization and expression in an unfolding activity' (ibid. 74). Second, individuals are immersed in ongoing environments, and it is in such institutionalized environments that individuals' knowingness and self-realization are actualized. In this sense, individuals are reflexive; they are both creators of, and created by, their environments.[6] Veblen theorized:

> The economic life history of the individual is a cumulative process of adaptation of means to ends that cumulatively change as the process goes on, both the agent and his environment being at any point the outcome of the last process.... Economic action is teleological, in the sense that men always and everywhere seek to do something. What, in specific detail, they seek, is not to be answered except by a scrutiny of the details of their activity. (Ibid. 74–5)

This conception of human nature inexorably and causally connects individuals and their environments, and makes both co-involved in life as 'an unfolding activity'. 'Cumulative causation' is what Veblen regarded as an evolutionary point of view. Such a point of view, he noted, 'leaves no place for a formulation of natural

[6] This thesis is one of the basic principles of pragmatism. William James made a similar statement in his first major publication, 'Remarks on Spencer's Definition of Mind as Correspondence' (1878).

laws in terms of definitive normality, whether in economics or in any other branch of inquiry' (1898*c*: 378).

If evolutionary economics does not seek law-like propositions based on economic normality, what is, then, the proper focus of economics? To this question, Veblen answered, '[A]n evolutionary economics must be the theory of a process of cultural growth as determined by the economic interest, a theory of a cumulative sequence of economic institutions stated in terms of the process itself' (1898*c*: 393).

16.2.3. The Interpersonal Nature of Consumption: Invidious Comparisons

At the same time that Veblen developed his critiques of orthodox economic theory, he was also working on developing a theory of the processes and logic of consumption. The fullest statement of this theory is found in *The Theory of the Leisure Class* (1899*b*), but antecedents are found in his earliest publications (1891, 1894). On the surface, Veblen's theory of consumption seems relatively simple and disconnected from the theories of modern capitalism that he developed in his later books. In fact, economists today seldom discuss *The Theory of the Leisure Class* when addressing Veblen's contribution to economics. As Becker noted, for his work on consumption, Veblen 'is classified as a sociologist' (1996: 163). A close reading of Veblen's works, however, shows considerable theoretical consistency throughout his writings. For Veblen, consumption in the form of emulation is a major factor that drives the growth of the modern 'business system'.

The classical and neoclassical schools of economics, Veblen wrote, both presume 'a theory of a process of valuation' (1948: 271). The laws of supply and demand and the equilibrium of normal market exchanges assume that hedonistic individuals react simply and consistently to 'pecuniary stimulus' (ibid.). In contrast, Veblen's own theory of value is based on an active process of valuation, and on the process that is both interpersonal in nature and rooted in economic institutions.

According to Veblen, the central characteristic of consumption is for individuals to establish, through the use of symbolic goods, one's 'self worth' in comparison to others in the same environment. Such 'invidious comparison is a process of valuation of persons with respect of worth' (Veblen 1899*b*: 34). In his first publication (1891) as an economist, written while he was still at Cornell University, Veblen outlined this process of valuation as follows: first, the most important concern for the individual is 'his standing in the esteem of his fellow-men'. In order to establish 'one's dignity—and to sustain one's self respect... it is necessary to display the token of economic worth'. In industrial society, people strive for economic success in order to earn esteem, but success alone is not enough to establish one's good name. One needs to display that success through the emulation of a 'standard of living'. Such a standard of living is 'of a very elastic nature, capable of an indefinite extension.... [I]n a general way... this emulation in expenditure stands ever ready to absorb any margin of income that remains after ordinary physical wants and comforts have been provided for, and, further, that it presently becomes as hard to give up that part of one's habitual "standard of living" which is due to the struggle for respectability, as it is to give up many physical comforts' (Veblen 1891: 62–3).

Veblen goes to great length in his early articles and in *The Theory of the Leisure Class* to show that these processes of emulation are not new, but are nearly as old as human societies themselves, but he maintains that capitalist society provides a new and greater force to propel these processes forward.

> The modern industrial organization of society has practically narrowed the scope of emulation to this one line [pecuniary emulation]; and at the same time it has made the means of sustenance and comfort so much easier to obtain as very materially to widen the margin of human exertion that can be devoted to purposes of emulation.... [T]he easier the conditions of physical life for modern civilized man become, and the wider the horizon of each and the extent of personal contact of each with his fellowmen, and the greater the opportunity of each to compare notes with his fellows, the greater will be the preponderance of economic success as a means of emulation, and the greater the straining after economic respectability. (1891: 64–5)

Capitalism does not supply the means to fulfill human dreams or to end human wants. Instead, 'no advance in the average well-being of the community can end the struggle or lessen the strain (or) quiet the unrest whose source is the craving of everybody to compare favorably with his neighbor' (ibid. 65).

16.2.4. The Evolution of Consumption

The nuances of pecuniary emulation in the capitalist era, in the forms of conspicuous leisure and conspicuous consumption, are spelled out in great detail in *The Theory of the Leisure Class*. The original subtitle of Veblen's first book, *The Theory of the Leisure Class: An Economic Study of the Evolution of Institutions*, was also making a theoretical point in the midst of his sardonic descriptions of the aberrations of upper-class bourgeois life. The premise of the book was that, although the underlying processes of invidious comparisons are commonplace, they are not an aspect of human nature. Instead, they are linked to social institutions that develop and that change over time. As such, invidious comparisons and the institutional context in which they occur co-evolve.

In the early chapters of *The Theory of the Leisure Class*, Veblen described this co-evolution in only the most general way and instead refers his readers to a series of articles (1898*a*, 1898*c*, 1899*a*) published in the *American Journal of Sociology* 'for a more explicit statement of the theoretical position' (Veblen 1899*b*: v). However, in these articles, Veblen provides only a crude outline of pre-industrial economic institutions. Without giving any historical specifics, he refers to primitive (savage), barbarian, feudal, and industrial societies. He does not give a theory of evolution, or even suggest whether or how societies evolve from one type to another. These are not the necessary elements of his 'theoretical position'. Instead, in these articles, as well as in the book, Veblen argues that it is human nature to be active and to create the world in which people are themselves created. This fundamental aspect of human nature Veblen (1898*b*) equates to the 'instinct of workmanship'. Invidious comparisons, accompanied by emulation and conspicuous consumption, arise only when social institutions develop that support them and make them socially meaningful. Similarly, the 'irksomeness of labor' (and hence the need to compensate the aversion to work with a wage of work) took shape only when the institutions of property arose and the institutions of property arose only when a sense of ownership emerged.

> Ownership is not a simple and instinctive notion.... It is not something given to begin with, as an item of the isolated individual's mental furniture.... It is a conventional fact and has to be learned; it is a cultural fact which has grown into an institution in the past through a long course of habituation, and which is transmitted from generation to generation as all cultural facts are. (1898*a*: 360)

Veblen claimed that the idea of ownership developed when warfare became a way of life in human societies. This is at the dawn of 'barbarian' societies, societies that internally became differentiated between those supplying the necessary goods and services (which Veblen called 'industrial employment') and those engaged in warfare, governments, and aggressive displays of prowess. Only in such differentiated societies did consumption as a social marker of self-worth arise for the first time. After this point in time, the institutions of ownership, control, property, emulation, and consumption evolved along with the people whose activities created those institutions.

16.2.5. Consumption, Advertising, and Salesmanship

Veblen's distinction between workmanship as a basic instinct, on the one hand, and invidious comparison and emulation as evolving social institutions, on the other hand, is a theme that runs throughout his writings. In his early work, Veblen used this theme, as a point of theoretical leverage, to critique economic theory and social behavior. In his writings after the publication of *The Theory of the Leisure Class*, the theme shows up again in his analysis of corporate America, but now it becomes more refined, even as it becomes more utopian.

Veblen morally disliked emulation, conspicuous consumption, and waste of any kind. He morally embraced workmanship and saw workmanship as inherently opposed to, and in tension with, invidiousness and emulation. After the turn of the twentieth century, Veblen began to write about corporate America using the same rhetorical technique, this time pitting the industrial arts and workmanship against corporate financial and marketing strategies aimed at selling products for the sake of conspicuous consumption. The contradictory trends of making useful products, on the one hand, and of selling and making a profit from conspicuously styled products, on the other hand, provided Veblen with much grist for his mill.

Veblen scorned advertising as 'absentee salesmanship', as an appeal to the fear of shame, of losing prestige, whereby advertisers make the consumer purchase unnecessary articles at inflated prices. Salesmanship is 'an attempt to get something for nothing'. It capitalizes on human credulity; it is 'trading on that range of human infirmities which blossom in devout observances and bear fruit in psychopathic wards' (Veblen 1923). In terms of the satisfaction of the material needs of the community, all marketing activities are wasteful, contributing nothing to material production and inflating prices of consumer goods. While in retrospect all this may sound like just another, largely misguided, indictment of 'manipulative' advertising, it should not be forgotten that Veblen's criticism was not only one of the first and most influential attacks on advertising but also represents a valiant attempt to incorporate the analysis of consumption practices into the core of economic theory. In this sense, Veblen's emphasis on the importance of advertising and salesmanship foreshadows later arguments by Chamberlin. Moreover, this emphasis also led him to develop rudimentary macroeconomic analysis, well before Keynes. Veblen clearly saw the possibility that advertising-induced consumption preferences may serve to drive the productivity growth and to narrow the gap between retail prices and production costs, although he preferred to focus on the darker, more problematic aspects of the lack of equilibration of supply and demand at the macroeconomic level.

In summary, Veblen's analysis of consumption was based on three crucial points, all very much at odds with the mainstream economics of his time, and, somewhat ironically, very much in line with the understanding of consumption in the emerging marketing profession whose skills and practices Veblen despised so much. First, Veblen saw consumption as an interpersonal and thus an inherently social, rather than individual, phenomenon. Second, he emphasized that consumption patterns are deeply rooted in social institutions and that they co-evolve with these institutions. Third, he analyzed both the microeconomic and macroeconomic consequences of the impact of marketing efforts on consumption.

16.2.6. The Tension between Industrial and Business Systems

Veblen emphasized the distinction between workmanship and salesmanship not just in order to criticize conspicuous consumption but also, and more importantly, as a way to advance a more general theoretical agenda. This agenda was to analytically separate the institutions and activities of the actual market economy of his time, what he called the 'business system' or the 'pecuniary economy', on the one hand, from the underlying industrial system, or the 'state of industrial arts of the community', on the other hand. The distinction between the two systems—one based on the laws of exchange, the price system, and pecuniary motives, and the other on industrial technology, production, and efficiency—is the central analytical and ideological theme in all his major works appearing after *The Theory of the Leisure Class*. It is expressed in terms of a series of dichotomies.

The business system (the pecuniary economy)	**The industrial system (the state of industrial arts)**
acquisition	production
pecuniary activity	industrial activity
invidious (ceremonial)	non-invidious (technological)
salesmanship	workmanship
vested interest	'the common man'
sabotage	community serviceability
conscientious withdrawal of efficiency	productive enterprise
competition	coordination
predatory	peaceful
businessman	engineer
intangible assets	technology

To a greater degree than most of his contemporaries, Veblen saw the advanced mass market economy that emerged in the United States at the beginning of the twentieth century as a differentiated system that follows its own laws. He also saw it as a regressive, predatory, parasitic, and exploitative system. He regarded the intense competition between businesses, the rise of advertising and salesmanship, and speculation in financial markets, as inherently wasteful and detrimental to the community.

At the same time, this intense animosity towards the pecuniary economy made Veblen one of its best and shrewdest observers. It allowed him to avoid the tendency of both classical and neoclassical economics to assume a fairly simple and direct grounding of the market economy in some non-economic reality, such as the factors of production, the productivity of labor, hedonistic and utilitarian psychology, or self-interest. In Veblen's view, the pecuniary economy and the economy of industrial production are so fundamentally different, that every such attempt at grounding is bound to fail. Veblen reiterates this point in numerous reviews of classical, Marxist, institutionalist, and neoclassical economists. From Adam Smith to Clark and Fisher, he states, the main goal of most economists was (1) to interpret the realities of industrial production as purely pecuniary, exchange-driven phenomena; and (2) to show that all pecuniary phenomena stand in a direct relation to some fundamental non-pecuniary realities and thus are 'natural' and generally beneficial to the community. In other words, all non-pecuniary phenomena related to production and consumption, the two activities that according to Veblen should constitute the core subject matter of economics, have been explained away in the mainstream economics as but reflections of the pecuniary economy.

This theoretical strategy thus endowed purely pecuniary phenomena, such as credit, interest, money, capital, salesmanship, etc., with some non-pecuniary function. In his reviews of Fisher's writings on the nature of capital (1907) and interest (1909*a*), as well as in an article written in the same period, 'On the Nature of Capital' (1908*b*), Veblen exposes the pitfalls of this strategy and at the same time offers a sophisticated analysis of the nature of 'intangible assets' of the modern corporation. Interest, Veblen emphasizes, does not relate to some non-pecuniary psychological reality, such as a supposed preference for present over future income. Rather, it is a feature of the mature business economy developed on the basis of credit transactions, a purely pecuniary phenomenon (1909*a*). Similarly, modern capital consists of intangible assets, not productive goods as tangible objects (1907). *Pace* Fisher, in the modern corporate economy, capital wealth, i.e. the physical capital comprised of productive goods, is not the same as capital value, which is based on pecuniary capital and intangible assets. The intangible assets are capitalizations of 'differential advantages', against other businesses, and, ultimately, against the community at large. This capital typically has little, if any relation to the underlying real productive assets. Moreover, Veblen insists, the expansion of intangible assets through common stocks, financial capital, and credit, is a wasteful, parasitic, and anti-industrial development that results in misallocation of resources, high prices, and recurrent economic crises:

> [U]nder the price system—under the rule of pecuniary standards and management—circumstances make it advisable for the business man at times to mismanage the process of industry, in the sense that it is expedient for his pecuniary gain to inhibit, curtail, or misdirect industry, and so turn the community's technological proficiency to the community's detriment. (1908*b*: 111)

The conclusion that the pecuniary economy is not just differentiated from the system of production but also anti-industrial and wasteful, increasingly became the dominant theme in all Veblen's writings after the turn of the century. The 'received preconceptions' of 'certified economists and substantial citizens' hold that

> credit is deferred payment, capital is assembled 'production goods,' business is the helper of productive industry, salesmanship is the facility of the 'middleman,' money is 'the great wheel of circulation' employed in a 'refined system of barter,' and absentee ownership is a rhetorical solecism. (Veblen 1923: 419)

But, in reality, the pecuniary economy is a closed system where the benefits accrue only to the capitalists themselves. Even worse, in relation to industry, it is a system of deliberate sabotage and restriction, where the underproduction of material necessities is counter-balanced by the ever-increasing costs of salesmanship. Towards the end of his life, Veblen grew increasingly vitriolic about the current state of the American economy, utopian about the potential of the fully planned industrial economy devoid of the wastefulness of the business system, and pessimistic about whether such potential will ever be realized. Much has been said of his ideas about the 'Soviet of technicians', his role in the emergence of the technocratic movement, and his radical ideological stance. Those, however, are not the most enduring aspects of his work, and they do not capture the importance of his distinction between business and industry. From our current perspective, the importance of this distinction is neither in establishing a moral primacy of a certain vision of how to address human 'material' needs nor in showing the pitfalls of the current economic system. Rather, it lies in emphasizing the process of differentiation, and the resulting tension, between production and consumption, on the one hand, and the market economy, on the other. As Veblen has shown, neoclassical economists, as well as their Marxist and even institutionalist counterparts, have too often assumed that economy is, ultimately, about production and consumption. But their theories of production and of consumption never fit well with their theories of how the market economy itself operates, and the tension between the two sets of categories persists even today in theoretical as well as policy discourse.

16.3. The Relevance of Veblen

16.3.1. Veblen: A Century Later

Veblen was not the sort of writer whom neoclassical economists would regard as a theorist, but he was a theorist nonetheless, a theorist of economic and social processes underlying the transformation through which America was going during his lifetime. That said, however, in most regards, his writings do not hold up as well as, for instance, Weber's writings do. Veblen was not a methodologist or a system-builder. His writings are highly polemical, his examples and references eclectic, and his major works, while often packed with unexpected and profound insights, usually lack a coherent structure. A few basic theoretical themes, subsumed under the master dichotomy between the pecuniary economy and the industrial system, recur in most of his works.

Therefore, we should not overstate the immediacy and relevance of his writings for our times, but should also recognize at the same time that he pointed to core issues that remain relevant to us a century after he first wrote them. Veblen has been correctly labeled an institutional economist. He critiqued other economists, not so much for ignoring the economy's institutional context, but rather for their seeing institutions and their relation to the economy as fairly simple, static, unproblematic, and, in short, taxonomic. This oversimplification, in turn, also led to a misrepresentation of the 'inner workings' of the market economy, as when, for instance, Clark and Fisher tried to portray purely pecuniary phenomena as being directly grounded in some non-pecuniary realities.

This type of criticism is as valid today as it was in Veblen's time because the elaboration of the relations between economy and society remains the least developed part of economic analysis. To a great extent, this gap in economic analysis is due to the particular trajectory the development of economic theory took in the decades after Veblen's death. Veblen expected mainstream economics to turn increasingly into the study of business practices, thus limiting itself solely to the study of the pecuniary economy. He did not foresee that the move away from institutional analysis within the discipline of economics would take the shape of reinforcing and rendering ever more abstract the neoclassical theory of his time. With this focus, neoclassical economists remained committed to shallow, unrealistic, and often trivial representations of the way the economy relates to its institutional context.[7] If economists dealt with the issue at all, they did so to extend the taxonomic models used in the study of the market economy to other social phenomena.[8]

As such, Veblen offers us a foundation upon which we can continue to build a fuller and more precise understanding of the co-evolving relationships between economy and society during the past century. Veblen's writings explicitly provide three important building blocks for this foundation: (1) a recognition that pecuniary and industrial systems are distinct and in tension with each other; (2) an analysis of consumption and the link between consumption and the pecuniary economic institutions that grew as an intrinsic part of capitalism in America; and (3) a critique of neoclassical economics and the endorsement of an evolutionary perspective emphasizing cumulative causation.

[7] Interestingly, those disciplines that look deepest into the 'real' functioning of the market have developed in those fields that emphasize the study of business practices, especially strategic management and marketing research. In this sense, Veblen's conviction that the economics of the pecuniary economy must be the economics of the business process, centered on salesmanship, is as valid as ever.

[8] As a side-effect of this development, theories of economic sociology took as their main task to contest such economic imperialism, typically by showing how all economic phenomena are rather directly 'embedded' in social relations, institutions, and practices, as opposed to creating a more nuanced picture of the interchanges between economy and society.

16.3.2. The Pecuniary and the Industrial Systems

Veblen wrote during the era of massive reorganization of the US economy, a reorganization that expanded the horizons of production and consumption well beyond what was deemed possible in the late nineteenth century. He observed closely its two major trends: the emergence of the modern corporate form, with its dependence on sophisticated financial markets, and the rise of mass marketing. Like many of his contemporaries, he held a negative stance towards both trends, placing them within the scope of the anti-industrial and socially wasteful 'business system'. Although he never specified the relation between the industrial and business systems in a theoretically satisfying manner, the virtue of his approach is that he also did not conflate these two systems.

For Veblen, the marketing activities of the firm are never simply auxiliary to the main task of production. Instead, they are a major source of profit and the basis for success in the pecuniary economy. Similarly, the tension between the production and marketing activities of the firm is not just an artifact of organizational malfunctioning, to be resolved practically in managerial terms, and analytically by defining all the firm's activities as 'productive'. Rather, such tension is inevitable and deep-seated because the two activities belong to different systems of the economy and operate on different principles, the former linking backward to the factors of production and the latter reaching forward to social and economic factors relating to consumption.

The dominant firms of Veblen's era internalized (and hence obscured) this tension between production and marketing by vertically integrating production and marketing activities in the multidivisional organizational structure that Chandler (1977) has described so well. Most of the major 'manufacturers' of this era followed this pattern of organization, such as Ford, General Motors, and Standard Oil, which owned or tightly controlled thousands of dealerships, and Procter and Gamble and American Tobacco, with their massive advertising budgets. But this organizational format was also no less true of those leading retailers of the era, such as A & P and Sears, which themselves led not only in advertising but also branched out into directly or indirectly controlling production in hundreds of plants, as well as into designing consumer products. All these corporate giants created both the supply and demand sides of the markets in which they were the major players. They pioneered new techniques of mass production and secured, often with government help, the land, labor, and capital needed to build and run their factories. Arguably of greater importance, however, they became market makers for the goods they manufactured. In this second role, they developed actual markets (the spaces for exchange, such as retail outlets) and market institutions (services for credit, insurance, mailing, as well as the actual retail formats) for selling products that never existed before (Petrovic 2005). They shaped, channeled, and generated demand for those products and developed new marketing techniques and new tools of marketing research (Marchand 1985, 1998). The era of mass marketing, first in the United States and then around the world, was built on the success of such firms. However, the very success of these vertically integrated firms in the opening phase of American capitalism masked the tension between making and selling products.

Nearly a century later, this tension is no longer obscured. Veblen's penetrating insight a century ago has become everyone's common knowledge today. Manufacturing and marketing are two quite distinct types of activities. The tendency of leading global firms to 'outsource' many if not all of their 'production' activities has led to a clearer recognition that the core competences of these firms are in making markets, including pricing, advertising, branding, and sales. The tension between the industrial and business aspects within interorganizational structures, such as supply chains, is only reinforced by the fact that today most 'production' activities are located in developing countries, while the firms from developed countries dominate advertising, branding, sales, and other market-making activities. Indeed, consumer marketing competence is the key strategic advantage that big buyers from the United States, Europe, and, to some extent, Japan have in comparison to producers from the developing world.

This common knowledge, however, has not made its way into theories of the economy. Economists and even many economic sociologists still view firms as primarily producers of goods and not market makers. With only a few exceptions (e.g. Gereffi 1994; Spulber 1998; Zelizer 2005; Feenstra and Hamilton 2006), a production bias is built into most theoretical perspectives, ranging in economic sociology from embeddedness, network, and rational choice approaches on the micro side (Granovetter 1985; White 2002; Nee 2005) to political economy and developmental state approaches on the macro side (Fligstein 2001, 2005; Evans 1995; Block and Evans 2005). 'Indeed,' as Zelizer notes, 'economic sociology grew up concentrating on production and distribution, rather than consumption' (2005: 336). This concentration is misplaced, for, when marketing is viewed as merely an auxiliary activity, the economy is linked to social institutions only through factors of production (inputs of land, labor, and capital) and not through factors relating to consumption. Veblen helps us understand that capitalism is not simply a supply-side system of production, but even more importantly a demand-side system of consumption, and that both systems, though closely connected, are also in tension with each other.

16.3.3. The Importance of Markets for Consumer Goods and of Consumption in the Contemporary Global Economy

Veblen wrote *The Theory of the Leisure Class* before the advances of mass marketing were fully evident. He, therefore, could not foresee the global spread of consumption that exemplified American society in his time. In retrospect, the twentieth century, as many historians have recently started to recognize, could be accurately characterized as the century of consumption and consumerism (Strasser, McGovern, and Judt 1998; Partner 1999; Jarausch and Geyer 2003). The creation of the first mass regime of consumption in the United States during the first half of the twentieth century was followed by its spread to Europe in the period after the World War II (de Grazia 2005), and then by its further spread to East Asia (Watson 1997; Davis 2000; Mathews and Lui 2001), and, to a somewhat lesser extent, to the rest of the global economy.

Moreover, as much as the Cold War was overtly about different models of industrialization and the concomitant military prowess, what eventually brought the Communist Bloc down was not its failure to keep up in the arms race, but rather its inability to deliver consumer goods to its citizens. For the citizens of the communist countries of Eastern Europe, exposure to Western consumer goods—some legally imported and sold at prestigious retail outlets, others smuggled in through variety of elaborate contraband channels—served as a daily reminder of the failure of their economies to catch up with the West. At the same time, the bleak prospects of communist economies were confirmed in every visit to the state-owned retail outlets, with their uninviting interiors, empty shelves, and long waiting lines. In other words, consumers in the communist countries were not only less affluent than their capitalist counterparts, but they were also prevented, by import and travel restrictions, as well as by the obsolescence of domestic retail structures, from participating in the global consumer markets even at the level they could afford.

The same process is unfolding in the developing world today. The globalization of consumption pertains not only to actual consumption but also to the diffusion of consumption norms and standards; these models of consumption are to a large extent carried by the spread of consumer goods markets, including the economic institutions on which these markets are based (e.g. malls, retail stores, credit cards). Consumers in developing countries, thus, define their aspirations today not just by combining traditional and global cultural representations of consumption but also in direct relation to the spread of institutions relating to consumption and to the actual global flow of objects of consumption, a part of which might be generated in their own backyard and a part of which trickles into the local market through both legal and illicit means.

This observation of the actual possibilities of globalized consumption redefines the meaning of progress and development that the governments of the developing world are supposed to promote, by providing a simple, yet effective standard by which the general public judges the performance of their own society compared to its neighbors and developmental peers. In developed, as well as developing countries, of course, the purchases of globally traded goods represent only a minor part of the total consumer spending on goods and services. Yet, it is those globally produced, tradable, and consumed goods that provide key consumption norms and symbols.

Similarly, the consumer revolution in China, triggered by Deng Xiaoping's 'open door policy', could well be one of the most massive social transformations in history, bringing hundreds of millions of Chinese into the orbit of global consumer goods markets (Davis 2000). While this process has so far generated little overt political trouble for the regime, in part due to China's massive economic growth, it has certainly changed the nature of both the economic and political aspirations of China's population.

In this sense, Veblen's invidious comparisons today operate on the global level (Olson 1998). As the global division of labor between national and regional economies advances, the 'developed world' becomes, more than anything else, a model of consumption, including, importantly, the consumption of cultural goods. Veblen's analyses of particular social mechanisms that shape consumption practices might have been superseded, both by newer scholarship (e.g. Bourdieu 1984) and by worldwide changes in consumption patterns. However, his general approach to observing consumption, which emphasizes the co-evolution and co-determination of the economic and social aspects of consumption, is as valid today as it was at the beginning of the last century. Social processes that influence consumer preferences—such as status comparisons, lifestyles, and self-realization concepts—are always complemented by and co-evolve with the efforts of major market makers to create specific market structures and thus reshape product worlds and consumer demands. Despite the recent proliferation of studies of consumption practices by historians, anthropologists, sociologists, and even economists, we are just at the beginning stages of developing a theoretical framework that would integrate these two sides of consumption.

16.4. Cumulative Causation: Towards a Theory of Economy and Society

Although neither referenced the other, Veblen and his contemporary, Max Weber, took the same general analytic approach. Both wrote that the analysis of capitalism should be directed towards the organizing processes of economic change, instead of the outcomes of those processes as conceived in essentialist terms. In contrast to the mainstream economists of their time, both thinkers thought that the proper subject matter of economic studies should be the relations between cultural and institutional development, what Veblen sometimes called the 'general scheme of life' and 'methods of dealing with the material means of life'. Veblen and Weber also adopted a very similar evolutionary or developmental conception of economic history, one which stressed in Veblen's term 'cumulative causation'.[9] Finally, both Veblen and Weber were very critical of the approaches taken by other economists. Weber (1949: 49–112) argued that many theorists made their models more real than the actual economies they studied, and Veblen (1898*c*) thought that the 'preconceptions of economic science' prevented the mainstream economists from developing a truly evolutionary standpoint, 'a theory of a cumulative sequence of economic events stated in terms of the process itself'.

Over a century later, most economists and economic sociologists are still searching for first-order generalizations about the nature of the economy and have largely ignored capitalism. 'Today's economic sociologists', Swedberg observes, 'have often taken capitalism for granted and have failed to develop a sociology of capitalism' (2003: 54). Instead, sociologists have been preoccupied with the nature of networks, organizational fields, institutions, and states—all of which are assumed to have independent effects on economic activity—as opposed to the organizing processes of capitalist activities themselves, activities that constantly co-evolve with the economic institutions that structure the activities themselves.

The first lesson that we should learn from rereading Veblen (as well as Weber) today is to analyze capitalism as a variegated, historical phenomenon. Capitalism is not, as Marx and many later writers believed, a fundamental historical object that can be rigorously defined and concretely analyzed once and for all time. We should take seriously Veblen's idea of cumulative causation and understand that this idea is unlike current notions of path dependence. Veblen's idea of cumulative causation was not to see change as emanating from some first cause, large or small, but rather was to see economy and society as being in constant processes of interacting and changing, with the actual interactions and the actual directions of change being contingent and, therefore, unpredictable from current patterns. Historical actors and the institutional environments they create co-evolve with 'both the agent and his environment being at any point the outcome of the last process' (1919*c*: 74–5).

Veblen's ultimate legacy, not unlike Weber's, is that he envisioned a historical and not a general theory of the co-evolution of economy and society. Looking back over the past century, we can see this historical co-evolution in motion. Both production and consumption have been transformed. Information technologies and global logistics have created profound reorganizations that have occurred across all national and local economies. These technologies, we (Petrovic and Hamilton 2006) have argued, have allowed retailers and brand-name merchandisers greater leverage in making both consumer and supplier markets, causing economies to become increasingly 'demand responsive', organized 'backwards' from point of sale (Feenstra and Hamilton 2006). All of these organizing processes of capitalism are

[9] For Weber's developmental conception of history, see Roth and Schluchter 1979.

now global. Although these processes certainly have profound local and national manifestations and consequences, they cannot be understood piecemeal, as simply being aggregations of what happens in local and national economies.

Adhering to structural and institutional perspectives, some analysts minimize the extent of this global reorganization. After all, they argue, states are still there; national economies are still important; big firms still have a lot of economic power and political pull. What is missing in this viewpoint is what Veblen and Weber can help supply. Their work of a century ago tells us that we should endeavor to understand and analyze the processes of capitalism and not the normative taxonomies that are the artifacts of our theoretical preconceptions. Our task going forward from their insights is to work out the details of, and give evidence for, secular theories of economic change, historical theories showing the processes of cumulative causation, so that we can come to terms with the fortunes and follies of our times.

References

Aspromourgos, T. (1986). 'On the Origin of the Term "Neoclassical"'. *Cambridge Journal of Economics*, 10: 265–70.

Becker, G. S. (1996). *Accounting for Tastes*. Cambridge, Mass.: Harvard University Press.

Berle, A. A., and Means, G. C. (1933). *The Modern Corporation and Private Property*. New York: Commerce Clearing House.

Blaug, M. (1985). *Economic Theory in Retrospect*. Cambridge: Cambridge University Press.

Block, F., and Evans, P. (2005). 'The State and the Economy', in Neil J. Smelser and Richard Swedberg (eds.), *The Handbook of Economic Sociology*. 2nd edn. Princeton: Princeton University Press.

Bourdieu, P. (1984). *Distinction: A Social Critique of the Judgment of Taste*. Cambridge, Mass.: Harvard University Press.

Brown, D. (ed.) (1998). *Thorstein Veblen in the Twenty-First Century: A Commemoration of* The Theory of the Leisure Class *(1899–1999)*. Cheltenham, UK; Northampton, Mass.: Edward Elgar.

Chamberlin, E. H. ([1933] 1962). *The Theory of Monopolistic Competition: A Reorientation of the Theory of Value*. 8th edn. Cambridge, Mass.: Harvard University Press.

Chandler, A. D., Jr. (1977). *The Visible Hand: The Managerial Revolution in American Business*. Cambridge, Mass.: Harvard University Press.

—— (1990). *Scale and Scope: The Dynamics of Industrial Capitalism*. Cambridge, Mass.: Harvard University Press.

Coase, R. (1984). 'The New Institutional Economics'. *Journal of Institutional and Theoretical Economics*, 140: 229–31.

Colander, D., Hold, R. P. F., and Rosser, J. Barkley, Jr. (2004). 'The Changing Face of Mainstream Economics'. *Review of Political Economy*, 16/4: 485–99.

Davis, D. S. (2000). *The Consumer Revolution in Urban China*. Berkeley: University of California Press.

de Grazia, V. (2005). *Irresistible Empire: America's Advance through Twentieth-Century Europe*. Cambridge, Mass.: Belknap Press of Harvard University Press.

Dorfman, J. (1934). *Thorstein Veblen and His America*. New York: Viking Press.

Evans, P. B. (1995). *Embedded Autonomy: States and Industrial Transformation*. Princeton: Princeton University Press.

Feenstra, R. C., and Hamilton, G. G. (2006). *Emergent Economies, Divergent Paths: Economic Organization and International Trade in South Korea and Taiwan*. New York: Cambridge University Press.

Fligstein, N. (2001). *The Architecture of Markets: An Economic Sociology of Twenty-First-Century Capitalist Societies*. Princeton: Princeton University Press.

—— (2005). 'States, Markets, and Economic Growth', in Victor Nee and Richard Swedberg (eds.), *The Economic Sociology of Capitalism*. Princeton: Princeton University Press.

Foss, N. J. (1998). 'The Competence-Based Approach: Veblenian Ideas in the Modern Theory of the Firm'. *Cambridge Journal of Economics*, 22: 479–95.

Gereffi, G. (1994). 'The International Economy and Economic Development', in Neil Smelser and Richard Swedberg (eds.), *The Handbook of Economic Sociology*. Princeton: Princeton University Press.

Gerschenkron, A. (1962). *Economic Backwardness in Historical Perspective*. Cambridge, Mass.: Harvard University Press.

Granovetter, M. (1985). 'Economic Action and Social Structure: The Problem of Embeddedness'. *American Journal of Sociology*, 91: 481–510.

Gruchy, A. G. (1958). 'The Influence of Veblen on Mid-Century Institutionalism'. *American Economic Review*, 48/2: 11–20.

James, W. (1878). 'Remarks on Spencer's Definition of Mind as Correspondence'. *Journal of Speculative Philosophy*, 12: 1–18.

Jarausch, K. H., and Geyer, M. (2003). *Shattered Past: Reconstructing German Histories*. Princeton: Princeton University Press.

Marchand, R. (1985). *Advertising the American Dream: Making Way for Modernity, 1920–1940*. Berkeley: University of California Press.

—— (1998). *Creating the Corporate Soul: The Rise of Public Relations and Corporate Imagery in American Big Business*. Berkeley: University of California Press.

Marshall, A. (1890). *Principles of Economics*. London: Macmillan.

Mathews, G., and Lui, Tai-lok (eds.) (2001). *Consuming Hong Kong*. Hong Kong: Hong Kong University Press.

Nee, V. (2005). 'The New Institutionalisms in Economics and Sociology', in Neil J. Smelser and Richard Swedberg (eds.), *The Handbook of Economic Sociology*. 2nd edn. Princeton: Princeton University Press.

Olson, P. (1998). 'My Dam is Bigger than Yours: Emulation in Global Capitalism', in Brown (1998).

Ozawa, T. (2004). 'Veblen's Theories of "Latecomer Advantage" and "the Machine Process": Relevancy for Flexible Production'. *Journal of Economic Issues*, 38/2: 379–88.

Partner, S. (1999). *Assembled in Japan: Electrical Goods and the Making of the Japanese Consumer*. Berkeley: University of California Press.

Penrose, E. T. (1959). *The Theory of the Growth of the Firm*. Oxford: Blackwell.

Petrovic, M. (2005). 'Market Makers and Market Making: The Evolution of Consumer Goods Markets in the United States, 1870–2000'. Ph.D. diss. University of Washington.

—— and Hamilton, G. G. (2006). 'Making Global Markets: Wal-Mart and Its Suppliers', in Nelson Lichtenstein (ed.), *Wal-Mart: The Face of 21st Century Capitalism*. New York: New Press.

Ringer, F. (1997). *Max Weber's Methodology: The Unification of the Cultural and Social Sciences*. Cambridge, Mass.: Harvard University Press.

Roth, G., and Schluchter, W. (1979). *Max Weber's Vision of History*. Berkeley: University of California Press.

Schluchter, W. (1989). *Rationalism, Religion, and Domination: A Weberian Perspective*. Berkeley: University of California Press.

Spulber, D. F. (1998). *Market Microstructure: Intermediaries and the Theory of the Firm*. Cambridge: Cambridge University Press.

Strasser, S., McGovern, C., and Judt, M. (eds.) (1998). *Getting and Spending: European and American Consumer Societies in the Twentieth Century*. Cambridge: Cambridge University Press.

Swedberg, R. (2003). *Principles of Economic Sociology*. Princeton: Princeton University Press.

Veblen, T. (1891). 'Some Neglected Points in the Theory of Socialism'. *Annals of the American Academy of Political and Social Science*, 2 (November): 57–74.

—— (1892). 'Bohm-Bawerk's Definition of Capital and the Source of Wages'. *Quarterly Journal of Economics*, 6 (January): 247–52.

—— (1894). 'The Economic Theory of Woman's Dress'. *Popular Science Monthly*, 46 (December): 198–205.

—— (1898*a*). 'The Beginnings of Ownership'. *American Journal of Sociology*, 4/3 (November): 352–65.

—— (1898*b*). 'The Instinct of Workmanship and the Irksomeness of Labor'. *American Journal of Sociology*, 4 (September): 187–201.

—— (1898*c*). 'Why is Economics Not an Evolutionary Science?' *Quarterly Journal of Economics*, 12/4 (July): 373–97.

—— (1899*a*). 'The Barbarian Status of Women'. *American Journal of Sociology*, 4/4 (January): 503–14.

—— (1899*b*). *The Theory of the Leisure Class: An Economic Study of the Evolution of Institutions*. New York: Macmillan.

—— (1899–1900). 'The Preconceptions of Economic Science', Part 1 (1899), Part 2 (1899), Part 3 (1900), *Quarterly Journal of Economics*, 13/2 (January): 121–50; 13/4 (July): 396–426; 14/2 (January): 240–69.

—— (1901). 'Industrial and Pecuniary Employments'. *Publications of the American Economics Association*, Series 3: 190–235.

—— (1904*a*). 'Review of Adam Smith's *Wealth of Nations*'. *Journal of Political Economy*, 13/1 (December): 136.

—— (1904*b*). *Theory of Business Enterprise*. New York: Scribner's.

—— (1906*a*). 'The Place of Science in Modern Civilization'. *American Journal of Sociology*, 11/5 (March): 585–609.

—— (1906*b*). 'Professor Clark's Economics'. *Quarterly Journal of Economics*, 20/2 (February): 147–95.

Veblen, T. (1906–7). 'The Socialist Economics of Karl Marx and His Followers', Part 1 (1906), Part 2 (1907), *Quarterly Journal of Economics*, 21/4 (August): 578–95; 22/2 (February): 299–322.

—— (1907). 'Fisher's Capital and Income'. *Political Science Quarterly*, 22/1 (March): 112–28.

—— (1908*a*). 'The Evolution of the Scientific Point of View'. *University of California Chronicle* (May): 396–416.

—— (1908*b*). 'On the Nature of Capital'. *Quarterly Journal of Economics*, 22/4 (August): 517–42; 23/1 (November): 104–36.

—— (1909*a*). 'Fisher's Rate of Interest'. *Political Science Quarterly*, 24/2 (June): 296–303.

—— (1909*b*). 'The Limitations of Marginal Utility'. *Journal of Political Economy*, 17/9 (November): 620–36.

—— (1915). *Imperial Germany and the Industrial Revolution*. New York: Macmillan.

—— (1919*a*). 'The Captains of Finance and the Engineers'. *Dial*, 14 June: 599–606.

—— (1919*b*). 'The Industrial System and the Captains of Industry'. *Dial*, 31 May: 552–7.

—— (1919*c*). *The Place of Science in Modern Civilization and Other Essays*. New York: B. W. Huebsch.

—— (1919*d*). *The Vested Interests and the Common Man*. New York: B. W. Huebsch.

—— (1923). *Absentee Ownership and Business Enterprise in Recent Times: The Case of America*. New York: B. W. Huebsch.

—— (1948). *The Portable Veblen*, ed. Max Lerner. New York: Viking Press.

Watson, J. L. (ed.) (1997). *Golden Arches East: McDonald's in East Asia*. Stanford, Calif.: Stanford University Press.

Weber, M. (1949). *The Methodology of the Social Sciences*. Glencoe, Ill.: Free Press.

White, H. C. (2002). *Markets from Networks: Socioeconomic Models of Production*. Princeton: Princeton University Press.

Williamson, O. E. (1994). 'Transaction Cost Economics and Organization Theory', in Neil J. Smelser and Richard Swedberg (eds.), *The Handbook of Economic Sociology*. Princeton: Princeton University Press.

Yonay, Y. P. (1998). *The Struggle over the Soul of Economics: Institutionalist and Neoclassical Economists in America between the Wars*. Princeton: Princeton University Press.

Zelizer, V. (2005). 'Culture and Consumption', in Neil J. Smelser and Richard Swedberg (eds.), *The Handbook of Economic Sociology*. 2nd edn. Princeton: Princeton University Press.

CHAPTER 17

THE SOCIOLOGY OF RACE

THE CONTRIBUTIONS OF W. E. B. DU BOIS

STELLA M. NKOMO

> The problem of the Twentieth Century is the problem of the color-line, the relation of the darker to the lighter races of men in Asia and Africa, in America and the islands of the sea . . .
>
> (Du Bois [1903] 1969: 54)

17.1. INTRODUCTION

DU Bois's observation in the epigraph that the problem of the twentieth century is the color line was prophetic when he wrote it in 1903. Race and racial ideas have always been in organizations and the workplace, even if they have not always been studied by organizational scholars (Nkomo 1992; Kurowski 2002; Nkomo and Proudford 2006). Historically, the earliest formally organized workforces in the United States were composed of African slaves, indentured servants, Native Americans, and convicts (Cooke 2003; Gutman 1977; Kurowski 2002). The rapid industrialization of the 1820s led to a phenomenal growth in the need for labor. This resulted in a large influx of immigrants from Europe and China (Takaki 1979). In Europe, residents of European colonies could enter under the quotas of their colonizing country (Kurowski 2002). So people from Africa, the West Indies, and India, for example, created a non-white presence in the labor forces of many countries in Europe. There have always been struggles and tensions emanating from race and ethnicity in the workplace with contestations over access to jobs and race relations between different race and ethnic groups (Gutman 1977; Takaki 1979).

While we can point to the explicit existence of race in organizations due to the physical presence of different racial and ethnic groups in the workplaces of the nineteenth century, the presence of race is also striking by its omission in the works of pioneering organizational scholars such as Taylor, Mayo, Barnard, and others (Nkomo 1992). These early scholars did not explicitly acknowledge or study race in their ideas and theories of organizations. Early management theorists advocated bureaucracy as the ideal form of organization and the goal was to develop universal theories that depersonalized social relations (Burrell 1994; Clegg 1990). Yet, a closer reading of the history of management and the works of these seminal scholars reveals the influence of prevailing ideas about race during the late nineteenth century (Kurowski 2002). Taylor's works were written during a time of heightened immigration in the United States, and the ethnicity of workers was carefully noted in his famous pig-iron loading experiments (Wrege and Perroni 1974). According to Kurowski (2002), Taylor adopted the racial/ethnic beliefs that prevailed at the time as his descriptions of the workers in his experiments bear testimony. There were also data in the famous Hawthorne studies relevant to differences in social relations grounded in ethnicity, gender, and age, but they did not become part of Mayo's theoretical formulations (Roethlisberger and Dickson 1939). The pioneering work of sociologists like Dollard (1937) and Hughes (1946) on issues of race, ethnic, and class differences did not find its way into organization studies (Nkomo and Stewart 2006). For example, Hughes's (1946) small-scale study of race relations in industry demonstrated how race affected individual and group dynamics on the factory floor. Hughes found that race and gender affected patterns of established labor–management relations, informal seniority among employees, and group control of individual productivity (Banton 1998). Because black women were not fully accepted by the white women on the factory floor, they were not subject to the full pressure to conform to the established output norms, and some of them exceeded production rates. At the time, Hughes urged sociologists 'to first understand the factory and then discover what ways customary attitudes were changed by the introduction of black workers (Banton 1998: 128). Ironically, Banton (1998) noted that sociologists were slow to follow Hughes's lead and the 'race problem' was perceived as a problem of group conflict but did not result in a modification of Mayo's human relations theory.

Significant explicit attention to race in organization studies began with the social movements of the 1960s that called for equal opportunities for racial minorities and women. The passage of Civil Rights legislation in the United States and similar legislation in certain parts of Western Europe turned the attention of organization studies scholars to understanding the effects of this legislation in the workplace. Nkomo (1992) identified two trajectories of the research. One stream focused on prejudice-reduction strategies, and the other centered on responses to the requirements of equal employment opportunity. The focus of most organizational scholarship was on documenting objective evidence of racial discrimination until the publication of Johnston and Packer's book, *Workforce 2000: Work and Workers for the 21st Century*, in 1987. With its forecast of 'an increasingly diverse workforce', the report implored organizations to respond urgently to this phenomenon. As Kurowski (2002) notes, racial diversity was presented as a novelty—something very new and never before present in the workplace. Consequently, the study of diversity and its management has largely subsumed the study of race in organizations (Nkomo and Stewart 2006; Prasad, Konrad, and Pringle 2006).

The purpose of this chapter is to review the seminal work of W. E. B. Du Bois—who has been proclaimed, 'the first sociologist of race' (Lewis 2000: 550)—and explore its relevance for organization studies. This review is done within the complex contours of today's global racial context. W. E. B. Du Bois wrote of race as the problem of the twentieth century and while Du Bois wrote primarily about race in the United States, he astutely recognized the problem was global in scope (Twine and Gallagher 2008). Globalization today has evoked two visions of how race and ethnicity manifest in the workplace (Robertson 1997). There is the positive vision of a multicultural global village in which people of different cultures intermingle across boundaries, use technology to bridge physical distance, exchange goods, and leverage capital and resources (Spickard 2005). In a contrasting vision, cultural harmony and integration remain elusive. Globalization produces a situation in which identities continue to be sources of conflict, marginalization, and political struggle (Castells 1997; Hirst and Thompson 1999).

A survey of the current state of race/ethnicity globally suggests one can safely say that race continues to be a problem in the twenty-first century, although the meaning and structure of race and racism in a post-civil rights, post-apartheid, and post-colonial world has changed (Winant 2006). Racially based social structures of inequality and exclusion persist not only in the United States but in many other countries and regions of the world despite the sentiment that we are now in a post-race era (Gilroy 2001). Scholars of race and ethnic studies assert the race concept is more problematic than ever before because of the discrepancies and contradictions between official racial rhetoric and the actual lived experience of race in a globalized world (Winant 2006; Essed and Goldberg 2002). Winant (2006: 987–8) points to four significant contradictions: (1) increased mobility of subaltern racialized groups coexists with ongoing patterns of exclusion and protection of national identities;

(2) post-colonial states have ushered in new leadership yet still display significant continuities with the transgressions of the old empire; (3) despite the rise of democracy in many nation states and the mantra of color-blindness in the United States, the life chances of racially marginalized populations have not improved significantly; and (4) the rise of multiculturalism has not altered patterns of racialized identity formation and cultural representation. In fact, alongside the expressed attraction for multiculturalism is what Grillo (2003) labeled the 'cultural diversity sceptical turn' or a weariness with the 'excess of alterity' (Sartori 2002). The latter has been particularly evident in Europe with heated debates about immigration, national identity, and the introduction of reactionary anti-immigration legislation (Grillo 2007). Accordingly, Winant (2006: 988) asserts 'the global racial situation remains volatile and undertheorized'. Race continues to permeate capitalism's economic and social processes that grossly favor the global north over the global south (Melamed 2006). In this chapter, I argue that race and its intersection with other markers of difference remains largely undertheorized in organization studies.

17.2. The Classical Contributions of W. E. B. Du Bois

Du Bois's ideas about the phenomenon of race were prescient and can perhaps provide organizational scholars with new ways of studying race in organizations. His contributions are not embodied in a single work but a series of books, articles, and monographs on race written over a period of nearly sixty-five years (Thompson 2005*a*). Du Bois was born three years after the end of the US Civil War in Great Barrington, Massachusetts and died on the eve of the historic Civil Rights March on Washington, DC, led by Martin Luther King, Jr. He also lived to see the beginning of the end of colonialism in many African countries. Du Bois earned his first BA degree from Fisk University, a historically black college, and then went on to earn a second BA from Harvard University in 1890, where he studied economics and social problems (Goodwin and Scimecca 2006). Du Bois received his Ph.D. in History from Harvard, where he undertook extensive coursework in sociology. During his doctoral studies, he spent one year at the University of Berlin, where he studied under Gustav Schmoller and became friends with Max Weber. His focus on sociology began in earnest in 1896 when he was asked by the University of Pennsylvania to conduct a study of the social and economic conditions of the Negro living in Philadelphia's seventh ward. The funding for the project was provided by Susan B. Wharton, a member of the wealthy Quaker family known for the founding of the Wharton School of Economics and Finance (Goodwin and Scimecca 2006: 244).

The published work, *The Philadelphia Negro*, appeared in 1899 and is considered to be one of the first examples of empirical urban studies scholarship as well as empirical sociology using multi-methods (Wortham 2005; Zuckerman 2004). Although Du Bois's central focus was on race, *The Philadelphia Negro* used a methodological lens that looked at the intersections of race, gender, age, and place of residence (rural–urban). At the time it was considered the definitive urban ethnography on African American quality of life covering everything from education to work and from religion to crime (Thompson 2005*b*).

Du Bois's methodology was consistent with his rejection of the grand theorizing that dominated the field in his day exemplified by the approaches of Émile Durkheim and Herbert Spencer (Zuckerman 2004). He argued that they were substituting metaphysical figures from their own imaginations for actual observation of human action. In a 1904 essay, *The Atlanta Conferences*, Du Bois set forth his conceptualization of sociology defining it as a discipline that 'seeks to know how much of natural law there is in human conduct' (Du Bois 1904, reprinted in Green and Driver 1978: 53). In other words, Du Bois saw sociology as a means to explain and understand human conduct empirically. He believed that in order to study social problems, sociologists could not stay inside of their offices but had to engage with the people about whom they wished to theorize, studying them first hand (Aptheker 1973: 75). Du Bois subscribed to the pragmatic philosophy that dominated the late nineteenth and early twentieth centuries and firmly believed scientific studies could debunk the hold that scientific racism had in explaining the plight of blacks in the United States (Goodwin and Scimecca 2006).

During his tenure at Atlanta University as a professor of sociology, he devoted his research to the study of the so-called 'Negro Problem' and created what became known as the Atlanta Sociological Laboratory (Dennis 1975; Wortham 2005). The laboratory focused on the social and economic conditions of 'Negroes', producing sixteen volumes of research.

Du Bois's voluminous scholarly output was related in some way to explaining, exploring, and deconstructing the so-called 'color line' not only in the United States but also globally (Zuckerman 2004: 5). Ironically, for many years his ideas and publications were never adopted in the canon of social theory nor did he form part of the cultural capital of sociology (Allan 2005). The exclusion of Du Bois's writing on race occurred despite the fact that the early sociology of race was concurrent with the birth of sociology itself in the mid-nineteenth century (Thompson 2005*a*). According to Seidman (1998), the very institutionalization of sociology in Europe and the United States in the late nineteenth and early twentieth centuries was accomplished through a serious of exclusions. As the study of race was marginalized in early mainstream sociology, so too was Du Bois.[1] Zuckerman (2004: 2) observed,

[1] Pettigrew (1980: xxv) observed that at the time of the founding of the American Sociological Society in 1905, critical work on race by scholars that included W. E. B. Du Bois, W. I. Thomas, and Charlotte Perkins Gilman was on the margins of mainstream sociological writing.

'The process of canonization invariably reflects political relations, racial fissures, class differences, national hierarchies, gender biases, and a host of other related balances of power, authority and access to the means of scholarly production, distribution, and recognition.'

Scholars who have worked to excavate Du Bois's scholarship within the field of sociology identify his major contributions as being in pioneering empirical studies of urban sociology, defining race and difference, illuminating the lived experience of exclusion and marginality, and standpoint theory (Allan 2005; Goodwin and Scimecca 2006; Lott 1999; Rabaka 2007).

17.3. The Idea of Race in Early Sociological Works

For the most part, when sociology emerged as an academic discipline in the 1890s, there was not a rush to study race (McKee 1993).[2] Yet, the 'race problem' was among the many social problems exacerbated by the political and industrial changes that were taking place at the beginning of the nineteenth century in both Europe and the United States (Thompson 2005*a*). The end of absolutism, the spread of capitalist competition, and the concomitant disorder they brought is said to have contributed to the creation of sociology (Tucker 2002). At the same time, there was much confusion and controversy surrounding the nineteenth-century idea of race and its influence on individuals, groups, and societies (Banton 1998: 92). Sustained efforts in Europe and the United States focused on providing scientific evidence for the idea of a qualitative rank ordering of the human races. An enormous amount of effort went into identifying racial traits by measuring various parts of the human body as well as research into the mechanics of genetic inheritance (McKee 1993). The latter referred to as the eugenics movement emerged in the early 1900s as a backlash against the flood of immigrants from eastern and southern Europe (ibid.).

Despite the emergence of Darwin's evolutionary theory that challenged the essentialist idea of race as type, efforts persisted to root racial differences in biological explanations (Banton 1998). Although some of the early sociologists adopted Darwin's theory, they believed non-white races were incapable of evolving as the white races had done (McKee 1993: 24). Among this group were founders of early sociology, such as Herbert Spencer and William Graham Sumner, who embraced Darwin's theory of evolution in the form of Social Darwinism (ibid.). They believed

[2] In the first five volumes of the *American Journal of Sociology* (1985–1900), there was only one article on race and one book review both about the races of Europe (McKee 1993: 29).

in the idea of evolving societies and civilizations but thought that societies change only very gradually. Spencer believed the minds of primitive races had all the limitations of the minds of children, except that their childhood of intellect was permanent (Gossett 1963: 149). In his most noted work, *Folkways*,[3] Sumner[4] commented on the confusion over nature and culture but at the same time insisted on the existence of racial inferiority and opposed suffrage for black people (McKee 1993: 26).

Thompson (2005*a*) identifies the work of George Fitzhugh as the earliest explicit sociological treatment of race in the United States. Fitzhugh defended slavery in his book, *Sociology for the South or the Failure of Free Society* (1854), as a system that was superior to socialism as a way of avoiding the social problems created by capitalism (Thompson 2005*a*). Domestic slavery in his analysis protected the weaker members of society (i.e. Negroes) and was a major reason for the stability of the South (Fitzhugh 1854). There were other prominent sociologists who were in concert with Fitzhugh's arguments. Franklin H. Giddings in his text, *Principles of Sociology*,[5] written in 1896, asserted the 'lower races' had accomplished less and did not have the same inherent abilities as the European races (McKee 1993).

The arguments of sociologists such as Giddings were bolstered by the eugenics movement in England led by Francis Galton, who wrote a book entitled *Hereditary Genius* in 1869 in which he argued that there were not only intellectual differences among men within each race but also in the grades of races.[6] Eugenics was also used to establish the inferiority of peoples from eastern and southern Europe. Although there were other prominent sociologists such as Lester Ward (1906) and Charles Horton Cooley (1902, 1909) who argued against the acceptance of the inferiority of the non-white races, they nevertheless evoked racial thinking (McKee 1993). The dilemma of sociologists like Ward and Cooley in many respects is still evident today as post-race proponents argue that in attempts to minimize the importance of race differences scholars continue to evoke the very concept of race. As will be noted later, Du Bois also struggled with the discourse of race. The tension between nature and nurture evident in the range of theoretical positions existing among sociologists at the time is in many ways indicative of the difficulties early sociologists had in maintaining a social analysis of differences among race and ethnic groups rather than retreating to essentialist explanations (Banton 1998).

[3] It should be acknowledged that his book, *Folkways* ([1906] 1959: Dover Publications), introduced the seminal concepts of folkways, mores, in-group, out-group, and ethnocentricism into the lexicon of sociology (Goodwin and Scimecca 2006: 272).

[4] William Graham Sumner is generally considered to be the father of American sociology (Goodwin and Scimecca 2006: 105).

[5] Giddings is credited with introducing statistics into sociology (Goodwin and Scimecca 2006: 293).

[6] Galton was a cousin of Darwin's. Eugenicists differed from Social Darwinians by advocating interventions to increase the influence of the upper classes and higher races (Gossett 1963: 158).

It is within this historical context that the pioneering work of W. E. B. Du Bois should be understood. Du Bois's life work represented an effort to refute racial explanations of what were often characterized as culturally inferior lifestyles of black Americans through empirical study of the historical, political, structural, and cultural factors creating inequalities among different groups (McKee 1993: 208).

17.4. Du Bois and the Idea of Race

17.4.1. Race Defined

Today it is commonly accepted that race is a social construction (Banton 1998) and few scholars would argue with this conclusion. Du Bois's conceptualization and contributions to the idea of race are contained in several of his writings. A chronological reading of these reflects the trajectory of the development and breadth of his thinking about race and its significance in society. In an early essay entitled, 'The Conservation of the Races' written in 1897, Du Bois interrogated the ontology and very meaning of race and posed the question: What is the real meaning of race? In the essay, he expressed skepticism about the essential physical differences in races propagated by scholars of his day who based definitions of race on physical characteristics (e.g. skin color, texture of hair, and cranial size). In the essay, Du Bois attempts to *de*construct and then *re*construct the concept of race (Rabaka 2007). He writes about the fallacy of so-called pure racial characteristics pointing to the intermingling of human characteristics; but most importantly he argues that so-called physical characteristics do not explain all the differences in the histories or status of the so-called races. Instead, he stresses the importance of understanding the structural and historical forces that account for any observed differences in the so-called races.

As noted earlier in this chapter, during this time scholars faced the paradoxical challenge of relying on essentialist racial categories while at the same time negating them. Du Bois's dilemma points to the ongoing tensions that organization studies scholars face in studying race. Race is a contested construct. By evoking and studying race, do we run the risk of perpetuating the belief in physical differences as markers of race? In other words, if we agree there is no such thing as race or as Montagu (1997: 44) points out 'race is one of the most dangerous myths of our time and one of the most tragic', then should we continue to study 'race'? Or placed within the current theoretical debates under the rubric of post-race talk we must ask: If race is an arbitrary sign used to divide up the human population, why do social constructionists continue to deploy the term at the same time as they refute its existence? (Nayak 2006: 415). Or—as Body-Gendrot (2004: 150) asks—'Has race become a word too much?'

Recently, prominent race and ethnic studies scholars have called for the very abandonment of the race construct and have labeled it a spurious and empty ideological construct (Gilroy 1998, 2001). Gilroy (2001) has been the most vocal proponent of post-race theory arguing that racisms would be better countered if scholars made a more consistent effort to de-nature and de-ontologize 'race'. Specifically, he called for scholars to step 'away from the pious ritual in which we always agree that "race" is invented but are then required to defer to its embeddedness in the world and to accept that the demand for justice nevertheless requires us to enter the political arenas that it helps to mark out' (Gilroy 1998: 842). Gilroy believes action against racial hierarchies and domination cannot proceed if the idea of race lingers.

Other scholars have noted and criticized the contradiction in Du Bois's early formulation of the race concept (Appiah 1992; Lott 1999). For example, Appiah (1992) challenged the social logic of Du Bois's idea that a common history defines race. He argued against the assertion of a unitary black experience rooted in history. But it is important to place Du Bois's conceptualization within the prominence of scientific racism at the time, even among well respected sociologists. Du Bois's goal at the time was to dispel the idea that race determined the status and behaviors of blacks. Not only in this essay but through his research, Du Bois systematically attempted to rebut the arguments proffered by scientific racism to justify racial discrimination and oppression (Rabaka 2007).

Yet, another of his objectives in the essay appears to be an argument for recognizing Negroes as a group of people with the potential to make a significant contribution to American society. He states, 'the fact still remains that the full, complete Negro message of the whole Negro race has not as yet been given to the world; that the messages and ideal of the yellow race have not been completed' (Du Bois 1897, reprinted in Green and Driver 1978: 243). Thus, he called for the valuing of different races in society, a message echoed loudly today by proponents of valuing diversity in organizations (Konrad, Prasad, and Pringle 2006) when he wrote, 'We believe that, unless modern civilization is a failure, it is entirely feasible and practicable for two races in such essential political, economic and religious harmony as the white and colored people of America, to develop side by side in peace and mutual happiness, the peculiar contribution which each has to make to the culture of their common country' (Du Bois 1897, reprinted in Green and Driver 1978: 248).

Du Bois was also keenly observant of the role of history in oppression, often referring to its role in legitimating oppressive social structures. His epoch book, *Black Reconstruction in America 1860–1880* published in 1935, offers a historical and empirical analysis of the role of American blacks in the post-Civil War Reconstruction period and the effects of the exploitation of black labor through the system of slavery on labor worldwide. His reconstruction was a *re*writing project to share the efforts and experiences of 'Negroes themselves' (Du Bois 1935: 1) and to point to the hypocrisy of America's grand narrative of democracy amidst its practice of human slavery.

In later writings, Du Bois expresses his doubts about racial categories. For example, in a short essay, entitled 'Does Race Antagonism Serve Any Good Purpose?' published in 1914 in *The Crisis* (the journal of the National Association for the Advancement of Colored People), 'race is a vague, unknown term which may be made to cover a multitude of sins. After all, what is a "race" and how many races are there?' (Du Bois 1914, reprinted in Zuckerman 2004: 30).

17.4.2. Interrogating Whiteness

Du Bois's groundbreaking interrogation of whiteness, 'The Souls of White Folk', a chapter written in *Darkwater* ([1921] 1975), prefigured contemporary treatments of whiteness. In the chapter, Du Bois explores the social construction of whiteness and its relationship to hegemony, exploitation, and the domination of others. He writes,

> Everything considered, the title to the universe claimed by White Folk is faulty. It ought, at least, to look plausible. How easy, then, by emphasis and omission to make children believe that every great soul the world ever saw was a white man's soul; that every great thought; that every great deed the world ever did was a white man's deed; that every great dream the world ever sang was a white man's dream. (Du Bois ([1921] 1975: 31, 42)

Du Bois ([1921] 1975: 29–30) referred to whiteness as a recent invention noting personal whiteness 'is a very modern thing—a nineteenth and twentieth century matter'. Contrasting the plight of blacks who were labeled a 'problem', he points out that being white is not a problem for Anglo-Americans; it bestows them with cultural power and privileges because of their assumed superiority over others. Du Bois discusses the ways in which the cultural power of whiteness manifests itself in economic and social institutions including the workplace (Tucker 2002). His critique of whiteness has major significance for organization studies, reminding scholars that what may appear to be neutral, natural organizational practices disproportionately benefit dominant group members while disadvantaging others. But more importantly, the culture of the dominant group is viewed as the most effective for organization functioning and success. Du Bois writing on the power of whiteness reminds us that cultural exclusion undergirds every oppressive structure (Allan 2005). The systematic exclusion of the contributions of black Americans and the general denigration of black culture was critical to the perpetuation of racism in US society. Du Bois's recognition of the role of culture and representation in oppression of non-dominant groups foreshadowed its contemporary explication (Allan 2005: 297). The study of representation has become a central theme in cultural analysis as exemplified in the work of scholars like Stuart Hall (2003).

17.4.3. Intersectionality

In his later years, Du Bois developed a more structural theory of poverty and racism, incorporating critiques of colonialism, capitalism, and sexism (Tucker 2002). His later work is clearly influenced by his readings of Marx and Hegel. Du Bois's attention to the intersection of race and class that emerged later is noteworthy because his earlier work has been criticized for its elitist tone. He had called for a 'Talented Tenth'—well-educated middle-class black Americans—to provide the vanguard leadership for the black community in overcoming oppression and racism (Rabaka 2007). In relation to Marxism, Du Bois offered insights into the relationships of capitalism, colonialism, and racism (Rabaka 2007). He argued that racism fractured the potential of white and black proletariats uniting against capitalism because the exploitation of black labor was essential to white labor's standard of living.

Du Bois wrote about the transformation in his thinking in a chapter entitled, 'The Concept of Race' in the book *Dusk of Dawn* published in 1940. He reflects upon his theories of race, highlighting his journey from his initial acceptance of the idea of social evolution but his steadfast rejection of the inferiority of Negro people to his awareness of the interdependent effects of race, class, and wealth on the plight of dark-skinned people around the world (Zuckerman 2004). He wrote,

> But one thing is sure and that is the fact that since the fifteenth century these ancestors of mine and their other descendants have had a common history; have suffered a common disaster and one long memory. The actual ties of heritage between the individuals of this group vary with the ancestors that they have in common, and many others; Europeans and Semites, perhaps Mongolians, certainly American Indians. But the physical bond is least and the badge of color relatively unimportant save as a badge; the real essence of this kinship is its social heritage of slavery; the discrimination and insult; ... I think it was in Africa that I came more to see the close connection between race and wealth. The fact that even in the minds of the most dogmatic supporters of race theories and believers in the inferiority of colored folk to white, there was a conscious or unconscious determination to increase their incomes by taking full advantage of this belief. And then gradually this thought was metamorphosed into a realization that the income bearing value of race prejudice was the cause and not the result of theories of race inferiority. (Du Bois 1940, reprinted in Zuckerman 2004: 41)

In another essay entitled, 'The Negro and the Warsaw Ghetto', written in 1952, he states,

> The race problem I was interested in cut across lines of color and physique and belief and status and was a matter of cultural patterns, perverted teaching and human hate and prejudice, which reached all sorts of people and caused endless evil to all men. So that the ghetto of Warsaw helped me to emerge from a certain social provincialism into a broader conception of what the fight against race segregation, religious discrimination and the oppression by wealth had become if civilization was going to triumph and broaden the world. (Du Bois 1952, reprinted in Zuckerman 2004: 46)

Du Bois was also explicit about the economic hegemony of the West in 1955 in a article that stated, 'Here then is the fundamental question of our day: How far can nations who are at present most advanced... keep their wealth without using the land and labor of the majority of mankind mainly for the benefit of the European world and not for the benefit of most men, who happen to be colored?' (Du Bois 1955: 939).

On race and gender, Du Bois expressed a concern with the plight of women in many of his writings and is quoted as making an analogy between the enslavement of blacks and the enslavement of women, 'The soul longest in slavery and still in the most disgusting and indefensible slavery is the soul of womanhood' (Zuckerman 2004: 145). He offered particularly astute insights into the stereotyping of black women well before those offered by a number of contemporary black feminist scholars (see e.g. Hill-Collins 1990; Hurtado 1989; Higginbotham 1992; and hooks 1981). In *The Black Mother* published in 1912, he wrote about the paradoxes of the adulation of the black mammy stereotype appearing in American media,

> But this appreciation of the black mammy is always of the foster mammy, not of the mother in her home, attending to her own babies. And as the colored mother has retreated to her own home, the master class has cried out against her. She is thriftless and stupid.... Let us hope that the black mammy, for whom so many sentimental tears have been shed, has disappeared from American life. She existed under a false social system that deprived her of husband and child. (Du Bois 1912, reprinted in Zuckerman 2004: 145)

He observed early on that the experience of gender for women was racialized. In a chapter entitled, 'The Damnation of Women' in the book *Darkwater*, he wrote of the differential position of white women and black women within American society:

> In other years, Women's way was clear: To be beautiful, to be petted, to bear children. Such has been their theoretic destiny... and partial compensation for this narrowed destiny the white world has lavished its politeness on its womankind,—its chivalry and bows, its uncovering and courtesies.... From black women of America, however, (and from some others, too, but chiefly from black women and their daughters' daughters) this gauze has been withheld and without semblance of such apology they have been frankly trodden under the feet of men. (Du Bois [1921] 1975: 181–2)

Some scholars, however, critique Du Bois as having privileged the plight of black men at the expense of attention to black women in foregrounding race in most of his work (Carby 1998).

17.4.4. Racial Identity

It is in the classic, *The Souls of Black Folks*, that Du Bois presents his conceptualization of racial identity. The title of this work emanates from a belief held by many whites at the time of its writing in 1903 that black people did not have 'souls' because they were utterly different beings from whites (Tucker 2002: 232). Throughout the book, Du Bois describes the lived experience of being black in the United States. Du Bois writes about the effects of oppression and racism on black people:

> While sociologists gleefully count his bastards and his prostitutes, the very soul of the toiling, sweating black man is darkened by the shadow of a vast despair. Men call the shadow prejudice, and learnedly explain it as the natural defence of culture against barbarism, learning against ignorance, purity against crime, the 'higher' against the 'lower' races.... But before that nameless prejudice that leaps beyond all this he stands helpless, dismayed, and well-nigh speechless; before that personal disrespect and mockery, the ridicule and systematic humiliation, the distortion of fact and wanton license of fancy, the cynical ignoring of the better and the boisterous welcoming of the worse, the all-pervading desire to inculcate disdain for everything black, from Toussaint to the devil. ([1903] 1969:50)

He illustrates how racial identity is not just self-defined but also shaped by others. In the opening lines of the book he writes,

> Between me and the other world there is ever an unasked question: unasked by some through feelings of delicacy; by others through the difficulty of rightly framing it.... They approach me in a half-hesitant sort of way, eye me curiously or compassionately, and then, instead of saying directly, How does it feel to be a problem: they say, I know an excellent colored man in my town; or, I fought at Mechanicsville; or, Do not these Southern outrages make your blood boil: At these I smile, or am interested, or reduce the boiling to a simmer, as the occasion may require. To the real question, How does it feel to be a problem? I answer seldom a word. And yet, being a problem is a strange experience,—peculiar even for one who has never been anything else, save perhaps in babyhood and in Europe.
>
> (Du Bois, [1903] 1969: 43–44)

He uses the metaphor of a veil and the concept of *double consciousness* to capture the essence of this feeling. Du Bois argued that a veil separates black and white worlds. Blacks in the United States live behind a veil and the self develops differently for blacks than for whites—the self for blacks is forced to be bicultural, embracing both black and white worlds.[7] Du Bois's conceptualization of how the self is constituted is similar to G. H. Mead's view on self and Cooley's looking-glass self (Rawls 2000; Goodwin and Scimecca 2006). Yet, blacks remain on the margins of white society because of their oppressed status. Lemert (2003: 336) cautions readers not to miss the subtlety of the underlying idea of the veil that separates blacks and whites. He points out that the color line impacts not only the psyche of blacks but also works on the souls of white folks: 'But the line they [whites] draw turns out to be a Veil with the reciprocal effect of imposing the blindness upon which their civilization depends. In attempting to cover their eyes, whites are doubly crippled. They are mute as well as blind, even though, everyone knows, we talk all the time about that which we do not wish to see.'

[7] For a contemporary discussion of biculturalism, see Bell 1990.

Double consciousness also captures the peculiar tension of being on the margins of society or as it is often labeled today as being an *outsider-within* (Hill-Collins 1990). Du Bois wrote, 'It is a peculiar sensation, this double-consciousness, this sense of always looking at one's self through the eyes of others, of measuring one's soul by the tape of a world that looks on in amused contempt and pity. One ever feels his twoness,—an American, a Negro; two souls, two thoughts, two unreconciled strivings; two warring ideals in one dark body, whose dogged strength alone keeps it from being torn asunder' (Du Bois [1903] 1969: 45). Du Bois's double-consciousness concept introduced the idea that identity is often fractured by numerous social identities within one individual and that these identities can be in conflict (Zuckerman 2004). It also recognizes that it is the social structure manifested in the inequality of power and social status that shapes the identities of marginalized groups (Goodwin and Scimecca 2006: 260).

According to Du Bois, double consciousness was not just a liability but also provided blacks with a profound understanding of human experience (i.e. a two-sightedness) because of their confrontation with slavery and oppression, and this situated knowledge should not be repressed. Du Bois is suggesting that blacks and other oppressed groups have a particular view of society that allows them to have insights about the social system that may escape members of dominant groups (Allan 2005). His views are consistent with Marx's idea of critical consciousness that only those outside of a system can critically view the system. Today the idea of double consciousness providing a second sight is embodied as *standpoint theory*. According to Pat Hill-Collins (1998: 193–4), '*standpoint theory* posits a distinctive relationship among a group's position in hierarchical power relations, the experiences attached to differential group positionality, and the standpoint that a group constructs in interpreting these experiences.'

17.5. Conclusion: Learning about Race from the Outsider Within

Despite his prolific contributions on race that appeared in both academic publications and popular outlets, W. E. B. Du Bois was not able to influence in a significant way the trajectory of the sociology of race in the twentieth century. Instead, the work of scholars like Robert Park (1935) and Gunnar Myrdal (1944) became the foundations upon which the sociology of race evolved (Morris 2007). Other sociologists associated with the structural-functionalist paradigm, including Talcott Parsons, viewed prejudice as a problem of values (Winant 2007). And Gordon Allport's (1954) study of prejudice took a decidedly social psychological perspective focusing on white attitudes towards blacks and racially different others. Attention to cultural oppression, structural inequality, and racism was largely pushed to the margins.[8]

According to sociologist James McKee (1993), the assumption by many early white sociologists of the biological inferiority of blacks, subsequently supplanted by a belief in their cultural inferiority, determined the questions asked, the concepts developed, and the body of knowledge produced (Morris 2007).[9] Consequently, white agency was theorized as front and center and research evolved from this perspective. It follows that research was dominated by studies of white prejudice, white attitudes towards blacks, and assimilation. Assimilation was viewed as the ultimate solution to the 'race problem'. Robert E. Park's (1935) seminal race relations cycle theory became a dominant analytical framework for understanding intergroup relations within a structural-functionalist paradigm.[10] His cycle included phases of contact, competition, conflict, and accommodation, whereby the dominant group finally accepts the assimilated minority group.

Organization studies research on race has largely followed this social psychological trajectory with a focus on cognitive prejudice and defining employment discrimination (Nkomo 1992; Goldman *et al.* 2006). However, there have been some notable efforts in recent years to offer more critical perspectives on race in organizations (e.g. Essed 1991; Ferguson 1994; McGuire 2002; Mirchandani 2003; Prasad, Konrad, and Pringle 2006). For example, Essed (1991) developed a theory of *everyday racism* as a means of connecting structural dimensions of racism and its associated practices with everyday situations in organizations. More recently, Dietch *et al.* (2003) used the concept of everyday racism to examine discrimination in the workplace. Other organization studies research that might be positioned within a Du Boisian frame include descriptive research on the lived experience of race/ethnicity in organizations (e.g. Bell 1990; Bell and Nkomo 2001; Thomas and Gabarro 1999; Livers and Caver 2003). These latter studies have attempted to provide insight into the barriers to equality in organizations faced by racial/ethnic minorities. Bell (1990) used Du Bois's concept of double consciousness in her study of the bicultural life experiences of black women managers. Her research

[8] There were notable black scholars who followed Du Bois's intellectual approach, but their work, while acknowledged, did not change the trajectory of mainstream sociological study of race. These scholars included Franklin E. Frazier who wrote *The Negro Family in Chicago* (1932) and Charles S. Johnson, author of *Shadow of the Plantation* in 1934. Both did their doctoral studies at the University of Chicago (Thompson 2005*a*).

[9] Some argue that James McKee's analysis is too harsh in terms of its condemnation of the failure of mainstream sociologists to anticipate the explosive black urban rebellions and Civil Rights Movement of the 1960s. Winant (2007) stresses the importance of social movements as a key force in paradigmatic shifts in the sociology of race.

[10] Interestingly, the pragmatist approach of Park and the students he developed took a decidedly sociocultural approach that stressed culture and the role of group conflict in race relations. They adopted some of Du Bois's methods, particularly ethnographic studies of the socio-historical environment in which race operated (Winant 2007).

demonstrated how the women developed the ability to navigate back and forth between their own culture and the dominant white male culture of the organizations within which they worked.

While there have been calls for greater attention to the study of whiteness in organization studies (Grimes 2001; Macalpine and Marsh 2005), little empirical work has appeared (for an exception, see Yanow 2003). This has largely occurred because of a tendency to equate the study of race in organizations with the study of 'others' and not the dominant group. As Du Bois observed, the ascription of race to those who were not white bestows cultural power and privilege to the dominant group.

Du Bois's writing focused on centering race as an important construct in the social world, in particular, foregrounding the effects of race on black Americans. Organizations scholars must embrace the core idea that organizations are critical locations for the production of racial inequalities. Such inequalities contribute to both local and global racial discrimination and disadvantage. Race cannot and should not be studied as something apart from our very understanding of organizations. Studying race should not be reduced to a study of discrimination in organizations but should also illuminate how race fundamentally structures social relations in organizations (Andersen 2008).

Du Bois's concepts of double consciousness and intersectionality suggest that he also understood that racial/ethnic identity is complex and multifaceted, interlocked with other categories of difference. Studies using an intersectional framework explicitly attending to race, gender, and class simultaneously are virtually absent from organization studies. The dominant pattern in organization studies has been to study race, gender, and class independently (e.g. Cockburn 1991; Ely and Meyerson 2000; Ridgeway 1997); or on some occasions race and gender are combined (e.g. Bell and Nkomo 2001; Bell *et al.* 2003; Ferdman 1999; Royster 2003; Shih 2006). Race cannot be studied without recognizing its interlocking and mutually reinforcing connections with gender and class embedded within complex social and historical relationships (Andersen 2005; Acker 2006). Research employing an intersectional framework can reveal important nuances in how inequality is experienced providing a more complicated understanding of how these interlocking categories of difference structure opportunity, disadvantage, and social interaction in organizations (e.g. Adib and Guerrier 2003). Adib and Guerrier (2003) explored the interlocking of gender with class, ethnicity, race, and nationality in hotel work. Their analysis revealed a negotiation of the many categories shaping identities at work rather than an identity construction of adding difference on to difference.

A partial reason for limited attention to intersectionality in organization studies may be the significant challenge of finding the appropriate methodology to study dynamic, mutually reinforcing systems of inequality presented by race, gender, and class (McCall 2005). Here, organizational scholars might draw viable approaches from other disciplines, especially feminist scholarship (Acker 2006; Andersen 2005; Weber 2001). For example, Acker (2006: 443) introduced the concept of 'inequality regimes' defined as loosely interrelated processes, actions, and meanings that result in and maintain racial, gender, and class inequalities within particular organizations. What kinds of inclusions and exclusion does a specific inequality regime produce? The shape and degree of inequality may vary according to organization type, structure of the work organization, job type, and relative presence of different categories of difference. Inequality regimes are viewed as being linked to inequality in society, politics, history, and culture (Acker 2006). The concept of inequality regimes has the potential to provide an analytical tool for enacting Du Bois's observation about the persistence of racial thinking despite a long-standing rejection of biological definitions of race. Organization studies scholars should also draw upon theorizations of intersectionality found in critical studies, critical race theories, and labor process theories.

Postmodern and post-structuralist thinking has pointed us to the importance of focusing on cultural fragmentation and complex identities in organizations. However, it is critically important to enfold race, gender, and class identity within our thinking about identity in organizations and not position them as peripheral or marginal to understanding individual identity in organizations. The very construction of identity scholarship should recognize race, gender, and class as fundamental to identity as individuals in organizations grapple with 'Who am I?' and 'How Should I Act?' (Alvesson, Ashcraft, and Thomas 2008).

In his later years, Du Bois began to write about race beyond the borders of the United States focusing on the effects of colonialism and the expansion of global capitalism on what he referred to as the 'dark nations' of the world. Gilroy (1993: 127) has described Du Bois's lens as embodying the three modes of thinking, being, and seeing: the first is racially particularistic; the second is nationalistic; and the third is diasporic or hemispheric, sometimes global and occasionally universalistic. The latter has major implications for how organization studies scholars might proceed in the interrogation of race/ethnicity in organizations in the twenty-first century.

Du Bois's legacy is a call for greater attention by organizational scholars to understanding and studying cultural oppression, incorporating post-colonial perspectives to interrogate the intersection of race, gender, and class in organizations globally. It is important to remember that no racial/ethnic category or group can be understood outside of the specific historical, geographical, and cultural processes that constitute it and the symbolic regimes of language that summon representations of race/ethnicity to life (Hall 2003). Current conceptualizations of race in organizations studies have been dominated by US racial history and race relations. There is a need to develop cross-national understandings of the meanings of race and ethnicity that are geographically specific (Aspinall 2007). 'Race' is still a preferred term in the United States but Canada prefers 'population groups' (ibid.), while in The Netherlands it is morally wrong to register according to race (Essed and Trienekens 2008). Post-colonial treatments of difference and the colonial aftermath can be particularly instructive in understanding the evolution of representations of race, gender, sexuality, culture, and body in global organizations (Loomba 2005) as well as surfacing the relationships between local and global inequalities. The imbrication of the national and the global is the hallmark of post-colonial studies that allows for an interrogation of the intertwined histories of the colonized and the colonizer (Melamed 2006; Özkazanç Pan 2008). Post-colonial scholars rely on Marxist traditions, postmodernism, and post-structuralist theories to critique Eurocentric and Western representations of non-Western societies and peoples (Özkazanç Pan 2008). Organizational scholars who have used post-colonial theories problematize the dominant Western knowledge base of organization studies as well as the colonial origins of management (e.g. Banerjee and Prasad 2008; Prasad 2003; Frenkel and Shenhav 2005; Westwood and Jack 2008).

Studying race/ethnicity in organizations is challenging given the current tensions in the sociology of race in what Winant (2007: 571) describes as post-racial political hegemonies that incorporate a color-blind view (Thernstrom and Thernstrom 1997) on the right as well as on the left (Gilroy 2001). Witness the growing scholarship in organization studies where the study of race has been largely eclipsed by diversity management and its variants (Nkomo and Stewart 2006). Too much of the diversity management literature has reduced race, gender, and other socially marked identities to being solely about a plurality of behaviors and experiences and how to leverage them for the benefit of organizational objectives, although critical treatments of it are also present (Litvin 1997; Lorbiecki and Jack 2000; Prasad *et al.* 1997; Prasad, Konrad, and Pringle 2006; Zanoni and Janssens 2004). For example, diversity management research often characterizes race as a 'surface' level difference among people ignoring its basis for inequality and subordination. Other work emphasizes the need to build a business case for diversity, linking the presence of different people in the workplace as a means to profitability (Litvin 1997). While writing this chapter, I did a quick search of major journals in organization studies using the word 'race' and found little, having more luck using 'diversity'. Du Bois's scholarship reminds us that race and other systems of domination can persist and reside alongside the turn to the discourse of valuing diversity. The terrain of the study of race in organizations has become more complex and contested. The recognition that race is socially constructed has failed to lessen the reality of the continued racialization of organizations. Inequalities rooted in race, gender, class, and other devalued differences keep the flawed logic of race in place or as Sharon P. Holland (2005: 406) states, 'Even as we pronounce the death of race, we cannot overlook the fact that our attempts to articulate it into oblivion, to pronounce the last word on race, simply have not worked!' Du Bois's work stresses the need for organizational scholars who study race to be reflexive in thinking about how our own racial identities, political beliefs, and social location influence how we engage the subject.

It has not been possible to do justice in this short chapter to the prolific scholarship of W. E. B. Du Bois. He has been described as both an academic and public scholar unrelentingly committed to using scholarship for social change (Morris 2007; Winant 2007). Hopefully, this chapter will inspire organizational scholars to read Du Bois's sociology of race and expand our ways of articulating race in organizations.

REFERENCES

ACKER, J. (2006). 'Inequality Regimes: Gender, Class and Race in Organizations'. *Gender & Society*, 20/4: 441–64.

ADIB, A., and GUERRIER, Y. (2003). 'The Interlocking of Gender with Nationality, Race, Ethnicity and Class: The Narratives of Women in Hotel Work'. *Gender, Work and Organization*, 10/4: 413–32.

ALLAN, K. (2005). *Explorations in Classical Sociological Theory: Seeing the Social World*. Thousand Oaks, Calif.: Pine Forge Press.

ALLPORT, G. (1954). *The Nature of Prejudice*. New York: Perseus.

ALVESSON, M., ASHCRAFT, K. L., and THOMAS, R. (2008). 'Identity Matters: Reflections on the Construction of Identity Scholarship in Organizations Studies'. *Organization*, 15/1: 5–28.

ANDERSEN, M. L. (2005). 'Thinking about Women: A Quarter Century's View'. *Gender & Society*, 19/4: 437–55.

—— (2008). 'Thinking about Women Some More: A New Century's View'. *Gender & Society*, 22/1: 120–5.

APPIAH, K. (1992). *In my Father's House: Africa in the Philosophy of Culture*. New York: Oxford University Press.

APTHEKER, H. (ed.) (1973). *The Correspondence of W. E. B. Du Bois*, Vol. 1. *Selection, 1877–1934*. Amherst, Mass.: University of Massachusetts Press.

—— (ed.) (1986). *Newspaper Columns by W. E. B. Du Bois*. Vol. 2. White Plains, NY: Kraus-Thomson Organization Limited.

ASPINALL, P. J. (2007). 'Approaches to Developing an Improved Cross-national Understanding of Concepts and Terms Relating to Ethnicity and Race'. *International Sociology*, 22/1: 41–70.

BANERJEE, S. B., and PRASAD, A. (2008). 'Introduction to the Special Issue on "Critical Reflections on Management and Organizations: A Postcolonial Perspective"'. *Critical Perspectives on International Business*, 4/2–3: 90–8.

BANTON, M. (1998). *Racial Theories*. Cambridge: Cambridge University Press.

BELL, E. (1990). 'The Bicultural Life Experiences of Career-Oriented Black Women'. *Journal of Organizational Behavior*, 11: 459–78.

—— and NKOMO, S. M. (2001). *Our Separate Ways: Black and White Women and the Struggle for Professional Identity*. Boston: Harvard Business School Press.

—— MEYERSON, D., NKOMO, S. M., and SCULLY, M. (2003). 'Interpreting Silence and Voice in the Workplace: A Conversation about Tempered Radicalism among Black and White Women Researchers'. *Journal of Applied Behavioral Science*, 39/4: 381–414.

BODY-GENDROT, S. (2004). 'Race a Word Too Much?', in J. Solomos and M. Blumer (eds.), *Race and Racism*. London: Routledge.

Burrell, G. (1994). 'Modernism, Postmodernism and Organizational Analysis 4: The Contribution of Jurgen Habermas'. *Organization Studies*, 15: 1–9.

Calhoun, C. (ed.) (2007). *Sociology in America: A History*. Chicago: University of Chicago Press.

Carby, H. (1998). *Race Men*. Cambridge, Mass.: Harvard University Press.

Castells, M. (1997). *The Power of Identity*. London: Blackwell.

Clegg, S. (1990). *Modern Organization: Organization Studies in the Postmodern World*. London: Sage Publications.

Cockburn, C. (1991). *In the Way of Women: Men's Resistance to Sex Equality in Organizations*. Ithaca, NY: ILR Press.

Cooke, B. (2003). 'The Denial of Slavery in Management Studies'. *Journal of Management Studies*, 40/1: 895–918.

Cooley, C. H. (1902). *Human Nature and the Social Order*. New York: Charles Scribner's Sons.

—— (1909). *Social Organization*. New York: Charles Scribner's Sons.

Dennis, R. M. (1975). 'The Sociology of W. E. B. Du Bois'. Ph.D. thesis, Washington State University.

Dietch, E. A., Barsky, A., Butz, R. M., Chan, S., Brief, A. P., and Bradley, J. C. (2003). 'Subtle Yet Significant: The Existence and Impact of Everyday Racial Discrimination in the Workplace'. *Human Relations*, 56: 1299–1324.

Dollard, J. (1937). *Caste and Class in a Southern Town*. New York: Doubleday.

Du Bois, W. E. B. (1897). 'The Conservation of the Races', in American Negro Academy, Occasional Papers, No. 2/2. Washington, DC. Reprinted in Zuckerman (2004).

—— (1898). 'The Study of the Negro Problem'. *Annals of the American Academy of Political and Social Science*, 11: 1–23. Reprinted in Green and Driver (1978).

—— ([1899] 1967). *The Philadelphia Negro: A Social Study*. New York: Schocken.

—— ([1903] 1969). *The Souls of Black Folk*. New York: Signet Classic.

—— (1904). 'The Atlanta Conferences'. *Voice of the Negro* (1 March), 1. Reprinted in Green and Driver (1978).

—— (1911). 'The First Universal Races Congress'. A paper presented at a conference in London. Reprinted in Zuckerman (2004).

—— (1912). 'The Black Mother'. *The Crisis*. Reprinted in Zuckerman (2004).

—— (1914). 'Does Race Antagonism Serve Any Good Purpose?' *The Crisis*. Reprinted in Zuckerman (2004).

—— ([1921] 1975). *Darkwater: Voices from the Veil*. Millwood, NY: Kraus-Thomson Organization Limited.

—— (1935). *Black Reconstruction in America: An Essay toward a History of the Part of which Black Folk Played in the Attempt to Reconstruct Democracy in America 1860–1880*. Cleveland, Ohio: World Publishing Company.

—— (1940). *Dusk of Dawn: An Essay toward an Autobiography of the Race Concept*. New York: Harcourt, Brace.

—— (1952). 'The Negro and the Warsaw Ghetto'. *Jewish Life*. Reprinted in Zuckerman (2004).

—— (1955). 'The Wealth of the West vs. A Chance for Exploited Mankind'. *National Guardian*, 28 November 1955. Reprinted in Aptheker (1986).

—— (1968). *The Autobiography of W. E. B. Du Bois: A Soliloquy on Viewing my Life from the Last Decade of its First Century*. New York: International Publishers.

Ely, R. J., and Meyerson, D. (2000). 'Advancing Gender Equity in Organizations: The Challenge and Importance of Maintaining a Gender Narrative'. *Organization*, 7: 589–608.

Essed, P. (1991). *Understanding Everyday Racism: An Interdisciplinary Theory*. London: Sage.

—— and Goldberg, D. T. (eds.) (2002). *Race Critical Theories*. Oxford: Blackwell Publishers Ltd.

—— and Trienekens, S. (2008). 'Who Wants to Feel White? Race, Dutch Culture, and Contested Identities'. *Ethnic and Racial Studies*, 31/1: 52–72.

Ferdman, B. (1999). 'The Color and Culture of Gender in Organizations: Attending to Race and Ethnicity', in G. Powell (ed.), *Handbook of Gender & Work*. Thousand Oaks, Calif.: Sage Publications.

Ferguson, K. (1994). 'On Bringing More Theory, More Voices and More Politics to the Study of Organization'. *Organization*, 1/1: 92–7.

Fitzhugh, G. (1854). *Sociology for the South or Failure of Free Society*. Richmond, Va.: A. Morris. Reprinted in Thompson (2005).

Frenkel, M., and Shenhav, Y. (2006). 'From Binarism Back to Hybridity: A Postcolonial Reading of Management and Organization Studies'. *Organization Studies*, 27/6: 855–76.

Gilroy, P. (1993). *Black Atlantic*. Cambridge, Mass.: Harvard University Press.

—— (1998). 'Race Ends Here'. *Ethnic and Racial Studies*, 21/5: 838–47.

—— (2001). *Against Race: Imagining Political Culture beyond the Color Line*. Cambridge, Mass.: Harvard University Press.

Goldman, B., Gutek, B., Stein, J., and Lewis, K. (2006). 'Employment Discrimination in Organizations: Antecedents and Consequences'. *Journal of Management*, 32/6: 786–830.

Goodwin, G. A., and Scimecca, J. A. (2006). *Classical Sociological Theory: Rediscovering the Promise of Sociology*. Belmont, Calif.: Thomson Wadsworth.

Gossett, T. F. (1963). *Race: The History of the Idea in America*. Dallas: Southern Methodist University Press.

Green, D. S., and Driver, E. D. (eds.) (1978). *W. E. B. Du Bois on Sociology and the Black Community*. Chicago: University of Chicago Press.

Grillo, R. (2003). 'Cultural Essentialism and Cultural Anxiety'. *Anthropological Theory*, 3/2: 157–73.

—— (2007). 'An Excess of Alterity? Debating Difference in a Multicultural Society'. *Ethnic and Racial Studies*, 30/6: 979–98.

Grimes, D. (2001). 'Putting our own House in Order: Whiteness, Change and Organization Studies'. *Journal of Organizational Change Management*, 14/2: 132–49.

Gutman, H. (1977). *Work, Culture and Society in Industrializing America*. New York: Vintage.

Hall, S. (2003). *Representation: Cultural Representation*. London: Sage Publications.

Higginbotham, R. B. (1992). 'African-American Women's History and the Meta Language of Race'. *Signs: Journal of Women in Culture and Society*, 17: 251–74.

Hill-Collins, P. (1990). *Black Feminist Thought: Knowledge, Consciousness, and the Politics of Empowerment*. New York: Routledge.

—— (1998). *Fighting Words: Black Women and the Search for Justice*. Minneapolis: University of Minnesota Press.

Hirst, P., and Thompson, G. (1999). 'Globalization—A Necessary Myth', in J. Bryson, N. Henry, D. Keeble, and R. Martin (eds.), *The Economic Geography Reader*. Chichester: Wiley.

Holland, S. P. (2005). 'The Last Word on Racism: New Directions for a Critical Race Theory'. *South Atlantic Quarterly*, 104/3: 403–23.

hooks, B. (1981). *Ain't I a Woman: Black Women and Feminism*. Boston: South End Press.

Hughes, E. C. (1946). 'The Knitting of Racial Groups in Industry'. *American Sociological Review*, 11: 512–19. Reprinted in E. C. Hughes and H. M. Hughes (1952). *Where Peoples Meet: Racial and Ethnic Frontiers*. Glencoe, Ill.: Free Press.

Hurtado, A. (1989). 'Relating to Privilege: Seduction and Rejection in the Subordination of White Women and Women of Color'. *Signs: Journal of Women in Culture and Society*, 14: 833–55.

Johnston, W. B., and Packer, A. H. (1987). *Workforce 2000: Work and Workers for the 21st Century*. Indianapolis, Ind.: Hudson Institute.

Konrad, A., Prasad, P., and Pringle, J. (2006). *Handbook of Workplace Diversity*. Thousand Oaks, Calif.: Sage Publications.

Kurowski, L. L. (2002). 'Cloaked in Culture and Veiled in Diversity: Why Theorists Ignored Early US Workforce Diversity'. *Journal of Management History*, 40/2: 183–91.

Lemert, C. (2003). 'W. E. B. Du Bois', in G. Ritzer (ed.), *The Blackwell Companion to Major Classical Social Theorists*. Oxford: Blackwell Publishing.

Lewis, D. L. (2000). *W. E. B. Du Bois: The Fight for Equality and the American Century, 1919–1963*. New York: Henry Holt.

Litvin, D. R. (1997). 'The Discourse of Diversity: From Biology to Management'. *Organization*, 4: 187–210.

Livers, A., and Caver, K. (2003). *Leading in Black and White*. San Francisco, Calif.: Jossey-Bass.

Loomba, A. (2005). *Colonialism/Postcolonialism*. London: Routledge.

Lorbiecki, A., and Jack, G. (2000). 'Critical Turns in the Evolution of Diversity Management'. *British Journal of Management*, 11: 17–31.

Lott, T. L. (1999). *The Invention of Race: Black Culture and the Politics of Representation*. Oxford: Blackwell Publishers.

Macalpine, M., and Marsh, S. (2005). 'On Being White: There's Nothing I can Say'. *Management Learning*, 36/4: 429–50.

McCall, L. (2005). 'The Complexity of Intersectionality'. *Signs: Journal of Women in Culture and Society*, 30: 1771–1800.

McGuire, G. M. (2002). 'Gender, Race, and the Shadow Structure: A Study of Informal Networks and Inequality in a Work Organization'. *Gender and Society*, 16/3: 303–22.

McKee, J. B. (1993). *Sociology and the Race Problem: The Failure of Perspective*. Urbana: University of Illinois Press.

Melamed, J. (2006). 'From Racial Liberalism to Neoliberal Multiculturalism'. *Social Text*, 24/4: 1–24.

Mirchandani, K. (2003). 'Challenging Racial Silences in Studies of Emotion Work: Contributions from Anti-Racist Feminist Theory'. *Organization Studies*, 24/5: 720–42.

Montagu, A. (1997). *Man's Most Dangerous Myth: The Fallacy of Race*. Walnut Creek, Calif.: AltaMira Press.

Morris, A. (2007). 'Sociology of Race and W. E. B. DuBois: The Path Not Taken', in Calhoun (2007).

Myrdal, G. (1944). *An American Dilemma: The Negro Problem and Modern Democracy*. New York: Harper and Brothers.

NAYAK, A. (2006). 'After Race: Ethnography, Race, and Post-Race Theory'. *Ethnic and Racial Studies*, 29/3: 411–30.

NKOMO, S. M. (1992). 'The Emperor Has No Clothes: Rewriting Race in Organizations'. *Academy of Management Review*, 17: 487–513.

—— and PROUDFORD, K. (2006). 'Race in Organizations', in A. Konrad, P. Prasad, and J. Pringle (eds.), *Handbook of Workplace Diversity*. Thousand Oaks, Calif.: Sage Publications.

—— and STEWART, M. (2006). 'Diverse Identities in Organizations', in S. R. Clegg, C. Hardy, T. B. Lawrence, and W. R. Nord (eds.), *The Sage Handbook of Organization Studies*. London: Sage Publications.

ÖZKAZANÇ PAN, B. (2008). 'International Management Research Meets "the Rest of the World"'. *Academy of Management Review*.

PARK, R. E. (1935). 'Social Planning and Human Nature', in E. W. Burgess and H. Blumer (eds.), *The Human Side of Social Planning*. Chicago: American Sociological Society.

—— (1950). *Race and Culture*. Glencoe, Ill.: Free Press.

PETTIGREW, T. F. (ed.) (1980). *The Sociology of Race Relations: Reflection and Reform*. New York: Free Press.

PRASAD, A. (ed.) (2003). *Postcolonial Theory and Organizational Analysis*. New York: Palgrave Macmillan.

PRASAD, P., KONRAD, A. M., and PRINGLE, J. K. (2006). 'Examining the Contours of Workplace Diversity: Concepts, Contexts and Challenges', in A. M. Konrad, P. Prasad, and J. K. Pringle (eds.), *Handbook of Workplace Diversity*. London: Sage Publications.

—— MILLS, A. J., ELMES, M., and PRASAD, A. (1997). *Managing the Organizational Melting Pot: Dilemmas of Workplace Diversity*. Thousand Oaks, Calif.: Sage Publications.

RABAKA, R. (2007). *W. E. B. Du Bois and the Problems of the 21st Century*. Lanham, Md.: Lexington Books.

RAWLS, A. W. (2000). '"Race" as an Interaction Order Phenomenon: W. E. B. Du Bois's "Double Consciousness" Thesis Revised'. *Sociological Theory*, 18/2: 241–74.

RIDGEWAY, C. L. (1997). 'Interaction and Conservation of Gender Inequality: Considering Employment'. *American Sociological Review*, 62: 218–35.

ROBERTSON, R. (1997). 'Glocalization: Time-Space and Homogeneity-Heterogeneity', in M. Featherstone, S. Lash, and R. Robertson (eds.), *Global Modernities*. London: Sage Publications.

ROETHLISBERGER, F. J., and DICKSON, W. J. (1939). *Management and the Worker*. Cambridge, Mass.: Harvard University Press.

ROYSTER, D. A. (2003). *Race and the Invisible Hand: How White Networks Exclude Black Men from Blue-Collar Jobs*. Berkeley: University of California Press.

SARTORI, G. (2002). *Pluralismo, Multiculuralismo e Etranei*. Milan: Rizzoli.

SEIDMAN, S. (1998). *Contested Knowledge: Social Theory in the Postmodern Era*. Malden, Mass.: Blackwell Publishers Inc.

SHIH, J. (2006). 'Circumventing Discrimination: Gender and Ethnic Strategies in Silicon Valley'. *Gender & Society*, 20/2: 177–206.

SPICKARD, P. (ed.) (2005). *Race and Nation: Ethnic Systems in the Modern World*. London: Routledge.

TAKAKI, R. (1979). *Iron Cages: Race and Culture in the 19th Century*. New York: Alfred Knopf.

THERNSTROM, S., and THERNSTROM, A. (1997). *America in Black and White: One Nation, Indivisible*. New York: Simon and Schuster.

Thomas, D. A., and Gabarro, J. J. (1999). *Breaking Through: The Making of Minority Executives in Corporate America*. Boston: Harvard Business School Press.

Thompson, K. (ed.) (2005*a*). *The Early Sociology of Race and Ethnicity*. Vol. 1. *Sociology for the South or the Failure of Free Society: George Fitzhugh*. Oxford: Routledge.

—— (ed.) (2005*b*). *The Early Sociology of Race and Ethnicity*. Vol. 3. *The Negro American Family (W. E. B. Du Bois), The Negro American Artisan (W. E. B. Du Bois and A. G. Dill); Efforts for Social Betterment among Negro Americans (W. E. B. Du Bois)*. Oxford: Routledge.

Tucker, K. H., Jr. (2002). *Classical Social Theory*. Oxford: Blackwell Publishers.

Twine, F. W., and Gallagher, C. (2008). 'The Future of Whiteness: A Map of the "Third Wave" '. *Ethnic and Racial Studies*, 31/1: 4–24.

Ward, L. (1906). *Applied Sociology: A Treatise on the Conscious Improvement of Society by Society*. Boston: Ginn and Company.

Weber, L. (2001). *Understanding Race, Class, Gender and Sexuality: A Conceptual Framework*. Boston: McGraw-Hill.

Westwood, R. I., and Jack, G. (2008). 'Manifesto for a Post-Colonial International Business and Management Studies: A Provocation'. *Critical Perspectives on International Business*, 3/3: 246–65.

Winant, H. (2006). 'Race and Racism: Towards a Global Future'. *Ethnic and Racial Studies*, 29/5: 986–1003.

—— (2007). 'The Dark Side of the Force: One Hundred Years of the Sociology of Race', in Calhoun (2007).

Wortham, R. A. (2005). 'The Early Sociological Legacy of W. E. B. Du Bois', in Anthony J. Blasi (ed.), *Diverse Histories of American Sociology*. Leiden: Brill.

Wrege, C. D., and Perroni, A. G. (1974). 'Taylor's Pig-Tale: A Historical Analysis of Frederick W. Taylor's Pig-Iron Experiments'. *Academy of Management Journal*, 17/1: 6–27.

Yanow, D. (2003). *Constructing 'Race' and 'Ethnicity' in America: Category-Making in Public Policy and Administration*. Armonk, NY: M. E. Sharpe, Inc.

Zanoni, P., and Janssens, M. (2004). 'Deconstructing Difference: The Rhetoric of Human Resource Managers' Diversity Discourses'. *Organization Studies*, 25/1: 55–74.

Zuckerman, P. (ed.) (2004). *The Social Theory of W. E. B. Du Bois*. Thousand Oaks, Calif.: Pine Forge Press.

CHAPTER 18

ORGANIZATIONS AND THE CHICAGO SCHOOL

ANDREW ABBOTT

Sociology's interest in organizations is customarily traced to three sources: the Harvard-based human relations school, the Weberian tradition descending from Parsons through Merton at Columbia, and the more formal and economic approach associated with March and Simon at Carnegie Tech. Omitted from these lineages is the dominant body of sociological thinking in the inter-war period, the Chicago School.[1]

To be sure, organizations play a small role in the canonical image of Chicago sociology. This absence did not involve any lack of interest in social organization more broadly, about which the Chicagoans wrote a great deal. But by 'social organization' they meant 'the organizing of social life': a gerund rather than a noun, a process rather than a thing. The study of fixed pieces of social structure such as bureaucracies and other formally enacted groups was not for the Chicagoans a separately delineated body of inquiry. They wrote about such things, as we shall see,

[1] Because this chapter refers to dozens of works, it could easily have consisted largely of bibliography. But I have listed only central or specifically quoted works. Where published versions of dissertations exist, I have used the published title rather than the dissertation title. Finally, to my knowledge, the only prior work on the topic of the Chicago School and organizations is Burns (1980). For some contemporary work explicitly in the Chicago theoretical tradition, see the various essays in Abbott (2001).

but not under the guise in which they are now familiar to us, as 'organizations' in the sense of given entities.

In this chapter I shall first sketch the Chicago School and the organizational world it confronted. I then turn to social and formal organization as they actually appear in the Chicagoans' writings. I close with a discussion of the lessons organization theory today might take from the Chicago sociological tradition.

18.1. School and Moment

The Chicago School was the dominant voice in American sociology from the 1890s until World War II. Already declining in the late 1930s, it was eclipsed in the war and post-war period by the 'grand theory' and survey-based sociology associated with Harvard and Columbia. The emerging orthodoxy came to view Chicago sociology and its descendants in characteristically political terms as a 'loyal opposition'. It was indeed this opposition status that led the inheritors of the Chicago tradition to decide that there had been such a thing as a Chicago School and to begin to write its history.

According to most versions of that history, the Chicago School proper endured from 1915 to 1935 and comprised Robert Park, Ernest Burgess, and a remarkable group of their graduate students whose dissertation books remain compelling reading today. Chicago sociology was rooted in three things: the Park and Burgess textbook of 1921 with its processual view of the social world, the concept of the city as a laboratory, and a methodology of direct, personal involvement with that laboratory via anything from ethnography to institutional analysis.

We now know that these Chicago themes began not with Park and Burgess but with the founders of Chicago sociology, Albion Small and Charles Richmond Henderson, and their first generation of students, in particular George Vincent and W. I. Thomas. In Thomas and Znaniecki's *The Polish Peasant in Europe and America*, published 1918–21 in five volumes, the Chicago School had a symbolically central work: substantively important, comprehensively theoretical, universally read, and enormously influential. It was indeed the reading of Thomas and Znaniecki that inspired the great students of the 1920s.

I shall therefore here use 'the Chicago School' to label the entire tradition of Chicago sociological thinking from Small and Henderson in the 1890s up through Thomas to Park, Burgess, and their students in the 1920s. All these had a unified and fairly cohesive view of social life. Social life consisted not of structures and roles and norms, but of groups and processes, perpetually pushing on each other in contact, conflict, and accommodation. Social facts were always local in time and space, always shaped or even determined by their context. Social organization, disorganization, and reorganization were perpetual processes, and groups were in perpetual turnover and transformation. 'The world', in the ringing phrase of the Chicagoans' philosopher colleague George Herbert Mead, 'is a world of events.'

The Chicagoans' methodological insistence on studying social life up close makes it puzzling that there are no works focused on bureaucracy and formal organizations in the usually accepted Chicago canon. After all, formal organization and bureaucratic experience were beginning to reach into average American life by the 1920s via postal banking, income taxes, military service, and vehicle registration. Yet average American experience remained free of formal organization. One-third of America's workers worked on farms, which averaged only 2.13 workers in 1920. The average 1920 textile establishment had only 130 workers, most of whom would have been subcontracted by foremen. Nor were non-work aspects of daily experience much more bureaucratized. In 1920, only 65 percent of children ages 5 to 19 were in school, and there remained over 190,000 one-teacher public schools. Most of the nation's 30,000 banks were small, local affairs. There was no health insurance beyond a few union and workplace programs.

By contrast, after World War II well over half the labor force could recall spending the war years in giant organizations: 16.5 million of them in the military, 19 million in large-scale war industries, and 3 million in the war-swollen federal government. Upwards of 70 percent of military-age white males enjoyed GI Bill benefits through the rapidly growing Veterans Administration, Housing and Urban Development, and other government bureaucracies. In the National Labor Relations Board, the New Deal had spawned an agency directly impacting the daily life of the majority of American workers. Bureaucratic employment regimes were now the norm, and unionization was rapidly increasing nationwide. The spread of health insurance and home ownership brought more and more of the population under the rule of claims, mortgages, and payments. That post-war America was such an extraordinarily bureaucratized society makes it unsurprising that bureaucracy and formal organization should then become focal topics of sociology. Modern organization theory grew and developed in that era because the thing it studied grew and developed in that era.

The relative absence of bureaucracy and formal organization from the Chicago canon may thus reflect their relative absence from American life during the heyday of the Chicago School. But on closer inspection, this argument fails. Chicagoans were prescient about urban disorganization, consumption patterns, ethnic and racial conflict, and revolutions in communications. Why did they miss bureaucracy and formal organization? As early as 1905, there were twenty-three railroads employing at least 10,000 employees apiece, ranging up to the Pennsylvania Railroad's 165,000 workers. Manufacturing concerns like the Ford Motor Company, Western Electric, and US Steel employed tens of thousands of workers apiece. The countryside was dotted with state-sponsored formal organizations such as prisons, universities, and mental hospitals. And government employment was enormous, from the hundreds of thousands working for the post office and for the military to the tens of thousands working for various state and local governments.

Moreover, the Chicago sociologists had large organizations right on their doorstep. In the 1920 census over half of Chicago's 403,942 manufacturing workers worked in the 259 establishments with over 250 workers apiece, and more than one-quarter in the forty-one establishments with over a thousand workers apiece. Indeed, Western Electric's Hawthorne works had passed 25,000 employees in 1917. The City of Chicago itself had 34,604 employees in 1923, its Board of Education alone employing 11,097 teachers for 452,257 students. The Archdiocese of Chicago, whose thousands of clergy ministered in 1915 to over a million Roman Catholics in 215 parishes, ran in addition dozens of hospitals and homes, hundreds of schools, academies, and colleges, and two universities. No one can say that Chicago lacked large organizations for the Chicago sociologists to study!

It turns out that on close inspection the Chicago School did indeed write a great deal about organizations. As we shall see, that work disappeared from the history of organization theory largely because the human relations school writers—Elton Mayo and Lloyd Warner in particular—seem to have consciously decided to set Chicago sociology aside. But the Chicagoans also connived at their own dismissal. For the post-war Chicagoans embraced their opposition status in sociology by founding their identity completely on the urban field research tradition, thereby themselves ignoring the important body of work their own predecessors had done on organization and organizations.

It is that work I aim to recover here. Because the Chicagoans lacked an explicit theory of organizations, it is useful to bear in mind, as we reread their work, three families of themes that can organize our reading: (1) static aspects of the interiors of organizations, (2) diachronic aspects of single organizations, and (3) aspects of relations among organizations. Under the first of these headings come topics like organization structure, line and staff issues, and executive function and decision making, as well as informal organization, the irrationality of bureaucracy, and the specific problem of professionals in bureaucracies. Under the second come the various versions of institutionalism, both the paleo-institutionalism of Selznick and the neo-institutionalism of Meyer. The focus on mimicry in the latter bridges directly to the third general family of themes, on relations among organizations. Under this heading come analyses of organizational fields and ecology, on the one hand, and of resource dependency—relation to external supports—on the other.

As we seek those themes in Chicago work, we shall find World War I a sharp dividing line, partly because of the war's own impact on American thinking about organizations, but more because the war marked the intellectual defeat of progressivism. Intimately linked with progressivism, pre-war social science derived much of its unity from its politics. The defeat of this unifying force led to sharper disciplinary lines as foundations invested in disciplinary social science, as the disciplines themselves matured, and as the new emphasis on 'science' made interdisciplinary differences more explicit (see Haber 1964; Ross 1991: ch. 10). All these forces mean that the pre-war and post-war constellations of 'organizational' ideas were quite different.

18.2. Organizations in Chicago Reform Era Sociology

In early social science, the themes just sketched out—static organizational analysis, dynamic and institutional analysis, and analysis of external organizational relations and fields—are scattered in various places. There is, to be sure, a literature on what by 1920 was called 'business administration' that had taken shape shortly after the turn of the twentieth century. This literature, which falls under the first of my themes, typically took a principal's eye view of the problem of structuring and running a business organization. It was to this audience that scientific management was in the first instance addressed. But there were other areas where organizational issues were debated, and two were particularly central in sociology: municipal and civil service reform and management–labor relations. The political slant of these literatures should be clear. Sociology's early view of organizations was thoroughly reformist, as the discontinuity between Taylorism and the sociological literature on management–labor relations makes clear. To be sure, as Haber (1964) and Nyland (1996) have shown, scientific management had its own ties to reformism and even at times to organized labor during the years before World War I. But scientific management had little impact in sociology: in the first thirty years of the *American Journal of Sociology*, only six articles have the word 'efficiency' in their titles.

In the eyes of pre-World War I social science, therefore, the issues that we think of as 'organizational' were largely perceived through the reform agenda. On these issues, the primary writers at Chicago, as elsewhere in academia, were outside the sociology department. Charles Merriam of Chicago's political science department wrote a definitive analysis of municipal financial systems in 1906 and a classic description of primary elections as political institutions in 1908. Merriam's position as a reform alderman made him Chicago's foremost authority on organization in government. On capital and labor issues, the leading Chicago writers were in economics. Department chair J. Laurence Laughlin's text gave a cursory handling of the labor question as a part of 'Descriptive Political Economy', but his younger colleague Thorstein Veblen's 1904 work on the theory of business enterprise coupled its revolutionary analysis of the new finance capitalism with an analysis of the impact of the machine process on workers. After Veblen left, his follower R. F. Hoxie wrote a long string of articles on labor issues from 1907 onward, culminating in a celebrated report of 1916 that condemned scientific management.

Within the sociology department, the chief writer on 'organizations' was neither Small, the general social theorist, nor Thomas, the social psychologist, but rather Charles Richmond Henderson, the Christian reformer. Henderson's explicit combination of religion and reformism with social theory has exiled him from the list of sociological classics, but in fact he wrote an enormous amount about organizational issues.

Like most of the Chicago sociologists, Henderson located what we now call organizations as one among many types of 'institutions'. The concept of institutions was general at the time, denoting any body of social behavior or structure dedicated to carrying out what we would now call a function of society. 'Crescive institutions' were our 'naturally-evolved' institutions like the family and the legal system, while 'enacted institutions' were our 'organizations' (more properly, 'organizational forms', see Sumner 1906: 53–4). Henderson was extremely explicit about organizational matters when he chose. He discusses in detail the advantages and disadvantages of various ways to administer charity in *The Needy and their Problem: An Introduction to the Study of the Dependent, Defective, and Delinquent Classes* (1893). Although Henderson does not see the topic as a theoretically unified body of inquiry, he considers a wide range of internal, synchronic organizational matters, embedding them within a reformist, evolutionary rhetoric that expects 'efficient' bureaucracy to solve most problems. In *Modern Methods of Charity*, a 1904 collection covering charity policies and systems in eighteen countries, Henderson (1904: 439 ff.) provides a detailed analysis of the function of charity organization societies. These precursors of modern social work were essentially coordination systems, bringing together relief organizations and needy clients. They should in Henderson's view not only identify needs, connect individuals with services, and sort out imposters but also organize services where they are lacking, pressure employers to provide welfare, and further the cause of municipal reform. Henderson was thus proposing a model of coordination that was neither the market coordination being extolled by the rising discipline of economics nor the bureaucratic rule structure of the continental systems of charity (ibid. 36 ff.), but something in between. We now know that this coordination would ultimately be turned into a professional expertise—social work—rather than an organizational form, losing its reformism in the process. But Henderson pre-dates this shift and hence proposes the charity organization societies as a model of a new organizational form combining rationality and 'morality' (that is, benevolence), and working not only to coordinate activities across complex boundaries but also to educate both the givers and the receivers of charity in the process. As an argument about social organization, this was sophisticated indeed.

Henderson's colleague Albion Small was less specific about organizations. Small and Vincent's textbook of 1894 took an evolutionist viewpoint, following 'the natural history of a society' from the family on the farm to the village, the town, and the city. In this, it followed the near universal experience of late nineteenth-century Americans. But the rest of the work was—in contemporary terms—largely functionalist and ignored organizations. Elsewhere, indeed, Small was at some pains to deny the reality of organizations altogether. There was only process:

> Association is activity, not locality. Like states of consciousness, it has to be known in terms of process, not in dimensions of space. (1905: 505)

> Institutions are but the shell of social activities. Analysis of them simply as institutions is necessary; but that sort of analysis is merely a step toward more real analysis of the place which they actually occupy in working social arrangements, and of the social content which their operation actually secures. (1905: 529–30)

That further analysis led Small to some quite radical strictures on capitalists ('The social problem of the twentieth century is whether the civilized nations can restore themselves to sanity after their nineteenth-century aberrations of individualism and capitalism', 1914: 440). But it never led him to investigate the nature of organizations for their own sake.

A more intimate sense of the early Chicago thinking about organizations comes from the dissertations done under Small and Henderson.[2] Of the thirty-one available, nine have some relevance to organizations.

Four of these are organizational censuses, three of them within communities. C. J. Bushnell's 1902 dissertation analyzes the stockyards community, giving as its main organizational content a discussion of the butchering and meat-processing system itself, which is compared to the military. Yet the welfare aspects of meatpacking firms are also discussed as are the churches and other local organizations. J. M. Gillette's 1901 dissertation discusses the various organizations in a steel community, with an interesting discussion of the 'straw boss' system of hiring and

[2] The department lacks a single master list of dissertations. The most comprehensive count (one including dissertations under Henderson in the Divinity School as well as in sociology) is forty-one dissertations before 1916. Of these, ten have disappeared. Among the others, I have scanned all with any relevance to organizations. The latter portion of the paper concerns dissertations up to 1935. I scanned all dissertations in that period (about another seventy) with possible relevance to organizations. I have also referred to a number of works generally taken to be in the Chicago canon that are not dissertations, e.g. Donovan's *The Saleslady* and Anderson's *The Hobo*.

a complete community census of churches, schools, fraternal and secret organizations, and so on. F. G. Cressey's (1903) dissertation is a questionnaire-based exploratory survey of the churches' methods for reaching young men. All three of these show an awareness of organizations and even to some extent of the ecology of organizations in a community. But that awareness is not central to their understanding of the organizations, which are seen mainly in terms of successful or unsuccessful performance, following the usual reform standard of 'efficiency'. 'Inefficiency', at least implicitly, was what would later be called 'bureaucratic irrationality' and under that name would obsess the literature on informal and formal relations in bureaucracy in the 1950s and 1960s. These dissertations thus combine work in the first and last of my thematic families: internal organizational functioning and interorganizational ecology.

A 'census' of a different kind is Fleming's 1906 study of all the magazines ever published in Chicago up to his time of writing. Although Fleming sees the issues that would later preoccupy Glenn Carroll and colleagues—the basics of organizational ecology—he provides only the statistics (on durations and foundings). He does not really conceive of the spread of magazines in the abstract as the development of an organization form or of an organizational population.

By contrast with all of these, the dissertations of Hannah Clark, Hector MacPherson, Samuel Reep, and Edwin Sutherland are recognizably modern organizational analyses. Clark's 1897 study of the Chicago school system recognizes the importance of organization charts and the flow of political power both through and around that structure. The problem of professionals (teachers) in organizations is also clearly recognized as such (Clark points out how teachers waste their time on 'elaborate bookkeeping'). The analysis of resource dependence is particularly interesting, the schools being supported partly by taxes under political control and partly by rental income from an enormous but decreasing real estate endowment. Hector Macpherson's 1910 analysis of the cooperative credit associations in the province of Quebec is an explicit study of the spread of an organizational form. Like many early dissertations, it bears the sign of progressivism; Macpherson clearly wants such associations to spread in the United States. But there is much attention to how and why a particular organizational form can work in a particular organizational and community environment.

With Samuel Reep's 1910 dissertation we come to an explicitly theoretical organizational analysis. Its title, 'The Organization of the Ecclesiastical Institutions of a Metropolitan Community', nicely captures the Chicagoans' processual use of the word 'organization', as opposed to their use of 'institution' where we would use 'organization'. Not only does Reep provide a denominational history of the city, he couples this with a questionnaire-based analysis of the polities, institutional activities, ecclesiastical and lay charities, and Sunday schools of the dozens of denominations in Chicago. He concludes with a theoretical chapter on 'ecclesiastical organization and the social process'. In that chapter, he argues that ecclesiastical structures that are dogmatic and centralized tend to be controlled by the past and by distant communities. Religious professionals in them acquire specific interests of their own in preservation of structure, and the means (the structure) gradually becomes an end in itself. This conflicts with the adaptability of the larger structure to new situations and places. This is a purely theoretical, thoroughly modern, argument about organizations.

Finally, Edwin Sutherland's (1914) thesis studies the entire field of employment agencies nationwide, explicitly contrasting public and private agencies in terms of their clienteles, missions, internal organization, and political determinants. Although Sutherland touches only lightly on internal matters, his analysis of the ecologies of these organizations, their competitive nature and their various resource dependencies is truly extraordinary. Sutherland is particularly deft in his discussion of unanticipated consequences and of the conflicts between trade-based unionism and the inter-occupational mobility necessary to effective placement of the unemployed and between locally provided relief and the need for inter-local mobility. Although not explicitly theoretical, his discussion is of an extraordinary, quite modern analytical subtlety.[3]

Like the work of the professors who supervised them, these dissertations betray a number of common themes vis-à-vis organizations. Although the synchronic issues of organizational chart irrationalities make an occasional appearance, the focus is much more on dynamics: institutionalization, ossification, change, and evolution. The second of my three families of themes (institutional dynamics) dominates, along with a considerable admixture of the third theme (interorganizational relations).

It is important to note, too, that with the exception of Bushnell's dissertation on the stockyards, Emory Bogardus's (1912) on industrial fatigue, and Sutherland's on employment organizations none of these early dissertations is even remotely about work and industry. The main organizations with which Chicagoans were concerned were those of charity and the city. Small was concerned with capitalism, but only abstractly, and he supervised no empirical work. The empiricist was Henderson, whose prime interest was charity organization. This is perhaps another reason for the invisibility of the Chicago tradition in later organizational analysis. The dominant organization of the post-World War II literature was the large corporation, whereas the organizational writings of the Chicago School mostly concerned non-commercial organizations—churches, employment agencies, schools, libraries, and so on.

[3] A good indicator of the loss of the Chicago organization tradition is the fact that Peter Blau's 1955 classic *Dynamics of Bureaucracy*, an internal synchronic study of one employment agency, does not cite Sutherland.

18.3. War and Transition

The 1910s were a period of great transition, both nationally and for Chicago sociology. Nationally, the decade brought the fruition of progressive urban reform in the commission/manager form of government and the concurrent triumph of civil service bureaucratization over machine politics (Schiesl 1977). By contrast, after a sudden vogue early in the decade, scientific management had relaxed after Taylor's 1915 death into a less visionary, more business-oriented program for industrial management (Haber 1964). Thus were the great foci of progressive thinking about organizations settled into the more comfortable framework of 'efficient management,' losing their connection with democracy and liberalism in the process. The war effort itself was viewed as a triumph of economic management, providing strong models for business in the 1920s. The 1919 Boston Police Strike and the echoes of the Russian Revolution brought a brief red scare. Politics moved decidedly to the right.

At Chicago too there were great changes, both in structure and in personnel. The crucial structural change was the founding of the School of Social Service Administration (SSA). SSA combined two ventures. One of these was the 'philanthropic section' of the College of Commerce and Administration (PSCCA; the college would later become the Graduate School of Business). This was a major for undergraduates planning to enter social work or charity administration, a major whose very existence testifies to the interest of the pre-war sociology department in organizations. Virtually all of the sociology faculty were on the PSCCA masthead, although Henderson and Bedford contributed the most courses. But PSCCA also involved extensive courses from political economy (Marshall and Hoxie) and political science (Merriam and Freund). The other ingredient of SSA was the Chicago School of Civics and Philanthropy (CSCP), a free-standing school dating from 1908 and run, to all intents and purposes, by Sophonisba Breckinridge and Edith Abbott, who were simultaneously long-standing Hull House reformers and Ph.D. faculty of the university in Household Administration and Sociology, respectively. SSA embodied the transition of social work from radical organizational form to delimited professional expertise.

The founding of SSA was closely tied to personnel changes in the sociology department. Charles Henderson died in 1915, and W. I. Thomas—another reform stalwart—was fired in 1918. That left Robert Park and Ernest Burgess as the dominant figures in the department, both of them inclined to 'scientize' sociology and loosen ties with reform. There had been changes elsewhere as well. In economics, a dominant voice of institutionalism was removed when Robert Hoxie committed suicide in 1916; Frank Knight, who would dominate the department intellectually, was much closer to the mainstream (Ross 1991: 424 ff.). In political science, recent graduate Leonard White emerged as the key voice on municipal institutions. Unlike

Merriam, he was not a reformer but a technocrat. This transition at Chicago echoed that of the social sciences nationally, as a generation without the unifying force of progressivism began to settle their research practices into a more permanently differentiated academic establishment.

In this new division of academic labor, a topic that did not go to the sociologists was organizations. The study of municipal bureaucracy at Chicago was, as elsewhere, located firmly in the department of political science, where it was dominated by Leonard White, who played the scientist to Merriam's continuing reformism. As late as 1933, Merriam was still hoping for a visionary reorganization of Chicago on a regional basis, but the younger White's masterful study of city managers (1926) was a more measured, dispassionate work. White's 1925 survey of morale in Chicago municipal employees is a recognizably modern analysis of a classic organizational problem, little different from Michel Crozier's book on French *fonctionnaires* forty years later.

Studies of work and industry (or of capital/labor, to give the area its progressive name) were located even more firmly in the department of political economy, which changed its name to economics in this decade. Coming to Chicago in the same year as Hoxie's death, Harry Millis in effect replaced Hoxie with another institutionalist labor economist. Millis's students produced a number of important dissertation studies in the 1920s: for example, on the Chicago Labor Federation (T. C. Bigham, 1925), on industrial relations in the Chicago building trades (R. E. Montgomery, 1927), on the Illinois State Federation of Labor (E. Staley, 1930), and on black workers in the slaughterhouses (A. Herbst, 1930). All of these are rich, finely textured ethnographic accounts of their topics, combined with quantitative and, in Herbst's case, extensive demographic analysis. To the modern reader, they look like the work the Chicago School sociologists could have done on industrial workers, but did not.

The theoretical side of this inquiry was also located in the economics department, where L. C. Marshall published in 1921 an enormous reader (*Business Administration*) in exactly the same format (and even the same typefaces) as Park and Burgess's famous *Introduction to the Science of Sociology* of the same year. This was Marshall's third such work; the first was an elementary economics reader in 1913 patterned after W. I. Thomas's *Source Book for Social Origins*, the second an enormous compendium of institutionalist economics (*Industrial Society*) in 1918. Marshall was thus the university's mainstream business administration theorist through this period.

Thus, the dominant topical areas in which organization concepts had been discussed during the progressive era fell in the post-war period into the jurisdiction of other departments. It is likely that the Chicago experience was paralleled at Columbia and other major training institutions. Indeed, the closeness of pre-war Chicago social science to reform may have kept Chicago sociologists closer to organizational topics than their peers. And in the event, a surprising amount of Chicago

School research in the 1920s bears on topics that today lie within organizational studies. It is to that research that I now turn.

18.4. The Park–Burgess Chicago School and Organizations

Students of the Chicago School examined a wide variety of organizations during the 1920s. They did not have a concept of 'organizations' per se, but they moved away from the absolute processualism of Small and began to recognize particular organizations as important entities, even though, as we shall see, their basic conception of these entities remained fundamentally dynamic.

The new faculty leaders had different interests from Small, Henderson, and Thomas. Robert Park was fascinated by the city as a phenomenon and in particular by the mixing of different cultures and races, by questions about communication both symbolic and practical, and by what we would now call the cultural structure—both emergent and individual—of the consumer society taking shape in that decade. Ernest Burgess was interested in the family and more broadly in how individuals evolved through the life course in the social world of modernity. Both of them seized on ecological metaphors to understand these various processes, with a consequent emphasis on geography, social location, and typical sequences of contact, conflict, and other social processes.

Chicago students were also strongly influenced by the teaching of Ellsworth Faris, who insisted on the detailed reading of Thomas and Znaniecki's *The Polish Peasant in Europe and America.* 'Organization'—in the Chicago sense of 'the task of organizing'—played a crucial theoretical role throughout that work. Social organization, disorganization, and reorganization were for Thomas continuous processes, happening at all times in all societies. Yet in this world of flux, Thomas was by no means silent on the topic of what we today would call organizations. The first part of volume 2 of *The Polish Peasant* contained long sections on the press and cooperative institutions in Poland, while the latter part (on America) discussed local organizations such as churches and the press, as well as more national organizations such as the Socialist Alliance and the Polish National Alliance. In the Wladek life history that concluded volume 2, literally dozens of workplaces and their internal structure (in Poland, where Wladek was an itinerant baker) were described. These organizations were, however, not judged in terms of their own internal logic, but in terms of their relation to their constituents, employees, and objects. In this sense, *The Polish Peasant* was continuous with much of the industrial psychology literature contemporaneous with it, only far more theoretically grounded and empirically broad. (The Hawthorne researchers' discovery of the embeddedness of work in society would not have surprised them had they bothered to read *The Polish Peasant.*)

The work for which the Chicago School is most prominently known comprises the dissertations written in this stimulating intellectual environment. Broadly speaking, there were three kinds of dissertations that touch on organizations: about kinds of events, about types of people, and about types of social institutions.

18.4.1. Dissertations on Types of Events

Dissertations about kinds of events are exemplified by works such as E. T. Hiller's *The Strike* (1928) and Lyford Edwards's *The Natural History of Revolution* (1927). Such dissertations located themselves absolutely within the department's processual world-view; as Edwards's title implies, both works are structured around the typical sequence of occurrences in the larger events they describe. Focused on images, beliefs, activities, and social control, Edwards's book says nothing about the organization of revolutionary groups beyond scattered comments on topics such as mobs, control of the military, and reformist organization of illegal governments. Hiller's analysis, by contrast, regularly pairs analysis of the symbolic and emotional unfolding of strikes with analysis of their organizational sources and consequences: organizations make and are made by the process of striking. Another dissertation loosely of this type—focusing on historical change—is John Mueller's 'The Automobile' (1928), which studies the effects of the automobile on traditional means of social control (e.g. illicit sex becomes easier because people can easily cross city lines). Aside from considering the new forms of social control aiming at these new forms of social disorganization, Mueller says little about organizations per se. In general, the 'event' dissertations are not strong contributors to the Chicago 'organizations' tradition.

18.4.2. Dissertations on Types of People

Organizations in the modern sense play only a slightly larger role in the large collection of Chicago work on types of people. Dissertations such as Samuel Kincheloe's 'The Prophet' (1929) and Everett Stonequist's 'The Marginal Man' (1930) work out the details of certain positions in the social structure, but do not study the organized section of that structure from which marginal men and prophets are excluded. Organizations are similarly tangential in the long (and famous) list of Chicago works about deviant types and social problems: Nels Anderson's *The Hobo* (1923), Ruth Cavan's *Suicide* (1928), Clifford Shaw's *The Jackroller* (1930) and *The Natural History of a Delinquent Career* (1931), Edwin Sutherland's *The Professional Thief*

(1937), and R. E. L. Faris and Warner Dunham's *Mental Disorders in Urban Areas* (1939). Some of these works give important views of organizations (prisons, missions, delinquent homes, and so on) as they are traversed by hobos and criminals. But in others (e.g. Cavan and Faris and Dunham) organizations are only part of the background, evidence of ongoing 'social organization' and 'disorganization' in their processual, Chicago senses.

Because their fascination with social disorganization led Chicagoans away from mainstream types, it was a peripheral member of the Chicago school who captured the explicit experience of bureaucratic employment. Frances Donovan was a widow who returned to school to complete an undergraduate degree at Chicago in 1918 (studying under Park among others) before becoming a full-time schoolteacher. In the summers, Donovan did participant observation as a waitress (*The Woman Who Waits*, 1919) and as a saleswoman (*The Saleslady*, 1928). She also eventually wrote up her own occupation (*The Schoolma'am*, 1938). While not sociologically theorized, these works are all fluent personal accounts of work in multiple settings with multiple types of people. Rewritten into separated quotes and larded with theory, they would be recognizable today as solid organizational ethnographies. But that is not their real place in the Chicago work of the time. The mainstream sociology of work would become a dominant theme of Chicago sociology only much later, under the post-war leadership of Everett Hughes. By contrast, Donovan's two earlier books were both about the consumption world that so fascinated Park. Their real importance is to yoke that consumption world to the experience of work, to give a social psychology of consumption work, and above all of women's place in that social psychology.

18.4.3. Dissertations on Institutions

The third general type of dissertation concerns what the Chicago school called institutions. As noted earlier, these were bodies of social organization the Chicagoans imagined as loosely related to certain kinds of social functions and necessities. There were really five types of such institutions: the family, entertainment institutions, communication institutions, communities, and, finally, organizations proper. The family dissertations—Ernest Mowrer's *Family Disorganization* (1927) and Franklin Frazier's *The Negro Family in Chicago* (1932)—like the Cavan and Faris and Dunham works, say almost nothing about organizations. Organizations in the modern sense are simply one part of the 'organization' and 'disorganization' (i.e. organizing and disorganizing) of the community that drive family demoralization, which is the focus of both books. Organizations are similarly absent from Herbert Blumer's *Movies and Conduct* (1933; Blumer's dissertation was purely theoretical), which simply asks about the social psychological effects of movies, another step in the Parkian analysis of the social psychology of modern consumption society.

By contrast, the other Chicago works on entertainment institutions—Paul Cressey's *The Taxi-Dance Hall* (1932) and Walter Reckless's *Vice in Chicago* (1933)—are first-rate organizational studies. Cressey's analysis of types of dance halls touches on the resource dependencies of the dance halls, the evolution of different types of halls, competition and specialization among them, and, of course, locational patterns. About the only main organizational topic not covered is the internal structure and executive difficulties of the dance hall, although the problem of maintaining a roster of good dancers is considered to some extent. Reckless's book on brothels is not quite as organizationally focused, but it has careful analyses of the emergence of the cabaret and the roadhouse as alternative organizational formats for prostitution. And like Cressey, Reckless does the organizational and locational ecology of brothels in great detail.

As a former journalist, Park had a specific interest in journalism, to which testify both his own monograph on *The Immigrant Press and Its Control* (1922) and a number of dissertations. Much of this work is focused purely on content. *The Immigrant Press*, as well as K. Kawabe's *Press and Politics in Japan* (1921) and F. G. Detweiler's *The Negro Press in the United States* (1922), all focus entirely or primarily on content. Detweiler and Park devote some attention to the basic ecology of newspapers—readership, external resource supports and alliances, rates of turnover, and so on—but these are not major foci. By contrast, H. E. Jensen's massive study of 'The Rise of Religious Journalism in the United States' (1920) analyzes the ecology of religious journalism in great detail. Jensen develops period mortality tables for religious journals, discusses resource dependency issues and imitation patterns, and concludes with a profoundly organizational interpretation of the effects of the press on denominationalism as an organizational system. Like Cressey's book, this too could pass muster as contemporary work.

A considerable number of Chicago dissertations can be thought of as studies of communities. Like the earlier community studies of the pre-1918 period, these nearly always list the organizations in their communities and sometimes go on to study particular aspects of organization. But their main focus is on the functions of organizations in constituting communities, a theme that would go underground until the Putnam social capital controversy of the 1990s. Thus, Harvey Zorbaugh's famous *The Gold Coast and the Slum* (1929) taxonomizes the rooming house as an organizational form, as well as the betterment organizations and missions that respectively characterize the gold coast and the slum of its title. But the main story is one of organizations fluctuating and developing within a community ecology. Louis Wirth's *The Ghetto* (1928) and Pauline Young's *The Pilgrims of Russian Town* (1932) both concern specialized types of communities as themselves a kind of organizational form, a social structure of defense against both threat and assimilation. D. Sanderson's 'The Rural Community' (1921) lists many of the organizations found in rural settings and considers how they contribute (or not) to the organizing (i.e. social organization in the Chicago sense) of rural life, but does not consider those organizational forms as interesting in themselves. Similarly, Albert Blumenthal's *Small Town Stuff* (1932), although an unsung classic, does not go beyond what is essentially a Parkian portrait of the social psychology (and social disorganization) of its author's home town.

A final work of this type is Edwin Thrasher's *The Gang* (1927), probably the ultimate Chicago statement of organizations as things that are always in transition. For Thrasher, gangs are rooted in communities, and thus are evidence of ongoing 'social organization'. But for us, Thrasher's study provides clear evidence that the organizations Chicagoans found most interesting were those that were the most transient. Again, one senses Robert Park's dominating interest in the evanescent social psychology of modern life. The same themes, in fact, characterize a work that a reader expects to be primarily organizational, Norman Hayner's 'The Hotel' (1923). Like Mueller's 'The Automobile', this dissertation is about an experience of modern living—in this case living in a hotel. Disappointingly, there is only minimal interest in the complex organization necessary to run the apartment hotel, then a revolutionary organizational form.

The Chicago School did, finally, write some work that would be recognized today as explicitly about organizations. Stuart Queen's *The Passing of the County Jail* (1920) is about the death of an organizational form, but is cast within the earlier reform rhetoric. I should also mention the only two Chicago sociology works that lie explicitly in the industrial relations tradition, Floyd House's 'Industrial Morale' (1924) and Walter Watson's 'The Division of Labor' (1930). The latter is a general review of the already huge literature on monotony coupled with some interesting data on loggers and reporters and their particularly intense job satisfaction, an early version of Csikszentmihalyi's concept of 'flow'. House's work is a broad and sophisticated review of everything then known about employee satisfaction, which it tries to theorize under the Chicago concept of 'social control', and then to merge with the war-born concept of 'morale', a buzzword of the 1920s roughly equivalent to 'human relations' in the 1950s. The work is sophisticated, even at times profound, in its grasp of the complexities of the organizational experience of work in America in the 1920s. But in the end, House does not have the tools with which to theorize the new economic world. He is unwilling to accept the employers' account of it, as would be Mayo and his followers. But he has no effective alternative.

On a less theoretical plane, Samuel Kincheloe's papers on the 'The Major Reactions of City Churches' (1928) and 'The Behavior Sequence of a Dying Church' (1929) are two classics of organizational ecology, which taken together precisely characterize the succession of organizational forms in the religious ecology of the city. W. A. Daniel's 'The Negro Theological Seminary Survey' (1925) delves into resource issues, considers problems in internal leadership, analyzes complex organizational environments, and nicely portrays a desperate ecology of failing organizations. It lacks the theoretical explicitness of Reep's earlier work but raises a whole agenda of familiar organizational issues. Everett Hughes's 'The Chicago Real Estate Board' (1931) is a more explicit study of organizational emergence. Like many of the Chicago studies, it looks at the 'organizing' of something, in this case land exchanges, rather than at the result of that organizing—the Chicago Real Estate Board itself. Much of the focus is on the complex of social organization surrounding land rather than on the board itself, and the work feels very descriptive. But it is, nonetheless, an explicit analysis of the emergence of a particular organization in the midst of a complex of relationships.

Finally, there are two Chicago works that are thoroughly modern in their explicit commitment to the theory of organizations and their mobilization of complex data to address theoretical questions about organizations. The first is E. T. Thompson's 'The Plantation' (1932), a quite surprising work that undertakes the historical sociology of colonial Virginia in a very modern style, drawing on an extraordinary breadth of secondary sources and a more limited quantity of primary ones. Thompson's theoretical aim is explicit throughout—to explain the emergence of a particular business and community form at a particular position in what we would today call the world system, as well as to theorize how that form in turn shaped the emergence of chattel slavery. It is a measure of the work's excellence that it cannot be summarized or easily characterized.

Even more extraordinary, however, is Ernest Shideler's 'The Chain Store' (1927). This is a comprehensive organizational analysis of the emergence of a new organizational form. The dissertation opens with a historical ecology of retail in the developing city, reviewing the forces that gradually led to the department store and the chain store. Shideler then distinguishes types of chains. He analyzes the spread of the chain form to different industries. He enumerates all the chains (and chain units) in Chicago. He considers the proportion of total Chicago business done with chains. He looks at the ecology of chains in a particular subcommunity. He analyzes the life history of a typical chain enterprise. He analyzes locational decisions. He analyzes the up- and downstream effects of the chain form in the economic system. He looks at the conflict between chains and department stores. He examines the impact of chains on communication, traffic, and even the social psychology of shoppers. The list goes on and on. This is organizational sociology of a comprehensiveness and theoretical sophistication that would not be seen again for another fifty years.

The writings and dissertations of the Chicago School thus show a consistent vision of social organization and disorganization as ongoing processes—a vision continuous from theorists like Albion Small in the 1890s to students like Wirth and Shideler in the 1920s studying the Chicago social landscape in the field. Above all, it focuses on organizing rather than organizations and on understanding change rather than stability. As a result there is relatively little Chicago writing on the internal processes of organizations, the first of my thematic families. About my second family (institutionalization and organizational dynamics), there is by contrast a quite considerable amount. And about the third family (organizational ecology, interorganizational relations, resource dependency, and the evolution of organizational forms), there is an enormous body of work. Indeed, one can argue that although we have some empirical advance beyond the Chicago work in this third area, we are not really very far beyond it theoretically.

18.5. Eclipse and Legacy

The Chicago vision was very much reduced after World War II. In part, this was a general transformation. For the first time, one could speak of a truly national, singular society, with national markets, national media, and a national persona. Social scientists both helped and chronicled this transformation, and it is little surprising that the theory of organizations—like all forms of post-war sociology—took its shape from the wartime experience and from the mass society and equally massive organizations that the war bequeathed. The conflictual, processual, local theories of the Chicago School made little sense in a world now conceived as grand, unified, and even static, a huge mechanism for steady expansion in a non-ideological, managed world. Not until the great conjunctural transformations of the late 1960s and 1970s would conflictual and processual theories of social life reemerge.

It is striking in this connection that most Chicago School studies of organizations involve small organizations like immigrant newspapers, brothels, churches, Negro seminaries, rooming houses, and taxi-dance halls. Only Shideler's 'The Chain Store' and Donovan's *The Saleslady* involve large-scale organizations. In part, this reflected Park's interests in communication and consumption, which were usually embodied in smaller organizations. In part, it reflected the inheritance of the progressive interest in churches and other community institutions. But as time went by, it also reflected a new reality. Large organizations had 'interiors' that could not be studied without permission; Western Electric, after all, had called in Mayo, not the other way around. Thus, for example, while there are a number of studies of particular churches and church ecologies in the Chicago tradition, there are no studies of the denominational hierarchies themselves nor of the enormous structure of Catholic, Lutheran, and Jewish eleemosynary organizations that blanketed the city.

But there were more specific causes for Chicago's decline as well. The late 1930s had brought to the Chicago sociology department Lloyd Warner, a

Radcliffe-Brownian functionalist fresh from L. J. Henderson's 'systems theory' seminar at the Harvard Business School. Among Warner's fellow seminarians had been Elton Mayo, a philosopher-turned-social-psychologist ignorant enough of sociology to think the discovery of social effects at Hawthorne revolutionary, and the young Talcott Parsons, whose post-war thinking would soon flower in the functionalist jargon of *The Social System* (on Mayo, see Gillespie 1991). Although the Chicago sociologists did not know it, Warner had himself torpedoed any involvement by them in the Hawthorne research (Gillespie 1991: 155–6). With Warner came colleagues and students who shared his functionalism and the managerial viewpoint that went with it. One was William Foote Whyte, whose *Street Corner Society* is often misread as a Chicago School gem, but who in fact drew his theory from the organization charts of the human relations school. Along too came Burleigh Gardner and Allison Davis, lead investigators on Warner's project on 'human relations' in Natchez, Mississippi. Gardner had also worked on Warner's Yankee City project, which Mayo's Rockefeller money funded because Warner thought the areas around the Hawthorne works too disorderly to be 'real' communities, and he would spend five years as a section head of the Personnel and Research Counseling Section at Hawthorne (Gillespie 1991: 233).[4]

Along with Everett Hughes, a Park student who returned to Chicago in the late 1930s, the Warnerians created at Chicago in 1943 a Committee on Human Relations in Industry. The committee's 1946 joint volume on *Industry and Society* (edited by Whyte) is essentially a management how-to volume. Whyte's *Human Relations in the Restaurant Industry* (1948), a sociological analysis of how best to run profitable restaurants, was funded by the National Restaurant Association and guided by 'the research program of the Western Electric Company' (Whyte 1948: 374). Indeed, Warner, Gardner, and others would soon create Social Research, Incorporated, a downtown business consulting firm that employed many of Chicago's post-war

[4] The central documents of the human relations school—Mayo (1933) and Roethlisberger and Dickson (1939)—make it quite plain that the absence of references to Chicago sociology is quite deliberate. In his 1933 classic, Mayo shows no sign of having read any Chicago work on organizations and rather strangely labels the Chicagoans he has read as Durkheimians (1933: ch. 6). Nor does he tell readers that the Harvard group decided to not to study the communities around the Hawthorne plant because they thought them to be pathologically disorganized. The only Chicago citation in Roethlisberger and Dickson is of Robert Park, for the somewhat uncharacteristic concept of social distance (1939: 359). The concept of 'attitude', which would have had to be cited to its Chicago inventors Thomas and Thurstone, was defined without citation (1939: 330). It goes without saying that dissertations like Floyd House's and Walter Watson's—both focused on topics with which the human relations school was centrally concerned—were overlooked by them. Yet despite his scuttling of Chicago School research in the communities around Hawthorne, Warner was polite about the Chicago School in the first volume of the Yankee City series (Warner and Lunt 1941: 4). Of course, by then, he had to be polite: they had hired him four years before. But the book itself has no trace of Chicago influence, even its chapters on community ecology being devoid of any reference to his new colleagues. The Chicagoans are seen only as analysts of social breakdown (ibid. 58). Warner's static, ahistorical approach would later make his work an easy target for Stephan Thernstrom's (1964) brilliant demolition.

graduate students on projects ranging from beer to automobiles (Karesh 1995). This was at a time when, as we now know, J. Edgar Hoover saw the retiring Ernest Burgess, along with W. E. B. Du Bois, as the two most dangerous Communists in American sociology.

The Chicago School itself went underground with McCarthyism, helping found the anti-establishment Society for the Study of Social Problems in 1950. Within the discipline, Chicago became identified with urban studies and ethnography and a kind of generic sympathy for underdogs, perhaps as reformist a line as was politically feasible in the early 1950s. The theoretical lineage of Chicago would not be re-established until Morris Janowitz came to the department in the 1960s.[5]

As for studies of formal organization more generally, the fog of structural-functional analysis descended with the human relations school, while Merton's students pursued the rather quixotic project of applying Weber's analysis of the Prussian civil service to mid-twentieth-century American commercial organizations. Even the Carnegie School had its roots in the wartime invention of operations research and control theory. It was not until the 1970s that population ecology reintroduced the kind of processual thinking characteristic of the Chicago School, of which it knew nothing other than what came through Amos Hawley, a student of Roderick McKenzie, a joint author with Park and Burgess of the 1925 classic *The City*.

What then are the lessons contemporary organization theory can learn from the Chicago organizations tradition and its vicissitudes? The most important lesson is that there is no necessary reason for seeing the social world as a world of organizations. The Chicago School's sublimation of organizations into an epiphenomenon of social processes reminds us that to see the social world in terms of organizational entities—as the human relations school did—is to take a quite historically specific view, one anchored firmly in the worldwide importance of large, stable bureaucratic structures in the years from about 1925 to 1975. Of that stable structure, the only real remnants today are national governments. The wartime army of eight million in which so many famous organizational sociologists served mustered only 400,000 effectives at the start of the Iraq affair. The gigantic commercial organizations of today are usually retail operations with transient labor forces and shallow divisions of labor. Since the great conjuncture of the middle 1970s—the end of Bretton Woods, the coming of OPEC, the legal transformations that led to globalization, the long-sought destruction of AT&T—we have in fact returned to the organizational world characteristic of the 1920s and earlier. It is

[5] Histories of the Chicago School often lay emphasis on George Herbert Mead, who was indeed a personal friend of Thomas, and whose courses (in philosophy) were routinely taken by students in sociology. But Mead's work was not relevant to the Chicago School 'organizations' work reported here, his popularity with such later organization theorists as Karl Weick notwithstanding.

a world of rapid turnover and change in organizations, a world of continuous organizational restructurings and financial prestidigitation, of networks and arm's length relationships, a world in which the employment and production structures that were laboriously built by scientific management and human relations have been deconstructed through outsourcing and offshoring, a world that deals with its human relations problems by denying and outrunning them. It is a world much better fitted to the ecological and processual 'organizing' theory of the Chicago School than to the organization theory we have inherited from the Warnerians and Mertonians.

If the Chicago School's first lesson is that the very idea of organization theory is historically contingent, its second is that what we used to call organizations must now be imagined as mere moments of processes. More than ever it is clear that an organization chart is just a fleeting snapshot of a structure perpetually in flux. It is tempting to think this revolution merely structural—a change of our basic idea of organization from bureaucracy to network. But we are not witnessing such a simple, synchronic transformation. The organizational world has changed because the new strategies of organizing activity aim at complex outcomes arrayed over extended periods. And the longer run forces that shape the system of commercial organizations—e.g. the location of cheap labor, the barriers of language and control, the varieties of governmental tax and benefit policies—all these things fluctuate steadily and strategically. In the new world, organizations respond to them not so much by changing organizational policies as by dismantling and reassembling what in mid-twentieth-century terms we would have called the organization itself: by selling it, loading it with debt, looting it, amalgamating it, spinning off parts, and so on. All this in order to lower labor force costs, or realize tax savings, or relocate profits to a new country, or shed pension obligations, or achieve technological returns to scale, or whatever. In many cases, it is not even clear what is the unit to which these various advantages are expected to accrue. Indeed, a crucial strategy of contemporary commercial organizations is to avoid accrual of resources in any one particular place because so located they become too easy to tax, expropriate, and so on.

All this creates a mathematical nightmare that organizational theory and its current major research paradigms cannot address because the changes involved are most often changes in the actual entities of the system. The assumption of constant units of analysis with fluctuating attributes—long a crucial fiction not only of organizational sociology but of sociology more generally—is simply nonsense in today's organizational world. It is difficult in such a world even to specify what is the right way to proceed, for most of us are uncomfortable with thinking about social systems in which there are no 'things', no ongoing actors. But such is the processual world we face. The Chicago School theorized about this, to be sure: 'Institutions are but the shell of social activity,' as Albion Small said. But they made only a beginning. The challenge remains.

References

Abbott, A. (2001). *Time Matters*. Chicago: University of Chicago Press.
Burns, L. R. (1980). 'The Chicago School and the Study of Organizational–Environment Relations'. *Journal of the History of the Behavioral Sciences*, 16: 342–58.
Gillespie, R. (1991). *Manufacturing Knowledge*. Cambridge: Cambridge University Press.
Haber, S. (1964). *Efficiency and Uplift*. Chicago: University of Chicago Press.
Henderson, C. R. (1904). *Modern Methods of Charity*. New York: Macmillan.
Karesh, M. (1995). 'The Interstitial Origins of Symbolic Consumer Research'. MA paper. University of Chicago.
Nyland, C. (1996). 'Taylorism, John R. Commons, and the Hoxie Report'. *Journal of Economic Issues*, 30: 985–1016.
Roethlisberger, F. J., and Dickson, W. J. (1939). *Management and the Worker*. Cambridge, Mass.: Harvard University Press.
Ross, D. (1991). *The Origins of American Social Science*. Cambridge: Cambridge University Press.
Schiesl, M. J. (1977). *The Politics of Efficiency*. Berkeley: University of California Press.
Small, A. W. (1905). *General Sociology*. Chicago: University of Chicago Press.
—— (1914). 'A Vision of Social Efficiency'. *American Journal of Sociology*, 19: 433–45.
Sumner, W. G. (1906). *Folkways*. Boston: Ginn.
Thernstrom, S. (1964). *Poverty and Progress*. Cambridge, Mass.: Harvard University Press.
Warner, W. L., and Lunt, P. S. (1941). *The Social Structure of a Modern Community*. New Haven: Yale University Press.

CHAPTER 19

AFTER JAMES ON IDENTITY

ARNE CARLSEN

More than anything, from a social perspective, organizations are sites for the production of human identities. People engage in practices that are imbued with a myriad individual and collective intentions, offering multiple potentials for development of self. Yet, theories of identity construction in organizations are curiously disconnected from conceptions of agency, and little of the substantial work on organizational identity gives any systematic attention to developments in value-creating activities, the specifics of what organizations deliver and what people do, or how the idiosyncrasies of everyday work experiences shape identity formation. The writings of William James (1841–1910) form a valuable source from which to address such shortcomings. James's foundational work on self is still radical in many more ways than what has been acknowledged by scholars investigating identity dynamics. It is indeed an example of a foundational source of knowledge that has largely been lost from view. Following after James on identity can, and should, inspire us to reopen the field and ask new questions.

Readers of the work of James have to resist seduction by elegant prose and a welter of brilliant asides, qualities that have caused commentators to warn against isolated quotes from his work (McDermott 1977). Identity scholars often use the following passage from James: '*a man has as many social selves as there are individuals who recognize him* and carry an image of him in their mind' (James [1890] 1950: i. 294, emphasis in original). While this quote certainly does not misrepresent James's stance on self, it does not give any hints about the center of his visions. This center starts in the placement of self in the stream of experience, the incessant flow of time. From that center springs the necessity to see self as inseparable from ongoing experience and to see agency as integral to self. By placing self in the stream of experience, James highlights its purposive, open-ended, and processual nature, the co-existence of the habitual with qualities of originality and novelty, as well as the importance of people's selective attention in rendering experience meaningful. By insisting on the agentic qualities of self, James highlights the projective capacities so central to how people experience their lives and their will to believe in the future. These are all qualities that point towards a need to ground conceptions of identity in organizations in the particulars of value-creating practice and the projects that people pursue.

James's philosophical project came to be in a historical period of evolutionism. As Darwin freed evolutionary thought from the idea of design by an almighty Creator, James freed social evolution from its determinist seal and reinstated human agency as its engine (Joas 1996: 134). James's (1880) early essay on Great Men was directed against the deterministic evolutionary theory of Herbert Spencer. Here James acknowledges the shaping force of 'social surroundings of the past and present hour' but insists that such shaping does not fully determine the paths of evolution, claiming that societies as well as individuals 'both at any given moment offer ambiguous potentialities of development'. James's conceptions of agentic selves were further developed in later writings, most of them focused on the individual, but had from the outset social change as their horizon. The conceptions are still radical, not so much as a stance against determinism but as an eye-opener to the idea that identity may be less about strictly defined social categories and more about multilevel processes of change.

The chapter has four main parts. First, I introduce some context on James and his work, point to strands of influence on organization studies, and discuss how his conceptions of self were shaped by historical circumstances and personal experiences. Second, I briefly overview key tenets of organizational identity theory and argue that it has been predominantly focused on the equivalence of what James called 'self-as-object'. Third, I give a treatment of what James meant by 'self-as-subject' and how we may understand that as collective processes of *authoring*, rooted in practice. Finally, I discuss two sets of the implications that follow from James's view of self: bringing identity into organizational practice and into social change.

19.1. William James and Pragmatism

William James was the oldest son of Henry James the elder, a religious writer of independent wealth and a literary associate of Oliver Wendell Holmes, Sr., and

Ralph Waldo Emerson (Murphy 1990). Henry James Jr., the famous novelist with a voluminous literary output, was William James's brother. The James family set an unusual stage for early exposure to intellectually advanced discussions on human affairs, as described in several rich biographies and commentaries (see the overview in McDermott 1977). In his youth William James took an interest in painting and the natural sciences, for which he received irregular formal education in top private schools during various stays in European cities. The contents of this education ranged from anatomy and physiology to philosophy and psychology, a mix of interests that were to mark James's later writings. James entered Harvard Medical School in 1864 and received his medical degree (the only one he ever achieved) in 1869 after a series of health problems and depressions. James began teaching physiology at Harvard in 1872 and psychology in 1874–75. His course proved very popular and became a turning point in his career. The publisher Henry Holt offered James a contract to write a textbook on psychology in 1878. The 1,200-page book, *Principles of Psychology*, took James twelve years to write. It is widely considered a masterpiece in many fields of social science and is the foundational text of modern psychology.

James's theories, and in particular his conceptions of agency and self, were profoundly colored by personal experiences. In one of his many inspiring introductions to the work of James, John McDermott (2000) refers to an episode from James's late twenties, according to the account in his diary. James had suddenly recalled the image of an epileptic patient from an asylum he had visited: 'a black-haired youth with greenish skin, entirely idiotic', who 'sat there like a sculptured Egyptian cat or Peruvian mummy, moving nothing but his black eyes and looking absolutely inhuman' (from James's diary, as quoted in McDermott 2000: 141). James was overcome by fear that such a condition could befall him:

> This image and my fear entered into a species of combination with each other. *That shape am I*, I felt potentially. Nothing that I possess can defend me against that fate, if the hour for it should strike for me as it struck for him. There was such a horror of him, and such a perception of my own merely momentary discrepancy from him, that it was as if something hitherto solid within my breast gave way entirely, and I became a mass of quivering fear. After this the universe was changed for me altogether. I awoke morning after morning with a horrible dread at the pit of my stomach, and with a sense of the insecurity of life that I never knew before, and that I have never felt since. (Ibid. 141, emphasis in original)

The episode precedes a state of suicidal depression, where James struggles with the deep awareness of the fragility of his sense of self and the doubt of the existence of an essential soul as a center of stability. James toils with the question of whether we have any control over the making of our own self. He eventually emerges from the personal experience with a deep conviction of the importance to believe in free will, not as a right to assume that everything we believe in is true, but as an embracement of the constitutive and creative character of self and of the possibility of future experience (McDermott 2000). These concerns were to be cardinal in James's philosophical project and in the philosophy of pragmatism.

Pragmatism is a philosophical tradition of American origin. Its followers argue that the truth of all beliefs, knowledge, and scientific concepts is provisional and defined by their pragmatic use in ongoing experience, not by correspondence with antecedent 'Truth' or 'Reality'. James's role as an originating force of pragmatism began in a series of discussions that started in the early 1870s, most famously in what was known as The Metaphysical Club (Menand 2001), an informal group of young Harvard-educated intellectuals usually meeting in the homes of James and Charles Sanders Peirce (1839–1914) in Cambridge, Massachusetts. The discussions dealt with what was perceived as a string of problems in modern philosophy and evolutionary thought, but few lines of agreement or any form of doctrine can be traced to these early years. Broadly formulated, however, the discussions gave rise to two interrelated streams of philosophical inquiry: theories of truth and theories of experience.

As a *theory of truth*, pragmatism rejects the separation between rational cognition and rational purpose (James [1907] 1977*b*; Murphy 1990: 39–57). People's beliefs and knowledge cannot be separated from contexts of use and possibilities for action. The world is out there, but our knowledge of it is always interpretive and *made* by people to cope with the worlds in which they find themselves, what James called 'teleological weapons of the mind' (James [1890] 1950: ii. 335). Accordingly, there are no privileged descriptions of reality that hold eternally, only conjectures from previous experiences to be tested in future experiences. Truth is provisional, always subject to fallibility by further inquiries. People do, however, have a right to believe in provisional truths according to their purposes, in everyday life as well as in science. The progress of science is defined with respect to advances in the conceptual apparatus created by a particular community of inquirers engaged in particular purposes, not progressions towards final truth. Questions of worth refer to how knowledge can have future consequences in improving human lives. As summed up by Rorty: 'If there is anything distinctive about pragmatism it is that it substitutes the notion of a better human future for the notions of reality, reason and nature' (2000: 27).

As a radical *theory of experience*, pragmatism considers experience plural, equivocal, and ongoing. The critical point here, most fully developed by James ([1890] 1950: vol. i, ch. 9; [1904] 1977*a*, see also McDermott 1977) and John Dewey ([1925] 1958), is that experience is considered an active, ongoing affair in which the experiencing subject and the experienced object constitute an integral relational unity. Experience does not come to us chopped up in small bits. Rather, we are immersed in a continuous stream of experience from which we choose what to attend to and make sense of. This stream contains no inner duplicity of the knowing consciousness and the known content (James [1890] 1950: vol. i, ch. 9). Consequently, dichotomies between experience and nature, experience and self, and experience and knowledge are negated. They all form part of a plural flow where there are no resting places or privileged positions for spectators, and all inquiry is in itself a felt experience. The world is in continuous flux, and selves, mind, knowledge, and social structures are best conceived as processes of becoming, not static being. Such a process theory of experience was inspired by Darwin's evolutionary theories (see also Dewey [1910] 1981) and has important parallel strands of theories in the work of two of James's contemporaries; Henri Bergson and Alfred North Whitehead. Process theory has been widely taken up in the social sciences, but is still, as we shall see, a radical position when speaking of matters of identity in organizations.

Pragmatism houses a number of theories and philosophies, some of which are conflicting[1]. In addition to James and Peirce, John Dewey (1859–1952) is usually also recognized as being a founder of pragmatism. James and Dewey both acknowledged a debt to the writings of Ralph Waldo Emerson (1803–1892). The processual view of reality is present in Emerson's writings as a source of influence but his main imprint on the philosophy of James seems to have been his emphasis on the innate creative powers of individuals and the importance of self-reliance. As formulated by James in his memorial address to Emerson: 'The point of any pen can be an epitome of reality; the commonest person's act, if genuinely activated, can lay hold on eternity. This is the headspring of all his outpourings' (James [1903] 2000: 16). A fourth pragmatist philosopher, George Herbert Mead (1863–1931), while not canonized to the same degree as Peirce, James, and Dewey, has had wide impact in the social sciences and complemented James's theory of self in important ways.

Much of the influence on organization theory from the work of William James has come indirectly through the work of his associates and followers within pragmatism (Carlsen and Mantere 2007). There is, for example, a heritage from James's theory of experience evident in Dewey's work on learning by doing, which in turn figures centrally in theories of organizational learning and action research, ranging from the work of Kolb (1984) on experiential learning, to the classical contribution from Argyris and Schön (1978), to more recent work by Elkjaer (Elkjaer 2004; Elkjaer and Simpson 2006), see also the chapter by Cohen in this volume. Aspects of James's work on self were continued and strengthened by Mead into symbolic interactionism (see Blumer 1969 and the chapter by Hallett, Shulman, and Fine, in

[1] A major rift is between the 'classical pragmatism' of James, Peirce, and Dewey and what has been called 'neopragmatism' (Diggins 1994; Hildebrand 2003) typically associated with the linguistic emphasis of Richard Rorty and others. While the linguistic view holds that nothing beyond language can be appealed to in a philosophical argument, critics like Hildebrand (2005) argue that 'experience' in the work of the classical pragmatists cannot be reduced to discourse. Experience includes body, knowledge, emotion, thinking, and action, and it is this whole that people both have and reflect upon (Dewey [1934] 1980). Provisional truth must be tested both in conversations and through experimental consequences in 'full experience'. See (Thayer 1981) on American versus European pragmatism and (Murphy 1990) for a stringent discussion of concepts of truth in pragmatism that draws out important distinctions between the work of James and Peirce. Haack (2004) offers a feisty contemporary overview that is highly critical of neopragmatism.

this volume). Likewise, James's conceptions of the stream of thought influenced Alfred Schütz in his pragmatic phenomenology and spread widely from there, for example, to ethnomethodology (Garfinkel 1967) and the interpretive branch of strategic management (Smirchich and Stubbart 1985). James's theories of truth linked to purposeful action have also had broad influence, from discussion of fallibility in the philosophy of science (Popper 1968) to ethics and purposes of organizational research (e.g. Wicks and Freeman 1998).

A clear exception to the overall pattern of indirect influence is a strong stream of process-oriented approaches to organizational life where leading researchers use James directly (e.g. Weick 1979, 1995; Chia 1997, 2003; Tsoukas and Chia 2002). In such contributions, re-engagement with James's theory of experience has been a source for pushing the frontiers of organizational research. Central here is the abandonment of the assumption that experience comes to us as a succession of discrete and finished states waiting to be found and that change means getting from one state to another. People are seen as being immersed in a buzzing and continuous stream of experience where habits of action and fields of meaning are always in the making. Weick's (1979, 1995) famous work on sensemaking is heavily influenced by James in describing how environments are enacted through selective attention in ongoing experience and people's faith in the future. Much less impact—also from pragmatist thought in general—can be seen in research on identity in organizations.

19.2. From Self-as-Object: 'Organizational Identities'

It is customary to refer to a paper by Albert and Whetten (1985) as the starting point of organizational identity research. The paper defines organizational identity as those characteristics of an organization that are considered *central* to internal stakeholders, *distinctive* in relation to other organizations, and *enduring* through time— all as evaluated by organizational members in response to the question 'who are we?' as an organization. It is fair to say that these are the definitional pillars on which most other contributions build (e.g. *Academy of Management Review* 2000; Whetten and Godfrey 1998). There are contributions adopting these premises that lay claim for corporate identities that have been unchanged for decades (Collins and Porras 1994) or even centuries (DeGeus 1997), thus invoking an essentialism that is anathema to James's philosophy (and most other conceptions of identity within the social sciences). However, it is important to recognize that (degrees of) social construction and malleability in identities were accounted for also in the early contributions. See, for example, the excellent paper by Dutton and Dukerich (1991), where organization members' sense of identity is conceived as being associated with skills and decision-making behavior undergoing change.

Organizational identity has traditionally been seen as a twin concept of image (Gioia 1998; Gioia, Schulz, and Corley 2000; Hatch and Schultz 2002). A main reason for invoking the concept is thus the legitimizing of external market positions, in a wide sense, by promoting a distinct and favorable image of the organization to clients, future employees, and other stakeholders. Distinction presupposes differentiation from salient out-groups. It can be seen as a source of enhanced self-esteem through fostering perceptions of connection (Dutton, Dukerich, and Harquail 1994) and individual belonging to a collective with prestigious qualities (Ashforth and Mael 1989). The related pursuit of internal sameness is motivated by intentions to build commitment to organizational goals and ease coordination, an alternative to technocratic modes of control (Alvesson 1993) by internalization of a shared and relatively stable 'cognitive structure of what the organization stands for and where it intends to go' (Albert, Ashforth, and Dutton 2000: 13). Other levels of analysis can be invoked from the same set of starting points, such as collective identification with a team (Van der Vegt and Bunderson 2005) or regional industrial identity (Romanelli and Khessina 2005).

Most of the research just cited derives a heritage from social identity theory (e.g. Tajfel and Turner 1985; Thoits and Virshup 1997), where in-group versus out-group categorizations figure centrally. Social identity theory, in turn, owes a heritage to Mead's ([1913] 1964) conceptions of the social self. Mead, more so than James, described how production of identities is always a social affair, presupposing otherness and actively taking the position of the other to define and negotiate conceptions of self. Mead ([1934] 2000), however, much as James ([1890] 1950: vol. i, ch. 10) before him, differentiated between the 'me' (thus an 'us'), self-as-object, and the 'I', self-as-subject. The 'me' self is the object of one's knowledge, a *content* aspect of self, whereas the 'I' self is the knower, a *process* aspect of self. For both James and Mead, the 'I' and the 'me' presuppose one another. The self-as-subject is necessary to account for initiative, emergence, and novelty, while the self-as-object is necessary to account for social reflexivity and the conditioning power of the succession of responses and attitudes of others. It is the self-as-subject that moves into the future, but always in response to a social situation that shapes the experience of the individual.

The principal move in this stream of theorizing was that James did away with the soul as a valuable concept for empirical investigation[2] by casting the 'I' self

[2] The manner by which James does away with the soul has been criticized. Both Mead ([1903] 1964: 47) and Dewey (1940) comment upon a vanishing subject in James's conception of the 'I'. Dewey's (1940) critique deals with an inherent dualism in how James describes the 'I' as pure thought and embodied organism. Johnson (1972) has pointed to the influence from James on 'stream of consciousness' style in fiction writing and a resulting tendency for the protagonist 'I' to be lost in experience, with

(self-as-subject) as an event in the flow of time, a judging Thought in passing, recollective of previous thoughts, and 'the only thinker which the facts require' (James [1890] 1950: i. 369). Rather than attributing to people (or collectives) souls that are independent of experience, James saw the processes of self-as-subject as having functions of self-awareness, self-continuity, and self-agency in relation to the self-as-object.

I shall return to what self-as-subject may imply for organizations. The main point for now is that the relative emphasis on identities as social characteristics found in organization identity theory, useful as it has been for many purposes, translates into an almost exclusive focus on self-as-object. It has resulted in strict separation between individual and organizational levels of analysis and a tendency to talk of identities as discrete objects existing independent of action. It is an approach to identity that has largely left out agency and the particulars of work experience.

Indicative of the focus on self-as-object is the curious neglect of Philip Selznick in organization identity theory. Selznick ([1957] 1983) introduced the concept of organizational character almost thirty years before the paper by Albert and Whetten but is seldom referred to in identity research (recent exceptions include Carlsen 2006; Birnholtz, Cohen, and Hoch 2007). Selznick conceptualized the formation of organizational character as a historical and dynamic process emerging from within 'critical experience' that 'reflects the "open-endedness" of organizational life' (Selznick [1957] 1983: 40). In Selznick's thought, identity formation included the formation of distinctive competence and the institutional embodiment of purpose. Unlike later conceptions, Selznick links character (self-as-object) directly to agency and to ongoing experience, thus implying a self-as-subject.

Since the work of Selznick—with some notable exceptions (e.g. Clark 1972; Czarniawska 1997; Nag, Corley, and Gioia 2007)—the primary attention of organization identity research has been on processes of defining, making sense of, conserving, and promoting the status quo. The active, creative, willing, believing, hoping self, which James and Mead attribute to the self-as-subject (see also Gecas 1982), is largely missing. Concentrating exclusively on self-as-object implies that people's identities at work, whether individual or collective, are independent of the particulars of what they are doing, what ends they pursue in what they do, and what hopes they have for their professional lives. Could we have a meaningful understanding of the identity of William James or pragmatist philosophers as a group based on social characteristics, differentiating qualities, and group affiliations alone? What if identity is primarily about change, and the will to change, not stability?

experience the subject and self the object. The interpretation of James given in this chapter sees him as not doing away with the subject in terms of denying a phenomenological existence of 'something' beyond passing thought, more so that it is purposeful to see the 'I' as process and that James by doing so firmly places self in the flow of time.

19.3. To Self-as-Subject: 'Collective Authoring'

The primary significance of reconnecting with the work of James in identity research is to shift the attention from self-as-object to self-as-subject. Attempting this shift, it is necessary to keep in mind that identity in James's writings is an individual level construct, and indeed, that James can be criticized for giving little attention to the social dimensions of self. Theories of self-as-object seem to scale more or less well from individual to collective levels of analysis (Thoits and Virshup 1997; Corley *et al.* 2006). We know much less about whether, and how, individual level theories of self-as-subject can be transported, reformed, and developed when used at a collective level of analysis. Luckily, though, when considering matters of agency and experience in identity formation, a whole arsenal of narrative theory comes into play. Narratives specialize in establishing meaning from sequences of human experiences and intentions through time (MacIntyre 1981; Sarbin 1986). Conceptions of identity within narrative psychology acknowledge narrative as the main device by which people continuously construe their life stories in times past and future (Polkinghorne 1988; Bruner 1990; McAdams 1993).[3] A narrative lens is necessary to understand self-as-subject as a collective process because narratives capture the temporality of experiencing (Crites 1971) and allows for multiple voices and interpretations in how people construct shared fields of meaning and engagement (Sarbin 2000; Brown 2006). Narratives also mediate how identities develop from the inside out—from individuals to culture—as well as from the outside in (Bruner 1990). I shall return to that point.

The notion of self-as-subject is closely related to agency. In James's thought, agency is a purposive and reflexive propensity to act upon the world and move into the unknown with belief in oneself and one's actions, thereby 'taking our life in our hands' (James [1896] 2000: 241). Key here are the notions that experience is open-ended, that people's conceptions of themselves are (also) future oriented and that the constitutive dimension of self requires *will* to *believe* and *act*, also in circumstances that are difficult and where there are tough choices to be made. When James decided he would have the will to believe, it was a will to hope for current thoughts and actions to be fruitful in future experience and for his sense of self not to be destroyed but enhanced by future experience (McDermott 2000). Belief or good intentions alone, however, are not sufficient. As formulated in James's famous chapter on *Habit*: 'No matter how full a reservoir of *maxims* one may possess, and

[3] Several leading scholars in this tradition—like Sarbin, Bruner, McAdams, Scheibe, and Polkinghorne—build upon the work of James. Sarbin's (1986) famous qualification of narrative as a root metaphor in psychology leans heavily on Pepper's (1942) world-view of 'contextualism', which again rests on James. Likewise, the work of McAdams, perhaps the leading identity scholar within psychology today, is deeply influenced by James (e.g. McAdams 1993, 1995, 1997).

no matter how good one's *sentiments* may be, if one has not taken advantage of every concrete opportunity to *act*, one's character may remain entirely unaffected for the better. With mere good intentions, hell is proverbially paved' ([1890] 1950: i. 125, emphasis in original).

From a narrative perspective, agency must be seen as integral to how people experience their lives and become active authors of individual and collective life stories (McAdams 1995), a defining property of self (Bruner 1994) that is seated in our will to believe and act.

To further unpack what an agentic, experiencing, self-as-subject may mean in organizations, let us start with considering James's conclusion to his long chapter 'The Consciousness of Self' in *Principles of Psychology*:

> The consciousness of Self involves a stream of thought, each part of which as 'I' can 1) remember those which went before, and know the things they knew; and 2) emphasize and care paramountly for certain ones among them as '*me*,' and *appropriate to these* the rest.... This me is an empirical aggregate of things objectively known. The *I* which knows them cannot itself be an [p. 401] aggregate, neither for psychological purposes need it be considered to be an unchanging metaphysical entity like the Soul, or a principle like the pure Ego, viewed as 'out of time.' It is a *Thought*, at each moment different from that of the last moment, but *appropriative* of the latter, together with all that the latter called its own.... *If the passing thought be the directly verifiable existent which no school has hitherto doubted it to be, then that thought is itself the thinker*, and psychology need not look beyond.
>
> ([1890] 1950: i. 400–401, emphasis in original)

In this passage James sums up his conception of self-as-subject (the 'I') as a stream of thought that selectively appropriates experience to self-as-object (the 'me'). Each thought is unique to its place in the incessant flow of 'pure experience' (James [1904] 1977*b*) but remembers previous thoughts. I propose that in organizational settings James's self-as-subject equates with a *stream of authoring acts*. Five sets of conjectures for our understanding of identity in organizations can be outlined from this: (1) that the organizational 'we' should be considered a collectively achieved authoring function, (2) that search for patterns of stability should be focused on this authoring process, since self-as-object has no independent ontological status, (3) that authoring is in itself a felt experience situated within the flow of time, (4) that authoring is a way of selectively attending to experience, and (5) that appropriation of experience may be addressed to several levels of self-as-object; individual me's within organizational us's within larger us's.

19.3.1. The Organizational 'We' as a Collectively Achieved Authoring Function

Following James, I propose that self-as-subject in organizations amounts to the selective appropriation of experiences, from within a perpetual stream of experiences, for the sake of constituting and synthesizing me's or us's. Then the organizational 'we' may be considered a collectively achieved authoring function, a stream of authoring acts that may or may not be patterned or show repeatable features in some way. The collective 'we' is similar to the individual 'I' in the sense that they are both *processes*—a subset of connections made within living experience and situated within the conditioning response of others. They are different in the sense that the various processes that make up the collective 'we' have no common referent of an organic body—the locus of the embodied self-as-subject does not exist for organizations. Neither can we assume a collective consciousness. Authoring acts will take place in different arenas of organizational life, some simultaneously, some coordinated, and many that are likely to be unaware of each other. There is no overall collective 'Thought' recollective of all previous thoughts, only a social process of assigning weight to some authoring acts over others.

Invoking this interpretation of James means an analytical focus on processes of identity construction as opposed to that which is construed. Following McAdam's (1997) interpretation of James, one may use the notion 'selfing' rather than self when talking about self-as-subject. I use the term 'authoring' to denote a continuous, polyphonic process where me's and us's are expressed and interpreted in multiple ways (McAdams 1995; Holland *et al.* 1998: 169–91) and to emphasize the agentic nature of the process. To 'self' is to grasp authorship, to enter into the condition of active authoring.

19.3.2. Shifting Sources of Stability from Object to Process

The field of organization studies has seen a growing recognition of process theory emphasizing activities over entities, process over steady states. A strong process theory goes further in that it denies the existence of social structures outside their constitutive events—action is seen as primary in constituting both human beings and social structures (Sztompka 1991). Thus, invoking a strong process theory from James implies not only that 'selves-as-objects' are seen as socially construed but also that they do *not exist outside their authoring acts*. How are we to understand that assertion? For practical purposes most people will assign a physical object, such as a car, a permanence that disregards it being in a constant process of construction or decay. There is certainly something there that undergoes change. Social structures are different. There are no identities (in the sense of self-as-object) at all outside authoring as there is no love outside loving. This does not exclude social conditioning. Each act of authoring and loving will be situated in a stream of experience where it may be heavily conditioned by previous acts of authoring and loving as well as the expectations of others, sometimes so shaped by the habits and patterns of its stream that the room for agency seems non-existent. Also, *conceptions* of identity and love are necessary as referential frames that give meaning to acts

(Clegg, Kornberger, and Rhodes 2005). Instead of referring to selves-as-objects as the factual and concrete dimension of identity, acts of authoring and patterns of authoring take center stage. It is a misunderstanding to infer from a strong process view or the notion of plurality of selves (also often attributed to James and Mead) that identity somehow loses its stabilizing function. Rather, questions of stability shift from object to process as people engage in ongoing efforts to maintain retrospective continuity and purpose (Clegg, Kornberger, and Rhodes 2005; Carlsen 2006). Claiming stability in identity for organizations over years or decades (as in Collins and Porras 1994) only makes sense as a claim to stability in authoring patterns. Following James, understanding organizational identity dynamics thus shifts from seeing patterns in differentiating qualities to understanding habits of authoring and their agential underpinnings.

19.3.3. Authoring is a Felt Experience Situated within the Flow of Time

When James asserted that an act of appropriating experiences to me's is in itself a felt experience, he situated self-as-subject in the flow of time and indirectly invoked temporality. Temporality is always felt in a present that extends backwards and forwards in time (James [1890] 1950: vol. i, ch. 13; Mead [1932] 2002) as our view of the past and our expectations for the future are continuously recast in light of new circumstances. As argued by Crites (1971), there are three times, a present of things present, a present of the things past, and a present of things future. To author is to experience oneself as agent in this threefold present. Authoring thus involves (1) retrospectively grasping present past experience as belonging to a 'me' or an 'us', (2) being deeply engaged in the present of the present (Csikszentmihalyi 1985), and (3) seeking experience within a horizon of some future pursuit (MacIntyre 1981; Carlsen 2008). The projective dimension of authoring is particularly important here as it tends to get overlooked. Rather than seeing more or less stable 'identities' as informing 'strategy', invoking self-as-subject implies exploring authoring of identities as part of what makes emergent strategy formation effective. Authoring of identities not only informs goal-directed behavior in organizations. It must be considered part of it, integral to *experiencing* in times past and future. This is not an argument that all processes of strategizing and authoring necessarily overlap, only that it is a failure to keep them strictly apart as they are intrinsically linked manifestations of the projective capacities of human agencies. As argued by Emirbayer and Mische, a sharp split between the two may have the effect that 'strategies are stripped of meaning and reflexivity while identities are temporally flattened out and shorn of their orienting power' (1998: 992). A move to integrate strategy and identity would follow in the footsteps of the strategy as management of meaning tradition (e.g. Smirchich and Stubbart 1985; Barry and Elmes 1997; Knights and Mueller 2004).

19.3.4. Authoring is a Way of Selectively Attending to Lived Experience

James rejected the idea that images, ideas, and events come to us as a priori discrete entities. People's experiencing is shaped by selective attention—as stated in the chapter 'Attention': 'Millions of items of the outward order are present to my senses which never properly enter into my experience. Why? Because they have no *interest* for me. *My experience is what I agree to attend to.* Only those items which I *notice* shape my mind—without selective interest, experience is an utter chaos' (James [1890] 1950: i. 402, emphasis in original). Authoring of identities is likely to take place in a plural flow of experience, a series of situations where many things are going on: working, conversing, making sense of everyday occurrences, suggesting future pathways of action, and so on. Following James, authoring must be understood as a subset of this stream, a specific way of attending to experience where people selectively perceive something as belonging to a 'me' or an 'us' and appropriate it as such, or let it 'fall into the bottomless abyss of oblivion' (James [1890] 1950: i. 643). That said, the phrase 'what I agree to attend to' does no justice to what necessarily must be a social process of shaping attention: what gets noticed and whose interests are given preference for what reason. Seeing *attending* as key to authoring of identities inevitably implies a need to ground studies of identity construction in everyday work practice. As I will return to in more detail, recurrent value creative activities at work may be seen as trajectories of experiencing, sometimes representing distinct traditions in themselves, at the very least mediating the collective purposes that shape what people notice and appropriate.

19.3.5. Experiences may be Appropriated to Multiple Me's and Us's

Focusing on self-as-subject opens up the possibility of multiple addressivity in how experiences are appropriated to self-as-object. Winning a medal at the Olympics or landing a large contract are types of experiences that are likely to be attributed to the protagonist individuals involved and may leave lasting imprints in their life stories. Such experiences may also be attributed to a team (e.g. swimming team, project team), an organization (e.g. a swimming association, an engineering firm), an industry, a tradition, or even a nation. It cannot be taken for granted that people operate with singular and clearly defined addressees in the way they appropriate experiences. Rather, me's may gain their social significance by being located in organizational us's that again are connected to larger us's of disciplinary traditions or societal causes beyond the organization (O'Conner 2000; Carlsen 2008). Seen from the viewpoint of self-as-subject, authoring of identities resists a clear separation between individual and collective levels of analysis. Again this is an argument for social practice as the unit of analysis. Whether authoring addresses individual me's or collective us's, it is experienced in collective activity and uses collective language resources.

19.4. Implications

Revisiting the legacy of James untangles the concepts of identity from the captivity of enduring characteristics and rigid levels of analysis and points to processes of authoring that have multiple addressees within and beyond organizations. In a Jamesian perspective, acts of authoring identity are less about defining and maintaining core values and more about what Shotter and Cunliffe (2003) have thoughtfully discussed as 'creating meaning from within ambiguous fields of experience'. To be more concrete: a field study of development processes in an IT consulting firm (Carlsen 2006), starting from the premises laid out here, showed that authoring can vary from charging practice with identity status ('these activities are what we are about', 'this is our core competence') to noticing and amplifying small events (e.g. 'this is really what we ought to be doing more of in this organization') to placing work activities within larger purposes and pursuits (e.g. 'the significance of what we do here is really not just programming, or IT systems applications, but being on the pathway to become another Microsoft'). Authoring of identities is seldom done in isolation as a deliberate reflexive exercise. Rather, authoring forms part of a plural flow of ongoing events where there is a mixture of identity-salient, strategy-salient, and learning-salient moments in which people make connections within experience to produce meaning and facilitate action. In what follows, I shall deepen this overall summation into two sets of implications.

19.4.1. Locating Authoring of Identity in Practice

If we accept James's premises of immersion in the stream of experience and selective attention, we must also accept that the specifics of what we do matter in identity formation. At a general level, this observation parallels the return to practice in the social sciences (e.g. Schatzki, Knorr-Cetina, and Von Savigny 2001; Wenger, McDermott, and Snyder 2002; Antonacopoulou 2007). In this tradition, especially within its anthropological branches, there is an increasing realization that identities are not mere psycho-social constructions that float above the ground of social practice (Dreier 1999). Rather, identities are achieved in social action and unfold along trajectories of social practice (Wenger 1998; Holland *et al.* 1998; Holland and Lave 2001). In this context I understand practice as 'embodied, materially [and symbolically] mediated arrays of human activity' (Schatzki 2001: 2), acknowledging that practice displays alternating phases of agential creativeness and structural determination (Sztompka 1991).

More specifically, work practices shape the way people attend to experience. Even small organizations may have many sets of recurrent activities with distinct deliverables, divisions of labor, and forms of knowledge being used. Work on crisis communication differs from strategic communication. Web design differs from development of large IT system solutions. Teaching differs from student counseling. The specifics of such differences will influence what is considered important in work—the activity specific goal structures—the variety of temporal rhythms in which work is performed, the disciplinary and occupational traditions being invoked and referred to, and the space for agency. These characteristics, in turn, may be important in how we are positioned in different streams of experience, how we perceive experience and how we appropriate experience to selves. Brown and Duguid (2001) have suggested that identities mirror practice in the sense that they will be social, dynamic, historical, and complex to the degree that the underlying practice displays such characteristics. One might thus investigate how the composition of value-creating activities forms an organizational equivalent to individual habits. If we are what we do, authoring of identity will in no small way mean a constant relating across participation in distinct activities.

While the habitual dimension of practice certainly shapes authoring, it cannot fully determine it. Practices are always open to change, from the imaginative extension of routines when encountering new circumstances (Tsoukas and Chia 2002) to seedlings for entirely new value-creating activities and business areas. Also, individuals and collectives will differ in how central they deem work experiences to their lives. A series of recent studies have taken issue with how changes in work practice may underpin positive identity construction. Roberts *et al.* (2005) have suggested a theory for how individuals narrate their reflected best-self portraits based on jolts in experience that create occasions for sensemaking. Ibarra (1999, 2003) has suggested several schemes (e.g. creating experiments with new roles and telling stories of past work experiences in ways that open up new development paths) by which people may foster fruitful imaginations of professional identities from their work experiences. Carlsen and Pitsis (2008) have shown how some projects build narrative capital that is repeatedly drawn upon for future-oriented purposes long after they have formally elapsed. Work experiences may be construed as 'identity exemplars' that simultaneously revitalize the life story of the organization, shape future practice, and contribute to growth (see also Carlsen 2006). All these examples are indicative of how we may investigate how authoring of identity takes shape from the novel aspects of practice—which brings us to change.

19.4.2. Bringing Authoring of Identity into Processes of Social Change

There is a sharp contrast between James's conception of self-as-subject and the overall attention to definition and maintenance of social categories in organization identity theory. Following after James means acknowledging the dimension of identity that not only is open to change but that may actively seek change. Rather than seeing change as threatening stability or ontological security (Giddens 1991), the lead from James opens up for consideration a range of forward-looking identity motives that form the basis for mobilizing collective engagement in change. Such motives range from a need to be self-determining (Ryan and Deci 2000) and experience causal control (Gecas 1991; Bandura 1997) when moving forward, to living with purpose (Bruner 1990; McAdams 1997), challenge (Csikszentmihalyi 1985), unpredictability (MacIntyre 1981), openness (McAdams 1993), and drama (Mattingly 1998; Carlsen 2008). Seen from the perspective of the agentic self, participation in social change may offer necessary relief from stagnation, boredom, and indifference. Change is not something one pursues as complete and finished actors—it forms the very basis for authoring of identities. Very few studies of identity dynamics in organizations incorporate the agentic and projective dimension (but see Roberts and Dutton 2009), whether we talk about the potential integration with strategizing or the small and large ideas that form the basis for creativity and bring hope to people's lives.

The lead from James also opens up for understanding how authoring of identities runs in confluence with change processes more broadly, also outside organizations. Partly, we may see the benefits of operating with self-as-subject as a promise to reach a more refined conception of agency, a concept increasingly given attention in fields such as population ecology (Amburgey and Rao 1996), neo-institutionalism (DiMaggio 1998; Seo and Creed 2002), and institutional entrepreneurship (Garud, Hardy, and Maguire 2007). Partly, James's dual push towards agency and experience—thus practice—in understanding self, reveals the failure of assuming that an organizationally confined 'us' is the only or most important addressee of authoring. While organizational practices offer sites for authoring of identity, the vital engagements (Nakamura and Csikszentmihalyi 2003) experienced in practice may not stop at organizational borders. A comparative study of authoring in four organizational settings (Carlsen 2008) identified enactment of positive dramas as a key authoring form. It was shown that these positive dramas achieve much of their significance by being placed in temporal-relational contexts outside the organization: the legacies left behind, the mysteries solved, the societal causes invoked, the psychological well-being provided to outside beneficiaries, the disciplinary traditions referred to. The study of identity dynamics in organizations needs to take onboard a fuller account of how individuals and collectives develop in tandem with larger societal changes. A full recognition of the agentic dimension is necessary to see identity as a social force (Gecas 2001). To paraphrase the path-breaking contribution of Holland and Lave (2001), seeing identity as the relationship between subjects' self-making, their participation in local practice, and the mediation of more enduring struggles in that practice, opens up for understanding 'social evolution in person'.

19.5. Conclusion

Following after James on identity reminds us that identities are lived as much as they are told and provides perspectives that are still radical in organization studies. In a nutshell, the heritage from James means a relative shift from social categories to experiencing. It means a shift from seeing selves predominantly as objects to an acknowledgement of the collective processes of selves as subject. I have suggested that these processes are best conceived as a form of authoring, a subset of ongoing experiencing where people author their individual and collective lives based on selective attention and their beliefs about the future. Such a move does not rule out the relevance of social categories or otherness, as they remain important referents when speaking of identity and doing research on identity. But it is a shift that goes beyond a mere turning to social construction and discourse, for it grounds identity construction in everyday work practice and makes it an inherent part of change processes. Identity must be seen as taking shape from both habitual and novel aspects of work practice. Authoring of identity must be considered as being oriented towards pursuits that may be part individual, part organizational, and part beyond.

More provocatively, and pointing well beyond pragmatism and the discussion attempted here, James's radical theory of experience (James [1904] 1977*a*, *b*) challenges our conventions of operating with established and segregated categories of inquiry—like identity, strategy, learning, power, or practice. In a Jamesian interpretation, these concepts should be conceived first of all as *functional attributes* of connections made within living experience.

Accepting that agency is an integral part of our identities, what sets up agency? The full power of James's writings on agentic selves may be that they suggest an orientation back towards life and what makes life significant, questions that are now given renewed attention within the burgeoning field of positive psychology

(Seligman and Csikszentmihalyi 2000; Snyder and Lopez 2002). James has much to offer an orientation towards the positive as he sensitizes us to the fragilities, despairs, and dangers that lurk behind greatness. In a series of essays towards the latter part of his life, James returned to a set of questions concerning the meaning of life, what makes for the strong life and why people are energized to break out of their habits and function on a higher level of power. His answers revolved around the presence of a duality in our strivings. On the one hand, according to James, people have a 'fundamental appetite for plunder' (James [1910] 1977: 661) to the degree that if 'war had ever stopped, we would have to re-invent it, on this view, to redeem life from flat degradation' (James [1910] 1977: 663). On the other hand, people also need to see their plunders and pluck as part of some form of ideal aspiration, so that danger and the ideal are married in some way (James [1899] 1977). Thus, asking how people manage to escape the 'habit of inferiority' to their full selves, reach their powers and contribute the most, James suggests the following: 'In general terms the answer is plain: Either some unusual stimulus fills them with excitement, or some useful idea of necessity induces them to make an extra effort of will. *Excitement, ideas, and efforts*, in a word, is what carry us over the dam' ([1907] 1977*a*: 674, emphasis in original)

Acknowledgments

This chapter has benefited much from the inputs of Paul Adler and four anonymous reviewers, as well as from critical readings and discussions with Elena Antonacopoulou, Stewart Clegg, Karl Halvor Teigen, Tord F. Mortensen, Kjersti Bjørkeng, and Tor Hernes. The effort has been sponsored by grant 187952/I40 of the Norwegian Research Council. I am also grateful for the inspirational guidance into the work of James by Ray McDermott, some years ago.

References

Academy of Management Review (2000). 'Special Topic Forum on Organizational Identity and Identification'. *Academy of Management Review*, 25/1: 13–152.

Albert, S., and Whetten, D. (1985). 'Organizational Identity', in L. L. Cummings and B. M. Staw (eds.), *Research in Organizational Behavior*, 7: 263–95.

—— Ashforth, B. E., and Dutton, J. E. (2000). 'Organizational Identity and Identification: Charting New Waters and Building New Bridges'. *Academy of Management Review*, 25/1: 13–17.

Alvesson, M. (1993). 'Cultural-Ideological Modes of Management Control: A Theory and a Case Study of a Professional Service Firm', in S. Deetz (ed.), *Communication Yearbook*, 16. London: Sage.

Amburgey, T. L., and Rao, H. (1996). 'Organizational Ecology: Past, Present, and Future Directions'. *Academy of Management Journal*, 39/5: 1265–86.

Antonacopoulou, E. P. (2007). 'Practice', in S. R. Clegg and J. R. Bailey (eds.), *International Encyclopedia of Organization Studies.* London: Sage.

Argyris, C., and Schön, D. (1978). *Organizational Learning: A Theory of Action Perspective.* London: Addison-Wesley.

Ashforth, B. E., and Mael, F. A. (1989). 'Social Identity Theory and the Organization'. *Academy of Management Review*, 14/1: 20–39.

Bandura, A. (1997). *Self-efficacy: The Exercise of Control.* New York: W. H. Freeman.

Barry, D., and Elmes, M. (1997). 'Strategy Retold: Toward a Narrative View of Strategic Discourse'. *Academy of Management Review*, 22/2: 429–52.

Birnholtz, J. P., Cohen, M. D., and Hoch, S. V. (2007). 'Organizational Character: On the Regeneration of Camp Poplar Grove'. *Organization Science*, 18/2: 315–32.

Blumer, H. (1969). *Symbolic Interactionism.* Berkeley: University of California Press.

Brown, A. D. (2006). 'A Narrative Approach to Collective Identities'. *Journal of Management Studies*, 43/4: 731–53.

Brown, J. S., and Duguid, P. (2001). 'Knowledge and Organization: A Social-Practice Perspective'. *Organization Science*, 12/2: 198–213.

Bruner, J. (1990). *Acts of Meaning.* Cambridge, Mass.: Harvard University Press.

—— (1994). 'The "Remembered" Self', in U. Neisser and R. Fivush (eds.), *The Remembering Self: Construction and Accuracy in the Self-Narrative.* Cambridge: Cambridge University Press.

Carlsen, A. (2006). 'Organizational Becoming as Dialogic Imagination of Practice: The Case of the Indomitable Gauls'. *Organization Science*, 17/1: 132–49.

—— (2008). 'Positive Dramas: Enacting Self-Adventures in Organizations'. *Journal of Positive Psychology*, 3/1: 55–75.

—— and Mantere, S. (2007). 'Pragmatism', in S. R. Clegg and J. R. Bailey (eds.), *International Encyclopedia of Organization Studies.* London: Sage.

—— and Pitsis, T. (2008). 'Projects for Life: Building Narrative Capital for Positive Organizational Change', forthcoming in S. R. Clegg and C. L. Cooper (eds.), *Handbook of Macro Organization Behavior.* Sage: London.

Chia, R. (1997). 'Essai: Thirty Years On: From Organizational Structures to the Organization of Thought'. *Organization Studies*, 18/4: 685–707.

—— (2003). 'Ontology: Organization as "World-Making"', in R. Westwood and S. Clegg (eds.), *Debating Organization: Point-Counterpoint in Organization Studies.* Oxford: Blackwell.

Clark, B. R. (1972). 'The Organizational Saga in Higher Education'. *Administrative Science Quarterly*, 17/2: 178–84.

Clegg, S. R., Kornberger, M., and Rhodes, C. (2005). 'Learning/Becoming/Organizing'. *Organization*, 12/2: 147–67.

Collins, J., and Porras, J. (1994). *Built to Last.* London: Random House Business Books.

Corley, K., Harquail, C., Pratt, M., Glynn, M., Fiol, C., and Hatch, M. (2006). 'Guiding Organizational Identity through Aged Adolescence'. *Journal of Management Inquiry*, 15: 85–99.

Crites, S. (1971). 'The Narrative Quality of Experience'. *Journal of the American Academy of Religion*, 39/3: 291–311.

Csikszentmihalyi, M. (1985). 'Emergent Motivation and the Evolution of the Self'. *Advances in Motivation and Achievement*, 4: 93–119.

Czarniawska, B. (1997). *Narrating the Organization*. Chicago: University of Chicago Press.

DeGeus, A. (1997). *The Living Company*. Boston: Harvard Business School Press.

Dewey, J. ([1910] 1981). 'The Influence of Darwinism on Philosophy', in J. J. McDermott (ed.), *The Philosophy of John Dewey*. Chicago: University of Chicago Press.

—— ([1925] 1958). *Experience and Nature*. 2nd edn. New York: Dover.

—— ([1934] 1980). *Art as Experience*. New York: Perigee Books.

—— (1940). 'The Vanishing Subject in the Psychology of James'. *Journal of Philosophy*, 37/22: 589–99.

Diggins, J. (1994). *The Promise of Pragmatism: Modernism and the Crisis of Knowledge and Authority*. Chicago: University of Chicago Press.

DiMaggio, P. (1988). 'Interest and Agency in Institutional Theory', in L. G. Zucker (ed.), *Institutional Patterns in Organizations, Culture and Environment*. Cambridge, Mass.: Ballinger.

Dreier, O. (1999). 'Personal Trajectories of Participation across Contexts of Social Practice'. *Outline*, 1/1: 5–32.

Dutton, J. E., and Dukerich, J. (1991). 'Keeping an Eye on the Mirror: Image and Identity in Organizational Adaptation'. *Academy of Management Journal*, 34/3: 517–54.

—— —— and Harquail, C. V. (1994). 'Organizational Images and Member Identification'. *Administrative Science Quarterly*, 39/2: 239–63.

Elkjaer, B. (2004). 'Organizational Learning: The "Third Way"'. *Management Learning*, 35/4: 419–34.

—— and Simpson, B. (2006). 'Towards a Pragmatic Theory of Creative Practice'. Paper presented at the Second Organizational Studies Summer Workshop.

Emirbayer, M., and Mische, A. (1998). 'What is Agency?' *American Journal of Sociology*, 103/4: 962–1023.

Garfinkel, H. (1967). *Studies of Ethnomethodology*. Englewood Cliffs, NJ: Prentice-Hall.

Garud, R., Hardy, C., and Maguire, S. (2007). 'Institutional Entrepreneurship as Embedded Agency: An Introduction to the Special Issue'. *Organization Studies*, 28/7: 957–69.

Gecas, V. (1982). 'The Self-Concept'. *Annual Review of Sociology*, 8: 1–33.

—— (1991). 'The Self-Concept as a Basis for a Theory of Motivation', in J. A. Howard and P. L. Callero (eds.), *The Self-Society Dynamic*. Cambridge: Cambridge University Press.

—— (2001). 'The Self as a Social Force', in T. Owens, S. Stryker, and H. Goodman (eds.), *Extending Self-Esteem Theory and Research*. Cambridge: Cambridge University Press.

Giddens, A. (1991). *Modernity and Self-Identity*. Stanford, Calif.: Stanford University Press.

Gioia, D. (1998). 'From Individual to Organizational Identity', in D. Whetten and P. C. Godfrey (eds.), *Identity in Organizations*. Thousand Oaks, Calif.: Sage.

—— Schultz, M., and Corley, K. G. (2000). 'Organizational Identity, Image and Adaptive Instability'. *Academy of Management Review*, 25/1: 63–81.

Haack, S. (2004). 'Pragmatism Old and New'. *Contemporary Pragmatism*, 1/1: 3–41.

Hatch, M. J., and Schultz, M. (2002). 'The Dynamics of Organizational Identity'. *Human Relations*, 55/8: 989–1018.

Hildebrand, D. (2003). 'The Neopragmatist Turn'. *Southwest Philosophy Review*, 19/1: 79–88.

—— (2005). 'Pragmatism, Neopragmatism, and Public Administration'. *Administration & Society*, 37/3: 345–59.

Holland, D., Lachiotte, W., Jr., Skinner, D., and Cain, C. (eds.) (1998). *Identity and Agency in Cultural Worlds*. Cambridge, Mass.: Harvard University Press.

—— and Lave, J. (eds.) (2001). *History in Person: Enduring Struggles, Contentious Practice, Intimate Identities*. Santa Fe: School of American Research Press.

Ibarra, H. (1999). 'Provisional Selves: Experimenting with Image and Identity in Professional Adaptation'. *Administrative Science Quarterly*, 44/4: 764–92.

—— (2003). *Working Identity: Unconventional Strategies for Reinventing Your Career*. Boston: Harvard Business School Press.

James, W. (1880). 'Great Men, Great Thoughts and the Environment'. *Atlantic Monthly*, 46: 441–59.

—— ([1890] 1950). *Principles of Psychology*. New York: Dover.

—— ([1896] 2000). 'The Will to Believe', in J. Stuhr (ed.), *Pragmatism and Classical American Philosophy: Essential Readings and Interpretive Essays*. 2nd edn. New York: Oxford University Press.

—— ([1899] 1977). 'What Makes a Life Significant', in J.J. McDermott (ed.), *The Writings of William James: A Comprehensive Edition*. Chicago: University of Chicago Press.

—— ([1903] 2000). '"Emerson," A Memorial Address', in J. Stuhr (ed.), *Pragmatism and Classical American Philosophy: Essential Readings and Interpretive Essays*. 2nd edn. New York: Oxford University Press.

—— ([1904] 1977*a*). 'Does "Consciousness" Exist?', in John J. McDermott (ed.), *The Writings of William James: A Comprehensive Edition*. Chicago: University of Chicago Press.

—— ([1904] 1977*b*). 'A World of Pure Experience', in J. J. McDermott (ed.), *The Writings of William James: A Comprehensive Edition*. Chicago: University of Chicago Press.

—— ([1907] 1977*a*). 'The Energies of Men', in J. J. McDermott (ed.), *The Writings of William James: A Comprehensive Edition*. Chicago: University of Chicago Press.

—— ([1907] 1977*b*). 'What Pragmatism Means', in J. J. McDermott (ed.), *The Writings of William James: A Comprehensive Edition*. Chicago: University of Chicago Press.

—— ([1910] 1977). 'The Moral Equivalent of War', in J. J. McDermott (ed.), *The Writings of William James: A Comprehensive Edition*. Chicago: University of Chicago Press.

Joas, H. (1996). *The Creativity of Action*. Cambridge: Polity Press.

Johnson, E. (1972). 'William James and the Art of Fiction'. *Journal of Aesthetics and Art Criticism*, 30/3: 285–96.

Knights, D., and Mueller, F. (2004). 'Strategy as a "Project": Overcoming Dualism in the Strategy Debate'. *European Management Review*, 1/1: 55–61.

Kolb, D. A. (1984). *Experiential Learning: Experience as the Source of Learning and Development*. Upper Saddle River, NJ: Prentice Hall.

McAdams, D. P. (1993). *The Stories We Live By*. New York: William Morrow.

—— (1995). 'Introduction: Narrative Construction of Emotional Life: Commentary'. *Journal of Narrative Life Histories*, 5/3: 207–21.

—— (1997). 'The Case for Unity in the (Post)modern Self: A Modest Proposal', in R. D. Ashmore and L. Jussim (eds.), *Self and Identity: Fundamental Issues*. New York: Oxford University Press.

McDermott, J. J. (1977). 'Introduction: Person, Process and the Risk of Belief', in J. J. McDermott (ed.), *The Writings of William James: A Comprehensive Edition*. Chicago: University of Chicago Press.

—— (2000). 'William James: Introduction', in J. Stuhr (ed.), *Pragmatism and Classical American Philosophy: Essential Readings and Interpretive Essays.* 2nd edn. New York: Oxford University Press.

MacIntyre, A. (1981). *After Virtue.* London: Duckworth Press.

Mattingly, C. F. (1998). *Healing Dramas and Clinical Plots: The Narrative Structure of Experience.* Cambridge: Cambridge University Press.

Mead, G. H. ([1903] 1964). 'The Definition of the Physical', in A. Reck (ed.), *Selected Writings: George Herbert Mead.* Chicago: University of Chicago Press.

—— ([1913] 1964). 'The Social Self', in A. Reck (ed.), *Selected Writings: George Herbert Mead.* Chicago: University of Chicago Press.

—— ([1932] 2002). *The Philosophy of the Present.* New York: Prometheus Books.

—— ([1934] 2000). 'The "I" and the "Me"', in J. Stuhr (ed.), *Pragmatism and Classical American Philosophy: Essential Readings and Interpretive Essays.* 2nd edn. New York: Oxford University Press.

Menand, L. (2001). *The Metaphysical Club: A Story of Ideas in America.* New York: Farrar, Straus and Giroux.

Murphy, J. P. (1990). *Pragmatism: From Peirce to Davidson.* Boulder, Colo.: Westview Press.

Nag, R., Corley, K. G., and Gioia, D. A. (2007). 'The Intersection of Organizational Identity, Knowledge, and Practice: Attempting Strategic Change via Knowledge Grafting'. *Academy of Management Journal*, 50/4: 821–47.

Nakamura, J., and Csikszentmihalyi, M. (2003). 'The Construction of Meaning through Vital Engagement', in C. L. M. Keyes and J. Haidt (eds.), *Flourishing: Positive Psychology and the Life Well-Lived.* Washington, DC: American Psychological Association.

O'Connor, E. (2000). 'Plotting the Organization: The Embedded Narrative as a Construct for Studying Change'. *Journal of Applied Behavioral Science*, 36/2: 174–92.

Pepper, S. (1942). *World Hypothesis.* Berkeley: University of California Press.

Polkinghorne, D. E. (1988). *Narrative Knowing and the Human Sciences.* Albany: State University of New York Press.

Popper, K. (1968). *Conjectures and Refutations.* New York: Harper Torchbooks.

Roberts, L. M., Dutton, J. E., Spreitzer, G., Heaphy, E., and Quinn, R. E. (2005). 'Composing the Reflected Best-Self Portrait: Building Pathways for Becoming Extraordinary in Organizations'. *Academy of Management Review*, 30/4: 712–36.

—— —— (eds.) (2009). *Exploring Positive Identities and Organizations: Building a Theoretical and Research Foundation.* New York: Psychology Press.

Romanelli, E., and Khessina, O. M. (2005). 'Regional Industrial Identity: Cluster Configurations and Economic Development'. *Organization Science*, 16/4: 344–58.

Rorty, R. (2000). *Philosophy and Social Hope.* New York: Penguin.

Ryan, R. M., and Deci, E. L. (2000). 'Self-Determination Theory and the Facilitation of Intrinsic Motivation, Social Development, and Well-Being'. *American Psychologist*, 55: 68–78.

Sarbin, T. R. (1986). 'The Narrative as a Root Metaphor for Psychology', in T. R. Sarbin (ed.), *Narrative Psychology.* Westport, Conn.: Praeger Publishers.

—— (2000). 'Worldmaking, Self and Identity'. *Culture & Psychology*, 6/2: 253–8.

Schatzki, T. R. (2001). 'Introduction: Practice Theory', in T. R. Schatzki, K. Knorr-Cetina, and E. Von Savigny (eds.), *The Practice Turn in Contemporary Theory.* London: Routledge.

—— Knorr-Cetina, K., and Von Savigny, E. (eds.) (2001). *The Practice Turn in Contemporary Theory*. London: Routledge.

Seligman, M., and Csikszentmihalyi, M. (2000). 'Positive Psychology: An Introduction'. *American Psychologist*, 55/1: 5–14.

Selznick, P. ([1957] 1983). *Leadership in Administration: A Sociological Interpretation*. Berkeley: University of California.

Seo, M., and Creed, D. (2002). 'Institutional Contradictions, Praxis, and Institutional Change as a Dialectical Perspective'. *Academy of Management Review*, 27/2: 222–47.

Shotter, J., and Cunliffe, A. (2003). 'Managers as Practical Authors: Everyday Conversations for Action', in D. Holman and R. Thorpe (eds.), *Management and Language*. London: Sage.

Smirchich, L., and Stubbart, C. (1985). 'Strategic Management in an Enacted World'. *Academy of Management Review*, 10/4: 724–36.

Snyder, C. R., and Lopez, S. J. (eds.) (2002). *Handbook of Positive Psychology*. New York: Oxford University Press.

Sztompka, P. (1991). *Society in Action: The Theory of Social Becoming*. Chicago: University of Chicago Press.

Tajfel, H., and Turner, J. C. (1985). 'The Social Identity Theory of Intergroup Behaviour', in S. Worchel and W. G. Austin (eds.), *Psychology of Intergroup Relations*. 2nd edn. Chicago: Nelson-Hall.

Thayer, H. S. (1981). *Meaning and Action: A Critical History of Pragmatism*. 2nd edn. Indianapolis: Hackett Publishing.

Thoits, P. A., and Virshup, L. K. (1997). 'Me's and We's: Forms and Functions of Social Identities', in R. D. Ashmore and L. Jussim (eds.), *Self and Identity: Fundamental Issues*. New York: Oxford University Press.

Tsoukas, H., and Chia, R. (2002). 'On Organizational Becoming: Rethinking Organizational Change'. *Organization Science*, 13/5: 567–82.

Van der Vegt, G., and Bunderson, J. S. (2005). 'Learning Behavior and Performance in Multidisciplinary Teams: The Importance of Collective Team Identification'. *Academy of Management Journal*, 48/3: 532–47.

Weick, K. E. (1979). *The Social Psychology of Organizing*. 2nd edn. New York: McGraw-Hill.

—— (1995). *Sensemaking in Organizations*. Thousand Oaks, Calif.: Sage.

Wenger, E. (1998). *Communities of Practice: Learning, Meaning, and Identity*. Cambridge: Cambridge University Press.

—— McDermott, R., and Snyder W. M. (2002). *Cultivating Communities of Practice*. Boston: Harvard Business School Press.

Whetten, D. A., and Godfrey, P. C. (eds.) (1998). *Identity in Organizations: Developing Theory through Conversations*. Thousand Oaks, Calif.: Sage.

Wicks, A. C., and Freeman, E. R. (1998). 'Organization Studies and the New Pragmatism: Positivism, Anti-Positivism and the Search for Ethics'. *Organization Science*, 9/3: 123–40.

CHAPTER 20

READING DEWEY

SOME IMPLICATIONS FOR THE STUDY OF ROUTINE

MICHAEL D. COHEN

In the last few years I have found myself drawn into a fairly extensive reading of the work of John Dewey, the American pragmatist philosopher who was a major figure in the first half of the twentieth century. I have not always been able to explain to myself or to others why I would turn to books such as *Art as Experience* or *Human Nature and Conduct* instead of spending the equivalent time reading recent research. But I have found Dewey's company hard to resist. When I have confessed this occasionally among professional friends, I have learned that there are others who have also developed a fascination with his work. Conversations with them have deepened my sense that there are important reasons why Dewey is appealing at the current juncture in the development of organization studies.[1]

[1] My fellow Dewey fans are not responsible for what I say here, of course. Indeed, almost every statement I want to make would prompt disagreement from at least one of them. Nonetheless, I am deeply grateful to this little network, which includes Karl Weick, Chuck Sable, Chris Ansell, Patricia Benner, Marc Ventresca, Carol Heimer, David Cohen, Paul Adler, and David Obstfeld. I am also grateful to the ICOS organization of the University of Michigan, for a small grant that allowed a number of us to get together and discuss our shared interest in Dewey's work in 2003, and to Adler, Ansell, and Yeheskel Hasenfeld for suggestions made during a workshop presentation of the paper. I thank as well Hari Tsoukas for encouraging the initial version of this chapter (Cohen 2007*c*), which has been reworked here with an eye to enlarging the treatment of the relation of routine to emotion as well as to habit.

20.1. Introduction

This chapter explores some of the reasons for Dewey's appeal by spelling out several difficulties that have plagued our efforts to understand routine activities and by suggesting how Dewey's point of view might be especially helpful in crafting an effective response to those problems. In recent years a large and varied set of scholars has been investigating what I will call 'recurring action patterns'. Frequently they have worked with the label 'routine' (Feldman and Pentland 2003; Kane, Argote, and Levine 2005; Nelson and Winter 1982), but they have also worked with closely related concepts such as 'practices' (Orlikowski 2002) or 'collective mind' (Weick and Roberts 1993), or even in apparently distinct subfields such as organizational culture or organizational identity (Martin 1992; Ravasi and Schultz 2006; Trice and Beyer 1993; Whetten and Mackey 2002). Work on this topic has deep roots in modern organization theory, going back to ideas about routines in Simon's *Administrative Behavior*, 'programs' in March and Simon's *Organizations*, and 'standard operating procedures' in Cyert and March's *A Behavioral Theory of the Firm*.

In my own research, and especially when teaching students in programs oriented towards professional practice, I have found that I am endlessly called upon to undo standing presumptions about recurring action patterns, most especially when the label 'routine' is in play. And I see much work by others interested in this area going into rebutting these same misleading presumptions.

A closely related observation is that, while there has been some advance in our efforts to understand routine, such as the application of quality management techniques in manufacturing, more general conceptual progress has been frustratingly slow. We are, for example, a long way from having an authoritative textbook for students in professional training who want to know how to create effective organizational routines in non-manufacturing settings, or how to modify them when they could be still better. I have asked myself many times why it has proven so difficult to give really useful, research-grounded answers to these questions about how routines arise, are maintained, change, or resist change.

In workplace conversation, in training of professionals, and in careful research, our thinking about routine seems to me to have encountered a set of fundamental intellectual difficulties that inhibit cumulative development of useful shared understanding. I think a fair portion of the difficulty can be attributed to four notions that are commonplaces of everyday thinking about routine but which undermine careful consideration. It is extremely easy to fall into assuming (1) that routines are rigid in their execution, (2) that they are mundane in content, (3) that they are isolated from thought and feeling, and/or (4) that their underlying action patterns are explicitly stored somewhere.

By saying that we may take routines to be *rigid*, I mean that we often suppose that a routine consisting of some particular pattern of actions—say, for purchasing a new round of office supplies—is identical or invariant on the multiple occasions of its execution. After all, the very reference to it as the routine for purchasing supplies implies that it is 'the same thing' over time, like my desk chair, or my copy of March and Simon.

By saying that we may take routines to be *mundane*, I mean that we often suppose that the actions we refer to as routine are likely not to be of major importance. So I often hear it said that less skilled workers are assigned to carry out the parts of a process that are 'merely routine'. When examples are given in this frame of mind, they might be for activities such as filing, cleaning, or assembling.[2]

By saying that we may take routines to be *mindless*, I mean that we often presume that routine actions are not tightly integrated with deliberation, reflection, or feelings. 'It's a routine matter' is often a way of indicating that not much reflection, commitment, or attention is required.

And finally, by saying that we may take routines to be *explicitly stored*, I mean that we often suppose that the 'recipe' for a routine action is encoded somewhere, such as in formalized standard operating procedures, in training session lectures, in memorized rules of behavior, or in artifacts such as production machinery or blueprints.

Dewey's writing began to fascinate me because he seemed to have worked out in the early 1900s a philosophical position that (1) makes each one of these presumptions to appear quite unnatural, and (2) suggests why in our own time we so frequently fall into them.

Although there have been some pockets of revived interest in Dewey, he seems still to be thought of in general academic circles mainly as someone who wrote about education, so the notion that his work suggests broad lines of reconstruction for research on organizational action might seem a bit surprising. However, he was a very important figure in the early decades of the twentieth century, one of the handful of philosophers who developed the position known as pragmatism (though he later preferred other names), a major contributor to early research in psychology who helped that field to branch off from philosophy to stand on its own (Dewey 1896; Manicas 2002), a co-founder and early president of the American Psychological Association, an active creator of social capital (the American Civil Liberties Union, the National Association for the Advancement of Colored People, the American Association of University Professors, and the New York Teachers Union), a towering public intellectual—of whom it was said 'for a generation no major issue was clarified until Dewey had spoken' (Commager 1950)—and, of course, the director (1902–4) of the enormously influential University of Chicago 'Lab School' (Menand 2001).

[2] Of course, these stereotypical examples themselves overlook how vital such activities are to organizational functioning.

20.2. Tripartite Views of Habit, Emotion, and Cognition

All Dewey's work is animated by a fundamental interest in learning—in the never-ending refinement of habits, feelings, and beliefs—at both the individual and collective levels, in domains as different as aesthetic perception (Dewey 1934), political mobilization (Dewey 1927), education (Dewey 1938*a*), and scientific inquiry (Dewey 1938*b*). This interest is crystallized in his *Human Nature and Conduct* (Dewey 1922). There he sets out his views of how we make use of what we have learned to shape individual and collective action, and to learn, in turn, from the results of what we undertake. Indeed, Dewey saw the classroom as preparation for the learning that must constantly go on in successful collective action, including both civic and organizational action.

Dewey views human beings as having three broad faculties: habitual, emotional, and cognitive. *Human Nature and Conduct* is organized into three sections corresponding to these faculties, and Dewey explains that he puts the discussion of habits first because they shape and empower the other two faculties. He says habits may seem individual but are fundamentally social. The native emotional impulses of an infant, in his view, acquire their meaning through interaction with the established customs and habits of surrounding adults. He says, in remarking on an insight of Gabriel Tarde's, 'all psychological phenomena can be divided into the physiological and the social, and that when we have relegated elementary sensation and appetite to the former head, all that is left of our mental life, our beliefs, ideas and desires, falls within the scope of social psychology' (Dewey 1916).

And habits are integral to thoughtful foresight and judgment. He conceives of habit as a kind of action disposition, rather than as the observable behavior to which it might give rise. Habits are deeply intertwined with emotion and cognition, but they have a primary role as basic building blocks of all our actions. So he writes (Dewey 1922: 88), 'Man is a creature of habit. Not of reason, nor yet of instinct', where by 'instinct' he means what we might term a basic emotional impulse. He assigns to deliberate thought (or we might say 'cognition') a continuous role of reflecting upon, analyzing, extending, and repairing habit.

The contrast between Dewey's stress on habit and our contemporary worldview of routine is quite sharp. He sees habit as integral to all action; therefore, it is the foundation of all skills and established collective practices, and an essential building block of improvisation in an ever-changing environment. He views habit as the basis of what we label 'routine', but he so strongly believes that habit is not rigid, mundane, mindless, or explicitly stored that, as we shall see, he declines to use the word 'routine' for fear of importing those conceptions (Dewey 1922: 51).

Elsewhere (Cohen 2007*a*), I have written about the shift in our thinking about these matters that can be seen during the early career of Herbert Simon, who cites Dewey's *Human Nature and Conduct* as a principal source of the psychology used in his earliest important work, *Administrative Behavior* (Simon 1947). Yet Simon begins his path-breaking book by announcing an explicit choice to emphasize decisions and their underlying cognitive processes, while de-emphasizing action. He reiterates this in the preface to the second edition, where he writes of his conviction that 'decision-making is the heart of administration, and that the vocabulary of administrative theory must be grounded in the logic and psychology of choice' (Simon 1957: xlvi). He was, in effect, asserting the preeminence of cognition over habit and emotion.

At the same time, Simon was moving towards positivism as a philosophy of science, away from the instrumentalism that Dewey had advocated. Thus, in *Administrative Behavior*, Simon begins by arguing that intellectual progress depends on making sharp distinctions between fact and value and between means and ends, where Dewey had argued that both pairs are defined in context and exhibit deep and subtle interdependence.

By the time the highly influential 'Carnegie School' that Simon initiated had developed into *A Behavioral Theory of the Firm* (Cyert and March 1963), decisions and anticipated consequences were very much in the foreground, so that standard operating procedures had become defined as 'bundles of decision rules', and habit, as Dewey understood it, had faded well into the background, relabeled as routine and sealed away in a presumption of mindless automaticity.[3]

Very roughly, we might picture both the Simon view and the Dewey view as tripartite, with each including cognition, emotion, and habit (see Fig. 20.1). But in the Simon version, which has so profoundly influenced all later organizational research, cognition is the top of the pyramid. Decisions are thoughtful problem solving—even if sharply bounded in their rationality—and as such they can be readily investigated with thinking-aloud protocols (Newell and Simon 1972). Emotions help determine the value of what decisions may accomplish. Habits may govern—or embody—the actions that will be triggered. Indeed, habit (by now, generally labeled 'routine') may provide a guarantee that the execution of choices will be pretty much automatic, further justifying that the crucial focus should be on decisions.

[3] Habits in something like Dewey's sense re-entered the picture when Nelson and Winter made them central to their *Evolutionary Theory of Economic Change* (Nelson and Winter 1982). But, revealingly, the marching banner of evolutionary economics as a 'school' has been 'routines as genes'. This often allowed theorists to reduce habits again to fixed action patterns whose 'phenotypic' variability could be set aside. In my view, the informal account of habit and routine in the Nelson and Winter book, which relies heavily on the work of Michael Polanyi, is quite a bit richer than the 'routines as genes' slogan might suggest. So is Winter's field-related work with various colleagues such as Gabriel Szulanski (Winter and Szulanski 2001).

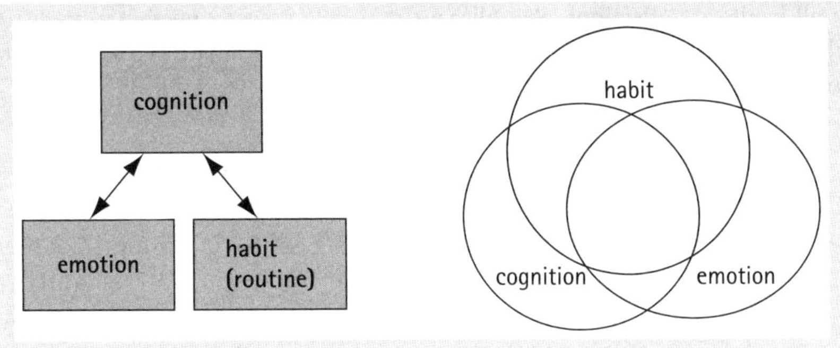

Fig. 20.1. The Simon perspective (left) compared to the Dewey perspective (right)

20.3. The Interactions of Habit, Thought, and Impulse

In Dewey's world, which was also the world of the brothers James (both William and his novelist sibling, Henry), the focus is on habit—along with its supporting mesh of emotional impulses—making it the leading aspect of the tripartite account. In this approach, effective action, individual or collective, always occurs through the operation of a biological system in which habit is integral. You can choose to eat a piece of cake, but only your arms, mouth, and intestines can accomplish the deed. As all parents know, these do their parts reliably only after months, or years, of training. And, as all adults know, they can sometimes accomplish the deed even when 'you' have decided you will not eat the piece of cake.

The four misleading presumptions about routine that I have described become more common when we lose sight of these habit-infused properties of human nature that we all recognize. The learning and ongoing dispositions that lie behind our embodied capabilities for an action, such as eating our cake, can disappear into the taken-for-granted status of normal functioning—until an arm is disconcerted (say by an injury or a stroke) and must learn anew, or until a diet forbids cake, and we may find it surprisingly challenging to comply despite the knowledge that it is in our best interest.

Dewey places considerable stress on these experiences with habit that we all have.

It is a significant fact that in order to appreciate the peculiar place of habit in activity we have to betake ourselves of bad habits.... When we think of such bad habits, the union of habit with desire and with propulsive power is forced upon us.... [When we think of positive habits, we] think of them as passive tools waiting to be called into action from without. A bad habit suggests an inherent tendency to action and also a hold, command over us.... A habit has this power because it is so intimately a part of ourselves.... [Bad habits] teach us that all habits are affections, that all have projectile power, and that a predisposition formed by a number of specific acts is an immensely more intimate and fundamental part of ourselves than are vague, general, conscious choices. (Dewey 1922: 21)

The actions we engage in despite our choices and resolutions seem to be mysteries or minor anomalies in a choice-centered world-view. Yet we enter a meeting room and head for the seat we occupied last time, not because it was optimal then and remains so now, but because now it is familiar. We may even feel some resentment if our seat has been 'taken' by someone else. Even for so-called 'knowledge workers', our work and daily life are mostly action, and (as Simon would agree) our capacity for careful reflection and choice is extremely slow and very limited in scope and depth. Unchosen action patterns therefore predominate in our lives, but they remain mere curiosities in a discourse on organization in which cognitively grounded decision is supreme.

In contrast, when action is taken as central and grounded in habit, the organism, or organization, is much more a historical being. The consequences of today's actions will be both today's consumption and tomorrow's skilled capabilities and acquired dispositions. Dewey makes this very clear in his work on education. His idea of education is just experience that is arranged to be both motivating in the moment and consequential for capabilities in the long run (Dewey 1938*a*).

All experience is in some sense educational. It always 'draws out' new potentialities—the root meaning of 'educate'—and leaves those who undergo it forever changed. We single out activities explicitly as educational when their longer term effects are predominant. But, for Dewey, experience is not likely to have the longer term effects that might be desired, if it is not also challenging and rewarding in the immediate doing.

Challenge arises when emotions are engaged by a task and established habits are insufficient to accomplish it. Cognitive powers are then mobilized to diagnose the reasons for breakdown and to redeploy capabilities in new combinations that may be expected to succeed. As we endlessly repeat this cycle of emotionally engaged perception and activity, periodically interrupted by breakdowns and cognitively intense repair work, it generates a vast repertoire of reasonably effective—and mutually coherent—habits.

In the Dewey three-part scheme, this dynamic interplay of habit, thought, and emotion is essential. He makes a deliberate effort not to modularize the system and define narrow interfaces between otherwise independent components. A deep example illustrating a number of these differences is in the treatment Dewey gives of the notion of character. He does not conceive of character as the espousal of lofty principles, but rather as expressed in the coherent patterning of recurring actions. Character is vitally important, but it is a matter mostly of emotionally charged habit built through experience and periodic reflection, rather than being centrally about explicit choices that consistently apply self-conscious goals to forecasts of consequences. Because he views all habits as continually active, he sees habits as shaping and supporting one another, and says 'Character is the interpenetration of habits' (Dewey 1922: 29).

In his view of character rooted in habit, he follows Aristotle, who writes in the *Nicomachean Ethics* (2.1):

For the things we have to learn before we can do them, we learn by doing them, e.g. men become builders by building and lyre players by playing the lyre; so too we become just by doing just acts, temperate by doing temperate acts, brave by doing brave acts. This is confirmed by what happens in states; for legislators make the citizens good by forming habits in them, and this is the wish of every legislator, and those who do not effect it miss their mark, and it is in this that a good constitution differs from a bad one.

Like Dewey's, Aristotle's is a formulation that relies on a sense of habit that is not common in our era and can therefore sound a bit strange to a contemporary ear. But perhaps this strangeness should alert us that a richer world-view, one that sees habit as fundamental to human action along with thoughts and feelings, may have become dangerously simplified in our own time.[4]

Because of his focus on the interactions of habit, thought, and impulse, habit is lively for Dewey, not dead. It suffuses both perception and reflection. It is triggered by and conveys emotion. It constitutes character and embodies morality. It definitely need not be rigid, mundane, mindless, or explicitly stored. As Dewey would have us use the term, habit is typically not routine. Some extended passages from *Human Nature and Conduct* may help to convey his approach and the distinctive language he uses to express it:

While it is admitted that the word habit has been used [here] in a somewhat broader sense than is usual, we must protest against the tendency in psychological literature to limit its meaning to repetition. This usage is much less in accord with popular usage than is the wider way in which we have used the word. It assumes from the start the identity of habit with routine. Repetition is in no sense the essence of habit. Tendency to repeat acts is an incident of many habits but not of all. A man with the habit of giving way to anger may show his habit by a murderous attack upon someone who has offended. His act is nonetheless due to habit because it occurs only once in his life. The essence of habit is an acquired predisposition to ways or modes of response, not to particular acts except as, under special conditions, these express a way of behaving. Habit means special sensitiveness or accessibility to certain classes of stimuli, standing predilections and aversions, rather than bare recurrence of specific acts. (Dewey 1922: 32)

How delicate, prompt, sure and varied are the movements of a violin player or an engraver! How unerringly they phrase every shade of emotion and every turn of idea! Mechanism is indispensable. If each act has to be consciously searched for at the moment and intentionally performed, execution is painful and the product is clumsy and halting. Nevertheless

[4] The virtual disappearance of the concept of habit from post-war American sociological discourse is nicely documented in Camic (1986).

> the difference between the artist and the mere technician is unmistakable. The artist is a masterful technician. The technique or mechanism is fused with thought and feeling. The 'mechanical' performer permits the mechanism to dictate the performance. It is absurd to say that the latter exhibits habit and the former not. We are confronted with two kinds of habit, intelligent and routine. All life has its élan, but only the prevalence of dead habits deflects life into mere élan. (Dewey 1922: 51).

> Habits are conditions of intellectual efficiency. They operate in two ways upon intellect. Obviously, they restrict its reach, they fix its boundaries. They are blinders that confine the eyes of mind to the road ahead. They prevent thought from straying away from its imminent occupation to a landscape more varied and picturesque but irrelevant to practice. Outside the scope of habits, thought works gropingly, fumbling in confused uncertainty; and yet habit made complete in routine shuts in thought so effectually that it is no longer needed or possible. The routineer's road is a ditch out of which he cannot get, whose sides enclose him, directing his course so thoroughly that he no longer thinks of his path or his destination. All habit-forming involves the beginning of an intellectual specialization which if unchecked ends in thoughtless action.
>
> Significantly enough this fullblown result is called absentmindedness. Stimulus and response are mechanically linked together in an unbroken chain. Each successive act facilely evoked by its predecessor pushes us automatically into the next act of a predetermined series. Only a signal flag of distress recalls consciousness to the task of carrying on. Fortunately, nature which beckons us to this path of least resistance also puts obstacles in the way of our complete acceptance of its invitation. Success in achieving a ruthless and dull efficiency of action is thwarted by untoward circumstance. The most skilful aptitude bumps at times into the unexpected, and so gets into trouble from which only observation and invention extricate it. Efficiency in following a beaten path has then to be converted into breaking a new road through strange lands. (Dewey 1922: 121)

In consequence of these views, Dewey uses 'routine habit' or 'routine' for the (often pathological) case in which action is mindless, or rigid. He uses 'habit' for the dispositions and skills of individuals and for their resulting actions, which can be sublime as well as mundane and improvised as well as scripted. He often uses 'custom' for habit-based recurring action at the collective level.

Dewey also has a distinctive vocabulary for discussing what contemporary research would call the emotional aspects of routine. As with his treatment of the word 'routine', it can be instructive to understand his choice of terms. Just as he uses 'routine' only for a special case, Dewey actually uses the word 'emotion' only rarely in *Human Nature and Conduct* and talks mostly of 'instincts' or 'impulses', which he uses almost interchangeably. When he does use 'emotion', it is to designate a generalized state of arousal or turmoil corresponding to the presence of many—usually contradictory—impulses to action. He does not speak of 'the emotions' or of 'the emotion of fear'. On the contrary, he insists that the impulses occurring in us are enormously varied by virtue of the habits and environmental contingencies with which they are entangled and that this multi-faceted engagement should be squarely in the foreground.

it is customary to suppose that there is a single instinct of fear, or at most a few well-defined sub-species of it. In reality, when one is afraid the whole being reacts, and this entire responding organism is never twice the same. In fact, also, every reaction takes place in a different environment, and its meaning is never twice alike, since the difference in environment makes a difference in consequences.... It is true enough that in all cases we are able to identify certain more or less separable characteristic acts—muscular contractions, withdrawals, evasions, concealments... [But these are interactions with the state of the organism and the environment, and so] there is no one fear having diverse manifestations; there are as many qualitatively different fears as there are objects responded to and different consequences sensed and observed. (Dewey 1922: 107)

This approach might seem strange. We are accustomed to thinking of a small number of principal 'states', such as anger, fear, or disgust—and perhaps a few others—each with its own cluster of neurological and hormonal responses. We take such basic emotions to be like the primary colors from which a skillful painter or a television set can mix up millions of subtle blends. But Dewey wants us to focus on the actual colors in the perceived scene, not the components into which they might be decomposed. His central concern is with the unfolding of action. The combinations of habit and impulse that actually occur are what are fused during experience, changing the actor in the process and constituting new 'primitive' resources for further action.

Merely knowing that a person is afraid might be too coarse a rendering of their condition. Will the person flee or attack? Fear could be part of either response, but accumulated dispositions associated with previous dangerous situations will have built the habits available in the present moment, and they will have built them in specific environmental conditions and with the actor in specific bodily states. The present habits of the person are crucial to the action taken. The impulses that will be evoked in encountering a situation will include complex mixtures of basic physiological responses. Those will be tied to the evoked habits that are the available potential action patterns. Together they will shape the action likely to occur. Indeed, Dewey often speaks of the combination of these impulse and action resources as the 'stock of activities'. Where 'activity' is understood as a potential effect derived from the person's nature, as in 'the activity of sulphuric acid' rather than as a realized action. The picture he conveys is of a large number of possible actions that might be appropriate to current circumstances, each yearning to be 'consummated' and hence to 'release' the associated impulses.

Fear [of a new situation like an aerial bomb] is just as much and just as little original and native as child's fear of a stranger. For any activity is original when it first occurs. As conditions are continually changing, new and primitive activities are continually occurring. The traditional psychology of instincts obscures recognition of this fact. It sets up a hard-and-fast preordained class under which specific acts are subsumed, so that their own quality and originality are lost from view. This is why the novelist and dramatist are so much more illuminating... than the schematizing psychologist....

When we recognize the diversity of native activities and the varied ways in which they are modified through interactions with one another in response to different conditions, we are able to understand moral phenomena otherwise baffling. In the career of any impulse activity there are speaking generally three possibilities. It may find a surging explosive discharge—blind, unintelligent. It may be sublimated—that is, become a factor intelligently coordinated with others in a continuing course of action. Thus a burst of anger may, because of its dynamic incorporation into disposition, become an abiding conviction of social injustice to be remedied.... Or again a released impulsive activity may be neither immediately expressed in isolated spasmodic action, nor indirectly employed in an enduring interest. It may be 'suppressed'. (Dewey 1922: 108)

Dewey's language of habit and impulse conveys a perspective that is subtly but importantly different in its emphases from the typical presumptions of post-World War II social science. Where a contemporary view might see emotional responses mainly as the bases of a preference function that would evaluate predicted outcomes of alternative actions, he focuses on impulses bound to habits and sees them as crucial to how the situation is perceived, and as linked directly to what actions will be taken, not just indirectly linked through possible consequences.[5]

20.4. Changes in our Research on Recurring Action Patterns

After living for quite a while with Dewey's stress on the fundamental role of habit and his efforts to integrate habit, emotion, and thought, I have found it a very satisfying alternative to the post-war enthronement of cognition. As a result, I have begun to consider some changes in the way we might go about our research on recurring action patterns. The suggestions I have come to—in some cases merely problem-framings—are speculative, and I certainly do not imagine that

[5] There is considerable recent psychological evidence consistent with many of Dewey's insights (Cohen 2007*b*). For example, the 'mere exposure effect' first demonstrated by Robert Zajonc has been replicated repeatedly (Zajonc 2001). He showed that subjects who had stimulus images secretly flashed at very high speed were not able to pick those images out when asked later which images in a larger collection they 'recognized'. But a comparable group that was asked which images they 'liked' were able to pick out the flashed images well above chance rates. A similar effect for action patterns rather than images was demonstrated by Gordon and Holyoak (1983). Antonio Damasio and his colleagues (Bechara *et al.* 2005) have shown that subjects playing a game in which cards are drawn from decks with differing frequencies of reward and punishment display physical symptoms of attraction and aversion, such as changes in skin conductance response, well before they can articulate hypotheses about which decks are favorable.

merely stating them will compel others to change their own approaches. At the same time, I see contemporary organizational research as having a pressing need for some deeply new—and, at the same time, inspiringly old—ideas, so perhaps the following suggestions will stimulate responses and eventually contribute to developments of some value.

1. **Modify our terminology of recurring action patterns to signal more clearly that we have in mind activity that is typically not rigid, mundane, mindless, or explicitly codified**

As we saw, Dewey's own suggestion in *Human Nature and Conduct* is to use 'routine' or 'routine habit' only for the pathological extreme ('dead habit') that does have these qualities. Weick and Sutcliffe (2006) take a similar stance when they wonder if perhaps the concept of routine has been stretched beyond the point of usefulness by efforts to re-conceive it as including elements of mindfulness. In a recent case study of the regeneration of recurring action patterns in a seasonal organization (Birnholtz, Cohen, and Hoch 2007), we ended up avoiding the term 'routine' except where discussing theories proposed by others. Instead we relied on 'disposition', a term Dewey often uses as a synonym for habit.[6]

Many researchers might not want to go so far. There are, after all, vibrant lines of research with 'routine' tightly woven into their fabric (Augier, Dosi, and Levinthal 2006; Nelson and Winter 1982; Feldman and Pentland 2003). And researchers such as Martha Feldman and Brian Pentland have worked hard to dispel the misconceptions that obscure a richer sense of routine action (Pentland and Feldman 2005). Another way to hold off the misconceptions might be by settling on a phrase for the mindless extreme—perhaps 'dead routine'. Levinthal and Rerup (2006) are in this same spirit when they argue (contra Weick and Sutcliffe) for characterizing routine as one form of 'less mindful' behavior.

I am not quite sure whether the right solution is (1) Dewey's sharp restriction of what is designated by 'routine' or (2) stretching the scope of routine and using a consistent modifier to distinguish the mindless extreme. With the second approach, it might be easier to keep the unqualified term for the larger body of patterned action on which so much research has been done, and still recognize that the activity can be flexible, important, and mindful though it recurs with enough similarity to deserve the label 'routine'. That is the sense in which I have been using 'routine' throughout this essay, as a term that should be understood without its common

[6] Pierre Bourdieu in developing his notion of *habitus* was one of the most notable exponents of this strategy of relying on notions of disposition and habit rather than routine. He wrote, 'I would say that the theory of practical sense presents many similarities with theories, such as Dewey's, that grant a central role to the notion of habit, understood as an active and creative relation to the world, and reject all the conceptual dualisms upon which nearly all post-Cartesian philosophies are based: subject and object, internal and external, material and spiritual, individual and social, and so on' (Bourdieu and Wacquant 1992: 122). Dewey had a considerable impact on French thought. He was also much admired by Émile Durkheim and has been a strong influence on Bruno Latour.

misconceptions. However, my opposing instinct is that as long as we use 'routine', its misleading connotations will linger perniciously in the background of our thinking. This line of argument leads to Dewey's solution, relying on 'habit' and 'custom' in general with 'routine' used just when the misconceptions actually are appropriate. While I am not sure which is the right approach, I am sure that we have to start making choices about this terminology, making them explicit in what we write, and sticking to them carefully.

2. Focus our research on the dynamic interplay of habit with other faculties

We could *avoid strictly counterposing improvisation to routine*, acknowledging instead that all (live) routine involves some amount of adaptation to prevailing circumstances and objectives. If we did, we might investigate the role played by earlier developed shared meanings and habits of interrelating when highly novel situations require unfamiliar actions. Fortunately, there are already examples of taking this direction, and of the informative results that are possible. Although he does not use quite the same vocabulary of habit and routine, Weick's work on aircraft carriers (Weick and Roberts 1993) and on fire-fighting techniques (Weick 1993) often reveals how well-established habits of relating become resources of improvising and sense-making.

We could understand that *emotional commitments form the matrix within which thought and habit play out*, and that those commitments are deeply social rather than strictly individual. If we did, we might revive lines of work on organizational leadership that stress the role that senior figures play in events that create and modify organizational character. Philip Selznick's *Leadership in Administration* (1957) was a striking example of this kind of work, but his treatment of organizational character had very little follow-on work.[7]

We could explore the implications of Dewey's view that *emotional impulses are tied to habits and not just to the consequences of action*—to actions themselves, not just to resulting 'states of the world'. This accords with the 'logic of appropriateness' sketched by March and Olsen (1989) as an alternative to the 'logic of consequences' that has been more influential in recent decades. They characterize that logic as an alternative frame of deliberation, typified by asking, 'what does a person like me do in a situation like this?' Dewey's approach extends further, suggesting that most 'appropriate' action (his word would be 'moral') is generated without conscious decision, via the interaction of the world with our habits that are themselves the impulse-infused products of prior deliberations.

Following Dewey's lead would take us beyond considering only the motivations of actors. He thought motives were most usefully conceived not as causes of actions, but as posterior analyses of them. 'A motive does not exist prior to an act and

[7] Selznick's book is very clear-sighted about trends in the research of its day. It begins by contrasting his own direction for studying administration (now largely overlooked) with Simon's, which was rather more influential (Ansell 2002; Birnholtz, Cohen, and Hoch 2007).

produce it. It is an act plus a judgment upon some element of it, the judgment being made in the light of the consequences of the act.... in short to build or destroy a habit' (Dewey 1922: 85). And it would also take us beyond 'the emotions' as dimensions of evaluation of outcomes, pushing us instead towards a view that more directly integrates feelings with perception and other forms of action.

The difference this might make can be illustrated from the recent work of Adler and Obstfeld (2007), which uses Dewey's tripartite scheme as a framework for exploring the role of emotions in organizational action. Although they do not cite Selznick's *Leadership in Administration*, their treatment of the strategic management of affect draws on the same pragmatic heritage as Selznick's and generates insights quite consistent with his. Adler and Obstfeld provide an illuminating perspective on the role of projects as a special form for generating organizational creativity, distinct from the organization's production routines and executive decision making. They arrive at a deep insight that project work is about constituting something genuinely new from the available habits and emotions of the organizational project members. Their result is one that Dewey foresaw:

> Impulses are the pivots on which the re-organization of activities turn, they are agencies of deviation, for giving new directions to old habits and changing their quality. Consequently, whenever we are concerned with understanding social transition and flux or with projects for reform, personal and collective, our study must go to analysis of native tendencies [i.e. impulses]. (Dewey 1922: 67)

We could pay closer attention to the *interplay of habit and emotion.* If we did, we might make progress in explaining the processes that reproduce organizational identity and culture (Birnholtz, Cohen, and Hoch 2007; Brooks 2004; Fiol, Hatch, and Golden-Biddle 1998; Hatch 1993; Martin 1992; Ravasi and Schultz 2006).

We could appreciate that *experience always generates some learning.* If we did, we might be led to investigate the kinds of organizational doing that generate the most learning. At the level of individual experience a great deal is being learned about the large cumulative effects of effortful, motivated, and reflective practice (Ross 2006). In some ways, specific techniques of organizational quality improvement might be understood as existing contributions already taking us in this direction.[8]

3. Increase the attention in organizational theorizing to contemporary psychology of emotion and habit

We have a long history of incorporating ideas from other fields into the study of organization. Herbert Simon personally bridged the study of organization and research on cognition (Newell and Simon 1972). Concepts from economics have

[8] Surprisingly, one of the most prominent examples of continuous improvement, the Toyota Production System, traces back to an American system called Training Within Industry that was developed by students of Dewey's from Columbia Teachers College (Adler 1999; Huntzinger 2002; Spear and Bowen 1999).

had a large effect on our understanding of organizational incentive systems and strategies, e.g. Gibbons (2005).

In contemporary psychology, there is enormous growth in the study of the procedural memory, the basis of habitual action (Squire and Kandel 1999; Cohen and Bacdayan 1994), and of emotions and feelings (Damasio 2003; Davidson 2001). For example, our sense of commitment to others is no doubt a matter in part of forecasting their future behavior based on past experience, as economic reasoning would lead us to suppose, but it may also be a matter of identifying with others by means of our newly discovered system of 'mirror neurons' (Dapretto 2006), and other physiological mechanisms of bonding (Brown and Brown 2006; Kosfeld *et al.* 2005).

If habit provides a flexible repertoire of action dispositions that can be customized to some extent as context may require, then we may be more interested to study how such dispositions are created and modified in field settings. Participant observation and classical organizational ethnography often provide access to the development of dispositions, but at very high costs per observation and with limited replicability. Extensions of random-interruption diary methods offer interesting complementary possibilities (Intille 2006), as do systematic analyses of video-recorded organizational micro-ethnographies (LeBaron 2005).

Economics itself is responding to the growth of these parts of psychology (Camerer and Malmendier 2007; Cohen 2007*b*). A nice example can be seen in a recent study (De Martino *et al.* 2006) of the role of the amygdala, an important center of emotion in the brain, in the frame switching that changes how subjects choose among alternatives with supposedly equal expected value.

4. Seek new representations of routine as pattern-in-variety

Seeing routine from a point of view strongly influenced by Dewey eventually leads to the questioning of some basic assumptions and methods that we use in our inquiring. What kind of thing is a routine (or a custom, or a practice)? Given the answer to that question, what are the most appropriate methods for investigating routines, and for representing what we may learn?[9]

Jeremy Birnholtz, Susannah Hoch, and I have argued (Birnholtz, Cohen, and Hoch 2007) that when we begin to break down the mistaken rigidity of our concept of routine we are led to confront the 'paradox of the (n)ever-changing world'. From one perspective (that of Heraclitus), 'one does not step into the same river twice'. Tsoukas and Chia (2002) argue the organizational importance of this point very forcefully. Yet from another perspective that is equally compelling (that of Ecclesiastes) 'there is no new thing under the sun'. For an established routine, the natural

[9] Connotations of the word 'thing' themselves reveal some of our difficulties. We often read 'thing' with a strong presumption of material object, but, as Bruno Latour points out (Weibel and Latour 2005), a root meaning of the word 'thing' is affair or transaction, and this includes public affairs such as legislating assemblies. Hence, the Norwegian parliament is still called the Storting.

fluctuation of its surrounding environment guarantees that each performance is different, and yet, being a routine, it is 'the same'. Somehow there is pattern in the action, sufficient to allow us to say the pattern is recurring, even though there is substantial variety to the action, variety sufficient to allow us to rule out any two occasions being exactly alike.

Some of the mystery of routine, and our consequent difficulty in studying it, derives from our lack of good representations for such patterns-in-variety, and of good methods to investigate their stability and fragility. We have many observations that there can be large variations in circumstances that leave an established pattern relatively undisturbed—as when new employees move into their roles and an organizational routine continues with little disruption. This is such a common occurrence that we hardly note it, but long-lasting organizations would be impossible if it were not usually reliable. We also have observations that a seemingly small variation in circumstances or behavior can bring a routine grinding to a halt—as when an unnoticed change at Intel from back-and-forth to circular polishing of a production mirror caused a semi-conductor factory to lose days of output.

Perturbations we take to be large (employee turnover) or small (mirror polishing motion) turn out not to have correspondingly large or small effects on the realized pattern of action. This is the hallmark of a complex, and probably nonlinear, system (Axelrod and Cohen 1999). But saying this only indicates a general direction for what may be a long conceptual journey. Dewey gets us started down this new road. With his help, we can say broadly that the patterning of action is recognizable as 'the same' because of the powerful shaping forces of human habits and emotions. They seem to provide the action repertoires of individuals and organizations with a coherent character that underlies their perceived sameness. His same framework also helps us to appreciate that our remarkable powers of thought let us reassemble our habit-rooted repertoires of action to cope with novel conditions. (Indeed, we often recognize conditions as 'something new under the sun' just when habitual responses do not suffice.) But, if we are to make substantial progress beyond the general insights he had formulated clearly in the 1920s, we need a much more detailed and systematic language for analysis of routine, a language with precise and fruitful primitives that help us to generate new insights and fend off interpretive errors. And, in tandem, we need a revised and enriched methodological arsenal, one that allows us to benefit from the extraordinary discernment of human observation and participation without losing the possibility of convincing disconfirmation.

Dewey understood that we needed improved conceptions of inquiry. His *Logic* (Dewey 1938*b*) was an effort, late in his career, to make 'an inquiry into inquiry' that might develop into the sort of tool we still need. The volume even closes with a chapter on the special needs of the social sciences. But Dewey's *Logic* de-emphasized mathematical inference and appeared at a moment in intellectual history that could hardly have been less favorable: just the same time in fact, when the young

Herbert Simon was taking a logic course from Rudolph Carnap and preparing the foundations of post-war organization theory. Bertrand Russell's review of the *Logic* was ferociously critical. Dewey's hopes that he could open a line of development that would yield precise tools for scientific inquiry into human affairs were not met. Recently, there has been some revival of interest in the work, including some effort to bring stronger mathematical structure to portions of it (Burke, Hester, and Talisse 2002; Modarres-Mousavi 2002). Whether or not it will play a direct role in meeting the current need for improved methodology, it serves as another of the many beacons he lit for us.

My aim in these concluding thoughts has been only to suggest the kinds of problems (and opportunities) that I think we are facing rather than to argue for specific solutions. I hope others may see the way forward more clearly, but for myself, I feel I have a lot more thinking to do. Although I do not expect Dewey's insights to suffice, I feel sure that his continuing intellectual company will be, as it has been, an enormous help along the way.

References

Adler, P. S. (1999). 'Hybridization of Human Resource Management at Two Toyota Transplants', in J. Liker, M. Fruin, and P. S. Adler (eds.), *Remade in America: Transplanting and Transforming Japanese Management Systems*. New York: Oxford University Press.

—— and Obstfeld, D. (2007). 'The Role of Affect in Creative Projects and Exploratory Search'. *Industrial and Corporate Change*, 16 (February): 19–50.

Ansell, C. (2002). 'Pragmatism and Organization'. Working Paper, Department of Political Science. Berkeley: University of California.

Augier, M., Dosi, G., and Levinthal, D. (2006). 'Introduction to Sidney G. Winter Special Section'. *Industrial and Corporate Change*, 15/1: 123–5.

Axelrod, R. M., and Cohen, M. D. (1999). *Harnessing Complexity: Organizational Implications of a Scientific Frontier*. New York: Free Press.

Bechara, A., Damasio, H., Tranel, D., and Damasio, A. R. (2005). 'The Iowa Gambling Task and the Somatic Marker Hypothesis: Some Questions and Answers'. *Trends in Cognitive Sciences*, 9/4: 159–62.

Birnholtz, J., Cohen, M. D., and Hoch, S. V. (2007). 'Organizational Character: On the Regeneration of Camp Poplar Grove'. *Organization Science*, 18/2: 315–32.

Bourdieu, P., and Wacquant, L. J. D. (1992). *An Invitation to Reflexive Sociology*. Chicago: University of Chicago Press.

Brooks, J. A. M. (2004). 'Presentations as Rites: Co-presence and Visible Images for Organizing Memory Collectively'. Ph.D. thesis, University of Michigan.

Brown, S. L., and Brown, R. M. (2006). 'Selective Investment Theory: Recasting the Functional Significance of Close Relationships'. *Psychological Inquiry*, 17/1: 1–29.

Burke, F. T., Hester, D. M., and Talisse, R. B. (2002). *Dewey's Logical Theory: New Studies and Interpretations*. Nashville, Tenn.: Vanderbilt University Press.

CAMERER, C., and MALMENDIER, U. (2007). 'Behavioral Economics of Organizations', in P. Diamond and H. Vartiainen (eds.), *Economic Institutions and Behavioral Economics: Proceedings of the Yrjö Jahnsson Foundation 50th Anniversary Conference*. Princeton: Princeton University Press.

CAMIC, C. (1986). 'The Matter of Habit'. *American Journal of Sociology*, 91/5: 1039–87.

COHEN, M. D. (2007*a*). 'Administrative Behavior: Laying the Foundations for Cyert and March'. *Organization Science*, 18/3: 503–6.

—— (2007*b*). 'Beyond Boundedly Rational Individuals: Remarks on Behavioral Organizational Economics', in P. Diamond and H. Vartiainen (eds.), *Economic Institutions and Behavioral Economics: Proceedings of the Yrjö Jahnsson Foundation 50th Anniversary Conference*. Princeton: Princeton University Press.

—— (2007*c*). 'Reading Dewey: Reflections on the Study of Routine'. *Organization Studies*, 28: 773–86.

—— and BACDAYAN, PAUL (1994). 'Organizational Routines are Stored as Procedural Memory: Evidence from a Laboratory Study'. *Organization Science*, 5/4: 554–68.

COMMAGER, H. S. (1950). *The American Mind: An Interpretation of American Thought and Character since the 1880s*. New Haven: Yale University Press.

CYERT, R. M., and MARCH, J. G. (1963). *A Behavioral Theory of the Firm*. Englewood Cliffs, NJ: Prentice-Hall.

DAMASIO, A. R. (2003). *Looking for Spinoza: Joy, Sorrow, and the Feeling Brain*. Orlando, Fla.: Harcourt.

DAPRETTO, M. (2006). 'Understanding Emotions in Others: Mirror Neuron Dysfunction in Children with Autism Spectrum Disorders'. *Nature Neuroscience*, 9/1: 28–30.

DAVIDSON, R. J. (2001). 'Toward a Biology of Personality and Emotion'. *Annals of the New York Academy of Sciences*, 935: 191–207.

DE MARTINO, B., KUMARAN, D., SEYMOUR, B., and DOLAN, R. J. (2006). 'Frames, Biases, and Rational Decision-Making in the Human Brain'. *Science*, 313/5787: 684–7.

DEWEY, J. (1896). 'The Reflex Arc in Psychology'. *Psychology Review*, 9 (July): 357–70.

—— (1916). 'The Need for Social Psychology' (Address on the 25th Anniversary of the Founding of the American Psychological Association), in *The Middle Works of John Dewey, 1899–1924*, ed. Jo Ann Boydston. Vol. 10. Carbondale, Ill.: Southern Illinois University Press.

—— (1922). *Human Nature and Conduct: An Introduction to Social Psychology*. New York: H. Holt & Company.

—— (1927). *The Public and its Problems*. New York: H. Holt & Company.

—— (1934). *Art as Experience*. New York: Minton.

—— (1938*a*). *Experience and Education*. New York: Macmillan Company.

—— (1938*b*). *Logic: The Theory of Inquiry*. New York: Holt, Rinehart & Winston.

FELDMAN, M. S., and PENTLAND, B. T. (2003). 'Reconceptualizing Organizational Routines as a Source of Flexibility and Change'. *Administrative Science Quarterly*, 48/1: 94–121.

FIOL, C. M., HATCH, M. J., and GOLDEN-BIDDLE, K. (1998). 'Organizational Culture and Identity: What's the Difference Anyway?' (sidebar commentary #2) in D. A. Whetten and P. C. Godfrey (eds.), *Identity in Organizations: Building Theory through Conversations*. Thousand Oaks, Calif.: Sage.

GIBBONS, R. (2005). 'What is Economic Sociology and Should Any Economists Care?' *Journal of Economic Perspectives*, 19/1: 3–7.

GORDON, P. C., and HOLYOAK, K. (1983). 'Implicit Learning and Generalization of the Mere Exposure Effect'. *Journal of Personality and Social Psychology*, 45: 492–500.

HATCH, M. J. (1993). 'The Dynamics of Organizational Culture'. *Academy of Management Review*, 18: 657–93.

HUNTZINGER, J. (2002). 'The Roots of Lean: Training within Industry: The Origin of Kaizen'. *Target*, 18/1: 6–19.

INTILLE, S. S. (2006). 'Technological Innovations Enabling Automatic, Context-Sensitive Ecological Momentary Assessment', in A. A. Stone, S. Shiffman, A. Atienza, and L. Nebeling (eds.), *The Science of Real Time Data Capture: Self-Report in Health Research*. Oxford: Oxford University Press.

KANE, A. A., ARGOTE, L., and LEVINE, J. L. (2005). 'Knowledge Transfer between Groups via Personnel Rotation: Effects of Social Identity and Knowledge Quality'. *Organizational Behavior and Human Decision Processes*, 96: 56–71.

KOSFELD, M., HEINRICHS, M., ZAK, P. J., FISCHBACHER, U., and ERNST, F. (2005). 'Oxytocin Increases Trust in Humans'. *Nature*, 435/7042: 673–6.

LEBARON, C. (2005). 'Considering the Social and Material Surround: Toward Microethnographic Understandings of Nonverbal Behavior', in V. Manusov (ed.), *The Sourcebook of Nonverbal Measures*. Mahwah, NJ: Lawrence Erlbaum Associates.

LEVINTHAL, D., and RERUP, C. (2006). 'Crossing an Apparent Chasm: Bridging Mindful and Less-Mindful Perspectives on Organizational Learning'. *Organization Science*, 17/4: 502–13.

MANICAS, P. T. (2002). 'John Dewey and American Psychology'. *Journal for the Theory of Social Behavior*, 32/3: 267–94.

MARCH, J. G., and OLSEN, J. P. (1989). *Rediscovering Institutions*. New York: Free Press.

MARTIN, J. (1992). *Cultures in Organizations*. New York: Oxford University Press.

MENAND, L. (2001). *The Metaphysical Club*. New York: Farrar, Strauss and Giroux.

MODARRES-MOUSAVI, S. (2002). 'Methodological Foundations for Bounded Rationality as a Primary Framework'. Ph.D. thesis, Virginia Polytechnic Institute and State University.

NELSON, R., and WINTER, S. (1982). *An Evolutionary Theory of Economic Change*. Cambridge, Mass.: Belknap Press of Harvard University.

NEWELL, A., and SIMON, H. A. (1972). *Human Problem Solving*. Englewood Cliffs, NJ: Prentice-Hall.

ORLIKOWSKI, W. (2002). 'Knowing in Practice: Enacting a Collective Capability in Distributed Organizing'. *Organization Science*, 13/3: 249–73.

PENTLAND, B. T., and FELDMAN, M. S. (2005). 'Organizational Routines as a Unit of Analysis'. *Industrial and Corporate Change*, 14/5: 793–815.

RAVASI, D., and SCHULTZ, M. (2006). 'Responding to Organizational Identity Threats: Exploring the Role of Organizational Culture'. *Academy of Management Review*, 49/3: 433–58.

ROSS, P. E. (2006). 'The Expert Mind'. *Scientific American*, 295/2: 64–71.

SELZNICK, P. (1957). *Leadership in Administration*. New York: Harper & Row.

SIMON, H. A. (1947). *Administrative Behavior: A Study of Decision-Making Processes in Administrative Organization*, with a foreword by Chester I. Barnard. New York: Macmillan.

—— (1957). *Administrative Behavior: A Study of Decision-Making Processes in Administrative Organization*. 2nd edn. New York: Macmillan.

SPEAR, S., and BOWEN, H. K. (1999). 'Decoding the DNA of the Toyota Production System'. *Harvard Business Review*, September–October: 96–106.

SQUIRE, L., and KANDEL, E. R. (1999). *Memory: From Mind to Molecules.* New York: Scientific American Library.

TRICE, H. M., and BEYER, J. M. (1993). *The Cultures of Work Organizations.* Englewood Cliffs, NJ: Prentice-Hall.

TSOUKAS, H., and CHIA, R. (2002). 'On Organizational Becoming: Rethinking Organizational Change'. *Organization Science*, 13/5: 567–82.

WEIBEL, P., and LATOUR, B. (2005). 'Making Things Public: Atmospheres of Democracy'. http://www.bruno-latour.fr/expositions/002_parliament.html.

WEICK, K. E. (1993). 'The Collapse of Sensemaking in Organizations: The Mann Gulch Disaster'. *Administrative Science Quarterly*, 38/4: 628–53.

—— and ROBERTS, K. H. (1993). 'Collective Mind in Organizations: Heedful Interrelating on Flight Decks'. *Administrative Science Quarterly*, 38/3: 357–81.

—— and SUTCLIFFE, K. M. (2006). 'Mindfulness and the Quality of Organizational Attention'. *Organization Science*, 17/4: 514–24.

WHETTEN, D. A., and MACKEY, A. (2002). 'A Social Actor Conception of Organizational Identity and its Implications for the Study of Organizational Reputation'. *Business and Society*, 41/4: 393–414.

WINTER, S., and SZULANSKI, G. (2001). 'Replication as Strategy'. *Organization Science*, 12: 730–43.

ZAJONC, R. B. (2001). 'Mere Exposure: A Gateway to the Subliminal'. *Current Directions in Psychological Science*, 10/6: 224–8.

CHAPTER 21

MARY PARKER FOLLETT AND PRAGMATIST ORGANIZATION

CHRISTOPHER ANSELL

ALTHOUGH Mary Parker Follett's reputation rises and falls with academic and management fashion, she has established a fairly secure place in the pantheon of organization studies. As many have noted, her contributions are sometimes difficult to classify because of her strong interdisciplinarity. Her writings range across political science, democratic theory, management, public administration, conflict resolution, social psychology, and organization theory, and she can be fairly claimed by all these fields. For many of us, it is precisely this interdisciplinarity that makes her an attractive and provocative figure. Her work is often seen as having a prescient or 'prophetic' quality, in that she anticipated developments in many of these fields that came to prominence much later (Graham 1996). The revival of interest in her work has often coincided with the attempt by these emerging fields to establish their intellectual pedigrees. In this chapter, I argue that what remains powerful and exemplary about Follett's work is her attempt to provide, and work through, the implications of a basic philosophical perspective for the social sciences. Follett read widely in philosophy and was influenced by a variety of philosophical traditions, but this chapter will emphasize the importance of pragmatist philosophy to her thinking. Since this philosophy has also been undergoing an important revival (Dickstein 1998), an exploration of Follett's pragmatism opens up broader possibilities for thinking about a pragmatist approach to organizations.

Follett's work is also of special interest because she is one of the few women regarded as a 'classical' organization theorist. As her biography makes quite clear, both the academic and management worlds inhabited by Follett were almost exclusively dominated by men (Tonn 2003). Her status as a 'management guru' to leading business leaders of the time was therefore a particularly extraordinary and unusual achievement (Parker and Ritson 2005). But in addition to being a highly successful woman in a male-dominated world, Follett is also regarded as having developed ideas now central to contemporary feminist theory. As Jane Mansbridge writes in her introduction to the reissue of Follett's *The New State*: 'As far as I know, Mary Parker Follett never called herself a "feminist." Yet one of her central insights on democracy and conflict, an idea that she called "power-with," has become a working part of feminist theory' (Follett [1918 1998: xvii). Morton and Lindquist (1997) argue that Follett's relational, anti-dualist ontology, her epistemology based on the experiential basis of knowledge, and an ethics that emphasized integration of differences and the cultivation of human relationships is consonant with contemporary feminist theory.

In organization studies, Follett's influence can be described as important, but somewhat fragmented. Parker, for example, argues that 'she contributed to the founding of two schools of thought about organizations—the behavioral and holistic (later to become systems).... In addition, she was one of the first writers to perceive interrelationships between behavioral and holistic perspectives' (1984: 738). Her work is often claimed as a guiding light for a number of specific subdisciplines within organization and management studies: organizational justice theory (Barclay 2005), empowerment research (Eylon 1998; Boje and Rosile 2001), and stakeholder theory (Schilling 2000). She is also claimed as having anticipated a number of different approaches to organization studies, such as complexity theory (Mendenhall, Macomber, and Cutright 2000). Fry and Thomas (1996) suggest that Follett's influence is seen directly in work on alternative dispute resolution and less directly in Deming's work on Total Quality Management. Child suggests that Follett anticipated the participative leadership models of Likert and McGregor, the effective teamwork principles of Peters, and the analysis of integration and differentiation developed by Lawrence and Lorsch (Child 1996: 89).

A return to the 'classics' for inspiration can pose some serious liabilities. First, classic authors sometimes write in an outmoded language that often sounds archaic or prescientific to contemporary ears. We are then placed in the awkward position of trying to translate between classical and contemporary languages. Often we search backwards from contemporary debates, exploring the genealogy of these debates and looking for support or inspiration from earlier authors. Often this search takes the form of identifying contemporary developments and then showing that they have a precursor in a classical theorist. Follett lends herself to this interpretation because it is common to argue that Follett was 'ahead of her time' and that she anticipated many contemporary management perspectives (Parker and Ritson 2005: 1345–6). For example, Mendenhall, Macomber, and Cutright (2000) point to the value of contemporary complexity theory and then argue that Follett provided a precursor to this kind of non-linear thinking. For these authors, Follett's anticipation of complexity theory helps to justify the borrowing of natural science concepts for use in the social sciences. Or Schilling describes how contemporary stakeholder theory shares the same premises with Follett and demonstrates the 'likeness' between the two (Schilling 2000: 230). Parker (1984) argues that Follett anticipated or articulated conceptions of control that would not reappear until the 1960s with the development of systems theory.

This approach to the classics is valuable to the extent that it establishes a genealogy of ideas. To the extent that we are concerned about knowledge accumulation in the social sciences, it is arguable that research 'traditions' provide the best framework for organizing knowledge. Yet the potential liability of indexing the classics by contemporary debates and developments is that it ultimately emphasizes the 'archaic' nature of classical work. The outmoded language is then merely pre-scientific groping towards the current state-of-the-art. Once the pedigree has been established, the classical author can offer little more. This is Calas and Smircich's (1996) objection to the description of Follett as a prophet because they argue that it only establishes her as a 'forerunner' of contemporary ideas, which have now evolved to a higher level. The hazard of this approach, they suggest, is that it makes Follett's ideas appear to be 'primitive'.

A somewhat different approach to the classics is to explore them as 'paths not taken'. For example, Barclay argues that Follett's work, while largely consistent with much of the work on organizational justice, suggests a different trajectory (2005). She argues that Follett's perspective on justice is more dynamic and process-oriented than much contemporary justice research and offers a corrective to current work that treats justice as a 'relatively static, context-free, universal phenomenon' (Barclay 2005: 744). For example, she argues that unlike current research, Follett does not treat emotions as merely an outcome of injustice but also as factors that 'accompany, infiltrate, and change justice perceptions' (2005: 746).

I will draw on both a genealogical and a 'paths not taken' approach to Follett's work in this chapter, but will emphasize a third approach to the classics that I call 'ontological'. I believe that we often return to the classics for inspiration when we are troubled by the basic philosophical premises of our contemporary theoretical and empirical work.[1] What is distinctive about Follett's work is how thoroughly she sought to ground her work in a consistent and systematic philosophy. That she is perhaps the most philosophical of classic organizational theorists

[1] Zald (1996) has argued that organizational studies has paid scant attention to its philosophical underpinnings.

helps us to understand both her relative neglect and her periodic revival. It also helps us understand something fundamental about the temper of her work. For example, while Chester Barnard was certainly sensitive to the broader intellectual currents of his day, his work is remembered because he sought to provide one of the first systematic frameworks for understanding organizations. Follett's theory of organization was not nearly as comprehensive as Barnard's.[2] Fox argues that Follett's work was not systematic: 'she threw out interesting ideas more or less randomly, and the thread of consistency is hard to find and harder to follow' (Fox 1968: 520–1). But I would argue that her work was systematic, if we understand it as working out the practical implications of a particular ontology. When she is read as working through the implications of a distinctive ontology, her work still reads as fresh and insightful—not archaic and outmoded. Yet Follett's fortunes as a classic theorist will also depend on collective sympathies for her ontological assumptions.[3]

21.1. Follett's Pragmatic Idealism

Follett's ontology was clearly influenced by idealism, and particularly Hegelian idealism, but her thought is most appropriately located within a transatlantic community of political and social thinkers who sought to break the shackles of traditional debates between idealism and empiricism (Kloppenberg 1986). Follett's idealism was 'grounded ... in strict factuality, making idealism and realism "meet in the actual"' (Graham 1996: 13). As Kloppenberg (1986) has argued, exploration of the terrain between idealism and empiricism in the United States was led by pragmatist philosophers such as William James and John Dewey.[4] 'Idealism and realism meeting in the actual' is, in fact, a rather good description of what pragmatist philosophy is all about.[5]

This chapter is certainly not the first work to point out the affinities of Follett's work with pragmatism. Stever (1986) and O'Connor (2000) both point out the

[2] In a search of the social science citation index between 1969 and 1990, her writings were cited in 148 articles, though only four of the articles were directly about Follett (Fry and Thomas 1996: 13). To put this in context, Chester Barnard has six times more citations. Herbert Simon has fifty times more citations. Fry and Thomas note that her work is distinctive in terms of the breadth of distribution of interest, ranging across management, psychology, sociology, political science, and public administration (Fry and Thomas 1996: 14).

[3] Calas and Smircich's (1996), for example, argue that Follett's work was not 'forgotten' until American business schools became dominated by positivism.

[4] Kloppenberg emphasizes the parallels between James and Dewey and the Cambridge political theorist Henry Sidgwick. Follett studied directly with Sidgwick at Cambridge (Tonn 2003: 61–4).

[5] This is actually a quote from Follett's essay 'Community is a Process' (Follett 1919: 587).

pragmatist influences in her work. Yet, with Graham, they also stress Follett's strong strain of idealism. O'Connor (2000) identifies Hegelian idealism as the dominant strand of Follett's work, while noting that Follett rejected an interpretation of Hegel that stressed the transcendence of the state. Follett was also strongly influenced by the idealist philosophy of Josiah Royce, and Royce and William James had a long-standing highly publicized debate. But Royce and James were also the best of friends and the debate influenced the thought of both of them, so that Royce later described his work as 'absolute pragmatism'. In fact, notwithstanding William James's antipathy for Hegel, pragmatism is better understood as a philosophy that sought to reconcile the competing philosophical traditions of idealism and empiricism. Stever (1986) argues that Follett's work was a hybrid of 'British idealism shorn of its metaphysics' and pragmatism (1986: 166).[6] And Mattson's introduction to Follett's reissued *The New State* argues that she saw herself as synthesizing idealism and pragmatism (Follett [1918] 1998: xliv).

In the pantheon of classic pragmatist philosophers, Follett's work bears the closest resemblance to the work of John Dewey, whose early philosophical formation was Hegelian and who retained strong idealist influences in his work. Scholars have seen Dewey and Follett as kindred spirits on a range of salient and divisive public topics, including pluralism (Stears 2002: 146–52; Smith 1964), participatory democracy (Mattson 1998: 87–104; Evans 1998), and the extension of democracy to the workplace (O'Connor 2000).

Any argument about the affinity of Follett's and Dewey's work (and by extension, Follett's relationship to pragmatism) is complicated by her pique with Dewey (Tonn 2003: 377). Although her vexation with Dewey may have been more personal than intellectual, it is useful to explore their intellectual similarities and differences.[7] The

[6] However, he argues that Follett's idealism and pragmatism often led her to conflicting conclusions. He suggests that 'she could not decide whether people had innate potential to be released within organizations or whether they were pragmatic objects to be socialized via language into organizational programs. At the organizational level, she could not decide whether administration was the art of releasing individual potential within collective situations or whether administration was a pragmatic science of educating individuals to suit organizational purposes' (Stever 1986: 171–2).

[7] My view is that Follett's irritation with Dewey may be partly linked to the difficulties that arose in her collaboration with Eduard Lindemann, a young scholar whose career Follett sought to promote. Follett successfully secured financial support for a Follett–Lindemann collaboration from a wealthy patron of progressive social causes, Dorothy Straight. As Tonn describes in detail, the collaboration proceeded well at first, but Lindemann grew increasingly uncooperative (Tonn 2003: 329–59). To Follett's great disappointment, they eventually published separate books with only limited cooperation. As Keith describes the book that grew out of Lindemann's collaboration with Follett: 'Lindemann's book reads like a philosophy of social science primer as conceived by John Dewey' (2007: 247). I suspect it was Dewey's influence on Lindemann that Follett refers to in her critical letter to Lord Haldane: 'Our young men have swallowed Dewey whole in the most deplorable way' (Tonn 2003: 377). She may have also been thinking of Herbert Croly, Alfred Sheffield, Henry Overstreet, and Ordway Tead. She had a close and productive affiliation with each of these four men and each of them, in turn, was strongly influenced by or connected to Dewey (Keith 2007: 101–3, 124; O'Connor 2000; Tonn 2003).

key difference is that Dewey, while implicitly retaining many idealist influences, followed James in critiquing both realism and idealism from a pragmatist perspective (Westbrook 1991: 120–30). By contrast, Follett, while remaining explicitly committed to idealism, sought to find a middle ground between idealism, realism, and pragmatism. In *Creative Experience*, Follett built directly, though not exclusively, on the Harvard neo-realist psychologist Edwin Holt. In a letter to Haldane, Follett wrote that 'Holt goes on calling himself a realist and does not quite like my making his psychology prove idealism' (Tonn 2003: 565 n. 37).[8] While remaining loyal to and self-conscious about her idealist roots, however, she also takes a stance between pragmatism and idealism at many points in her work. In her essay, 'Community is a Process', Follett writes, 'Our alternative is not between Royce's finished absolute and James's strung-alongness' (1919: 584). Her intermediate stance between idealism and pragmatism is a cornerstone of her social philosophy and undergirds her position on the debate between 'monists' and 'pluralists' that she first took up seriously in *The New State* (Tonn 2003: 292–6, 304). While Follett could often play the idealist card against the pragmatists, her position on this key debate was actually very close to Dewey's, who also retained certain idealist elements in his approach to pluralism (Stears 2002: 146–53).

Dewey and Follett were both steeped in neo-Hegelian thought, but they eventually developed different stances towards Hegel. Dewey started off his philosophical career firmly in the neo-Hegelian camp, but gradually moved away from idealism towards pragmatism. Indeed, he moved far enough away from Hegel to attribute growing German militarism to the absolutist idealism inherent in Germany culture (Westbrook 1991: 198; Kloppenberg 1986: 110). By contrast, in moving towards pragmatism, Follett defended Hegel, while interpreting him in a more empiricist and pluralist light.[9] In *The New State*, Follett wrote: 'The political pluralists are fighting a misunderstood Hegelianism.... When they accept the compounding of consciousness taught by their own master, James, then they will see that true Hegelianism finds its actualized form in federalism' ([1918] 1998: 266–7).

While the differences between Dewey and Follett were not trivial, their commonality ran far deeper. With James and Royce, Dewey and Follett shared a philosophical tradition shaped by New England Calvinism and by Emersonian transcendentalism (Greenstone 1993; West 1989; McDermott 1986: 29–43). All of them shared the fundamental Emersonian premise that 'the experimental makings, workings, and doings of human beings have been neither adequately understood nor fully unleashed in the modern world' (West 1989: 16).

[8] Moreover, she directly critiqued the pragmatist conception of verification, which she saw as overly linear (Tonn 2003: 376–7).

[9] Hoopes (1998) contrasts Dewey's 'implicit nominalism', which he argues undercut his ability to offer a full-fledged communitarian liberalism, with Follett's idealist rejection of nominalism.

21.2. Follett's Ontology of Organization

One of the remarkable things about Follett's work was how well she could move back and forth from philosophical reasoning to practical application. This often leads some commentators to regard her 'philosophy' as inductively derived from her social work and management consulting. Yet her biographer demonstrates how deeply steeped she was in current philosophical and political debates in both the United States and Britain. Perhaps one of the most striking 'ontologies' that she advanced consistently and forcefully throughout her later works is her emphasis on applying 'processual' and 'relational' thinking to organizational life. Her processual and relational approach to understanding groups is perhaps best put forward in her chapter on 'circular response' in her book, *Creative Experience*. She summarizes her argument about the 'behavior process' as follows:

> We have now, to repeat in summary, three fundamental principles to guide us in our study of social situations: (1) that my response is not to a rigid, static environment, but to a changing environment; (2) to an environment which is changing because of the activity between it and me; (3) that function may be continuously modified by itself, that is, the activity of the boy going to school may change the activity of the boy going to school. (Follett 1924: 73)

Follett uses this idea of a 'circular response' to show how 'subject' and 'object' are not two separate, static things, but related in a dynamic way. Mendenhall, Macomber, and Cutright argue that 'The foundational assumption that undergirds Follett's model of social systems is that of interdependence between subject and object' (2000: 196). This idea is absolutely at the heart of most of her other insights about how authority and constructive conflict work and about how individual and groups are interrelated.[10] This attempt to overcome subject–object dualism was also at the core of Dewey's work, as most fully developed in his *Experience and Nature.* Anti-dualism was, as Hans Joas puts it, 'one of the leitmotifs of pragmatism' and the same can be said for Follett (Joas 1993: 72; Boje and Rosile 2001).

In developing this idea of the circular response, Follett draws heavily on the work of Edwin Holt, a Harvard psychologist. In his discussion of the circularity of stimulus and response, however, Holt was in turn strongly influenced by the ideas of William James and functional psychology.[11] Follett does indeed cite James

[10] She sums up her argument later in *Creative Experience* as follows: 'The full acceptance of life as process gets us further and further away from the old controversies. The thought I have been trying to indicate is neither conventional idealism or realism.... It is now possible to rid ourselves of these more partial views; we have now given to us new modes of thinking, new ways of acting' (Follett 1924: 90).

[11] Edwin Holt, *Encyclopedia Britannica.* http://www.britannica.com/eb/article-9040837/Edwin-B-Holt. Accessed 25 November 2007. See also Tonn's description of Holt's influence on Follett (2003: 367–72).

briefly in a footnote in this discussion. However, she does not at all mention the most well-known paper of this period on the circular relationship of stimulus and response: Dewey's 1896 paper, 'The Reflex Arc Concept in Psychology', which was also heavily indebted to James (Phillips 1971). Moreover, drawing on his Hegelian background, Philips points out that Dewey emphasized that the 'arc' was a 'circle' or a 'circuit'—an interpretation very close to Follett's. Both Dewey and Follett sought to replace a mechanistic 'stimulus-response' approach to behavioralism with a more evolutionary approach (Bredo 1998).

Follett argues that there are three aspects of process—interacting, emerging, and unifying. Interaction leads to emergence, which leads to unity: 'Functional relating is the continuing process of self-creating coherence' and notes that '[m]ost of my philosophy is contained in that sentence' (Follett 1941: 200). Mendenhall, Macomber, and Cutright (2000) are indeed right to point to out that Follett can be regarded as a progenitor of complexity theory in social science. Her 'philosophy' as she puts it, states the basic idea of what complexity theory now calls 'self-organizing systems'. Perhaps the most novel aspect of her argument for the time in which she wrote is her explicit recognition of 'emergence', which she draws from biology and from Whitehead's process philosophy. She describes emergence as 'the something new, the progressive feature of the process', which is formed through interaction (Follett 1941: 198–9). Pragmatists like George Herbert Mead, who was heavily influenced by both Dewey and Whitehead, had a strikingly similar view of emergence.

A *relational ontology* is one in which social entities are to be understood in terms of their relationships rather than in terms of their inherent (essential) characteristics. Follett's work is thoroughly *relational* in its approach to the Organizational phenomena. In her first book, *The New State*, she drew heavily upon what she calls 'The New Psychology' to talk about the relationship between the individual and the group:

> By the 'new psychology' I mean something now in the making: I mean partly that group psychology which is receiving more attention and gaining more influence every day, and partly I mean that feeling for a new conception of *modes of association* which we see in law, economics, ethics, politics and indeed in every department of thought. It is a short way of saying that we are now looking at things not as entities but in relation.
>
> (Follett [1918] 1998: 13)

This relational thinking distinctly shaped her thinking about organizations, as Follett notes when she writes that 'my key word of organization is relatedness' (Follett 1941: 258).

In his *Essays on Radical Empiricism* (1912), James had already given voice to this relational way of understanding: '*Radical empiricism*, as I understand it, *does full justice to conjunctive relations*, without, however, treating them as rationalism always tends to treat them, as being true in some supernal way, as if the unity of things and their variety belonged to different orders of truth and vitality altogether' (James 1977: 196). Dewey had also made a relational perspective the heart of his psychology, as he declared in *How We Think*: 'To grasp the meaning of a thing, an event, or a situation is to see it in its relations to other things: to note how it operates or functions, what consequences follow from it, what causes it, what uses it can be put to' (1910: 137). Recently, Emirbayer (1997) has drawn heavily on Dewey and pragmatism as inspiration for a relational sociology in his 'Relational Manifesto for the Social Sciences'.

Follett's emphasis on 'experience' as a central perspective from which to understand human relations was influenced directly by James. In *The New State*, she writes: 'James brought to popular recognition the truth that since man is a complex of experiences there are many selves in each one' ([1918] 1998: 20). As more fully developed later in her book *Creative Experience*, the concept of experience served several purposes for Follett, as it did for the pragmatists. First, it allowed her to adopt an empirical perspective on human behavior and get down beneath more idealist conceptions of political and social life. In the introduction to *Creative Experience*, for instance, she writes, 'The conceptions of politics, economics and sociology should be studied—while they are still living in the lives of men. We need to study not the "conception" of a general will but concrete joint activity' (1924: 1).

Follett also used the concept of experience to privilege the knowledge and perspectives of ordinary people. Chapter 1 of *Creative Experience* is subtitled 'Vicarious Experience: Are Experts the Revealers of Truth?' In this chapter, she is arguing against Walter Lippman and others who had earlier argued for government by experts and elites and for the value of science to resolve societal conflicts. Although Follett makes it clear that she is not against an important role for either experts or science, she claims that experts cannot resolve these conflicts through the use of science. Her argument, of course, closely parallels Dewey's argument about the role of experts in *The Public and its Problems*.

Experience also represented for Follett a way to bring together a holistic and historical view of the subject. For Follett—as for Dewey—experience is encoded in habit (Follett 1941: 51). One implication of this, she suggests, is that attitudes have to be 'built up'—a claim identical to Dewey's claim in *Human Nature and Conduct* ([1922] 1957) about the importance of character, which later influenced Philip Selznick's concept of organizational character (1957). Like the work of Dewey and Mead, in particular, her approach to experience is social psychological.

Follett's processual and relational ontology and her emphasis on concrete experience led her to privilege activity over social structure. As Fox writes, critically, 'She was concerned only with the activity of people and with processes that take place when people interact with each other, quite apart from any formalized circumstances that may surround them' (1968: 527–8).[12] Her work is, in fact, in the same spirit as what Rochberg-Halton calls pragmatism's concern with 'qualitative immediacy' and what White terms the 'anti-formalism' of pragmatism (Rochberg-Halton 1986; White 1949). Both Follett and Dewey placed stress on immediate circumstances—the 'situation' for Follett and the 'problem' for Dewey. However, while they both insisted on focusing analytical attention on the specific context in which activity was occurring, they both also treated that situation holistically (Parker 1984: 741). Elsewhere, I have described pragmatism's combination of analytical specificity and holism as *analytical holism*, and it is a description that could equally be used to characterize Follett's work (Ansell 2007).

A process ontology and a focus on experience also led Follett to stress the importance of experiential and reflexive learning, much as Dewey did in his well-known work on education. She argues, for instance, that we have to take a reflexive attitude towards our own experience: 'What I urge is not that you adopt my principles, but that you stop to think what principles you are acting on' (Follett 1941: 50). One important implication of this reflexivity, as both Dewey and Follett advocated, is that we should adopt an experimental approach to learning: 'We should try experiments,' Follett writes, 'and note whether they succeed or fail and, most important of all, why they succeed or fail' (ibid. 51). She advocated for experiential and reflexive learning at the organizational, as well as the individual level. For instance, Follett called for systematic data-gathering to 'compare experience', while arguing that 'we should deliberately experiment' (ibid. 128). Follett also emphasized the creative element of experience and learning, as she developed in *Creative Experience*. Her emphasis on creativity is, in fact, very compatible with pragmatism, which Hans Joas has described as 'a theory of situated creativity' (Joas 1996: 133). Follett's theory of creativity, in which she emphasized the need for a creative response to a situation, is quite similar to Dewey's whole argument about problem-solving.

Another striking similarity between Follett and the pragmatists was their effort to break down strong dichotomies between individualism and collectivism (Ryan and Rutherford 2000). At the core of Follett's social psychological perspective was her insistence on seeing individuals in the context of group processes (and vice versa). Fox (1968) suggests that her ideas for a 'healthy group process' came out of her work on the Boston community center movement, which she first elaborated in *The New State* and later refined in *Creative Experience*. But again, her distinctive approach to the relationship between individuals and groups is shaped by philosophical considerations. As Follett wrote:

[12] Fox writes, 'She has nothing useful to tell us about organizational structures or administrative devices, and it is a question that we will have to leave open as to how much her own ideal of integration may have depended on certain structural characteristics that she took for granted' (1968: 527).

> It is impossible, however, to work most effectively at co-ordination until you have made up your mind where you stand philosophically in regard to the relation of parts to the whole. We have spoken of the relation of departments—sales and production, advertising and financial—to each other, but the most profound truth that philosophy has ever given us concerns not only the relation of parts, but the relation of parts to the whole, not to a stationary whole, but to a whole a-making. (Follett 1941: 91)

Much as does Mead in his description of the evolution of the social self or Dewey does in his revision of the 'liberal' view of individuality, Follett argues for a reciprocal influence between the whole and its parts: 'Production policy, sales policy, financial policy, personnel policy, influence one another, but the general business policy which is being created by the interweaving of these policies is all the time, even while it is in the making, influencing production, sales, financial, and personnel policies' (Follett 1941: 195). In keeping with her emphasis on process and activity, she insists that groups—as wholes—are the result of the 'interweaving' of individuals: 'Unity is always a process, not a product' (ibid.).

Although Follett was a social behavioralist, she was also, like the pragmatists, an institutionalist. For instance, she wrote: 'You can be for labour without being against capital; you can be for the institution' (Follett 1941: 82). Follett does not use the term 'institution' often, but I believe it had a particular meaning for her that was related to her idea of 'integrative unity'. For Follett, the institution is, as Commons put it, a 'going concern'.[13] Her institutionalism comes through most clearly where she talks about how business should become professionalized by developing a service ethic, collective standards and traditions, and even 'style' (Follett 1941: ch. 5).[14] In arguing that business is not merely the pursuit of profit but also the development of ideas and style, she is making an argument very close to Dewey's claim that all experience has an artistic element (Dewey 1934). Organization, she argues, requires artistry: 'Organization is what separates mediocre endeavor from high endeavor' (Follett 1941: 144).

Finally, although Follett is perhaps less direct than the pragmatists in emphasizing communication as a core process of social interaction, she certainly sees deliberative communication as being at the heart of fruitful conflict resolution. She argues that conflict has to be transformed from 'fighting' to 'conferring' (Follett 1941: 73–7). At various points in her writings, she calls this the 'conference method' and she uses it to describe the importance of engaging in an exchange of perspectives, experience, and knowledge. Moreover, like the pragmatists, she emphasizes the symbolic intermediation of interaction. She is highly sensitive to the way that language shapes our understanding of our own interests and she suggests many times that constructive conflict requires attention to the use of language: 'You will notice that to break up a problem into its various parts involves the examination

[13] Follett had clearly read Commons, though her comments on his work are primarily critical (see e.g. Follett 1941: 83).

[14] She cites Whitehead at length on 'style' as a characteristic of all organized activity.

of symbols, involves, that is, the careful scrutiny of the language used to see what it really means' (ibid. 41).

21.3. Follett's Pragmatist Organization

I have argued that Follett's ontology is informed by a pragmatist idealism, but why is this important? One reason is that despite the breadth of the pragmatist vision, particularly Dewey's, it does not have a very well-grounded notion of how pragmatist organization and authority might work in practice. In fact, John Patrick Diggins (1994) has argued that the weak link in pragmatism is its lack of a practical theory of power and authority. The same criticism cannot be leveled against Follett, who develops a sophisticated model of how power and authority operate in certain kinds of organizations. In her Introduction to *Creative Experience*, Follett asks, 'What is the central problem of social relations?' And she answers, 'It is the question of power; this is the problem of industry, of politics, of international affairs.' It is clear, of course, that Follett was not comfortable with naked power. Her whole work is devoted to civilizing and transforming naked power in a constructive fashion. Organization is one of the key ways in which she proposes to do this. Follett is often as seen as advancing an argument against traditional hierarchical (command and control) models of organization (Parker 1984). Fry and Thomas write that 'Follett's approach to organizational behaviour challenged the then dominant model of the organization as a co-operative entity rounded on a harmony of interests, relying on hierarchical control mechanisms, and employing a 'rational-choice approach' to decision making' (1996: 11). When taken together, Follett's discussions of control, authority, power, and conflict can contribute significantly to a pragmatist theory of organization.

Before proceeding to her ideas, it is useful to put her work on organization in historical context. Parker and Ritson (2005) argue that Follett was one of the earliest 'management gurus', but that her work has been 'stereotyped' and consequently obscured. They argue that Follett has been misinterpreted, either by lumping her with Taylor's scientific management school or with Mayo's human relations school. They argue that Follett's work was fundamentally opposed to both approaches: 'Then during the human relations era of the 1930s, Follett's work was mis-interpreted in the shadow of Elton Mayo as her philosophy of industrial democracy became a license for managers to lead others to their own predetermined point of view, while her approach to control was represented as and reduced to a mere management technique' (Parker and Ritson 2005: 1344). In comparing

Mayo and Follett, however, Child argues that Mayo's approach was much more a vision of 'paternalistic, top-down management' than Follett's (Child 1996: 88). He also argues that Follett's belief in constructive conflict differed from Mayo's more harmonious vision of the workplace. But it would be wrong to treat Follett as simply 'anti-hierarchical'. Her model of organization is certainly a major departure, as Child suggests, from 'paternalistic, top-down management', but she is no anarchist or even a guild socialist, as indicated by her discussions of control and the giving of orders. Follett's model of organization suggests that 'obedience' and 'liberty' can be reconciled (Follett 1941: 64–5).[15]

So what are the major elements of Follett's vision of organization? Certainly, hers is a non-linear perspective. Mimicking her theory of organization, her ideas have a circular (though not teleological) quality, reinforcing each other in a complex fashion. Perhaps the best place to start is with her intermediate position in a debate that once raged between 'monists' and 'pluralists'. Searching for a way to reconcile the 'finished absolute' of Royce and the 'strung-alongness' of James, Follett finds the resolution of the monism–pluralism debate in the idea of 'community as process'. The problem of hierarchy, according to Follett, is that it makes us think in static, structural terms: 'We must develop the language which will express continuous qualitative change. Those who speak of hierarchy deal with the quantitative rather than the qualitative: they jump from the making to the thing that is made; they measure quantitatively the results of the unifying principle' (1919: 582). She argued that a dynamic model of federalism was the key to understanding community as process. Both James and Hegel, she claimed, converged on a federal model of society (Follett [1918] 1998: 264–70). For Follett, dynamic federalism promised a synthesis of 'collective' (monist) and 'distributed' (pluralist) sovereignty.

Follett claims that sovereignty is an achievement of people coming together in groups to create a collective will. Federalism appears when the collective will of smaller groups is fused together into a larger collective will. As she repeatedly stresses, her conception of federalism is not based on the idea of a 'separation of powers' (Follett [1918] 1998: 297). Rather, federalism represents the fusion of the powers of its constituent groups. This fusion is always an active unifying process and not a static achievement. By focusing on the process of unifying, the hierarchical notion that either the whole or the parts come first could be overcome. In a circular unifying process, the whole infuses the parts while the parts reciprocally infuse the whole (ibid. 284).

The core of the unifying process for Follett is what she calls 'integration'. She assumes conflict is the basic state of affairs, but the basic question for her is how individuals and groups address this conflict. She describes three distinctive modes of conflict resolution: domination, compromise, and her preferred strategy, integration. Her most important distinction here is between compromise and integration.

[15] In this discussion, she argues directly against 'guild socialists'.

Compromise occurs when each side gives up something in a negotiation in order to reach a solution that each side can accept, though it will not be the preferred solution of either side. By contrast, integration demands some kind of 'invention' that transcends the original position of either side by finding a solution that does not require either side to compromise. Follett argued that compromise was only a temporary form of conflict resolution; lasting conflict resolution requires integration. Conflicts between distributed and collective sovereignty must ultimately be reconciled through integration, which is a dynamic process of unifying diverse interests.

Follett argues that the first rule of integration is to bring conflict out into the open so that it can be scrutinized and, ultimately, 're-evaluated' (Follett 1941: 38). She argues that 'A business should be so organized (this is one of the tests for us to apply to our organization) that full opportunity is given in any conflict, in any coming together of desires, for the whole field of desire to be viewed' (ibid. 39). Follett's argument is not that people do not have interests; rather, these interests are malleable and can be revised in the light of examination. Follett's claim is not only very similar to the pragmatist emphasis on reflexivity as a basis for learning but also similar to current perspectives about 'reframing' as a basis for resolving intractable conflict (Schon and Rein 1994). To re-evaluate our interests, she suggests that we have to break them down into their constituent parts and examine their symbolic dimension. Ultimately, integration requires a creative response. As Fox summarizes: 'Follett's message is that within every total, evolving situation of interpenetrating circular responses there are many powerful factors operating to erode established interests, positions, and prejudices; to effect changes in the direction of wishes; and to make possible the unifying of previously separated elements into new and integrated wholes' (1968: 524).[16]

Many concepts in contemporary negotiation theory bear a strong similarity to Follett's concept of integration: positive sum games, Pareto optimality, mutual gains, or integrated bargaining. It would take too long to investigate specific similarities and differences between these concepts, but suffice it to say that Follett saw integration as joint discovery of new options that were unifying.[17] This concept has been a particular inspiration to those advocating strategies of 'alternative dispute resolution'. Organizational justice researchers have also been inspired by Follett's concept of integration. Barclay (2005) suggests that Follett's notion of integrative unity can help to demonstrate how the perspectives of both managers and employees together contribute to perceptions of fairness. Fry and Thomas, however, argue that a limitation of Follett's work is that it does not propose concrete measures for transforming group processes in a more constructive fashion (1996: 17). I believe

16 This summary provides a good description of what I mean by Follett's analytic holism.

17 Integration is, in other words, the 'emergent' aspect of the conflict process. Dewey and Bentley (1949) made a similar kind of claim about 'transactions' that John Commons picked up to talk about 'transaction' economics (Commons 1934).

this is a little unfair because she did make concrete suggestions for how to encourage constructive conflict (see the previous paragraph). But they may be right that a serious limitation of her work is that she did not consider when 'integrative solutions' are possible and what to do when they are not.

At the heart of integration is what Follett calls 'circular response', described above as a reflection of Follett's processual and relational ontology. For Follett, 'circular response' summed up the complex phenomenon of dynamic and reciprocal influence between individuals or groups. Today, organization studies might refer to circular response as 'coevolution', but note her specific analysis of this: 'Do we mean all the ways in which A influences B, and all the ways in which B influences B? Reciprocal influences means more than this. It means that A influences B, and that B, made different by A's influence, influences A, which means that A's own activity enters into the stimulus which is causing his activity' (Follett 1941: 194).[18]

Integration and circular response are at the core of many of her other ideas about how authority and coordination work in organizations. Among her most famous essays is 'The Giving of Orders', in which she lays out a model of authority that requires integration between supervisor and subordinates. She argues that 'I should say that the giving of orders and the receiving of orders ought to be a matter of integration through circular behavior' (Follett 1941: 54). Follett argues that the extremes of what she calls 'bossism' (linear command) and no orders at all (anarchism) are to be avoided (ibid. 58). She asks us to understand the 'experience' that employees have when they are issued a linear order, which undercuts both their independent judgment and their motivation.

To achieve that balance between top-down command and bottom-up initiative, she articulates what she calls the 'law of the situation'. The key to the law of the situation is to 'depersonalize the giving of orders' (Follett 1941: 58): 'One *person* should not give orders to another *person*, but both should agree to take their orders from the situation' (ibid. 59). For Follett, the situation has 'authority'. The law of the situation is very much an expression of the idea of 'situated creativity', as described in the previous section. In arguing for depersonalizing the giving of orders, she clarifies that the goal is not actually to depersonalize organization, but rather to repersonalize the relationship by stripping it of personalized control. She argues that the goal is 'fact-control' rather than 'man-control' (ibid. 295). Like Dewey, Follett emphasized the importance of 'face-to-face' relations and the immediacy of the specific situational context. Face-to-face relations are important because they facilitate the 'joint' study of the situation.

Follett also suggests that people can develop the 'habit' (the attitude) for joint study of the situation and for obeying the law of the situation. She is clear, however, that training is not to be used to produce the attitude to accept orders; rather

[18] Barclay (2005) argues that the idea of circular response can provide a framework for understanding the dynamic evolution of perceptions of fairness and justice.

you are using training to produce the habit of joint study of the situation (Follett 1941: 61). The key to authority and consent is, therefore, to stress the 'jointness' of the activity of managers and employees rather than the vertical status ordering of one over the other. Although Follett's view of the law of situation emphasizes the importance of employees having discretion, she emphasizes that she is not advocating the independence of workers in decision making. As I will point out later in discussing Follett's concept of leadership, she is not rejecting the idea that some form of structural hierarchy is necessary for complex coordination. Rather, she is suggesting a transformation of the way those vertical positions fundamentally relate to one another.

Follett's revision of the concept of authority, as expressed by the law of the situation, is closely related to the stress she lays on the idea of responsibility. 'How can you expect people merely to obey orders,' she writes, 'and at the same time to take that degree of responsibility which they should take?' (Follett 1941: 63). Follett argues that authority and responsibility are derived from tasks (function) and not from position in the hierarchy (ibid. 147). Authority should follow knowledge and experience. She argues against a principal–agent model of authority in which 'the President *delegates* authority and responsibility' (ibid. 148). Instead, she insists that 'legitimate authority flows from co-ordination, not co-ordination from authority' (ibid. 150). Moreover, responsibility is difficult to fix, and hence assign, because it grows organically out of the process of interweaving the task situations of different people. Although she recognizes the need to assign authority and responsibility a priori and to hold people accountable, she observes that 'In the ideal organization authority is always fresh, always being distilled anew' (ibid. 151). Her goal is draw attention to the authority and responsibility of people lower in the organizational hierarchy.

To clarify, Follett does not object to the idea of authority, as such, but only to the idea of 'ultimate' authority, from which lesser authority is derived (Follett 1941: 154). She proposes that instead of thinking about 'ultimate' authority, we ought to think about 'cumulative responsibility' (ibid. 154–5). Thus, some people do have more cumulative responsibility than others.[19] But, she writes:

> The best method of organization is not that which works out most meticulously or most logically the place for 'finals' and 'ultimates,' but that which provides possibilities for a cumulative responsibility, which provides for gathering together all the responsibility there actually is in the plant, which provides for making various individual and group responsibilities more effective by the working out of a system of cross-relations.
>
> (Follett 1941: 159–60)

What I find most valuable about Follett's conception of authority is that it rejects a model of either centralization or decentralization. 'That centralization and

[19] I do not find her description of cumulative responsibility very clear, but I give my best interpretation here.

decentralization are not opposed is,' she writes, 'the central lesson for business administration to learn' (Follett 1941: 80). Clearly, she favors a form of decentralization because she writes that 'I know no one who believes more strongly in decentralization than I do, but I believe that collective responsibility and decentralized responsibility must go hand in hand' (ibid. 79). She provides multiple examples of the benefit of pushing initiative down into the operational ranks and she argues that there should be no 'sharp line' between planning and executing (ibid. 88).

To fully see how Follett would overcome the pulls of centralization and decentralization, we have to further investigate her analysis of power and leadership. Complementing her 'law of the situation', Follett suggests a distinction between 'power-over'—as exemplified by traditional command relationships—and 'power-with', which is a 'co-active' or 'joint' power (Follett 1941: 100). Follett regards 'legitimate power' as power-with and she sees it as produced through the circular relations of integration. Like her contrast between compromise and integration, Follett distinguishes the idea of 'balance of power' from the idea of 'power-with' or joint power (e.g. power-with is a form of integration). A balance of power constrains the power of each party through countervailing power. By contrast, Follett argues in favor of increasing the power of each party by increasing their joint power (ibid. 110). Furthermore, she argues that power cannot be delegated because it is a capacity (ibid. 109).[20] She writes: 'To confer authority where capacity has not been developed is fatal to both government and business' (ibid. 111).

Follett's concern with the capacity of employees to assume responsibility makes her a very relevant figure to contemporary empowerment research. As Follett wrote: 'The manager cannot share his power with division superintendent or foreman or workmen, but he can give them opportunities for developing their power' (Follett 1941: 113). Boje and Rosile (2001) argue that Follett transcends the debate between empowerment and disempowerment perspectives. In distinguishing delegation from power, Follett argues that power is a capacity and therefore cannot be delegated. With respect to employees, they are not 'delegated' power, but rather have to have the opportunity to develop their own capacity. Eylon argues that 'the paradox of empowerment is that the very existence of circumstances that place one group in a position to "provide" another group with power implies that power is a finite commodity controlled by a sub-set within the organization' (1998: 21). Eylon suggests that Follett's concept of building up 'co-active' power (power-with) helps to address the limitations of conceiving of empowerment as 'sharing' power. The important thing is not how to divide power, but how to organize joint power.

What is the role of leadership in Follett's model of organization? Obviously, she vigorously rejects the idea that the leader's role is to command and the follower's role is to obey. Instead, she stresses that the role of leaders is to help to achieve

[20] Power is the 'blossoming of experience' (Follett 1941: 111).

integration in the organization or, as she puts it, the role of the leaders is to 'organize experience' (Follett 1941; 258). The leader does this through articulating the common purpose of the enterprise, thus helping the various moving parts of the organization to know how they fit together. This argument anticipates Selznick's more elaborate argument about the role of leaders in shaping organizational missions (Selznick 1957). 'The great leader', she writes, 'is he who so relates all the complex outer forces and all the complex inner forces that they work together effectively' (Follett 1941: 265). Arguing against a command-oriented view of leadership, she writes that 'Group activity, organized group activity, should aim: to incorporate and express the desires, the experiences, the ideals of individual members of the group.' What Follett's idea tries to prepare the way for is a situation in which employers would not fear increasing the power of their employees. She goes on to say that 'leadership rightly understood increases freedom as it heightens individuality' (ibid. 275).[21]

A concept of leadership that emphasizes its integrative role suggests a more general point about Follett's model of organization. Her model of organizations stresses the modes of horizontal coordination as much as she does modes of vertical coordination. The complements to Follett's integrative conception of leadership and a distributed conception of responsibility are her emphasis on coordination and control. Her sense of coordination is typically a form of collegial governance, often through the organizational vehicle of committees.[22] She repeatedly emphasizes the importance of cross-functional coordination and organization (Follett 1941: 157–8). Critically, she stresses that early and continuous coordination are essential.[23] Ultimately, integration can only be successful if it builds up from organic coordination among separate tasks.[24] Control, she argues, arises out of the interactive coordination that produces unity: 'The activity of self-creating coherence *is* the controlling activity' (ibid. 204). The implication, she tells us, is that the more 'highly integrated' an organization is, the more control it will have (ibid. 205).[25] However, this does not imply that the group controls the individual (recall the discussion of whole–part relationships above). Rather, an integrated group encourages a form of self-control, which is what Follett means by responsibility. Parker summarizes

[21] 'The essential task of the leader is to free' (Follett 1970: 138).

[22] For example, she writes, 'One of the tests of conference or committee should be: are we developing genuine power or is someone trying unduly to influence the others?' (1941: 103).

[23] 'Four fundamental principles of organization are:

coordination by direct contact of the responsible people concerned;
coordination in the early stages;
coordination as the reciprocal relating of all the factors in a situation;
coordination as a continuing process' (Follett 1941; 297).

[24] Essentially, she is expressing here the idea later called 'simultaneous engineering'.

[25] 'The aim of organization engineering', she writes, 'is control through effective unity' (Follett 1941: 184).

Follett's theory of control: 'The group-oriented process of shared self-control therefore constituted the major aspect of the Follett behavioral model of control' (Parker 1984: 740). Parker identifies both 'behavioral' and 'holistic' models of control in Follett's work, but stresses the importance of 'self-control' in both models. '[T]he synthesis of individualism and collective control', Follett writes, 'is collective *self*-control' (Follett 1941: 308).

Yet it is not simply self-control at work in integrative groups. She also writes that 'central control is coming more and more to mean correlation of many controls rather than a superimposed control' (Follett 1941: 295). Follett writes that the 'correlation of many controls' means the 'gathering up of many authorities found at different points in the organization' (ibid. 296). She talks about planning as a 'horizontal' rather than a 'vertical' process (ibid. 301). Nor are planning and operations separate processes: 'Thus planning remains an integral part of the management of the self-governing units' (ibid. 302).[26]

Although I find Follett's description of control ultimately a little vague, her analysis suggests a very different model of organization. Building on the core concepts of integration and circular response, Follett describes a model of organization strikingly similar to the 'organic' model of organization described by Burns and Stalker in the 1960s. Whereas it is easy to read Burns and Stalker's organic organization, however, as a model of decentralization—in contrast to what they call a 'mechanistic' organization—Follett is quite clear about arguing for a combination of centralization and decentralization.

21.4. Conclusion

Mary Parker Follett was a remarkable scholar of organizations. Whether or not it is useful to think of her as a 'prophet of management', it is clear that she anticipated many ideas that would later become important concepts in organization and management studies. I have argued that Follett was among the most 'philosophical' of organization and management scholars and that is one of the reasons that we periodically return to her to read her afresh. She shows us how a certain ontological position can be translated into a practical understanding of how organizations work. While acknowledging that she was strongly influenced by idealism, I have argued that her idealism was strongly tempered by pragmatism. With the pragmatists, she shared a processual and relational ontology, a focus on experience, habit, and activity, and a stress on learning, experimentation,

[26] In doing this, she draws on an organic view of the organization as an integrated whole (Follett 1941: 185).

creativity, and communication. In part, the pragmatists—particularly the work of William James—directly influenced her work. But as a contemporary of Dewey's and Mead's, she also shared the same intellectual environment and wrestled with similar kinds of social and political problems. I make this claim about the link between pragmatism and Mary Parker Follett not to establish a veritable intellectual history of her work, but rather to demonstrate an intellectual complementarity that I believe strengthens both of them. Pragmatism lacks a practical conception of everyday authority and power that Follett provides, while a pragmatist interpretation of Follett's deepens our understanding of the philosophical basis of her claims about organizations. To the extent that Follett is understood as a pragmatist, the contemporary revival of pragmatism as a major philosophical perspective increases our appreciation of the originality and importance of her work.

Acknowledgments

I would like to thank Paul Adler, Margaretha Breese, Michael Cohen, Giuseppe Di Palma, Steve Hoffman, Satoshi Miura, Erik Schneiderhan, and Klaus Weber for advice and encouragement with this chapter.

References

Ansell, C. (2007). 'Pragmatism and Action Research', in Gunner Gjestrop and Eva Sorenson (eds.), *Public Administration in Transition: Theory, Practice, Methodology*. Copenhagen: DJØF Publishing.

Barclay, L. (2005). 'Following in the Footsteps of Mary Parker Follett: Exploring How Insights from the Past can Advance Organizational Justice Theory and Research'. *Journal of Management History*, 43/5: 740–60.

Boje, D. M., and Rosile, G. A. (2001). 'Where's the Power in Empowerment?: Answers from Follett and Clegg'. *Journal of Applied Behavioral Science*, 37/1: 90–117.

Bredo, E. (1998). 'Evolution, Psychology, and John Dewey's Critique of the Reflex Arc Concept'. *Elementary School Journal*, 98/5: 447–66.

Calas, M. B., and Smircich, L. (1996). 'Not Ahead of her Time: Reflections on Mary Parker Follett as Prophet of Management'. *Organization*, 3/1: 147–52.

Child, J. (1996). 'Follett: Constructive Conflict', in Pauline Graham (ed.), *Mary Parker Follett: Prophet of Management*. Cambridge, Mass.: Harvard Business School Press.

Commons, J. (1934). *Institution Economics*. New York: Macmillan.

Dewey, J. (1896). 'The Reflex Arc Concept in Psychology'. *Psychological Review*, III.

—— (1910). *How We Think*. Lexington, Mass.: D. C. Heath.

DEWEY, J. ([1922] 1957). *Human Nature and Conduct: An Introduction to Social Psychology.* New York: Random House.

—— (1934). *Art as Experience.* New York: Perigee Books.

—— and BENTLEY, A. (1949). *Knowing and the Known.* Boston: Beacon Press.

DICKSTEIN, M. (ed.) (1998). *The Revival of Pragmatism: New Essays on Social Thought, Law, and Culture.* Durham, NC: Duke University Press.

DIGGINS, J. (1994). *The Promise of Pragmatism: Modernism and the Crisis of Knowledge and Authority.* Chicago: University of Chicago Press.

EMIRBAYER, M. (1997). 'Manifesto for a Relational Sociology'. *American Journal of Sociology,* 103/2: 281–317.

EVANS, K. (1998). 'Governance, Citizenship, and the New Science: Lessons from Dewey and Follett on Realizing Democratic Administration'. Ph.D. thesis, Virginia Polytechnic Institute and State University.

EYLON, D. (1998). 'Understanding Empowerment and Resolving its Paradox: Lessons from Mary Parker Follett'. *Journal of Management History,* 4/1: 16–28.

FOLLETT, M. P. (1919). 'Community is a Process'. *Philosophical Review,* 27: 576–88.

—— ([1918] 1998). *The New State: Group Organization the Solution of Popular Government.* University Park: Pennsylvania State University.

—— (1924). *Creative Experience.* New York: Longmans, Green and Co.

—— (1941). *Dynamic Administration: The Collected Papers of Mary Parker Follett,* ed. H. Metcalf and L. Urwick. Bath: Management Publications Trust.

—— (1970). 'The Teacher–Student Relation'. *Administrative Science Quarterly,* 15/2: 137–48.

FOX, E. M. (1968). 'Mary Parker Follett: The Enduring Contribution'. *Public Administration Review,* 28/6: 520–9.

FRY, B., and THOMAS, L. (1996). 'Mary Parker Follett: Assessing the Contribution and Impact of her Writings'. *Journal of Management History,* 2/2: 11–19.

GRAHAM, P. (ed.) (1996). *Mary Parker Follett: Prophet of Management.* Cambridge, Mass.: Harvard Business School Press.

GREENSTONE, J. D. (1993). *The Lincoln Persuasion: Remaking American Liberalism.* Princeton: Princeton University Press.

HOOPES, J. (1998). *Community Denied: The Wrong Turn of Pragmatic Liberalism.* Ithaca, NY: Cornell University Press.

JAMES, W. (1977). *The Writings of William James: A Comprehensive Edition.* Chicago: University of Chicago Press.

JOAS, H. (1993). *Pragmatism and Social Theory.* Chicago: University of Chicago Press.

—— (1996). *The Creativity of Action.* Chicago: University of Chicago Press.

KEITH, W. M. (2007). *Democracy as Discussion: Civic Education and the American Forum Movement.* Lanham, Md.: Lexington Books.

KLOPPENBERG, J. (1986). *Uncertain Victory: Social Democracy and Progressivism in European and American Thought, 1870–1920.* New York: Oxford University Press.

MCDERMOTT, J. (1986). *Streams of Experience: Reflection on the History and Philosophy of American Culture.* Amherst: University of Massachusetts Press.

MATTSON, K. (1998). *Creating a Democratic Public: The Struggle for Urban Participatory Democracy during the Progressive Era.* University Park: Pennsylvania State University.

MENDENHALL, M. E., MACOMBER, J. H., and CUTRIGHT, M. (2000). 'Mary Parker Follett: Prophet of Chaos and Complexity'. *Journal of Management History,* 6/4: 191–204.

Morton, N. O'R., and Lindquist, S. A. (1997). 'Revealing the Feminist in Mary Parker Follett'. *Administration & Society*, 29/3: 348–71.

O'Connor, E. S. (2000). 'Integrating Follett: History, Philosophy and Management'. *Journal of Management History*, 6/4: 167–90.

Parker, L. D. (1984). 'Control in Organizational Life: The Contribution of Mary Parker Follett'. *Academy of Management Review*, 9: 736–45.

—— and Ritson, P. (2005). 'Fads, Stereotypes and Management Gurus: Fayol and Follett Today'. *Management Decision*, 43/10: 1335–57.

Phillips, D. C. (1971). 'James, Dewey, and the Reflex Arc'. *Journal of the History of Ideas*, 32/4: 555–68.

Rochberg-Halton, E. (1986). *Meaning and Modernity: Social Theory in the Pragmatic Attitude*. Chicago: University of Chicago Press.

Ryan, L. V., and Rutherford, M. A. (2000). 'Mary Parker Follett: Individualist or Collectivist? Or Both?' *Journal of Management History*, 6/5: 207–23.

Schilling, M. (2000). 'Decades Ahead of Her Time: Advancing Stakeholder Theory Through the Ideas of Mary Parker Follett'. *Journal of Management History*, 6/5: 224–42.

Schon, D., and Rein, M. (1994). *Frame Reflection: Toward a Resolution of Intractable Policy Controversies*. New York: Basic Books.

Selznick, P. (1957). *Leadership in Administration: A Sociological Interpretation*. Berkeley: University of California Press.

Smith, D. G. (1964). 'Pragmatism and the Group Theory of Politics'. *American Political Science Review*, 58/3: 600–610.

Stears, M. (2002). *Progressives, Pluralists, and the Problems of the State: Ideologies of Reform in the United States and Britain, 1909–1926*. Oxford: Oxford University Press.

Stever, J. A. (1986). 'Mary Parker Follett and the Quest for Pragmatic Administration'. *Administration & Society*, 18/2: 159–77.

Tonn, J. C. (2003). *Mary P. Follett: Creating Democracy, Transforming Management*. New Haven: Yale University Press.

West, C. (1989). *The American Evasion of Philosophy: A Genealogy of Pragmatism*. Madison: University of Wisconsin Press.

Westbrook, R. (1991). *John Dewey and American Democracy*. Ithaca, NY: Cornell University Press.

White, M. (1949). *Social Thought in America: The Revolt Against Formalism*. New York: Viking Press.

Zald, M. N. (1996). 'More Fragmentation? Unfinished Business in Linking the Social Sciences and the Humanities'. *Administrative Science Quarterly*, 41/2: 251–61.

CHAPTER 22

PEOPLING ORGANIZATIONS

THE PROMISE OF CLASSIC SYMBOLIC INTERACTIONISM FOR AN INHABITED INSTITUTIONALISM

TIM HALLETT
DAVID SHULMAN
GARY ALAN FINE

Contemporary social theory seems to have strayed far from its proper task. Theorists spend whole careers marginalizing classic texts. . . . But the classic thinkers themselves—Marx, Durkheim, Weber, Thomas, and so on—were up to their necks in empirical data: Documents, surveys, statistics and histories, describing dozens of different people and processes. These were not votaries of 'classic problems' invented by their predecessors. They wrote theory to explain empirical realities they saw. And they worried less about giving specific answers, about specific theories of why specific things happened, than they did about creating vocabularies for framing theories, ways of asking questions.

Andrew Abbott, *The System of Professions: An Essay on the Division of Expert Labor* (1988: 326)

22.1. Introduction

Our professional climate compels—or at least encourages—theories and research orientations to be bound to particular communities of thought. This compartmentalization of scholarship, particularly in organizational studies, comes at the cost of neglecting classic theorists perceived as outside the ivied walls of one's invisible college. Paul Adler suggests, in his introduction to this volume, that reacquainting ourselves with the concerns, insights, and open-mindedness of classic thinkers can push organizational studies in new directions. Revisiting the classic *interactionist* thinkers provides that push, as they embody the virtues Abbott describes—they created distinct vocabularies, generated theories from empirical observations, and asked questions that have provided lasting insights into the social world.

While epistemic communities have always existed, those that we now define as classic transcended the narrow boundaries that separate current disciplinary perspectives. Interactionism began as a melding of traditions in philosophy, psychology, and the emerging discipline of sociology. Herbert Blumer coined the term 'symbolic interaction' in a textbook chapter in 1937, but the approach originated in George Herbert Mead's theories of social behaviorism.[1] Mead was a philosopher, but he was responding to the behavioral psychology of John Watson (Mead 1934). Generations of sociologists attended his lectures (Lewis and Smith 1980), and his analyses of minds, social selves, and societal institutions appealed to graduate students at the University of Chicago who were looking for an epistemological charter

[1] The term 'symbolic interaction' is a label of convenience and provides a depiction of scholars who might not have embraced the label as descriptive of their own work. Given Blumer's origin of the term in 1937, neither Charles Horton Cooley (who died in 1929) nor Mead (who died in 1931) would have known that they were 'symbolic interactionists'. The rivalry between Blumer and Hughes in the Chicago Department of Sociology (Abbott and Gaziano 1995) suggests the term originally referred to Blumer's approach, developed from Mead, as opposed to Hughes's orientation, which was more closely linked to Park and Burgess. The label 'symbolic interaction' was not widely utilized until the 1960s, when opposition movements to functionalist dominance in sociology emerged, culminating in the publication of Blumer's collection of papers, *Symbolic Interactionism* (1969). Goffman never labeled himself a symbolic interactionist; for others the term provided a convenient label that represented a perspective or a group of colleagues as opposed to a defined set of premises. Whenever possible, we use the more general term 'interactionism', but we rely upon intellectual placements of these writers to do so, rather than depending upon the murky distinctions they made.

for their own studies of everyday life. Connections were also strong between sociologists and anthropologists at the University of Chicago, including links between Robert Redfield, Everett Hughes, and W. Lloyd Warner, the latter two mentors of Erving Goffman.

While rereading canonical texts can reacquaint us with forgotten insights, there is also a danger: we must be wary not to resuscitate ideas that have been deservedly transcended. In our case, we must identify the contributions of interactionist thinking without overselling the relationship interactionism has had with organizational studies. Interactionists have long focused on what goes on within organizations—thus their scholarly importance as researchers of work. However, they have avoided conceptualizing organizations as such until quite recently. Their primary concerns are the relationships among individuals and how people create meanings and social relations. Structures and institutions, while never denied, receive secondary attention. Interactionists have made their most significant advances studying interpersonal realms, not in their investigations of 'institutions' or 'society'.

We argue that the value of the interactionist approach for organizational research exists in its emphasis on how interaction and meaning provide a foundation for thinking about the constitutive role of people in organizations. The 'peopled' perspective of symbolic interaction stands in stark contrast to the 'un-peopled' view that has often characterized organizational sociology. Over fifty years ago, Gouldner (1954: 16) asserted:

> The social scene described has sometimes been so completely stripped of people that the impression is unintentionally rendered that there are disembodied forces afoot, able to realize their ambitions apart from human action. This has colored some analyses of bureaucracy with funereal overtones, lending dramatic persuasiveness to the pessimistic portrayal of administrative systems.

Gouldner (1955: 498) described this fatalistic structural sentiment that robs organizational theory of life as a 'metaphysical pathos'.[2] Twenty years ago DiMaggio expanded Gouldner's critique to argue: 'institutional theorists often employ selectively assertions about actor interests on an ad hoc basis; and their writings are frequently laden with "metaphysical pathos"—specifically, a rhetorical defocalization of interest and agency' (1988: 3). A decade ago, borrowing from DiMaggio, Colomy criticized 'new' institutionalism for its 'metaphysical pathos', portraying institutions as 'disembodied structures acting on their own volition while depicting actors as powerless and inert in the face of inexorable social forces' (1998: 267).

Although much has changed in organizational sociology over the past fifty years, the tendency to treat people as inconsequential remains. In contrast, consider a

[2] Gouldner adapted and modified this term from Arthur O. Lovejoy, a historian of ideas. Lovejoy (1948: 11) described 'metaphysical pathos' as the implicit, unstated sentiments that are attached to ideas, sentiments that theorists become committed to when they subscribe to an idea.

vision for organizational sociology that Blumer (1947: 277) articulated in a 1946 address to the American Sociological Society:

> It [organizational sociology] must visualize human beings as acting, striving, calculating, sentimental and experiencing persons and not as the automatons and neutral agents implied by the more dominant of our current scientific ideologies and methodologies.... It must embrace the complicated behavior of these collectivities, particularly as they act and prepare to act toward one another.

Blumer's words are prescient. We believe that reengaging the interactionism of Mead, Blumer, Hughes, and the Second Chicago School (Fine 1995) works by Goffman, Becker, and Strauss promotes a distinctive institutional analysis that 'brings people back' as a key focus for organizational research.

22.2. The Interactionist Credo

Although classic interactionists did not theorize the organization proper, they often analyzed work and work settings. This research tradition poses the questions:

- How do workers interpret the work that they do?
- How do they identify with or disavow work in connection to their sense of 'self'?
- How do they do things together?
- How do they strategize their actions as 'calculating and experiencing persons' within a set of formal and informal expectations for performance?
- How do patterns of interaction constitute negotiated orders that shape how work is accomplished?

Work is viewed as locally constituted through institutional arrangements and cultural assumptions, and practiced through the facilitation of group dynamics. Although formal bureaucratic relations and rules may determine the form of work, interactionists explore how people, with all the attendant messiness of lived experience, define, negotiate, and do (or shirk) their work in practice.

Three themes, then, capture the relevance of interactionism for organizational studies. First, interactionism prioritizes how the *interpretive meanings workers attach to work* affect how they conduct their work. Second, interactionists originated theories, methodological approaches, and conceptual vocabularies, including *dignifying rationalizations*, *negotiated order*, and *total institutions*, which analyze *how people work and are affected by work*. These thinkers examined work inside organizations as meaningful, identity-forming, influential in constructing the organization to outside monitors, and as a set of reflexive processes between workers. Third, they created distinctive methodological approaches, grounded in their theoretical concerns, emphasizing that the *discovery of knowledge must be a joint project* between empathetic researcher and committed informant. Taking the role of the other is not only a theoretical concept, but also a methodological one.

By addressing these themes, these early thinkers contribute to an 'inhabited' institutionalism (Scully and Creed 1997; Fine 1996; Hallett and Ventresca 2006; Binder 2007) that recognizes the obdurateness, limitations, and constitutive role that institutions and organizations place on behavior, but is also suffused with groups, interaction, and meanings. These meanings are not simply the by-product of larger forces, but are a resource and result of local interactions that are consequential to organizational outcomes. Instead of treating 'institutions' and 'interactions' as oppositional, inhabited institutionalism views them as mutually constitutive and recursively linked, just as Giddens (1984) views social structure as both the medium and outcome of human agency.

In providing a cure for the metaphysical pathos of organizational sociology, this interactionally inspired, inhabited institutionalism exhibits optimism about human possibilities and our potential to overcome the challenges that organizations create, 'iron cage' be damned. Drawing extensively from pragmatist philosophy, the early interactionists were not simply interested in ideas for their own sake, but as a means to promote social change. If we recognize how social systems work, and if we reject their effects, we can change them because, in the final analysis, they are not the result of 'inexorable social forces', but rather 'people doing things together' (Becker 1986). An important misinterpretation of symbolic interactionism is that it ignores the larger structural forces that impinge on action. Mead and those who followed did not ignore such things, but their humanistic ideas, conceptualization of mind, self, interaction, and meaning envision the possibility of social change. What is currently defined (if not stigmatized) as 'public sociology' was central to early interactionists.

We now outline the development of interactionist themes through a chronological discussion of its relevance for organizational studies. Although we cannot discuss every important contributor, we assess several key figures, starting with George Herbert Mead, followed by the mid-century contributions of Herbert Blumer and Everett Hughes, and concluding with the contributions of Erving Goffman, Anselm Strauss, and Howard Becker.

22.3. George Herbert Mead: The Promise of Mind and Self for Conceptualizing People in Organizations

A peopled organizational sociology can draw inspiration from George Herbert Mead (1863–1931) and his influential analysis of human intelligence (what he called 'mind') and the self. These ideas are central to Blumer's conceptualization of symbolic interaction and the possibility of an interactionally engaged, inhabited institutionalism.

Mead's goal was to develop a pragmatist theory of mind grounded in an understanding of human behavior and its implications (Morris 1962: xii). For Mead, what distinguishes humans from other animals is the capacity for reflexive thinking—the ability to take ourselves as an object (instead of subject) of our own behavior—or what he called 'mind' (Mead 1934: 73, 134). At the most basic level, mind is the ability to step outside oneself as a means to reflect on one's actions. At the most developed level, mind represents the highest functioning of the self when people assume the attitudes of an abstract community. Although mind is a human capacity, it does not exist a priori. Rather, it develops from social interaction (ibid. 49–50). Our capacity for vocal (as opposed to merely physical) gestures and the development of language as a system of 'significant symbols' with shared meaning across interactants is essential: when we use language to convey shared meaning, we can appreciate the attitudes of others because such speech 'calls out in the individual making it the same attitude toward it (or toward its meaning) that it calls out in the other individuals participating with him in the given social act, and thus makes him conscious of their attitude toward it (as a component of his behavior) and enables him to adjust his subsequent behavior to theirs in light of that attitude' (ibid. 46). Mind develops from interactions based on shared meanings. It is in these interactions that we step outside of ourselves, see ourselves as objects by taking the attitude of others, imagine their responses to us, and modify our behavior accordingly.

Mead's conception of mind was innovative in challenging the simplistic, Watsonian, behaviorist assumption that human action could be understood as simple chains of stimulus–response interactions (Mead 1934). The reflexivity of mind enables us to intervene and reflect before responding to stimuli, providing a measure of self-control over our actions, and in turn providing a measure of control over our environment (ibid. 245–7). Mead offered a conceptualization of mind that was premised on, and developed from, an understanding of social interaction and not a Cartesian mind/body dualism. Hence, his student Charles W. Morris titled Mead's posthumously published compilation of lectures *Mind, Self, and Society* ***from the Standpoint of a Social Behaviorist*** (emphasis added).

According to Mead, the self develops in tandem with mind, and once again, the key mechanism is the ability to take the attitude of others. Via the process of language acquisition and the play and game stages of childhood socialization (all of which involve taking the attitude of others and taking one's self as an object—Mead 1934: 150–64), we acquire what Mead called a 'generalized other', a sense of the collective attitudes of our community (ibid. 90). This generalized other is internalized in one part of Mead's dialectical conceptualization of the self, the 'me'. Via the generalized other and the me, Mead introduces a dose of social control—as we respond to environmental stimuli and interact with others, we take ourselves as an object and respond with the me (ibid. 210). However, we also respond with an 'I', a more impulsive, novel response to a situation. The self is composed of both 'I' and 'me'. Mead describes the self as an ongoing social process in which the 'I' and 'me' continually respond to each other in relation to the stimuli of a situation:

> The self is not something that exists first and then enters into relationship with others, but it is, so to speak, an eddy in the social current and so still a part of the current. It is a process in which the individual is continually adjusting himself in advance to the situation to which he belongs, and reacting back to it. So that the 'I' and the 'me,' this thinking, this conscious adjustment, becomes then a part of the whole social process (ibid. 182)

Via the 'I' and the 'me', human action is characterized by both creativity and social control, and consistent with the writings of Cooley and W. I. Thomas, Mead emphasized reflexivity—the ability to develop a sense of self by perceiving oneself in the reactions of others.

Fitting squarely into the legacy of pragmatism, Mead's account of action is humanistic, and though Mead did not analyze organizations directly he wrote about organizations within the parameter of pragmatism—as someone working in an age of progressive reformists, like his close friend Jane Addams (Miller 1973: xxxi), to promote change on behalf of labor unions, settlement houses, and industrial education. Mead's orientation was that of the progressive who saw organizations as external forces, potentially for good, introduced into a system of interaction.

Mead's activist writings took the form of speeches to public, professional, and union audiences that were transcribed and published in forums such as the *Union Labor Advocate* and *Elementary School Teacher*. In these writings, Mead analyzed contemporary social problems with conclusions that might be defined either as prescient or as naive. For example, Mead offers an analysis of the alienation of labor akin to the concerns of progressive intellectuals regarding the decline in an ethic of craftsmanship, a point Thorstein Veblen (1898) emphasized during the same period: 'The more the machine accomplishes the less the workman is called upon to use his brain, the less skill he is called upon to acquire. The economics of the factory, therefore, calls for a continual search for cheaper and therefore less skilled labor' (Mead 1908–9: 370–1). Mead's analysis of alienated labor can hardly be called astructural, and it further deflates the misplaced argument that interactionists ignore the larger structural forces that impinge on action.

To address such structures, Mead advocated for educational reform:

> The curriculum should also contain the study of the social community into which the graduated apprentice will go. He should comprehend the central and state government not only, but the legal and administrative features of the city within which he is to labor. He should understand the laws that protect him as well as those which threaten him with pains and penalties. (1908–9: 382)

More broadly, Mead argued: 'In the bill of rights that a modern man may draw up and present to the society, which has produced and controls him, should appear the right to work with intelligent comprehension of what he does, and with what interests' (ibid. 378).

Because organizations and their structures both constrain and enable our humanity, Mead advocated for organizations that could foster civil society by helping us express our common humanity. He called for 'international mindedness' (Mead 1934: 270) and organizations that would facilitate a 'global' generalized other, arguing that 'What is essential is the development of the whole mechanism of social relationship which brings us together, so that we can take the attitude of the other in our various life processes' (ibid. 272). Mead (ibid. 326) considered the ability to take the attitude of others as essential to good citizenship, which he hoped would reach a zenith of 'expression in the League of Nations, where every community recognizes every other community in the very process of asserting itself' (ibid. 287). He envisioned democracy as a common political language, 'an attitude' that 'goes with the universal relations of brotherhood' (ibid. 286).

In these moments, Mead moved towards a more philosophical, political, and normative ideal. This is where his sociology is at its weakest and is perhaps why few scholars realize that a third of his famous set of lectures consisted of an examination of 'society' based primarily on an analysis of institutions (Athens 2005, 2007). To define institutions, Mead stated: 'When we call out that response in others, we can take the attitude of the other and then adjust our own conduct to it. There are, then, whole series of such common responses in the community in which we live, and such responses are what we term "institutions" ' (1934: 261). Mead's view of institutions reflected a larger abstraction and stabilization of the interactional process of attitude taking. For Mead, institutions are stabilized components of the generalized other that call forth common responses. Although there is some room for creativity as our selves (particularly the 'I') interact with institutions, these institutions structure activity, thereby assuring order and allowing for more complex forms of society (Mead 1934: 260–1). Thus, in engaging the whole of his work, it is hard to argue that his theory is astructural. However, Athens (2007) has made the respectful but energetic criticism that Mead's theory of institutions and society is premised on an assumption of sociality that, while appropriate for examining interaction and the development of minds and selves, falters if expected to serve higher explanatory purposes in understanding institutional behaviors.

It is somewhat unfair to decontextualize Mead's work from the intellectual, political, and social context of his time by criticizing it through a present-day lens. Yet, as Mead himself argued in his brilliant but neglected theory of time (1932), any vision of the past necessarily exists in the context of the present and is inevitably distorted by that present. Despite the shortcomings of Mead's analysis of institutions and society, his approach is alive with people and their possibilities, and free of metaphysical pathos. His groundbreaking work on mind and self as interactional processes provide a vantage point for thinking about what the actors in a 'peopled' organizational sociology might look like: reflective and dynamic, and yet constrained by the boundaries of interaction and the attitudes of other people and the community. The implications of these contributions emerge more fully in Blumer's efforts to establish the basic premises of symbolic interactionism.

22.4. The Promise (and Peril) of Blumer's Premises of Symbolic Interaction

While Mead placed people and interaction at the heart of his analysis, Herbert Blumer (1900–1987) went further, developing a framework of symbolic interaction based on the type of mind and self that Mead described.[3] Blumer, who became a member of the faculty at the University of Chicago in 1931, coined the term 'symbolic interactionism' in 1937 and sought to advance Mead's thought by 'tracing the implications of the central matters which he analyzed' (1966: 535). Blumer was first exposed to Mead's ideas as a graduate student at Chicago during course work with Ellsworth Faris, 'who had been a foremost student of Mead' (Blumer 1977: 286). Blumer then took Mead's 'Advanced Social Psychology' course and became his research assistant. When Mead fell ill before his death, he requested that Blumer teach his class (ibid.).

Blumer developed principles that led to a more programmatic approach to symbolic interactionism, and at a time when the discipline was small, his ideas diffused through graduate students who took his classes, particularly among students who later made up the influential 'Second' Chicago School (Gusfield 1995; Fine 1995). By the time his collection of essays *Symbolic Interactionism: Perspective and Method* was published in 1969, Blumer's ideas were already known and influential (Abbott 1999: 71).

Based on the assumption that people have the kinds of minds and selves Mead outlined, Blumer argued that much of human life takes the form of 'symbolic interaction', that is, interaction in which we interpret the acts of others and the meanings of objects, and then respond on the basis of those interpretations and meanings (1936: 518; 1966: 537). Equipped with mind, we can insert our reflexive selves into the 'stimulus–response couplet... which implies some checking of immediate reaction, and leads, as suggested, to directed response upon the basis of the meaning assigned to the actions of another or the relevant object' (1936: 518).

[3] Mead's legacy has generated considerable debate among microsociologists. See Stryker (1980) for an important alternative formulation.

Blumer contrasted symbolic interaction with 'non-symbolic interaction', a state characterized by the 'unconscious responses that one makes to the gestures of others' (1936: 519). In non-symbolic interaction people are 'spontaneous, direct, and unwitting' (ibid.). Without denying that non-symbolic interaction occurs, Blumer argued that symbolic interaction is the 'characteristic mode of interaction' in human life (1969: 9).

The most concise statement of this framework is found in Blumer's three premises of symbolic interaction:

1. 'Human beings act towards things on the basis of the meanings that the things have for them.'
2. 'The meaning of such things is derived from, or arises out of, the social interaction that one has with one's fellows.'
3. 'These meanings are handled in, and modified through, an interpretative process used by the person in dealing with the things he encounters.' (1969: 2)

An interactionist guidebook for organizational research becomes evident if we substitute the word 'things' with the word 'organizations' in these premises. Or take the following passage from Blumer's 1966 exegesis of Mead, in which we replace the word 'object(s)' with 'organization(s)':

> There are several important points in the analysis of [organizations]. First, the nature of an [organization] is constituted by the meaning it has for the person or persons for whom it is an object. Second, this meaning is not intrinsic to the [organization] but arises from how the person is initially prepared to act toward it.... It follows that [organizations] vary in their meaning.... Third, [organizations]—all objects—are social products in that they are formed and transformed by the defining process that takes place in social interaction. The meaning of the [organization]... is formed from the ways in which others refer to such [organizations] or act toward them. Fourth, people are prepared or set to act toward [organizations] on the basis of the meanings of the [organizations] for them.... Fifth, just because an [organization] is something that is designated, one can organize one's action toward it instead of responding immediately to it; one can inspect the [organization], think about it, work out a plan of action toward it, or decide whether or not to act toward it.
>
> (Blumer 1966: 539)

Replacing the word 'organization' in this passage with any keyword in organizational studies—'bureaucracy', 'institutions', 'isomorphism', 'professions'—sensitizes us to Blumer's approach. This vision emphasizes that organizations are comprised of people, and their meanings and activities matter, because it is based on those meanings that people work and pursue organizational goals.

Although interactions and meanings are paramount in Blumer's approach, he limits social construction: 'the empirical world can "talk back" to our pictures of it or assertions about it—in the sense of challenging and resisting our images or conceptions of it. This resistance gives the empirical world an obdurate character that is the mark of reality' (Blumer 1969: 22). Blumer labeled any sociology that rejected structure 'ridiculous': 'There are such matters as social roles, status positions, rank orders, bureaucratic organizations, relations between institutions, differential authority arrangements, social codes, norms, values and the like' (1966: 543). However, he emphasized, 'they are important only as they enter into the process of interpretation and definition out of which joint actions are formed' (ibid.). Thus, instead of assuming that structures have a determinant role, the researcher's task is to demonstrate empirically how these realities impinge on the process of symbolic interaction (1969).

Blumer confronted this obdurate reality in his work as a labor arbitrator. In 1946 he spent much of his time working to solve a very real Pittsburgh steel strike (Abbott 1999: 47). He was also 'Deputy Director of the Latin American Center for Research in the Social Sciences' for UNESCO (Blumer 1990: ix), which inspired a line of research on the connection between industrialization and social change (1960, 1990[4]). This work demonstrates the applicability of the symbolic interactionist framework for examining macrosociological strains. Instead of reifying industrialization as a mystical force, Blumer emphasized points at which industrialization came into contact with group activity. He argued that industrialization does compel social change, but is 'neutral' in the sense that it is 'indifferent to what follows socially in its wake' (1960: 9). The ultimate form that social change takes, whether disruptive or beneficial, depends on a host of local factors. This is necessarily so because industrialization—or any organizational or institutional process—'consists of people, individually and collectively, adjusting to situations' (Maines and Morrione 1990: xiii).

Whereas Mead provides an optimistic view of institutions, Blumer provides a neutral one: institutions provide for a range of responses, but do not constitute those responses. The metaphysical pathos that characterizes much organizational research has been enabled by an underlying assumption that human activity is largely irrelevant. Implicitly, this view conceptualizes people as non-symbolic actors. This is true whether the analysis is guided by the assumption that people act based on a priori interests or whether they act habitually according to the institutionalized schemata of the organizational environment (DiMaggio 1997). In the latter view, common to 'new' institutionalism, people are merely 'carriers' of institutional processes (DiMaggio 1988; Scott 2001: 79). At its best, this view is over-socialized (Fligstein 2001). At its worst, it treats people as institutional dopes (Hirsch and Lounsbury 1997).

Blumer's actors are not dopes. Yet taken too far, his three premises can lead to a different but equally distorted extreme. Symbolic interactionism does not contend that meanings are always up for grabs. But it is true that, in his emphasis

[4] The 1990 volume *Industrialization as an Agent of Social Change: A Critical Analysis* was published posthumously. It is estimated that Blumer first drafted the manuscript in the early 1960s.

on symbols and interaction, Blumer 'simultaneously illuminates and obscures by directing conceptual light on some aspects and principles of social action rather than others' (Snow 2001: 368). By emphasizing symbolic interaction, even as he admitted the occurrence of non-symbolic interaction (Blumer 1936), Blumer provides a limited analysis of human life. Herein lays the peril of Blumer's approach as it pertains to organizations. Blumer downplays 'the extent to which symbols and the meanings they convey are often, perhaps routinely, embedded in and reflective of existing cultural and organizational contexts and systems of meaning' (Snow 2001: 371). In other words, habituated non-symbolic behavior might be usefully examined as institutionalized behavior. Moreover, to the extent that meanings can become reified and institutionalized (Zucker 1977), institutions can be experienced as external forces that shape symbolic interaction, limiting the dynamism of Blumer's second and third premises while recognizing the importance of the first premise.

These criticisms of institutionalism and symbolic interactionism suggest that, instead of being incommensurable, they are different sides of the same coin (Hallett and Ventresca 2006). The pivot point for an inhabited institutionalism that takes people, interaction, and groups seriously is not if action is 'symbolic' or 'non-symbolic', but rather when do actors respond with symbolic interaction? Under what conditions are responses non-symbolic in nature? What do both of these kinds of responses tell us about institutions as an obdurate feature of the organizational environment?

These questions are beyond the scope of Blumer's foundational work. Blumer's most influential writings were theoretical and methodological critiques of sociological practice (Blumer 1931, 1954, 1956, 1969). Even when his work was based on empirical observations, he wrote at a high level of abstraction and did not directly present his data, a contrast to Everett Hughes and the students who later comprised the Second Chicago School (Fine 1995).

22.5. Everett Hughes: The Conceptual Promise of Embedded Research on 'Peopled' Work

Many of the best-known interactionists are associated with a set of prominent concepts—Goffman with dramaturgy, Becker with labeling, Mead with the 'I' and 'me'. Hughes (1897–1982) is perhaps less known today, but he made substantial conceptual contributions to the study of work. As just one example of Hughes's influence, Andrew Abbott, in his landmark study *The System of Professions*, used Hughes as a touchstone and point of departure: 'The Hughes school felt that professions evolved, to be sure, but that their evolution was interactional, negotiated by the group in an environment.... The present model arises, essentially, by extending the Hughes logic to its limit and focusing on jurisdictional interactions themselves' (1988: 112).

For those invested in organizational studies, Hughes must be interpreted as a scholar whose original writings pioneered the exploration of how occupations attempt to become professions, how workplaces function as racial crossroads, and how workers mitigate the stigma of doing dirty work; as well as for his mentorship of generations of graduate students.[5]

Hughes took investigating the agency of workers as a mission that called for serious ethnographic engagement. Within the interactionist tradition, Hughes spurred a methodological reorientation from Blumer's modus operandi of reflecting on organizations more abstractly to studying interaction in work as an empirical imperative. Although Hughes did not object to quantitative work, he noted, 'the meanings of work are many, not all included in the usual questionnaires and classifications' ([1952] 1984: 299). He argued that researchers must be embedded in work situations in order to learn how people interpret their work. Hughes supervised a wave of fieldwork dissertations that covered occupations ranging from janitors to jazz musicians. The dissertations, articles, and books that flowed from his students established ethnography as a legitimate means for studying organizations.

Hughes prioritized the importance of interaction in researching organizations by defining work situations as 'Systems of interaction, as the setting of the role, drama of work, in which people of various occupational and lay capacities, involved in differing complexes of *lebenschancen*, interact in sets of relationships that are social and technical' ([1959] 1984: 294). He called for a broad approach to the sociological study of work, identifying generic organizational activities that occur across work sites, such as mistakes, professionalization, secrets, status, and maintaining the respectability of one's work. Hughes also emphasized the importance of comparing and contrasting different types of work across history, geography, peoples, and nations, an argument that became important in the 'constant comparative method' of grounded theory (Glaser and Strauss 1967). Hughes believed in the value of induction, a cornerstone of the ethnographic method. He argued that researchers could develop generalizable concepts that touched on multiple professions by examining the details of a single profession, as obtained through in-depth observation.

Hughes's comparative investigations often generated Weberian ideal-type descriptions of work and work roles. For example, Hughes wrote of the 'straw boss' who 'understands the language, the symbols and meanings of the industrial world

[5] Hughes taught at the University of Chicago from 1938 to 1961.

and translates it into symbols which have meaning to people from another culture who live in a different set of life-chances' ([1949] 1984: 83). Hughes's 'straw boss' was hired to translate the bureaucratic dictates of industrialists to local workers. The straw boss was a necessary figure of control in settings where work involved people from different cultural backgrounds. In this regard, Hughes presciently addressed a mode of worker control in imminent globalization—the person who can get across the industrial language of the first world to control and manage poor workers from the second and third worlds. The 'straw boss' gives flesh to vague processes of 'coercive' and 'mimetic' isomorphism through which industrial pressures compel organizations to conform to their environments, and, in doing so, promotes homogeneity across organizations—a key concern of organizational sociology in the 'new institutional' idiom.

Hughes warrants rereading on the basis of his early, astute identifications and analyses of issues that are contemporary sociological concerns, such as race and human rights. He emphasized the connection between race and work, presaging later sociological involvement in civil rights issues. Hughes was ahead of the times in studying these issues empirically, and he examined exploitation by race, ethnic, and religious divisions in locales as diverse as South Africa, Canada, the United States, and pre- and post-war Germany.

Hughes also developed the idea of 'bastard institutions', a term that describes illegitimate distributors of many illegal goods and services. His call to investigate the actual functions of such institutions as a form of work presages a present renaissance in that topic, most notably in the recent bestsellers by Stephen Dubner and Steven Levitt (*Freakonomics*) and Sudhir Venkatesh (*Off the Books: The Underground Economy of the Urban Poor*), that expose the underground economy of drug dealers, prostitutes, and gang members—bastard institutions of our day.

Hughes also focused attention on moral agency among individuals within organizations. He recognized that work is constituted through a local culture that is separated from the public and emphasized how the desire to see one's work, occupation, and organization as moral and upright shapes what information is shared with others. Having to organize a moral presentation of one's work is also necessary because all occupations require some 'dirty work'. Hughes addressed the necessity of doing and legitimating dirty work as a generic feature of all occupations: 'It is hard to imagine an occupation in which one does not appear, in certain repeated contingencies to be practically compelled to play a role of which he thinks he ought to be a little ashamed morally' ([1951*b*] 1984: 343). As a result of this universal need to legitimate stigmatized actions, Hughes wrote, 'People do develop collective pretensions to give their work, and consequently themselves, value in the eyes of themselves and others.' Hughes referred to this practice as offering *dignifying rationalizations* (ibid. 340). Hughes directly addressed the need to legitimate discrediting work as an interpretive exercise with consequences for the status and moral standing of workers. His argument foreshadows Goffman in noting, 'There goes with prestige a tendency to preserve a front which hides the inside of things' (ibid. 342).

In 'Good People and Dirty Work', Hughes asked the important question: 'Are pariahs who do the dirty work of society... really acting as agents for the rest of us?' ([1962] 1984: 93). Here Hughes operated at his most macrosociological level, focusing on how social groups can exculpate themselves from moral responsibility for horrible dirty work by ignoring their silent connivance in encouraging a class of workers to commit that work. Hughes raised this issue in an attempt to understand German complicity in and reaction to genocide. Hughes felt that there was nothing inherent about Germans or 'German-ness' that explained the practice and motives of genocide. Instead, Hughes argued that there is inevitably a class of people in societies who do 'dirty work', sometimes with the knowing and deliberately ignorant consent of others. Hughes emphasized that organizations have a seedy underside. This became a major theme of interest for Goffman and to symbolic interactionist studies of organizations in general, and it is regaining attention in contemporary work (Morrill, Zald, and Rao 2003; Shulman 2007; Vaughan 1999). Not only are organizational backstages inevitable, they are necessary in that they preserve the public good name of the organization (and the occupation) while preserving the efficient and competent doing of work. Work requires a public front that places the best face on the activity, while ensuring that the audience lacks full knowledge of how work gets done, preserving a measure of controlled expertise as well as 'a desired conception of one's work and hence of one's self' ([1951*b*] 1984: 340).

Hughes addressed a classic dilemma that emerges from workers self-identifying with their work roles. The desired conceptions of self that they wish to take from their work are subject to external mechanisms of social control that determine how individuals can work. As a consequence, the meanings workers attach to their work are not solely of their own making; they are subordinate to interpretations that organizations and other actors impose. Hence, workers are in constant battle with managers, clients, the public, and the state, over control of the interpretive meanings and environment of their work, and how others perceive them.

An ultimately critical theme for Hughes was to explore the informational control and autonomy of workers. How do workers structure and present the meaning of their work to others? How do organizations extend control over the interpretation and nature of organizational tasks? These questions represent the classic interactionist approach to organizations as one where sites of work are transformed analytically into interactions that reveal hidden agendas and the dynamics and meanings of presenting images to others. Goffman picked up and further developed these threads of control and organization of information in work settings, particularly in his work *Asylums*.

22.6. Erving Goffman and the Total Institution

Goffman (1922–1982) is arguably the most influential American sociologist of the twentieth century (see Manning 1992; Fine and Manning 2000; Burns 1992). As a microsociologist, his work, dripping with sensitizing concepts, engaging metaphor, and sarcasm is without peer, treating social interaction as a cross between ballet and drama. Throughout his career, Goffman attempted to understand how social life was possible, postulating the idea of an 'interaction order'. However, despite Goffman's explorations of the 'organization of everyday life', his work was not primarily concerned with how organizations operate. Goffman would, on occasion, discuss how individuals behave within organizations, but he was relatively unconcerned with how organizations behave. Goffman focused his lens on the dynamics of interactions: temporary, fleeting, evanescent. One could not fairly suggest—as one could not suggest of Mead, Blumer, or Hughes—that he established a rigorous set of organizational theories. At best Goffman provided the rudiments for an organizational sociology that others developed.

The one book of Goffman's in which organization per se plays an explicit and central role is *Asylums* (1961). In 1955 Goffman began fieldwork at St Elizabeths hospital in Washington, DC, a massive mental hospital, housing some 7,000 patients. Installed as the assistant to the athletic director, Goffman roamed the hospital grounds without attracting undue attention. The choice of St Elizabeths was propitious: the mental hospital provided Goffman with a highly structured setting in which he could associate with a sequestered group of organizational clients. Through his connections with the patients, Goffman could snipe at institutionalized authority and, in a Hughesian way, invert traditional hierarchies. Goffman focused on the characteristics of 'total institutions': settings where the staff seems to fully control the time and space of inmates.

St Elizabeths allowed Goffman to collect data for a critique of an institutional order. Manning (1997) has referred to *Asylums* as not simply an ethnography of St Elizabeths, but as an 'ethnography of the concept of the total institution'. As Fine and Martin (1990) note, Goffman gives no account of a typical day, and there is little information about the day-to-day operations of St Elizabeths. Instead, Goffman's observations explain how individuals carve out a modicum of freedom in the face of organizational control.

Asylums is foremost a comparative and theoretical work. Goffman's primary goal is to understand the organization of total institutional life, of which St Elizabeths is an example. *Asylums* consists of four essays. The first three are interrelated; they all examine the ordinary experiences of patients or inmates in total institutions. However, the fourth essay is quite different and sits uncomfortably with the other contributions. This essay is a theoretical examination of professional–client interaction. In it, Goffman isolates the unique elements of psychiatrist–client interaction, in order to show the 'grotesque' predicament of the mentally ill under organizational constraint.

Most of *Asylums* deals with the pre-patient and in-patient phases. In the second essay, Goffman offers a subtle account of the process whereby a person who behaves 'strangely' can become a candidate for institutionalization. Although he does not provide a clear empirical basis for his argument, Goffman persuasively discusses the 'betrayal funnel' through which unwitting pre-patients discover that the people in whom they have invested the most trust are the same people who report their actions to institutional authorities. This moment is filled with pathos for pre-patients because they witness their families and friends hanging up the phone when they walk in the room, changing topics, and meeting secretly. This informal network of concerned people benignly deceive the pre-patient, refusing to talk to him or her openly, often until they recommend to the pre-patient that a visit to a doctor might be helpful, unable even then to avoid this euphemistic reference to a psychiatrist. The unintended consequence of the behavior of concerned friends is that the old adage that 'just because you're paranoid doesn't mean they're not out to get you' rings true. Ultimately pre-patients are passed on to a 'circuit of agents'—social workers, officers of the criminal justice system, psychiatrists, and others—who assess the viability and desirability of institutionalization.

Once institutionalized, patients are exposed to 'batch living' and the tightly regimented life typical of any total institution. The staff has extensive control of time and space, upheld with carefully planned schedules and surveillance. The result is *civil death* (1961: 25) or as Goffman sometimes puts it a *mortification of self* (1961: 31). New patients are efficiently transformed from civilian outsiders into hospital products: they are supplied with clothes, familiar names are dropped, and they are disciplined so as to accept the authority of staff members. At St Elizabeths, a ward system punished uncooperative patients by confining them to poor living conditions, from which they could only move gradually to a ward that afforded them a greater comfort.

Over time, St Elizabeths, like other total institutions, offered privileges to patients who accepted their diminished roles. These consisted of minor rewards, such as cups of coffee or access to newspapers. The result 'is that cooperativeness is obtained from persons who often have cause to be uncooperative' (1961: 54). An unintended consequence is that patients had a diminished sense of self-worth, as they discovered that they would accept trivial rewards to upgrade to moderately oppressive conditions. In this sense, the total institution accomplished its mission as a 'forcing house' for changing persons because outside its walls patients would be unlikely to cooperate in return for small-time rewards. In different ways and means, both the mortification of self and the privilege system undermine the patients' sense of self. In many different total institutions ranging from concentration camps to monasteries, neophytes experience severe attacks on their core self-conception.

In response, patients learn to resist the pull of the total institution without directly confronting it. Goffman identified four strategies of resistance, which he referred to idiomatically as 'playing it cool'. The first strategy, situational withdrawal, involves intensive daydreaming as a means of escaping or absenting oneself from the total institution. The second strategy is to establish an intransigent line that if breached triggers uncooperative behavior. This is a means whereby inmates demonstrate a measure of control over their lives by telling themselves (if no one else) that they can only be pushed so far. The intransigent line is always provisional and subject to revision. At its limit, it may involve a hunger strike, but Goffman points out that staff may try to break the intransigent prisoner—in a mental hospital doing so may take the form of electro-shock treatment (1961: 62). The third strategy is colonization, during which inmates play up whatever positive features they can identify in the total institution. Goffman indicates that inmates who have experienced several different total institutions reapply familiar adaptive techniques, whereby a home of sorts is made of a restrictive environment. Although these types of practices do not threaten the institutional order, they 'allow inmates to obtain forbidden satisfactions' and a sense of self-autonomy (1961: 54). In contrast, the fourth strategy, conversion, involves either the inmate's acceptance or the pretense of acceptance of the institution's ideology: 'the inmate appears to take over the official or staff view of himself and tries to act out the role of the perfect inmate' (1961: 63).

Goffman argued that the similarities between inmate experiences in different total institutions are both glaring and persistent (1962: 115), such that the apparent antics of the institutionalized mentally ill are misunderstood as symptoms of underlying disorders and better understood as extensively practiced adjustments to trying and threatening circumstances. Goffman made this point forcefully:

> The impression may be given, therefore, that patients throughout the day fitfully engaged in childish tricks and foolhardy gestures to better their lot, and that there is nothing inconsistent between this pathetic display and our traditional notions of mental patients being 'ill'... in actual practice almost all of the secondary adjustments I have reported were carried on by the patient with an air of intelligent down-to-earth determination, sufficient, once the full context was known, to make an outsider feel at home, in a community much more similar to others he has known than different from them. (1961: 266)

Asylums demonstrates both the power of organizations and the power of an interactionist analysis of their operation and outcomes. Yet, *Asylums* is not a critique of an organization as such. It examines how organizational actors create and avoid local status and meaning systems. A detailed consideration of *Asylums* demonstrates the variety of outcomes that the give-and-take between individual autonomy and organizational control can have. In the inhabited institutional approach, the limits and possibilities of agency under organizational control are complex, and in total institutions individual agency confronts strict organizational limits and either adjusts or collapses.

Goffman's analysis was so powerful, in fact, that some argue that it (along with Fredrick Wiseman's 1967 documentary film *Titicut Follies*) was instrumental in deinstitutionalization. This was ironic because Goffman was famously unconcerned with using his critiques of social order to improve the lot of his fellow citizens. Goffman once asserted,

> The analysis developed does not catch at the differences between the advantaged and disadvantaged classes and can be said to direct attention away from such matters. I think that is true. I can only suggest that he who would combat false consciousness and awaken people to their true interests has much to do, because the sleep is very deep. And I do not intend here to provide a lullaby but merely to sneak in and watch the way the people snore.
>
> (1974: 14)

Goffman's mantra could not differ more from Mead's, but his cynicism went further to awake the masses than did Mead's optimism.

Intentions aside, Goffman's contribution to organizational theory was to show how institutions could impact our actions and selves. Goffman replaces Blumer's 'neutral' view of institutions with a potentially oppressive one, and yet, in the next moment he skillfully demonstrates that those ostensibly under institutional control have resources left to them, providing for what later was described under the rubric of 'weapons of the weak' (Scott 1987). Even total institutions are never totalizing in their effects. This point provides an enduring basis for analyzing how people and their interactions *inhabit* organizations, ranging from mental hospitals to elementary schools.

22.7. Strauss, Becker, and *Boys in White*

An account of the utility of classic interactionism, even one as cursory as ours, must include some discussion of the contributions of Anselm Strauss and Howard Becker. Interactionists have been fortunate in the longevity of their theorists; they start publishing early in their careers and continue throughout their work lives. Anselm Strauss contributed to sociology for over a half-century and Howard Becker for close to sixty years without an end in sight. But more than longevity, these writers have been a font of conceptual development, far more than we can do justice to here. Becker and Strauss both take the interactionist tack of seeing organizations as arenas that produce and constrain actions and are shaped by them. They developed concepts that address how organizations label those who respond in inappropriate ways (Becker 1963)—and the effects that such labeling has on the future opportunities of those so labeled, as well as how organizations control information to shape the responses of those under their control, providing awareness contexts for organizational control (Glaser and Strauss 1965).

Given space constraints, we examine a single work, *Boys in White: Student Culture in Medical School*, a collaborative ethnography by Becker, Blanche Geer, Hughes, and Strauss (1961). This classic ethnography provides an exceptionally fruitful instance of how interactionists approach the analysis of organizations as behavioral and cultural systems. Working with the University of Kansas Medical School, the authors explored how student cultures, as generated through the requirements set by the institution and their own expectations, created patterns of behavior that were unexpected in light of the institution's publicly held values. In particular, the authors address the 'fate of idealism', asking how institutional pressures transformed the moral imaginings of the students into pragmatic choices and transformed them as individuals into laborers who had to discover strategies for coping with a workload that they—and often their mentors—felt was unmanageable. Students were forced to create make-dos and work-arounds, which altered their idealism into a sometimes brittle cynicism, but allowed them to see that, following Hughes, medicine involved dirty work and created backstage awareness contexts: information became a resource, a form of power. Medicine, at this time in the 1950s, was premised on the fact that doctors and families could access knowledge from which patients should be shielded.

What makes this analysis so powerful is that these students came into medical school with the naive hopefulness of the patient, only to learn that this was not—entirely—how doctors had to manage their professional life: doing it efficiently took priority over doing it right. The organizational task then was to create the conditions under which the students could regain some of their idealism while, simultaneously, practicing medicine as it needed to be practiced given institutional demands. An ongoing struggle existed between the forces that demand conformity and those that counsel individual action. These approaches are very much in accord with the perspective of Hughes and of Goffman (and those of Davis 1963 and Roth 1963).

The reality that these aspiring doctors could be broken and then reassembled—moral but practical—indicates the power of institutions to shape selves, not less than the mental institutions described by Goffman. And yet, as with Goffman, social interaction remains as a font of creativity, as it was in their interactions with each other that the medical students created a peer culture suited for organizing their experiences and dealing with the problem of an oppressive workload. The medical student culture consisted of three perspectives that evolved over time: the initial perspective (an effort to 'learn it all'), the provisional perspective ('you can't do it all'), and the final perspective ('what they want us to know'). These students were not institutional dopes, and this classic analysis forces us to rethink contemporary models of professional socialization that are top-down and deterministic. Instead, *Boys in White* suggests a model similar to Corsaro's (2005) interactionist analysis of interpretive reproduction in childhood: socialization was not something that happened to these students; rather, it was a process in which the students interacted, created their own peer cultures, and eventually reproduced the medical profession. Professional socialization is also an inhabited arena.

22.8. Conclusion

As invigorating as it is to re-engage classic texts, we temper our zeal by acknowledging the shortcomings of classic interactionism. For all of his strengths, Mead's optimism about human action became manifest in a rather naive discussion of institutions in the 'society' portion of his famous lectures, *Mind, Self, and Society*. For all of the face validity of Blumer's three premises of symbolic interactionism, he is mostly known for his polemic against the macrostructuralism of his day (Blumer 1931, 1954, 1956, 1969). Blumer was a trenchant critic, and his tone may have done more to stigmatize symbolic interactionism than to validate it, perhaps marginalizing subsequent works by Anselm Strauss and Howard Becker (associated today with the 'negotiated order' or 'social worlds' approach) that have not received their due in organizational studies (Barley 2008).[6] For all of his pioneering empirical studies of work, his rich concepts, and his mentoring of students, Hughes neglected to build a holistic theory of organizations. Finally, despite his virtuoso analyses of asylums and total institutions, Goffman is mostly known for his provocative, if not cynical, discussion of the self and its presentation, robbing his legacy of a more prominent place in organizational sociology. His unwillingness to engage with either macrosociologists or agents of change placed the Goffmanian oeuvre outside of the boundaries of organizational sociology.

The organization is both an independent and autonomous shaping force and an arena for action. It is the relationship between these two elements that provides for a rich analysis of organizational life. If the interactionist tradition primarily focused upon the latter of these two elements, it provided as rich an interpretation of that element as has been suggested, and in this way it stands as essential, if incomplete. Interactionists have long been interested in what goes on within organizations, and from this feature of the interactionism of the past, we can continue to build an inhabited institutionalism for the future.

[6] Barley makes a persuasive case for the utility of this later interactionist work for current organizational studies.

Acknowledgments

We thank Howard Becker and Lonnie Athens for their comments.

References

Abbott, A. (1988). *The System of Professions*. Chicago: University of Chicago Press.

—— (1999). *Department and Discipline: Chicago Sociology at One Hundred*. Chicago: University of Chicago Press.

—— and Gaziano, E. (1995). 'Transition and Tradition: Departmental Faculty in the Era of the Second Chicago School', in G. A. Fine (ed.), *A Second Chicago School?* Chicago: University of Chicago Press.

Athens, L. (2002). ' "Domination": The Blind Spot in Mead's Analysis of the Social Act'. *Journal of Classical Sociology*, 2/1: 25–42.

—— (2005). 'Mead's Lost Conception of Society'. *Symbolic Interaction*, 28: 305–25.

—— (2007). 'Radical Interactionism: Going Beyond Mead'. *Journal for the Theory of Social Behavior*, 37/2: 137–65.

Barley, S. R. (2008). 'Coalface Institutionalism', in R. Greenwood, C. Oliver, R. Suddaby, and K. Sahlin-Andersson (eds.), *The Sage Handbook of Organizational Institutionalism*. Newbury Park, Calif.: Sage.

Becker, H. (1963). *Outsiders*. Glencoe, Ill.: Free Press.

—— (1986). *Doing Things Together*. Evanston, Ill.: Northwestern University Press.

—— Geer, B., Hughes, E. C., and Strauss, A. L. (1961). *Boys in White*. Chicago: University of Chicago Press.

Binder, A. (2007). 'For Love and Money: Organizations' Creative Responses to Multiple Environmental Logics'. *Theory and Society*, 36: 547–71.

Blumer, H. (1931). 'Science without Concepts'. *American Journal of Sociology*, 36/4: 515–33.

—— (1936). 'Social Attitudes and Nonsymbolic Interaction'. *Journal of Educational Sociology*, 9/9: 515–23.

—— (1940). 'The Problem of the Concept in Social Psychology'. *American Journal of Sociology*, 45/5: 707–19.

—— (1947). 'Sociological Theory in Industrial Relations'. *American Sociological Review*, 12/3: 271–8.

—— (1954). 'What is Wrong with Social Theory?' *American Sociological Review*, 19/1: 3–10.

—— (1956). 'Sociological Analysis and the "Variable" '. *American Sociological Review*, 21/6: 683–90.

—— (1960). 'Early Industrialization and the Laboring Class'. *Sociological Quarterly*, 1/1: 5–14.

—— (1966). 'Sociological Implications of the Thought of George Herbert Mead'. *American Journal of Sociology*, 71/5: 535–44.

—— (1969). *Symbolic Interactionism: Perspective and Method*. Berkeley: University of California Press.

—— (1977). 'Comment on Lewis' "The Classic American Pragmatists as Forerunners to Symbolic Interactionism" '. *Sociological Quarterly*, 18/2: 285–9.

BLUMER, H. (1990). *Industrialization as an Agent of Social Change*. New York: Aldine de Gruyter.

BURNS, T. (1992). *Erving Goffman*. New York: Routledge.

COLOMY, P. (1998). 'Neofunctionalism and Neoinstitutionalism: Human Agency and Interest in Institutional Change'. *Sociological Forum*, 13/2: 265–300.

CORSARO, W. A. (2005). *The Sociology of Childhood*. 2nd edn. Thousand Oaks, Ill.: Pine Forge Press.

DAVIS, F. (1963). *Passage through Crisis: Polio Victims and their Families*. Indianapolis: Bobbs-Merrill.

DIMAGGIO, P. (1988). 'Interest and Agency in Institutional Theory', in L. Zucker (ed.), *Institutional Patterns and Organizations: Culture and Environment*. Cambridge, Mass.: Ballinger.

—— (1997). 'Culture and Cognition'. *Annual Review of Sociology*, 23: 263–87.

FINE, G. A. (1995). *A Second Chicago School?* Chicago: University of Chicago Press.

—— (1996). *Kitchens: The Culture of Restaurant Work*. Berkeley: University of California Press.

—— and MANNING, P. (2000). 'Erving Goffman', in G. Ritzer (ed.), *Blackwell Companion to Major Social Theorists*. Oxford: Blackwell.

—— and MARTIN, D. D. (1990). 'A Partisan View: Sarcasm, Satire, and Irony as Voices in Erving Goffman's *Asylums*'. *Journal of Contemporary Ethnography*, 19: 89–115.

FLIGSTEIN, N. (2001). 'Social Skill and the Theory of Fields'. *Sociological Theory*, 19: 105–25.

GIDDENS, A. (1984). *The Constitution of Society*. Berkeley: University of California Press.

GLASER, B. G., and STRAUSS, A. L. (1965). *Awareness of Dying*. Chicago: Aldine Publishing Company.

—— —— (1967). *The Discovery of Grounded Theory*. New York: Aldine de Gruyter.

GOFFMAN, E. (1961). *Asylums*. New York: Doubleday.

—— (1974). *Frame Analysis*. Boston: Northeastern University Press.

GOULDNER, A. (1954). *Patterns of Industrial Bureaucracy*. Glencoe, Ill.: Free Press.

—— (1955). 'Metaphysical Pathos and the Theory of Bureaucracy'. *American Political Science Review*, 49: 496–507.

GUSFIELD, J. R. (1995). 'Preface', in G. A. Fine (ed.), *A Second Chicago School?* Chicago: University of Chicago Press.

HALLETT, T., and VENTRESCA, M. (2006). 'Inhabited Institutions: Social Interactions and Organizational Forms in Gouldner's *Patterns of Industrial Bureaucracy*'. *Theory and Society*, 35/2: 213–36.

HIRSCH, P. M., and LOUNSBURY, M. (1997). 'Putting the Organization Back into Organization Theory: Action, Change, and the "New" Institutionalism'. *Journal of Management Inquiry*, 6/1: 79–88.

HUGHES, E. C. ([1949] 1984). 'Queries Concerning Industry and Society Growing Out of Study of Ethnic Relations in Industry', in Hughes (1984).

—— ([1951*a*] 1984). 'Mistakes at Work', in Hughes (1984).

—— ([1951*b*] 1984). 'Work and Self', in Hughes (1984).

—— ([1952] 1984). 'The Sociological Study of Work: An Editorial Foreword', in Hughes (1984).

—— ([1959] 1984). 'The Study of Occupations', in Hughes (1984).

—— ([1962] 1984). 'Good People and Dirty Work', in Hughes (1984).

—— ([1970] 1984). 'The Humble and the Proud: The Comparative Study of Occupations', in Hughes (1984).

—— (ed.) (1984). *The Sociological Eye: Selected Papers.* New Brunswick, NJ: Transaction Press.

Lewis, J. D., and Smith, R. (1980). *American Society and Pragmatism.* Chicago: University of Chicago Press.

Lovejoy, A. O. (1948). *The Great Chain of Being.* Cambridge, Mass.: Harvard University Press.

Maines, D. R., and Morrione, T. J. (1990). 'On the Breadth and Relevance of Blumer's Perspective: Introduction to his Analysis of Industrialization', in D. R. Maines and T. J. Morrione (eds.), *Industrialization as an Agent of Social Change.* New York: Aldine de Gruyter.

Manning, P. (1992). *Erving Goffman and Modern Sociology.* Cambridge: Polity Press.

—— (1997). 'Erving Goffman', in J. A. Garrity and M. C. Carnes (eds.), *American National Biography.* Oxford: Oxford University Press.

Mead, G. H. (1908–9). 'Industrial Education, the Working-Man, and the School'. *Elementary School Teacher,* 9: 369–83.

—— (1932). *The Philosophy of the Present.* Chicago: London Open Court Publishing Company.

—— (1934). *Mind, Self, and Society.* Chicago: University of Chicago Press.

Miller, D. L. (1973). *George Herbert Mead: Self, Language, and the World.* Chicago: University of Chicago Press.

Morrill, C., Zald, M. N., and Rao, H. (2003). 'Covert Political Conflict in Organizations: Challenges from Below'. *Annual Review of Sociology,* 29: 391–415.

Morris, C. W. (1962). 'Introduction: George H. Mead as Social Psychologist and Social Philosopher', in C. W. Morris (ed.), *Mind, Self, and Society.* Chicago: University of Chicago Press.

Roth, J. A. (1963). *Timetables: Structuring the Passage of Time in Hospital Treatment and Other Careers.* Indianapolis: Bobbs-Merrill.

Scott, J. C. (1987). *Weapons of the Weak.* New Haven: Yale University Press.

Scott, W. R. (2001). *Institutions and Organizations.* Thousand Oaks, Calif.: Sage Publications.

Scully, M., and Creed, D. (1997). 'Stealth Legitimacy: Employee Activism and Corporate Response during the Diffusion of Domestic Partner Benefits'. Paper presented at the Academy of Management Meetings, Boston, August.

Shulman, D. (2007). *From Liar to Hire: The Role of Deception in the Workplace.* Ithaca, NY: Cornell University Press.

Snow, D. A. (2001). 'Extending and Broadening Blumer's Conceptualization of Symbolic Interactionism'. *Symbolic Interaction,* 24/3: 367–77.

Stryker, S. (1980). *Symbolic Interactionism: A Social Structural Version.* Menlo Park, Calif.: Benjamin/Cummings.

Vaughan, D. (1999). 'The Dark Side of Organizations: Mistake, Misconduct, and Disaster'. *Annual Review of Sociology,* 25: 271–305.

Veblen, T. (1898). *Theory of the Leisure Class.* New York: Macmillan.

Zucker, L. G. (1977). 'The Role of Institutionalization in Cultural Persistence'. *American Sociological Review,* 42: 726–43.

CHAPTER 23

JOHN R. COMMONS

BACK TO THE FUTURE OF ORGANIZATION STUDIES

ANDREW H. VAN DE VEN
ARIK LIFSCHITZ

THE resurgence of interest in the design and change of institutions has increased the importance of the institutional theory of John R. Commons.[1] Recognized as a founder of both institutional economics (Chamberlain 1963; Rutherford 1983) and industrial relations (Barbash 1989; Kochan 1980), John R. Commons was a pioneer of ideas that merit serious consideration by organizational scholars. Commons contributed original ideas for developing a pragmatic and volitional theory of institutions that addresses: (1) the role of institutions in structuring social behavior between interdependent and conflicting individuals, (2) the micro–macro link of how the purposes and actions of individuals construct and are constrained by collective action, and (3) how institutional change emerges not from environmental forces, nor simply for efficiency considerations, but from resolutions to strategic problems in social relationships between individuals and between groups of individuals based on a collectively defined norm of prudent, reasonable behavior.

[1] This chapter is an extension of a review of the institutional theory of John R. Commons by Van de Ven (1993) and an application of Commons's work to contemporary issues in organizational theory. We greatly appreciate useful comments on an earlier draft from Paul Adler, Paul Hirsch, Thorbjorn Knudsen, and Sean Safford, as well as helpful editorial assistance from Julie Trupke.

Born in 1862, Commons began his graduate studies at the age of 26 at Johns Hopkins University working as an assistant to Richard T. Ely. Although he never actually completed a Ph.D., the experience at Johns Hopkins left a lasting mark on Commons's future work. 'At Johns Hopkins I learned a lot about political economy,' writes Commons in his autobiography. 'I had always supposed that political economy was a deductive science of economic theory.... But Professor Ely set me at work visiting the building and loan association in Baltimore, and joining the Charity Organization Society as a "case worker"'. Commons goes on to describe how he spent a year getting a pension for an ailing Civil War veteran: 'I visited the pension office, interviewed lawyers, attached myself to the Democratic congressman from Baltimore where the sympathies were with the Confederate soldiers. I got the pension. Was this political economy?' (Commons 1934*b*: 42–3).

Commons's career before and after this event suggests that to him the answer was a resounding 'yes'. During the next years, Commons taught at various universities until he joined the University of Wisconsin in 1904. At Wisconsin, Commons trained a host of prominent students, many of whom shared his dissent against static, deductive economic thought (Harter 1965). But Commons did not limit his ideas to the classroom. He was an engaged scholar who ventured into an amazing variety of fields in his ever-expanding roles as a printer, union member, investigator, administrator, and counselor to public officials during his career. His contributions on legislation and public policy involved civil service reform, factory legislation, workers' compensation, unemployment insurance, small-loan interest-rate control, rural credit and taxation measures, inheritance taxation, property assessment laws, immigrant laws, and monetary policy, in addition to his better known industrial relations contributions of labor history, labor conciliation, and industrial commissions.

Out of this vast treasury of experiences and engagements, Commons developed a grounded and novel institutional perspective. His work shares many commonalities with that of Thorstein Veblen and other institutionalists, but differs from them in important ways. Like Veblen and other pragmatists of his era, Commons considered the importance of habits and customs in stabilizing economic action. However, while Veblen emphasized the inertial nature of economic institutions, Commons believed that institutional adaptation is constant, if incrementally so, as a result of a volitional, cooperative process. Commons highlighted the role of conflict—and its collective resolution—in the generation and adaptation of institutions. Many decades after its inception, Commons's unique view of institutional change has yet to receive the attention it deserves among organizational scholars. Our hope is that this chapter will encourage others to revisit some of these powerful ideas to further the field of organization studies.

This chapter focuses on a review of *The Economics of Collective Action* (first published posthumously in 1950 with the editorial assistance of Kenneth H. Parsons). It is logically the first book in understanding Commons's thought, for in it Commons presented a simplified statement of issues that he had argued more fully in *The Legal Foundations of Capitalism* (1924) and *Institutional Economics* (1934*a*). Although complex and difficult to comprehend in a single reading, the work of Commons provides a treasury of suggestions for those who seek insight and inspiration in dealing with issues of institutional innovation and change. This chapter presents our interpretation of the work of John R. Commons and its relevance for current developments in organization studies. The first part of the chapter summarizes Commons's pioneering perspective on institutions and institutional change, as we understand it. Based on this review, we discuss some implications of Commons's ideas for advancing contemporary approaches to the study of organizations.

23.1. Commons's Perspective on Institutions and Institutional Change

In *The Economics of Collective Action* (1950), Commons portrayed society as a complex social organization rather than as an organism or a mechanism driven either by natural external forces or an automatically self-correcting system. A social organization, Commons argued, consists of purposeful individuals whose wills conflict and whose actions are interdependent under conditions of scarcity. Accordingly, a central problem of collective action is control of the differential powers of participants to exercise their individual wills on others. In the absence of institutionalized constraints, conflicts will be resolved by private violence to the detriment of productive efficiency and human justice. Order and security of expectations are achieved by devising *working rules* (i.e. institutions) that define the limits within which individuals and firms may exercise their own wills and powers. Historical customs, common practices, and laws of 'prudent reasonable behavior' are used to collectively devise these institutions. Without an institutionalized system of rules to create a degree of order and certainty or 'security of expectations', there could be 'little or no present value, present enterprise, present transactions, or present employment' (Commons 1950: 104).

For Commons, individual actions within collective action were the core phenomena to be explained. Individuals are not self-sufficient, independent entities, and society is not the summation of individual members. The organized forms of collective action include the states, political parties, courts, firms, unions, churches, and the like. The norms, customs, and laws that regulate and provide security of expectations to the actions of individuals and organizations are the 'working rules of collective action'. These working rules pertain to the rights and duties of individuals and organizations. 'An institution is collective action in control, liberation, and expansion of individual action' (Commons 1950: 21). Collective action controls individual action through physical, moral, or economic sanctions. Institutions do not simply constrain; they also liberate and expand individual action. Liberation for some individuals (e.g. from coercion, duress, or discrimination) may be achieved by constraining the acts of others. Commons emphasized that individual freedom is not a natural right; he viewed it as a collective achievement. 'The only way in which "liberty" can be obtained is by imposing duties on others who might interfere with the activity of the "liberated" individual.... Thus, collective action is literally the means to liberty' (Commons 1950: 35).

But just as institutions constrain, liberate, and expand individual action, individuals construct and change institutions. As discussed further in the implications section, Commons rejected natural selection and replaced it with *artificial* (i.e. 'purposeful') *selection*, noting that individuals adapt their environments to their own needs and purposes. He argued that individuals have capabilities, in their own nature, of molding natural and institutional forces around them. As a consequence, institutional evolution is subject to individual volition, purpose, and morality.

Commons provided three amazingly operational concepts for examining the human will in action: *performance*, *avoidance*, and *forbearance*. 'In choosing, which includes acting, the will is purposeful—forward looking. The will is always up against something. It is always performing, avoiding, forbearing, that is, always moving along lines... with a purpose looking toward the future' (Commons 1950: 79). An individual performs by undertaking a behavioral act, which is limited or constrained by avoidance and forbearance. Avoidance is a choice to omit all alternative courses of action other than the one chosen. Although some alternatives may be avoided because of institutional rules or constraints of nature, the individual has the freedom to choose from a remaining set of alternatives available to him or her. Within the direction of the alternative chosen, performance is further modified by forbearance (or the degree of power exercised at the 'right' time, place, and degree). Forbearance is self-restraint in action either with nature or in transactions with others. 'The human will does not override natural laws, but makes use of them in accomplishing its purposes' (Commons 1950: 193). Unlike physical forces (e.g. gravity) that always go to the limit, individuals place constraints on their performances by avoiding and forbearing in the exercise of their full power, except in times of crises. In Commons's framework, these times of crises revolved around exceptional cases that triggered opportunities for institutional change. They occurred when individuals were engaged in strategic (i.e. novel or disputed) transactions to gain control over 'limiting factors' (i.e. the crucial resources or procedures that prevented otherwise routine transactions from working to bring about the results they intended).

Commons offered a dialectical and pragmatic view of institutional change. As in common law and jurisprudence, Commons viewed institutional change (i.e. new or modified working rules of a society) as produced by an accretion of numerous pragmatic decisions and temporary procedures for resolving disputes between conflicting parties. Institutional working rules change incrementally over time as a result of precedents. These precedents are established when the validity of transactions among contesting parties is questioned and judged by arbitrators or courts of law to be legal or illegal, given what a 'prudent reasonable man' would do under the new set of circumstances. Procedures for due process and appeal not only resolve disputes between plaintiffs and defendants, but they also (and more significantly) set precedents for resolving future similar disputes. Precedents thereby become the customs and the laws for the repetition of activities by which expectations are made secure.

The detailed analysis of how individual and collective actions lead to and are constrained by institutional changes is contained in Commons's treatment of transactions. To motivate an appreciation of transaction as the basic unit of analysis, Commons addresses the pragmatic question: How can individuals go about making a living in a world of scarcity, interdependence, and conflict of interest? He answers by observing that '[t]his is an age of collective action. Most individuals must work and live collectively as participants in organizations in order to earn a living. In this collective process, persons engage in [transactions], for this is the way individual wills meet and become a part of the collective will' (Commons 1950: 23).

Thus, out of the great seamless web of activities and social relationships among persons in society, Commons fixed upon the *transaction* as the elemental unit of analysis. A transaction joins the three inescapable elements of conflict of interest (arising out of scarcity), interdependence of interests (arising out of the need for exchange), and order or compromise (arising out of the need for establishing a system of working rules and expectations as the basis for exchange). As Chamberlain (1963: 73) observed, 'Scratch any social relationship, and you will find that it involves all of these three elements.' In contrast to economists' traditional focus on the product as the basic building block, or an individual's pleasure–pain sentiments regarding it, Commons took his cue from common law and the courts, where economic decisions start with a conflict of interest between transactors that has to be resolved by an appeal to social rules.

Commons took a process view of transactions by examining the actions of parties as they negotiate, make commitments to, and administer their 'deals'. Table 23.1 illustrates these processes in three kinds of transactions. In the *negotiations* stage, joint (not individual) valuations are made by the parties through persuasion, argumentation, and threats in evaluating alternatives. In the *commitment* stage, 'the wills' of the parties meet by agreeing on the terms, conditions, and rules of a relationship. Finally, in the *administrative* stage, the rules of action are carried into effect; the parties give orders to their subordinates, buy materials, pay the amounts agreed upon, and otherwise administer whatever is needed to execute the agreement. Although these stages may occur almost simultaneously in simple transactions, the duration of each stage varies with the complexity and uncertainty of the

Table 23.1. Scope of transactions

Time sequence	Kinds of transactions (status of participants)		
	Bargaining (legal equals)	Managerial (legal superior and inferior)	Rationing (legal superior and inferior)
1. *Negotiational psychology* (inducements, intentions, purpose)	Persuasion or coercion	Command and obedience	Command and obedience
2. *Commitments for future action* (agreement, contracts, obligations, rules of action)	Debts of performance and payment	Production of wealth	Distribution of wealth
3. *Execution of the commitments* (administration, management, sovereignty)	Prices and quantities	Input and output	Budgets, taxes, price-fixing, wage-fixing

Source: Commons 1950: 57.

issues involved in the transaction and the nature of the working rules developed to govern the transaction among parties. Each stage of transacting requires conjoint valuations regardless of the form of the legal relationship the parties have with one another.

Bargaining transactions are used to deal with the transfer of property rights between parties who are equal before the law, but who may have greatly unequal economic or social power. In bargaining transactions (also commonly known as *market transactions*), the central issues of reasonableness relate to the question of how much coercion and disparity in social or economic power is tolerable between the parties.

Managerial transactions occur between parties who stand in the legal relations of superior and subordinate; the superior has the legal right to hire and fire, whereas the subordinate has the right to serve or quit at will. Also called a *hierarchical transaction*, this is a command-and-obedience relationship for the creation of economic goods and wealth. In this case, questions of reasonableness focus on the protection and enforcement of collectively defined rights for subordinates by the imposition of duties on the superior and vice versa.

Rationing transactions pertain to the distribution of benefits and burdens of the joint production of wealth among legal inferiors by command of a monopolized power without specific individual consent and bargaining. Reasonableness of rationing transactions is based on the equitable enforcement of taxes, budgets, and levies imposed by a sovereign power (the state) or its delegated agency (e.g. the board of directors of a firm).

Commons viewed these different forms of transactions as highly interdependent; they are separable only for analytical purposes. Bargaining (market) and managerial (hierarchical) transactions are related as limiting and complementary factors, respectively. 'As a bargainer, the modern wage earner is deemed to be the legal equal of his employer, induced to enter the transaction by persuasion or coercion; but once he is permitted to enter the place of employment he becomes legally inferior, induced by commands which he is required to obey' (Commons 1950: 353). Also, Commons stated that rationing transactions are executed by means of managerial transactions. 'Collective action in control of individuals becomes a hierarchy of collective action in control of the bargaining, managerial, and rationing transactions of individuals' (Commons 1950: 56–7).

Commons developed a far more dynamic and encompassing view of transactions than admitted to by current formulations of transaction cost theory. As his diagram of the scope of transactions illustrates (Table 23.1), Commons combined ideas from law, economics, and psychology to examine the temporal stages of negotiations, commitment, and execution for three types of transactions in which the standings between parties are of different legal status.

Commons used four key concepts or principles to link this formulation of transactions with a dynamic view of institutional change: scarcity, futurity, limiting factors, and reasonable value. Organizational scholars often have difficulty understanding these four concepts because few of them have training in common law and jurisprudence. In law and jurisprudence the meanings of the four concepts are embedded in a deep history and rich context of literature and practice. When these concepts are transferred and adopted by a different scholarly discipline, their meanings often do not transplant easily. The adopting community (in this case, organization institutional scholars) needs to gain an understanding of the context in which the concepts originated in order to appreciate their meanings. This requires a psychological attitude of tolerance and a behavioral motivation to study the source context of new concepts and their potential meaning and application in a new domain.

'*Scarcity* in economics is property in jurisprudence, and the rights and duties of property are the working rules of sovereignty in control of scarcity' (Commons 1950: 89). Commons traces the historical evolution of the meaning of property from the original common law conception of a physical corporeal thing held for one's own use to its current meaning of 'intangible property' in law, that is, withholding rights from others or what they need but do not own. This distinction between the thing itself and ownership of the thing being exchanged is central to an institutional analysis of property. The thing itself may be scarce (have value) in a physical sense, but it takes a property right to endow it with institutional scarcity. As Chamberlain (1963: 81) pointed out, 'A stolen object or asset is no less scarce for being stolen rather than purchased, but in a going society it acquires institutional meaning only when a transfer of title has been legalized.' Property rights are the social relations that the state vests in the owner of property. These rights are created by the imposition of duties upon other persons. To the extent that duties have been imposed upon other persons with respect to my property, I am in the status of security; their conformity gives me security commensurate with my rights to the property. But if other persons are under no obligation or duty to respect my property, I am exposed to their liberty to do as they please. Thus, when I buy property, I am really buying rights to property, which are expectations that the state will use its powers to support my claims to the property when and if my rights are violated. Again, these rights are institutionally defined and vested by the state in the owner of property.

The principle of *futurity*, which is central to Commons's volitional theory, relates to expectations and human willfulness. Negotiations among parties to alienate and acquire rights to property are based on expected values at a future time when the use value or exchange value of the property will be realized. More generally, Commons argued that purposes, values, and expected consequences are the grounds for human choices, which are made in the present to be realized in the future. If people are to enter into present commitments to engage in future courses of action (e.g. making investments, accepting jobs, making contracts, or paying taxes), they need some security or insurance that the terms of their transactions are enforceable. This security is necessary because in Commons's volitional theory, effects precede their cause—this is unlike the formula in the physical sciences where cause precedes effect. Transactions require parties to negotiate and commit to achieving expected consequences (the effects) in the present by undertaking a line of behavior (the cause) in the future. Enforcement of collective working rules provides individuals with a security of expectations. These working rules focus on the repetition of activities in which institutions create order and stabilize the wills of participants by defining the rights and duties of each. It is the similarity of activity in custom, norms, and law by which expectations are made secure.

The presence of a collective institutional order within which all transactions take place is easy to forget because most transactions are routine, repetitive, and not contested; hence, the potential intervention of institutional rules and enforcement agencies does not become obtrusive. For Commons, though, the test of his process framework for institutional change was not in these routine transactions; the test was in the *limiting factors*, when new transactions are negotiated or when disputes occur among transacting parties. Transactions involving the limiting factors incite human action—they are strategic; those that recur without attention are routine. In the flow of time for a firm, first one transaction and then another becomes strategic, only to pass over into routine for some period of time.

Commons emphasized strategic transactions, for they are the generative mechanisms for establishing customs, resolving conflicts of interests, and establishing working rules. The strategic transaction represents the dynamic element, the transaction that alters the set of incentives or constraints that affect routine transactions. Commons observed that although a static equilibrium analysis might focus on the efficiency of alternative forms of routine transactions within existing institutional arrangements, a dynamic analysis of strategic transactions centers attention on the wills, social psychology, and power of contesting parties as they attempt to affect and alter the working rules of collective action. Individuals and firms do not necessarily accept the legal or institutional status quo. They are active and attempt, through strategic transactions, to exercise their wills to increase their expectations of beneficial routine transactions, whether managerial, bargaining, or rationing in nature (Rutherford 1983).

Commons brings these concepts of scarcity, futurity, and limiting factors together when he uses *reasonable behavior* (discussed in the next section) as the criterion for evaluating transactions. Scarcity and a resulting conflict of interest are Commons's basic premises. Scarcity finds its expression in property title, and conflict between individuals and groups takes the form of negotiations over the terms on which the title will be transferred (except in those situations where legal authority determines the issue by rationing transactions). Thus, property ownership involves the power to withhold goods or services from use by others, a power that can be employed to win concessions of other parties to a potential transaction.

Commons pointed out that any bargaining transaction actually involves five parties: two potential buyers and two sellers to determine the future value of a transaction plus an institutional authority—a manager, an arbitrator, a court—that will apply and enforce a standard of reasonable behavior to circumscribe the limits of opportunities and powers of exchanging parties (Leblebici 1985). Because any transaction involves future values and future behavior, and because the transacting parties are assumed to be self-interested participants with conflicts of interest and uncertain foresight, an agreement reached by the parties may lack the needed quality of being self-enforcing. Commons recognized the crucial role of a fifth party, a sovereignty, an institutional actor who is the ultimate guarantor for deciding and settling disputes by applying a standard of 'prudent reasonable behavior'.

For Commons, the line between reasonable and unreasonable behavior was not drawn from any broad social philosophy or public principle. It was 'hammered out' pragmatically on a case-by-case basis in the resolution by an arbitrator, an executive, a board, or (and this for Commons was crucial) finally, by the courts of law up to the Supreme Court. After private parties failed to resolve an issue, the judicial authority of the state would resolve the question. Thus, for Commons, reasonable value was ultimately determined in a court decision of what is a fair and equitable settlement to a dispute between a plaintiff and a defendant.

In law, reasonableness must meet some uniform, collective standard of conduct. This standard is external and objective in the sense that it is determined with reference to a community valuation and must be the same for all persons, 'since the law can have no favorites' (Prosser 1971: 150). However, provisions are made in the standard for the risk apparent to the actor, that is, his or her capacity and competence to meet the standard and the normal or extenuating circumstances under which the act occurs.

In the appendix to *The Economics of Collective Action*, Kenneth Parsons concluded that

> as a theory of valuation, this is a radical departure.... Instead of individual valuation, we have social valuation. Instead of valuation at the limit of perfect competition, we have valuation in the zone of private power. Instead of valuation of resources in terms of incremental values to one individual or concern, we have valuations between two individuals or concerns within an institutional framework. (Commons 1950: 362)

23.2. Implications of Commons's Ideas for Advancing Organization Studies

John R. Commons had an obscure and difficult writing style, which may have limited the influence of his work and contributed to the wide variety of opinions on the nature and value of his theoretical contributions. These opinions range from 'naive, unsophisticated, [and] inherently uninteresting' (Seckler 1975: 5, 130) to 'a tangled jungle of profound [or] naked insights' (Boulding 1957: 12; Chamberlain 1963: 93). Problems of exposition aside, the substance of Commons's work has a number of serious omissions because it lacks systematic treatment of the limitations of the state to enforce institutional working rules, the costs to conflicting parties of appealing to the state to litigate their disputes, the importance of mutually negotiated safeguards for the internal governance of relational transactions among parties, and the potential for stalemates between several sovereignties in resolving disputes among transacting parties from different nation states. Subsequent treatments of some of these issues have elaborated, but not altered, Commons's overall framework on institutions and institutional change.

Despite these problems and omissions, we concur with Rutherford (1983) that Commons provided a more general, coherent, and valuable theoretical contribution to institutional theory than has been recognized. Commons's ideas deserve careful study, particularly because his volitional and pragmatic theory of institutions and institutional change anticipates significant areas for expanding the scope of current perspectives on organizations. Especially worthy of emphasis are his (a) dynamic views of institutions as a response to scarcity and conflicts of interest; (b) original formulation of the transaction as the basic unit of analysis; (c) part–whole analysis of how collective action constrains, liberates, and expands individual action in countless numbers of routine transactions; (d) treatment of individual wills and power to gain control over limiting or contested factors provide the generative mechanisms for institutional change; and (e) historical appreciation of how customs, legal precedents, and laws of a society evolve to construct a collective standard of prudent reasonable behavior for resolving disputes between conflicting parties in pragmatic and ethical ways. We believe that these ideas have potentially far-reaching consequences for advancing the field of organization studies.

Space considerations require us to limit our discussion below to immediate implications for three streams within the field: institutional theory, social movements, and organizational ecology. We integrate and expand some of these themes in a concluding discussion of Commons's theory of valuation as it applies to the study of organizations. We also discuss some methodological implications of Commons's work that may challenge and inspire contemporary organizational scholars.

23.2.1. Institutional Theory

Commons is routinely credited as one of the three founders of institutional economics (the others being Mitchell and Veblen). It is an irony, fitting perhaps but disturbing nonetheless, that these ritualistic nodes are usually decoupled from any substantive attention by contemporary institutionalists. We feel that this is unfortunate, since Commons's work has the potential to enrich—perhaps even transform—new approaches to organizational institutional theory.

Commons's version of institutionalism differed from neoclassical economic models in that it promoted a socially embedded, historically and culturally contingent view of economic behavior. Commons emphasized the importance of understanding the similarities but also the differences that exist in empirical data. In contrast, some new institutional economists follow a radically different approach that is based on deductive reasoning, the search for regularities, and the pursuit of generalizability. This latter approach too often results in a decontextualized definition of institutions, one that is ahistorical as well as culturally and socially empty.

A case in point is the concept of transaction, introduced by Commons and elaborated by Coase (1937) and Williamson (1985). Contemporary transaction costs economics has made an important contribution to the study of interorganizational relations. It developed clear, testable predictions regarding the choice of transaction modes under different conditions. It did so, however, using economic efficiency as its only criterion, underplaying the role of social relations in the decision-making process (Granovetter 1985). As illustrated in Table 23.1, Commons's treatment of transaction, in comparison, seems significantly more comprehensive and nuanced. To Commons, transactions should not be evaluated solely in terms of the self-interests of individual parties; they are joint relationships and must therefore be assessed in terms of the joint values of the parties involved. These joint valuations are based on a collectively constructed standard of prudent reasonable behavior; not simply in terms of the self-interests of the most powerful party to a relationship.

Among contemporary institutional economists, it is perhaps North (1990) who advanced a conception of institutions that most closely follows that of Commons. Both have viewed institutions as working rules that emerge to address human problems and that change through the interaction of agents. Commons and North both have described institutional change as gradual, incremental, and deliberate, occurring through processes of collective action that resolve conflicts among individuals that are brought into opposition by resource scarcity. Both have also argued that ideas and not just material conditions can bring about dialectical change, and related to this, both have elaborated on the role of the state in limiting the opportunities and powers of conflicting parties.

Regarding this last point, to Commons, the state (through the court system) is a key institutional actor in every transaction. This follows from his distinction between the legal transfer of property rights and the physical transfer of the thing owned. Whereas the physical aspect of a transaction is handled directly between sellers and buyers, the legal aspect of it also involves a government, which is responsible for devising the underlying structure of property rights in society. Although Commons acknowledged the importance of historical customs, common practices, and shared norms in structuring economic behavior, it is the direct involvement of the state—the sovereignty—in specifying and enforcing property rights that is highlighted throughout his work. This is especially true with regards to what Commons referred to as 'strategic transactions', those non-routine transactions that are the generative mechanisms of new working rules.

Compared to this focus on formal rules and regulatory processes, the new institutionalism in organization studies is characterized by an emphasis on the normative and—even more so—the cognitive pillars of institutions (Hirsch 1997). Even works dedicated to the investigation of the legal environment of organizations have usually taken-for-granted the central role of the state in forming and organizing a sustainable legal regime. Instead, they tend to look at more peripheral regulation, particularly in the area of labor laws, and even then pronounce the impact of the state as 'weak' and heavily mediated by other actors (e.g. Dobbin *et al.* 1993; Edelman 1992).

The few exceptions to this cognitive turn so far have typically dealt with historical (Ingram and Simons 2000) or international (Zhao 2006) contexts, characterized with unstable legal institutions. These efforts, we believe, must extend beyond the boundaries of research on economic history and international management and into the mainstream of institutional research in organization studies. After all, the involvement of the state does not end with the enactment of an ordered institutional framework. Rather, such frameworks are constantly reshaped, often at the initiative of powerful economic actors. Different actors may well vary in their access to, influence of, and compliance with seemingly uniform rules. According to Commons, it is these differences in political power, more than the impersonal forces of supply and demand, that ultimately determine the production of wealth and the distribution of income (Kaufman 2003).

Recently, some new institutional scholars have begun to take a design perspective on institutional change, albeit with a focus on the cognitive rather than on norms and values (Suddaby *et al.* 2007). For them, designed institutional change is not so much about the need to address social problems and remedy injustices, as Commons emphasized, but instead occurs when actors question taken-for-granted 'scripts'. Unfortunately, this cognitive analysis reduces institutions to 'scripts' that are examined from a rhetorical perspective that leaves the 'guts' out of institutional theory (Stinchcombe 1997). To Commons, institutional theorizing was grounded in the pervasive human dilemma of scarcity, interdependence, and conflict among people, and the need to develop institutional working rules that society considers reasonable and fair in settling disputes and preventing a 'war of all against all'. Addressing these problems requires more than an analysis of cognitive and normative dimensions of collective action; it requires systematic consideration of the full repertoire of institutional mechanisms (regulative, normative, and cognitive) for achieving social order and making life predictable. Moreover, it requires moving outside of the current neo-institutional 'echo chamber' of discourse and engaging with other institutional perspectives, as found in law, political economy, and international relations.

In this sense, Commons has succeeded where many contemporary institutionalists have failed—the development of an integrative theory of institutions based on their multiple facets. He did so by carefully attending to the historical evolution of institutions and the significance of part–whole relationships in this process. Commons maintained that the organized forms of collective action in the modern-day capitalist economy—the market, private firms, nonprofit organizations, and state agencies—evolved historically through customs, habits, and common law patterns for executing bargaining (market), managerial (hierarchical), and rationing (distributions of benefits and burdens) transactions. They were carved out and institutionalized over many centuries through the accretion of numerous decisions to adjust the institutions of society to ever-changing conditions.

This explanation for the historical evolution of alternative forms of transactions and the kinds of organizations engaged in them is consistent with the views of contemporary institutional scholars who see the nature and origin of social order as a process of institutionalization. In this case, 'social order is based fundamentally on a cognitively shared social reality which, in turn, is a human construction, being created in social interaction' (Scott 1987: 495). Because of his appreciation of the dialectical relations between the parts (individual action) and the whole (collective action), Commons took the explanation one step further.

The process of institutionalization cannot be solely an emergent product of the shared cognitive belief systems of interacting individuals. In a society of scarcity, interdependence, and conflict, this emergent product could produce an unworkable world of irreconcilable belief systems. To bring order to the institutionalization process, Commons argued, also requires collective sovereign action. The state and its delegates (officials, courts, boards, and police) can exercise their monopoly powers (including violence) in direct and indirect ways without specific individual consent. It can directly constrain, liberate, and expand certain belief systems through its collective working rules. Indirectly, it can promulgate and enforce its own belief system of the 'official collective will.'

This institutionalization process illustrates the enabling and constraining effects of part–whole analysis that can be described as top-down and bottom-up views. From the bottom-up, individuals may indeed socially construct institutional frames and over time begin to take them for granted as Berger and Luckmann (1966) discussed. From the top-down, this process is enabled and constrained by the institutional working rules of sovereignty. Dictatorships may squelch and democracies may enable the expression of institutional designs by individuals. For Commons, part–whole relationships are not simply different units of analysis, they serve as checks and balances in creating working rules.

23.2.2. Social Movements and Collective Action

In addition to being a seminal institutional scholar, Commons was also a pioneering scholar of social movements, and in particular the development of due-process procedures for collective bargaining in addressing labor–management disputes. He was actively engaged in creating collective institutional 'working rules' for the labor movement—the major social movement of his time. He was a key intellectual architect and promoter of Wisconsin's pioneering unemployment insurance and workers' compensation laws that were signed by Governor Philip La Follette in 1932[2]. This state law became the model adopted by Congress and is still the current labor law of the land.

Unfortunately, sociological social movement scholars seldom cite these contributions of Commons. In fact, in the thirteen chapters of Davis *et al.* (2005) by leading scholars of 'social movements and organization theory', Commons is not cited even once. This is unfortunate, for his analysis of conflict, power, and politics is central to explaining processes of collective action in social movements. Such a processual perspective is importantly needed to move beyond the structuralist causal models that dominate contemporary views of social movements, as evident in Davis *et al.* (2005). *Conflict* is the core generating mechanism of institutional change; *power* is a necessary condition for the expression of conflict; and *political behavior* is the means for activists and incumbents to engage in social movements in order to gain or maintain the power needed for expressing their conflict.

[2] Courtesy of the State Historical Society of Wisconsin a picture enacting this institutional innovation is available on the web at http://www.dwd.state.wi.us/dwd/DWDHistory/uc_law.htm

Much of the literature on social movements tends to focus on the conditions that support or hinder the realization of a given agenda among conflicting groups engaged in a social movement (McAdam, McCarthy, and Zald 1996). While this work has certainly generated some important insights, it neglects to address the early stages of the emergence of social movements. Commons's view, in comparison, is more comprehensive and gives serious consideration to the sources of conflict and the motivation to organize. Once again, the notion of reasonableness is invoked to explain these fundamental issues. In particular, Commons maintained that market forces are at play only to the extent that prices and rates pass the test of reasonable value. Put differently, market failures are not limited to inefficient allocations of goods but also involve considerations of fairness and social justice. When expectations of fairness are violated, people will organize through collective action—resulting in the rise and growth of dedicated social movements—to change the equilibrium. With this, Commons outlined a promising link between neoclassical economics and social movement research, a link that could advance contemporary scholarship in both areas.

Conflict entails direct confrontation and struggle among opposing parties within institutional constraints. Societies prohibit the use of violence or physical force among conflicting parties but permit parties to engage in social and economic conflict within reasonable institutional boundaries. Conflict is the means by which dialectical tensions play out. A necessary condition for conflict to be expressed is that the opposing parties have sufficient power to confront each other and engage in struggle. Conflict tends to remain latent or to be squelched by dominant actors until challengers can mobilize sufficient power by engaging in political strategies and tactics of collective action to gain support for their demands. The relationship between conflict, power, and political behaviors and institutions is recursive; just as conflict, power, and politics are central to institutional change, so too institutions shape the forms that conflict, power, and politics take (Hargrave and Van de Ven 2006). Conflict and power relations become institutionalized and are reproduced through taken-for-granted arrangements and routine behaviors.

The view of conflict as latent, yet ever-present, and as a source of creativity is at the core of Commons's original perspective on institutional change. This perspective makes clear that the 'taken-for-grantedness' of institutions will inevitably be shattered and that change is ongoing. Commons portrayed institutional history as a process of willful, pragmatic selection of one set of institutional rules over other sets, given the circumstances and organization of conflicting interests. Collective action—as it is manifested by the activities of the government, corporations, and labor unions—plays a key role in this historical evolution of institutions.

Power is another concept that is central to collective action processes. As already noted, the concept of power is intimately bound up with the concept of conflict in the sense that conflict cannot become manifest unless opposing parties have sufficient power to confront each other. Just as power shapes the course of institutional change, so power also derives from institutions. Institutions provide the framework in which power struggles play out. The resources that one controls and that are a source of one's power may have as their source a law, norm, or widely taken-for-granted belief. Commons argued that institutions enable and constrain the exercise of individual power and action. Liberation for some actors is achieved by establishing institutional constraints (rights and duties) on others. During his time, much of the labor union and collective bargaining movement focused on creating institutions that would protect workers as legal equals to employers in negotiating their employment contracts, given the overwhelming economic and social power of corporations over individual workers.

The outcomes of collective action processes are not foreordained; politics are central to processes of institutional innovation. An assessment of social movements suggests that history may have turned out differently had particular political strategies and tactics not been used. Just as political behaviors influence the course of institutional change, so also the reverse: political tactics are influenced by the institutional working rules of collective action.

In sum, models of social movements could benefit from a recognition that conflict, power, and politics both shape and are shaped by institutions. Just as actors exert their power and engage in conflict and political behaviors to influence the institutional environment, so too existing institutions govern the exercise of power, the form that conflict takes, and the political behaviors that are viewed as appropriate. There is a relationship of mutual co-production between conflict, power, and politics, on the one hand, and institutional change, on the other.

23.2.3. Organizational Ecology

Despite preceding the rise of the field of organizational ecology by many decades, the work of John R. Commons should prove valuable for contemporary organizational ecologists. As with other research areas surveyed here, Commons's influence on organizational ecology research has thus far been negligible. Nevertheless, we believe that revisiting Commons's rich and nuanced discussion of the concepts of scarcity, valuation, and selection could extend research on organizational ecology in novel and productive directions.

On first reading, Commons's approach to the study of economic activity seems to be in clear conflict with views held by modern-day organizational ecologists. Commons was highly critical of neoclassical economic theories for their use of mechanical analogies to the physical sciences. Such theorizing, he argued, erroneously assumes that behavior is propelled by external forces only and leaves no room for human will or agency. Organizational ecology is based on one such analogy—the biological metaphor of environmental selection and in that sense seems to be equally problematic. Hannan and Freeman (1977), in their foundational contribution to the field, asserted that a full understanding of the evolution of organizational populations must account for both environmental selection and organizational adaptation. Much of the subsequent research, however, did not follow this recommendation and assumed the primacy of selection processes over adaptive processes. Even when exploring organizational change, ecological accounts have tended to emphasize random grouping and inter-firm imitation rather than calculated strategic action (Baum and Shipilov 2006). Reflecting on Commons's caution about the limited value of importing models from the physical sciences to explain economic activity, this state of affairs is hardly surprising. By clinging to its biological root metaphor, organizational ecology had to develop into a theory that severely limits the significance of organizational adaptation and human agency more generally.

But Commons's work offers much more than a polemic against organizational ecology and similar approaches to organizations. Contemporary organizational ecologists may, in fact, draw inspiration from his work to expand and enrich their theory. Of particular relevance is Commons's treatment of the concept of scarcity. Commons distinguished between three aspects of scarcity: biological scarcity, psychological scarcity, and proprietary scarcity. The biological aspect of scarcity corresponds most closely with current ecological models of the economy. Biological scarcity is based on the principle of natural selection as developed by Darwin and involves five simplified assumptions, namely heredity, variability, multiplication, struggle for life, and survival of the fittest. While acknowledging the relevance of biological scarcity, Commons maintained that it is neither the only nor the most fundamental aspect of scarcity in the analysis of economic activity.

Another aspect of scarcity Commons considered is psychological scarcity, which has its roots in the Austrian School and utility theory. The notion of psychological scarcity implies that the pleasure of consumption will be most intense when the object wanted is scarce. Increasing abundance, on the other hand, should result in diminishing satisfaction. In this way, scarcity has as much to do with human psychology as with environmental selection. Commons further contrasted Darwin's natural selection model with Malthus's (who preceded and inspired Darwin) model of moral selection. The latter 'introduces ethical ideas of fitness—the ethical ideas of right and duty, goodness and badness, justice and injustice—and these ideas are limits set by sovereignty and other collective action on the methods of success' (Commons 1950: 91).

When divorced from its theological roots, the idea of moral selection is closely related to the concept of proprietary scarcity, which is at the core of Commons's novel contribution. The recognition of proprietary scarcity came with the development of the judicial concept of property rights and the distinction between the physical thing held and the ownership of that thing. Proprietary scarcity, Commons argued, is not related to the quantity of a given good, nor is it created by individuals restricting the available supply of that good by means of physical force. Rather, scarcity adheres to property rights as established and enforced by sovereignty. This aspect of scarcity is thus defined and enforced by institutional working rules of government and by the collective action of corporations and labor unions. Proprietary scarcity is still a function of selection, but this selection is neither natural nor purposeless, but rather artificial and purposeful.

As the focus on the different selection criteria may indicate, the preceding discussion may offer important insights for advancing contemporary organizational ecology research. Organizational ecologists have been criticized for spending too little time on the conceptual development of the notion of selection, focusing instead on the empirical study of population dynamics (Donaldson 1995). The natural selection model, suggested by the founders of the paradigm (Aldrich 1979; Hannan and Freeman 1977), is by now taken for granted by their followers. However, as Commons suggested, it is not the only selection model available. There are, in fact, multiple selection criteria, each of which may or may not be appropriate in different contexts. For instance, the Darwinian natural selection model may be a viable model in unregulated, highly competitive industries. Most contexts, however, are characterized by some collectively defined standard of prudent reasonable behavior, which are better described with an artificial or purposeful selection model.

By closely following the natural selection model, research on organizational ecology has evolved into a paradigm that is theoretically coherent and empirically rigorous (Pfeffer 1993). These strengths have come at a high cost, however, namely the neglect of context and of values. Ecological models typically assume organizations to be equally susceptible to environmental pressures. This assumption underpins some of the fundamental models in the field including the age, size, and density dependence models. However, as a few studies have shown, these general models may not hold in certain contexts. For example, institutional linkages may protect young and small organizations from the liabilities of newness and smallness (Baum and Oliver 1991; Miner, Amburgey, and Stearns 1990). These studies have departed from the usual treatment of selection as a blind process, forwarding instead a more purposeful model of selection. Further research embodying richer conceptions of organizational contexts and their respective selection criteria is clearly needed. Such a research emphasis will help develop a fuller and more realistic understanding of the evolution of organizational populations.

Implicit in the notion of purposeful selection is the idea that individuals may reshape their institutional environments to their own needs and purposes. This molding of the environment is achieved through collective action, as conflicts between interdependent groups are resolved in the modification of existing institutions or the creation of new ones. In other words, selection is neither random nor rational. Rather, selection criteria are constantly changing and are socially constructed according to what is collectively perceived as reasonable. The emphasis on collective action here may prove significant, as it may help reorient the effort of reconciling selection and adaptation accounts. Past attempts to integrate these two classes of explanations have focused on the study of organizational change and have had a limited effect on the literature. Indeed, many of these studies have only strengthened the hold of selection-based explanations by depicting organizational change as infrequent, difficult, and risky. A shift in the level of analysis, from the organization to the community of organizations, from individual action to collective action, may prove useful. Thus, it may be the case that the same organizations that fail to adapt to their environments may act collectively to change their environment so that individual-level adaptation will not be necessary. This direction may provide the field of organizational ecology with new research opportunities and, perhaps more importantly, help integrate it with other traditions within organization studies.

23.2.4. Theory of Valuation: Prudent Reasonable Behavior

Once it is accepted that change is not controlled by natural selection or some random environmental force, then change must be addressed in terms of human experience and values. Normative value judgments and ethics are unique to human experience. Rational self-interest is the most widely used human value in models of management and economics. But because people have different experiences and interests, private resolution of conflicts among rationally self-interested individuals, if left unchecked, could result in a 'war of all against all'. There is no pragmatic recourse but to collectively construct a reasonable standard of human value to negotiate and settle disputes among self-interested individuals.

Fortunately, de novo solutions to recurring conflicts are not necessary in an ongoing society. Historical customs, common practices, and precedents established to settle prior disputes are relied upon to settle the vast majority of immediate conflicts among individuals. Only a small fraction of all conflicts—those dealing with limiting factors in strategic transactions—require new or modified interpretations of institutional working rules to achieve resolution. Thus, Commons saw institutional change as a process of cumulative modification of collective 'working rules' for solving new problems and conflicts among willful and powerful individuals.

To say that individual and collective action are produced by human volition and conscious decision processes is not to say that everything that happens is comprehensible, intended, or under human control. Indeed, a volitional theory is indeterminate. Because social conflicts are complex, some solutions produce outcomes that are unintended, accidental, or may appear random. Knowledge is fallible, and the 'best' or rationally preferred practices at a specific time will change as knowledge and beliefs change. Individual intentions often are not realized because joint—not individual—valuations are required among transacting parties. In 'getting to yes' (Fisher and Ury 1981), transactions often produce compromises and win–lose outcomes for the involved parties. Finally, less-than-optimal institutional arrangements persist over time either because the existing arrangements are pragmatically good enough for society to putter along, or because individuals or groups have chosen to avoid and forbear in the exercise of their wills by not contesting the issues that require change. There are no ideal or final solutions. Institutions are dynamic; they are not held together by a 'natural' or an 'expectable' equilibrium. They are contrived and transient solutions to problems and conflicts.

Thus, Commons's conception of decision making is experimental and pragmatic—a process of trial and error in search of workable solutions. For Commons, institutions can be conceived as a constantly changing patchwork of repairs. Commons did not deny that technological change would play a role in institutional change, but his work does not lead to the position that technology is the only, or even the major, source of change. Commons's primary concern was with the resolution of problems and conflicts, whatever their source, and his analysis is of human choice, of artificial selection, of judicial and political processes through which disputes are resolved.

Commons also was obviously aware of efficiency considerations in evaluating alternative transactions. However, compared to the strong assumptions of rationality that characterize modern conceptualizations of transaction costs (Coase 1937; Williamson 1985), Commons approached questions of efficiency within a broader context that emphasized power relationships, distribution, and the need for a 'reasonable' framework of institutional rules. Although courts consider efficiency and scarcity aspects, ethical criteria of justice, equity, and fairness are equally present. Therefore, institutional assessments of transactions are not simply based on reducing transaction costs; instead, they are based on a collective standard of prudent reasonable behavior.

With this, Commons advanced a novel theory of valuation, which represents a true alternative to valuation theories based on random environmental events or rational self-interest. As discussed throughout this chapter (and as summarized in Table 23.2) Commons's theory departs from previous treatments on multiple dimensions. Rather than profit maximization or environmental survival, Commons employed the rule of law—based on the standard of reasonable behavior as determined by the courts—as the final rule of valuation in his theory. He replaced evolutionary processes and rational decision making models with the temporal stages of contractual negotiations, contract commitment, and contract administration when describing economic action. Commons emphasized the power of sovereignty in structuring conflicts between interdependent groups of individuals, compared to other theories that tolerate significant power asymmetries between conflicting parties.

Commons did not follow the Austrian economists by shifting from system-level analyses based on the biological model of natural selection to individual-level subjective, psychological, and moralistic models. Rather, he found inspiration in legal scholarship and practice, introducing the transaction as the unit of analysis

Table 23.2. Theories of valuation

	Random	Rational	Reasonable
Rule	Rule by nature Survival of fittest	Rule by man Maximize self-interests	Rule by law Jurisprudence
Action	Evolutionary stages of 1. Variation 2. Selection 3. Retention	Choice of stages of 1. Dissatisfaction 2. Search and screen 3. Choice of an alternative	Temporal stages of 1. Contractual negotiations 2. Contract commitments 3. Contract administration
Power	Nature	Elite rulers	Sovereignty
Unit of analysis	Environment	Man	Transaction
Scarcity	Biological	Psychological Hedonistic	Proprietary
Selection	Natural	Purposeful	Sovereign
Ethic/ultimate basis of value	Natural laws	Moral laws Individualistic right and wrong	Sovereign laws Collective working rules Rights and duties

and delineating a theory of valuation based on sovereign selection and proprietary scarcity. For Commons, value is not governed by natural laws or by individualistic judgments of right and wrong. Instead, valuation is a social process performed by two parties within an institutional framework—based on reasonable standards of rights and duties defined collectively and protected by sovereign laws.

23.3. Conclusion

This chapter has reviewed the seminal work of John R. Commons. His pioneering ideas merit serious consideration by contemporary organizational scholars. In particular, we have focused on four areas that are relevant to advancing current organization studies.

1. Commons introduced a novel and pragmatic theory of institutional design and change. This theory is based on an appreciation of dialectical part–whole relationships between individual action and collective action and how they enable and constrain each other and the overall process of institutionalization. It anticipated treatments of the action-structure paradox by organizational sociologists (Coleman 1986) and their reciprocal relations in structuration theory (Giddens 1979). Compared to recent treatments of institutions in economics and organization studies, Commons's approach seems remarkably rich and comprehensive. Commons promoted a view that was socially and

culturally embedded and that seriously considered the full repertoire of institutional mechanisms, including regulative, normative, and cognitive systems.

2. Commons was also a pioneering scholar of social movements. His detailed analysis of the social movements of labor unionization and monopoly busting showed how institutional working rules are created to address disputes and injustices among conflicting parties with unequal power and diverse interests. Commons's historical analysis of the labor movement prefigured by many years the relatively recent recognition by organizational scholars of the complementary relations between organizational institutional theory and social movements (Davis *et al.* 2005; Hargrave and Van de Ven 2006).
3. Commons's replacement of natural selection with artificial selection has the potential of turning the field of organizational ecology on its head. Instead of adopting Darwin's biological evolutionary theory of natural selection as has been done by organizational ecologists (Aldrich 1979; Hannan and Freeman 1977), Commons developed a volitional theory that emphasized artificial (purposeful) selection. He emphasized collective rather than individual artificial selection. Solutions to conflicts among parties should not be based on an individual standard of rational self-interest for that would produce unjust solutions favoring the more powerful parties. Instead, Commons argued that just and equitable solutions are based on a collective 'artificial' standard of prudent reasonable behavior. A straightforward implication of Commons's argument is that collective standards of prudent reasonable behavior govern the procedures that appear to reflect the natural selection of a population of organizational forms.
4. Commons's collective standard of prudent reasonable behavior represents a major alternative theory of valuation to that based on individual rational self-interests as well as random environmental events. Commons emphasized that institutions are pragmatic temporary solutions to conflicts among transacting parties. Civilized societies do not base these solutions on random natural processes in the environment nor on rational individual self-interests. Commons pointed out that solutions based on random environmental forces and rational self-interest are often unjust or unethical. Commons took his cue from law and jurisprudence to propose a dramatic alternative theory of valuation—one that is based on collective standards of prudent reasonable behavior.

In addition to these substantive contributions for advancing organization studies, it is fitting to conclude with some insights organizational scholars can gain from the methods of engaged scholarship that Commons used in his investigations. These methods reflect an appreciation of the comparative method of analysis among social scientists and practitioners and the roles of a social scientist.

Commons adopted a comparative method of reasoning in linking theory and practice. This method focused on identifying significant similarities and differences between cases examined, in contrast to deductive methods that were usually employed in social science (and for Commons, economics in particular). He noted that the conflict between deductive and comparative reasoning is evident when social scientists (economists) work with practitioners (public administrators). The social scientist and the practitioner often speak different languages—each may be appropriate in its own field. The social scientist starts with a single assumption and reasons deductively that all individual cases are similar. The practitioner starts with all circumstances and must give appropriate weights to each in the volitional result. Commons noted that by getting academics and practitioners together in conference, they were forced by necessity of action to reach an agreement. This negotiated agreement was often a kind of 'weighted average' or balanced emphasis of different viewpoints that served as guides to workable rules of action for the circumstances of time and place. He noted that negotiated conclusions between social scientists and practitioners were achieved through 'the comparative method of searching for similar or common ground amid the multitudes of differences' (Commons 1950: 125).

Selig Perlman notes that for Commons, 'scholarship and practical statesmanship were forever inseparable' (1945: 785). Commons's genuine personal modesty went hand-in-hand with unusual intellectual courage. He never shrank from taking risks with his reputation when his personal interpretation loomed among a variety of tentative interpretations of a body of factual material. But Commons appreciated that in developing a science of working rules among collective and conflicting interests, the scientist is not likely to be successful by going it alone; instead the investigator will be more successful when he or she works in a group and tries to understand their conflicts and bring them together in the actual situations where the conflict takes place. As Commons put it, 'understanding and conciliation, and not mere facts, are the goals of social investigation' (Commons 1950: 188).

References

Aldrich, H. (1979). *Organizations and Environments*. Englewood Cliffs, NJ: Prentice-Hall.

Barbash, J. (1989). 'Commons, John R.—Pioneer of Labor-Economics'. *Monthly Labor Review*, 112/5: 44–9.

Baum, J. A., and Oliver, C. (1991). 'Institutional Linkages and Organizational Mortality'. *Administrative Science Quarterly*, 36: 187–218.

—— and Shipilov, A. V. (2006). 'Ecological Approaches to Organizations', in S. Clegg, C. Hardy, T. B. Lawrence, and W. R. Nord (eds.), *The Sage Handbook of Organization Studies*. London: Sage Publications Ltd.

Berger, P. L., and Luckmann, T. (1966). *The Social Construction of Reality: A Treatise in the Sociology of Knowledge*. Garden City, NY: Doubleday.

Boulding, K. (1957). 'A New Look at Institutionalism'. *American Economic Review*, 47: 1–12.

Chamberlain, N. W. (1963). 'The Institutional Economics of John R. Commons', in C. E. Ayres, N. W. Chamberlain, J. Dorfman, R. A. Gordon, and S. Kuznets (eds.), *Institutional Economics: Veblen, Commons, and Mitchell Reconsidered*. Berkeley: University of California Press.

Coase, R. (1937). 'The Nature of the Firm'. *Economica*, 4: 386–405.

Coleman, J. S. (1986). 'Social-Theory, Social-Research, and a Theory of Action'. *American Journal of Sociology*, 91/6: 1309–35.

Commons, J. R. (1924). *The Legal Foundations of Capitalism*. New York: Macmillan.

—— (1934*a*). *Institutional Economics*. New York: Macmillan.

—— (1934*b*). *Myself*. New York: Macmillan.

—— (1950). *The Economics of Collective Action*. Madison: University of Wisconsin Press.

Davis, G. F., McAdam, D., Scott, W. R., and Zald, M. N. (2005). *Social Movement and Organization Theory*. New York: Cambridge University Press.

Dobbin, F. R., Sutton, J. R., Meyer, J. W., and Scott, W. R. (1993). 'Equal Opportunity Law and the Construction of Internal Labor Markets'. *American Journal of Sociology*, 99/2: 396–427.

Donaldson, L. (1995). *American Anti-Management Theories of Organization: A Critique of Paradigm Proliferation*. Cambridge: Cambridge University Press.

Edelman, L. (1992). 'Legal Ambiguity and Symbolic Structures'. *American Journal of Sociology*, 97: 1531–76.

Fisher, R., and Ury, W. (1981). *Getting to Yes: Negotiating Agreements without Giving In*. Boston: Houghton-Mifflin.

Giddens, A. (1979). *Central Problems in Social Theory: Action, Structure, and Contradiction in Social Analysis*. Berkeley: University of California Press.

Granovetter, M. (1985). 'Economic Action and Social Structure: The Problem of Embeddedness'. *American Journal of Sociology*, 91: 481–510.

Hannan, M. T., and Freeman, J. (1977). 'The Population Ecology of Organizations'. *American Journal of Sociology*, 82/5: 929–64.

Hargrave, T. J., and Van de Ven, A. H. (2006). 'A Collective Action Model of Institutional Innovation'. *Academy of Management Review*, 31/4: 864–88.

Harter, L. G. (1965). 'John R. Commons: Social Reformer and Institutional Economist'. *American Journal of Economics and Sociology*, 24/1: 85–96.

Hirsch, P. M. (1997). 'Sociology without Social Structure: Neoinstitutional Theory Meets Brave New World'. *American Journal of Sociology*, 102/6: 1702–23.

Ingram, P., and Simons, T. (2000). 'State Formation, Ideological Competition, and the Ecology of Israeli Workers' Cooperatives, 1920–1992'. *Administrative Science Quarterly*, 45: 25–53.

Kaufman, B. E. (2003). 'The Organization of Economic Activity: Insights from the Institutional Theory of John R. Commons'. *Journal of Economic Behavior & Organization*, 52/1: 71–96.

Kochan, R. A. (1980). *Collective Bargaining and Industrial Relations*. Homewood, Ill.: Irwin.

Leblebici, H. (1985). 'Transactions and Organizational Forms—A Re-Analysis'. *Organization Studies*, 6/2: 97–115.

McAdam, D., McCarthy, J., and Zald, M. N. (1996). 'Introduction: Opportunities, Mobilizing Structures, and Framing Processes—Toward a Synthetic, Comparative Perspective on Social Movements', in D. McAdam, J. D. McCarthy, and M. N. Zald (eds.), *Comparative Perspectives on Social Movements: Political Opportunities, Mobilizing Structures, and Cultural Framings*. Cambridge: Cambridge University Press.

Miner, A. S., Amburgey, T. L., and Stearns, T. M. (1990). 'Interorganizational Linkages and Population Dynamics: Buffering and Transformational Shields'. *Administrative Science Quarterly*, 35: 689–713.

North, D. C. (1990). *Institutions, Institutional Change and Economic Performance*. Cambridge: Cambridge University Press.

Perlman, S. (1945). 'John Rogers Commons 1862–1945'. *American Economic Review*, 35/4: 782–6.

Pfeffer, J. (1993). 'Barriers to the Advance of Organizational Science: Paradigm Development as a Dependent Variable'. *Academy of Management Review*, 18/4: 599–620.

Prosser, W. L. (1971). *The Law of Torts*. 4th edn. St. Paul, Minn.: West.

Rutherford, M. (1983). 'J. R. Commons's Institutional Economics'. *Journal of Economic Issues*, 17/3: 721–44.

Scott, W. R. (1987). 'The Adolescence of Institutional Theory'. *Administrative Science Quarterly*, 32/4: 493–511.

Seckler, D. (1975). *Thorstein Veblen and the Institutionalists*. Boulder, Colo.: Associated University Press.

Stinchcombe, A. L. (1997). 'On the Virtues of the Old Institutionalism'. *Annual Review of Sociology*, 23: 1–18.

Suddaby, R., Elsbach, K., Greenwood, R., Meyer, J., and Zilber, T. (2007). 'Academy of Management Journal Special Research Forum Call for Papers: Organizations and Their Institutional Environments: Bringing Meaning, Culture, and Values Back In'. *Academy of Management Journal*, 50/2: 468–9.

Van de Ven, A. H. (1993). 'The Institutional Theory of John R. Commons: A Review and Commentary'. *Academy of Management Review*, 18/1: 139–52.

Williamson, O. E. (1985). *The Economic Institutions of Capitalism: Firms, Markets, Relational Contracting*. New York/London: Free Press/Collier Macmillan.

Zhao, M. Y. (2006). 'Conducting R&D in Countries with Weak Intellectual Property Rights Protection'. *Management Science*, 52/8: 1185–99.

CHAPTER 24

THE PROBLEM OF THE CORPORATION

LIBERALISM AND THE LARGE ORGANIZATION

ELISABETH S. CLEMENS

LIBERAL political theory is populated by individuals: they have natural rights, enter into social contracts, and retain the right of revolution against sovereign power (Locke [1690] 1952). Formulated in opposition to monarchical rule, this liberal vision informed the political constitution of what came to be the industrial democracies, polities entwined with economies dominated by large organizations rather than individual entrepreneurs and small enterprises. The result was a problematic combination of political commitments and economic practices that infused debates—both academic and electoral—over the proper form of twentieth-century democratic society. The dilemma was captured in the words of the Fund for the Republic, a 1950s project dedicated to 'clarifying fundamental questions concerning freedom and justice that emerge when the forms and principles developed by Eighteenth Century America meet the ideas and practices of today's highly developed industrial society'.[1] How could a liberal constitution, designed for a polity of rights-bearing natural individuals, accommodate the rise of very large organizations legally endowed with many of those same rights?

[1] From the series description preceding Berle (1957).

Without a doubt, this is a big question. And, quite often, big questions generate responses that come to be recognized as classics. As Murray Davis has argued, classic social theorists (including Marx, Durkheim, Weber, Simmel, and Freud) set themselves 'the task of specifying the factor that disrupted the previous society's equilibrium to create modern society's disequilibrium' (1986: 288). For liberal polities, the rise of the large corporation potentially represented just such a challenge to their foundations in a world of rights-bearing individuals embedded in a market society of small enterprises. Yet, contrary to expectations, some of the greatest social theorists of the 1930s and 1940s did not simply ignore the problem but actively marginalized it. Unlike the Chicago sociologists of the 1910s and 1920s, who paid little attention to formal organizations precisely because most of the people they observed still lived their lives in other settings (see the chapter by Abbott, in this volume), those who looked at the political and economic organization of the world just a decade or two later encountered a very different picture: mass production industries, mobilized in the war effort and ready to serve a new consumer market once peace was secured. Millions were mobilized into the warring militaries, which would be the exemplars of bureaucracy for a post-war generation of organizational sociologists (Abbott and Sparrow 2007). Yet some of the most important works of political economy of this period—notably Karl Polanyi's *The Great Transformation* (1944) and Friedrich Hayek's *The Road to Serfdom* (1944)—looked piercingly into the political economy of the inter-war period, but still saw primarily markets and the state rather than the large corporation. The problem of the large organization and liberalism was left as a classic waiting to happen.

This puzzling non-classic constitutes what social reformers would term 'an object lesson'. Although most of the chapters in this volume explore how classical social theory can help to frame important questions and compelling research, such theoretical traditions can also make it difficult to see a process even when it is empirically unmistakable. Although it was difficult for some theorists to see the tensions between large corporations and liberal democracy, others struggled to reframe the question so that broader publics would recognize what these individual authors discerned as a major threat and promise for modern society.[2] A diverse set of American scholars—including the legal theorist Adolph Berle, the journalist and popular social scientist W. H. Whyte, and the economist Kenneth Boulding—all struggled in different ways with the big question of what the rise of large organizations meant for the well-being of modern society and how the tensions between corporations and democracy could be resolved or, at least, minimized. Their efforts, however, remained a subsidiary current, overshadowed by the dominant poles of 'free market' and 'centralized planning'. And even those who focused on the corporation as a factor in social change were often intent on discovering how its potential effects

[2] Without this commitment to liberalism, and the historical equation of the corporation with the individual, other theoretical traditions were not so constrained in their analysis of the rise of the large firm.

were contained or re-equilibrated. Consequently, the question of the relationship of the large corporation to liberal democracy is with us still.

24.1. A Problem Unseen

Why was it so difficult or unappealing to think through the implications of the large organization for liberal democracy, even in the context of efforts to understand the rise of fascism and communism, both understood as social systems built upon hierarchical social organization? A central element of the problem lay in the artificial character of the corporation or, indeed, of any large organization with legal standing. Once granted charters, a decision highly contested and constrained by early American state and federal constitutions (Berle 1957: 4), corporations became actors in a polity that was understood to be constituted by natural persons. In legal terms, this fictive personhood gave corporations rights to hold property, to sue and be sued, just 'as if' they were natural persons.[3] This stretching of the legal framework was the camel's nose under the tent, allowing large corporations to develop within the framework of classical liberalism. A product of late nineteenth-century judicial decisions, the opening preceded much of the growth of national railroads, the emergence of large publicly traded corporations (Roy 1997), and the growing prominence of large companies as sites of employment and production (Berle and Means [1932] 1934).

While this transmutation of large organizations into fictive persons solved legal issues, it created a durable problem for political and social theory. Specifically, classical liberalism had been strongly allied to a vision of market society, informed by Adam Smith's case for the invisible hand. In an argument that can be traced back to the eighteenth century and Bernard Mandeville's *The Fable of the Bees*, private vice or passion could be harnessed to produce good (Hirschman 1977: 18). In a famous passage found early in Smith's *The Wealth of Nations*, technological improvements were credited to a lazy boy seeking to avoid the effort of his assigned task (Smith [1789] 1976: 13–14). Thus, the aggregation of individual behavior, even slothfulness, generated overall improvements in social well-being. As passion and vice (including sloth) were replaced by rational self-interest, the model relating private motives to

[3] This equation of corporations with individuals also created puzzles for economic governance. Even Friedrich Hayek was puzzled as to 'the rationale or justification of allowing corporations to have voting rights in other corporations of which they own shares. So far as I can discover, this was never deliberately decided upon in full awareness of all its implications, but came about simply as a result of the conception that, if legal personality was conferred upon the corporation, it was natural to confer upon it all powers which natural persons possessed. But this seems to me by no means a natural or obvious consequence' (Hayek 1960: 112–13).

public outcomes remained compelling. Because individuals could be trusted to find the optimal method of advancing their own well-being, the collective pursuit of individual interests would produce public benefits.

This formulation accommodated both the rights-bearing individual of liberal political theory and the profit-maximizing individual of market society. Assuming this economic foundation, private individual decisions operating both through the market and democratic institutions would aggregate into social goods—that 'universal opulence' promised in *The Wealth of Nations.* Faced with the rise of larger firms, defenders of market capitalism invoked the equivalence of individuals and corporate entities. Reflecting on the competing claims for pre-eminence in corporate decision making, Friedrich Hayek explained that 'the traditional reconciliation' of the competing interests of 'owners of equity and the public at large' built on 'the assumption that the general rules of law can be given such form that an enterprise, by aiming at long-run maximum return, will also serve the public interest best' (1960: 104). Thus, whether the primary economic actors were individuals or corporations mattered not; the operation of markets would continue to spin universal opulence out of private interest.

Yet as individual proprietors gave way to small enterprises, which were then overshadowed by large corporations, the economic grounding for this vision of a liberal society was brought into question. If the operation of the invisible hand rested on the aggregated decisions of rational self-interested individuals, then the changing contexts that shaped choices could have deleterious effects, unwinding the transformation of private interests into public good. An individual's capacity to maximize the return to his investments or labor might be constrained by the presence of monopolies over key supplies or market opportunities (Hayek 1994: 46–7) or the fact that a single large employer effectively set the terms of exchange for wage labor. To the extent that these large organizations also developed political influence unimagined within classical liberal theory, the links between rational individuals pursing their self-interests and the production of universal opulence was further strained. Although natural persons might still be important stockholders in large corporations, providing key investments of capital, the decisions governing the uses of those resources were no longer directly governed by the property owner (Berle and Means [1932] 1934; the problem of agency theory is discussed in Tolbert and Hiatt's chapter on Robert Michels, in this volume). As a result, many key decisions were located in neither the market nor the polity, but in the private, more often hierarchical, relationships of management within complex organizations. Benefits might accrue to some members of the organization while costs were imposed on others. These changes posed an important question for modern polities: What sort of liberal democracy would be possible after the organizational revolution?

This question, however, was not readily answered. Challenges to liberalism mounted during the twentieth century, and, even in the United States, the political order was sufficiently shaky in the late 1930s that Gallup regularly asked respondents if they would prefer to live under fascism or communism. Yet even within this context, some theorists looked away from the dilemmas posed to liberal democracy by the large organization, focusing instead on relationships between state and market, the latter in terms largely congruent with the vision of Adam Smith. For all their manifest differences, this duality of state and market was central to both Friedrich Hayek's fierce critique of state planning in *The Road to Serfdom* (1944) and Karl Polanyi's (1944) eloquent case for state intervention as a necessary 'double movement' to contain the 'cascades of social dislocation' produced by capitalism.

For the question of the place of the corporation in democratic society, therefore, the classic arguments by theorists such as Hayek and Polanyi represent not a hoard of forgotten insights so much as a lesson in the difficulties of posing the question in the first place. In their masterworks, as well as in many contributions far less known, the role of the large organization in a liberal society was repeatedly simplified in terms of the limiting case of monopoly on the operations of a market society. Thus, the disengagement of organizational studies from core questions of political sociology has been driven not only by the insularity of the former (Augier, March, and Sullivan 2005) but also by the decided disinterest of the latter, which during the post-war decades framed the big questions in terms of market and state, individualism and collectivism. In these dichotomies, there was no place for corporations and large organizations as non-market collectivities often organized through conscious rather than market coordination.

Despite the potential for the rise of very large organizations to provoke a 'classic' social theory, a fundamental reassessment of social order did not follow. For reasons that had much to do with the Cold War's looming opposition of state socialism and market democracy (Ciepley 2006), the broader political and theoretical implications of the growing role of large corporations were not fully appreciated. But, in the wake of World War II, an increasing number of American scholars and commentators addressed the issue of whether a 'society of organizations' could be meaningfully democratic or at least compatible with democratic institutions. Whereas political economists, such as Hayek and Polanyi, framed their questions in terms of state and market, relegating the corporation to a marginal status, a varied set of lawyers, economists, journalists, and sociologists directly explored the implications of the large organization for how we live and how we should live. Deeply informed by the experience of the Depression and the New Deal, these inquiries were shot through with normative and political sensibilities, sensibilities that would be largely excised by the self-constitution of organizational studies during the decades that followed World War II (Augier, March, and Sullivan 2005).

Alongside these often neglected normative concerns and questions of grand theory, however, there were also a set of analytical issues with the potential to inform ongoing research in organizational studies. Adolf A. Berle, in particular, conforms to Davis's (1986) criteria for a 'classic'; he begins by identifying a key factor as the source of social disruption or change. Just as Polanyi had historicized the market as a political project and the source of subsequent 'cascades of social dislocation', Berle and others framed the 'organizational revolution' as a transformation of basic social institutions, a shift of the same order as communist revolutions. The corporation, they argued, represented a new constellation of power, analogous to the modern nation state or the Catholic Church. If so, how could one trace out the implications of these new organizational arrangements? Intriguingly, however, the modal response was to identify some other factor or process that would moderate the potential threat: moral leadership (Boulding 1953), decentralized organization (Drucker 1946), due process (Berle 1957), and countervailing powers (Galbraith 1952). Each of these represented either a means of aligning the corporation with the public good or limiting its capacity to act to its detriment. So while these arguments possessed the first element of a classic—that key factor—they explored how these disruptions could be contained or stabilized rather than looking for signs of transformation.

24.2. The Heavy Hand of Adam Smith

The development of a political sociology of the modern corporation was blocked by the welding of political and economic individualism as the legitimating foundation of liberal democracy. Sympathetic critics of classical nineteenth-century liberalism—the version of liberalism that crystallized in the doctrine of laissez-faire—repeatedly sought to disentangle the elements borrowed from John Locke and from Adam Smith. For the former, private property functioned both as a source of value but perhaps more importantly as a bulwark against the power of the monarch and the centralized state. For the latter, however, private property was the ticket for admission to the market and, thereby, to participation in a system of exchange that would harness the self-interest of individuals to the production of generalized prosperity. As John Dewey explained in his reconstruction of the history of liberalism, in the nineteenth-century laissez-faire variant (which provided a foundation for twentieth-century conservatism):

> The concern for liberty and for the individual, which was the basis of Lockean liberalism, persisted; otherwise the newer theory would not have been liberalism. But liberty was given a very different practical meaning. In the end, the effect was to subordinate political to economic activity; to connect natural laws with the laws of production and exchange, and

to give a radically new significance to the earlier conception of reason. The name of Adam Smith is indissolubly connected with initiation of this transformation. ([1935] 2000: 18)[4]

By using Smith as the foundation of their economic understanding, nineteenth- and twentieth-century theorists of liberalism and democracy had elided the problems of durable concentration of wealth and power, specifically as these durable concentrations become embedded in large organizations and legal institutions such as the corporation.

The imagery of society as market society obscured the ways in which large firms differed from individual economic actors and how experience working within large organizations could reshape natural persons. What we want, what we know, how we think about how to get what we want on the basis of what we know—all these are shaped by the individual's location and experience in social life. As that social life is increasingly structured by large organizations, whether primarily economic in character or otherwise (Riesman [1950] 1961; Whyte 1956), the constitution of political citizens and their capacities or motivations to act politically are also shaped by organizational experience in addition to their experience of culture and community (Clemens 2006).

Tocqueville, famous as a theorist of associations (see Swedberg, in this volume), acknowledged at least some of the potentially troubling implications of larger economic entities for democracy. Starting from the observation that a love of equality will fuel a greater desire for goods and thus a turn from agriculture to industry, he recognized that the employment relationships within manufacturing tended to reduce workers to their capacity for labor. Faced with turmoil in the market, 'today's manufacturing aristocracy, having impoverished and brutalized the men it uses, abandons them in times of crisis and turns them over to public assistance to be fed' (2004: 652). Yet this very callousness of manufacturers also represented a protection for democracy; absent ties of loyalty between employer and employee, manufacturers lacked the social material for constituting themselves as a durable aristocracy, and, therefore, the membership of this class would be volatile and unable to exert collective leverage over political institutions (2004: 650–2). Thus, Tocqueville provides an early example of the characteristic evasiveness of liberal theory when confronted with the corporation or large enterprise. Even when this new feature of economic life is recognized, its consequences are diminished by

[4] Polanyi made much the same point concerning the fusion of economic and political liberalism: 'All types of societies are limited by economic factors. Nineteenth-century civilization alone was economic in a different and distinctive sense, for it chose to base itself on a motive only rarely acknowledged as valid in the history of human societies, and certainly never before raised to the level of a justification of action and behavior in everyday life, namely, gain. The self-regulating market system was uniquely derived from this principle.' He recognized, however, that the full force of nineteenth-century ideology incorporated a shift from the humanistic foundations of Smith's *Theory of Moral Sentiments* to a more thoroughly biological understanding of competition and equilibrium associated with Malthus and Ricardo ([1944] 2001: 31, 120).

appealing to some other, countervailing, feature: for Tocqueville, the evanescence of any particular manufacturing aristocracy guaranteed that the development of large enterprises would not threaten democracy through the consolidation of an economic elite even as the elaboration of the division of labor eroded the capacities of workers for full citizenship.

Writing in the 1830s, informed by his encounter with an American economy still dominated by independent proprietors and small enterprises, Tocqueville might be forgiven for minimizing the implications of the large, durable economic firm. He recognized that the master 'comes more and more to resemble the administrator of a vast empire' while the worker comes 'to resemble a brute' (2004: 650). Yet this analysis of his treatment of the corporation—as situational and evanescent rather than reflecting some deeper difficulty with liberal theory—is more difficult to sustain in the face of a robust pattern of evasion evident in arguments for liberalism made over a century later, as the large corporation became the dominant feature of the economic landscapes of both Europe and the United States. As Adolf Berle, who had long railed against the entrenched presumption of market society, argued in 1957:

> No doubt the American system is the child of that [French] revolution. Certainly the Jeffersonian ideal was a country in which everyone had private property, no one was very rich, no one was very poor. In order to make this system work, however, a companion theory was needed—that economics worked automatically. The self-interest of men leveraged against each other and controlling each other through competition resulted in a splendid ethical balance wheel which was the open market. This leveled out inequalities, eliminated the inefficient and through competition prevented an undue concentration of power.
>
> Adam Smith's *Wealth of Nations* consecrated the theory. Smith said that this strange animal 'the corporation' could never be a major factor in economics because in it men worked for other men, and obviously no man would ever pay as much attention to other men's affairs as he would to his own. Therefore, such a collective enterprise could never play a major role in society. Its inefficiency would always be such that the workings of the market would eliminate it. Thus the corporation was merely an agency of the state for specialized purposes, and those suspect. (1957: 3–4)[5]

So long as laissez-faire ideals were taken as an accurate account of how the world really worked, an adequate appreciation of the rise of an organizational society was impossible.

Nowhere is this invisibility of the modern corporation more striking than in the classic set piece that emerged from World War II: Karl Polanyi vs. Friedrich Hayek. For all their many differences, of both diagnosis and prescription, both shared a fundamental understanding of social organization as oscillating between the alternatives of state and market. Even Polanyi, celebrated by economic sociologists for his analysis of 'social embeddedness', paid little attention to perhaps the most distinctive locus of embedding of economic relationships in the twentieth century:

[5] For an extended version of the argument, see Berle 1954.

the large organization. In his classic analysis of 'the double movement', the expansion of markets (themselves the creation of political project) produces cascades of social dislocation, disrupting the webs of social relationships that support and sustain individuals. In response, spontaneous protective reaction resulted in labor legislation, social welfare, and other forms of state intervention that slowed the process of market dislocation so that new forms of adjustment could develop. These public programs would sustain the relational worlds of family, neighborhood, and community during a period of adjustment to a new economic order. In this analysis, state and market are the major protagonists; corporate organization appears only as one of the forms of self-protection, in this case of business itself, against the instabilities and disturbances following from market exposure ([1944] 2001: 138, 154).

Polanyi's relative inattention to the corporation as a fundamental ordering element of economic life is telling,[6] not least because so many of the terms of his analysis are sensitive to the implications of institutional innovations. Yet this attention to innovation stops at the market's edge: 'Once the market organization of industrial life had become dominant, all other institutional fields were subordinated to this pattern: the genius for social artifacts was homeless' ([1944] 2001: 126). Even where new efforts at organization occurred, they were suppressed in order to preserve the fundamental character of the self-regulating market:

> Theoretically, laissez-faire or freedom of contract implied the freedom of workers to withhold their labor either individually or jointly, if they so decided; it implied also the freedom of businessmen to concert on selling prices irrespective of the wishes of the consumers. But in practice such freedom conflicted with the institution of a self-regulating market, and *in such a conflict the self-regulating market was invariably accorded precedence.* In other words, if the needs of a self-regulating market proved incompatible with the demands of laissez-faire, the economic liberal turned against laissez-faire and preferred—as any antiliberal would have done—the so-called collectivist methods under the conditions of modern industrial society than the fact that even economic liberals themselves regularly used such methods in decisively important fields of industrial organization. (ibid. 155).

For Polanyi, therefore, the market itself is the moving force of social development. Large organizations, and corporations in particular, are only temporary shelters against market pressures, shelters that can be smashed by either state intervention in aid of the market or by the market directly. How can this position then be squared with the obvious existence and considerable durability of large corporations? This puzzle points to the inadequacy of theory and moral ideas: 'With the liberal the idea of freedom thus degenerates into a mere advocacy of free enterprise—which is today reduced to a fiction by the hard reality of giant trusts and princely monopolies. This means the fullness of freedom for those whose

[6] In characterizing the peak of market expansion circa 1914, Polanyi does acknowledge 'huge fictitious bodies called corporations' ([1944] 2001: 136).

income, leisure, and security need no enhancing and a mere pittance of liberty for the people, who may in vain attempt to make use of their democratic rights to gain shelter from the power of the owners of property' ([1944] 2001: 265). Polanyi notices the dominance of the large corporation, with its accompanying economic elite, only as a prelude to a call for a new and fuller understanding of liberty. The large firm functions as a boundary marker, designating both the hypocrisy and the brutality of market ideologies, but is itself not subject to sustained analysis. So while it is clear that Polanyi concludes that state intervention against economic concentration is necessary for reconstitution of a more authentically liberal and democratic society, he largely fails to explore the implications of a world dominated by complex organizations for democracy.

For all their striking disagreements, this inattention to corporations and complex organizations is an intriguing point of convergence between Polanyi and Friedrich Hayek whose 1944 publication of *The Road to Serfdom* provided a rallying point for opponents of centralized state planning and champions of a revivified market society. Hayek located the origins of the threat to liberal freedoms in the hubris of those intent on correcting all the shortcomings of market society at once. This hubris, he argued, led to an embrace of a technocratic utopia of rationalized planning that would supplant economic and political freedoms in the name of equality and security. Here again, the stylized opposition of market and state dominates the analysis. Economic organizations oscillate midfield: more market-like when small so that property is widely distributed and possibilities for individual choice are preserved, more state-like when large.[7] Furthermore, Hayek attributes the emergence of monopolies and near-monopolies not to immanent features of economic life (such as the advantages of scale), but rather to suspect forms of political collusion, either between firm and state or between firm and union, which put 'the consumer at the mercy of the joint monopolistic action of capitalists and workers in the best organized industries' ([1944] 1994: 46).[8]

[7] This effort to make corporations as 'market-like' as possible infuses one of Hayek's later essays, 'The Corporation in a Democratic Society'. He advocated both enhancing the control of individual stockholders over corporate investment decisions by allowing them 'annually and individually to decide what part of his share in the net profits he was willing to reinvest in the corporation' while also arguing that the corporations should not be expected to 'serve the public good' in any way other than its central mission of maximizing returns to shareholders within the bounds of the 'rule of law' (1960: 110).

[8] Hayek explicitly rejects the argument that increases in the scale of organization (which he consistently refers to as 'monopoly') can be attributed to technological advances. His conclusion rests on the claim that these arguments consistently ignore the ways in which technological advances may also increase the efficiency of market coordination, a countervailing force to managerial coordination. In support of his dismissal of claims for the greater efficiency of large organizations, Hayek cites the 1941 conclusions of the Temporary National Economic Committee, which was established by FDR and Congress. Rather than technology, the growth of monopoly 'is largely the result of a deliberate collaboration of organized capital and organized labor where the privileged groups of labor share in the monopoly profits at the expense of the community and particularly at the expense of the poorest, those employed in the less-well-organized industries and the unemployed' ([1944] 1994: 218).

The relocation of decisions within monopolies, Hayek argues, violates the fundamental principle of liberalism 'that in the ordering of our affairs we should make as much use as possible of the spontaneous forces of society, and resort as little as possible to coercion' ([1944] 1994: 21). While he acknowledges that some may prefer 'the hierarchical order of military life ... the security of the barracks' (ibid. 140), no liberal society can be preserved if the state itself takes on the centralized direction of economic life. This would give the state enormous power over individuals, resting the practices of coordination in a complex society firmly on methods of coercion rather than the decentralized, spontaneous mechanism of the price system in a competitive market. Thus, in his project of defending market freedom, Hayek ultimately treats the large organization, specifically the corporation, much in the same way as does Polanyi: either as a little bit of state in economic life or a little bit of economic activity within the state. Regardless of the author's conclusions for political theory, the large organization is elided from the problematic of sustaining liberal democracy in an organizational society.

Underlying all the differences between Polanyi and Hayek is a similar focus on the self-equilibrating qualities of society. For Polanyi, the very spontaneity of the double movement—which he documents by pointing to absences of social movements and legislative ideologies—attested to the homeostatic, equilibrating role of moral reactions against the ravages of too-rapid expansion of market relations. For Hayek, the price mechanism functioned as an equivalent social thermostat, guaranteeing that—at least in the long run—distortions in the market would be remedied as prices conveyed information to rational economic actors. In both cases, however, there is a unity to the observer and the actor—moral and political man for Polanyi, rational and economic man for Hayek. So long as those who bore the effects of current arrangements (or current prices) also had the capacity to act, then any distortions and disequilibria would be counteracted.

The influence of Hayek's and Polanyi's theoretical imagery remains powerful. Within political and economic scholarship, rational actor theories begin from an essentially Smithian understanding of politics and economies as market arrangements. This imagery has been exported to innumerable policy domains as 'choice' has become the banner for a 'market model' of social provision. Driven by the informed choices of innumerable 'citizen consumers', choice in education or health care or anything else will generate competitive pressures that will improve the quality of overall provision and, if we are to believe the claims of candidates from across the political spectrum, lead to a decline in the overall cost of these programs (Suleiman 2003). Yet just as Hayek and Polanyi 'black-boxed' the corporation in their reflections on inter-war economic and political turmoil, so contemporary debates foreground the pseudo-markets created by public policies while paying little attention to the organizations that populate them.

24.3. Theorizing the Corporation

How can we think ourselves out of this black box and get to that unrealized classic? To this end, it may help to return to the inter-war years, before the Cold War effectively cemented the opposition of free market and state planning. Although, as Andrew Abbott has discussed in his chapter on the Chicago School, the organizational sensibility of the social sciences was not yet developed (and would not be until a cohort of veterans returned to the academy from that biggest of all bureaucracies, the American military), key theorists were delineating how modern social organization was eroding the foundation of both liberalism and market economics in methodological individualism. At the same time, a few heterodox economists were confronting the limits of that Smithian vision of the market—limits represented by the puzzling existence of firms.

Insofar as the corporation appears only at the margins of many economic analyses, as an illegitimate exercise of economic power or a deviant form of coordination, then the large organization could be treated as an exception in theoretical terms. The viability of this approach was threatened, however, insofar as the development of organization was recognized as a necessary rather than a deviant component of market exchange. While many political economists and legal theorists continued to reject the inevitability of economic concentration and to embrace a vision of small enterprise and competition,[9] others increasingly focused directly on the puzzle of the large organization, specifically the for-profit corporation. The challenge, as stated by R. H. Coase, was 'to discover why a firm emerges at all in a specialized exchange economy' (1937: 390). The answer, he argued, lay in the costs associated with market transactions. By recognizing the costs of information, negotiation, and uncertainty, Coase expected 'that a firm will tend to expand until the costs of organizing an extra transaction within the firm become equal to the costs of carrying out the same transaction by means of an exchange on the open market or the costs of organizing in another firm' (1937: 395).[10] In addition, he recognized that the advantages of transacting with a firm would be increased to the extent that government taxed market transactions but not those internal to organizations; firms would also be expected to grow in size as technological inventions and improvements in managerial technique reduced the costs of organization in comparison to the

[9] Supreme Court Justice Louis Brandeis was often identified as the leading advocate of this position (Leuchtenberg 1963: 148).

[10] A third mode of coordination can be added to Coase's pair of market and firm-based forms: political coordination. Then it is possible to conceptualize the locus of decisions moving from one form of coordination to another, not necessarily constrained by the substance of the decision itself. For example, what were once public services (e.g. within that peculiar firm known as government) may be contracted-out to private firms, shifting activities from military mobilization to primary education into modified forms of market coordination.

costs of transaction within a market.[11] This argument did not directly challenge the core assumptions of the Smithian world—the rational individual in pursuit of gain, motivated by that fundamental propensity to 'truck, barter and exchange'—but rather explained how the pattern of behavior that followed from this understanding of human nature would result in an economic landscape quite different from a system of market exchange among individuals and small enterprises.

Thus, the development of an economic theory of the firm explained why the large organization—the firm or more specifically the corporation—would emerge out of an economic system described by assumptions that could be traced back to Adam Smith. But if this solved the puzzle for academic economists, the central issue for political theorists was to understand the implications of a society of large organizations for the possibility of liberalism. If nineteenth-century liberalism had been grounded in analogies to market society, what would change with the recognition that the large firm was not a deviation from market principles but a predictable outcome of their operation?

A key bridge between the economic theory of the firm and the political implications of an organization society was provided by Adolf A. Berle, Jr. and Gardiner Means in 1934 with the publication of *The Modern Corporation and Private Property*.[12] Whereas academic economists addressed the emergence of the firm in terms of the dynamics of market exchange, Berle and Means also recognized the corporation as a distinctive legal form or institution. From this perspective, the critical market was found in the supply of capital for investment rather than of goods produced for markets. In their analysis, the rise of the large firm represented not simply the marginal costs of coordination by managerial control versus market exchange, but a fundamental shift in the organization of economic power:

> In its new aspect the corporation is a means whereby the wealth of innumerable individuals has been concentrated into huge aggregates and whereby control over this wealth has been surrendered to a unified direction. The power attendant upon such concentration has brought forth princes of industry, whose position in the community is yet to be defined. The surrender of control over their wealth by investors has effectively broken the old property relationships and has raised the problem of defining these relationships anew. The direction of industry by persons other than those who have ventured their wealth has raised questions of the motive force back of such direction and the effective distribution of the returns from business enterprise. (1934: 2)

[11] Boulding makes a similar argument for limits to the scale of the corporation, pointing to the limits imposed by communications capabilities and fear of public opinion/anti-trust (1953: 136–7).

[12] Berle figures in the 1930s as both analyst and political actor. Shortly after the publication, with Gardiner Means, of *The Modern Corporation and Private Property*, Berle would participate as a member of Roosevelt's 'brain trust' between the 1932 election and FDR's inauguration in March 1933. Informed by the Social Gospel of his father, a minister, Berle hoped to 'evangelize the businessman rather than resort to the naked power of the state' (Leuchtenberg 1963: 35).

This shift followed from a decomposition of the attributes of economic man as envisioned by Smith. Whereas that version of *homo economicus* both deployed assets (whether capital or simply his own labor) and enjoyed the returns of those efforts, his modern heir—the stock owner—took a passive role, supplying investment capital but ceding control over decision making to a growing cadre of professional managers. Whereas defenses of this arrangement argued that stockholders retained ultimate control as principals over managerial agents, Berle and Means explained in painstaking detail the many techniques by which managers could redirect corporate gains away from stockholders to their own advantage. The result was the increasing autonomy of corporate management over an economy in which the 200 largest non-banking corporations already controlled approximately one half of corporate wealth (1934: 32). With this increasing control of wealth, large corporations were further liberated from the potential control of stockholders and raised more and more of their investment capital from retained earnings. The implications of this development ranged far beyond the organization of business itself:

> the huge corporation, the corporation with $90,000,000 of assets or more, has come to dominate most major industries if not all industry in the United States. A rapidly increasing proportion of industry is carried on under this form of organization. There is apparently no immediate limit to its increase. It is coming more and more to be the industrial unit with which American economic, social, and political life must deal. The implications of this fact challenge many of the basic assumptions of current thought. (ibid. 44)

So whereas Coase's analysis found a limit to corporate expansion in the relative marginal costs of transactions within the firm compared to market exchange, Berle and Means portrayed an economy ever more dominated by corporate organizations of increasing size, autonomy, and influence.

If so, the corporation represented a fundamental dilemma for liberal democracy. On the one hand, 'if modern civilization and technical development require enterprises of size to provide the standard of living the American community expects, they require precisely this split of property into its component attributes, assigning the receptive attributes to the group of shareholders, and gathering the creative attributes in a single command' (Berle 1954: 32). The large corporation with its complex division of labor was, therefore, necessary to produce the 'universal opulence' foreseen by Smith and to overcome the conditions of poverty that would fuel class conflict. Yet, on the other hand, the emergence of these new 'princes of industry' clearly represented one threat to the ideal of liberal democracy, constituting a form of private power that potentially constrained the choices that could be made by individual citizens. Furthermore, the growing autonomy of management from the consequences of their decisions for the stockholders threatened the operation of the feedback mechanisms that harnessed private interest to public good. As economic activity concentrated into the affairs of a few large firms in each industry, competition no longer served to drive out inefficiencies. Instead, the 'result of great corporations fighting each other is either consolidation, or elimination, of one of the units, or acceptance of a situation in which the place of each is approximately respected' (ibid. 45).[13]

24.4. Making Corporations Safe for Democracy

If the routine workings of market society would not limit the size and power of corporations, how were these large private organizations to be kept compatible with the rights of individual citizens? One response focused on the character of the leaders of these ascendant large corporations. If modern society no longer conformed to the classic liberal requirement for wide distribution of property and a meaningful link between ownership and the returns to ownership, then these guarantees would need to be relocated within these clearly non-democratic, non-liberal organizations. In *The Twentieth Century Capitalist Revolution*, Berle explicitly subjects the corporations to the requirements of a system of political rule, using the right of subjects to appeal to the monarch as the basis of an extended analogy. The specifics of the analogy were particularly timely, focused on the question of the rights of an employee charged with Communist associations. After working through the cases where firms are under contract to government (and arguing that to ask firms to enforce government rules against employing Communists is an unacceptable delegation of power), Berle asked:

> But suppose there is no underlying contract, and there is no government pressure: the corporation, considering its operations and the public interest, makes a rule proscribing as unemployable Communists or persons accused of Communism who take refuge behind the privilege against self-incrimination. Has an individual affected by such a rule any rights?
>
> In classical theory, he does not. The business corporation has discretionary power (subject to the limitations imposed by a few Fair Employment Practices Acts in some states) to select and reject employees at will, as a part of the kit of rights going with private property and management power. Yet the classic theory seems somehow not satisfactory. It was made for a time when there were many thousands of employers, and the act and policy of the most powerful of them could relate only to a tiny fragment of the economic complex. The same act or policy carried out by one or two large corporations, controlling a substantial percentage of the employment in a region or industry, has a vastly different effect.
>
> (1954: 103)[14]

[13] On firms' efforts to insulate themselves from risk and competition, see Fligstein 2001.

[14] On the more general extension of due process jurisprudence after World War II, see Ciepley 2006.

Accompanying calls for corporations to respect individual rights were arguments that, like governments, corporations would be judged by their contributions to the public good. 'Twentieth-century capitalism', Berle argued, 'will justify itself not only by its out-turn product, but by its content of life values' (1954: 114). In part, this would entail an extension of guarantees of due process to the individual within the corporation, but more importantly it would demand a change of perspective on the part of business leaders:

> the really great corporation managements have reached a position for the first time in their history in which they must consciously take account of philosophical considerations. They must consider the kind of a community in which they have faith, and which they will serve, and which they intend to help construct and maintain. In a word, they must consider at least in its more elementary phases the ancient problem of the 'good life,' and how their operations in the community can be adapted to affording or fostering it. (1954: 166–7)

Thus, the response to the erosion of market society, and the disempowerment of the Smithian individual, would be to imbue the corporation through its leadership with a clear moral vision. In a sense, new forms of corporate social responsibility[15] would substitute for the classic liberal guarantees of freedom and self-interest.[16] Although corporations did not, Berle asserts, seek political power, 'the corporation, almost against its will, has been compelled to assume in appreciable part the role of conscience-carrier of twentieth-century American Society' (1954: 182). Thus, the spontaneous workings of classic liberalism would give way to the moral leadership of corporate executives.

A further piece of the argument focused on the conditions that would allow individuals within corporations to act morally. In *The Organizational Revolution*, Kenneth Boulding contrasted the realm of ethical behavior with domains of coercion. This framing mapped on to the familiar opposition of market and state; thus efforts to protect a classic market society (against the organization of labor, farm, and business interests) would maximize the possible domain for ethical or uncoerced behavior. Interestingly, however, Boulding minimizes the degree of hierarchy or coercion—both inimical to ethical behavior—internal to corporations: 'Within the sheltering framework of a large corporation formed by the merger of many small ones, the component units frequently keep a good degree of independence, and in its structure the large corporation may be something like a coral colony of a number of semi-independent departments knit by a common financial skeleton' (1953: 133). This line of argument resonated with claims for the efficiency of decentralization as

[15] Note that Berle incorporates a discussion of corporate philanthropy at this point in the discussion (1954: 167–75).

[16] Boulding, by comparison, argues that 'We have seen already that competition is a substitute for political process in the control of power, in that if it is effective the inefficient holders of power lose their positions through the adverse impact of the market on their organizations. There is fear, however, that big business may grow to the point where it can control the competition which is the only effective check on its power' (1953: 142–3).

a form of corporate organization, an argument famously linked to Peter Drucker's *Concept of the Corporation* (1946). Here again, morality met the invisible hand—one could do well by doing good.

While Berle and Boulding argued that corporations and their leaders could be infused with concern for the public good and respect for individual rights, other theorists looked to democratic processes as effective constraints upon destructive corporate self-interestedness. Corporations had both created the conditions for such governance and would be subject to it. For the American philosopher John Dewey, the key change was the triumph over scarcity. As he argued in 1935, 'the problem of democracy becomes the problem of that form of social organization, extending to all the areas and ways of living, in which the powers of individuals shall not be merely released from mechanical external constraint but shall be fed, sustained and directed' ([1935] 2000: 40). Dewey argued that the practice of governance should be reconceived so that it enhanced the full development of the individual, as both means and ends of democratic life. Yet to achieve this goal, it was necessary to recognize not only the overall abundance of economic production but the problems stemming from the concentration of ownership of resources as well as control of enterprise: 'It demands no great power of intelligence to see that under present conditions the isolated individual is well-nigh helpless. Concentration and corporate organization are the rule. But the concentration and corporate organization are still controlled in their operation by ideas that were institutionalized in eons of separate individual effort' (ibid. 65). Economic liberals had, Dewey asserted, 'completely failed to anticipate the bearing of private control of the means of production and distribution upon the effective liberty of the masses in industry as well as in cultural goods. An era of power possessed by the few took the place of the era of liberty for all envisaged by the liberals of the early nineteenth century' (ibid. 43–4).

The growing dominance of the large corporation in the American economy mattered as a vehicle for the concentration of power among elites and thus the capacity of individual citizens to enjoy 'actual liberty' and therefore meaningful development as fully human selves. The remedy would be to cultivate a countervailing power in a democratic state directed not by technocrats but instead by participatory politics organized through 'the cooperative experimental method', a method that might be practiced by 'occupational groups' ([1935] 2000: 74). This imagery of countervailing powers would be famously developed by John Kenneth Galbraith in *American Capitalism* (1952). Galbraith began by invoking the now familiar trope of the mismatch between American ideas about how the economy worked and the ways in which it actually did work. 'It is told', he opened, 'that such are the aerodynamics and wing-loading of the bumblebee that, in principle, it cannot fly' (1952: 1). Similarly, both conservatives and liberals alike looked at the post-war economy and saw a system in fundamental violation of either the Smithian principles of market society or the liberal vision of a society of political equals. Galbraith, by contrast, argued that government and unions provided adequate counterweights to corporate self-interest; countervailing powers thus replaced competition as a control upon organizational excesses.

While Dewey was sensitive to the role of the corporation in the concentration of wealth and power, his eventual focus on the countervailing power of the state foreshadowed how the debate over the organization of capitalist democracy would unfold during and after World War II. Rather than achieving a reconstruction of liberalism through corporations, the moral solution advocated by both Berle and Boulding, the path led to some form of state intervention (here, no doubt, Dewey's argument reflects its moment in time, the height of the New Deal effort): 'Organized social planning, put into effect for the creation of an order in which industry and finance are socially directed in behalf of institutions that provide the material basis for cultural liberation and growth of individuals, is now the sole method of social action by which liberalism can realize its professed [aims]' ([1935] 2000: 60).

If the arguments for corporate responsibility and countervailing powers focused on what corporations might do to society, different lines of argument traced what life within corporations might do to the individual, the foundation of both classic liberalism and neo-classical economics. Without denying the possible exercise of corporate power to shape policy, these analyses pointed to the more subtle ways in which the mid-century corporation eroded the cultural, indeed the psychological, requisites for a liberal polity. The corporate leader exerted moral influence not only through the ethical qualities of his own decisions but also by shaping the context in which other selves were constituted: 'the organizer who creates roles, who creates the holes that will force the pegs to their shape, is a prime creator of personality itself. When we ask of a man, "What is he?" the answer is usually given in terms of his major role, job, or position in society; he *is* the place that he fills, a painter, a priest, a politician, a criminal' (Boulding 1953: 80). In his popular volume, *The Organization Man* (1956), William H. Whyte, Jr. captured something of the repressed tension between organizational structure and individual character. At the level of discourse, the formal ideology of the American corporation was insistently individualist:

> It is the corporation man whose institutional ads protest so much that Americans speak up in town meeting, that Americans are the best inventors because Americans don't care that other people scoff, that Americans are the best soldiers because they have so much initiative and native ingenuity, that the boy selling papers on the street corner is the prototype of our business society. Collectivism? He abhors it, and when he makes his ritualistic attack on Welfare Statism, it is in terms of a Protestant Ethic undefiled by change—the sacredness of property, the enervating effect of security, the virtues of thrift, of hard work and independence. Thanks be, he says, that there are some people left—e.g., businessmen—to defend the American dream.

> He is not being hypocritical, only compulsive. He honestly wants to believe he follows the tenets he extols, and if he extols them so frequently it is, perhaps, to shut out a nagging suspicion that he, too, the last defender of the faith, is no longer pure. Only by using the language of individualism to describe the collective can he stave off the thought that he himself is in a collective as pervading as any ever dreamed of by the reformers, the intellectuals, and the utopian visionaries he so regularly warns against. (1956: 5)

So just as political economists looked at modern society 'as if' it exemplified Smithian principles, individuals lived within that society 'as if' they were still the rugged, self-reliant characters associated with life on the frontier.[17] Yet these hymns to individualism sat uneasily with a corporate culture which celebrated 'human relations' or getting along.[18] This tendency was evident in the practices of corporate training programs, the processes of 'personality testing' and promotion, as well as in the preferences of college graduates for positions in corporations rather than entrepreneurial careers. Within corporations, the most desired positions were in personnel and public relations, as managers of others yet not leaders of all. For these new cohorts of organizational men (almost all men, with wives and children in tow), the corporation shaped their pilgrimages through life, from one position to another, from one new suburb to another. In the process, Whyte observed, these organization men did not become so much rootless as they developed new kinds of roots with distinctive implications for political life.[19] While their 'new roots' allowed them to engage easily in what social movement theorists would term the 'modular' forms of community life—committees, boards, nonprofit organizations—they lacked the more durable connections to social worlds fundamental to more classic communitarianism or the secure grounding in independent property that guaranteed the individual freedoms of classical liberalism.

[17] Although the specific implications of human relations were new, the consequences of new forms of enterprise for character and socialization had been evident to Tocqueville (2004) more than a century before. These discussions appear in volume 2 of *Democracy in America*, which was written after a long visit to Britain in 1835, after the publication of volume 1. In this section of the analysis, Tocqueville recognized the effects of the division of labor on individuals, anticipating some of the post-war debate over organizational man. The worker, Tocqueville explained, 'belongs not to himself any longer but to the occupation he has chosen.... As the principle of division of labor is more thoroughly applied, the worker becomes weaker, more limited, and more dependent. The art progresses, the artisan regresses' (Tocqueville 2004: 649–50). Thus, the division of labor undermines the self-sufficient rational individual of liberal theory.

[18] For his discussion of Mayo, see Whyte 1956: 35. In the emphasis of personnel programs on cultivating a particular 'company type', Whyte saw a long-term source of weakness (ibid. 195).

[19] Whyte developed this analogy by quoting at length from the 1954 Musser Forests' Catalogue: 'Stock is transplanted in our nurseries from one to four or more times. Each time, the longer, more easily damaged roots are reduced so that more small feeder roots develop near the stem. The more feeder roots, the more quickly the tree is established on your land. Also, the resulting compact mass of small feeder roots makes the tree easier to plant. Every year in the spring and summer, we transplant hundreds of thousands of seedlings to build more feeder roots. Results prove extra cost is repaid many times over' (1956: 289).

This line of analysis resonated with the broader public, an appeal evident in the success of not only Whyte's *Organization Man* but also David Riesman's best-selling *The Lonely Crowd*. In Riesman's argument, the other-directedness characteristic of contemporary life (and exemplified in the popularity of human relations as an occupational choice and the rise of a 'new middle class' represented by 'the bureaucrat, the salaried employee in business'; Riesman [1950] 1961: 20) led to a new kind of political disengagement characterized by indifference.[20] These 'new-style' indifferents, Riesman argued, 'have some education and organizational competence and since they are neither morally committed to political principles nor emotionally related to political events, they are rather easily welded into cadres for political action—much as they are capable of being welded into a modern mechanized and specialized army' (ibid. 171). Whether disengaged and insulated by apathy or mobilized by political entrepreneurs, this type of civic character no longer fulfilled the equilibrating role of the ideal-typical liberal society, for whom choices and consequences were tightly linked.

24.5. Towards a New Political Sociology of the Large Organization

Although the emergence of large organizations represented a challenge to the premises of liberal democracy, that encounter did not generate a classic analysis, an argument that would meet Davis's twin criteria of identifying a central factor and linking it to an explanation of social disruption and change. In part, this non-event in social theory reflected the enduring strength of the entwined ideologies of liberal democracy: Smithian market economics and the classical liberalism of John Locke. Both grounded in the primacy of the independent and rational individual, these imageries could encompass the rise of large organizations only by treating the new corporations 'as if' they were individuals. Thus, instead of provoking a debate over the role of the large corporation in liberal democracy, the key stakes in political economy were posed by the opposition of centralized state planning and free markets. For those few theorists who struggled to draw attention to the implications of the large corporation for liberal democracy, notably Adolf Berle and Gardiner Means (1932), they attributed their role as voices in the wilderness to the durability of philosophical ideas, a variant on cultural lag theories developing more generally in the social sciences (Ogburn 1922). Dewey offered a similar analysis,

[20] Writing only a few years earlier, Arendt made the point that as a social type, the 'bureaucrat' was easily unmoored from moral reflection and thus a recruit to project that dehumanized others (Arendt [1948] 1968).

arguing that this 'lag in mental and moral patterns provides the bulwark of the older institutions; in expressing the past they still express present beliefs, outlooks, and purposes. Here is the place where the problem of liberalism centers today' ([1935] 2000: 80). This opposition was cemented by the climate of the Cold War, during which each of these social imageries was powerfully linked to values of freedom, social justice, equality, human liberation, and so forth. Whereas it had been difficult to think beyond the melding of Smith and Locke in the inter-war years, in the wake of World War II it became still more challenging to question the alliance of free market economics and democratic freedoms.

Yet despite the strength of this ideological-analytic complex, at least the handful of American scholars discussed here did grapple directly with the adequacy of the Smithian understanding of the economy and the implications of the growth of large corporations. In many cases, however, these analyses identified the many ways in which the rise of the corporation was at odds with the premises of liberal democracy, but then pointed to additional factors or new equilibrating forces that contained the challenge to existing political institutions. Even Adolf Berle, who had warned of the 'new princes' of corporate management in the early 1930s,[21] would look back from 1960 with satisfaction at the extent to which the domesticating reforms of the New Deal had contained business hostility to government (1960). Like many other post-war analyses that did grapple directly with the implications of large organizations, the conclusion was relief that what appeared to be a disrupting challenge to liberal democracy could be contained or mitigated.

What, then, do these scattered engagements with the corporation provide by way of guidance for rethinking the implications of the corporation for liberal democracy? The proper response would be to scuttle debates over the relationship of the abstract individual to an equally abstract society. Instead, the development of social knowledge must turn on 'inquiry into the *consequences* of some particular distribution [of freedom, personal rights, and social obligations], under given conditions, of specific freedoms and authorities, and for inquiry into what altered distribution would yield more desirable consequences' (Dewey [1927] 1954: 193). More precisely, the problem of the formation of an effective public in modern society stemmed from the complexity and fragmentation of the indirect effects of the action of others.

The key question, then, was which contexts provided the greatest possibility for the emergence of publics grounded in shared knowledge of the indirect effects of the action of others. Although Dewey himself contended that 'democracy must

[21] If this concentration of wealth—and particularly the concentration of control in the hands of professional managers rather than stockholders—was a predictable outcome of the corporate form, could a society of large organizations sustain a liberal and democratic polity? An influential lineage of critical sociologists traced how networks of the powerful, the wealthy, and the powerful as well as wealthy controlled many key decisions despite the persistence of the institutions of electoral democracy (Mills 1956; Domhoff 1967).

begin at home, and its home is the neighborly community' ([1927] 1954: 213), he also recognized that the 'ties formed by sharing in common work' (ibid. 212) could contribute to the emergence of new publics. The challenge, however, was enormous:

> Indirect, extensive, enduring and serious consequences of conjoint and interacting behavior call a public into existence having a common interest in controlling these consequences. But the machine age has so enormously expanded, multiplied, intensified and complicated the scope of the indirect consequences, has formed such immense and consolidated unions in action, on an impersonal rather than a community basis, that the resultant public cannot identify and distinguish itself. And this discovery is obviously an antecedent condition of any effective organization on its part. Such is our thesis regarding the eclipse which the public idea and interest have undergone. There are too many publics and too much of public concern for our existing resources to cope with. The problem of a democratically organized public is primarily and essentially an intellectual problem, in a degree to which the political affairs of prior ages offer no parallel. (Dewey [1927] 1954: 126)

In contemporary societies, large organizations provide important contexts for the formation of selves and the development of publics (Sennett 1998). Organizations are also important targets for political mobilization, constituting an effective polity if not a formally recognized one (Davis *et al.* 2005). So although market fundamentalism endures, exemplified by Hayek's *The Road to Serfdom*, endorsed by the linkage of freedom and market by Kenneth Boulding, and later revivified by Milton Friedman and his disciples, the recognition of the corporation as a central feature of contemporary society remains a potential object of organizational inquiry and reflection on the ethics and political possibilities of mid-century liberalism. A classic might yet be written.

Acknowledgments

I am grateful to Pam Tolbert, Jay Chok, and Paul Adler for their comments and constructive criticism.

References

Abbott, A., and Sparrow, J. T. (2007). 'Hot War, Cold War: The Structures of Sociological Action', in Craig Calhoun (ed.), *Sociology in America: A History*. Chicago: University of Chicago Press.

Arendt, H. ([1948] 1968). *The Origins of Totalitarianism.* New York: Harcourt.

Augier, M., March, J. G., and Sullivan, B. N. (2005). 'Notes on the Evolution of a Research Community: Organization Studies in Anglophone North America, 1945–2000'. *Organization Science*, 16/1: 85–95.
Berle, A. A., Jr. (1954). *The Twentieth Century Capitalist Revolution.* New York: Harcourt, Brace & Co.
—— (1957). *Economic Power and the Free Society: A Preliminary Discussion of the Corporation.* New York: Fund for the Republic.
—— (1960). 'The Corporation in a Democratic Society', in M. Anshen and G. L. Bach (eds.), *Management and Corporations 1985.* New York: McGraw-Hill.
—— and Means, G. D. ([1932] 1934). *The Modern Corporation and Private Property.* New York: Macmillan Company.
Boulding, K. E. (1953). *The Organizational Revolution: A Study in the Ethics of Economic Organization.* New York: Harper & Brothers.
Ciepley, D. (2006). *Liberalism in the Shadow of Totalitarianism.* Cambridge, Mass.: Harvard University Press.
Clemens, E. S. (2006). 'The Constitution of Citizens: Political Theories of Nonprofit Organizations', in W. W. Powell and R. Steinberg (eds.), *The Nonprofit Sector: A Research Handbook.* 2nd edn. New Haven: Yale University Press.
Coase, R. H. (1937). 'The Nature of the Firm'. *Economica*, 4/16: 386–405.
Davis, G. F., McAdam, D., Scott, W. R., and Zald, M. N. (eds.) (2005). *Social Movements and Organization Theory.* New York: Cambridge University Press.
Davis, M. (1986). ' "That's Classic!" The Phenomenology and Rhetoric of Successful Social Theories'. *Philosophy of the Social Sciences*, 16: 285–301.
Dewey, J. ([1927] 1954). *The Public and Its Problems.* Athens: Ohio University Press.
—— ([1935] 2000). *Liberalism and Social Action.* Amherst, NY: Prometheus Books.
Domhoff, G. W. (1967). *Who Rules America?* Englewood Cliffs, NJ: Prentice-Hall.
Drucker, P. F. (1946). *Concept of the Corporation.* New York: John Day Company.
Fligstein, N. (2001). *The Architecture of Markets: An Economic Sociology of Twenty-First-Century Capitalist Societies.* Princeton: Princeton University Press.
Galbraith, J. K. (1952). *American Capitalism: The Concept of Countervailing Power.* Boston: Houghton Mifflin Company.
Hayek, F. A. ([1944] 1994). *The Road to Serfdom.* Chicago: University of Chicago Press.
—— (1960). 'The Corporation in a Democratic Society: In Whose Interest Ought It and Will It Be Run?' in M. Anshen and G. L. Bach (eds.), *Management and Corporations 1985.* New York: McGraw-Hill.
Hirschman, A. O. (1977). *The Passions and the Interests: Political Arguments for Capitalism Before Its Triumph.* Princeton: Princeton University Press.
Leuchtenberg, W. E. (1963). *Franklin D. Roosevelt and the New Deal, 1932–1940.* New York: Harper and Row.
Locke, J. ([1690] 1952). *The Second Treatise of Government.* Indianapolis, Ind.: Bobbs-Merrill.
Mills, C. W. (1956). *The Power Elite.* New York: Oxford University Press.
Ogburn, W. F. (1922). *Social Change with Respect to Culture and Original Nature.* New York: B. W. Huebsch, Inc.
Polanyi, K. ([1944] 2001). *The Great Transformation: The Political and Economic Origins of Our Time.* Boston: Beacon.
Riesman, D. ([1950] 1961). *The Lonely Crowd.* New Haven: Yale University Press.

Roy, W. G. (1997). *Socializing Capital: The Rise of the Large Industrial Corporation in America.* Princeton: Princeton University Press.

Sennett, R. (1998). *The Corrosion of Character: The Personal Consequences of Work in the New Capitalism.* New York: Norton.

Smith, A. ([1789] 1976). *An Inquiry into the Nature and Causes of the Wealth of Nations.* Chicago: University of Chicago Press.

Suleiman, E. (2003). *Dismantling Democratic States.* Princeton: Princeton University Press.

Tocqueville, A. de (2004). *Democracy in America*, trans. Arthur Goldhammer. New York: Library of America.

Whyte, W. H., Jr. (1956). *The Organization Man.* New York: Simon and Schuster.

CHAPTER 25

BUREAUCRATIC THEORY AND INTELLECTUAL RENEWAL IN CONTEMPORARY ORGANIZATION STUDIES

MICHAEL REED

25.1. Introduction

BETWEEN the late 1940s and the early 1960s, a number of case studies on the dynamics of bureaucratic power and control were published. The studies focused on substantive themes and theoretical debates that were to shape the development of organizational studies during the second half of the twentieth century. These 'modern classics' underwent a cycle of imaginative interpretive reformulations during the 1960s to 1980s that reflected the wider socio-political and cultural context in which organization studies evolved as a recognizable, if contested, field of study.

The objective of this chapter is to revisit this classical body of theoretical and empirical work on the dynamics of bureaucratic power and control and to reassess its significance for the intellectual renewal and regeneration of contemporary organization studies (Perry 1979). First, I will examine the strategic sociological, political, and ethical issues that these works were responding to during a historical period of deep-seated structural changes—that is the period between the Great Depression in the 1920s and 1930s and the rise of the 'corporate state' between the 1940s and 1960s. Second, I will consider the cycle of imaginative reformulations that these modern classics have experienced as the intellectual dominance of structural functionalism and systems theory between the late 1940s and 1960s gave way to the much more theoretically open and contested trajectory that organization studies followed from the 1970s onwards. Third, I will evaluate the major theoretical debates that have emerged out of the modern classics and continue to frame the intellectual agenda constitutive of organization studies in the twenty-first century. In short, I will identify the key intellectual continuities that indelibly link the modern classics with contemporary work and thus provide a vital resource for intellectual renewal and revitalization in contemporary organizational analysis and research.

25.2. From the Iron Cage to Vicious Circles

Selznick's book, *The TVA and the Grass Roots*, was published in 1949 (with a second edition in 1966). Gouldner's *Patterns of Industrial Bureaucracy* and its sequel *Wildcat Strike* were both published in 1954. Blau's *Dynamics of Bureaucracy* was published in 1955 (with a second edition in 1963). Crozier's *The Bureaucratic Phenomenon* was published in 1964.

Taken together, these studies document the emergence of new forms of bureaucratic power and control that are symptomatic of pivotal shifts in the institutional formations that define modern, industrial capitalist political economies and the underlying structural mechanisms that generated them (Mouzelis [1967] 1975; Perry 1979). Collectively, they also served to challenge the analytical, theoretical, methodological, and empirical basis on which Weber diagnosed the key structural features of rational bureaucracy and offered a prognosis of a 'shared organizational fate' dominated by bureaucratic rationalization and the 'iron cage' of bureaucratic control that it instigated (Clegg 1994). Unintentionally, they also convincingly illuminated the inherent explanatory weaknesses and limitations of a form of structural-functionalist theorizing and analysis that traded on a model of the organization as a natural system internally adapting to externally imposed needs and demands (Silverman 1970).

25.2.1. Selznick

Selznick's study examines the operation of the Tennessee Valley Authority (TVA), which was established by Congress in 1933 to plan the sustainable use, conservation, and development of the natural resources of the Tennessee River drainage and its adjoining territory. His analysis traces the process whereby the TVA's administrative leadership adapted the agency's program and structure to meet the demands of local interest groups and thereby met the organization's core functional needs for long-term survival and growth. This process of evolutionary adaptation in the agency's policy goals and organizational practices depended on skillful manipulation, by bureaucratic elites, of the official 'grass roots' ideology that had legitimated its creation within an often suspicious, if not downright hostile, institutional field. It also depended on the emergence of an administrative mechanism of 'informal co-optation' that ensured the representation of these locally influential vested interests by way of internally generated and sustained 'administrative constituencies'. Selznick's analysis of this complex administrative-cum-political process draws on a creative synthesis of elitist bureaucratic theory and structural-functionalist theory in order to understand how the behavior of certain key individuals and groups becomes adapted 'to the needs and structure of the organization as a living social institution' (Selznick 1966: 14).

The main substantive focus of Selznick's study is the processes of political manipulation and administrative micro-management through which the putatively radical philosophy and ideology of 'grass roots' participation and control were reinterpreted in order to ensure policy outcomes of a far more conservative and restricted nature (Colignon 1997). The key bureaucratic mechanism through which the TVA's elite administrative management achieved this strategic political objective was the process of 'co-optation'—that is, 'the process of absorbing new elements into the leadership or policy-determining structure of an organization as a means of averting threats to its stability or existence' (Selznick 1966: 13). Selznick identifies two forms of 'co-optation': 'formal' and 'informal'. Formal co-optation entails overtly and publicly absorbing new interests into the policy-determining structure as a way of protecting and potentially enhancing the legitimacy and stability of the organization's existence, status, and role. Informal co-optation involves the covert and tacit absorption of potentially threatening and recalcitrant individuals and groups within the wider community into the internal decision-taking process in a way that preserves the form, if not the content, of its founding ideology. Such a form of co-optation, Selznick maintains, necessitates a redistribution of political power within the organization and its wider institutional field. Newly co-opted interest groups come to exert a real impact on policy-making processes and outcomes in a way that unavoidably dilutes the political and cultural force of the founding ideology. Bureaucratic elites are more than prepared to risk a significant degree of 'organizational capture' by powerful external interest groups, if this is deemed necessary, by them, in the longer term 'institutional interests' of the organization.

In the case of the TVA, Selznick contends, the increasing reliance on the mechanism of 'informal co-optation' as a means of absorbing and neutralizing the threat posed by large-scale farming interests inevitably resulted in a substantial dilution of the political influence of small-scale farmers, ethnic minorities, and conservation groups within local communities. As Selznick puts it, 'My conclusion was not merely that the TVA trimmed its sails in the face of hostile pressure. *More important is the fact that a right wing was built inside the TVA*. The agricultural program of the agency was simply turned over to a group that had strong commitments, not only to a distinct ideology but to a specific constituency' (1966: xiii, emphasis added). The TVA was very much an organizational expression of the New Deal era and Roosevelt's drive to promote and support forms of integrated planning and management of regional and local areas that were suffering from the ravages of long-term rural neglect and decay. This had been exacerbated by the catastrophic material and social consequences of extended economic recession and social deprivation. In order to achieve this strategic goal of nationally led economic planning and development for economically and socially depressed areas, the federal government, under Roosevelt's leadership, promoted the passing of legislation to create 'a corporation clothed with the power of central government but possessed of the flexibility and initiative of private enterprise' (Selznick 1966: 5).

But this classic 'organizational hybrid' was highly constrained, ideologically, politically, and administratively, in what it could do, how it could do it, and why its continued existence was deemed to be acceptable by a sufficient range of interest groups located at national, state, and local levels (Colignon 1997). The legislation setting it up gave it little or no direct power and authority to engage in large-scale regional planning and development. The delegated powers that it enjoyed were very specific in nature and scope, relating to the major problems of flood control, navigation, fertilizer production and distribution, and energy production and distribution. Yet, its managerial elites were allocated significant administrative discretion, if not complete autonomy, in designing and delivering a wide range of policies and programs aimed at improving the economic and social well-being of seriously disadvantaged groups. Thus, the bureaucratic leadership within the TVA very quickly adjusted the agency's structures, policies, and programs to the existing pattern of interorganizational power relations at state and community levels, while justifying this move in terms of the ideology of 'grass roots' control that had initially legitimated its inception to a sometimes wary and suspecting audience of stakeholder interests. Consequently, the 'political realism' of the TVA's bureaucratic elites—particularly among a younger cadre of senior officials whose career prospects were intimately tied to the organizational fate of the agency—became reflected in the combination of structural mechanisms and administrative practices that they selected to sustain it over a difficult period and beyond. This may have politically disenfranchised low-income small farmers and reinforced the economic and political domination of large-scale land-owning and farming interests. But the administrative leadership calculated that this was an economic price and political sacrifice that was worth paying if it meant that the long-term survival and expansion of the organization could be virtually guaranteed.

The agency found itself increasingly exposed to the political struggles and organizational conflicts, occurring at national, state, and local levels, within and between New Deal agencies that were being forced to align themselves with either central government or local elites. Eventually, the TVA aligned itself with local elites, so fundamentally transforming its organizational culture and identity from a conservation agency originally charged with utilizing publicly owned land and material resources for ecological sustainability and socio-economic progress into a business enterprise dominated by commercial priorities and market discipline. Organizational viability and growth had been secured but at the cost of undermining the moral foundations and political authority of its institutional mission and cultural identity within American society. The agency's bureaucratic elites and managerial cadres had expertly turned the ideology of 'grass roots' control to instrumental political and administrative ends for their own reasons and cloaked these within a patina of technical necessity and ethical neutrality.

Throughout his analysis, Selznick juxtaposes his theoretical commitments and substantive conclusions with those emerging from Weber's analysis of bureaucratic administration and control. Weber, Selznick suggests, is methodologically and theoretically committed to a form of ideal-typical analysis that focuses on the formal structures and mechanisms through which bureaucratic power and control are authorized and allocated. This leads him to focus narrowly on the officially explicated rules and regulations that bureaucratic behavior is meant to follow rather than what bureaucrats actually do, how they do it, and with what long-term consequences for the organization and the values and interests that it is meant to serve. The broader implications of this argument for the study of bureaucratic behavior, organization, and change are quite clear: 'Though official statements and theories are important, an undue concentration upon what men [*sic*] say diverts attention from what they do.... it is precisely to the realm of actual behavior and its significance for evolving structures and values that we must move if this kind of inquiry is to realise its possibilities' (Selznick 1966: 9). Indeed, it is exactly this point that Selznick (1966: 9) picks up on in his suggestion that the study of actual bureaucratic behavior and practice should focus on the 'recalcitrance of the tools of action'. This focus would provide a leitmotif for subsequent studies of the dynamics of bureaucracy and their wider implications for our understanding of organizational restructuring and institutional change. It would also provide an analytical

'Trojan horse' for new theoretical approaches to the study of organizations and organizing that fundamentally and irrevocably broke with structural-functionalist theorizing and the ontological presuppositions on which it had been developed.

25.2.2. Gouldner

The institutional context and organizational locale for Gouldner's study exhibited many similarities to those evident in Selznick's study of the TVA. In both cases, we have relatively isolated and traditional rural communities in the throes of rapid agricultural industrialization and mechanization that reinforces the dominance of the commercial interests of large-scale farming and further weakens and destabilizes the viability and legitimacy of localized forms of social solidarity based on a paternalistic ideology. In Gouldner's study, we also have an industrial sector, the gypsum industry, experiencing severe competition in both its product and labor markets in ways that intensify the pressure on management and labor to increase productivity and reduce overhead, particularly labor, costs. In turn, these interrelated economic, social, and cultural transformations occurring within the wider institutional environment strengthen forms of social stratification based on class power and domination and their articulation within the micro-politics of workplace struggles over the 'frontier of control'. It is within this context of the dynamic interplay between larger structural conditions or forces and the creative responses of social actors to these developments that Gouldner analyzes the process of bureaucratization and its longer term implications for the organization.

Through a very rich and detailed ethnographic account, Gouldner describes the move from 'mock or paternalistic' to 'punishment-centered' to 'quasi-representative' forms of bureaucracy (1954*b*: 119–20). Thus, the virtual destruction of the paternalistic ideology underpinning the 'indulgency pattern' within the plant and the form of 'mock bureaucracy' that it legitimated and its eventual replacement with a much more instrumental and rational form of bureaucratic control is explained in terms of the complex interplay between changing material conditions, social relations, and moral orders and the attempts of social actors to cope with these momentous developments as best they can. But Gouldner's major explanatory focus throughout the study is on the power and control struggles between key socio-political groups (located at different levels of socio-economic organization) and the various structural mechanisms through which they conduct these conflicts and strive to realize their interests and protect the moral values on which they rest.

The emergence of a, relatively, more rational and representative form of bureaucracy following the wildcat strike created as many problems, for both management and workers, as it solved (Gouldner 1954*b*: 119). It generated increased centralization of decision-making power within both management and labor hierarchies, extended the range of formalized rules and controls, legitimated an instrumental and commercially driven corporate culture, and destroyed what remained of the moral force and significance of the old 'indulgency pattern'. The underlying moral and social stability facilitated by the indulgency pattern and the 'mock bureaucracy' that it legitimated was gone forever; it had been replaced by a more instrumental, but transient and unstable, set of understandings and relationships that would prove to be rather weak and ineffective in coping with succeeding control struggles and organizational conflicts.

Gouldner also echoes Selznick's critique of Weber's over-reliance on formalistic ideal-typical analysis and his consequent lack of interest in the complex socio-political processes whereby the practical legitimacy of and operational consent to changing forms of bureaucratic power and control can be, however temporally, secured. Yet again, he reinforces Selznick's argument that the inherent 'recalcitrance of the tools of action' has to be the major explanatory focus for any theoretical approach to the study of bureaucratization and bureaucracy that aspires to account for such a dynamic and complex social process and phenomenon. It also reinforces the key point that any such account will need to encompass multi-level, comparative case study and historical organizational research that is analytically and methodologically equipped to deal with the emergence of new organizational forms and the innovative repertoires of control strategies and design practices that they make available to elite groups (Clark 2000). These themes and arguments are reflected with some force in Blau's and Crozier's studies of changing forms of bureaucratic power and control in very different institutional environments.

25.2.3. Blau

Blau's intensive case studies of one department of a state employment agency and another department within a federal enforcement agency—the latter having been established under the auspices of New Deal ideology, policy, and programs—focuses on the complex interplay between changing functional needs and shifting micro-level power structures embedded within their wider institutional fields. In this way, intra-organizational changes in bureaucratic structures and practices are linked both to the everyday micro-politics of organizational life and to the more enduring macro-politics of interorganizational restructuring and development. Consequently, micro-level innovations in bureaucratic rules and practices—such as the introduction of new control mechanisms as exemplified in statistical performance records and formalized case-processing procedures—have unanticipated and unintended consequences that have to be understood and explained. Once this explanatory move is introduced, then the role of pivotal macro-level structural mechanisms—such as class, race, ethnicity, and gender—in shaping the fate of innovations in micro-level bureaucratic control mechanisms, Blau concludes, can be more properly and fruitfully integrated into the theoretical frameworks that we rely on to account for these changes and their effects. Only in this way can we begin to more clearly understand and appreciate the theoretical and practical significance of the fact that

> The co-existence of democratic and bureaucratic institutions in a society [however] poses a paradox. Bureaucracies seem to be necessary for, and simultaneously incompatible with, modern democracy. In a mass society democracy depends on bureaucratic institutions, such as a complex machinery for electing representatives and efficient productive units that make a high standard of living for all people possible. Yet, by concentrating power in the hands of a few men in business and government, bureaucracies threaten to destroy democratic institutions. (Blau 1963: 265)

Herein lies the intractable dilemma or paradox that was at the heart of Weber's analysis (Ray and Reed 1994). But Blau's study, as that of Selznick and Gouldner before him, shows that whatever the inherent analytical and substantive limitations of Weber's work on bureaucratization and bureaucracy, it serves to remind us of the even greater weaknesses and lacunae in structural-functionalist analysis. Indeed, the evident inability of structural-functionalist analysis to theorize power relations and to analyze their impact on organizational forms and practices consistently recurs in the three modern classics we have reviewed so far in this chapter. It is only by breaking free of the theoretical shackles imposed by structural-functionalist orthodoxy that Blau, Selznick, and Gouldner are able to construct explanatory accounts of the processes and phenomena that they identify and to relocate them within a neo-Weberian tradition of sociological theorizing, in which the interplay between pre-existing power structures and innovative forms of collective agency emerges as the central explanatory focus. This becomes particularly clear in all three case studies when their authors attempt to describe and explain the dynamics of intraorganizational control struggles and their complex interaction with institutionalized power relations and structures. These simply cannot be forced into the theoretical straitjacket imposed by structural-functionalist orthodoxy. This is even more clearly revealed in Crozier's analysis of bureaucratic 'vicious circles' and their implications for the reproduction and elaboration of bureaucratic power structures.

25.2.4. Crozier

Crozier's analysis of the 'bureaucratic phenomenon' is formally developed within a structural-functionalist theoretical framework that has to be analytically modified to account for the general social process that he perceives as underlying organizational change and development—that is, the intensifying power struggles over 'areas of uncertainty'. This is an inevitable outcome of the failure of bureaucracy to provide a universal solution to the 'problem of control' (Crozier 1964: 1–9).

The organizational case studies that provide the empirical basis for Crozier's theoretical analysis were embedded in highly structured institutional environments in which their administrative elites and managers were constantly subjected to surveillance and 'control-at-a-distance' exercised by senior officials located within the French central government bureaucracy. The first case study ('The Clerical Agency') examines the hierarchical and operating routines of a Parisian branch of the French giro system; the other case study ('The Industrial Monopoly') involves an in-depth analysis of three Parisian plants (and a general questionnaire survey of twenty provisional plants) of a French state-owned tobacco monopoly. The major focus for the first case centers on mapping and explaining the underlying mechanisms that generate and sustain a highly formalized and routinized pattern of decision making that protects the power and status interests of occupationally based work groups. The second case is focused on the mechanisms that link the formal structure of bureaucratic surveillance and control to the complex network of intraorganizational power relations and processes that form between groups located at managerial and shop-floor levels. Both cases are also analyzed in the wider societal and institutional context of French history and society with particular regard to the established norms for dealing with authority relations and group power struggles. Here, Crozier gives particular emphasis to the fact that the latter stress the overriding importance of avoiding face-to-face conflicts and the transparent exercise of power in superior/subordinate transactions. At the same time, Crozier argues that these established institutional structures and cultures are coming under increasing strain and pressure from the accelerated economic and social development of the French political economy and society during the 1950s and 1960s (Crozier 1969).

The wider theoretical implications of these empirical studies are identified in three interrelated concepts that Crozier develops to understand and explain his findings: (1) the concept of 'parallel power relations', which emerges from his analysis of the crucial interplay between power and uncertainty in organizational life; (2) the concept of 'bureaucratic vicious circles', which develops out of his interpretation of 'parallel power relations' and the political processes that sustain them; and (3) his concept of 'strategic bureaucratic organization' and its critical explanatory role in contextualizing 'parallel power relations' and 'bureaucratic vicious circles'. Taken as a complete theoretical package, Crozier's study provides an extremely powerful analytical synthesis of the central themes, concepts, and conclusions that emerge from his progenitors' work.

For Crozier, 'power' is the central problem in the study of organizations. It is a concept that has been consistently neglected by mainstream organizational theory—particularly in North America—because of its individualist/reductionist methodological predilections and its near obsession with socio-psychological processes such as 'motivation' and 'leadership'. 'Power', he argues, is most appropriately conceived as a concept that describes a form of social relationship that is neither uni-dimensional nor predictable; nor is it possible to cleanse the concept of its ideological, political, and moral connotations. Rather, the most appropriate way to proceed in analyzing power relationships within and between organizations is to link it to the 'areas of uncertainty' that inevitably emerge in bureaucratic systems that cannot eliminate them—no matter how hard they might try through various forms of technological, administrative, and cultural rationalization:

> Since it is impossible, whatever the effort, to eliminate all sources of uncertainty within an organization by multiplying impersonal rules and developing centralization, a few areas of uncertainty will remain. Around these areas, parallel power relationships will develop, with the concomitant phenomena of dependence and conflict. Individuals or groups who control a source of uncertainty in a system of action where nearly everything is predictable, have at their disposal a significant amount of power over those whose situations are affected by this uncertainty. (Crozier 1964: 192)

Two major forms of power, Crozier continues, will emerge from this pattern of 'parallel power relations': 'expert power' (e.g. the maintenance crews in the 'industrial monopoly') and 'managerial power' (e.g. the engineering line managers in the 'industrial monopoly'). Consequently, this complex dialectical interplay between 'rationalization' and 'resistance' provides Crozier with the underlying power dynamic through which he can identify 'parallel power relations' and their explanatory significance in accounting for the processes through which 'strategic bureaucratic organization' is reproduced.

This analysis of power relations is then linked to his concept of 'bureaucratic vicious circles'. Bureaucratic vicious circles, Crozier contends, have four interrelated components: (1) highly centralized decision making and control; (2) a framework of rules and regulations emphasizing strict conformity to impersonalized modes of social interaction; (3) the social and organizational isolation of various groups located at different levels within the institutional hierarchy; and (4) the crystallization of parallel power relations around the inevitable 'areas of uncertainty' that the formal system cannot eliminate. While the dysfunctional consequences of bureaucratic vicious circles can be alleviated in various ways (e.g. by the introduction of more open and transparent decision-making procedures) they cannot, Crozier insists, be eradicated. New sources of uncertainty, ambiguity, and unpredictability will inevitably emerge—often as a result of the implementation of innovative rationalization strategies and practices designed and implemented by management. In turn, this will provide the impetus for new rounds of technical, organizational, and cultural rationalization that will reinforce the institutional status quo.

This leads Crozier to the third and final concept in his theoretical triptych: the concept of 'strategic bureaucratic organization'. As in the case of Selznick, Gouldner, and Blau, this is directly juxtaposed with Weber's ideal type of 'rational' or 'mechanistic bureaucracy'. In particular, Weber, once again, stands accused of drastically underestimating the innate resistance of social actors to bureaucratic rationalization and of developing a model of bureaucratic organization that, at best, marginalizes the explanatory significance of dynamic political processes and the changing pattern of power relations emerging from them. In stark contrast, Crozier argues, the model of 'strategic bureaucratic organization' recognizes the fundamental explanatory importance of interorganizational and intraorganizational political processes and power relations (and the crucial strategic and operational interdependencies between them), as they shape and reshape the institutional structures that these action strategies have generated (Crozier 1974; Crozier and Frieberg 1980).

By the time we reach Crozier's analysis of 'the bureaucratic phenomenon', we have moved a long way—philosophically, theoretically, methodologically, and substantively—from the core domain assumptions of structural-functionalist analysis and its implications for conceptualizing and explaining the key features of bureaucratization and bureaucracy. While the public display of functionalist respectability may be preserved—and would be renewed with some vigor as this body of work became creatively reinterpreted through the emerging orthodoxy of systems/contingency theory during the 1960s and 1970s—it increasingly looks like an empty theoretical husk with little or no substantive explanatory capacity or power.

25.3. Imaginative Reformulations

Throughout the 1960s and for much of the 1970s and early 1980s, systems-based contingency theory—with its philosophical roots in empiricist ontology and positivist epistemology—strove to establish itself as the dominant intellectual position in organization studies (Burrell and Morgan 1979; Clegg and Dunkerley 1980; Reed 1985, 1992; Donaldson 1985, 1995, 1996; Reed and Hughes 1992). A crucial component of this attempted strategy to establish the intellectual hegemony of systems-based contingency theory during this period entailed the initial incorporation and eventual assimilation of the modern classical studies of bureaucratization and bureaucracy into the emerging orthodoxy's theoretical core and program. However, as might be expected, this was a highly selective process of theoretical incorporation and absorption that denuded these modern classics of most of their conceptual creativity and explanatory power.

The pivotal text in achieving this initial 'incorporation and assimilation' is March and Simon's *Organizations* (1958). It detects a structural convergence of Merton's, Selznick's, and Gouldner's analyses around the core theme of organizational rules as a socio-psychological response to the 'need for control' on the part of organizational leaders or elites and the unintended and unanticipated 'dysfunctional learning' on the part of work groups that this generates. In this way, a sociological analysis of the dynamics of power and control within bureaucratic organizations operating in highly complex socio-political and economic contexts is reduced to a set of independent and dependent socio-psychological variables that can be accommodated within a systems model of the organization and a behaviorist model of the social actor.

As Perry notes (1979), March and Simon's interpretation became one of the 'received orthodoxies' of the organization studies literature throughout the 1960s and 1970s; it identified the 'dysfunctional school of bureaucratic theory' in a very distinctive, if highly tendentious, way and legitimated an interpretation of it that was entirely consistent with an emerging systems orthodoxy that would come to dominate the field intellectually from the late 1950s onwards. March and Simon's socio-psychological reinterpretation of the bureaucratic classics would be given a more 'radical twist' in the work of, say, Perrow (1970, 1972, 1979, 1986, 2002). But their highly selective 'reworking' would continue to be the primary point of reference for interlocutors as diverse as Thompson (1967) and Burrell and Morgan (1979).

Thompson's (1967) attempted synthesis of the 'classical' and 'modern' traditions in organization theory played a pivotal bridging role in absorbing the work of the 'dysfunctions of bureaucracy school' into an emerging 'administrative science' paradigm. He conceptually and theoretically embraces the 'newer tradition' of open-systems theorizing with its analytical focus on coping with 'uncertainty'. Crozier's work is deftly appropriated as providing theoretical legitimacy and empirical support for this 'newer tradition', which 'starts from the bureaucratic position [but] focuses on coping with uncertainty as its major topic' (Thompson 1967: 10).

Later on in his book, Thompson praises the work of Selznick, Gouldner, and Blau for enhancing our understanding of the underlying dynamics of organizational control and the mechanisms through which more complex forms of control can emerge and become institutionalized. But, yet again, his exposition and interpretation of their work and its wider explanatory implications are contained within a highly formalized administrative science approach seeking to generate and test empirical hypotheses in such a way that they can be translated and codified into abstract theoretical propositions. Thus, for example, Crozier's complex and rich analysis of 'parallel power relations', 'bureaucratic vicious circles', and 'strategic bureaucratic organization' is conceptually rendered down into a small subset of formal propositional statements about the potential logical and substantive links between 'managed uncertainty' and 'power dependency' (Thompson 1967: 129–31).

Nearly twenty years after the publication of Thompson's book, Donaldson (1985) would attempt a similar 'stripping down', 'incorporation', and 'assimilation' of the modern classics in a way that legitimates positivistic organization theory and systems-based contingency theory as the, by now somewhat intellectually worn and tarnished, dominant philosophical and theoretical orthodoxies within the field. So, 'the now classic studies of bureaucratic dysfunctions' (Donaldson 1985: 30) are paraded to negate the 'accusation' that structural functionalism and systems theory are necessarily theoretically wedded to crude and simple models of 'system equilibrium':

> Each of these [classic studies of bureaucratic dysfunctions] postulate pathological cycles, detrimental to efficient goal attainment. Note in passing that each offers causal explanations of how people and structures interact to produce consequences contrary to the intentions of the actors. It is axiomatic to structural functional analysis that contrasts between states of equilibrium and disequilibrium can identify ineffective designs and illuminate change processes. (Donaldson 1985: 30)

By the mid-1980s, as Donaldson clearly recognized, other 'imaginative reformulations' of the nature and legacy of the 'classic studies of bureaucratic dysfunctions' had emerged that departed from the underlying tenets of structural functionalism. Thus, from the late 1960s to early 1970s onwards, a steady stream of publications emerged that gave the modern classics a very different 'spin' from that provided by their positivist/systems-based interlocutors and began to map out a very different intellectual and ideological path for the 'sociology of organizations' to follow (Albrow 1968, 1970; Mayntz 1964; Perrow 1970, 1972, 1979; Silverman 1968, 1970, 1975; Elger 1975; Burrell and Morgan 1979; Clegg and Dunkerley 1980). The lines of intellectual and ideological lineage that these anti-positivist/systems interlocutors identified and drew on were grounded in a very different set of 'domain assumptions' (Reed 1985) than those prioritized by Donaldson and the tradition of organizational theorizing and analysis that he represented. They were expressly locating their work with the 'sociology of control', as opposed to the 'sociology of order' (Dawe 1970, 1979; Haddon 1973; Abrams 1982), and in so doing they were reasserting their view that 'the problematic of human agency' provided the conceptual key to understanding the unresolved, and ultimately irresolvable, tensions that lay at the core of organization studies (Reed 1988). Consequently, their reinterpretation and reformulation of the modern classics were poles apart from those offered by those writers and researchers locating themselves full-square in the 'sociology of order'.

The writers associated with this 'second wave' of reinterpretation and reformulation strongly identified with the modern classics' focus on organizations and societies as 'structures of power and decision-making' (Haddon 1973: 26). This call for a 'sociology of control', which rejected the philosophical, theoretical, and technological determinism inherent in positivism, structural-functionalist analysis, and systems theory, reworked the modern classics as exemplary illustrations of a 'sociology of social action in action'. The inherent creativity, contingency, autonomy, inconsistency, and unpredictability of human agency could be reclaimed and restored to its proper place as the central problematic or dilemma in organization studies (Reed 1988, 1997, 2003, 2005, 2006).

Thus, each of the modern classics can now be reinterpreted as illuminating the endemic contradictions and tensions between 'structure' and 'agency' as they work their way through emerging organizational forms and practices. Collectively, they provide a penetrating analysis of the contradictions and tensions between the reality of the material conditions and institutional configurations that agents inherit from the past and the promise of social innovation and change that agency always contains for the future. It is in these terms that the modern classics speak to a new and rising generation of scholars whose substantive concerns and theoretical tools are focused on organizations as arenas of social action and on organizational change as a complex social process necessarily shaped by the emergent interplay between structural constraints and action strategies.

Yet, for some (Benson 1977*a*, *b*; Burrell and Morgan 1979; Clegg and Dunkerley 1977, 1980; Clegg 1975, 1977; Littler and Salaman 1982; Thompson 1983), it is increasingly clear by the late 1970s and early 1980s that this social action-based reinterpretation and reworking of the modern classics had not gone far enough. The latter may have radically modified, but it had not entirely broken with, the conservative roots of the structural-functionalist/systems-theory tradition through which the reformulation of the modern classics has proceeded. In particular, it has consistently failed to confront its inherent limitations in coming to grips with the institutionalized forms of, essentially class-based, power that largely determine collective action strategies and their fundamental impact on long-term organizational change. In time, this emerging critique of the work of social action theorists and researchers would provide further impetus to the development of forms of labor-process-based theory and analysis in organization studies that drew on the modern classics to achieve an innovative conceptual synthesis between selected elements of neo-Weberian and neo-Marxist strands of sociological theorizing.

It is in these terms that Clegg (1977: 32) contrasts 'the naturalist and a-historical tendencies that find expression in current versions of the organization as a natural system' with an emerging approach that 'poses an understanding of the organization as the locus of domination of a specific form of life'. This dovetails neatly with Burrell and Morgan's (1979: 184–9, 207–9) interpretation of the modern classics as holding out the possibility of a radical break with functionalist orthodoxy and the development of an alternative approach, which could have established the basis for a 'radical organization theory' that is focused on macro-level power structures and their role in shaping and reshaping changing organizational forms and practices. However, in Burrell and Morgan's view, this potential is never realized because all forms of social action theorizing and analysis, including those evident within the modern classics, remain trapped within the philosophical, theoretical, and ideological orthodoxies characteristic of the functionalist paradigm in social and organization theory. As such, they can be located on the outlying borders of the functionalist paradigm, but they have failed to make the transition into the radical structural paradigm because they are unable to make a clean break with the core domain assumptions on which the functionalist paradigm is founded.

Finally, we come to the imaginative reformulation of the nature, standing, and influence of the modern classical studies of bureaucratization and bureaucracy that has emerged from the arrival and progression of 'the new institutionalism in organizational analysis' (Scott 1987, 1995, 2001; Powell and DiMaggio 1991; Zucker 1988; Tolbert and Zucker 1996; Barley and Tolbert 1997; Hirsch and Lounsbury 1997; Jennings and Greenwood 2006; Lounsbury and Ventresca 2003; Lawrence and Suddaby 2006). It is here that we might reasonably expect that the line of intellectual descent between the modern classics and contemporary organization studies will be most direct and explicit, given the critical role that Selznick's work, in particular, has played in the development of neo-institutional theory and analysis. Jennings and Greenwood (2006: 195, emphasis in original) draw the contrast between 'old institutionalism' and 'new institutionalism', as exemplified in Selznick's work, and, to a lesser extent, Gouldner's work, in the following manner:

While many variants of the new wing of institutional theory—'new institutionalism'—exist, all are distinguished by this shift to a stress on human agency from an older, more structurally inert institutionalism.... Older institutionalism has been a compelling perspective because it says rationalization and bureaucratization appear inexorable in the modern world and because it says that normative (moral), cognitive, and regulative (authority-based) forces push towards rationality and cognitive complexity. But older institutionalism also says that to understand the construction of the iron cage of bureaucracy, a theorist must assess its creation in context, a context that includes power, interest, and conflict over alternative modes of organizing and ways of understanding the world. Newer institutionalism is even more compelling because it points to fields and networks of actors (especially organizations) as the locus of action. New institutionalism connects these fields both with the long-term macro-development of culture, forms and archetypes, *and* with more micro, short term interactions among actors in the fields, especially as they seek to make sense of these fields.

However, the extent to which new institutionalism has fully recognized the philosophical and theoretical significance of 'agency' has been seriously questioned by a growing number of contemporary organization theorists (Hoffman and Ventresca 2002), who feel that new institutionalism remains ontologically and analytically wedded to a form of cultural and historical determinism in which powerful environmental forces that collectively push in the direction of institutional isomorphism are unlikely to be resisted, much less redirected, by agents.

This assessment of the significance of 'old institutionalism' for 'new institutionalism' suggests that the former played a critical role in opening up the issue of the 'organization/environment' relationship in a way that connected the analysis of normative systems to the political interests and power relations that they served. Thus, Selznick's study of the TVA is regarded as a classic illustration of the complex ways in which long-term organizational development has to be analyzed in the light of changing 'legitimation needs' emerging in the wider political and cultural environment in which organizations are embedded. This argument is then absorbed as a core assumption within 'new institutionalism' but is reworked and reframed in various ways that lead to a more precise conceptual delineation of the structural mechanisms through which organizational change is generated and of the cultural processes through which that change occurs. Within this emerging analytical framework, the focus of the classics on long-term organizational survival as a, if not 'the', primary outcome of complex institutionalization processes has been sustained in contemporary research conducted by organizational ecologists and institutional theorists (Baum and Shipilov 2006).

25.4. Thematic Continuities

In this penultimate section of the chapter, I identify and review a number of recurring themes emerging from the body of work bequeathed by the modern classics on bureaucratization and bureaucracy—themes that continue to inform and shape the agenda in contemporary organization studies.

First, there is the *agency/structure* dilemma or paradox and its continuing analytical, philosophical, and ethical significance for contemporary organization studies. Second, one can identify the *dialectic of power and control* as a dominant motif that is as central to us today as it was to the modern classicists in the middle of the previous century. Third, there is the focus on the ever-changing balance between *organizational dynamics and statics* and its implications for our understanding of the emergence, diffusion, institutionalization, and deinstitutionalization of innovative organizational forms and practices.

25.4.1. The Agency/Structure Dilemma

Previous exposition and evaluation of the modern classics on bureaucratization and bureaucracy has consistently highlighted the enduring significance of the agency/structure dilemma or paradox and its fundamental importance for contemporary organization studies (Dawe 1970, 1979; Giddens 1979, 1984, 1990; Reed 1985, 1988, 1997, 2003, 2006; Layder 1993, 1994; Archer 2000, 2003; Stones 2005; Manicas 2006). The agency/structure dilemma or paradox is, at root, an ontological issue that has far-reaching consequences for how we understand and explain social phenomena, such as organizations. At its core lies the fundamentally paradoxical nature of social life and existence—that creative interventions on the part of human beings to improve 'their lot' are always bound by pre-existing structural constraints and always result in unanticipated and unintended consequences for themselves and for future generations. As social scientists and students of organization, we must find intellectual means, resources, and tools that fully recognize the inherently paradoxical or dualistic quality of social life and existence. We need theoretical tools that can equip us to engage with Layder's (1994: 4) crucial question of 'how creativity and constraint are related through social activity—how can we explain their co-existence?'

As should be clear by now, the works of the modern classicists on bureaucratization and bureaucracy provide vital intellectual resources for how Layder's question might be responded to by students of organization. They imaginatively call our attention to the complex interplay between agency and structure as it works its way through successive phases of organizational restructuring and their longer term implications for material and social outcomes. In many respects, the overall tenor of their analyses is relatively pessimistic in that they collectively identify an interlocking set of 'bureaucratic vicious circles' that are extremely difficult, if not impossible, to counteract, much less to break out of into more virtuous circles. But this overlying pessimism, and the strong analytical and theoretical emphasis that it gives to inherent structural constraint and limitation, is qualified by an underlying optimism that the creative and dynamic force of human agency will always reassert itself in ways that will not and cannot be 'rationalized out' by any conceivable bureaucratic control regime and system.

Indeed, all of the case studies reviewed in this chapter are illustrations of Perry's (1979: 270) particular assessment of Selznick's damning moral evaluation of the TVA—that they are all 'bureaucratic successes but political failures as well'. In turn, this illustrates the strong voluntaristic undertones of the analyses that Selznick, Gouldner, Blau, and Crozier proffer and of their commitment to a form of analysis in which 'the organizational' and 'the political' are analytically synonymous in that they both necessarily partake 'in *de facto* power relationships and their consequences' (Perry 1979: 266, emphasis in original). This consistent emphasis on voluntarism highlights the necessary contradictions and contingent tensions between agency and structure and serves to identify the potential sources of future dynamic momentum and change.

25.4.2. Dialectic of Power and Control

The previous evaluation of the modern classics has revealed a consistent focus on the dynamic interaction between 'structural or systemic power' and 'relational or agentic power' and its impact on the emergence, elaboration, and transformation of control regimes within work organizations. Whereas the former concept identifies a form of power that is regarded as a structurally determined capacity that is accumulated and stored in institutions and positions, the latter concept refers to power as a contingent relation or capacity that is always potentially reversible depending on the outcome of particular strategic struggles and tactical engagements (Clegg 1989; Fincham 1992; Sibeon 2004; Lukes 2005).

The complex interweaving and interpenetration between 'structural' and 'relational' power is consistently revealed throughout each of the modern classics and stands testimony to the enduring significance of what Giddens (1990: 138–9) calls the 'dialectic of control'—that is, the endemic contradiction between forms of power and control that are mobilized in support of institutionalization strategies aimed at stabilizing and sustaining established regimes and those mobilized to resist, even challenge, the latter. In this context, Giddens's focus on the power struggles between 'experts' and 'non-experts', and their impact on the appropriation and reappropriation of scarce knowledge and skills vital to maintain or change existing power structures and control relations, is anticipated in the modern classics. Within the latter, the strategic power/control dynamic is generated by the struggle between 'the manager', as the primary agent of rationalization/institutionalization, and the 'expert' (such as Crozier's maintenance engineers or Gouldner's gypsum miners), as the primary agent of uncertainty, indeterminacy, and autonomy. As agents of rationalization/institutionalization, managers are seen to have a range of strategies at their disposal, such as technological and organizational rationalization, but the new 'areas of uncertainty' that they unavoidably generate will provide a focus for expert strategies aimed at reappropriating new knowledge and skill.

However, it is vitally important to note that these 'organizational level' power and control struggles, which provide the major focus for the modern classics, are always embedded—ontologically, analytically, and historically—within the 'societal level' structures of domination from which they take their significance and meaning. Indeed, as recent contributors (Sibeon 2004; Stones 2005; Lukes 2005; Edwards 2006) to the ongoing debate over the complex interplay between 'power as domination' and 'power as strategy' have reflected, this raises fundamental questions about the nature of and links between 'power', 'ideology', 'interests', and 'control'. Much of this interest has, of course, been stimulated by Foucault's (2005) work on 'disciplinary regimes' and its implications for the development of a more dynamic, ascending, or capillary conception of power as reflected in a great deal of organizational research and analysis over the last two decades or so.

Whatever the relative merits of these different approaches to the 'dialectic of power and control', they remind us of one of the enduring lessons we can take from the modern classics—that is, the need to focus on the wide range of mechanisms through which power and control can be generated and sustained in contemporary organizations and on the highly complex and dynamic interplay between them. As Lukes (2005: 171, emphasis added) puts it when responding to some of his critics and defending his view that the power of agents, individual and collective, should be conceptualized in terms broad enough to encompass the full range of social mechanisms through which power may be generated, stabilized, and mobilized:

Power, in other words, does not, when it is at work, need to involve deliberate and strategic manipulation.... Viewing power in this broader way, one *is significantly less inclined* to see social arrangements that induce powerlessness and failures to solve collective action problems as unconnected to the powerful, as merely structural or attributable to 'luck' though sometimes one may conclude they are.

In turn, the theme of the 'dialectic of power and control' in organizational life is linked to the issue of the relative explanatory emphasis that is given to 'organizational dynamics and statics' in organizational analysis.

25.4.3. Organizational Dynamics and Statics

Over the last two decades or so, there has been a very definite theoretical shift towards a much more dynamic conception of 'organization' in which a concern with the underlying processes through which change, innovation, and development occur have come to dominate organizational research and analysis (Westwood and Clegg 2003; Tsoukas and Knudsen 2003; Clegg *et al.* 2006). However, some have warned that this, relatively positive and productive, theoretical shift can result in a situation where a 'process-based ontology' and its analytical architecture come to so intellectually dominate the field that any concern with the more enduring and constraining features of 'organization' are, at best, marginalized and, at worst, totally excluded from view (Clark 2000; Reed 2003, 2005; Sibeon 2004). As a result, organizational research and analysis may be in danger of overestimating the capacity of agents to transform the material conditions and structural contexts under which they act and, correspondingly, of underestimating the extent to which such individual and collective forms of action result in the reproduction and elaboration of pre-existing institutional and organizational forms. In short, that a greatly exaggerated emphasis on 'process' or 'dynamics' has been purchased at the cost of substantially weakening our theoretical capacity to deal with 'structure' or 'statics' and its central explanatory role in accounting for organizational change.

This need to sustain a sensible balance between a focus on 'dynamics' and 'statics' in organizational analysis is clearly expressed in the key contribution of the modern classics to our understanding of the process of 'organizational hybridization' and its implications for the emergence and development of new organizational forms. The latter has become a major theme in contemporary organizational analysis and finds its clearest, but by no means only, expression in current debates about the 'post-bureaucratic organization' and the importance attached to 'network-based' forms of organizational design at all levels of contemporary socio-economic and political activity (Clegg 1990; Adler and Borys 1996; Adler 2001; Castells 2000; Hecksher and Donnellon 1994; Child and McGrath 2001; Thompson 2003; Reed 2005, 2006; Sennett 2006).

Much of the current debate about the emergence and significance of organizational hybrids—logics of organizing and organizational forms combining contrasting, and often conflicting, rationales and principles that have to respond to a multiplicity of ideologically mediated interests and demands—is presaged in the modern classics. Within the latter, there is a recurring emphasis on organizational change and innovation as a complex response to changing economic, political, cultural, and ethical conditions that cannot be accommodated within uni-dimensional organizational forms and practices. Thus, for example, Selznick's analysis tries to convey how innovative the TVA was as an organizational form and how it attempted to combine private-sector flexibility and public-sector consistency within an integrated framework of institutional arrangements. His work also documents the inherent flexibility and adaptability of bureaucratic organization in the face of threats to its viability and survival—capacities that depend on the discipline and continuity so often criticized in more orthodox analyses of the 'bureaucratic phenomenon' (Selznick 1992; Du Gay 2000). His concept of 'administrative constituency' presages Child's concept of 'dominant coalition' (Child 1972, 1973, 1997) and the pivotal role that it would play in the development of the 'strategic choice' approach to organizational analysis during the 1970s and 1980s (Perry 1979; Clark 2000).

The modern classics also warn us about the over-optimism that often accompanies analyses of the emergence and diffusion of 'new' or 'hybrid' organizational forms because it is mindful of the unintended and unanticipated consequences of social action and of the inherent capability of established power structures and dominant groups to reassert their control—even in situations where there seem to be substantial threats to their dominance. Thus, once again, Selznick's analysis of the TVA reminds us how easily voluntary associations and groups, often seen as the best hope for the re-establishment of more participatory and democratic organizational forms in which social capital can be rebuilt and revitalized (Adler 2001), can become 'an extension of the state's apparatus, created by it for administrative purposes and available for use as an agency of control' (Perry 1979: 268). This reminder may be particularly apposite in an era during which the ideological, political, and organizational power of 'managerialism' has grown exponentially since the end of World War II.

25.5. Conclusion

As an exercise in intellectual recovery and renewal, this chapter has focused on the enduring contribution that the modern classical studies of bureaucratization and bureaucracy have made to our understanding of organizational change in its wider historical and societal context. The chapter has been conceived and constructed in keeping with the spirit and substance of Perry's (1979: 269, emphasis in original) injunction that

> The contemporary relevance of these authors is not limited to their attempts to recover history and to monitor the relation between organizational transformations and changes in social structure. It lies rather in their willingness to link this to a concern for the direction and content of organizational action, the effort to provide a politics *of* organization that is not reducible to the study of politics *in* organization. In so doing, they are obliged to transcend their own initial premises and their works move at the points of intersection between distinct levels of abstraction and discrete theoretical orthodoxies. Thus held by chains of ambivalence they exemplify what Gellner (1964: 50 *et seq*) might call metamorphosis—the position of authors who have had the skids put below them and who are trying, with some skill and ingenuity, to both interpret that fact and to change it.

Looked at in this way, the modern classics bequeathed an intellectual inheritance and an ideological legacy that has, in many ways at least, been diluted and narrowed by successive phases of imaginative reformulation (over a period of three decades or more) that have allowed their, relatively parochial and exclusionary, concerns to dominate the reinterpretations that they proffered. Yet, as Perry (1979: 269, emphasis added) also notes, the latter have not managed to extinguish the fact, however hard they may have tried, that 'organization is no longer conceived as a purely technical problem but becomes a social and political one, *with a potentiality for tension in the relation between the principles of legitimacy and the pattern of operation*'. Indeed, as we have seen, this fundamental tension has become the analytical focus and substantive concern for a succession of theoretical perspectives in organizational studies that have consistently and firmly rejected the intellectual constraints and ideological limitations imposed and policed by a, no longer dominant, positivist/functionalist orthodoxy.

Reconsidered in this light, we can see that the modern classics played an absolutely vital role in breaking the intellectual power and control of that orthodoxy—even though their work had originally been conceived and legitimated within the philosophical, theoretical, and ideological terms of reference laid down by that very same orthodoxy. To invoke Perry's phrase once more—they knew they 'have had the skids put beneath them' but they attempted, pretty successfully, to deal with this reality by confronting it and responding to it with some considerable theoretical skill and ingenuity. As Selznick (1992: 265–88) himself notes, the modern classics reminded us of 'the *dynamic* aspects of bureaucracy' and of the threat that it inevitably poses—'the energies released by the vested interests it creates'—to instrumental or purposive rationality as the ideological lynchpin of Weberian 'legal-rational bureaucracy'. In reminding us of the inherent moral and practical limits of bureaucracy, the modern classics also revived and renewed our interest in more open and participatory forms of organization that resonate with 'a post-modern spirit of openness, adaptation, participation and problem-solving' (Selznick 1992: 287). In short, they recovered and retrieved that endemic tension between 'organization' and 'community' that has been central to organization theory's intellectual development since the latter half of the nineteenth century (Wolin 2004). But they also caution against a too easy acceptance of these postmodern ideas:

> Enthusiasm for openness, negotiation, and self-affirming consent invites excessive optimism; and the virtues we associate with form and discipline are easily misunderstood and too readily disparaged. It is not likely that bureaucracy can be wholly transcended.... Rather, the new, non-bureaucratic forms will be essential leaven in the bureaucratic dough.
>
> (Selznick 1992: 287)

References

Abrams, P. (1982). *Historical Sociology*. Ithaca NY: Cornell University Press.

Adler, P. (2001). 'Market, Hierarchy and Trust: The Knowledge Economy and the Future of Capitalism'. *Organization Science*, 12/2: 215–34.

—— and Borys, B. (1996). 'Two Types of Bureaucracy: Enabling and Coercive'. *Administrative Science Quarterly*, 41/1: 61–89.

Albrow, M. (1968). 'The Study of Organizations—Objectivity or Bias?' in J. Gould (ed.), *Penguin Social Sciences Survey*. Harmondsworth: Penguin.

—— (1970). *Bureaucracy*. London: Pall Mall.

Archer, M. (2000). *Being Human: The Problem of Agency*. Cambridge: Cambridge University Press.

—— (2003). *Structure, Agency and the Internal Conversation*. Cambridge: Cambridge University Press.

Barley, S., and Tolbert, P. (1997). 'Institutionalization and Structuration: Studying the Links between Action and Institution'. *Organization Studies*, 18/1: 93–117.

Baum, J., and Shipilov, A. (2006). 'Ecological Approaches to Organizations', in S. Clegg, C. Hardy, T. Lawrence, and W. Nord (eds.), *The Sage Handbook of Organization Studies*. 2nd edn. London: Sage.

Benson, J. K. (1977*a*). 'Innovation and Crisis in Organizational Analysis'. *Sociological Quarterly*, 18: 229–49.

—— (1977*b*). 'Organizations: A Dialectical View'. *Administrative Science Quarterly*, 22/1: 1–23.

Blau, P. (1955). *The Dynamics of Bureaucracy*. Chicago: University of Chicago Press.

—— (1963). *The Dynamics of Bureaucracy*. 2nd revised edn. Chicago: University of Chicago Press.

Burrell, G., and Morgan, G. (1979). *Sociological Paradigms and Organizational Analysis*. London: Heinemann.

Castells, M. (2000). *The Rise of the Network Society*. 2nd edn. Oxford: Blackwell.

Child, J. (1972). 'Organization Structure, Environment and Performance: The Role of Strategic Choice'. *Sociology*, 6/1: 163–77.

—— (1973). 'Organization: Choice for Man', in J. Child (ed.), *Man and Organization*. London: Allen and Unwin.
—— (1997). 'Strategic Choice in the Analysis of Action, Structure, Organizations and Environment: Retrospect and Prospect'. *Organization Studies*, 18/1: 43–76.
—— and McGrath, R. (2001). 'Organizations Unfettered: Organizational Form in an Information-Intensive Economy'. *Academy of Management Journal*, 44/6: 1135–48.
Clark, P. (2000). *Organization in Action: Competition between Contexts*. London: Routledge.
Clegg, S. (1975). *Power, Rule and Domination*. London: Routledge.
—— (1977). 'Power, Organization Theory, Marx and Critique', in S. Clegg and D. Dunkerley (eds.), *Critical Issues in Organizations*. London: Routledge.
—— (1989). *Frameworks of Power*. London: Sage.
—— (1990). *Modern Organizations: Organization Studies in the Postmodern World*. London: Sage.
—— (1994). 'Weber and Foucault: Social Theory for the Study of Organizations'. *Organization*, 1/1: 149–78.
—— and Dunkerley, D. (1977). *Critical Issues in Organizations*. London: Routledge.
—— —— (1980). *Organization, Class and Control*. London: Routledge.
—— Hardy, C., Lawrence, T., and Nord, W. (eds.) (2006). *Sage Handbook of Organization Studies*. 2nd edn. London: Sage.
Colignon, R. A. (1997). *Power Plays: Critical Events and the Institutionalization of the Tennessee Valley Authority*. New York: State University of New York Press.
Crozier, M. (1964). *The Bureaucratic Phenomenon*. Chicago: University of Chicago Press.
—— (1969). *The Stalled Society*. New York: Viking Press.
—— (1974). 'Recent Trends and Future Trends for Sociology of Organizations', in M. Archer (ed.), *Current Research in Sociology*. Paris: Mouton Hague.
—— and Frieberg, M. (1980). *The Actor and the System*. Chicago: University of Chicago Press.
Dawe, A. (1970). 'The Two Sociologies'. *British Journal of Sociology*, 21/2: 207–18.
—— (1979). 'Theories of Social Action', in T. Bottomore and R. Nisbet (eds.), *A History of Sociological Analysis*. London: Heinemann.
Donaldson, L. (1985). *In Defence of Organization Theory*. Cambridge: Cambridge University Press.
—— (1995). *Anti-American Theories of Organization*. Cambridge: Cambridge University Press.
—— (1996). *For Positivist Organization Theory*. London: Sage.
Du Gay, P. (2000). *In Praise of Bureaucracy*. London: Sage.
Edwards, P. (2006). 'Power and Ideology in the Workplace: Going Beyond Even the Second Version of the Three-Dimensional View'. *Work, Employment and Society*, 20/3: 571–81.
Elger, T. (1975). 'Industrial Organization: A Processual Perspective', in J. B. McKinlay (ed.), *Processing People: Cases in Organizational Behaviour*. New York: Holt, Rinehart and Winston.
Fincham, R. (1992). 'Perspectives on Power: Processual, Institutional and "Internal" Forms of Organizational Power'. *Journal of Management Studies*, 26/9: 741–59.
Foucault, M. (2005). *Society Must be Defended*. London: Allen Lane, Penguin Press.
Gellner, E. (1964). *Thought and Change*. London: Weidenfield and Nicholson.

GIDDENS, A. (1979). *Central Problems in Social Theory: Action, Structure and Contradiction in Social Analysis*. London: Macmillan.

GIDDENS, A. (1984). *The Constitution of Society: Outline of a Theory of Structuration*. Cambridge: Polity Press.

—— (1990). *The Consequences of Modernity*. Cambridge: Polity Press.

GOULDNER, A. (1954*a*). *Patterns of Industrial Bureaucracy*. New York: Collier Macmillan.

—— (1954*b*). *Wildcat Strike*. New York: Antioch Press.

GREENWOOD, R., and HININGS, R. (1996). 'Understanding Radical Organizational Change: Bringing Together the Old and the New Institutionalism'. *Academy of Management Review*, 21: 1022–54.

HADDON, R. (1973). Foreword to *Industrialism and Industrial Man* by C. Kerr, J. T. Dunlop, F. Harbison, and C. A. Myers. Harmondsworth: Penguin.

HECKSHER, C., and DONNELLON, A. (eds.) (1994). *The Post-Bureaucratic Organization: New Perspectives on Organizational Change*. Thousand Oaks, Calif.: Sage.

HIRSH, P., and LOUNSBURY, M. (1997). 'Ending the Family Quarrel: Towards a Reconciliation of "Old" and "New" Institutionalism'. *American Behavioural Scientist*, 40/4: 406–18.

HOFFMAN, A., and VENTRESCA, M. (2002). Introduction in A. Hoffman and M. Ventresca (eds.), *Organizations, Policy and the Natural Environment: Institutional and Strategic Perspectives*. Stanford, Calif.: Stanford University Press.

JENNINGS, P., and GREENWOOD, R. (2006). 'Constructing the Iron Cage: Institutional Theory and Enactment', in R. Westwood and S. Clegg (eds.), *Debating Organization: Point-Counterpoint in Organization Studies*. Oxford: Blackwell.

LAWRENCE, T., and SUDDABY, R. (2006). 'Institutions and Institutional Work', in S. Clegg, C. Hardy, T. Lawrence, and W. Nord (eds.), *Sage Handbook of Organization Studies*. 2nd edn. London: Sage.

LAYDER, D. (1993). *New Strategies in Social Research*. Cambridge: Polity Press.

—— (1994). *Understanding Social Theory*. London: Sage.

LITTLER, C., and SALAMAN, G. (1982). 'Bravermania and Beyond: Recent Theories of the Labour Process'. *Sociology*, 16/2: 251–69.

LOUNSBURY, M., and VENTRESCA, M. (2003). 'The New Structuralism in Organizational Theory'. *Organization*, 10/3: 457–80.

LUKES, S. (2005). *Power: A Radical View*. 2nd edn. London: Palgrave Macmillan.

LYNN, B. (2006). 'Breaking the Chain: The Anti-Trust Case against Wal-Mart'. *Harper's Magazine*, July.

MANICAS, P. (2006). *A Realist Philosophy of Social Science: Explanation and Understanding*. Cambridge: Cambridge University Press.

MARCH, J., and SIMON, H. (1958). *Organizations*. New York: Wiley.

MAYNTZ, R. (1964). 'The study of organizations. A trend report and bibliography'. *Current Sociology*, 13/3: 95–156.

MERTON, R. (1968). *Social Theory and Social Structure*. Enlarged edn. New York: Free Press.

MOUZELIS, N. ([1967] 1975). *Organization and Bureaucracy*. 2nd edn. London: Routledge.

PERROW, C. (1970). *Organizational Analysis: A Sociological View*. London: Tavistock Publications.

—— (1972). *Complex Organizations: A Critical Essay*. Dallas, Tex.: Scott, Foresman and Company.

—— (1979). *Complex Organizations: A Critical Essay*. 2nd edn. Dallas, Tex.: Scott, Foresman and Company.

—— (1986). *Complex Organizations: A Critical Essay*. 3rd edn. Dallas, Tex.: Scott, Foresman and Company.
—— (2002). *Organizing America: Wealth, Power and the Origins of Corporate Capitalism*. Princeton: Princeton University Press.
PERRY, N. (1979). 'Recovery and Retrieval in Organizational Analysis'. *Sociology*, 13: 259–73.
POWELL, W., and DIMAGGIO, P. (eds.) (1991). *The New Institutionalism in Organizational Analysis*. Chicago: University of Chicago Press.
RAY, L., and REED, M. (eds.) (1994). *Organizing Modernity: New Weberian Perspectives on Work, Organization and Society*. London: Routledge.
REED, M. (1985). *Redirections in Organizational Analysis*. London: Tavistock.
—— (1988). 'The Problem of Human Agency in Organizational Analysis'. *Organization Studies*, 9/1: 33–46.
—— (1992). *The Sociology of Organizations: Themes, Perspectives and Prospects*. Hemel Hempstead: Harvester Press.
—— (1997). 'In Praise of Duality and Dualism: Rethinking Agency and Structure in Organizational Analysis'. *Organization Studies*, 18/1: 21–42.
—— (2003). 'The Agency/Structure Dilemma in Organization Theory: Open Doors and Brick Walls', in H. Tsoukas and C. Knudsen (eds.), *The Oxford Handbook of Organization Theory: Meta-Theoretical Perspectives*. Oxford: Oxford University Press.
—— (2005). 'Reflections on the Realist Turn in Organization and Management Studies'. *Journal of Management Studies*, 42/8: 1621–44.
—— (2006). 'Organizational Theorizing: A Historically Contested Terrain', in S. Clegg, C. Hardy, T. Lawrence, and W. Nord (eds.), *The Sage Handbook of Organization Studies*. 2nd edn. London: Sage.
—— and HUGHES, M. (1992). *Rethinking Organization: New Directions in Organization Theory and Analysis*. London: Sage.
SCOTT, W. (1987). 'The Adolescence of Institutional Theory'. *Administrative Science Quarterly*, 32/4: 493–511.
—— (1995). *Institutions and Organizations*. Thousand Oaks, Calif.: Sage.
—— (2001). *Institutions and Organizations*. 2nd edn. Newbury Park: Sage.
—— and CHRISTENSEN, S. (eds.) (1995). *The Institutional Construction of Organizations: International Longitudinal Studies*. Thousand Oaks, Calif.: Sage.
—— and MEYER, J. (1994). *Institutional Environments and Organizations: Structural Complexity and Individualism*. Thousand Oaks, Calif.: Sage.
SELZNICK, R. (1949). *The TVA and the Grass Roots*. Berkeley: University of California Press.
—— (1966). *The TVA and the Grass Roots*. 2nd edn. New York: Harper and Row.
—— (1992). *The Moral Commonwealth: Social Theory and the Promise of Community*. Berkeley: University of California Press.
SENNETT, R. (2006). *The Culture of the New Capitalism*. New Haven: Yale University Press.
SIBEON, R. (2004). *Rethinking Social Theory*. London: Sage.
SILVERMAN, D. (1968). 'Formal Organizations or Industrial Sociology: Towards a Social Action Analysis of Organizations'. *Sociology*, 2: 221–38.
—— (1970). *The Theory of Organizations*. London: Heinemann.
—— (1975). 'Accounts of Organizations—Organizational "Structures" and the Accounting Process', in J. McKinlay (ed.), *Processing People: Cases in Organizational Behaviour*. London: Holt, Rinehart and Winston.
STONES, R. (2005). *Structuration Theory*. London: Palgrave Macmillan.

Thompson, G. (2003). *Between Hierarchies and Markets: The Logic and Limits of Network Forms of Organization*. Oxford: Oxford University Press.

Thompson, J. (1967). *Organizations in Action*. New York: McGraw-Hill.

Thompson, P. (1983). *The Nature of Work*. London: Macmillan.

Tolbert, P., and Zucker, L. (1996). 'The Institutionalization of Institutional Theory', in S. Clegg, C. Hardy, and W. Nord (eds.), *The Handbook of Organization Studies*. London: Sage.

Tsoukas, H., and Knudsen, C. (eds.) (2003). *The Oxford Handbook of Organization Theory: Meta-Theoretical Perspectives*. Oxford: Oxford University Press.

Westwood, R., and Clegg, S. (eds.) (2003). *Debating Organization: Point-Counterpoint in Organization Studies*. Oxford: Blackwell.

Wolin, S. (2004). *Politics and Vision*. Expanded edn. Princeton: University of Princeton Press.

Zucker, L. (1988). *Institutional Patterns and Organizations: Culture and Environment*. Cambridge, Mass.: Ballinger.

CHAPTER 26

THE COLUMBIA SCHOOL AND THE STUDY OF BUREAUCRACIES

WHY ORGANIZATIONS HAVE LIVES OF THEIR OWN

HEATHER A. HAVEMAN

This chapter focuses on the work of three scholars, Robert K. Merton and his students Alvin W. Gouldner and Peter M. Blau, who were part of Columbia University's sociology department, Merton as professor, Gouldner and Blau as students. Together with Philip Selznick, Seymour Martin Lipset, James Coleman, and Martin Trow (Selznick 1949, 1957; Lipset 1950; Lipset, Trow, and Coleman 1956), these scholars were the core of the Columbia School of organizational sociology. Along with sociologists and political scientists scattered across America and Europe who studied public administration (e.g. Gulick and Urwick 1937; Anderson and Gaus 1945), and sociology and business professors at Harvard who studied industrial organization (Mayo 1933; Roethlisberger and Dickson 1939), these Columbia sociologists pioneered the sociological study of organizations.

The work of the Columbia School was rooted in Weberian ideas about bureaucracy, but moved in directions that Weber might not have expected. Rather than focusing on the technical rationality inherent in bureaucracy as celebrated by Weber, these scholars studied the unanticipated consequences of organizational design; in particular, the dysfunctions of bureaucratic organizations that arise from goal displacement. They highlighted conflicts that ensued both within organizations and between organizations and their surroundings. They saw organizations as the crucible of institutionalization: over time, organizations become valued in and of themselves, far beyond the technical merits of the things they do.

Sociologists and scholars in nearby disciplines, such as business and political science, have built extensively on the Columbia School's work, extending our knowledge of organizations in myriad ways. Notwithstanding the many theoretical, methodological, and empirical advances that have been made in the six decades since these men started publishing, their work still resonates. Most notably, reading this work reminds us that although people create organizations to achieve goals that require the joint, sustained, and coordinated efforts of many individuals, these social tools are highly recalcitrant: organizations take on lives of their own and so behave in ways that often surprise, even confound, the men and women who design and manage them (Selznick 1949: 10).

I begin by discussing an essay written by Merton that greatly influenced his students' research. I then examine closely two books that grew out of dissertation research by Gouldner and Blau.[1] Both books respond to Merton's call for developing and testing sociological theories of the middle range, which he defined as logically interconnected sets of propositions derived from assumptions about essential facts that yield empirically testable hypotheses and that deal with delimited aspects of social phenomena (Merton 1968: 39–72). Both books develop, using a mixture of deduction and induction, middle-range theories of organizations. Not surprisingly, given their common intellectual origins, these theories are related, notably by an explicit concern for understanding conflict. But each offers a distinct lesson for contemporary organizational scholars: Gouldner reminds us that culture (meaning the ideas organizational members have about what is good and bad, what is valued and ignored, what should and should not be done) mediates the meaning of all purportedly 'technical' phenomena, including bureaucratic rules,

[1] I originally planned to review books by three of Merton's students, the third being Philip Selznick's (1949) *TVA and the Grassroots*. But I found the chapter growing far too long. I decided to sacrifice breadth for depth. I chose to drop Selznick because his work has been covered by Dick Scott in all editions of his widely used texts on organizational theory (Scott 1981, 1987, 1992, 1998, 2002; Scott and Davis 2007) and institutional analysis (Scott 1995, 2001). For those who seek an introduction to the Columbia School and their impact on organizational sociology that is painted with a broader brush, Mike Reed's chapter in this volume offers a lovely complement to this chapter.

and highlights the importance of the physical world, while Blau shows us the unanticipated consequences of organizational design and demonstrates the prevalence of organizational change that is endogenous, stemming from the shortcomings of bureaucracies themselves rather than from external stimuli.

26.1. Robert Merton: Bureaucratic Structure and Personality

In his essay titled 'Bureaucratic Structure and Personality', Merton described the Weberian ideal-typical bureaucracy and noted its many functional merits—precision, expertise, reliability, and efficiency. (For more on Weber, see the chapters by Clegg and Lounsbury, and du Gay, in this volume.) Merton then pondered what Weber ignored—namely, the *dysfunctions* of bureaucratic organizations, meaning the things they do badly, often for precisely the same reasons that make them so good at other things. Merton called the primary bureaucratic dysfunction *goal displacement*, by which he meant that the members of organizations—officials—inevitably come to value rules and the behavior required by those rules over the objectives that the rules were intended to achieve. Because officials come to value means over ends and rules over performance, they often fail to achieve organizational goals. Merton's own elegant words provide the best explanation of this phenomenon:

> [T]his very emphasis... develops into rigidities and an inability to adjust readily. Formalism, even ritualism, ensues with an unchallenged insistence upon punctilious adherence to formalized procedures. This may be exaggerated to the point where primary concern with conformity to the rules interferes with the achievement of the purposes of the organization, in which case we have the familiar phenomenon of the technicism or red tape of the official.
>
> (1940: 563)

Why are ideal-typical Weberian bureaucracies and bureaucrats prone to goal displacement? Merton's explanation is as follows: if bureaucracies are to be effective, they must be reliable. Reliability, in turn, requires strict devotion to rules. Over time, devotion to rules leads bureaucrats to treat rules as absolutes rather than instruments: rules come to be conceived as things valued for their own sake rather than as things created to achieve an objective, as symbolic rather than strictly utilitarian. No matter how thoughtful the designers of bureaucracies are, they cannot conceive of all possible circumstances that bureaucracies and their members might face, so they cannot draw up rules that will yield efficient and effective performance under all circumstances. When circumstances change, as they inevitably do, bureaucrats who value rules for their own sake may not recognize the change because they are narrowly focused on rules, not environments or their organization's performance in its environment. Alternatively, bureaucrats may recognize the change in circumstances but be unwilling to adjust valued rules to suit the new situation. In either case, the very thing that makes bureaucracies perform well—devotion to rules—can make them perform poorly once circumstances change. Moreover, bureaucrats are unlikely to realize that their bureaucracies are not fulfilling their goals, either because they focus on rules rather than the outcomes of following rules, or because they conceive of rules as more important than performance.

Goal displacement is fostered by several features of ideal-typical Weberian bureaucracies. First is the fact that officials expect to make careers—to remain in one bureaucracy for a large part of their work lives, rising through the ranks by following rules, developing expertise, and performing well. Anticipation of a long career increases the value placed on rules—sometimes to the level of sanctifying them—and thus increases conformity to rules. Second, officials come to share a sense of common destiny because they do not compete for promotions: in the ideal-typical Weberian bureaucracy, promotion depends on seniority and technical merit. The group mentality generated by such promotion rules leads officials to reinforce each other's tendencies to value and conform. Members who break rules, specifically by substituting personal for impersonal treatment, even if they do so to improve performance, are resented and chastised by their fellows. Third, the sharp distinction drawn between organizational positions and the people who hold them not only reduces bureaucrats' sense of ownership of their positions, it also reduces their sense of personal responsibility for the consequences of their actions.

Merton concluded by suggesting that sociologists study organizations and the personalities and actions of officials, paying attention to the effects of variations in organizational features, such as different systems of recruitment or different mechanisms for formalizing rules and roles. His students took his suggestion to heart. These pioneering organizational sociologists immersed themselves in a variety of complex organizations and conducted rigorous analyses that were driven by existing theories of organizations. The results of their investigations revolutionized those theories. They all fulfilled Gouldner's (1954*a*: 9) stated goals: (1) to use Weber's theory of bureaucracy, which had been based on Weber's analysis of the nineteenth-century Prussian army and state bureaus, to shed light on many kinds of twentieth-century organizations, including industrial enterprises, and (2) to use 'data bearing on [bureaucratic] processes' to 'help us to evaluate the theory, to modify and redirect it'. In this regard, Merton's students sought to develop several theories of the middle range—theories that might be specific to the kinds of organizations they studied, in the times and places they studied them—rather than grand theories that had universal applicability.

26.2. Alvin Gouldner: Patterns of Industrial Bureaucracy

Gouldner shared Merton's skepticism of rationality in bureaucracies and his insistence that bureaucracy was not as simple and manifestly functional as proposed by many other interpreters of Weber. Gouldner was interested in three things. First, he wanted to understand how bureaucracy came to be—in particular, how formal rules developed over time. Second, he wanted to know how, in different environments, organizations' goals and everyday operations combined to produce differing levels of bureaucracy. Third, he wanted to understand how bureaucracy was perceived by workers and supervisors. To understand these things, Gouldner and several students interviewed and directly observed workers and supervisors in one plant in an industrial firm, which he called the General Gypsum Company. They also pored over plant and company archives. Most commentaries (e.g. Burawoy 1982; Chriss 2001) have emphasized the dynamic aspect of Gouldner's text. I will seize this opportunity to rebalance our attention and examine both the dynamic and the comparative parts of this study.

26.2.1. Bureaucracy in Dynamic Perspective

The first part of the book examines the aftermath of managerial succession. Before the succession event, the culture in the plant was an 'indulgency pattern', a coherent set of judgments and values that disposed workers to appreciate and trust their supervisors. Central to this culture was the value of 'leniency', which had five behavioral manifestations. First, supervisors did not ride the backs of workers, as long as they kept up with demand; instead, supervisors let workers set their own pace. Supervisors disciplined workers primarily to increase efficiency and workers accepted such discipline without complaint. Second, workers were given second chances: they were rarely fired, never without repeated warnings, and they were often rehired after quitting to take jobs at other plants. Third, workers were allowed to move from job to job, either to experiment until they found one they liked best or to gain the experience needed for promotion. Fourth, injured workers were cared for above and beyond the letter of employment law, by being given physically easy tasks. Fifth, workers were allowed to take materials from the plant to do home repairs. In all these ways, managers gave workers something they did not have to. For their part, workers appreciated these manifestations of leniency as something above and beyond what was rightfully theirs.

The new plant manager instituted many changes that expanded the bureaucracy, primarily by developing new rules and standardized forms. These changes had the intended consequence of restricting workers' freedom and the unintended consequence of destroying the indulgency culture, in large part by obliterating manifestations of leniency. The opening shot in the war against leniency was to fire a worker who took company materials for personal use, even though his foreman had given him permission. The new manager's approach went far beyond this single decision. He interpreted all plant rules literally and rigorously; for instance, penalizing absenteeism and restricting workers from moving around the plant during rest periods. He also increased formalization through paperwork; for example, by requiring daily and weekly supervisory reports or by developing standardized forms to warn employees of behavioral problems such as disobedience or absence, which created a paper trail that could later justify demotion or firing. He demoted several supervisors, replacing them with new hires who were less socially connected to workers and who therefore tended to view themselves as workers' superiors rather than as their peers or neighbors. Finally, he stopped allowing injured men to work at physically easy tasks, instead forcing them to stay home and take sick pay, which was less remunerative than pay for the physically easy tasks. Not surprisingly, workers responded poorly to this impartial bureaucratization and to the curbing of the freedoms and privileges that the indulgency culture had given them.

The new plant manager did not institute these changes randomly; neither did he do so, Gouldner reported, because he was innately cruel. Instead, the new manager was guided by explicit objectives given to him by headquarters: to increase productivity, which was essential to meet greatly increased post-war demand. Since he came from a plant in another region, the new manager had no ties to the community in which the plant was situated, and thus no social ties to workers. For that reason, he viewed the plant and its employees dispassionately. Indeed, if he had any bias, it was towards the suspicion sown by his superiors in company headquarters that the plant and its workers were not producing at as high a level as they could. Because he was a stranger, the new manager ignored invisible and informal aspects of the organization (its culture) and relied instead on more visible and formal aspects (the bureaucracy he elaborated and tightened) to drive his productivity-focused changes. Gouldner's judgment that the new manager did not act randomly or cruelly is consistent with Hodson's (2001) conclusion, based on a meta-analysis of 156 organizational ethnographies, including Gouldner's, that management is far more often incompetent than evil. (For more on managerial incompetence, see Pfeffer 2007.) Because the new plant manager ignored the plant's existing culture and because workers shared close social ties that made it easy for them to coordinate their actions, workers not only resented the changes he made but also were able to mount a debilitating strike, which Gouldner reported in a companion volume (Gouldner 1954*b*).

Gouldner's analysis of the impact of bureaucratization on this plant highlighted omissions and tensions in Weber's model of bureaucracy. First, Weber never considered that responses to bureaucracy might be different for organizational members in different ranks. But Gouldner found that the gypsum plant's new manager and the new men he hired to report directly to him viewed increases in bureaucracy as efficient and just; workers, however, viewed these new managers as usurping their previously granted privileges. Second, Weber did not consider that the effectiveness of bureaucracy might depend on the way rules were put in place—that is, by imposition from above or agreement among all affected parties. Gouldner's analysis suggested that process matters: participative and consultative decision-making styles are more likely to produce compliance than authoritative styles. Third, Weber did not consider bureaucracies as dynamic systems whose evolution was subject to path dependence. Gouldner's study revealed that rules have a history: who initiates them, why, and how determines how, and how well, they are understood and accepted.

26.2.2. Bureaucracy in Comparative Perspective

The plant Gouldner studied contained two distinct units: a factory on the surface that manufactured wallboard and a mine underground that provided the basic raw material, gypsum ore. Gouldner's analysis highlighted many not-so-subtle differences between the tasks, structures, and cultures of these two units, which allowed him to assess the extent of bureaucratization in the cross-section as well as before and after managerial succession.

The mine was a much less formally structured workplace than the factory and so had a much less formal culture. There were four main differences in structure and attendant culture between mine and factory. First, the hierarchical distance between workers and supervisors was less in the mine than in the factory; indeed, Gouldner (1954*a*: 108) reported that miners looked on their supervisors 'in much the manner that the stars of a show look upon the stagehands'. Miners often enlisted each other's help on complicated tasks without consulting supervisors; such circumvention of official channels of command almost never happened in the factory. Second, miners' spheres of competency were more diffuse than those in the factory. Miners often repaired the machines they used; in the factory, such work was done only by maintenance mechanics, who jealously guarded their specialty. Miners also relieved each other for lunch and coffee breaks, and so frequently worked at many different jobs; factory workers did not, unless they were searching for better-fitting jobs or augmenting their skills to ensure promotion. Third, miners were overtly hostile to rules, including planning and work schedules; factory workers were much more rule-bound, although, as explained above, they were seldom held to the letter of these laws, at least before the new plant manager arrived. In other words, the zone of indifference or acceptance, meaning the range within which each worker would willingly accept orders without consciously questioning authority (Barnard 1938; Simon [1946] 1976), was larger for plant workers than for miners. Fourth, relations between men in the mine were far more personal than those between men in the factory. All miners, up to and including the mine's general manager, were given nicknames derived from their speech, behavior, or appearance; in contrast, very few factory workers, and certainly no supervisors, were called by nicknames. Taken together, these differences in structure and culture led miners to develop a far greater feeling of social solidarity and group cohesion than factory workers.

Comparing the extent of bureaucratization over time (before and after the new manager arrived) and in the cross-section (between the factory and the plant) allowed Gouldner to highlight an important ambiguity in Weber's conception of bureaucracy. Weberian bureaucracy, Gouldner pointed out, was Janus-faced: it was both a consensual social unit and a coercive instrument. The impact of bureaucracy on both workers and supervisors hinged on this distinction. When bureaucracy was perceived as consensual, following rules and procedures was a means to an end that was attuned to all organizational members' personal preferences and goals. But when bureaucracy was perceived as coercive, following rules and procedures was an end in itself, disconnected from (at least some) organizational members' personal preferences and goals.

26.2.3. Summary

Gouldner argued that Weber's conception of bureaucracy was ambiguous because Weber conflated two distinct bases of power in bureaucracy: expertise in the form of specialized knowledge and training, and discipline in the form of rewards and punishments. Expertise was the driving force of consensual bureaucratic systems—those that were accepted by both workers and supervisors. Discipline, in contrast, was the engine of coercive bureaucratic systems—those that were often accepted by supervisors but not by workers, and more rarely accepted by workers but not by supervisors.

Gouldner concluded that there are three types of bureaucracy—representative, punishment-centered, and mock—that can be distinguished in terms of who creates them, whose values they incarnate or violate, how deviations are understood, and what effects they have on bureaucrats' status. Representative bureaucracy arises from pressure by supervisors and workers, and incarnates values of both supervisors and workers. Deviation from such rules and procedures is understood as intentional ignorance or unintentional error that harms both supervisors and workers. As a result, representative bureaucracy generates little, if any, conflict and is maintained by tacit agreement among supervisors and workers. Punishment-centered bureaucracy, in contrast, arises from pressure by either supervisors or workers, but not both. Accordingly, it legitimates the values of one group and violates the values of the other. Deviation is attributed to deliberate (malicious) intent and is perceived as harming the status of the group whose values are legitimated. As a result, punishment-centered bureaucracy generates a great deal of conflict between supervisors and workers, and is likely to be undermined by the actions of the group whose values are violated and whose status is impaired. Finally, mock bureaucracy arises from neither group, but rather from outside pressures, and violates the values of both groups. Deviation is viewed as inevitable, as the result of human nature, and enhances the status of both workers and supervisors. This form of bureaucracy engenders little conflict within the organization, but may engender conflict between the organization and the external observers who value and promote it.

26.3. Peter Blau: The Dynamics of Bureaucracy

Blau conducted a highly refined study of work groups, focusing on how they responded behaviorally to changes in bureaucratic rules and procedures, and in the process developed a parallel, informal organization that subtly reshaped the formal bureaucracy. Like Gouldner, Blau built on Merton's formulation of functional analysis (Merton 1968: 73–138), which held that researchers must probe the consequences of social phenomena, not just their origins. Blau sought to determine the consequences of bureaucracy, meaning formal organizational structure, for workers and for later incarnations of the structure itself. He also sought to determine the causal mechanisms, specifically the social interactions, through which changes in bureaucracy engender changes in behavior and structure. Blau's third goal was to highlight and understand the unanticipated consequences of intentional bureaucratic change (Merton 1936), which lead organizations and their bureaucracies to evolve in unforeseen directions. In conducting this functional analysis, Blau wanted to understand unofficial practices and structures, which casual observers might perceive as irrational or irrelevant to official rules or goals. In other words, he wanted to understand just how informal organization (that is, power relations and culture) arose from the accumulation of formal bureaucratic elements and from behavioral responses to those elements, and thus how this informal organization became institutionalized—that is, became an accepted and enduring part of organizational goals, activities, and structures. In this way, Blau could demonstrate and explain endogenous change in organizational structures and the behavior of organizational members. In his own words, Blau demonstrated that bureaucracy 'contains the seed, not necessarily of its own destruction, but of its own transformation' (1955: 9).

In contrast to Gouldner, Blau focused on behavior within white-collar settings rather than blue-collar settings. His research site had two parts, both government agencies: a state employment agency that referred workers to firms in the clothing industry and a federal law-enforcement agency that oversaw businesses' relations with their employees. Like Gouldner, Blau used multiple methods to gather data to investigate ideas that he deduced from extant sociological theory and to refine that theory. Blau not only directly observed workers in the two government agencies, he also interviewed workers and supervisors, had workers and supervisors fill out surveys and record behavior as they occurred, and pored over agency records.

26.3.1. Bureaucracy in the Employment Agency

Blau studied one department in a state agency that interviewed job seekers and sought to match them to job openings. He observed that how work was done in this department differed from what was laid out during the agency's new-employee training: this department largely eschewed the formal documentation that was prescribed for other departments. This happened, Blau explained, because the department served a single industry (apparel manufacturing) that needed help filling jobs in a handful of low-skilled occupations and that had a particular work rhythm (alternating periods of frenzy and doldrums) dictated by the industry's cycles of demand. When industry demand peaked, workers had to be matched to job openings in a single day; when industry demand ebbed, workers were not needed at all.

Official procedures were modified in three ways—through adjustment, redefinition, and amplification—to suit prevailing industry conditions. Adjustment allowed more efficient operation, given both conditions in the apparel industry and the agency's own performance objectives. The most obvious adjustment was that interviews were extremely brief and most paperwork was eliminated to ensure very quick referrals; moreover, the department focused on the number, rather than the quality, of placements, and so ignored some tasks altogether (e.g. counseling those who were seeking employment). Procedural redefinition was one unintended consequence of procedural adjustment: the original objective of a procedure (e.g. maximizing the fit between referred workers and jobs) was deliberately sacrificed in the service of a different objective (e.g. maximizing the number of placements). Another example of procedural redefinition played out when clients who were receiving unemployment-insurance benefits refused job offers. Department officials notified the state's unemployment-insurance bureau as a threat, to induce clients to accept the jobs offered them and thereby maximize the number of placements, rather as a simple sign of interagency cooperation. Finally, procedural amplification involved placing more emphasis on some bureaucratic elements, in order to keep some procedural redefinitions from interfering with organizational goals. For instance, supervisors reviewed every notification of the unemployment-insurance bureau, set explicit rules governing when notifications must be sent, and required their subordinates to explain to job seekers that such notifications did not, after all, disqualify them from receiving unemployment-insurance benefits.

When procedures were modified, their meanings often changed. The department head elaborated formal reporting in way that was similar to what Gouldner observed in the gypsum plant. Rather than recording just the number of job-seeker interviews conducted, the department head began to record also the number of application forms filled out by job seekers, the number of job seekers referred to employers, the number of placements, and the number of notifications of job-offer refusals sent to the sister unemployment-benefits office, as well as the proportion of interviews that led to referrals and placements, and the proportion of referrals that led to placements. As with the gypsum plant's employees, the department's employees came to view increased bureaucratization as a direct mechanism of control, which contrasted sharply with their previous perception of formal statistics as tools to facilitate agency administration; for instance, by allowing the department head to even out workloads by redistributing personnel.[2]

After formal reporting was elaborated, the placement rate (specifically, the percentage of job openings filled by job seekers) increased dramatically, as intended, even though the number of job openings declined. Blau went on to highlight the unintended consequences of this bureaucratic change, both functional (i.e. beneficial to organizational objectives and/or to employees' welfare) and dysfunctional (i.e. harmful to those objectives or to employees' welfare). One unexpected functional consequence was that relations between supervisors and interviewers improved. The statistics-laden formal reports offered seemingly objective justification for any negative performance feedback that, in the past, might have been attributed to supervisor whimsy. Indeed, the formal reports obviated most corrective conversations, thereby increasing the efficiency of operations. As one supervisor explained, 'I just let [the numbers] speak for themselves' (Blau 1955: 43).

Alas, Blau also observed many unexpected dysfunctional consequences, most of which stemmed from the fact that competition among the department's employees heated up when individual performance was made visible in the reports. The supervisor of one section within the department relied heavily on these reports in evaluating subordinates' performance. Those subordinates began to compete more and to cooperate less with each other. As a result, aggregate section performance, in terms of placement rates, declined. The supervisor of a second section based performance evaluations on other factors than just the formal reports, so her employees were less moved to compete to look good in the formal reports. As a consequence, aggregate performance improved in the second section. Finally, both sections began to cooperate less with a third section that depended on them for information about job openings—the section that matched handicapped workers to job openings. It took an informal adjustment of procedures—allowing employees in the first

[2] Another example of how meanings changed in the wake of procedural change is that when the department head stopped gathering data on counseling services for the unemployed, her subordinates came to offer such services less and less often. Thus, Blau documented both how people attend to what is measured and how they ignore what is not measured.

two sections to refer uncooperative job seekers to employees in the handicapped section—to restore a reasonable balance of power-dependence relations, which again made employees in the first two sections willing to provide information about job openings to employees in the handicapped section.

Another important dysfunctional consequence of the elaboration of bureaucracy was that the things that the reports measured did not precisely capture the phenomena they were intended to measure, so they could be 'gamed'. In making this observation, Blau echoed Merton's discussion of goal displacement and foreshadowed Marshall Meyer's thinking on what he termed the 'performance paradox': the tendency of all performance measures to become less informative over time as employees learn how to work the system (Meyer and Gupta 1994).

In sum, the elaboration of bureaucracy in this department of the employment agency created quantitative data on performance that made it possible for departmental employees (and their supervisors) to compare employees, which engendered competition between individuals in each section. In turn, increased competition had a series of unintended consequences that reduced the department's efficiency: making employees less willing to cooperate with each other, even though cooperation was essential for effective performance for each section and the department as a whole, and pushing employees to behave in time-wasting ways that allowed them to 'cook' the numbers. Thus, Blau demonstrated the dilemma of bureaucracy: formal structures that are intended to solve one problem often give rise to other problems. He also demonstrated that the informal organization, specifically subgroup culture, moderates the impact of bureaucratic change. In the first section, a competitive culture developed as departmental employees vied to increase their individual placement statistics in the formal reports, which determined their performance evaluations. In contrast, in the second section, a more cooperative culture developed that was less disrupted by bureaucratic elaboration because performance evaluations did not depend solely on the statistics in the formal reports. Blau may have been the first person to explain the oft-noted managerial folly of rewarding one behavior while hoping for an entirely different behavior (Kerr 1975).

26.3.2. Bureaucracy in the Law-Enforcement Agency

The second organization Blau studied was a department that inspected businesses to ensure that they complied with two new federal employment laws; violations led to negotiations over adjustments to business practices or, in severe cases, to lawsuits. This bureaucracy was replete with formal rules and regulations, many of which were gathered in a 1,000-page manual. Most rules focused on the quality (according to legal standards) of employees' work, specifically their decisions regarding compliance or noncompliance by the businesses they inspected, and their ability to get businesses to voluntarily make amends. In contrast, there were few rules concerning the process by which employees achieved these results. In addition, all decisions and actions were checked twice, by supervisors and by a review section.

Despite the high degree of formality of work rules in this organization, Blau noted several informal work practices that, when followed, made workers secure members of a valued social milieu and that, when ignored or flouted, rendered them social outcasts. First and most strikingly, agents consulted with one another about the cases each handled, even though their supervisor prohibited such discussions. Blau recorded who consulted with whom and how often, and analyzed the manifest (explicitly intended) and latent (implicit or unintended) reasons for them. The manifest cause was that consultations with fellow agents obviated the need for consultations with the supervisor, and so kept employees from earning black marks for demonstrated ignorance. The latent causes were numerous. Consultations reduced employees' social isolation; without such interactions, employees would work alone almost all the time, with their only social contact being their supervisor and the businessmen they investigated. Thus, consultations created group solidarity and a cohesive professional culture, both of which were valued by agents. Consultations also heightened employees' interest in their jobs. Finally, consultations forestalled conflict between employees by reflecting and thus honoring very real differences in level of expertise. Of course, there were latent dysfunctions, too: consultations not only honored differences in expertise, they also reinforced those differences, and made it difficult for agents who were perceived as poor performers to improve; they flouted and thus weakened the supervisor's authority; and they worsened employees' perceptions of the supervisor's competence relative to that of the expert peer advisors.

In addition to informal work practices, Blau noted that informal social events—the annual Christmas party, the practice of buying gifts for coworkers to celebrate birthdays, weddings, and children's births, as well as to commiserate illnesses—served as a social glue. Because these events were bureaucratized—committees managed them and everyone participated simply by virtue of working in the department—they came to symbolize and valorize membership in the group. One unexpected function of these social events was to increase agents' effectiveness at work by decreasing their anxiety about their ability to perform their often-difficult assignments and by relieving the emotional tensions inherent in the delicate negotiations they undertook with the men whose businesses were under investigation.

The third informal aspect of work relations that Blau analyzed was a series of workplace norms. First and foremost were restrictions on work output. The departmental supervisor set a production quota for each agent: investigate eight cases per month, find violations in half of these, and persuade the managers of businesses found in violation of the law to make voluntary adjustments so as to become compliant without having to be taken to court. Agents competed to meet this standard, as they all sought to be ranked high relative to their coworkers. But norms about quota restrictions curbed agents' natural competitive tendencies. Rate busters were teased and consistent rate busters were socially ostracized. What Blau described with these white-collar workers largely echoed what Roethlisberger and Dickson (1939) found in their study of blue-collar workers in a Western Electric manufacturing plant, and what Donald Roy (1952) found in his study of a machine shop, but there were interesting differences. Many agents responded to these inconsistent pressures—to meet or exceed the production quota *versus* to comply with the quota-restriction norm—by concealing their accomplishments from their peers. And although quota restrictions occasionally chafed, agents justified them as necessary for professional performance: they deemed it impossible to achieve both quantity and quality, as quality was expected to suffer if quantity rose very high.

A second important norm revolved around limits on the formal authority that was vested in the supervisor and the section of the agency that reviewed agents' work. In Blau's (1955: 208) own words, the supervisor 'extended his authority... by voluntarily surrendering parts of it'. This meant that supervisors bent their behavior to reduce overt reliance on formal authority and to expand subordinates' zones of indifference or acceptance (Barnard 1938; Simon [1946] 1976). This was especially pronounced among supervisors who had frequent social interactions with subordinates. Such supervisors give more high and fewer low performance ratings than did supervisors who had few social interactions with subordinates—yielding precisely 'the Lake Wobegon effect' chronicled in Garrison Keillor's tales of the mythical Minnesota town 'where all the children are above average'. Supervisors also allowed agents to break minor rules, such as spending more than the prescribed time at lunch. Why would supervisors willingly limit their authority by granting subordinates leeway in work process and catering to subordinates' desires for high performance ratings? Blau explained that the answer lay in the mutual dependence that bound supervisors to subordinates just as tightly as it bound subordinates to supervisors. To put it simply, supervisors relied on agents to cooperate willingly with their requests. By abrogating part of their formal authority and offering subordinates things that were above and beyond what was prescribed by written rules and formal operating procedures, supervisors made subordinates dependent on them, which ensured obedience. Positively skewed performance ratings and acceptance of minor infractions of workplace regulations were privileges that supervisors could easily grant or withhold; subordinates depended on supervisors' goodwill to maintain these privileges and so cooperated with them. The mutual give-and-take between supervisor and subordinates became crystallized in prevailing, albeit unofficial, practices. This analysis of white-collar workers echoes Gouldner's (1954*a*) analysis of the indulgency pattern among blue-collar workers in a gypsum plant, but it goes further to appreciate the causes of such patterns. This analysis also foreshadows Blau's ([1964] 1992) later work on power and exchange relations, as well as work on power and dependence by Richard Emerson (1962).

Supervisors were not the only bureaucrats to surrender part of their authority in order to wield it more effectively. The men who worked in the review section did the same. This section checked the reports filed by agents for factual, procedural, and legal correctness, and returned problematic cases to agents for revision. Reviewers rotated into this section from field assignments in one of the law-enforcement agency's operating departments; after six months, they returned to those departments. Blau found that the same informal social constraints that prevented supervisors from exercising their full formal authority affected reviewers. When reviewers sent problematic cases back to agents, these problems were noted in the agents' personnel files, which adversely affected their performance ratings. Agents, quite understandably, disliked having cases returned for errors and vilified reviewers for doing so. Shrinking from conflict with their once and future colleagues, reviewers developed an informal alternative: 'walking back' problematic cases to the agent who handled them, so he could revise the cases without any official notice being taken. This happened frequently despite the fact that walking back cases, and thus reporting fewer than the expected number of problematic cases, harmed reviewers' own performance ratings. Nonetheless, reviewers who had close social relations with agents tended to sacrifice their own performance ratings in order to mitigate the negative impact on their relationships with fellow agents: reviewers who interacted frequently with agents walked back two-thirds of problematic cases, a much higher fraction than more socially isolated reviewers.

In sum, Blau revealed that the employees of this law-enforcement agency reshaped formal bureaucratic elements—rules and regulations, hierarchical relationships, and evaluation criteria—to serve their own interests. Such endogenous changes also engendered a rich set of highly value-laden informal arrangements, in the form of potent norms concerning 'professional' (i.e. good) behavior. Endogenous change was not haphazard; rather, it flowed from imperfections in formal structure—tensions between goals, unexpected difficulties in achieving goals, and misfits between formal structure and new external contingencies.

26.3.3. Summary

Blau's analysis demonstrated that change in bureaucratic elements—the introduction of new rules or procedures—can lead to either functional changes, which shift conditions in the direction of socially valued objectives or contribute to the attainment of those objectives, or dysfunctional changes, which shift conditions in the direction opposite to socially valued objectives or impede the attainment of those objectives. He further demonstrated that when conditions change—for instance, when new demands are placed on an organization—several different outcomes are possible. First, the new demands may not be met. Second, the new demands may disappear or be transformed as a result of workers' and/or supervisors' adjustment in value orientations; that is, as workers and/or supervisors learn new values and discard old ones, new demands are transformed from disruptive threats into stimulating challenges. Third, new demands may give rise to new structures and behaviors that meet the demands. Which outcome actually occurs depends partly on who benefits and who loses—on the relative power of organizational members in different units and at different levels in the hierarchy—and partly on the prevailing culture (or subcultures), as pre-existing values and norms shape perceptions of new demands, making organizational members conceive of some outcomes as possible and others as impossible.

Blau showed us that bureaucracies change all the time—change may not be inevitable in vending machines, but it is in organizations. He also showed us that bureaucrats often welcome, rather than resist change (*pace* Hannan and Freeman 1984). Moreover, he proposed that bureaucrats often have favorable attitudes towards social change, rather than resisting any change in external conditions. He went further than merely offering existence proofs of organizational flexibility by inducing a theory of the conditions under which organizations are more or less rigid (or, conversely, flexible); in doing so, he modified Merton's (1940) theory of bureaucratic dysfunction. Blau predicted that social insecurity, rather than overly strong identification with rules and consequent goal displacement, engenders inefficient rigidity. Perhaps most striking is the finding that the process by which subunit and individual performance is appraised—the things that are and are not taken into consideration, and their relative weights—has a huge impact on bureaucratic inertia (or flexibility). When changes to organizational structures and operations, whether designed or emergent, threaten to make subunit or individual performance look bad, bureaucrats will resist change. But when changes promise to make performance look good, bureaucrats will invite (nay—insist on) change. In addition to anxiety concerning performance appraisals, Blau demonstrated that threats to important social relations at work (with coworkers and clients, not just with supervisors) also induce rigidity.

26.4. Conclusion: What Can We (Re)learn for a Twenty-First-Century Organizational Sociology?

A close rereading of Merton, Gouldner, and Blau reveals several lessons for contemporary organizational theorists. Let me discuss each in turn.

26.4.1. Culture Determines How Organizational Members Respond to Bureaucracy

Workers and their supervisors do not perceive bureaucratic structures and practices as neutral stimuli. Instead, their understanding and acceptance of bureaucratic elements is developed by viewing them through lenses that vary by culture (i.e. by pre-existing systems of meaning). Gouldner invoked three levels of culture—societal, community, and organizational—and argued that organizational culture was enmeshed in the cultures of the national society and the local communities in which workers lived. At the societal level, Gouldner pointed out the egalitarian ethos that pervades the United States and argued that within this egalitarian culture, direct supervision (rather than supervision through rules) can be perceived negatively, as a form of punishment. At the community level, Gouldner noted that the workers and supervisors he studied came mostly from small towns characterized by fairly flat social-status hierarchies, political conservativism, and long-established populations. The cultures of these communities engendered friendly and highly egalitarian informal relations between supervisors and workers; they also engendered distrust and suspicion of outsiders.

Within the nested system of societal, community, and organizational cultures, Gouldner concluded that the 'usefulness' of bureaucratic elements (primarily rules, but also forms, job descriptions, and standard operating procedures) depends on five factors: who initiates the bureaucratic elements (insiders or outsiders, workers or managers or both), whose values are legitimated or violated by them (workers or managers or both), the perceived nature of deviations from bureaucracy (human nature, out of human or organizational control, good intentions, accidents, or deliberate bad intentions), and the effects of bureaucratic elements on status (enhances both workers and managers, impairs both, or enhances one at the expense of the other). In a similar vein, Blau's analysis of the fallout from the elaboration of formal (statistical) reports of production output and process in the employment agency demonstrated that reward systems shaped organizational culture (pushing it to be more or less individualistic and competitive), which in turn determined employees' responses to this bureaucratic change.

Surprisingly, the idea of bureaucracy as a contingent element of organizational design appears in few subsequent studies. One excellent example is Paul Adler and Bryan Borys's (1996) analysis of the coercive *versus* enabling impact of the ways new production technologies are designed—either to force employee effort and compliance with official rules or to improve employee mastery of their assigned tasks. They identified factors that discourage and encourage both bureaucratic orientations.

26.4.2. The Inevitable (but Often Forgotten) Link between Induction and Deduction

Gouldner and Blau amply fulfilled Gouldner's (1954*a*: 9) stated goals, which were to use Weber's theory of bureaucracy to shed light on organizational behavior and then to use data bearing on that behavior to evaluate the theory, to modify it, and to push it in new directions. These scholars mixed induction and deduction in a way that cemented the connection between theory and data. They started with ideas from Weber, Merton, and other sociologists, and used those ideas to guide their data-gathering and data-analysis efforts. That research strategy is quite common among contemporary inductive researchers—those who infer existence proofs and causal patterns from empirical observation. But Gouldner and Blau went far beyond what most contemporary inductive researchers do and so offer a crucial lesson for them. Gouldner and Blau induced, based on a combination of extant theory and analysis of their own data, explicit statements of hypotheses that could be tested in other settings; they also developed typologies of organizational structures and processes. More than this, Gouldner and Blau wove typologies and hypotheses into theories of the middle range (Merton 1968: 39–72). In other words, they offered general, abstract ideas that could guide future research, ideas that when tested, and revised by post-testing reflection, might cumulate into a scientific approach to the study of organizations. This act of 'closing the loop' between induction and deduction is seldom seen in contemporary inductive research on organizations. Attention to explication of abstract, general predictions would facilitate building bridges between inductive and deductive researchers, who tend to form insular camps, and would help us accumulate facts and interpretations of those facts in a more systematic, scientific manner.

Contemporary deductive researchers—those who formally 'test' hypotheses, often using statistical techniques, sometimes using qualitative techniques like Mill's (1872) method of agreement and difference—can learn important lessons from Gouldner and Blau. Virtually all hypothetico-deductive papers are developed through a combination of deduction from extant research and induction from data. Notwithstanding this fact, most studies are written as if all ideas were in place before any data were gathered, certainly before data were analyzed. Reviewers and editors are complicit in this charade: they tend to behave as if prior knowledge of the data being analyzed—looking at univariate statistics and bivariate correlations, estimating different versions of multivariate models, adding or dropping cases in comparative case analyses—has no bearing on what authors predict. Instead, reviewers and editors tend to behave as if what authors predict is based solely on prior theory and evidence—purely on deduction, not at all on induction. Gouldner and Blau demonstrate that the scientific study of organizations can indeed allow for explicit recognition of the inevitable intertwining of deduction and induction. Greater honesty about the important role that induction plays in the hypothetico-deductive research process would make it easier to write clearly about what we (both authors and readers) learn, when we learn it and from what data, and why what we learn matters for the specific cases we study versus any general social science of organizations. In other words, explicit recognition of induction would allow us to specify more clearly boundary or scope conditions for the theories we test and to propose contingencies for purportedly general theories.

26.4.3. Gouldner: Physical Conditions Matter as Much as Cultural and Political Factors

Within the plant he studied, Gouldner learned that there were huge differences in subunit culture: the highly informal, close-knit, mutually helpful culture of the subsurface mine contrasted sharply with the semi-formal but still cohesive and benevolent culture of the surface factory. He attributed these differences in structure and culture between mine and factory to differences in conditions. The mine was darker, dirtier, louder, more physically taxing, more dangerous, and more unpredictable than the factory. Moreover, the cultural distance Gouldner observed between the two units—they had little real contact and their members stereotyped each other—developed and persisted in part because they were separated by considerable physical distance. This part of Gouldner's analysis highlights factors that are still largely missing from sociological analyses of organizations. He showed that the physical environment—its size or spatial distance, aesthetic qualities, privacy, level of discomfort or danger, and extent to which it is unpredictable or uncontrollable—has fundamental effects on organizational tasks, structures, and cultures. This part of Gouldner's analysis shows that, contrary to the well-known 'Hawthorne effect', which attributed the impact of physical changes in the workplace to social-psychological forces (Mayo 1933; Roethlisberger and Dickson 1939), physical conditions per se affect organizational design and social-interaction patterns.

The importance of organizations' physical environment has not been entirely lost on later scholars. For instance, in his survey and synthesis of organizational theory, Pfeffer (1982) argued passionately and eloquently for researchers to pay attention to the physical structures that house organizations, which literally structure interactions. But alas, few organizational theorists have heeded Pfeffer's call; even fewer have gone further to consider other aspects of the physical environment. Perhaps it is time we built a bridge to other fields, such as architecture, physiology, and cultural geography, which focus on physical systems, and adapt their theories of physical conditions to develop sociologically informed theories of the physical conditions surrounding organizations and their employees. I see hope in a few scattered studies. One notable example is Brian Lande's (2007) ethnography of the

Reserve Officer Training Corps at a western American university. Reflecting on his own experiences and those of his fellow recruits, Lande revealed how particular socialization routines and training procedures taught recruits to 'breathe like a soldier', so they literally came to 'embody' the culture of the army. He concluded that through this socialization and training, recruits literally became different people.

26.4.4. Blau: An Interest-Driven Theory of Organizational Change and Inertia

Blau noted that the common belief that bureaucracies and bureaucrats resist change stems from the (generally implicit) assumption that bureaucratic structures are in perfect equilibrium, meaning that bureaucracies meet their goals and fit their environments perfectly, and so any change is a disturbance. Blau disagreed with this assumption of perfect adjustment and adaptation. Instead, he pointed out many examples of imperfect adjustment and adaptation in these two government agencies. He further noted that the employees of these imperfect bureaucracies recognized their agencies' shortcomings. For that reason, the members of both bureaucracies constantly wrestled with situations that limited their efficiency and effectiveness, as well as members' own economic and social-psychological well-being. Instituting new procedures and structures was welcomed, rather than resisted, as long as these procedures and structures were perceived as serving the interests of organizational members. (This concern with the interests of organizational members echoes Gouldner's.)

Contrast Blau's notion that organizational change is commonly driven by the combination of structural misalignment (externally, with the organizations or individuals served, or internally, with other organizational goals and procedures) and the economic and psychological goals of members with recent thinking by organizational ecologists on organizational identity and change (Pólos, Hannan, and Carroll 2002; Hannan, Pólos, and Carroll 2007), and recent discussions by institutionalists concerning organizational change and persistence (Clemens and Cook 1999). Both groups of contemporary scholars assume, again generally implicitly, that organizational structures are in some sort of steady state, if not at perfect equilibrium. That is why they perceive that dislodging bureaucracies from the status quo is a problem, something that reduces operating efficiency and external legitimacy. Contemporary scholars would do well to reconcile Blau's theory of interest-driven organizational change with the ecological theory of adaptive (that is, evolutionary beneficial) organizational inertia and the institutionalist prediction that change is a puzzle, not an inevitable part of organizational life. Blau's (1955: 247) conclusion that 'social insecurity breeds rigidity' merits rigorous testing.

Acknowledgments

I thank Andy Abbott and Brayden King for their kind and helpful comments. I also thank participants at the Classics of Organizational Studies Conference for their suggestions.

References

Adler, P. S., and Borys, B. (1996). 'Two Types of Bureaucracy: Enabling and Coercive'. *Administrative Science Quarterly*, 41: 61–89.

Anderson, W., and Gaus, J. M. (1945). *Research in Public Administration: Parts 1 and 2*. Chicago: Public Administration Service.

Barnard, C. I. (1938). *The Functions of the Executive*. Cambridge, Mass.: Harvard University Press.

Blau, P. M. (1955). *Dynamics of Bureaucracy: A Study of Interpersonal Relations in Two Government Agencies*. Chicago: University of Chicago Press.

—— ([1964] 1992). *Exchange and Power in Social Life*. New Brunswick, NJ: Transaction Publishers.

Burawoy, M. (1982). 'The Written and Repressed in Gouldner's Industrial Sociology'. *Theory and Society*, 11/6: 831–51.

Chriss, J. J. (2001). 'Alvin W. Gouldner and Industrial Sociology at Columbia University'. *Journal of the History of the Behavioral Sciences*, 37/3: 241–59.

Clemens, E. S., and Cook, J. M. (1999). 'Politics and Institutionalism: Explaining Durability and Change', in K. Cook and J. Hagan (eds.), *Annual Review of Sociology*, 25: 441–66.

Emerson, R. M. (1962). 'Power-Dependence Relations'. *American Sociological Review*, 27: 31–41.

Gouldner, A. W. (1954*a*). *Patterns of Industrial Bureaucracy*. New York: Free Press.

—— (1954*b*). *Wildcat Strike*. Yellow Springs, Ohio: Antioch Press.

Gulick, L., and Urwick, L. F. (eds.) (1937). *Papers on the Science of Administration*. New York: Institute of Public Administration, Columbia University.

Hannan, M. T., and Freeman, J. (1984). 'Structural Inertia and Organizational Change'. *American Sociological Review*, 49: 149–64.

—— Pólos, L., and Carroll, G. R. (2007). *Logics of Organization Theory: Audiences, Codes, and Ecologies*. Princeton: Princeton University Press.

Hodson, R. (2001). *Dignity at Work*. New York: Cambridge University Press.

Kerr, S. (1975). 'On the Folly of Rewarding A, while Hoping for B'. *Academy of Management Journal*, 18: 769–83.

Lande, B. (2007). 'Breathing like a Soldier: Culture Incarnate'. *Sociological Review*, 55: 95–108.

Lipset, S. M. (1950). *Agrarian Socialism: The Cooperative Commonwealth Federation in Saskatchewan*. Berkeley: University of California Press.

Lipset, S. M., Trow, M. A., and Coleman, J. S. (1956). *Union Democracy: The Internal Politics of the International Typographical Union*. New York: Free Press.

Mayo, E. (1933). *Human Problems of an Industrial Civilization*. New York: Macmillan Co.
Merton, R. K. (1936). 'The Unanticipated Consequences of Purposive Social Action'. *American Sociological Review*, 1: 894–904.
—— (1940). 'Bureaucratic Structure and Personality'. *Social Forces*, 18 (May): 560–8.
—— (1968). *Social Theory and Social Structure*. Enlarged edn. New York: Free Press.
Meyer, M. W., and Gupta, V. (1994). 'The Performance Paradox', in B. Staw and L. Cummings (eds.), *Research in Organizational Behavior*, 16: 309–69. Greenwich Conn.: JAI Press.
Mill, J. S. (1872). *System of Logic*. 8th edn. London: Longmans, Green, Reader, and Dyer.
Pfeffer, J. (1982). *Organizations and Organizational Theory*. New York: Pitman.
—— (2007). *What Were They Thinking? Unconventional Wisdom about Management*. Boston: Harvard Business School Press.
Pólos, L., Hannan, M. T., and Carroll, G. R. (2002). 'Foundations of a Theory of Social Forms'. *Industrial and Corporate Change*, 11: 85–115.
Roethlisberger, F. J., and Dickson, W. J. (1939). *Management and the Worker*. Cambridge, Mass.: Harvard University Press.
Roy, D. (1952). 'Quota Restriction and Goldbricking in a Machine Shop'. *American Journal of Sociology*, 57: 427–42.
Scott, W. R. (1981). *Organizations: Rational, Natural, and Open Systems*. 6th edn. Upper Saddle River, NJ: Prentice-Hall. 2nd edn. 1987, 3rd edn. 1992, 4th edn. 1998, 5th edn. 2002.
—— (1995). *Institutions and Organizations*. Thousand Oaks, Calif.: Sage. 2nd edn. 2001.
—— and Davis, G. F. (2007). *Organizations and Organizing: Rational, Natural, and Open Systems Perspectives*. Upper Saddle River, NJ: Prentice-Hall.
Selznick, P. (1949). *TVA and the Grassroots*. Berkeley: University of California Press.
—— (1957). *Leadership in Administration: A Sociological Interpretation*. Berkeley: University of California Press.
Simon, H. A. ([1946] 1976). *Administrative Behavior: A Study of Decision-Making Processes in Administrative Organization*. 3rd edn. New York: Free Press.
Weber, M. (1978). *Economy and Society: An Outline of Interpretive Sociology*, trans. and ed. Guenther Roth and Claus Wittich. Berkeley: University of California Press.

CHAPTER 27

PARSONS AS AN ORGANIZATION THEORIST

CHARLES HECKSCHER

27.1. Introduction

Talcott Parsons was America's most influential sociologist in the 1950s and 1960s—bringing Max Weber's work to America, building a multidisciplinary social sciences approach at Harvard, and developing a highly integrated and complex theory of social action. Even before his death in 1979, however, his star had greatly dimmed; today his work is rarely read. And that, I will argue, is unfortunate, because he still has far more to say than anyone before or since on the core concepts of sociology: trust, values, commitment, and other 'normative' aspects of behavior. I will also argue, by using his model to think through the current growth of collaborative systems in business firms, that it still generates many fruitful avenues for organization theory.

From his college days, Parsons battled the neoclassical economic paradigm that believed it could predict behaviors by assuming a universal orientation of rational self-interest. He argued that there is far more to life than that—that social life includes orientations such as solidarity, value commitments, power, and cultural expression that were far from the 'code' of individual utility-maximization. The difficulty of social analysis is to understand how these complex and vastly different orientations can come together in lasting relations.

Parsons was through-and-through a voluntarist: he believed that people have choices. Sociological explanation can therefore not be predictive in the way that we predict the behavior of billiard balls. What sociologists can do is (1) to understand the situation from the point of view of the actors and (2) to understand how those points of view interact with each other in a system. From these understandings, we can analyze constraints on choice, fundamental problems that must be faced, and ways in which the interplay of expectations and perspectives steers the possibilities for action—though without being able to predict any particular action. In this sense, Parsons essentially agrees with Marx's famous view that 'Men make their own history, but they do not make it as they please' (1852).

Parsons sought to understand how social order is possible, but he was not a Hobbesian seeking ways to maintain order at any cost. He was deeply committed to a Kantian ideal of human development (Munch 1981). Yet he also rejected 'mere' individualism, adhering to the fundamental sociological premise that individual choice and development are inconceivable outside of social interaction, that society creates degrees of capability and freedom that no individual could ever approach. His core problem always focused on this classic tension: how to reconcile voluntary action with social coherence. The growing complexity of society and its increasing differentiation were for him not merely a means to increased functional capacity but also a road to human freedom: more complex forms of exchange enable an expansion of diversity without threatening the basis for social relations.

This 'humanist' underpinning for Parsonian theory is less explicit in his later, more technical work, but it is always a major point of orientation. In this respect Parsons traces, if one may be allowed a bit of irony, the same path as Marx, who is often similarly accused—and equally falsely, I believe—of abandoning his early voluntarist ideals in his later economic analyses.

Finally, Parsons was a systematizer. His passion was not the understanding of any particular aspect of society, but rather the grasping of everything within a single coherent theoretical framework. In his long career he wrote about everything from religious symbolism to the organization of cognition, from racial integration in America to the limitations of the Roman Empire, from the cultural ordering of time and space to the social ordering of status. All these subjects he sought to approach with the same parsimonious set of concepts—in their final form, they boiled down to four functional categories and the interactions among them. He sought always to make the case for

> the virtues of theoretical 'holism' in attempting to tie together an immense variety of phenomena.... The essential theoretical background throughout is the theory of the social system, treating the concrete system not as an empirically integrated whole, but as a system the problems of which must be analysed in terms of an integrated conceptual scheme. Only by following this path can the various problems associated with the common categories of 'structure', of 'function,' of 'process,' of 'conflict,' and of 'change' be related to each other. (Parsons 1960*b*): 13.

I argue that these neglected virtues—the analysis of normative aspects of action, the attempt to reconcile voluntarism and social coherence, the effort to create a systematic and embracing analytic framework—can greatly help in understanding the current development of business organizations, and that Parsons's categories are both precise and fruitful for this domain.

27.2. Parsons on Organizations

The whole of Parsons's writings specifically on organizations is not large: two 1956 articles in *Administrative Science Quarterly* and a follow-up chapter (Parsons 1956*a*, 1956*b*, and 1958). In analyzing Parsons as an organization theorist, therefore, one needs to consider not only what he actually said about the subject but also what he might have said had he continued to explore the implications of his theoretical model for this field. The first of these perspectives is merely suggestive: though he packed into his three papers on organization a wealth of ideas and proposals, he never followed them up enough to provide a solid target of analysis. The second opens very interesting pathways, and it is worthwhile following up at least a few of them to see where they lead.

I will focus on the later, most developed articulation of Parsons's sociology, the so-called 'general theory of action'. The core of this work, from the early 1950s on, is the claim that any aspect of human action can be analyzed as an open system that needs to fulfill four basic functions. He extended his analysis not only to social systems but also to personalities and cultures; for the sake of manageability, I will focus on social systems, which were his main starting point and which received most of his attention.

The four functions, as is typical of Parsons's work, are derived simultaneously from specific cases and broad theory. On the 'inductive' side, he was inspired by his association with Robert Freed Bales's studies of small group interactions, which had led Bales to a quite down-to-earth, empirically derived set of four behavioral categories (Parsons, Bales, and Shils 1953). On the 'deductive' side, Parsons drew on a set of general philosophical and methodological categories, including the open systems view, cybernetic theory, and Kantian epistemology. Thus, the four functions are an almost breathtaking integration of concrete research with abstract concepts.

The functions divide on two fundamental axes: internal vs. external, and latent vs. consummatory. The internal–external divide is based on the notion that actors maintain some form of 'internal life' that is distinct from, and stable in relation to, their environment. This is a central feature of open systems approaches and also central to the criticism of utilitarian-economic types of social theory. Maintaining the internal life, the *identity* of the system, requires one set of processes and orientations, and interacting with the environment requires another. Action, in this view, is a constant state of tension between opening to the outside and consolidating the inside, and it requires a continual set of exchanges—including dynamic learning—to keep the two aspects in harmony.

The second dimension, latent vs. consummatory, distinguishes the maintenance of *general* resources from the processes of *committing* them to particular uses. The first resulting pair, on the 'inside' of the social system, constitutes the distinction between universal values, shared by all members of a system, and the specific norms that define particular roles. This pairing is clearly influenced by Kant's distinction between hypothetical imperatives, which depend on the identity of the proposer, and categorical imperatives, which are universal. At the social system level, an example where this difference plays out clearly is in law: the Supreme Court has become the arbiter of the unifying universal principles represented by the Constitution, and the legal system as a whole involves continual two-way interchanges between these general principles and their specification to particular cases. In social theory, this distinction is also reflected in Durkheim's concepts of organic and mechanical solidarities: mechanical solidarity is based on strong shared values, while organic gives increasing room to individual differences while still providing a basis for people to trust each other. Parsons's terms for the two internally oriented subsystems of societies are the 'fiduciary system', for institutions that maintain universal values, and the 'societal community', for institutions that coordinate particular solidarities.

The second pair of latent–consummatory functions, on the external side, distinguishes between 'adaptive' institutions that provide generalized mastery of the environment and 'goal-attainment' institutions that mobilize for specific collective purposes. For the social system the former is the function of the economy, which turns 'raw material' into products generally useful to members of the system; and the latter is the polity, which defines particular collective goals and mobilizes actors when necessary.

The 'four-function paradigm' (adaptation and goal attainment on the external side, integration and pattern maintenance on the internal) is shown in Figure 27.1.

Since these functions are necessary to all action systems, they apply at any level. Within the economy, for example, there are also four sets of functional institutions. Organizations as institutional forms specialize in goal attainment: thus the goal-attainment subsystem of the economy is performed by economically focused organizations, in particular the business firm; the goal-attainment function of the value sphere (L) is performed by value-focused organizations such as churches and schools; and so on. Each of these organizations is in turn itself a system with four functions; we will shortly analyze the business firm as such a system.

	Consummatory	*Latent*
Internal	I Integration *The societal community*	L 'Latency'—pattern maintenance *The fiduciary system*
External	G Goal attainment *The polity*	A Adaptation *The economy*

Fig. 27.1. The four functions and social-system institutions

An underlying empirical, though abstract, proposition is that increased differentiation among these functions results in higher adaptive capacity of the system. Just as the division of labor increases economic capacity, action systems generally work better when particular institutions and processes specialize in one of the functions rather than mixing them. Thus, there is a continual tendency, as systems face new challenges and learn to perform better, to differentiate along functional lines. A major historical example is the differentiation of the polity (G) from the Church (L), which started during the Reformation: by distinguishing values from political authority, societies were able to be far more inclusive and flexible than before (Parsons 1964, 1966).

Functionally based institutions are characterized by distinct orientations, or 'ways of seeing'. From the economic point of view, for example, the primary value is utility; from that of the polity, it is effectiveness; for the community, it is solidarity; and for the value sphere, it is integrity. It is intuitively evident that these orientations can often conflict: decisions made from the orientation of pure utility may well pull against solidarity or integrity.[1] The point is that a successful social system must maintain and develop all these orientations—it can survive neither in the absence of economic utility nor in the absence of solidarity—and so must find ways of working through and overcoming such tensions.

[1] The 'pattern variables' were Parsons's formalization of these varieties of orientation (e.g. Parsons 1960*a*). But this is too detailed a level for our purpose here, and Parsons himself rarely used the pattern variables after formalizing the four-function model. I have used here his 'value principles' as presented in *The American University* (Parsons and Platt 1973: 434 and elsewhere).

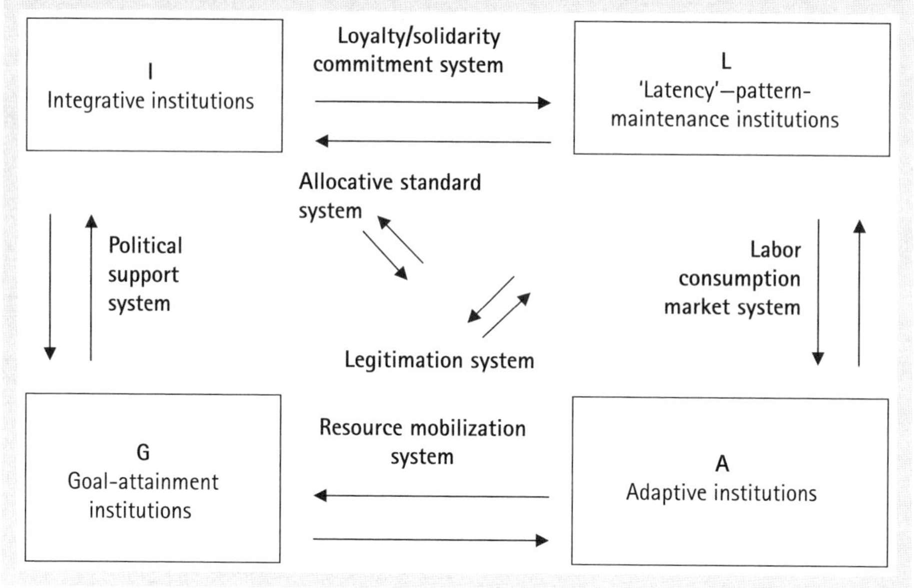

Fig. 27.2. The interchange paradigm (Parsons and Platt 1973: 426)

This led Parsons to the further step of analyzing interchanges among the subsystems (see Figure 27.2). To take one interchange as an example: political actors need value-based institutions, as Weber showed, to secure their legitimation; Parsons conceptualizes this as an input from the value sphere (L) to the polity (G). Legitimation becomes more effective in supporting power if the two spheres are relatively differentiated from each other. This means that if, for example, the Church is merely an appendage of the State and is not seen as maintaining an independent orientation, it will not create trust among social system members by approving of political acts; but if the Church is seen as effectively representing the independent value stance of integrity, then its approval will make a real difference in members' willingness to obey commands from political leaders.

On the other side of the exchange, the value sphere in turn needs an input from the polity that Parsons calls 'moral responsibility for collective interest'. If political actors fail to assume moral responsibility—to make the link between their actions and generalized values—then the value sphere itself is weakened and becomes less able to provide effective legitimation.

This I–L interaction is one of six major exchanges among the functions, each of which could inspire reams of studies (as the concept of legitimation has already done). Together, these exchanges mediate the differing priorities of the system's parts and, through a dynamic process of dialogue or negotiation, maintain a relative balance among them. To the extent that this balance is achieved, it provides a set of answers to the fundamental question of every actor: Why should I trust this system and the actors in it?

It is worth emphasizing again that these are exchanges of expectations, or norms. Parsons interprets labor power, for example, not in terms of its physical base but as an input of commitment to the economy. If a firm receives only physical labor from its workers it will function badly; it will be able to generate more utility to the extent that it can generate broad commitment to economic and firm values. Parsons does not in any sense deny the existence of force or 'mere' incentives; but from his perspective, any system that relies on these to motivate action will be very constrained. His analytic mission is to understand how a system can build far more generalized forms of trust that enable people to act both freely and with coordination.

Since the subsystems have differing orientations, communication among them raises problems of translation: each of the four sets of institutions requires a 'language' capable of symbolizing its value in a way that is understandable to others with a different orientation. This led Parsons to the development of media theory, which has become one of the most influential parts of his approach (see Chernilo 2002). He began with *money*, which he treated as a medium symbolizing economic value, then identified three analogous media grounded in each of the other functional subsystems as ways of symbolizing their value. For the goal-attainment system, the medium is *power*; for integration, *influence*; for pattern maintenance, *value commitments*. The legitimation process, for example, involves an exchange mediated by power and value commitments.

This is an unusual view of power, to take just one of these four. Parsons is claiming that power is not just a way of making someone else do what you want; rather, it is a way of communicating the system's need for collective mobilization so that people will willingly obey. It 'works' only to the extent that it is exchanged for value commitments, so that it is viewed as legitimate, and also for influence and economic resources. In the absence of such a generalized medium of power, the system is limited to the use of mere force, which makes it far less effective.

A further important refinement is that when the exchanges break down, the media undergo processes similar to inflation and deflation of money. There is inflation when actors trust a medium too much—believe overmuch in what it can deliver: for example, power inflation typically occurs at times of system crisis, when everyone wants to believe that those with political authority have the answers. Inflation is frequently followed by a deflationary reaction, when people withdraw their trust and demand hard results (Parsons 1963; Coleman 1963).

This framework is built from a very few concepts and yet is enormously rich in distinctions and relations. To continue with the much-vexed concept of power: as Parsons notes at the start of his article on the subject (Parsons 1963), most uses of the term are very diffuse and inconsistent. This framework gives it a relatively precise meaning—or rather, breaks it into an array of precise meanings. All four of the media of exchange might be called, in the usual vague parlance, 'forms of power', in that they are ways of getting others to do things; yet they operate very differently. Power based on political authorization is very different from 'moral authority' based in the value sphere, or from influence based on appeals to solidarity. Moreover, we can better understand distortions: political power in a deflated form moves towards coercion, while in inflated form it is easily manipulated as a kind of 'false consciousness'. The paradigm provides, in short, systematic leverage on these complex issues involving social norms and orientations, which are generally treated idiosyncratically, diffusely, and disconnectedly.

27.3. Applying the General Theory: The Development of Collaborative Organizations

This tour through Parsons's general theory now allows us to explore the question: Does it provide any insight on organizations beyond what Parsons himself said in the 1950s? In order to best use my own knowledge I will focus this discussion on one kind of organization—the business firm. I will try not only to elaborate on certain aspects of Parsons's first analysis but also to understand a major and often-confusing empirical development in the last few decades: increased use of cross-boundary collaboration. My evidence will be drawn primarily from two cases: the mod IV product development team at Honeywell (Margolis and Donnellon 1990), and a unit of Citibank responsible for developing an e-commerce capability in the early 2000s (see Heckscher 2007: ch. 3). The first of these was an early and troubled exemplar of the move to cross-functional collaboration; the latter was more successful and developed.

Traditional large firms—through about the 1970s—were based around strong cultures of loyalty: the organizations offered high security, but asked in return diffuse commitment and deference to authority. This normative structure was a basis for strong trust, loyalty, and security, which was for many very attractive. In the last few decades, however, this traditional corporate community has been challenged by a set of problems that it is unable to master: increasingly rapid technological change, heightened competition as a result of globalization, changing consumer expectations, and so on. These challenges have 'broken' the old normative structure and forced dramatic, but poorly justified, waves of downsizing and restructuring.

The resulting debate has gone in several directions. A large number of writers have implicitly or explicitly advocated a return to loyalty; this is especially common in the popular press but includes some academic writers who focus on worker satisfaction or who tout the Japanese model (e.g. Ouchi 1981; Gordon 1996). Others have, to the contrary, celebrated the 'liberating' effects of breaking the old system: it frees productive forces from (they argue) the constraints of employment security guarantees; at the same time, it frees employees by providing opportunities for increased diversity and choice (Arthur and Rousseau 1996; Bradach 1997).

From a Parsonian perspective, the first of the reactions just described reflects a desire to return to the comfort of the familiar system; the other reflects a desire to break it. In effect these options pose a choice between the traditional form of community and no community at all. Both, however, are severely problematic. Lack of community leads to mistrust, fundamentally undermining the ability to interact. Traditional loyalty is a normative framework that provides trust, but it has major limitations: it relies on a concrete level of conformity and homogeneity that limits the ability to adapt and innovate (Kanter 1977; Mills 1951; Jackall 1988). (Figure 27.5 is my attempt to formalize the traditional firm in Parsonian terms.)

Parsons would invite us to explore a third alternative, one with a greater adaptive capacity than the traditional form, built on a higher level of differentiation and more generalized and flexible exchanges—and therefore more flexible relations of trust. A small group of scholars has begun to explore such an alternative, calling it variously 'network', 'trust', or 'community' (Thorelli 1986; Bradach and Eccles 1989; Powell 1990; Sabel 1993; Adler 2001; Adler and Heckscher 2006). This alternative believes in the need for normative integration, trust, and commitment, but suggests there is an emergent form different from the community of loyalty. Such a shift would require a basic restructuring of expectations and normative exchanges.[2]

In this view, the continuing development of capitalist economic production puts the traditional 'paternalist-bureaucratic' structure of relationships under severe pressure because it demands a wider and more flexible circle of trust. A very well-explored concrete example of the problem is the automobile design process. Traditionally designers have 'thrown' products 'over the wall' to manufacturers with very little communication. As consumers have become more demanding, it has become evident that it is much more effective for the two functions to sit in the same room and talk openly. Yet this apparently sensible innovation is in fact very hard to implement because of the lack of integration—in Parsons's normative sense—between these functions. Multifunctional teams, even late in the first decade of the twenty-first century, regularly run into problems of misaligned expectations and values-based problems of 'territorial' defensiveness, cultural misunderstandings,

[2] Among the longest and most elaborate efforts to define a new form of organizational community is Adler and Heckscher (2006). Paul Adler approached the problem from a largely Marxian framework, while I worked mostly from Parsons. The following remarks in effect sketch my version of the theoretical background to that essay and of my subsequent book, *The Collaborative Enterprise* (2007).

and conflicting priorities (Clark and Fujimoto 1989; Donnellon 1993; Heckscher 2007).

At a wider level, companies find it increasingly necessary to plug in to worldwide networks of knowledge development and to form relations that cross firm borders far more than before—in the form of alliances, partnerships, involvement in open-source processes, and many other mechanisms. These problems make it imperative to solve the basic Parsonian problem at a higher level: to include more different orientations and to allow more scope for independent and voluntarist action, while still maintaining a coherence that allows the system to function rather than spiraling into a cycle of mistrust and loss of coordination.

The four-function paradigm draws our attention to a set of problems involved in this 'adaptive upgrading'. The starting problem we have pointed to is the elaboration of the methods of integration among more diverse and specialized actors. This is an issue that had already drawn Parsons's attention as early as the 1950s: the need to incorporate differences in capability, especially in knowledge, that 'break' the chain of authority. But because social exchange consists of balancing expectations, this elaboration in turns puts strain on the relation to other parts of the system—creating a whole set of problems of trust, which can be traced systematically through the analysis of the interchanges. If a manufacturer tries to reach out in a new way to involve a marketer in broad dialogue around customer needs, the marketer is likely to respond from an established, 'narrower' point of view that protects his function. How should the roles be redefined so that both sides can trust the relationship? How will that then affect the way they think about making collective commitments? How will it affect the definition of their shared values?

I will illustrate a Parsonian analysis through the systematic exploration of the development of integrative systems in collaborative enterprises, and its effects on the three sets of interchanges centered on integration. This will necessarily be very brief, and will leave out further necessary analyses. (For a diagrammatic version of the following analysis, see Figures 27.3–27.7.)

27.3.1. The Internal Development of Integrative Institutions

The first and most direct requirement for collaborative systems is for a set of norms that define appropriate behaviors for the differentiated actors in situations that call for influence rather than power—that is, where the central problem is to combine diverse knowledge or capabilities. How are marketers supposed to act in a cross-functional team or process? When is it appropriate for them to insist on their particular expertise, and when should they defer to other members? How should the group go about defining and modifying its shared purpose? How important is it for people to know and like each other personally beyond the task requirements?

Who should define tasks? When there are conflicts, what are the proper responses and procedures for resolution? How should they handle slackers and other deviants? These questions, and many others, come to the foreground in a new way in teams and processes that are not merely extensions of hierarchical relations of power.

Such problems have been the center of a remarkable wave of innovations in the last few decades that Paul Adler and I have summarized under the term 'interdependent process management' (Adler and Heckscher 2006: 43 ff.). This consists of the elaboration of routines and roles for coordinating differentiated specialists without putting them under a stable hierarchy of command. At the simplest level, the idea that peers should begin projects by reaching agreement on roles and responsibilities is now routine in many organizations, but it was virtually unknown twenty years ago, when the roles were simply defined by the person in authority. The techniques of managing interdependent processes now go far beyond that simple starting point; they involve elaborate procedures for managing information and flows, setting goals, and maintaining accountability—all without the direct use of formal power.

A crucial part of this development is the creation of effective reputational systems. Reputation in the paternalist firm is very unreliable—one can say, with proper precautions, that the 'market' in reputation is very limited. Most information about performance and capability circulates very little, and the superior authority has a monopoly on the public definition of reputation. This limited market is easily distorted: whispering campaigns, water-cooler conversations, and partial impressions often become the dominant currency. By contrast, in successful collaborative firms, there are many sources of information about capability: informal exchanges are seen as legitimate and valid, and are therefore much more open, and they are generally supplemented by formal mechanisms of multi-source feedback (Heckscher 2007: chs. 3 and 6, esp. 95 ff.)

27.3.2. Integration in Relation to Goal-Attainment: Influence and Power

The development of this associational dimension enormously increases the ability of people to work together flexibly and effectively across organizational boundaries, going far beyond the hit-or-miss network of informal contacts. But it also puts strain on relations to other aspects of the organization and requires the development of more complex interchanges at all its boundaries.

The most obvious one is the relation between the elaborated set of associational institutions based on influence and the hierarchy of power. The tension is fundamental: power used inappropriately can undermine the conditions for effective integration of capabilities by suppressing essential knowledge and demotivating contributors; on the other hand, purely collaborative processes can go on forever without reaching binding decisions. The Harvard Business School case study of the Mod IV Product Development Team documents the struggles of a team and their hierarchical boss at Honeywell in redefining their relationship. The latter says:

> We have several problems going on right now, and I'm not really happy about them, but no one expects me to be happy about them. But I know all those people are really working hard to resolve the problems. Now if you jump in there and shout, or accuse, then what you're basically saying is you don't have faith in the people you've assembled to get the job done, or you don't think that they're giving it their best effort. We may lack some skills in the technology we're in, but basically I think we have a good set of people, and I think they're working really hard. My job is to support them rather than shout at them.
>
> (Margolis and Donnellon 1990: 11)

This executive is manifestly caught between the 'power' problem of mobilizing people effectively around a clear policy—he is 'not happy' with their performance—and building their integrative capability by giving them the space to build teamwork, to work out the issues on their own with full engagement. He is looking for ways of communicating his needs—an example of what Parsons would call a medium of exchange—that moves beyond 'shouting' and enables a more effective balance between those orientations.

For this particular interchange between goal-attainment and integration, using power and influence, I will go to one more level of detail. Parsons's complete theory, drawing on economic models, specified each interchange as a double exchange, one of factors and one of products. Without going too deeply into the logic of factors and products,[3] we can begin with Parsons's sketch of the double set of interchanges between integrative and goal-attainment institutions at the level of the social system.

Our focus requires looking at the same interchange, but specifying it in two ways. First, we are focusing on the economic subsystem rather than on society as a whole. Second, we are analyzing not economic organizations in general, but a particular stage of their development with relatively complex integrative institutions and a highly symbolized medium of influence. In this particular setting, the 'problems' that the interchanges need to bridge are specifications of the Parsonian categories.

The first input from integration to goal attainment involves assertions by the differentiated actors that they have some crucial basis of influence that the power system would do well to heed. At the societal level, Parsons identifies this input with

[3] The factors are in effect 'resources' that are used by the institutions of the receiving functional subsystem and that are communicated in the medium of the sending system: thus, the integrative system uses factors valued through money, power, and value commitments, and it provides factors valued through influence. The products are 'returns' that provide support for the receiving functions and are valued in the medium of the receiving system.

		Medium		Exchange	
G Polity	Factors	*Influence*	←	Interest demands	I Societal community
		Power	→	Policy decisions	
	Products	*Power*	←	Political support	
		Influence	→	Leadership responsibility	

Fig. 27.3. Parsons's definition of societal I–G interchanges (Parsons and Platt 1973: 432)

interest demands, which are exchanged for policy decisions. Within a collaborative firm, however, what the policy makers need to pay attention to is not interests as such but the relevance of particular *capabilities* to the firm's goals. Such influence is based on the ability to deliver expertise effectively to build the team's success. The credible assertion of these capabilities depends heavily on effective reputational systems as mentioned above—preferably based on well-organized multi-source feedback.

The Mod IV leader, like many caught in the transition from simpler paternalist hierarchies, was not very clear about what he needed. He emphasized that the people on the cross-functional team, though perhaps 'lack[ing] some skills in the technology we're in', were 'good people' who were 'working really hard'. Because he lacked sufficient input of assertions of capability, he did not have a good sense of whether these were the right people for the job in terms of their particular competence and knowledge, nor were mechanisms available to bring in new capabilities at the proper moments. This lack of data and confidence contributed greatly to the leader's dilemma about whether and how to intervene in the team's functioning.

The authorities' reciprocal input to the integrative sector is what Parsons calls 'policy decisions' that shape its functioning. I suggest a specification that I call

		Medium		Exchange	
G Collaborative leadership	Factors	*Influence*	←	Assertions of capability	I Interdependent process management
		Power	→	Guidance of processes	
	Products	*Power*	←	Collaborative accountability	
		Influence	→	Support for capabilities	

Fig. 27.4. I–G interchanges in collaborative enterprises

'guidance of processes'. The problem here is that the integrative institutions that bring together differentiated capabilities need a fair amount of autonomy to function properly, but they also need guidance about what to focus on in terms of the firm's goals and mission. This tension has given rise to the concept of 'chartering'—another innovation of recent years—in which the leadership defines essential responsibilities and tasks but leaves considerable openness about who will be involved and what resources will be required. People in such contexts talk about wanting a 'clear *direction*'—rather than a clear *directive*. As a Citibank e-Solutions employee put it, 'Focusing on the alignment and focusing on value-generation... is the way you get trust.' Chartering is just the first step in a process of guidance involving periodic realignment between the integrative process and the system goals. All this is, of course, sharply different from the bureaucratic process of monitoring performance of job tasks, which essentially ignores the integrative aspects and assumes that performance can be entirely managed by power.

The reverse side of the exchange, the return of power to the executive function, comes in the form of what I call 'assumption of collaborative responsibility' (see the contrast of the I–G exchanges in Figures 27.5–27.7).

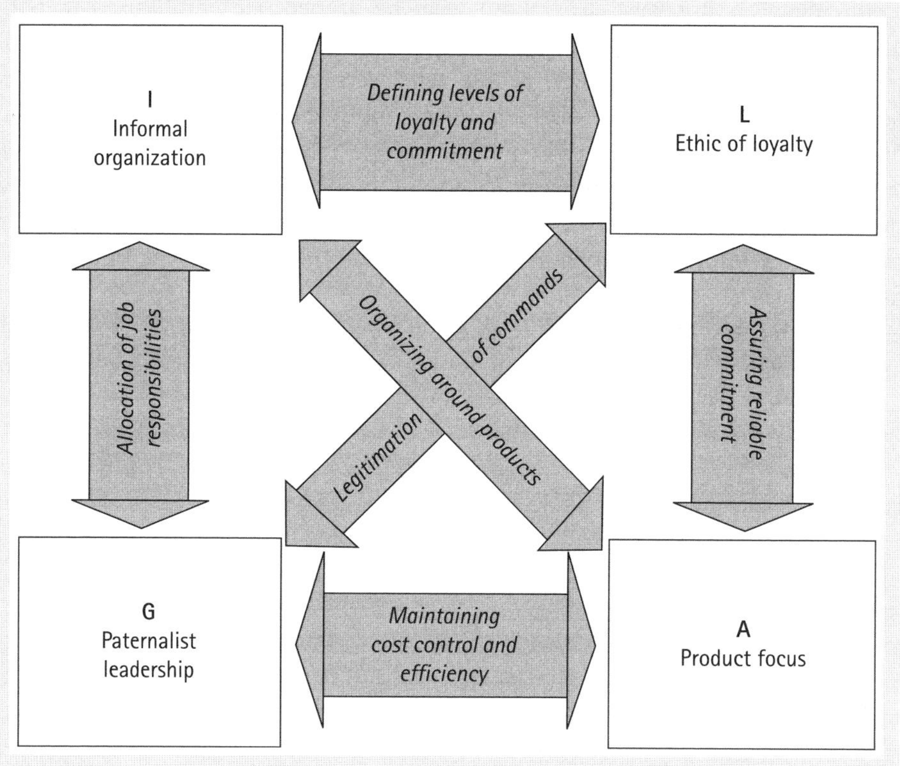

Fig. 27.5. Exchanges in paternalist bureaucracies

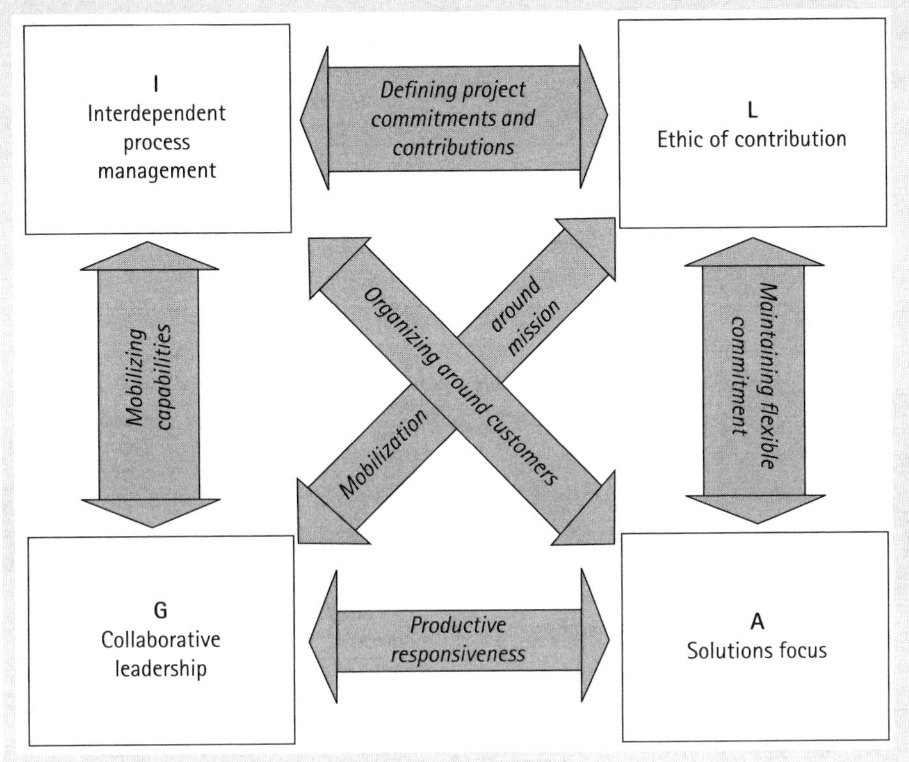

Fig. 27.6. Exchanges in collaborative enterprises

Responsibility is the organizational version of Parsons's term, drawn from political science, 'electoral support': it is the way in which authority gains the trust, or degrees of freedom, that it needs to define the goals for the system. In the bureaucratic form, lines of accountability correspond closely to lines of authority, but in a collaborative organization accountability gets much more complicated. People are no longer expected to simply do what they are told, and they do not expect to be told specifically what to do; the notion of accountability becomes—in true Parsonian manner—more abstract and mediated. At Citibank e-Solutions, people said things such as:

> I have five or six bosses, with one direct boss and dotted lines to all the global heads. My evaluation will be managed with their input.... The feedback given by some of my dotted-line bosses sometimes doesn't mix; so I get them on the phone and they resolve it. They say, 'Don't allow yourself to be pulled in different directions.'

Here the accountability involves not a passive acceptance of orders, but active responsibility involving use of influence to 'resolve' the multiple demands of power. Such accountability serves to increase the power of the organization as a whole—its

L Ethic of contribution	Factors	*Influence*	←	Assessments of value of contributions	I Interdependent process management
		Commitments	→	Commitments to teams and processes	
	Products	*Commitments*	←	Commitments to common mission	
		Influence	→	Legitimation of claims to contribution	

G Collaborative leadership	Factors	*Influence*	←	Assertions of capability	I Interdependent process management
		Power	→	Guidance of processes	
	Products	*Power*	←	Assumption of collaborative responsibility'	
		Influence	→	Participatory leadership responsibility	

A Solutions focus	Factors	*Money*	→	Assertion of claims to resources	I Interdependent process management
		Influence	←	Standards for allocation of resources	
	Products	*Influence*	→	Solutions-based grounds for justification of claims	
		Money	←	Solutions-focused ranking of claims—budgeting	

Fig. 27.7. Detailed exchanges in collaborative enterprises—integrative focus

ability to get things done—and is much less directly dependent on the power of individual bosses.

For the final piece of the exchange, the return of influence to the integrative institutions, the question is: In what way does line authority contribute to supporting the associational institutions?[4] The Mod IV leader found this very difficult: he feared that any action on his part would instead undermine the operation of the team. He understood vaguely that using his power constructively required that he 'support them rather than shout at them'. We can be more precise: the problem identified in the interchange model is to strengthen the ability of the functions to interact with each other.

[4] Parsons's term here at the societal level, 'leadership responsibility', is obscure to me, and he does not say much about it.

This is an area that remains difficult to pin down. There is a literature on 'participatory leadership', but it generally fails to make a central distinction that is highlighted by this framework: between leaders who merely encourage their subordinates individually, in a paternalistic way, in order to strengthen the boss–subordinate bond, and those who increase associational capabilities. In my own interviews, even in relatively developed organizations, people struggle to put this into words. One e-Solutions leader said, 'You are being put in a position which is asking you to take your own authority and your own value and spread that around.' Most people in that organization described boss–subordinate relationships as a matter of discussion and negotiation—'more of a dialogue around the business proposition'.

In general, considerable progress has been made on one side of the I–G interchange, but less on the other. Much has been learned about how influence can contribute to power—how executives can mobilize differentiated capabilities for the organization's goals; but there is less understanding of how power can contribute to the strengthening of influence, the ability to create effective teams of differentiated capabilities. Since this is an exchange, the imbalance restricts the overall capacity of the system. In general, the picture is still one in which 'pockets' of successful influence relationships have developed within many corporations—areas where people work together relatively easily across lines and can build on the differences in their knowledge—but there is insufficient system-level understanding of how senior leaders can encourage this.

27.3.3. Integration in Relation to Latency and Adaptation: Money and Value-Commitments

Each of the exchanges involved in the development of collaboration raises problems that cry out for entire streams of studies. The scope of a chapter does not allow analysis of the other interchanges around the integrative problem at the level of detail I just applied, though briefly, to the I–G interface. Rather than trying to break these interchanges down into their components, I will only point to some of the broad issues in the relations between integration and the value system, on the one hand, and the adaptive system on the other (see Figure 27.6).

The significance of the L–I exchange—the relation of the value system to collaboration—is often missed by the large coterie of scholars who have focused on the development of 'networks'. As Richard Munch noted long ago, the 'American creed' in sociological theory has regularly overemphasized the power of pure self-regulation among autonomous agents (Munch 1986), which in Parsonian terms is integration without value unity. Such mere horizontal integration is very fragile, however, easily producing 'chain reactions' of misunderstanding and conflict.

Attention to shared values acts as a kind of regulator to maintain alignment across shifting networks of interactions.

The values of paternalist bureaucracies centered on the notion of loyalty, a pattern of stability, deference, and reliability. But this value complex is too concrete and narrow to unify complex networks that cross boundaries of functions, levels, firms, and countries. Loyalties attach to particular firms, units within firms, and leaders, creating limited spheres within which people cooperate fairly well but outside of which they are mistrusting. These loyalties therefore become a barrier to integrating capabilities on the increasingly broad scale required in a knowledge economy.

Thus, one of the processes that goes on in the move towards extended collaboration is what Parsons called 'value upgrading', a phenomenon that has received almost no attention. Most analysts have focused on the negative side, the dismantling of the value of loyalty. What they have not noticed, but to which the Parsonian framework draws attention, is that there has been significant development of a more abstract, universalistic set of values that define a broader business community beyond firms. This involves an increasing commitment to a generalized 'capitalist' or market orientation seen as good, not just by the captains of industry but by middle managers and below. These levels are much less likely to define themselves as 'General Motors men' and much more likely to see themselves as 'good business men'—and, of course, women, since the broader orientation also requires less emphasis on concrete similarity and conformity as a basis for trust. (See the contrast of the I–L exchanges in Figures 27.5–27.7.)

This value upgrading has been supported by a societal and indeed international growth of educational systems developing business orientations. Prior to the 1980s, most employees assumed that financial planning would get taken care of by the companies they worked for, and they could just focus on doing their jobs; they typically did not know much about money market funds or retirement financing. Today the level of general business literacy, and commitment to the values that attach to it, is much higher: the popular business press, daily business sections of newspapers, hourly stock market updates on popular radio increasingly provide a universally understood language and orientation that enables people to work together across organizational boundaries.

The application of this general business orientation to the firm is what Adler and I have called the 'ethic of contribution' (Adler and Heckscher 2006: 39 ff.; Heckscher 2007: ch. 4). The defining aspect is that value is attached to contribution to the firm's business purpose. Other aspects of interaction—niceness, conformity, shared friendships—which were central to the culture of loyalty are now treated as secondary or extraneous. There are many components to this pattern of contribution that are markedly different from those of the loyalty pattern: in particular, a positive embracing of diversity of capabilities, and of dialogue, conflict, and criticism. These value orientations are increasingly institutionalized above the level of firm and function, through more general cultural mechanisms of the media and schooling.

A new set of processes are needed to bridge the gap between these general value orientations and the operation of specific teams, task forces, and other associational mechanisms. A crucial problem at this L–I boundary is that people's commitment to teams is no longer 'given' as a result of a boss's command, but must be negotiated: in organizations like Citibank e-Solutions, individuals have considerable choice in what projects they join, and they typically juggle a half dozen commitments or more that are not simply aligned with the authority of a single executive. Thus, people have to learn how manage their own commitments to projects, and how to persuade others to join with them in developing new opportunities, by referring to the broad values just discussed rather than to particular loyalties. This requires a long process of detailing new expectations and patterns of interaction, which one can summarize by reference to the exchanges between I and L: people need to agree on appropriate arguments for this persuasion, of acceptable standards for acceptance or refusal, of the kinds of commitment one can legitimately ask for, and so on. Furthermore, for full functioning of this commitment exchange, it has to contribute as well to strengthening both the value-maintaining and the integrative functions—both the overall commitments to the firm's mission and the institutions for coordinating the multiple projects.

Finally, here is an even briefer word about the third interchange around the integrative function, that with adaptation. I suggest that the move to collaborative organization is linked to a broad increase in the complexity of organizations' adaptation to the environment, captured in a strategic shift from product focus to solutions focus (Heckscher 2007: ch. 1) (see the contrast of the I–A exchange in Figures 27.5 and 27.6). A product focus is relatively simple, focusing largely on internal development and then trying to 'push' products out to the market; a solutions focus involves a more complex, interactive relationship with customers, seeking to understand their problems in depth and to mobilize the firm's resources around them. This is a major driver of the elaboration of cross-boundary collaboration, but it, of course, also creates new problems of coordination. The hierarchy of authority is once again too restricted: no one branch of hierarchical offices covers enough scope to manage the provision of resources to the solutions teams. Thus, there is a need for differentiated processes cutting across the hierarchy. One widespread manifestation is the new and increasingly important role of 'Customer Relationships Manager', cutting across the formal authority structure, responsible for bridging between the internal capabilities of the firm and the demands of customers.

27.3.4. The Firm in Relation to Other Social Institutions

So far my analysis has been on (part of) the internal functioning of the firm. But a major significance of Parsons's work is that it also draws attention to, and enables us to think systematically about, external exchanges across boundaries. The firm, as mentioned earlier, is focused on the goal-attainment function within the economy; all the changes we have explored in firm structure thus will have ramifications on wider economic institutions. Even a cursory scan of this next level of analysis brings into focus a number of these problems.

The relation of firms to the *integrative* sphere of the economy, for example, highlights the evolution of inter-firm relations from a relatively simple model of competition to complex patterns of alliances, collaboration around standards, and so on—sometimes summarized under the rubric of 'co-opetition' (Nalebuff and Brandenburger 1996; Tsai 2003). These developments have put into question some of the most fundamental norms of economic interaction, creating new choices and new difficulties manifested in an explosive growth in the complexity of contractual relations.

The relation of the firm to the *value* sphere of the economy—and through it, to that of the wider society—involves some of the most important and difficult problems in the firm's external exchanges. The 'ethic of contribution', legitimated by a wider social emphasis on economic values, works well enough within the firm; but the value of capitalist enterprise represents only one aspect of a fully functioning society. Its incompleteness is evident in the growing tension around other social values, especially around the inclusion of diverse identity groups and the role of religion in society. The ethic of contribution assumes that economic value is sufficient to unify everyone; but there is a danger, from the point of view of the organization, that the severe value splits in the wider society may penetrate the firm and make it harder to agree on what contributions have value and what the purpose of the firm should be. Such disagreements would greatly undermine collaborative institutions.

27.3.5. The Problem of Change

I have described an emergent system of collaborative organization and the problems that it needs to resolve to function effectively. This analysis supports, in a more systematic way than usual, the popular business view that such an organization is better than the older model of paternalist hierarchy, in the sense that it has a higher adaptive capacity—it can mobilize more resources more flexibly across a wider range of external conditions. Yet despite this argument, companies are not simply moving smoothly forward; the process has been advancing for a long time, since at least the 1970s, and is very far from being completed yet.

Parsons's approach illuminates many aspects of the dynamic process of change. The difficulty is that any process of social change requires changing mutual expectations: in Parsons's framework, the two sides of the interchange paradigm must balance. If just one party to a transaction shifts to a new set of norms, the other will not know how to respond appropriately. Thus, change of this kind always involves a great deal of risk-taking and trial and error. To illustrate with one small example from the large (and still very incomplete) set of problems sketched above, the development of the Customer Relationship Manager role, though widely seen as crucial for responding to customer demands, has been marked by many failures and misunderstandings. Traditional executives see the role as encroaching on their turf, siphoning off resources that they control, tempting 'their' people into projects that are not in the job description. Those who are approached by Customer Relationship Managers to participate in developing customer solutions are naturally reluctant, even when they personally believe in the projects, because they do not know how such a commitment will play out in terms of their careers, their compensation, or their reputations. They will not be able to develop real confidence in these outcomes, even under the best conditions, until the whole effort has gone on long enough that they can observe its effects.

In these circumstances, the system is in a fix: the old pattern of norms regulating interaction is evidently too narrow and rigid for the organization's problems, and a new one is far from functional; yet at the same time external pressure has been ratcheted up by increased competition from globalized markets. Thus, in many companies the demands on normative institutions—both integrative and value maintaining—outstrip their capacity to respond. That is the very definition of *deflationary* pressure: influence and value commitments suffer a withdrawal of trust, a downward spiral of skepticism about their worth.

In their stead, in many cases, power and money gain. In system crises members commonly want to believe that their leaders can solve the problems for them, and they expect too much—the very definition of *inflationary* pressure on power. Thus, enormous levels of trust are placed in CEOs' transformational abilities, far beyond their ability to deliver, rather than into the more difficult development of new levels of community. Money is also inflated relative to influence: leaders increasingly place unjustified faith in the power of incentives to regulate complex behaviors. One of the interesting themes in my interviews across a number of collaborative companies is the bemused feeling of middle managers that the incentive system is growing simultaneously more complex and less relevant to the real problems they face.

The inflationary trend of power and money is also manifest in the fact that there is constant pressure to use them in ways that diminish rather than increase the power of collaborative systems. Thus, executives under pressure for quick results frequently restructure (a power move) and change incentive systems (a money move) in ways that diminish support for cross-boundary solutions processes. This is, I would argue, one reason why the overall trend of white-collar productivity has been so poor, and why so few corporate restructurings and downsizings have paid off (Gittell, Cameron, and Lim 2004).

Parsons only began to sketch the analysis of inflation and deflation of the media; this is one of many areas where it would be of great value to extend the theory. He offered no real guidance for thinking through imbalances of this sort, though it is clear that he would expect them to lead to system crises. There are also no suggestions about why some organizations, like e-Solutions, seem to manage to build in a more balanced way. All this would require much more detailed technical analysis of media and their interaction than has been done to date.

The imbalances in the current phase have so far not spiraled into uncontrolled inflation or deflation. There is some evidence, though not universally accepted, of significant loss of employee confidence in their managers, but nothing like a major collapse. It appears that the contrary currents are partially canceling each other—that the pressure for increased responsiveness is driving continued innovation and development in associational institutions despite the opposing 'regressive' forces.

27.4. Conclusion

The great achievement of Parsons's framework is that it enables us to systematically explore and categorize the complex patterns of expectations and values needed to maintain trust in developed social systems. Most analysts focus (at best) on one or another problem—on utilitarian exchanges, perhaps, or on issues of legitimation, or on the conditions for group solidarity. Parsons is the only one to put these and other crucial sociological problems together in a single coherent paradigm, enabling us to view the complete set of problems and interactions involved in social systems. In analyzing change, it enables us to trace out the consequences of new capabilities in any one area of social action—how particular shifts will impact other norms and expectations throughout the system, and the types of problems that will be posed.

The approach does a remarkably good job of squaring the crucial circle of action theory: offering considerable rigor by specifying the systemic nature of interactions, without reducing action to a mechanical calculus. It generates not predictions, but rather a sharpened understanding of the conditions and constraints that shape choices. Part of this power lies in the fact that it does not deny the richness of the 'internal life' of human beings, as economists do in their search for analytic rigor; Parsons faces issues of values and relations and commitments directly, but he analyses their interplay systematically and rigorously.

There are certainly important holes in the theory. One that I have found particularly significant is the developmental process sketched by Parsons; his sequence of differentiation, inclusion, value generalization, and adaptive upgrading is useful as a starting point but remains too general for many purposes. My effort in this chapter to specify the interchange model at particular developmental stages goes beyond what Parsons himself did in his work.

Second, as I have indicated, the understanding of the dynamics of inflation and deflation of the media also remains preliminary. The concept of inflation drawn from economics reflects a relation between the medium of money and its underlying 'use value'; but Parsons would like to use the same notion quite differently, to analyze imbalances between money and other media, such as power or influence. He never adequately explored the implications of this novel use of the concepts.

These and other weaknesses, however, can most fruitfully be addressed by building on the substantial scaffolding already in place. A major failure of the sociology of norms, in seeking to go beyond behavioral descriptions and empirical correlations, is that it has almost completely failed to build cumulatively; when analyzing trust or commitment, each author generally starts from scratch, or at best picks up a small thread from a previous author. Parsons has pulled together a large body of work, including that of Weber and Durkheim and many other theorists, into a foundation which should support more weight.

Substantively, Parsons was notable in the 1950s for seeing, long before most of his contemporaries, the growing importance of horizontal 'professional' relations within the bureaucratic hierarchy. In this respect he pointed the way to an extension of the Weberian approach, with its strong emphasis on social norms and meaning, to the growing complexity of late twentieth-century organizations. For analysts today, Parsons still provides, in my view, one of the clearest ways of thinking about why the growth of collaboration is likely to triumph over pure bureaucracy, by tracing the ways it increases the scope of organizations' adaptive capability. He can also help us to understand the enormous difficulties in making the change—the tensions between value orientations and developing associational relations, the delicate balance of power and influence, and so on—which lead so easily to conflict and error.

But the potential of this analytic method remains largely unfulfilled. The general failure to employ this framework and to explore the rich potential of the concepts has several causes. Parsons's own execrable writing style is certainly a contributing factor; but more fundamentally, the trend towards utilitarian-economic modes of analysis in all the social sciences has made it unfashionable to dig deeply into the realms of norms and meaning. Moreover, those who do operate in the broadly Weberian tradition, and certainly in the Parsonian, cannot assume their readers' familiarity with the concepts. So they either address each other, with a tendency to focus on the concepts in themselves rather than on any empirical field; or, if they do empirical studies, they hide their conceptual apparatus. Thus, the theory becomes increasingly divorced from research and real social phenomena and justifies the critics' view of it as arid abstraction.

Like any normative pattern, this one cannot change easily; but I believe that it would be of great value for scholars to begin to address and argue about what the Parsonian interchanges would mean for particular organizational problems, and how to extend the theory so as to bring new problems within a coherent conceptual field. I have surely not gotten all the interchanges right in my treatment of collaborative organization, and debates about them would clarify the phenomenon. Pushing further, the elaboration of Parsons's sketchy developmental model and his notions of inflation and deflation of media could be particularly powerful in helping us to understand the dynamics of change, resistance, and conflict in the enormous organizational transformations we are experiencing.

References

ADLER, P. S. (2001). 'Market, Hierarchy, and Trust: The Knowledge Economy and the Future of Capitalism'. *Organization Science*, 12/2: 214–34.

—— and HECKSCHER, C. (2006). 'Towards Collaborative Community', in C. Heckscher and P. Adler, *The Firm as a Collaborative Community: Reconstructing Trust in the Knowledge Economy*. Oxford: Oxford University Press.

ARTHUR, M. B., and ROUSSEAU, D. M. (eds.) (1996). *The Boundaryless Career: A New Employment Principle for a New Organizational Era*. Oxford: Oxford University Press.

BRADACH, J. L. (1997). 'Flexibility: The New Social Contract between Individuals and Firms?' Boston: Harvard Business School Division of Research Working Paper 97-088, May 1997.

—— and ECCLES, R. G. (1989). 'Markets vs Hierarchies: From Ideal Types to Plural Forms'. *Annual Review of Sociology*, 15: 97–118.

CHERNILO, D. (2002). 'The Theorization of Social Co-ordinations in Differentiated Societies: The Theory of Generalized Symbolic Media in Parsons, Luhmann and Habermas'. *British Journal of Sociology*, 53/3: 431–49.

CLARK, K. B., and FUJIMOTO, T. (1989). 'Overlapping Problem Solving in Product Development', in K. Ferdows (ed.), *Managing International Manufacturing*. North Holland: Elsevier.

COLEMAN, J. S. (1963). 'Comment on "On the Concept of Influence" '. *Public Opinion Quarterly*, 27/1: 63.

DIMAGGIO, P. J., and POWELL, W. W. (1983). 'The Iron Cage Revisited: Institutional Isomorphism and Collective Rationality in Organizational Fields'. *American Sociological Review*, 48/2 (April): 147–60.

DONNELLON, A. (1993). 'CrossFunctional Teams in Product Development: Accommodating the Structure to the Process'. *Journal of Product Innovation Management*, 10: 377–92.

GITTELL, J. H., CAMERON, K., and LIM, S. (2004). 'Relationships, Layoffs, and Organizational Resilience: Airline Industry Responses to September 11th'. Annual Meeting of the Academy of Management, New Orleans, La., August.

GORDON, D. M. (1996). *Fat and Mean: The Corporate Squeeze of Working America and the Myth of Managerial 'Downsizing'.* New York: Free Press.

HECKSCHER, C. (1995). *White-Collar Blues: Management Loyalties in an Age of Corporate Restructuring.* New York: Basic Books.

—— (2007). *The Collaborative Enterprise: Managing Speed and Complexity in Knowledge-Based Businesses.* New Haven: Yale University Press.

JACKALL, R. (1988). *Moral Mazes: The World of Corporate Managers.* New York: Oxford University Press.

KANTER, R. M. (1977). *Men and Women of the Corporation.* New York: Basic Books.

LAWRENCE, P. R., and LORSCH, J. W. (1967). *Organization and Environment.* Boston: Harvard Business School.

MARGOLIS, J., and DONNELLON, A. (1990). 'Mod IV Product Development Team'. Case N9-491-030. Boston: Harvard Business School.

MARX, K. (1852). 'The Eighteenth Brumaire of Louis Napoleon'. *Die Revolution*, 1/1.

MILLS, C. W. (1951). *White Collar: The American Middle Classes.* London: Oxford University Press.

MUNCH, R. (1981). 'Talcott Parsons and the Theory of Action. I. The Structure of the Kantian Core'. *American Journal of Sociology*, 86/4: 709–39.

—— (1986). 'The American Creed in Sociological Theory: Exchange, Negotiated Order, Accommodated Individualism, and Contingency'. *Sociological Theory*, 4: 41–60.

NALEBUFF, B., and BRANDENBURGER, A. (1996). *Co-opetition.* New York: Doubleday.

OUCHI, W. G. (1981). *Theory Z: How American Business can Meet the Japanese Challenge.* Reading, Mass.: Addison-Wesley.

PARSONS, T. (1956*a*). 'Suggestions for a Sociological Approach to the Theory of Organizations I'. *Administrative Science Quarterly*, 1/1: 63–85.

—— (1956*b*). 'Suggestions for a Sociological Approach to the Theory of Organizations II'. *Administrative Science Quarterly*, 1/2: 225–39.

—— (1958). 'Some Ingredients of a General Theory of Formal Organization', in E. Halperin (ed.), *Administrative Theory in Education.* New York: Macmillan.

—— (1960*a*). 'Pattern Variables Revisited: A Response to Robert Dubin'. *American Sociological Review*, 25/4: 467–83.

—— (1960*b*). *Structure and Process in Modern Societies.* Glencoe, Ill.: Free Press.

—— (1963). 'On the Concept of Political Power'. *Proceedings of the American Philosophical Society*, 107/3: 232–62.

—— (1964). 'Evolutionary Universals in Society'. *American Sociological Review*, 29/3: 339–57.

—— (1966). *Societies: Evolutionary and Comparative Perspectives.* Englewood Cliffs, NJ: Prentice-Hall.

—— (1968). 'Professions', in *International Encyclopedia of the Social Sciences.* New York: Crowell Collier and Macmillan.

—— and PLATT, G. M. (1973). *The American University.* Cambridge, Mass.: Harvard University Press.

—— BALES, R. F., and SHILS, E. (1953). *Working Papers in the Theory of Action.* Glencoe, Ill.: Free Press.

PFEFFER, J., and SALANCIK, G. R. (1978). *The External Control of Organizations.* New York: Harper and Row.

POWELL, W. W. (1990). 'Neither Market nor Hierarchy: Network Forms of Organization'. *Research in Organizational Behavior*, 12: 295–336.

SABEL, C. F. (1993). 'Studied Trust: Building New Forms of Cooperation in a Volatile Economy'. *Human Relations*, 46/9 (September): 1133–70.

SCOTT, W. R. (2001). *Institutions and Organizations*. Thousand Oaks, Calif.: Sage Publications.

THORELLI, H. B. (1986). 'Networks: Between Markets and Hierarchies'. *Strategic Management Journal*, 7/1 (January/February): 37–51.

TSAI, W. (2003). 'Social Structure of "Coopetition" within a Multiunit Organization: Coordination, Competition, and Intraorganizational Knowledge Sharing'. *Organization Science*, 13/2: 179–90.

PART IV

AFTERWORD

CHAPTER 28

SOCIOLOGICAL CLASSICS AND THE CANON IN THE STUDY OF ORGANIZATIONS

GERALD F. DAVIS
MAYER N. ZALD

A distinctive feature of many parts of sociology, including organizational sociology, is their impulse towards classicism and their evident veneration of the ancestors. In an oft-quoted quip attributed to Jim Davis, sociologists seeking to publish a finding need to cite a dead German who said it first. Some influential neoclassical scholars manage to get this requirement out of the way in the very first sentence (e.g. DiMaggio and Powell 1983), while others wait until the literature review. Still others find that the current stock of dead Germans (or other venerated sociologists) is not sufficient for their purposes and seek to trace a lineage to an eminent theorist and convert them to sociology retroactively. Baudrillard's standing in sociology, for instance, was undoubtedly aided by Veblen's posthumous conversion (Kellner 1989). Authors in this volume find overlooked ancestors in organizational sociology to include Tocqueville, Tarde, and Commons, and make a compelling case for their continuing relevance.

In some scientific domains outside of sociology, one could win a Nobel Prize without ever having perused that field's classic works. The great majority of psychologists can safely ignore William James even if they are housed in a building bearing his name, as at Harvard—and how many economists have made it past chapter 3 of *The Wealth of Nations*? Yet few sociologists can afford to be unfamiliar with Max Weber, who apparently said that Protestantism was important for capitalism. This observation suggests that sociology is indeed part science and part humanities (Zald 1991–2, 1993). Like humanists, sociologists believe they can do better work when informed by how the luminaries of the past have done it—or at least those currently considered luminaries when prelim exam committees draw up their reading lists. But why do they think that? Why do sociologists care about the classics, and why should we read a book about the classics?

Art Stinchcombe (1982) gave an influential answer to the first question when he described six functions of classics (see Thornton, in this volume, for a more extended discussion). The first function is to serve as examples of excellence that we can hope to emulate. The second is to provide developmental tasks to make minds more complex—in particular, the minds of graduate students as we prepare them to enter the profession. A third function is to act as shorthand for identifying one's tradition in the first paragraph of a paper, so that the readers know how to read the rest of it (or whether they want to). Fourth, the classics help us to understand the genealogy of fundamental ideas in a field, the lineage from the trunk to the branches (to mix metaphors). Fifth, the classics can be used as a source of hypotheses that have not yet been fully explored. Finally, the classics have a ritual function to bind together the profession and give it a sense of shared history. Stinchcombe's point was that 'classics' need not meet all of these criteria—they can be classic in one way (e.g. as a shorthand for identifying the literature one hopes to contribute to) without being classic in another (e.g. as a source of unplumbed empirical insights), and it is best not to confuse these functions by imagining that exemplars of one function are also necessarily exemplary in the other ways.

We could add some other functions for a book about sociological classics of organization studies. The first is to provide CliffsNotes; or, how to talk about books you have not read. Many American sociologists, for instance, may not be familiar with the works of Norbert Elias, and a Cook's tour can be a good introduction (and, ideally, an impetus to read the originals). The second function is to introduce great unread (or under-read) authors (e.g. Gabriel Tarde; see Czarniawska, in this volume) whose works deserve to be in the canon. A third function is to revise how we think of great *misread* authors. Max Weber, for instance, first became known to most North American sociologists through Talcott Parsons's translations, yet these translations often included a clear Parsonian inflection that may be at odds with what Weber intended (see Clegg and Lounsbury, and du Gay, in this volume). Finally, a book about classics can help us understand authors in their social context. It is enlightening to know that Follett and Dewey were not just contemporaries, but familiar and even adversarial (see Ansell, in this volume).

This book accomplishes all of these ends, although the authors vary on which function they emphasize. In this brief commentary, we want to meditate a bit about classics and the canon—how and why works enter and exit required reading lists for certified sociologists, what 'canon studies' might tell us, and what we might still learn from classic works about how to theorize more fruitfully today.

28.1. The Classics and the Canon: Entry and Exit

The chapters in this volume have largely not told a story of how the classic authors became classic; instead, the chapters have assumed that the classics deserve to be more widely used, or have been neglected in recent years and ought to be resurrected, or that other works by the authors of classics deserve attention. Many of the chapters assume that the classical authors were widely acknowledged as important in their own time, and it is only that we are currently provincial or uneducated that has led to their neglect.

While it is useful to re-examine the works of the great authors of classics and attempt to educate the current generation of scholars about what from the past might be useful now and in the future, it is also useful to step back from this somewhat ahistorical and unsociological approach and ask a set of broader questions: How are the classics constructed? What is the intellectual, social, and disciplinary context in which the classic works are written and why are they seen in their time as important, or, if neglected, unimportant? What is the process by which the canonical works are established as part of the foundational writings for a field or subfield? Are there aspects of the classic works that are given a specific interpretation or reading, so that later generations use the work in a somewhat different manner than earlier uses? Why are some authors added to the list of what is considered canonical? And why do some authors, or works of particular authors, get excluded at a later point in time?

These questions suggest a broad agenda for thinking about the classics. The classics may be important for the insight they can give to particular lines of research. But it is also important to see the role they play in shaping the definition and image of what the discipline or sub-discipline is about. What are the orientations—intellectual, social, and political—that the set of works that are widely viewed to be central, less central, and, at the extreme, ignored tell us are the focal points for analysis in the living canon of the current generation of scholars?

Note that reading and thinking about the classics is not usually done in the natural sciences. Very few physicists today read Newton; rather they are taught the distilled and what are believed to be useful parts of his work, with little revisiting of early formulations or attention to the parts of his work that were dismissed as the scientific revolution took hold. (Newton was famously committed to alchemy.) Attention to the classics and the canon is more common in the humanities than in natural sciences. The curriculum in some parts of the humanities, especially in literature departments, but also in art history, and to some extent in philosophy, has been substantially devoted to interpreting past exemplars, the works seen as great. It is also recognized that classics are in some sense 'constructed' as critics, teachers, and readers (of literature or poetry) and viewers (of art) engage in acts of using and evaluating the works. Works become part of the canon as they achieve high valuation, and their reputation is carried forward in the curriculum and in the consuming public (whether passive audience or active researchers and critics).

The distinction between a classic and the canon is important, but not widely noted in sociology and social science. Indeed, until the 1970s, scholars in the humanities largely assumed the canon, rather than asking how and why it was created, although there were debates about the criteria for inclusion of specific kinds of work. But the radicalization of the curriculum and the pressure from suppressed groups for recognition of 'their' classics forced an examination of how the canon was constructed, why some forms of literature or art were included, and others excluded, why few women and African-American authors or artists were included in the then acceptable curricula. In *Cultural Capital: The Problem of Literary Canon Formation* (1993), professor of comparative literature John Guillory develops a sociologically sophisticated analysis of how the canon was created in the study of English literature in the United States. The book draws heavily on Pierre Bourdieu and Marxist analyses of the superstructure. The canon is created as part of the game of developing cultural capital in the sphere of distinguishing literary, aesthetic, and moral elites. Writers, critics, scholars, and teachers contest criteria of evaluation. They do this at an abstract level, but also in producing anthologies of poetry and short stories, and required novels to meet the needs of a standardized curriculum for high schools, colleges, and universities. Debates about the canon have implications for publishing houses, for students, and for careers. The intent was to hold up exemplars of literary taste, which demonstrated aesthetic, moral, and spiritual value for whites of the upper and middle class. The purpose of developing the canon was to elevate the standards of what counted as being educated. The standards were developed with the assumption that works included fit the needs of a homogeneous elite. Racial, ethnic, and alternative gender identities were submerged and ignored. The canon defined the kinds of literary works (e.g. poetry and drama, and, later British and European novels) and within these forms, the specific works that were believed to have the most aesthetic and substantive value. It is well to remember that it was only fifty years or so ago that recently published novels began be studied in university curricula in the United States, and 150 years ago, most students in universities learned Latin and Greek. When novels first appeared and reached mass audiences, they were read and discussed outside of university settings (Graff 1987).

Classics can be seen as the exemplary works of a particular kind. In the social sciences, they are the foundational studies and their descendants provide answers to substantive and methodological problems. The canon is the collection of surviving classics; some earlier ones eliminated as interests shift and as more 'satisfactory' forms of analysis are adopted by academic communities. The relation of classics to the canon can be seen as analogous to the relationship of species of trees to the forest; the ecology of the canon makes certain kinds of classics less likely to survive; in fact, although a rebirth may occur (similar to a long hibernation, to mix metaphors), shifts in the intellectual, social, and political environment and in the approved forms of persuasive rhetoric (e.g. hypothetical-deductive, mathematical, objective language, formal, reflective, literary) shape the distribution of species in the canon. And in some cases, the species is eliminated.

The study of the classics in organizational theory is a study of the genealogy of particular types of exemplary interpretations for a range of phenomena and the successive important iterations on the themes of the foundational exemplars as perceived by scholars working in a somewhat similar domain at later periods. The study of the canon would focus on the reasons that certain kinds of theories are selected at one point in time, while they are excluded at a later one. To study the genealogy of the classics is to focus on one line of analysis at a time. To study the transformation of the canon requires us to look over time at what is included or excluded. For instance, one could look at the shifting reading lists of graduate courses on organization theory. It is our impression that the works of Alfred DuPont Chandler, Jr. (1962, 1977) are no longer widely included. Yet, thirty years ago, they were. Chandler stands as the exemplar of the structural analysis of the large corporation; the decline in his use and of others of a structural persuasion represents a change in the canon. (We expand on this change in the next section). Similarly, the fact that Weber on bureaucracy is used in a more ceremonial way, rather than substantively, is also related to the declining relevance of the analysis of the structure of organizations and the organization of offices. Of course, it is worth noting that Weberian emphases on bureaucratic rationality are still very relevant for the study of public administration, especially in the context of developing countries (Evans and Rauch 1999, 2000). On the other hand, Simmel becomes more important, as network and relational analysis, within and between organizations, becomes a focal point of social and economic processes (see Scott, in this volume).

Other canon changes can be noted: in the 1950s hardly any courses in the sociology of organizations, whether in departments of sociology or schools of management, had syllabi dealing with leftist and Marxist works. Indeed, in the United States, discussion of Marxist theory was politically suppressed in the public sphere, and intellectually denigrated in many academic circles. As calls for the transformation of society and organizations increased in the 1960s and 1970s, works that had a Marxist tinge, whether dealing with labor process or class domination and conflict, became more widely read. By the end of the century, Marxist works had not been suppressed, but are clearly less widely used. Although 'critical' analysis can be seen as a descendant of both Marxist and Frankfurt approaches, the Foucauldian turn gives it a quite different inflection.

Note, too, that because organizational studies is partly both a scientific and humanistic enterprise, the surrounding societal and intellectual culture has a greater impact upon local canons than would be found in disciplines such as mathematics or geology. Marxist, critical, and discourse-based approaches have a greater role even at elite institutions in Europe and Australia than in America. We know of no American management school that recruits explicitly for 'critical' scholars, although that occurs regularly in Canada and England.

28.2. Why Now? The Renewed Relevance of 'Classics'

As already mentioned, an important reason to read the classics and contemplate the canon draws on Stinchcombe's 'exemplar' function. Stinchcombe notes that Claude Lévi-Strauss used to read a few pages of the *18th Brumaire* to remind himself of how it was done when it was done well. Some classics provide a (perhaps) achievable standard of excellence that we might hold in our mind in setting our own aspirations as theorists. We would argue that there is a specific sense in which we need examples of 'doing it well' now. Many of the great social theorists read by organizational sociologists can be seen as documenting and grappling with the birth of a society of organizations (or more acutely, a society of corporations) out of the previous system of competitive capitalism (e.g. Clemens, in this volume). By some accounts, we are currently observing the death throes of that system, as signified by terms such as post-industrial, post-Fordist, post-statist, globalized capitalism. The study of the classics can inform contemporary theorists not so much by providing ideas to be tested (e.g. does Google conform to the core features of bureaucracy identified by Weber?), but as styles of theorizing when you are not sure what your object is yet.

Several classics of organizational sociology covered in this book were explicitly or implicitly concerned with making sense of the rise of corporate industrial capitalism. During the period in which many of our theorists wrote, Western economies were in transition from agriculture to mass production manufacturing. In the

United States, for instance, 42 percent of the working population was spread among six million farms at the end of the nineteenth century. Within two generations, nearly half the labor force worked in manufacturing. New forms of work and social organization were arising and spreading, particularly Fordist mass production and the social forms that arose around it. Peter Drucker wrote in 1949 that 'the representative, the decisive, industrial unit is the large, mass-production plant, managed by professionals without ownership-stake, employing thousands of people, and organized on entirely different technological, social, and economic principles' from the enterprises of competitive capitalism (1949: 22). Moreover, 'The big enterprise is the true symbol of our social order.... In the industrial enterprise the structure which actually underlies all our society can be seen' (ibid. 29). The principles of mass production had spread beyond the factory to engulf research, education, medicine, warfare, and public administration. Yet Drucker had the benefit of seeing the 'society of organizations' in its adolescence, when its main contours had already been worked out. The early twentieth-century theorists were there at its birth.

In hindsight, it is clear that large corporations were en route to becoming the dominant social structures in society in the late nineteenth and early twentieth centuries. The broad outlines of the new 'corporate system' were evident by the early 1930s, when Berle and Means wrote their famous book. By that point, the largest 200 corporations controlled half of industry's assets, and almost half of these firms were under the control of professional managers. The result was a new kind of social system. 'The economic power in the hands of the few persons who control a giant corporation is a tremendous force which can harm or benefit a multitude of individuals, affect whole districts, shift the currents of trade, bring ruin to one community and prosperity to another. The organizations which they control have passed far beyond the realm of private enterprise—they have become more nearly social institutions' (Berle and Means [1932] 1991: 46). By mid-century it was widely believed by American social scientists of various stripes that corporations and other large-scale organizations had absorbed much of American society. Economist Carl Kaysen wrote in 1957 that 'The whole labor force of the modern corporation is, insofar as possible, turned into a corps of lifetime employees, with great emphasis on stability of employment' (1957: 312), and as a result 'membership in the modern corporation becomes the single strongest social force shaping its career members' (ibid. 318). Complex organizations evidently merited their own distinct sub-discipline. Thus, March and Simon described the individual organization as 'a sociological unit comparable in significance to the individual organism in biology' (1958: 4), yet one about which little was known systematically. Organizational sociology took it from there.

The idea of 'society' as a unit of analysis was also still relatively new and contested, but further ratified by processes around the time of industrialization. Espeland and Stevens (1998) describe how the evolution of statistics in its original sense in the

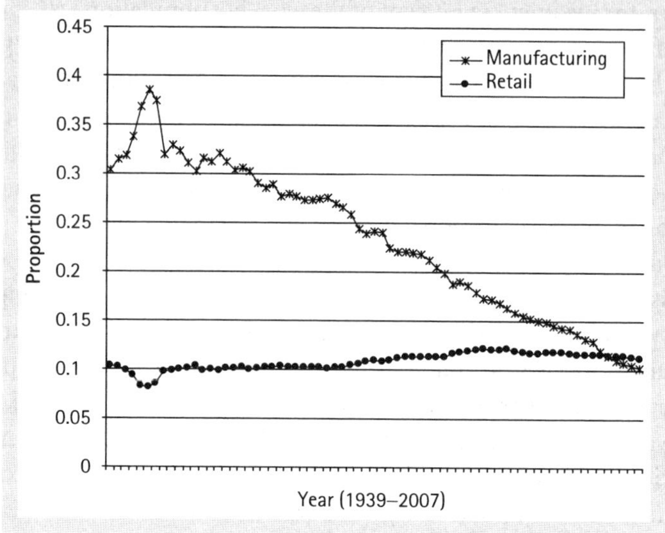

Fig. 28.1. Proportion of the US non-farm labor force employed in manufacturing and retail, 1939–2007

Source: US Bureau of Labor Statistics

1820s and 1830s—of counting entities, such as persons—enabled the discovery of regularities in things such as suicide rates. It also induced the discussion of units of analysis of which the rates were a property, such as 'society' or the nation-state. The notion of societies that were coherent and separate from other societies and were roughly coterminous with contemporary nation-states—entities that had a comprehensible structure and trajectory (e.g. determined by class struggle)—was relatively new, and it made a discipline that studied such units plausible.

But in the past few decades many of the transitions that sociological classics addressed have been transcended. The idea of a society of organizations made sense in Kaysen's time, when industrial corporations sought to cultivate career 'members' and pay them pensions when they retired. But by the mid-1990s, more Americans worked in retail than in all of manufacturing, and Wal-Mart had replaced GM as the largest private employer (Scott and Davis 2007). Figure 28.1 shows the secular decline in manufacturing employment as a proportion of the non-farm labor force from 1944 until 2007. It takes little imagination to project where the trend is headed: just since the start of the Bush administration in 2001, over 3.6 million manufacturing jobs—20 percent of that sector's employment—have been lost. The shift to post-industrialism has meant that organizations no longer envelop the social lives of their members and structure their careers, and even the notion of 'membership' is suspect given the relatively short attachments between employees and firms in the predominant service organizations. To give a recent example: in 2006 there were 400,000 mortgage brokers working in 50,000 firms in the United States. The business of intermediating between home borrowers and lenders—an industry that was virtually non-existent two decades previously, when banks and S & Ls wrote mortgages—employed more Americans than the entire textile industry. Moreover, in light of the 2007 mortgage meltdown, the industry is likely to be nearly non-existent again in 2009.

As legal fictions, corporations are still powerful actors, but they are no longer the encompassing entities contemplated by the 'society of organizations'. And much the same can be said about states. Michael Burawoy (2005) pointed out in his ASA Presidential Address that 'Globalization is wreaking havoc with sociology's basic unit of analysis—the nation-state—while compelling deparochialization of our discipline.' We cannot take for granted that a society is coterminous with a nation-state (or states). Following the lead of corporations, states have found that they can use offshore providers for some revenue-generating functions (e.g. licensing corporations and ships, in the case of Liberia), and even outsource some of their most basic functions (e.g. paramilitary violence against unarmed civilians, in the case of Blackwater). States are now just one vendor among many competing for the custom of their (corporate and other) consumers. A post-nation-state, post-corporate world requires new ways of theorizing about social structure, different from the ones in which we were trained.

Examining the classics might help us theorize our contemporary transition away from a society of organizations. We can learn much by appreciating the context of ideas, for instance, the link between American pragmatism and the rise of stock markets and large-scale industrial capitalism in the United States. The social history of ideas gives useful clues, for example, the parallels between Marx and Darwin in their imageries of change are perhaps analogous to the widespread use of network imagery in contemporary natural and social science. Many ideas from prior theorists lie fallow and then become revived due to their new applicability. Industrial districts and the continuing centrality of geography for economic activity, for instance, were largely ignored by American theorists between the time of Alfred Marshall (1920) and that of Piore and Sabel (1984). And Veblen's most famous idea, of conspicuous consumption, went from a peculiarity of the wealthy at the turn of the twentieth century to a dominant social motif at the turn of the twenty-first century.

The authors of several chapters point to particular styles of theorizing that have regained their relevance, namely, how to understand organizing and extra-organizational processes. For roughly a decade, many organizational theorists have gradually begun to classify themselves as economic sociologists, which is further reflected in the dominance of neo-institutional and network approaches to theory. Organizations, in other words, need no longer be the predominant object of organizational research, as many of the processes of interest transcend particular organizations. As described by Abbott (in this volume), the old Chicago School also studied the organizing of human activities without focusing on formal organizations as distinct objects. Schumpeter unpacks the structures for entrepreneurial action inside and outside organizations (Becker and Knudsen, in this volume). And Elias provides a model of examining large-scale evolutionary processes linking the micro to the macro (see van Iterson, in this volume).

28.3. Conclusion

The chapters in this volume present a feast for reflection on the continuing relevance and sometimes irrelevance of past works. The classics and the canon evolve. Unlike the elimination of species that occurs in biotic evolution, the evolution of the canon allows for the recall, possibly in reinvigorated forms, of what were once classics, or had been published in some form. It is at least possible that the classics of tomorrow may have had little fame or reputation when they first appeared. We have no idea whether there are hidden jewels out there, just waiting for some scholar to make claims about their importance for current or future thinking. It is easiest to suppose that some work of an eminent scholar that had little resonance in its time deserves contemporary currency. When the 'cultural turn' in sociology and organizational studies occurred, scholars turned to Durkheim's *The Elementary Forms of the Religious Life* ([1912] 1965). When population ecology approaches to organizations flourished in the 1970s, Amos Hawley's book (1950), largely unknown to students of organizations without grounding in human ecology, became a foundational text. It is very unlikely that a work from the past by a long dead and rarely or never cited author could suddenly be trumpeted as a classic. A work without a well-known sponsor would be a kind of virgin birth! When Thomas Kuhn discovered in its original German language form Ludwig Fleck's *The Genesis and Development of a Scientific Fact* ([1935] 1979), only Robert K. Merton had previously read it in Harvard's Widener Library. Fleck, a Polish microbiologist, had developed the idea of a thought collective and can be seen as taking a constructionist approach to science, long before the sociology of science took that turn. Fleck showed how the diagnosis of syphilis emerged from the welter of assumptions, classifications, and research of the community of microbiologists. An annual award in Fleck's name is now given by The Society for the Social Study of Science.

This Handbook has largely focused on the classics and the canon for theoretical interpretations of important organizationally and sociologically substantive issues. Of course, there are also classics for methodological and analytic forms as well. There are exemplars of quantitative methods and exemplars of analytic styles. Durkheim's *Suicide* (1951) is known not largely because of its findings about rates of suicide, but for its enunciation of a sociological level of analysis not, apparently, reducible to psychology. Case studies of organizations have exemplars that can be called classic, as can comparative studies with a small number of cases.

Although the study of organizations changes partly in response to changes in organizations as they respond to their societal and organizational context, the changes in what from the past is seen as foundational also responds to the chaotic and fractal processes within and between academic disciplines (Abbott 2001). Thus, we return to classics and reinterpret them in the context of a transformed academic discourse.

REFERENCES

ABBOTT, A. D. (2001). *The Chaos of Disciplines*. Chicago: University of Chicago Press.

BERLE, A. A., and MEANS, G. C. ([1932] 1991). *The Modern Corporation and Private Property*. New Brunswick, NJ: Transaction.

BURAWOY, M. (2005). 'For Public Sociology'. *American Sociological Review*, 70: 4–28.

CHANDLER, A. D., JR. (1962). *Strategy and Structure: Chapters in the History of the Industrial Empire*. Cambridge, Mass.: MIT Press.

—— (1977). *The Visible Hand: The Managerial Revolution in American Business*. Cambridge, Mass.: Harvard University Press.

DIMAGGIO, P. J., and POWELL, W. W. (1983). 'The Iron Cage Revisited: Institutional Isomorphism and Collective Rationality in Organizational Fields'. *American Sociological Review*, 48: 147–60.

DRUCKER, P. F. (1949). 'The New Society, I: Revolution by Mass Production'. *Harper's Magazine*, September: 21–30.

DURKHEIM, É. ([1912] 1965). *The Elementary Forms of the Religious Life*. Chicago: Free Press.

—— (1951). *Suicide: A Study in Sociology*, trans. J. Spaulding and G. Simpson. Glencoe, Ill.: Free Press.

ESPELAND, W. N., and STEVENS, M. L. (1998). 'Commensuration as a Social Process'. *Annual Review of Sociology*, 24: 313–43.

EVANS, P. B., and RAUCH, J. (1999). 'Bureaucracy and Growth: A Cross-National Analysis of the Effects of "Weberian" State Structures on Economic Growth'. *American Sociological Review*, 64/5: 748–65.

—— —— (2000). 'Bureaucratic Structure and Bureaucratic Performance in Less Developed Countries'. *Journal of Public Economics*, 75: 49–62.

FLECK, L. ([1935] 1979). *The Genesis and Development of a Scientific Fact*, ed. and trans. T. J. Truen and R. K. Merton, with a foreword by T. S. Kuhn. Chicago: University of Chicago Press.

GRAFF, G. (1987). *Professing Literature: An Institutional History*. Chicago: University of Chicago Press.

GUILLORY, J. (1993). *Cultural Capital: The Problem of Literary Canon Formation*. Chicago: University of Chicago Press.

HAWLEY, A. (1950). *A Theory of Community Structure*. New York: Ronald Press.

Kaysen, C. (1957). 'The Social Significance of the Modern Corporation'. *American Economic Review (Papers and Proceedings)*, 47/2: 311–19.

Kellner, D. (1989). *Jean Baudrillard: From Marxism to Postmodernism and Beyond*. Stanford, Calif.: Stanford University Press.

March, J. G., and Simon, H. A. (1958). *Organizations*. New York: Wiley.

Marshall, A. (1920). *Principles of Economics*. 8th edn. London: Macmillan.

Piore, M. J., and Sabel, C. F. (1984). *The Second Industrial Divide: Possibilities for Prosperity*. New York: Basic.

Scott, W. R., and Davis, G. F. (2007). *Organizations and Organizing: Rational, Natural, and Open System Perspectives*. Upper Saddle River, NJ: Pearson Prentice Hall.

Stinchcombe, A. L. (1982). 'Should Sociologists Forget their Mothers and Fathers?' *American Sociologist*, 17: 2–11.

Zald, M. N. (1991–2). 'Sociology as a Discipline: Quasi-Science, Quasi-Humanities'. *American Sociologist*, 22: 5–27.

—— (1993). 'Organizational Studies as a Humanistic Discipline: Notes on the Foundations of the Field'. *Organization Science*, 4: 513–28.

Index

Figures, notes and tables are indexed in bold.